Probability, Logic, and Management Decisions

Probability, Logic, and Management Decisions

Jerome D. Braverman
Associate Professor of Statistics
Temple University

McGraw-Hill Book Company

New York St. Louis San Francisco Düsseldorf Johannesburg
Kuala Lumpur London Mexico Montreal New Delhi Panama
Rio de Janeiro Singapore Sydney Toronto

Probability, Logic, and Management Decisions

Library of Congress Catalog Card Number 75–148979

07–007345–7

1 2 3 4 5 6 7 8 9 0 M A M M 7 9 8 7 6 5 4 3 2 1

This book was set in Times Roman, and was printed and bound by The Maple Press Company. The designer was Marsha Cohen; the drawings were done by John Cordes, J. & R. Technical Services, Inc. The editors were Richard F. Dojny and Barry Benjamin. John A. Sabella supervised production.

To
Judy, Amy, Tom,
and my parents

CONTENTS

PREFACE

The past several years have seen the publication of many excellent books on statistical decision theory at all levels from the most elementary to the most abstract. Many of the applied works stem from Schlaifer's outstanding effort, "Probability and Statistics for Business Decisions." Consequently, most of these books have certain similarities in approach, although each attempts to achieve a slightly different presentation or viewpoint from that of its predecessors. This book is no exception. I am deeply indebted to authors such as Schlaifer, Savage, Wald, and numerous others for the ideas and theories upon which this book is based. I have, however, attempted to take my own approach in viewing the general decision problem in its entirety and looking at the bayesian techniques as only the final step in achieving a solution.

In most practical situations, the formulation of the problem represents one of the most difficult tasks of the decision maker. Furthermore, those problems for which the decision theoretic solution is the most rewarding relate generally to situations of the greatest complexity. The simpler the decision situation, the more straightforward the solution and the easier it is for the decision maker to achieve a relatively satisfactory result without resorting to lengthy statistical or mathematical procedures.

In teaching these procedures it is necessary to begin with simple situations that lend themselves to straightforward solutions in order that the student may grasp the basic principles. However, students taking courses in decision theory seldom become aware of the actual complexities usually encountered in real life situations. Furthermore, those students who may have had courses in basic statistics, probability, operations research, and other disciplines rarely understand how the various techniques and disciplines fit together in the formulation and solution of complex decision problems.

All decision problems in the real world primarily involve stating the problem in clear, unambiguous terms, defining the relationships of all parts and facets of the problem to one another and to the whole; collecting and analyzing data, drawing inferences from the data; assessing probabilities, and only then utilizing decision theory to reach some optimum conclusion. Hence, this book has been divided into four parts: Logic, Probability, Statistical Analysis, and Decision Theory.

My purpose was to approach the complex management decision situation as a problem requiring the application of various techniques for solution and to integrate all these techniques into an orderly system for decision making. Consequently, a complex decision situation is first analyzed from a logical standpoint, and the concepts of probability and bayesian decision theory are introduced to show how they can be used to contribute toward a more optimal solution. Statistics and statistical inference are considered first as a method of analyzing data and providing inputs to the decision model and then in the context of classical decision-making techniques. I attempted to relate every topic to the problem of decision making rather than to treat each topic as an isolated element.

This text was prepared with the intention of its being suitable for a self-contained, two-semester course in decision theory for a student with little or no background in probability and statistics. For a course of this type the entire book should be covered and the sequence of topics maintained.

For students who have already had one or possibly two courses in basic statistics, this book would be suitable for a one-semester course in statistical decision theory which would cover Part I on Logic, Chapters 8 and 9 from Part II on Probability, and the entire Part IV on Decision Theory.

For a more conventional approach to the topic of decision theory, Part I might be eliminated together with Chapter 8 on probability networks and the rest of Part II; all of Parts III and IV would be suitable for a two-quarter sequence in basic probability and statistics with emphasis on the modern approach to decision theory.

The choice of topics included is relatively broad and, needless to say, the individual professor can make his own selection of topics to meet the requirements of his particular course.

The mathematical prerequisites have been kept to a minimum although familiarity with intermediate algebra and some finite mathematics is highly recommended. Certain sections, particularly those relating to continuous probability distributions, utilize some concepts of the calculus, but these can easily be omitted without affecting the student's comprehension of the rest of the book.

I am grateful to the ladies of the Cochran Research Center, and especially to Miss Nancy Cliff and Mrs. Grace Tappert for the typing of the manuscript. I am indebted also to the students of my Statistics 611 course, whose suggestions are reflected in many of the examples used in the text.

Jerome D. Braverman

Probability, Logic, and Management Decisions

1 Introduction

Managers, from the middle organizational level up to and including the highest level, are continually faced with the necessity for making decisions with respect to highly complex situations. Indeed, if any single function can be said to characterize the job of the manager, it is that of decision making.

As the pace of business and industry quickens, the drive for higher sales, greater efficiency, larger market shares, more reliable products, etc., achieves ever-higher levels of intensity, and the manager, at all levels, is required to make more numerous decisions in even less time than before. Because of the increasing size of the average business or industrial organization and the increasing complexity of the environment in which it operates, wrong decisions are likely to be more costly to the organization, and indirectly to society, than at any previous time in history. But more than ever before, the factors involved in decision making, the problems and subproblems for which solutions must be found and implemented, have also increased in number and complexity.

The manager, then, is confronted with an increasingly large number of increasingly more complex problems or situations with ever-mounting frequency, for which solutions must be found and decisions made in less and less time. This situation is not likely to improve with time, but on the contrary is almost certain to get worse. What an awesome prospect indeed for the present or future manager to face!

With ever-increasing numbers of problems requiring solution and situations requiring decisions, the manager requires new and more numerous sources of data upon which to base his decisions; and the data are available. Volumes and volumes of data are being generated in the modern business and industrial environment. The problem of the astronomical increase in the generation of data or information has frequently been discussed. Terms such as "information explosion" and "data revolution" have been attached to the problem. To assist him in the assimilation of all these data, the manager and others have turned to the large-scale computer and all its associated equipment. But let us face the facts. The computer, or the electronic data processor (EDP), has not solved or even alleviated the problem. It has in many instances made it more severe. EDP does not solve problems for the manager; it merely reduces the vast amount of data, which may or may not bear on the manager's specific problem, to a form that makes them more intelligible.

Before the advent of EDP, the data were so massive and so diffuse that the manager might justifiably ignore them on the basis that they were unintelligible or in unusable form. This excuse is no longer valid. Now the manager must use the elegantly reduced data in his decisions or be remiss as a manager. But how should the data from all sources be integrated and applied to the decision problem with which the manager is faced? The overall, integrated approach to management problem solving and decision making is the subject of this book.

We shall attempt to provide a guide or framework suitable for any type of decision problem faced by a manager in business or industry. We shall discuss and explain the problem-solving tools which are available, show how they relate to one another and to the decision problem, and demonstrate their use in the process that begins with the definition of the problem and ends with the decision made. A brief description of the manner in which the general decision problem will be approached follows.

A complex problem requiring a solution is really a collection of smaller problems or subproblems, the solutions of which bear on the final solution of the larger primary problem. A complex problem of this type, which we shall label the primary problem, can be compared with the operation of a complex system. The operation or state of the system is dependent upon the operation or state of its subsystems or components, just as the solution to the primary problem is dependent upon the solutions of the many related subproblems.

Take as a simple example the problem of developing, producing, and marketing some new product *X* which faces the president of an industrial organization. To market or not to market, which shall it be? The solution to this problem depends upon the solutions to myriads of smaller, secondary problems which could include some of the following factors:

1. The potential demand for the product
2. The existence and strength of competitive products
3. The costs of developing, manufacturing, and marketing the product
4. The availability of facilities, personnel, and raw materials
5. The availability of capital and the cost of money

And the list could go on and on.

The decision as to whether to develop, produce, and market product *X* will depend upon whether the solution to the primary problem, which happens to be the outlook for the success of the venture, is good or bad. We would equate a *good* solution or outlook with a YES decision, and a *bad* solution or outlook with a NO decision.

If we look upon the total primary problem as a system with many interacting facets or components, the state of the system, good or bad, is a direct consequence of the states of the various components, either good or bad.

For example, the potential market might be determined to be very large, which is good, but many competitive products exist, which is bad. Personnel and raw materials are available, which is good, but new facilities would have to be acquired, which is bad, and so on down the list. After determination of these states of all the components, it is still necessary to determine the state of the overall system. That is, in view of the pattern of the component states, good and bad, is the system state good or bad in the context of the primary problem? And this is the problem facing the manager. How does one integrate data about all the many components or subproblems into an evaluation of the system state or primary problem solution?

Almost any scientist or operations research analyst will explain that, having defined the problem to be solved, the first step toward a solution is to construct a model to represent the system under consideration.

A model is, in fact, a representation of some subject of interest or inquiry. It is synthetic in the sense that it reduces the object or system of interest, which exists in the real world, to a more easily viewed and handled and generally simplified, even though synthetic, representation by eliminating the nonessential and the unimportant. Models take many shapes and forms, but all can generally be classified as iconic, analog, or symbolic. An iconic model represents certain aspects of a system visually or pictorially, as a model airplane represents the original. An analog model utilizes some set of characteristics to represent another set of characteristics possessed by the object of interest. A symbolic model utilizes symbols to represent properties of the entity being studied.

The symbolic model is the class of models that will be referred to here. If the symbols used are mathematical symbols, we would refer to the model as a mathematical model. If other types of symbols, not specifically mathematical, are used, we might refer to the model as graphical. In either case, the system model, whether graphical or mathematical, is simply a convenient device for expressing the relationships of the system components to one another and to the system as a whole. And, as has been discussed previously, the state of the system (solution to the problem) is a function of the states or conditions of all its component parts.

If the graphical model of the system depicts the logical relationships of all the system components to each other and to the system, we shall call the model a *logical model.* The construction of an accurate logical model of the system is one of the most important steps in this entire process of decision making. Given the states, good or bad, of all system components, the logical model provides a means for determining the state of the system, good or bad. Without going any further, a preliminary answer to the problem can be found by referring to the logical model of the system. It may not provide an optimum solution, but, nevertheless, it does provide a solution. Because of the importance of constructing accurate logical models of the decision system under consideration, a discussion of symbolic logic and several extensions of this basic subject are included.

If probabilities can be assigned to the possible states of the components in the logical model, then the probability of the system being in some specific state can also be determined. The addition of probabilities to the logical model essentially makes it into what could be called a "probability model," since a probability model can be defined as a model by means of which the probability of some specific system state or outcome can be determined.

The determination of the probabilities of the various component states relies on probability theory and classical statistical inference in the treatment of data referring to the component characteristics of interest.

By transforming the logical model into a probability model, the manager, rather than having to be satisfied with a gross estimate of system state in terms of *good* or *bad*, can now estimate the system state with some probability statement attached. Once this point has been reached in the decision sequence, statistical decision theory can be employed in the process by incorporating the state probabilities as well as the economic consequences of wrong decisions in an attempt to select the optimum decision under the given circumstances.

In this rather lengthy total-decision process, we have employed symbolic logic, probability theory, statistical inference, and statistical decision theory. All these general areas, as well as specific pertinent topics in each, will be discussed subsequently.

These several major topics have all received extensive treatment previously as separate entities. This book will, however, treat each one as a significant component of an integrated management decision process in an attempt to assist the manager in the process of making optimal decisions.

part one

Logic

2
Symbolic Logic and Boolean Algebra

In the first chapter of his work on mathematical logic* that resulted in the algebra which bears his name, George Boole wrote:

> The design of the following treatise is to investigate the fundamental laws of those operations of the mind by which reasoning is performed; to give expression to them in the symbolical language of a Calculus, and upon this foundation to establish the science of Logic and construct its method, ...

The purpose of beginning a book on decision making with an introduction to symbolic logic and boolean algebra is somewhat more prosaic. Decision problems are originally expressed in the language of the field or fields of application in which they occur. In order to apply a systematic and logical method to the solution of these problems, it is necessary to express the

* George Boole, "An Investigation of the Laws of Thought," p. 1, Dover Publications, New York.

pertinent elements of the decision situation in a manner which lends itself to analysis by the technique to be applied.

While Boole investigated the fundamental laws of the operation of the human mind and gave expression to them in a symbolic language, we shall attempt to use that language and those laws in such a way as to facilitate the solution of certain problems facing human beings in management situations. Just how they will be used is the subject of this and several following chapters.

2.1 SYMBOLIC LOGIC

In the search for an effective decision-making process we are faced with the necessity of defining a problem or describing a situation in terms which are unambiguous and unequivocable. The English language, or any language for that matter, though providing an extremely useful and effective means of communication, is still ambiguous in many instances and falls short of providing an ideal or even efficient approach to problem solving.

The language of pure mathematics, on the other hand, is certainly unambiguous and precise but is somewhat limited for describing lifelike situations and those types of problems with which managers are frequently beset.

We can, however, turn to the discipline of logic for a language that helps to bridge the gap between pure mathematics and the human situation. Although not perfect, and still limited in its application, symbolic logic helps to fill this gap.

The purpose of this chapter is not to present a complete course or even a comprehensive summary of symbolic logic or boolean algebra. Its intent is simply to present those ideas and concepts that will prove useful in relation to the major undertaking of this book, which is to develop a comprehensive decision-making procedure.

In developing the basic and pertinent techniques which will be useful in the decision process, the following symbols will be utilized:

$\vee$ the logical OR as in $A \vee B$, read A or B
$\wedge$ the logical AND as in $A \wedge B$, read A and B
$'$ (prime) the logical negation as in A', read not A

One other symbol will be utilized during the ensuing discussion. The $\vee$ symbol above is called the *inclusive* OR and is defined to mean "A or B or both" when used in an expression such as $A \vee B$. There is, however, another symbol which stands for what is called the *exclusive* OR and is defined to mean "A or B but not both." The symbol used for the exclusive OR is $\underline{\vee}$.

We shall define a *simple statement* as a statement which conveys a single idea or fact. For example, "I am cold" is a simple statement. "I am hungry" is a simple statement. However, "I am cold and hungry" is not a simple statement. It is a compound statement which combines two simple statements and the ideas conveyed by both of them.

We shall let a capital letter represent a simple statement. Suppose A represents the simple statement "I am cold," and B represents the statement "I am hungry." Then A and B, which we would write $A \wedge B$, using the symbols previously defined, would represent the compound statement "I am cold and hungry."

The symbols $\vee$, $\wedge$, and $\underline{\vee}$ are called *connectives* in symbolic logic because they are used for joining simple statements and making them into compound statements conveying some specific idea or ideas. If we construct a compound statement out of simple statements and connectives, the validity or *truth* of the compound statement is dependent upon the validity or truth of its components and their relationship to one another. By "components of the compound statement" we refer, of course, to the simple statements and the connectives used to link the components into the compound statement.

The compound statement can be either true or false. We shall refer to the truth or falsity of a compound statement as its *truth state* or simply as its *state*. The dependence of the truth state of the compound statement on that of its components means that the state of the compound statement can be uniquely determined by the state of its components, also either true or false. This statement should be modified somewhat since the connective does not have a truth state, only a function. Therefore, let us say that the state of the compound statement can be uniquely determined by the states of its component simple statements and by the nature of the connectives linking them.

A simple way of depicting this relationship between the state of the compound statement and that of its components is by means of a *truth table*. A truth table is simply a listing of all possible states of the component statements and the resulting state of the compound statement for the given connectives. For example, let us construct the truth table for the compound statement $A \wedge B$. We shall construct a table with three columns, one for each simple statement and one for the compound statement. Under the simple statements we shall list all possible combinations of their states using the letters T for True and F for False. Since there are two simple statements and each can have one of two possible states, we shall need four rows to list all the combinations. In general, we can determine the number of rows required in a truth table for any number of simple statements to be compounded, provided only two states are possible, very simply. If there are n simple statements, each of which is capable of being in one of two states, the number of rows required in the truth table is 2^n.

Table 2.1 Truth table for the compound statement $A \wedge B$

A	B	$A \wedge B$
T	T	T
T	F	F
F	T	F
F	F	F

After listing all the possible combinations of states for the simple statements, the next step is to determine the state of the compound statement for each of the combinations and enter that state in the proper column. This is done in Table 2.1.

The entries under the $A \wedge B$ column were determined by this reasoning. If both A and B are true, then $A \wedge B$ must be true. But if either A or B or both are false, the compound statement $A \wedge B$ must be false.

Let us look at the statement $A \vee B$ which says that *at least* one of the two statements is true. The truth table for this compound statement is given in Table 2.2.

We can see that the compound statement $A \vee B$ is true if either of its simple statements is true and is false *only if* both of its simple statements are false.

There is, however, a more useful way of designating the truth states of statements than the T and F used in these two previous tables. Useful, that is, in the context of, and for the purpose expressed in subsequent material. We shall allow only two states, true or false. If a statement is true we shall assign to it a truth value of 1. If it is not true, then it must be false, and we assign to it a truth value of zero. Then for the states listed in the truth

Table 2.2 Truth table for the compound statement $A \vee B$

A	B	$A \vee B$
T	T	T
T	F	T
F	T	T
F	F	F

Table 2.3 Truth table for the compound statement $A \wedge B$

A	B	$A \wedge B$
1	1	1
1	0	0
0	1	0
0	0	0

tables of Tables 2.1 and 2.2 we would use 1s and 0s instead of T's and F's. Tables 2.1 and 2.2 would then appear as they do in Tables 2.3 and 2.4.

The difference between the inclusive and exclusive OR would be worth illustrating at this point. The illustration also serves to show how ambiguities in the language can be reconciled by the use of logic symbols. Suppose, as before, that A stands for the simple statement "I am cold," while B stands for "I am hungry." If we compound the two simple statements into "I am cold or I am hungry," there are the following obvious possibilities regarding my state of being which are logically true. These are:

1. I am cold but not hungry.
2. I am hungry but not cold.

However, the statement does not make it clear whether or not I can be both cold and hungry at the same time. If I can, that is, if I mean by the above statement that I am either cold or hungry or both, then the inclusive OR is called for and the statement in logic symbols should be written $A \vee B$. If, however, I mean that I am either cold or hungry but not both at the same time, then the exclusive OR is used, and the statement is $A \veebar B$. When the

Table 2.4 Truth table for the compound statement $A \vee B$

A	B	$A \vee B$
1	1	1
1	0	1
0	1	1
0	0	0

Table 2.5 Truth table for the compound statement $A \veebar B$

A	B	$A \veebar B$
1	1	0
1	0	1
0	1	1
0	0	0

simple statements are compounded by the use of logic symbols, there is no doubt as to the meaning of the statement.

The truth table for the exclusive OR appears in Table 2.5.

We have so far considered the combination of two simple statements into a compound statement utilizing a single connective. There are, of course, more complicated compound statements than those illustrated, resulting from the use of several connectives. For example, let us consider the statement $A \wedge B'$. The truth table is given in Table 2.6.

The first step in constructing this truth table is to set down side by side the two simple statements involved. In this case the simple statements are A and B. Underneath the two simple statements indicate all the possible combinations of truth states just as in the previous truth tables. This is shown in the first two columns of the truth table in Table 2.6. The second step is to define the state of B' for all states of B. This is done in the third column of the table. The states of B' or not B are just the opposite of the states of B. Finally, the connective $\wedge$ is evaluated for the compound statement $A \wedge B'$.

The basic rule to remember is that the effect of *each* connective on the simple statements to which it applies must be defined or evaluated in a specific order. The order requires that the connectives be evaluated from

Table 2.6 Truth table for the compound statement $A \wedge B'$

A	B	B'	$A \wedge B'$
1	1	0	0
1	0	1	1
0	1	0	0
0	0	1	0

Table 2.7 Truth table for the compound statement $(A \vee B') \wedge A'$

A	B	B'	$A \vee B'$	A'	$(A \vee B') \wedge A'$
1	1	0	1	0	0
1	0	1	1	0	0
0	1	0	0	1	0
0	0	1	1	1	1

the inside out in the same way that algebraic expressions are simplified. In the previous example, the effect of the negation was determined before the effect of the $\wedge$ since the negation affected only the statement B while the $\wedge$ affected both A and B.

A more complicated statement is $(A \vee B') \wedge A'$. The truth table for this statement is given in Table 2.7.

The procedure is similar to that used in the previous example. The two simple statements and the combinations of their possible states are set down in the first two columns. Then each connective is evaluated, working from the inside out. First, the prime, which affects the B inside the parentheses, is defined in column 3, then the $\vee$ inside the parentheses which connects the truth states of the statement A and the statement B'. Third, the prime affecting the A outside of the parentheses is evaluated, and finally the $\wedge$ connecting the parenthetic expression with A'. Whenever a compound expression is repeated in the truth table for the purpose of evaluating a connective, the truth values of that statement resulting from the last connective evaluated should appear in a column under *that* connective so that it is apparent which connective results in the truth values obtained. This was done in the previous examples.

This procedure being followed, the evaluation of each connective proceeds from left to right in the truth table. To avoid repeating very complicated expressions in the truth table every time the effect of another connective is determined, it would be convenient and proper to head a column simply with the connective evaluated, rather than with the entire statement affected. The statement $[(A \wedge B') \vee (A' \wedge B)]'$ is evaluated in Table 2.8. Here, the last two columns are headed only by the connective evaluated in that column. The last column is, of course, the truth state of the entire compound statement. It will be left to the reader to follow through all the steps in evaluating the compound statement and to verify the correctness of the truth table.

Just as it is not necessary to limit oneself to a single connective in forming a compound statement from two simple statements, it is also not

Table 2.8 Truth table for the compound statement $[(A \wedge B') \vee (A' \wedge B)]'$

A	B	B'	$A \wedge B'$	A'	$A' \wedge B$	$\vee$	$'$
1	1	0	0	0	0	0	1
1	0	1	1	0	0	1	0
0	1	0	0	1	1	1	0
0	0	1	0	1	0	0	1

necessary to limit oneself to two simple statements. Three or more simple statements can be linked, but of course the more simple statements and connectives used in forming the compound statement, the larger and more complex will be the truth table. As an example, we shall construct the truth table for a compound statement which consists of the three simple statements A, B, and C.

The compound statement is $[A \vee (B \wedge C')]$. Its truth table is given in Table 2.9. It should be noted that with three simple statements, there are now a total of 2^3 or eight possible combinations of truth states. These are listed in the first three columns of the table.

We have so far discussed how a complex statement of a state or a condition can be broken down into its simple components and expressed unambiguously by use of logic symbols. We have also seen how we can determine the state of the compound statement for each and every state or combination of states of its components by constructing a truth table. We can now think of both the compound statement expressed in logic symbols

Table 2.9 Truth table for the compound statement $[(A \vee B \wedge C')]'$

A	B	C	C'	$B \wedge C'$	$\vee$	$'$
1	1	1	0	0	1	0
1	1	0	1	1	1	0
1	0	1	0	0	1	0
1	0	0	1	0	1	0
0	1	1	0	0	0	1
0	1	0	1	1	1	0
0	0	1	0	0	0	1
0	0	0	1	0	0	1

and the truth table as models of the condition that exists. Both the statement itself and the truth table are logical models since they express the logical relationship of all components to each other and to the overall statement of condition.

2.2 BOOLEAN ALGEBRA

That there is a close relationship between symbolic logic and the boolean algebra will become very apparent as this section continues. That there is also a close relationship between symbolic logic, boolean algebra, and set theory will also become apparent in the following chapter.

We shall define a *set* here as any collection of identifiable objects or elements. We shall define an *algebra* as a set upon whose elements are defined certain operations.

Let S be a set of elements upon which the following operations are defined: the $\wedge$, the $\vee$, and the $'$. Set S, under these operations, also satisfies the following properties:

Axiom 1, closure: If $x \in$ (is contained in) S, and $y \in S$, then $x \wedge y \in S$, and $x \vee y \in S$.

Axiom 2, commutation: $x \wedge y = y \wedge x$, and $x \vee y = y \vee x$.

Axiom 3, association: $x \wedge (y \wedge z) = (x \wedge y) \wedge z$, and $x \vee (y \vee z) = (x \vee y) \vee z$.

Axiom 4, idempotency: $x \wedge x = x$, and $x \vee x = x$.

Axiom 5, absorption: $x \wedge (y \vee x) = x$, and $x \vee (y \wedge x) = x$.

Axiom 6, distribution: $x \wedge (y \vee z) = (x \wedge y) \vee (x \wedge z)$, and $x \vee (y \wedge z) = (x \vee y) \wedge (x \vee z)$.

Axiom 7, complementation: For every $x \in S$ there exists another element called the complement of x, $x' \in S$, such that:
$x \vee x' = 1$,
$x \wedge x' = 0$.

Axiom 8: There exist in S special elements called 0 and 1 such that:
$0 \wedge x = 0$ for all $x \in S$, and
$1 \wedge x = x$ for all $x \in S$, and
$0 \vee x = x$ for all $x \in S$, and
$1 \vee x = 1$ for all $x \in S$.

We can call set S a boolean algebra, and properties 1 to 8 can be called the axioms of this boolean algebra.

By using these properties or axioms, various theorems about S can be derived. For our purposes, however, two useful theorems will be stated without proof. These theorems are called DeMorgan's laws and are as follows:

Theorem 2.1

$$(x \vee y)' = x' \wedge y' \qquad (x \vee y \vee z)' = x' \wedge y' \wedge z'$$

Theorem 2.2

$$(x \wedge y)' = x' \vee y' \qquad (x \wedge y \wedge z)' = x' \vee y' \vee z'$$

These eight axioms and two theorems will enable us to simplify some complicated boolean expressions which will be encountered later. It should be obvious at this point that boolean *operations* are analogous to the symbolic logic *connectives*.

2.3 BOOLEAN POLYNOMIALS AND FUNCTIONS

Several definitions necessary to this development will make their appearance in this section. A *boolean minterm* will be defined as a group of symbols representing elements of set S and operations on these elements, except that the operation OR is excluded. A minterm corresponds to the *conjunction* of simple statements, which may or may not be negated, in symbolic logic. For example, $x \wedge y$, $x' \wedge y$, $x \wedge y' \wedge z'$ are minterms.

A *boolean polynomial* is a group of minterms connected by the OR symbol. An example of a boolean polynomial would be $(x \wedge y \wedge z') \vee (x' \wedge y) \vee (y \wedge z)'$.

A *boolean function* of the variables $x_1, x_2, \ldots, x_n$ is an expression which is obtained from the variables x_i by using a finite number of operations $\vee$, $\wedge$, and $'$. An example of a boolean polynomial of the variables x, y, and z would be $(x' \wedge y \vee z)' \vee [(x \vee y) \wedge (y \vee x')]'$.

A boolean function, when expressed in the form of the example given above, can become very complicated. It is certainly desirable to be able to simplify an expression of that type whenever possible, and indeed it is always possible to express a boolean function as a polynomial consisting of minterms OR'd together. A boolean function expressed in this manner is said to be in *canonical* form.

A complex boolean function may be simplified by the application of the axioms and theorems discussed previously. As an example, let us simplify the following function: $(x \wedge y)' \wedge (y \vee x)$. The procedure is essentially to first use DeMorgan's laws to remove negations which apply to more than one variable at the same time, then use the distributive laws to remove parentheses. The simplification of the above function is accomplished in the following steps.

Step 1: Apply Theorem 2.2 to the first parenthetical expression and obtain $(x' \vee y') \wedge (y \vee x)$.

Step 2: Apply the distributive law to get $x' \wedge (y \vee x) \vee y' \wedge (y \vee x)$ and again to get $(x' \wedge y) \vee (x' \wedge x) \vee (y' \wedge y) \vee (y' \wedge x)$.

Step 3: By Axiom 7 $x' \wedge x = 0$, $y' \wedge y = 0$; therefore, we have $(x' \wedge y) \vee 0 \vee 0 \vee (y' \wedge x)$.

Step 4: Remove the zeros and get $(x' \wedge y) \vee (y' \wedge x)$.

The simplified expression now consists of two minterms OR'd together and is in canonical form.

As boolean functions become more complex, their simplification by the applications of the axioms and basic theorems becomes more difficult. Fortunately, there are easier ways of simplifying the functions and converting them to canonical form. Probably the simplest method is the tabular method. Let us look at the expression $(x \wedge y)' \wedge (y \vee x)$ which was simplified above and which we shall designate the boolean function $f(x,y)$; that is, $f(x,y) = (x \wedge y)' \wedge (y \vee x)$. We allow each variable to have one of two possible states, zero and 1, and we list all the possible combinations of the states of x and y in Table 2.10.

We want to determine the state of $f(x,y)$ for each possible state of the variables x and y, and we would proceed just as we did previously in the construction of a truth table in symbolic logic by evaluating each operation or connective and working from the inside out. In the last column, instead of repeating the entire function in the heading of that column, we simply write $f(x,y)$. We proceed from the truth table to the canonical form of the function as follows.

If a simple statement in symbolic logic was true, we assigned to it the value 1. If it was false, we assigned to it the value zero. Therefore, if the statement $A = 1$, the complement of A, $A' = 0$. The variables in boolean algebra are not limited to being statements of a condition, and, therefore, the terms *true* or *false* are really not applicable. However, if the state of a variable x is 1, then its complement x' would be in state zero and vice versa. In Table 2.10 we shall let the 1s in the columns under the variables correspond

Table 2.10 Truth table for boolean function $f(x,y) = (x \wedge y)' \wedge (y \vee x)$

x	y	$x \wedge y$	$(x \wedge y)'$	$y \vee x$	$f(x,y)$
1	1	1	0	1	0
1	0	0	1	1	1
0	1	0	1	1	1
0	0	0	1	0	0

to the variable itself, and we shall let the zero correspond to its complement or opposite state, which in the function is expressed by the negation symbol of prime ($'$). In deriving the canonical form of the function from its truth table, we shall adopt the convention that each combination of states of the variables listed in the initial columns of the table represents a minterm, that is, the variables ANDed together. The state of the variable, either zero or 1, tells us whether to write the variable itself or its complement. In the case of Table 2.10 where both x and y are 1, as in the first row, we write the minterm as $x \wedge y$. Where both variables are zero as in the fourth row, we write the minterm as $x' \wedge y'$. Where one variable is zero and the other is 1 as in the second row, the minterm is $x \wedge y'$. We shall also specify that the only minterms which should appear in the canonical form of the function are those for which the value of the function is 1. Therefore, we shall write the canonical form of $f(x,y)$ utilizing only those minterms for which the corresponding entry in the column under $f(x,y)$ is 1.

Referring to Table 2.10, we see that the minterms corresponding to rows 1 and 4 of the table will be eliminated, since $f(x,y)$ for these rows is zero. We would write the minterms of rows 2 and 3 and connect them with the OR symbol. The boolean function $(x \wedge y)' \wedge (y \vee x)$ in canonical form is obtained from the truth table in Table 2.10 by ORing rows 2 and 3 together according to the conventions just presented. Row 2 provides $x \wedge y'$. Row 3 provides $x' \wedge y$. ORing these two terms together, we get $x \wedge y' \vee x' \wedge y$, which is identical with the expression which we obtained by manipulating the function according to the axioms and theorems stated previously.

To summarize, a complicated boolean function can be transformed to canonical form from its truth table by ORing together those minterms for which the value of the function is 1. In terms of symbolic logic, the canonical form of an expression is formed as the disjunction of the basic conjunctions of simple statements. Remember that a zero in a column under a boolean variable corresponds to the negation of that variable.

2.4 FINDING FUNCTIONS FROM TRUTH TABLES

The truth table development used in symbolic logic has provided a convenient method for determining the state of a complex statement, given the truth states of its components and the connectives joining them together. The relationship between the truth table and the canonical form of a boolean function has provided another useful procedure.

It is now possible to construct a truth table which illustrates a desired relationship between the individual variables and the function and, by use of the procedure discussed just previously, determine what that function must be. Since the boolean function and the complex statement are analogous, and the boolean variables and simple statements are also analogous, this method applies to complex statements as well as to functions and can also be extrapolated to include the concept of complex systems and their components.

For example, suppose we have two variables x and y and we wish to be able to write the function $f(x,y)$ which provides that when $x = y$, $f(x,y) = 0$, but when $x \neq y$, $f(x,y) = 1$. The truth table for this function would be as shown in Table 2.11.

This truth table was constructed by listing the possible combinations of the states of the variables in the first two columns as has been done in all previous truth tables. However, the entries under the function column are the states desired for the as yet unknown function. We now find the desired function by following the procedure discussed for writing the canonical form, which was described previously. We eliminate those minterms for which $f(x,y)$ is zero and OR together those minterms for which $f(x,y) = 1$. In this case, $f(x,y) = (x \wedge y') \vee (x' \wedge y)$.

In terms of symbolic logic, if x and y were actually the simple statements A and B, the truth table in Table 2.11 would indicate that we want to combine them into a complex statement which is false when both A and B have the same truth value, that is, when they are both true or both false. However, the complex statement would be true when A and B have different truth values. The desired complex statement which meets these conditions would be $(A \wedge B') \vee (A' \wedge B)$.

To illustrate this with actual simple statements and the complex statement which would result from combining them according to the form resulting from the truth table, suppose that the simple statements are as follows:

Statement A: I am hungry.
Statement B: I have eaten my fill.

Then, if A is true and B is also true, the minterm $A \wedge B$ would translate to

I am hungry and I have eaten my fill.

Table 2.11 Truth table for specified function

x	y	$f(x,y)$
1	1	0
1	0	1
0	1	1
0	0	0

If both A and B are false, the minterm $A' \wedge B'$ would translate

I am NOT hungry and I have NOT eaten my fill.

Both of these complex statements are logically contradictory when each simple statement is taken at face value. However, the minterms $A \wedge B'$, $A' \wedge B$ are logically consistent as in the compound statement $A \wedge B' \vee A' \wedge B$ which would translate to

I am hungry AND I have NOT eaten my fill.

OR

I am NOT hungry AND I have eaten my fill.

The compound statement is logically true.

It should now be quite evident that symbolic logic and boolean algebra are essentially the same. However, where symbolic logic was developed in terms of simple and compound statements only, the boolean algebra was discussed in terms of variables which could represent a wide range of elements both physical and abstract. Since the decision process with which we shall be concerned must on occasion deal with varied situations involving both physical and abstract elements, it is probably the more appropriate for our purpose. Some examples of applications of boolean algebra to physical systems and components appear in the following two sections.

2.5 PHYSICAL APPLICATION: SWITCHING

A continuous path is necessary for electric current to flow in a circuit. If it is desired that current flow from some point P_1 to some other point P_2, then the path P_1P_2 must be uninterrupted. Although the electrical analogy is used here, it should be apparent that many other situations are similar, and that liquid flowing through a network of pipes, for example, represents an identical situation with valves used instead of switches.

A switch inserted in the path or circuit can interrupt current flow or allow current to flow depending upon whether the switch is open or closed. When the switch is closed, the path for the current is unbroken. When the switch is open, the path is broken, and the current cannot flow.

In the simplest case let the network appear as shown in Fig. 2.1.

Whether or not current flows from P_1 to P_2 is dependent upon the state of switch x, either open or closed. We can therefore say that the state of the network P_1P_2 is a function of switch x. Now let us assign the value 1 to the state "switch closed" or equivalently to the state "current flows," and the value zero to the opposite state "switch open." The system or network

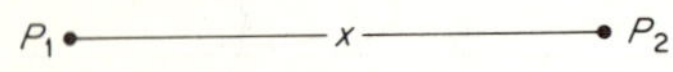

Fig. 2.1

Table 2.12 Truth table for simple switching network

x	$f(x)$
1	1
0	0

state can also be either zero or 1 depending upon whether current flows from P_1 to P_2.

Since there is only a single variable in this situation which can have either of two states, the truth table for the network of Fig. 2.1 is given in Table 2.12. The function is simply $f(x) = x$.

A slightly more complicated network is shown in Fig. 2.2. Here we have two switches, x and y, in series in the path P_1P_2. In this case, both x and y must be closed in order for current to flow from P_1 to P_2. If either x or y is open, no current will flow.

The truth table for Fig. 2.2 is shown in Table 2.13.

Table 2.13 Truth table for series switching network

x	y	$f(x,y)$
1	1	1
1	0	0
0	1	0
0	0	0

For this network, $f(x,y) = x \wedge y$, which means that *both* x AND y must have the value 1 (closed) in order for the network to have the value 1 (current flows from P_1 to P_2). If the reader will refer back to the discussion relating to Table 2.3, he will see that the truth tables are identical.

It is possible to have a two-switch network that has a different configuration than the one illustrated in Fig. 2.2. Figure 2.3 shows a two-switch network with the switches arranged in what is called a *parallel* configuration.

In this network current will flow from P_1 to P_2 if *either* switch x is closed or switch y is closed or if both switches are closed. The only way in

Fig. 2.2

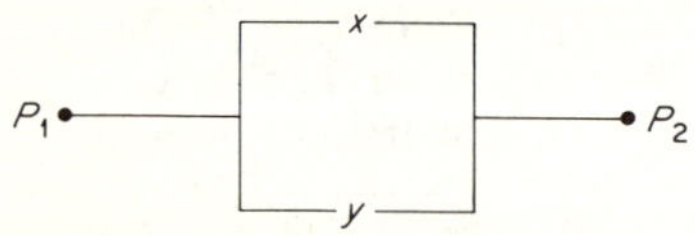

Fig. 2.3

which the current can be kept from flowing is if *both* switch x and switch y are open. The truth table for this network is given in Table 2.14. For this network, $f(x,y) = (x \wedge y) \vee (x \wedge y') \vee (x' \wedge y)$. The reader will also note that the truth table in Table 2.14 is identical with that given in Table 2.4 for the compound statement $A \vee B$. Since this is so, and substituting x and y for A and B, $x \vee y$ should be equivalent to $(x \wedge y) \vee (x \wedge y') \vee (x' \wedge y)$. This is indeed so, by definition, since $x \vee y$ is defined as meaning: either x and not y, or not x and y, or both x and y.

Table 2.14 Truth table for parallel switching network

X	Y	$F(X,Y)$
1	1	1
1	0	1
0	1	1
0	0	0

It seems appropriate at this time to add another rule or axiom to those discussed previously; we shall state it as follows:

Axiom 9: Functions having identical truth tables are identical to each other.

Let us illustrate one other switching network which is slightly more complex than the ones previously shown. In this network a single switch x is in parallel with two other switches y and z which are in series with each other. This is shown in Fig. 2.4.

In this network current will flow if either switch x is closed or if both switches y and z are closed or if all three switches are closed. The truth

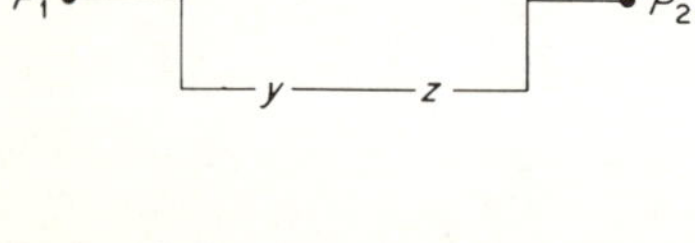

Fig. 2.4

Table 2.15 Truth table for three-switch network

x	y	z	$f(x,y,z)$
1	1	1	1
1	1	0	1
1	0	1	1
1	0	0	1
0	1	1	1
0	1	0	0
0	0	1	0
0	0	0	0

table for this network is given in Table 2.15. For this configuration of switches,

$$f(x,y,z) = (x \wedge y \wedge z) \vee (x \wedge y \wedge z') \vee (x \wedge y' \wedge z) \vee (x' \wedge y \wedge z)$$

2.6 PHYSICAL APPLICATION: COMPUTER CIRCUITS

Electronic digital computers use electric pulses or signals to represent numbers. In the binary number system utilized in digital computers, the only digits used are zero and 1. A 1 could be represented by an electric signal, and a zero could be represented by the absence of a signal. In reality, zeros and 1s are represented by signals at different voltage levels. In this application, the variables or elements of the system with which we are concerned are electric signals which can take on a state characterized by the value zero or 1.

These signals can be combined or operated upon by means of electronic devices called *gates*. We shall consider three types of gates which will be called AND GATES, OR GATES, and INVERTERS, and which have the following characteristics.

An AND GATE receives several inputs having values either zero or 1. The output is 1 only if ALL the inputs are 1; otherwise the output is zero. This operation resembles the logical AND previously discussed.

An OR GATE receives several inputs having values either zero or 1. The output is 1 if ANY of the inputs is 1. The output is zero only if ALL the inputs are zero. This operation resembles the logical OR.

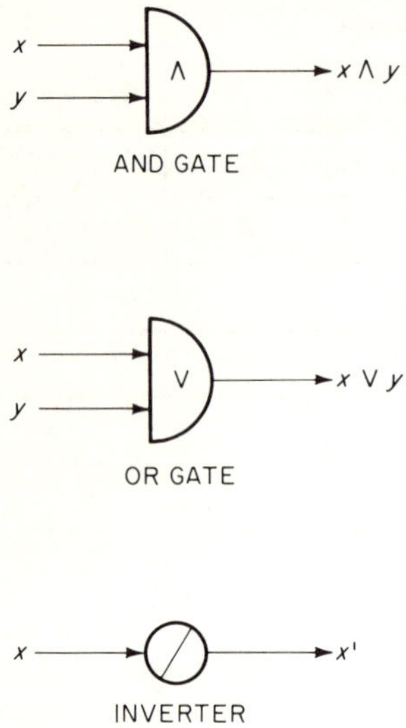

Fig. 2.5

An inverter receives a single input having a value either zero or 1, and its output is the opposite of its input. This operation corresponds to the NEGATION or NOT operation previously discussed.

The gates used to perform these operations are represented diagrammatically as shown in Fig. 2.5.

Our problem here is somewhat different from that described in the switching application where a switching network was given and the truth table and function were derived from the given network. Here we want to design a circuit having certain characteristics which we shall describe by constructing a truth table first, then we shall derive the function that satisfies the desired characteristics from the truth table, and finally we shall draw the corresponding circuit.

Table 2.16 Truth table for computer circuit

x	y	$f(x,y)$
1	1	0
1	0	1
0	1	1
0	0	0

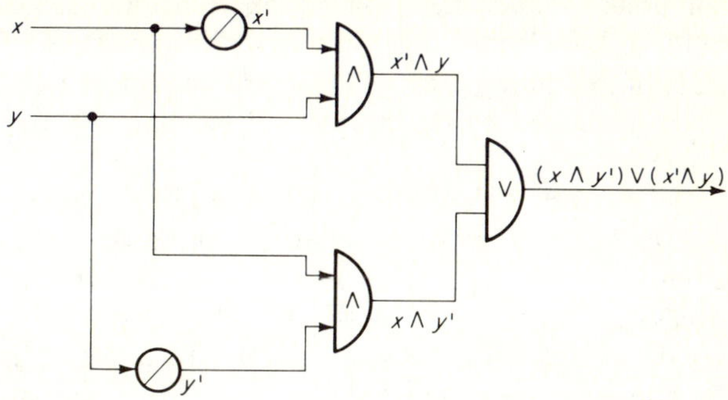

Fig. 2.6

Suppose we wish to design a circuit such that when the inputs are the same, the output is zero, and when the inputs are different, the output is 1. We would begin by constructing the truth table in Table 2.16.

The reader should note that Table 2.16 is identical with Table 2.11, and therefore the function is also the same. That is, $f(x,y) = (x \wedge y') \vee (x' \wedge y)$. Since the ANDs are represented physically by AND GATES, the ORS by OR GATES, and the NEGATIONS by INVERTERS, the circuit would contain two AND GATES, one OR GATE, and two INVERTERS. This can be determined simply by counting the connectives and negations in the function. All that is required is to follow the directions provided by the function to construct the circuit. The function says that an x input and a y' input are put through an AND GATE while another y input and an x' input are put through another AND GATE. Then the outputs of both AND GATES are put through an OR GATE. Whenever the function indicates that a negated variable is required as an input to some other gate, we simply put the required variable through an INVERTER. The required circuit is shown in Fig. 2.6.

2.7 SUMMARY

In searching for an unambiguous way of describing conditions and situations, we have adopted the conventions and symbols of logic or boolean algebra. By utilizing these symbols, rules, and associated techniques, we have devised a useful way for translating statements of both abstract and physical conditions into an unambiguous form which is, in fact, a logical model of the situation or condition with which we are concerned. We can also use the general terms *system* and *components* in referring to the situation or condition which we are modeling and which requires that a decision be made. Since the state of a complex system is uniquely determined by the states of its components and their logical relationships to one another, these logical models provide a means for determining the state of the system for any given state of its components. They also provide a means for working backward from a desired system state to determine the required states of the components.

We found that we can work in either direction, beginning either from a given system configuration and going to the logical relationships among its components or from a set of desired logical relationships and going to the necessary system configuration. This transition, back and forth, is facilitated by means of the truth table. In a broad sense, the truth table, the functional expression, and the diagrammatic representation of the system can all be considered logical models.

PROBLEMS

2.1. Let A stand for the simple statement "John is a good student." Let B stand for "John is a fast worker." Let C be "Mary is helping John." Write the following statements symbolically:

(*a*) John is a good student and a fast worker.
(*b*) John is a good student but he is slow.
(*c*) Either John is a good student or Mary is helping him.
(*d*) Either John is a good student or he is a poor student and Mary is helping him.
(*e*) John is a good student but Mary is helping him.
(*f*) John is not a good student and he is slow but Mary is helping him.

2.2. Let A represent the simple statement "It is cold." Let B represent the simple statement "It is snowing." Write the following statements in symbolic form.

(*a*) It is cold and it is snowing.
(*b*) It is cold but it is not snowing.
(*c*) It is not cold but it is snowing.
(*d*) It is either cold or it is snowing.
(*e*) It is either cold or it is not snowing.
(*f*) It is not cold and it is not snowing.
(*g*) It is either not cold or it is snowing.

2.3. Let A represent the simple statement "Frank is thirsty." Let B represent the simple statement "Frank is hungry." Translate the following symbolic statements into ordinary language.

(*a*) $A \wedge B'$
(*b*) $A \vee B$
(*c*) $(A \wedge B)' \vee (A \vee B)$
(*d*) $(A' \vee B') \vee (A \vee B)$
(*e*) $(A \wedge B') \vee (A' \wedge B)$
(*f*) $(A \vee B') \wedge B$

2.4. If A is the simple statement "Costs are rising" and B stands for "Profits are higher than last year" and C is "Sales are good this year," write the following statements in symbolic form:

(*a*) Sales are good but costs are rising.

(*b*) Costs are rising but profits are higher than last year.

(*c*) Either profits are down from last year or sales are bad or costs are rising.

(*d*) Either profits are down from last year or sales are down and costs are rising.

(*e*) Either sales are good and costs are rising or costs are not rising but sales are down.

2.5. Suppose A represents the statement "All the tickets have been sold" and B is the statement "There are empty seats." Provide a verbal translation for the following symbolic expressions:

(*a*) $A \wedge B$

(*b*) $A \wedge B'$

(*c*) $A' \wedge B$

(*d*) $A \veebar B$

(*e*) $(A \wedge B)'$

2.6. Let A represent the simple statement "The market is good." Let B represent the simple statement "Interest rates are high." Let C represent the simple statement "Labor is scarce." Write the following statements in symbolic form:

(*a*) The market is good and labor is not scarce but interest rates are high.

(*b*) Either the market is good and labor is not scarce or interest rates are high.

(*c*) Either the market is good or labor is scarce and interest rates are high or the market is good and interest rates are high and labor is scarce.

(*d*) The market is not good and interest rates are high or interest rates are not high and labor is scarce or the market is good and labor is scarce.

2.7. Let A, B, and C represent the same statements as given in Prob. 2.3. Translate the following symbolic statements into ordinary language.

(*a*) $A \vee B \vee C'$

(*b*) $A \wedge B' \vee C$

(*c*) $(A \wedge B) \vee C'$

(*d*) $(A \wedge C)' \vee (B \wedge C')$

(*e*) $[(A' \vee C)' \wedge B] \vee (A \vee B \wedge C)$

2.8. Let A stand for "The output is unsatisfactory." Let B stand for "The operator is skilled." Let C stand for "The machine needs adjustment." Provide verbal translations for the following:

(*a*) $A \wedge (B' \vee C)$

(*b*) $(A \wedge B)' \vee C$

(*c*) $A' \vee (B' \wedge C)$

(*d*) $A \vee (B \wedge C')$

2.9. Construct truth tables for each of the following compound statements:

(*a*) $A \wedge B'$

(*b*) $A \wedge B' \vee C$

(*c*) $A' \vee B' \vee C$

(*d*) $(A' \wedge B') \wedge (B \vee C')$

(*e*) $A \veebar B$

(*f*) $A' \veebar B \vee C$

(*g*) $(A \vee B)' \vee (A \wedge C)$

2.10. Use a truth table to find the canonical form of the following boolean polynomial:
$x \wedge y' \vee (x \wedge y)'$

2.11. Use a truth table to find the canonical form of the following expression:
$(x' \wedge y) \vee (x' \wedge z)' \vee (y \wedge z)$

2.12. Given the following truth table, find the corresponding boolean function:

x	y	z	$f(x,y,z)$
1	1	1	0
1	1	0	1
1	0	1	1
1	0	0	0
0	1	1	1
0	1	0	0
0	0	1	0
0	0	0	0

2.13. It is desired to design a switching network consisting of three switches, x, y, and z, such that x must be closed in order for the current to flow but either y or z (but not both) may be open. Find the boolean function and draw the network.

3
Logical Networks

The concept of a network has been used in many types of applications. As a management tool networks are frequently used as aids to the planning, scheduling, and controlling of many types of activities. One of the most common applications of networks in project management is in PERT, which stands for Program Evaluation and Review Technique. In a more technical environment, networks are utilized in the analysis of certain types of problems which occur in communications and electrical engineering.

Basically networks are used to illustrate dependencies or relationships between elements of a system. These elements can be electric or electronic devices, machines, jobs, events, people, and/or combinations of any or all the foregoing, depending upon the application for which the network is intended. The networks to which we shall address ourselves are simply another form of graphical model. They are a useful tool for analyzing the total decision problem by breaking it into its component parts and for providing a visual representation of the logical relationships between the parts and the total problem.

If the decision situation is not particularly complex, we might discard the network representation and work directly with truth tables or functions. However, as the problem increases in complexity, the network affords a comprehensive view of the problem which cannot be achieved either by truth tables or mathematical expressions. Furthermore, the transition from logical model to probability model to decision model is probably easier to effect by means of the network.

The network considered in this chapter is called a *logical network* since it represents a logical model of the total system. That is, it is assumed that each component can assume only one of two states, good or bad, and that these states are completely determinable for each component. The network, as for any logical model, determines the system state resulting from any combination of component states, or, conversely, by working backward from a desired system state, determines the required component states.

When component states are not completely determinable, which is usually the case, they can be expressed in terms of probabilities. The *probability network* will be examined later, after a study of the elements of probability theory. Recognition of the rather obvious fact that the component states need not always be either absolutely good or absolutely bad will also be considered later in a discussion of value networks or decision trees. This latter discussion will appear in Part 4 of this book, which covers decision theory and in which the economic consequences resulting from the decision acts will be considered as part of the decision model.

3.1 COMPONENT STATES AND STATES OF NATURE

The components of a decision problem are essentially those external factors and conditions which are beyond the control of the decision maker but which influence or affect the consequences of a decision. In later chapters on statistical decision theory, these factors are referred to as "states of nature." In the simpler decision theory problems, there is generally a single category of nature which can assume one of two or more states and which must be evaluated by the decision maker. For example, in some elementary problems nature might be the national economy and its states a high level of economic activity versus a low level. Nature might be the demand for a particular product during some specified time period, and its states would correspond to the actual numbers of the product demanded in that time period. In other situations nature might be the capability of a manufacturing process to produce good or defective parts, and its states would then be various values of the proportion of such parts which are defective.

In these and similar situations, decisions are based on the particular value of the single category of nature which is pertinent to the problem at hand. Complex decision problems which face management, however, are generally not limited to a single category of nature but involve many so-

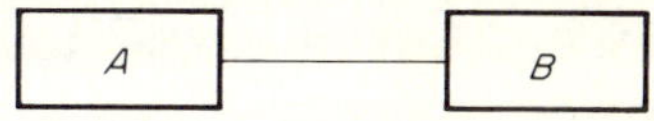

Fig. 3.1

called states of nature. Demand for a product may be only one factor bearing on a particular decision. Process capability may be another, economic conditions a third, competitors' actions a fourth, etc.

The logical model or network discussed here is simply a method for identifying all such component states of nature which are pertinent to the problem and relating them to one another and to the overall decision situation in such a way that the state of this overall decision situation can be evaluated.

3.2 SYMBOLS AND NOTATION

Let us, at this point, describe the graphical symbols which will be used in developing the logical network. The total system of states will be designated S. The states of the system and its components are limited here to either *good* or *bad*, and, where it assists the analysis and the decision process, the good state will be given the arbitrary value 1, and the bad state the value zero. Therefore, $S = 1$ implies that the system is good, $S = 0$ implies that the system is bad.

System components will be identified by capital letters A, B, C, etc. We must also provide for the possibility of major components of the system, of minor components, which are themselves components of the major components, of subminor components which make up the minor components, and so on, down to whatever level of detail appears practical for evaluation. These various levels will be identified by subscripts.

If A is a major component of S, then A_i represents a component of A, A_{ij} represents a component of A_i, and A_{ijk} is a component of A_{ij}. Finer distinctions can be made, if necessary, by the use of additional subscripts.

Since the logical OR is roughly equivalent to the addition process in standard algebras, we may use the plus sign to replace the $\vee$ when there is no danger of misunderstanding what is intended. Therefore, $A \vee B$ could be written $A + B$.

Also, since the logical AND is roughly equivalent to multiplication, we may use a dot instead of the $\wedge$, so that $A \wedge B$ could be written $A \cdot B$ or simply AB.

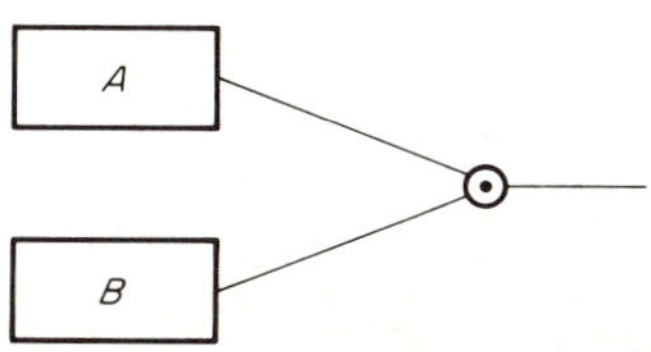

Fig. 3.2

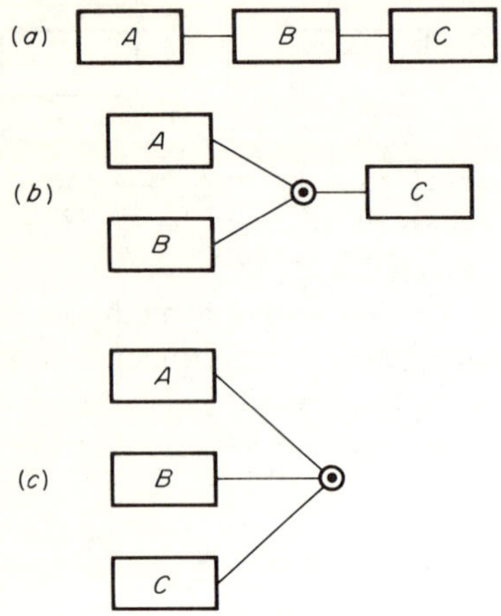

Fig. 3.3

In the network representation, components will be represented by rectangular boxes. A component *A* would appear as $\boxed{A}$.

If two components, say *A* and *B*, are both required to be in the good state in order for the system to be good, they can be represented by the diagram in Fig. 3.1 in which the boxes are in series.

Any number of components can be drawn in series; however, as the network becomes complicated, the stringing out of boxes in a horizontal line becomes awkward. In this case, an alternate and preferred representation

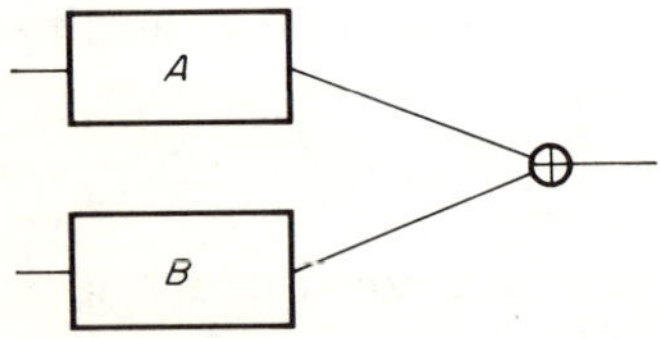

Fig. 3.4

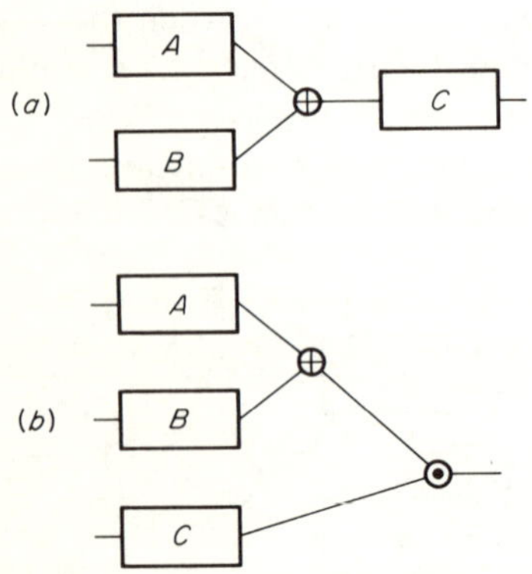

Fig. 3.5

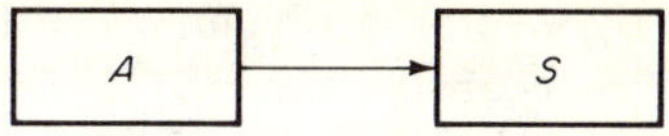

Fig. 3.6

is shown in Fig. 3.2, in which the ⊙ stands for the logical AND and both diagrams represent A AND B.

A AND B AND C could be shown in either of the ways illustrated in Fig. 3.3.

If either A or B or both would suffice in order for the system to be good, the representation in Fig. 3.4 is used.

Three or more components OR'd together would be represented by that number of boxes leading into the ⊕ symbol.

The similarity between these diagrams and the switching networks illustrated in Chap. 2 should be noted.

The configurations illustrated in Fig. 3.5 are equivalent to either A or B or both and then C, that is $(A + B)C$ or alternatively $(A \vee B) \wedge C$.

One final symbol is needed at this stage of the process to aid in the representation. This symbol is the arrow, used as shown in Fig. 3.6. The arrow simply means that A belongs to or is a part of S; that is, A is one of the components of S. The arrow in the network context is equivalent to the symbol $\in$ in symbolic logic. For example, in the network Fig. 3.7, the arrow simply shows that components A_1, A_2, and A_3 all belong to A, which is the next higher-level component in the network. It does not indicate that A_3 is in series with A.

3.3 PROBLEM FORMULATION

Given a complex decision problem which is dependent upon the answers to an interrelated series of subproblems, or, to use the convention adopted here, given a complex system the state of which is dependent upon the state of its components, we are faced with the difficult task of developing a suitable model. The more complex the system, the more complex the model. As is the case with any complex problem, the solution is facilitated by identifying the components and the subcomponents until a level is reached at which individual solutions can be derived and then recombined into a solution to

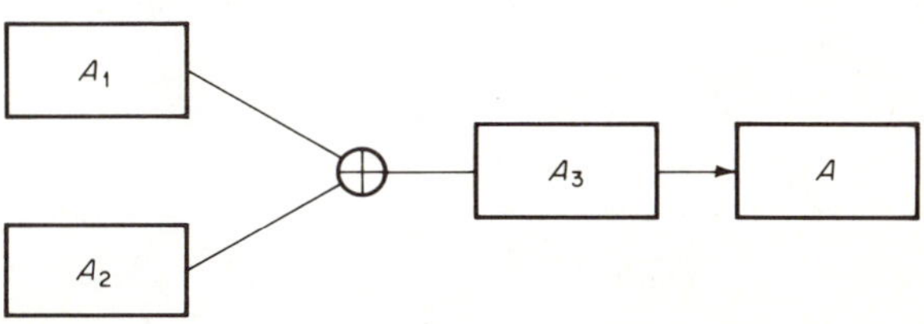

Fig. 3.7

the overall problem. The process then becomes one of reduction followed by reconstruction.

In analyzing the total problem system, interest must center on those components whose states do indeed affect the system state. For example, suppose we consider two components, A and B. We judge, at least from the standpoint of the logical model, that both A and B should be good in order for the system to be good, but after further consideration we decide that if A is good the system could be considered good even if B is bad. (The more reasonable situation is one in which a scale of values is allotted to both A and B and the system is good if A is very good and B is not too bad; however, this type of situation will not be considered at this point.)

The logical relationship between A, B, and the system S would then be represented by the equation

$$S = (A \wedge B) \vee (A \wedge B')$$

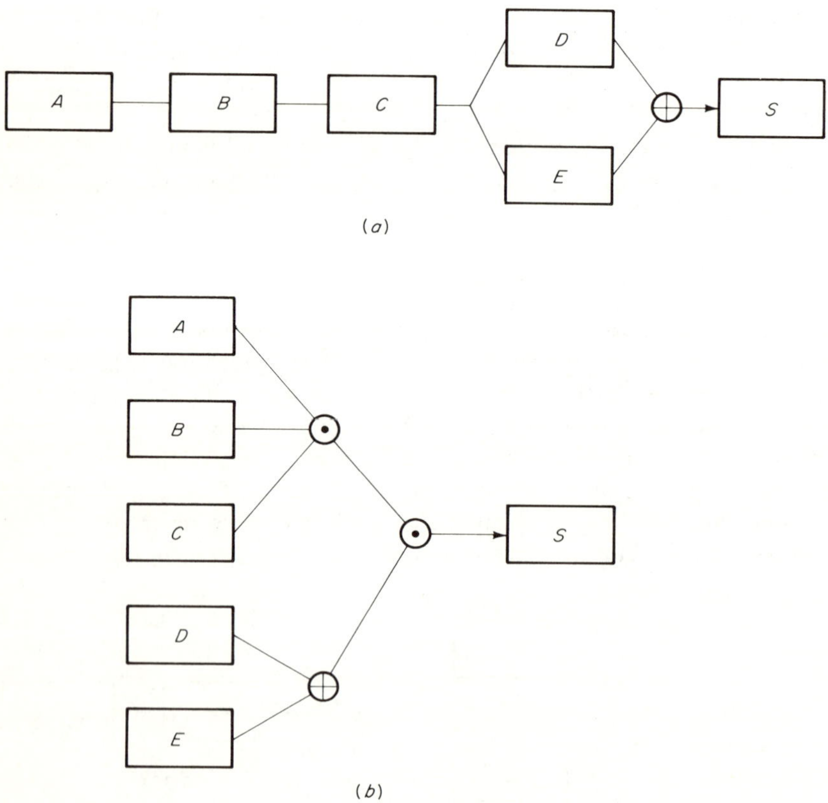

Fig. 3.8

By algebraic simplification this reduces to

$$S = A \wedge (B \vee B')$$

but $B \vee B' = 1$ by axiom 7 of the boolean algebra and $S = A \wedge 1 = A$ by axiom 8. Therefore, $S = A$, which shows that the system state is dependent on A above and independent of B. B can therefore be eliminated from the model.

Suppose a decision must be made based on the state of system S. Analysis shows that S consists of five major components, A, B, C, D, E. The system is good if A, B, and C are all good and if either D or E is good. That is, $S = f(A,B,C,D,E)$, and, specifically, $S = (A \wedge B \wedge C) \wedge (D \vee E)$.

The network at the major component level is simple and can be shown either as Fig. 3.8*a* or *b*. The latter presentation is preferred since it tends to group components which are of the same level of importance.

The next step in the modeling process would consist of examining each of the major components to determine its minor components and their logical relationships. In this illustration we would examine major component A first. Suppose we identify four components of A which we label as A_1, A_2, A_3, and A_4. It may be difficult to determine immediately the function relating A to the A_i, and we might take the truth table approach to clarify the relationship and develop the function and, subsequently, the network. Since there are four components of A, there are $2^4 = 16$ possible combinations of component states. These are listed in the truth table in Table 3.1. The column under $A = f(A_i)$ is completed by considering each of the 16 possibilities and determining whether A is good or has the value 1 in each case. For row 16, where all four components are zero, A is obviously zero. Only a thorough knowledge of the system can lead to the evaluation of the state of A for every combination of states of its components.

The procedure which is followed here is essentially that which was described previously in Sec. 2.4.

After the $A = f(A_i)$ column is completed, we can write the function in canonical form by ORing all those terms for which $f(A_i) = 1$. This produces

$$(A_1 \wedge A_2 \wedge A_3 \wedge A_4) \vee (A_1 \wedge A_2 \wedge A_3 \wedge A_4') \vee$$
$$(A_1 \wedge A_2 \wedge A_3' \wedge A_4) \vee (A_1 \wedge A_2 \wedge A_3' \wedge A_4') \vee$$
$$(A_1 \wedge A_2' \wedge A_3 \wedge A_4') \vee (A_1 \wedge A_2' \wedge A_3 \wedge A_4).$$

By combining terms according to the axioms and theorems of boolean algebra, the canonical form of the function can be converted to

$$A = f(A_i) = A_1 \wedge (A_2 \vee A_3)$$

which indicates that the function A is not dependent upon A_4, which can be eliminated. The logical network for component A can be drawn as shown in Fig. 3.9.

Table 3.1 Truth table for evaluating component A

A_1	A_2	A_3	A_4	$A = f(A_i)$
1	1	1	1	1
1	1	1	0	1
1	1	0	1	1
1	1	0	0	1
1	0	1	1	1
1	0	1	0	1
1	0	0	1	0
1	0	0	0	0
0	1	1	1	0
0	1	1	0	0
0	1	0	1	0
0	1	0	0	0
0	0	1	1	0
0	0	1	0	0
0	0	0	1	0
0	0	0	0	0

The other major components can be approached in the same manner resulting in, let us say,

$$B = B_1 \wedge B_2$$
$$C = (C_1 \wedge C_2) \vee C_3$$
$$D = (D_1 \vee D_2) \wedge (D_3 \vee D_4)$$

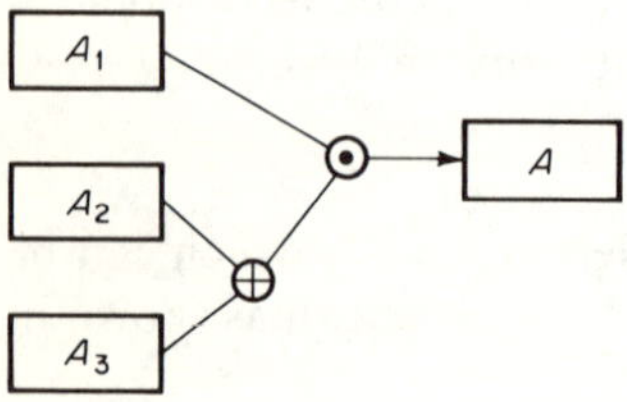

Fig. 3.9

and

$$E = E$$

That is, there are no pertinent components of E.

Each of the minor components of the A_i, B_i, C_i, and D_i must also be approached in the same way. Let us assume that this results in the following functions:

$$A_1 = A_1, A_2 = A_{21} \wedge A_{22}, A_3 = A_{31} \vee A_{32}$$
$$B_1 = B_{11} \wedge B_{12}, B_2 = B_2$$
$$C_1 = C_1, C_2 = C_{21} \vee C_{22}, C_3 = C_{31} \vee C_{32}$$
$$D_1 = D_{11} \wedge D_{12}, D_2 = D_2, D_3 = D_3, D_4 = D_{41} \vee D_{42}$$

And again all the A_{ij}, B_{ij}, C_{ij}, and D_{ij} must be considered for pertinent components if applicable. Let us say that in this case only B_{12} need be subdivided further and that $B_{12} = B_{121} \wedge B_{122}$.

The total system logical network would appear as shown in Fig. 3.10. The reader should verify that the network accurately depicts the functional or logical relationships listed above. The logical network provides a visual representation of the total system. All components representing the same level in the system appear in the same vertical segment of the chart. The decision maker can tell at a glance the data inputs which are required and the relationship of each component to every other component and to the system. Given the status of every component in the network, the state of the system is uniquely determined. Granted, this could also be determined from the logical equations themselves. However, a series of equations fails to provide the visual information which can be derived from the network representation.

3.4 SYSTEM EVALUATION FROM THE LOGICAL NETWORK

Consider the network in Fig. 3.10. Starting at the lowest-level component of the system, a value zero or 1 is assigned depending upon whether that component is good or bad. The determination of the state of the component is based on investigation, data, judgment, or a combination of all three. Suppose the following values have been assigned:

For major component A, it has been determined that

$$A_1 = 1$$
$$A_{21} = 1, A_{22} = 1$$
$$A_{31} = 0, A_{32} = 1$$

Then

$$A_2 = A_{21} \wedge A_{22} = 1$$
$$A_3 = A_{31} \vee A_{32} = 1$$

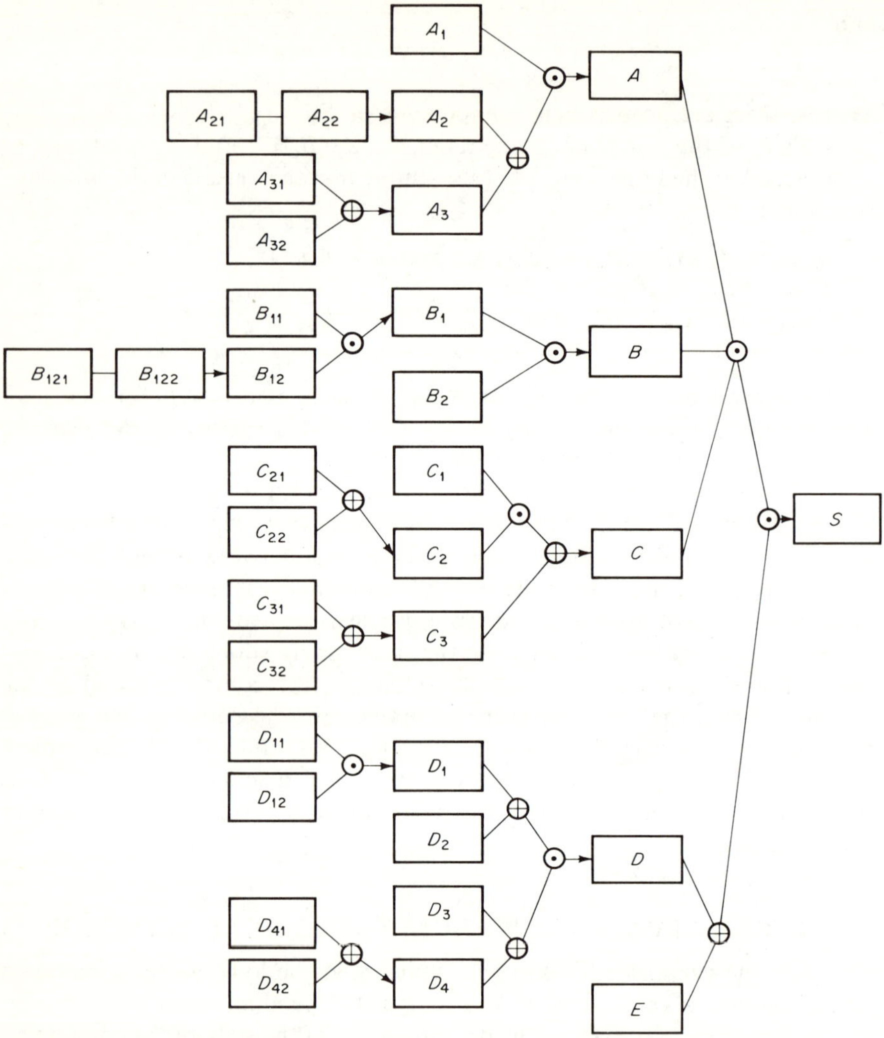

Fig. 3.10 Logical network.

and

$$A = A_1 \wedge (A_2 \vee A_3) = 1$$

For major component B, it has been determined that

$$B_2 = 1$$
$$B_{11} = 1$$
$$B_{121} = 1, B_{122} = 1$$

Then

$$B_{12} = B_{121} \wedge B_{122} = 1$$
$$B_1 = B_{11} \wedge B_{12} = 1$$

and

$$B = B_1 \wedge B_2 = 1$$

For major component C, it has been determined that

$$C_1 = 1$$
$$C_{21} = 1, C_{22} = 0$$
$$C_{31} = 0, C_{32} = 0$$

Then

$$C_2 = C_{21} \vee C_{22} = 1$$
$$C_3 = C_{31} \vee C_{32} = 0$$

and

$$C = (C_1 \wedge C_2) \vee C_3 = 1$$

For major component D, it has been determined that

$$D_{11} = 1, D_{12} = 0$$
$$D_2 = 0$$
$$D_3 = 1$$
$$D_{41} = 1, D_{42} = 0$$

Then

$$D_1 = D_{11} \wedge D_{12} = 0$$
$$D_4 = D_{41} \vee D_{42} = 1$$

and

$$D = (D_1 \vee D_2) \wedge (D_3 \vee D_4) = 0$$

It has been determined that

$$E = 1$$

Therefore, for system S

$$S = A \wedge B \wedge C \wedge (D \vee E) = 1$$

On the basis of the logical network and the component states, the system state is good.

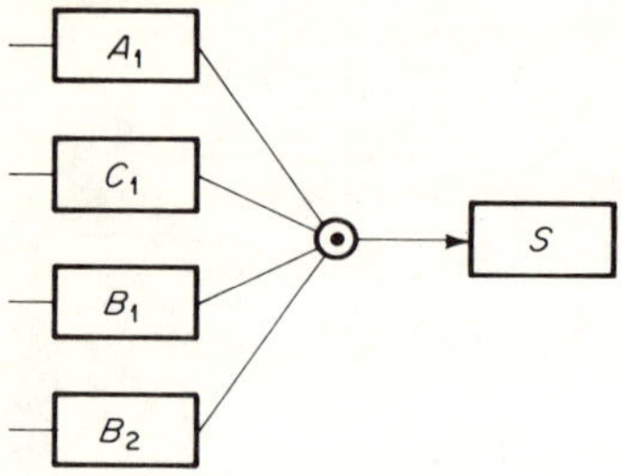

Fig. 3.11

3.5 INTERDEPENDENCE OF COMPONENTS

It is quite conceivable that some one component could affect more than one higher-level component. Consider a system $S = A \wedge B$ in which both A and B are dependent upon some other component. Since this third component affects S only indirectly through A and B, it cannot be considered to be on the same level as A and B but is, in effect, a component of both A and B. Let us call this third component C_1. Suppose

$$A = A_1 \wedge C_1$$

and

$$B = B_1 \wedge B_2 \wedge C_1$$

Then

$$S = A \wedge B = (A_1 \wedge C_1) \wedge (B_1 \wedge B_2 \wedge C_1) = A_1 \wedge B_1 \wedge B_2 \wedge C_1$$

and could be diagrammed as shown in Fig. 3.11.

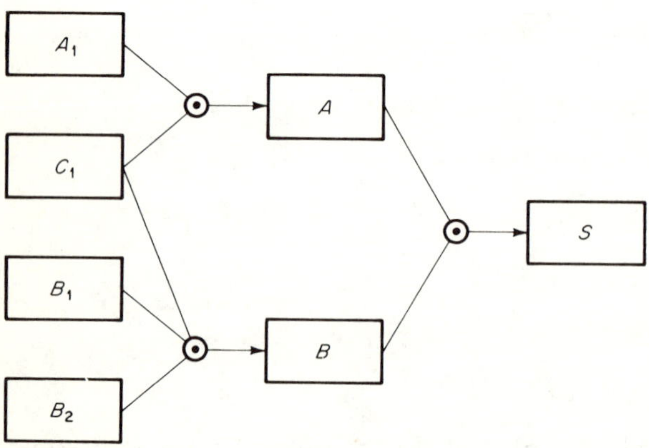

Fig. 3.12

Table 3.2

B_1	B_2	A_1	A_2	A_3	$B_1 \wedge B_2 \wedge A_1$	$A_1 \wedge A_2$	$A_1 \wedge A_2 \vee A_3$	S
1	1	1	1	1	1	1	1	1
1	1	1	1	0	1	1	1	1
1	1	1	0	1	1	0	1	1
1	1	1	0	0	1	0	0	0

But since we wish to show that C acts on S through A and B, the diagram that would better illustrate the relationship is Fig. 3.12, which shows that C_1 affects both A and B.

As another illustration, again let $S = A \wedge B$. Let $A = (A_1 \wedge A_2) \vee A_3$, and $B = (B_1 \wedge B_2) \wedge A_1$. Then $S = [(A_1 \wedge A_2) \vee A_3] \wedge B_1 \wedge B_2 \wedge A_1$.

Let us use the truth table to clarify these relationships. Since we have five components, we would need $2^5 = 32$ rows in the truth table. However, it is obvious from the equation $S = [(A_1 \wedge A_2) \vee A_3] \wedge B_1 \wedge B_2 \wedge A_1$ that in order for $S = 1$, B_1, B_2, and A_1 must all equal 1. Therefore, we can construct a partial truth table where we use only those rows where A_1, B_1, and B_2 are 1. This is done in Table 3.2.

The function in canonical form is then

$$\begin{aligned} S &= A_1A_2A_3B_1B_2 \vee A_1A_2A_3'B_1B_2 \vee A_1A_2'A_3B_1B_2 \\ &= A_1B_1B_2(A_2A_3 \vee A_2A_3' \vee A_2'A_3) \end{aligned}$$

and since the expression in parentheses is simply $A_2 \vee A_3$,

$$S = A_1B_1B_2(A_2 \vee A_3)$$

The logical network could then be drawn as given in Fig. 3.13.

However, since this fails to show the manner in which A_1 affects the system, the preferable representation would be as shown in Fig. 3.14.

The recognition of the interdependence of certain components within the system also allows for the consideration of time phasing of certain activi-

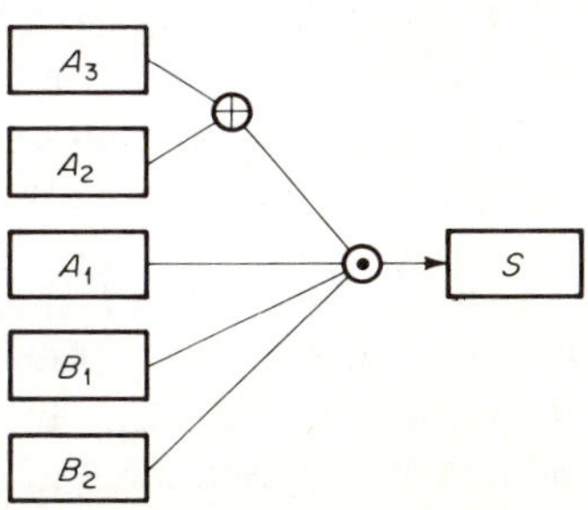

Fig. 3.13

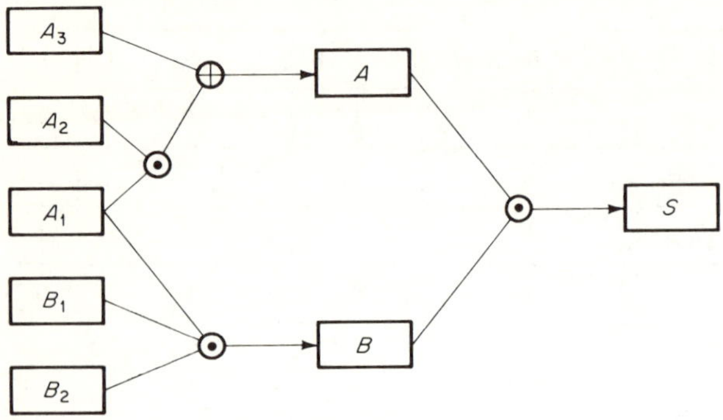

Fig. 3.14

ties. Since, in the first illustration, both major components, A and B, were dependent upon C_1, this particular logical relationship might indicate that work leading to the evaluation of C_1 should precede any work involved in the evaluation of A and B. If C_1 is bad, value zero, then A and B are both bad regardless of the value of any of their components.

3.6 SEQUENTIAL LOGICAL DECISIONS

The network we have considered so far leads to a single decision about the state of the system, or, to be more precise, an evaluation of the state of the system which leads to a single decision. In a practical situation, it is quite likely that the problem is such that several decisions are made in sequence. In other words, the final decision regarding the major problem or system is made only after several intermediate decisions are made. The intermediate decisions are probably sequential in a time domain so that some portions of the total system are evaluated, a decision made as to whether or not to proceed further, and, if so, how; then the next portion evaluated, another decision made, etc.

Any intermediate decision can provide two or more alternatives. Depending upon the state of the system up to that decision point, the decision made could be to stop, that is to cancel, the project or to continue. If the decision is to continue, it may be necessary to make a selection between alternative courses of action.

This factor of intermediate decisions does not affect the approach described in the least. The network leading to each sequential decision point is constructed and evaluated as shown previously. When the first decision is made, then a new network is constructed leading to the second decision point, etc. If a decision point is reached after the evaluation of major component A, we shall label this decision α. If decision α has two alternatives, we shall call them α_1 and α_2. Each alternative can lead to a different course of action; let us say α_1 leads to an evaluation of major component B, while α_2 leads to an evaluation of major component C. If a decision is to be made after B is evaluated, this decision will be labeled β. The decision based on the state of C is labeled γ.

The state of the total system S is arrived at in successive steps as each sequentially occurring major component is evaluated in succession.

In order to illustrate the occurrence of sequential decision points in the network, we shall introduce one new symbol which we shall call a *decision box*, drawn as a small square, and identified with a Greek letter as shown below.

$\boxed{\alpha}$

If the decision box follows A and represents a choice between two alternatives, the diagram would be as given in Fig. 3.15.

The α decision box indicates that the state $A = 1$ leads to decision α_1, while the state $A = 0$ leads to α_2. Obviously, $A = 0$ is equivalent to $A' = 1$.

If the decision α is a decision to continue the project or cancel it, then α_1 leads to the next set of components to be evaluated if the program continues, while α_2 leads to cancellation.

On the other hand, if α is a choice between two alternative approaches, both α_1 and α_2 lead to different sets of components to be evaluated.

Suppose α_1 leads to major component B while α_2 leads to C. Then α_1 and α_2 are both starting points for a logical network to B and C. If the decision α_1 is made, then the system $S = AB$. If α_2 is made, then $S = A'C$. Which of these is the true system state cannot be known until that portion of the system leading up to decision box α is evaluated.

If B and C each consist of numerous components, the network beginning with decision α and leading to B or C should most conveniently be drawn separately rather than attempting to show A, B, C, and any subsequent component networks in detail as one sheet. If the major components are relatively few in number and not too complex, the related networks might be drawn as shown in Fig. 3.16.

Keep in mind that all logical networks ultimately lead to a decision box. In evaluating system state, when the system is good, a decision is made to act in one way. When the system is bad, a decision is made to act in another way. This could be shown as in Fig. 3.17.

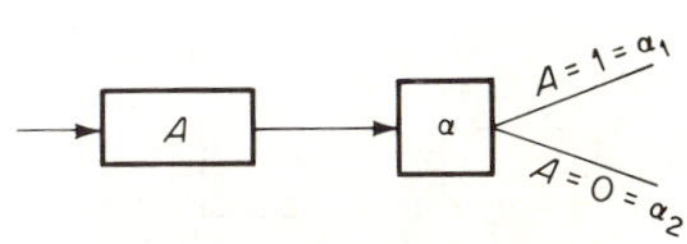

Fig. 3.15

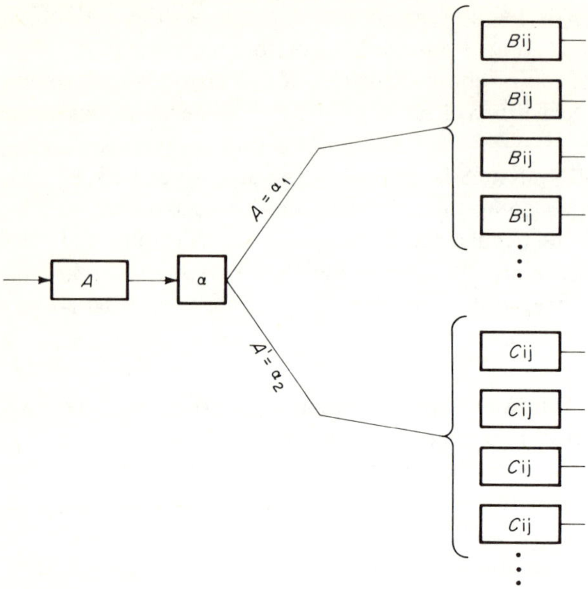

Fig. 3.16

3.7 SUMMARY

The development of a logical network to facilitate the decision process stems readily from the theoretical foundations established in the previous chapter. Truth tables, boolean functions, and the network itself work together to provide the decision maker with a comprehensible representation of the total decision problem. This particular network is, of course, limited to a two-state evaluation of the problem, but even so, it is not unlikely that situations may arise where complex decisions must be made in the absence of information other than the good-bad, go-no-go evaluations for which this model is suited.

The graphical symbols used in the network presentation have been described, and the processes of problem formulation in network terms and network evaluation have been illustrated. Attention has been devoted to the incorporation of sequential decisions into the network, and it has been shown that the matter of sequential decisions does not affect the basic approach to the network development in this type of situation.

Fig. 3.17

Probability networks in which the probability of a component being in either state will be discussed subsequently. However, a consideration of the elements of probability theory must be a prerequisite. Before looking into the theory of probability, however, we shall first consider a hypothetical case study which relates the methodology of this chapter to a practical situation.

PROBLEMS

3.1. Construct a logical network for components *A*, *B*, *C*, and *D* showing that either *A* and *B* or *C* and *D* must be good in order for the system to be good.

3.2. Construct a logical network for components *A*, *B*, *C*, and *D* such that the system is good if either *A* or *B* is good or both *C* and *D* are good.

3.3. Consider a system consisting of three major components, *A*, *B*, and *C*. *A* consists of two components, either one of which must be good for *A* to be good. *B* consists of two components both of which must be good in order for *B* to be good. *C* consists of three components; if C_1 is good, *C* is good even though C_2 and C_3 are bad. If C_1 is bad, both C_2 and C_3 must be good. If *A* is bad, the system is bad regardless of the states of the other two major components. However, if *A* is good, the system is good if either *B* or *C*, but not both, is bad.

3.4. For the system described in Prob. 3.3, given the following component states, determine the system state.

(*a*) $A_1 = 1, A_2 = 0, B_1 = 0, B_2 = 0, C_1 = 0, C_2 = 1, C_3 = 1$
(*b*) $A_1 = 0, A_2 = 0, B_1 = 1, B_2 = 1, C_1 = 1, C_2 = 1, C_3 = 1$
(*c*) $A_1 = 0, A_2 = 1, B_1 = 1, B_2 = 1, C_1 = 1, C_2 = 0, C_3 = 1$
(*d*) $A_1 = 0, A_2 = 0, B_1 = 1, B_2 = 1, C_1 = 1, C_2 = 1, C_3 = 0$
(*e*) $A_1 = 1, A_2 = 0, B_1 = 1, B_2 = 0, C_1 = 1, C_2 = 1, C_3 = 1$
(*f*) $A_1 = 1, A_2 = 1, B_1 = 1, B_2 = 1, C_1 = 0, C_2 = 0, C_3 = 1$

3.5. Given the following relationships and the partial truth table below,

(*a*) Complete the truth table.
(*b*) Write the system equation in canonical form.
(*c*) Draw the logical diagram as simply as possible.

$A = A_1 \vee A_2 \qquad B = A_2 \wedge B_1 \qquad S = A \wedge B$

A_1	A_2	B_1	A	B	S
1	1	1			
1	1	0			
1	0	1			
1	0	0			
0	1	1			
0	1	0			
0	0	1			
0	0	0			

3.6. Consider the system in Prob. 3.5. Suppose A_1 consists of components A_{11} and A_{12} such that either A_{11} or A_{12} must be good in order that A_1 be good. Suppose B_1 consists of B_{11} and B_{12} such that both B_{11} and B_{12} must be good in order that B_1 be good. There are no components of A_2. Given the following states, determine the system state.

(*a*) $A_{11} = 0, A_{12} = 0, B_{11} = 1, B_{12} = 1, A_2 = 1$
(*b*) $A_{11} = 1, A_{12} = 1, B_{11} = 1, B_{12} = 1, A_2 = 0$
(*c*) $A_{11} = 1, A_{12} = 0, B_{11} = 0, B_{12} = 0, A_2 = 1$
(*d*) $A_{11} = 0, A_{12} = 1, B_{11} = 1, B_{12} = 0, A_2 = 0$
(*e*) $A_{11} = 0, A_{12} = 0, B_{11} = 0, B_{12} = 1, A_2 = 1$
(*f*) $A_{11} = 0, A_{12} = 1, B_{11} = 1, B_{12} = 1, A_2 = 1$

3.7. A decision must be made with respect to some system S consisting of subsystems A, B, and C. A consists of components A_1, A_2, and A_3 such that in order for A to be good, A_1 and either A_2 or A_3 must be good. Subsystems B and C have no components. It has been decided to evaluate subsystem A first. If A is bad, the program will be canceled immediately. If A is good, subsystems B and C will be evaluated. If both are good, S is good, meaning the project will be implemented; otherwise, it will be canceled. Construct a logical network showing the components and decision boxes involved.

3.8. Consider the system in Prob. 3.7. For the component states listed below, will the project be implemented or canceled, and at what stage?

(*a*) $A_1 = 0, A_2 = 1, A_3 = 1, B = 1, C = 1$
(*b*) $A_1 = 1, A_2 = 0, A_3 = 0, B = 1, C = 0$
(*c*) $A_1 = 1, A_2 = 1, A_3 = 0, B = 0, C = 1$
(*d*) $A_1 = 1, A_2 = 1, A_3 = 0, B = 1, C = 1$
(*e*) $A_1 = 1, A_2 = 0, A_3 = 1, B = 1, C = 1$
(*f*) $A_1 = 1, A_2 = 1, A_3 = 0, B = 0, C = 1$

4
Case Study: Logical Decisions

This case study and others which follow are hypothetical. They are based on information taken from various sources and pertain to real situations but are developed in such a way as to best illustrate the procedures and techniques discussed without introducing complicating details of little significance. The decision situations in the case studies are simplified for the same reasons. These case studies are designed to illustrate major points of the theory. If this can be done simply, there is no reason to introduce undue complexities.

The reader is cautioned, however, that real-life situations are seldom as simple as those illustrated. The world has a way of clouding issues with many seemingly insignificant details. The techniques illustrated here are just as effective regardless, but it is incumbent upon the decision maker to identify those features which are significant, separate them from those that are not, and apply the proper techniques to the former.

A real decision situation, no matter how complicated, can, with patience, be broken down into its component parts to any level of detail desired, a process of reduction; solutions then can be found for the individual components; and the overall solution can be achieved by a continued application of the logic process.

4.1 THE PENNWOOD CASE

The Pennwood Corporation is a manufacturer of heating and air conditioning systems. The major portion of its business consists of sales to building contractors who install Pennwood systems in newly constructed homes. Pennwood also sells smaller room air conditioners, which are marketed by department stores and appliance stores, but this product represents a relatively small proportion of their sales.

Sales of central heating and air conditioning systems are heavily influenced by the housing market, and Pennwood can predict future business with a reasonable degree of accuracy on the basis of building permits issued during some previous period plus several other factors. The procedure used for this prediction or forecast is that of a multiple regression analysis.*

Engineers in Pennwood's engineering development division have been working for some time on the heat pump principle. This is a single unit which would both heat and cool a structure and would be controlled from a single thermostatic device. The major obstacle to widespread use of the heat pump has been its cost, which was so high as to prohibit its use in all but the most expensive of residences. Pennwood engineers have been working to reduce the cost in order to make it feasible for use in less expensive houses. Their goal was to develop a unit that would cost the homeowner about $2,600 installed. Considering the typical markup required by contractors, this would require that the unit be sold to the contractor for $1,400.

Pennwood's engineering development division has finally come up with a new design. The estimated manufacturing cost of the newly designed unit is either $900 or $1,050. At this time, the engineers cannot be more specific about cost because the final cost is dependent upon the future price of a basic material that will be required in the manufacture of the heat pump, and this price will be dependent upon the result of labor negotiations soon to begin in that basic industry. If labor negotiates a substantial wage increase, then the price of the material is sure to rise. If labor and management fail to reach an agreement by the contract expiration date, labor is very likely to strike, causing a cessation in production, a subsequent scarcity of the material, and a rise in its price. If either of these eventualities occurs, the manufacturing cost of the heat pump will be $1,050. If an agreement is reached in the basic industry which does not include an immediate large wage increase, then the $900 cost of manufacture would be feasible.

* See Chap. 14.

If the cost of manufacture is $900 per unit, and Pennwood sells each unit at $1,400, then each sale would contribute $500 to profit. If, on the other hand, cost is $1,050 per unit, each sale would contribute only $350 to profit.

If Pennwood decides to manufacture and market the heat pump, a considerable investment in the project would be required. Management estimates that $300,000 would be required for expansion of facilities, tooling, etc., resulting in a production capacity of 1,200 units per year. An additional $100,000 would have to be spent on advertising, promotion, and the training of salesmen. This amounts to a total investment of $400,000. The money previously spent on research and development would not be considered since this has already been spent and would have no bearing whatsoever on any decision made at this point as to whether to market the product.

Since Pennwood management is forced to make a decision whether to manufacture and market the new product, some criterion or goal must be established by which to measure the success or failure of the proposed venture. Management had previously adopted such a criterion by which other proposals were evaluated, and the criterion was that in order to be successful the project would have to recover the company's initial investment within 1 year.

Based on this criterion and the estimated cost figures, it is easy to see that in order for the project to be successful, it would be necessary to sell 800 units the first year if cost is $900 per unit, but if cost turns out to be $1,050 per unit, it would be necessary to sell 1,143 units. These conclusions result from dividing the total investment of $400,000 by the profit per unit resulting from each of the estimated cost figures.

It is apparent at this point that manufacturing capacity will not preclude success since capacity would be 1,200 units per year and in the worst cost situation only 1,143 units would be required in order to recover the initial investment in one year. There is, however, still another question which must be answered. That question is what other factors bear on success or failure of the project. This question can be answered by the single word "sales."

The number of units sold during the first year and the profit contribution per unit will determine whether or not the project is successful. A preliminary analysis by the marketing research department indicates that there are two main factors bearing upon sales of the heat pump. These are, first, economic conditions for the coming year relating to new housing starts and, second, competition.

Because of the price of the heat pump, about $2,600, the marketing division estimates that the potential market exists only for houses in the price range of $50,000 and up. Preliminary market research indicates that of all houses constructed to sell in this price range, approximately 3 percent of the owners would install the heat pump if it were available at a price of $2,600. Considering the state of the housing component of the problem as either good or bad, market research estimates that good economic conditions will result in the construction of 60,000 residences in this price range, but if economic conditions are bad, only 40,000 new residences will be constructed in this price range.

It is quite easy to convert the above estimates into market estimates for heat pump units. Three percent of 40,000 equals 1,200 units if conditions are bad, while 3 percent of 60,000 results in a market for 1,800 units if economic conditions are good.

There is, however, another factor bearing on the market for heat pumps. This factor is the presence or absence of competition. It is known that a competitive company is also interested in the heat pump idea, but it is not known whether it will attempt to market one during the coming year. If the competition does bring a competitive model onto the market, it is expected that the two competitors will share the available market equally. If not, Pennwood could expect to get the entire market.

The management of the Pennwood Corporation, faced with this information, must now make the decision whether or not to commit the required dollars to the project and proceed with the manufacture and marketing of the new heat pump.

4.2 THE ANALYSIS

The basic analysis of this problem will be a logical analysis. The decision to be made is a choice between two acts, a_1 (market the product) and a_2 (do not market the product). This analysis does not consider a priori the consequences of the acts, but rather a priori the state of the decision system. If the state of the system is good or favorable, management will select a_1; if bad or unfavorable, management will select a_2. The decision system, or the state of nature, is allowed only two states, good or bad. In order to determine the overall system state, however, various component states which affect the system state must be considered. This is a three-stage process. First, the pertinent component states must be identified. Second, their relationship to each other and to the overall state of the system must be determined. Third, the state of each component must be assessed. The assessment of system state results from the application of the appropriate algebraic rules to the system components.

The Pennwood Corporation has established a criterion for assessing the state of the system relating to the proposed project with which their decision is involved. This criterion is "contribution to profit in 1 year equal to initial investment" or in this specific case "contribution to profit of $400,000 or more during the first year of the project." In other words, the system state is good if the project contributes $400,000 or more to profit during the first year; otherwise it is bad. This overall system state is difficult to assess directly since it depends upon the states of other factors or components which act upon one another and the overall system in various ways. The more component states are involved, the more difficult it becomes to determine their effect on the system state. A model of the system, in this case a logical model, assists in studying and analyzing these relationships.

The first step is, of course, to identify these pertinent components. In this situation, we *might* identify them simply as the cost of manufacture and sales. Sales, however, can be broken down into the two factors of economic conditions in the housing construction market and competition. Therefore, instead of considering sales as a single component or factor with its state determined by economic conditions and competition, let us eliminate sales as a separate component and use economic conditions and competition as two components, each one affecting profit contribution or system state directly. This model construction could be done either way and, as a matter of fact, in many different ways; however, the logical relationship between components must be determined carefully and correctly. Let us identify the component "competition" with the letter C and "economic conditions in the housing market" with the letter B. "Cost of manufacture," the third major component, we shall label A. The state of component A is, however, dependent upon other factors, namely, the results of negotiations in a basic materials industry. We shall consider these factors as second-level components leading into major component A. That is, A is good if negotiations result in an agreement at no immediate large wage increase. Let us assign A_1 to the condition "strike," A_2 to the condition "settlement at a substantial wage increase," and A_3 to the condition "settlement at no great immediate wage increase."

Let us begin the analysis, however, considering only the major components A, B, and C for the time being and ignoring the second-level components A_1, A_2, and A_3.

The conditions constituting the *good* and *bad* states of each of the major system components and the overall system are shown in Table 4.1.

Having identified the major components of the system and having also determined what characterizes their state or condition, we find it necessary to establish the logical relationships between the components and the overall system. Since there are three major components and two states of each,

Table 4.1 Pennwood Corporation major component states

Component	*Good state*	*Bad state*
A: Cost of Manufacture	\$900	\$1,050
B: Economic Conditions	60,000 homes	40,000 homes
C: Competition	No	Yes
S: System	Profit $\geq$ \$400,000	Profit $<$ \$400,000

good and *bad*, there will be eight logical possibilities of components and states. We must examine each possibility and determine the system state for each as follows:

Possibility 1: All components are in the *good* condition: $A \cdot B \cdot C$.

If A is good, the cost of manufacture is \$900, and profit contribution per sale is \$500.

If B is good, 60,000 homes will be constructed in the proper price range, and the market for the heat pump will be 3 percent of 60,000 or 1,800 units.

If C is good, there will be no competition, and Pennwood will sell 1,200 units, which uses up its total manufacturing capacity.

Contribution to profit in state $A \cdot B \cdot C$ would, therefore, be \$500 × 1,200 = \$600,000.

Since \$600,000 > \$400,000, the system state is good, and $S = A \cdot B \cdot C = 1$.*

Possibility 2: A and B in *good* state but C in *bad*: $A \cdot B \cdot C'$.

If A is good, manufacturing cost = \$900 and per unit profit = \$500.

If B is good, 60,000 homes will be constructed, and the market will be 1,800 units.

If C is bad, there will be a competitive product on the market, cutting Pennwood's market share to one-half of 1,800, or 900 units.

Contribution to profit if $A \cdot B \cdot C'$ would be \$500 × 900 = \$450,000. Since \$450,000 > \$400,000, the system state is good, and $S = A \cdot B \cdot C' = 1$.

Possibility 3: A and C are good, but B is bad: $A \cdot B' \cdot C$.

If A is good, manufacturing cost = \$900, and per unit profit = \$500.

If B is bad, only 40,000 homes will be constructed in the right price range, and the market for the heat pump will be 3 percent of 40,000 or 1,200 units.

If C is good, there will be no competition, and Pennwood will sell all 1,200 units.

* Recall that 1 represents the *good* state and zero represents *bad*.

Contribution to profit if $A \cdot B' \cdot C$ would be \$500 × 1,200 = \$600,000.

Since \$600,000 > \$400,000, the system state is good, and $S = A \cdot B' \cdot C = 1$.

Possibility 4: A is bad but B and C are good: $A' \cdot B \cdot C$.

If A is bad, per unit manufacturing cost is \$1,050, and per unit profit = \$350.

If B is good, there will be a market for 1,800 units.

If C is good, there will be no competition, and Pennwood will sell 1,200 units.

Contribution to profit if $A' \cdot B \cdot C$ would be \$350 × 1,200 = \$420,000.

Since \$420,000 > \$400,000, the system state is good, and $S = A' \cdot B \cdot C = 1$.

Possibility 5: A is good but both B and C are bad: $A \cdot B' \cdot C'$.

If A is good, per unit profit will be \$500.

If B is bad, there will be a market for only 1,200 units.

If C is bad, Pennwood will sell one-half of the market or 600 units.

Contribution to profit if $A \cdot B' \cdot C'$ would be \$500 × 600 = \$300,000.

Since \$300,000 < \$400,000, the system state is bad, and $S = A \cdot B' \cdot C' = 0$.

Possibility 6: A and C are both bad but B is good: $A' \cdot B \cdot C'$.

If A is a bad, per unit profit is \$350.

If B is good, there will be a market for 1,800 units.

If C is bad, Pennwood will sell one-half of the market or 900 units.

Contribution to profit if $A' \cdot B \cdot C'$ would be \$350 × 900 = \$315,000.

Since \$315,00 < \$400,000, the system state is bad, and $S = A' \cdot B \cdot C' = 0$.

Possibility 7: A and B are bad but C is good: $A' \cdot B' \cdot C$.

If A is bad, per unit profit is \$350.

If B is bad, there will be a market for 1,200 units.

If C is good, Pennwood will sell all 1,200 units.

Contribution to profit if $A' \cdot B' \cdot C$ would be $350 × 1,200 = $420,000.

Since $420,000 > $400,000, the system state is good, and $S = A' \cdot B' \cdot C = 1$.

Possibility 8: A, B, and C are all bad: $A' \cdot B' \cdot C'$.

The per unit profit will be $350.

There will be a market for only 1,200 units.

Pennwood will sell one-half of 1,200 or 600 units.

Contribution to profit would be $350 × 600 = $210,000.

Since $210,000 < $400,000, the system state is bad, and $S = A' \cdot B' \cdot C' = 0$.

This information about A, B, and C and their relationships with each other and with the system state can be summarized in a truth table.

Table 4.2 Truth table for Pennwood case

Component				*System*
Possibility	*A*	*B*	*C*	*S*
1	1	1	1	1
2	1	1	0	1
3	1	0	1	1
4	0	1	1	1
5	1	0	0	0
6	0	1	0	0
7	0	0	1	1
8	0	0	0	0

Keep in mind that a 1 represents the good state and a zero represents the bad state of a component or system. A 1 under column A means that the component A is in the good state; a zero under A leads us to A' or not A, meaning that component A is in the bad state. A boolean polynomial of A, B, and C leading to "system in good state" is obtained by ORing all the minterms for which $S = 1$ as follows:

$$S = ABC + AB'C + A'B'C \tag{4.1}$$

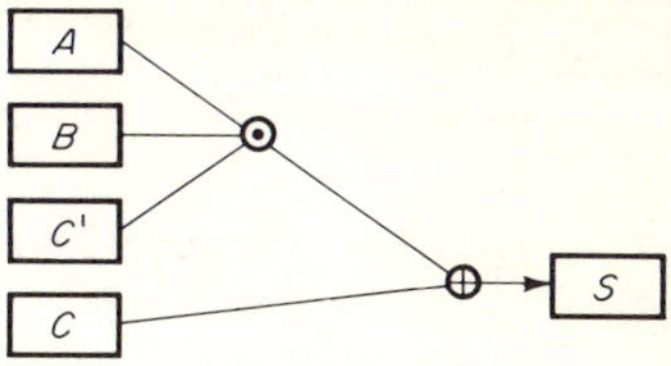

Fig. 4.1

This represents the function $S = f(A,B,C)$. In order to construct a graphical model of the system, the functional form in Eq. (4.1) should be simplified.

For example, Eq. (4.1) reduces to

$$C(AB + AB' + A'B + A'B') + ABC'$$

Since the expression in the parentheses includes all combinations of A, B, A', and B', it is equal to 1, and Eq. (4.1) reduces to

$$S = C + ABC' \tag{4.2}$$

This means that if C is good, the system is good regardless of A and B. If C is bad, then both A and B must be good. The graphical model is simply constructed as in Fig. 4.1.

We have so far neglected the subcomponents of A. These can be approached in the same manner as were the major components with respect to the total system. A is in the bad state if there is a strike, that is, if no wage agreement is reached. Let us go directly to the truth table and fill in the values from what is known about the effects of A_1, A_2, and A_3 on A, the cost of manufacture. For one thing, if $A_1 = 1$, that is, if a strike occurs, $A = 0$ since the cost of manufacture goes up if a strike causes a scarcity of the product. Therefore, the only rows of the truth table that are needed are those rows in which $A_1 = 0$, representing no strike.

If $A_2 = 1$, $A_3 = 0$, and vice versa, by the definition of these two subcomponents. Therefore, a truth table with only two rows will suffice, as shown in Table 4.3. The column headed A results directly from the following reasoning. If $A_2 = 1$ and $A_3 = 0$, that means that a wage increase occurs and $A = 0$. If $A_2 = 0$ and $A_3 = 1$, by the same reasoning $A = 1$. The expression for $A = 1$, that is, A being in the good state, is simply

Table 4.3 Reduced truth table for component A Pennwood Corporation case

A_1	A_2	A_3	A
0	1	0	0
0	0	1	1

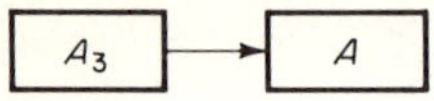

Fig. 4.2

$A = A_1'A_2'A_3$. However, since A_3 implies A_1' and A_2', this can be written $A = A_3$. In graphic form this is shown in Fig. 4.2.

The total logical network for the system appears in Fig. 4.3.

The third step in the logical analysis is simply the assignment of values to all the components. In order to determine or to estimate the states of the components, it is generally necessary to collect data and subject the data to some form of statistical analysis. Component B, for example, represents the market for heat pumps based on new housing starts in a given price range. It was mentioned previously that forecasts of the housing market were made by Pennwood based on a multiple regression analysis utilizing the number of building permits issued as well as other factors. The topic of correlation and regression is taken up in Chap. 14. Frequently state estimates can be based on statistical estimation techniques or on statistical tests of hypotheses. Both of these topics are also discussed subsequently. In some situations, however, where statistical data is not available, management may be forced to use subjective estimates of the component states. With regard to the components representing a wage settlement in a basic material industry and the possible actions of a competitor, subjective assessments of these events are likely to be necessary. It is to be hoped that these subjective assessments or estimates are more than mere guesses or hunches. Possibly data can be acquired on the progress of negotiations, the attitude of the parties involved, etc. Intelligence may be collected regarding the competition, its financial status, other commitments, etc. This information, although possibly not lending itself to quantification or statistical analysis, can still be utilized to arrive at state judgments. Once judgments are made as to the various component states, the system state is determined directly from the logical relationships.

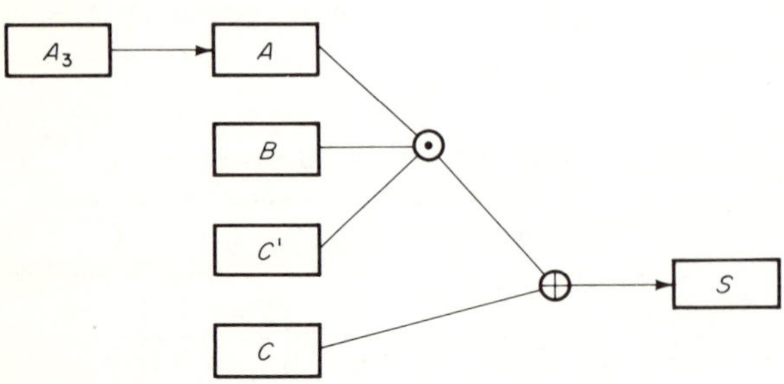

Fig. 4.3

Assume that Pennwood management assigns the following state values to the components:

$$A_3 = 0 \therefore A = 0$$
$$B = 1$$
$$C = 1$$

Then, from Eq. (4.2),

$$S = C + A \cdot B \cdot C'$$
$$S = 1 + 0 \cdot 1 \cdot 0$$
$$S = 1 + 0$$
$$S = 1$$

and the system state is assumed to be good. The obvious decision would then be to market the heat pump.

4.3 SUMMARY

The model assumed here is a model for the states of nature, or, in the terminology used heretofore, for the decision system. Neither probabilities nor economic consequences of wrong decisions are explicitly included; however, they must be a part of the decision maker's judgmental processes in determining success criteria and in assigning state values to the components. Whether a decision maker would or should be satisfied with a simple logical decision model such as the one illustrated is problematical. However, keep in mind that probably nine out of ten management decisions are based on a process far less systematic and objective than this one.

To be more specific, the typical decision maker faced with the Pennwood Corporation decision would listen to or read reports from engineering, marketing research, etc., assign subjective success criteria, and make a go or no-go decision without objectively relating the parts to the whole. The logical analysis at least provides an objective and consistent method for relating the various states of nature or of the system to the overall decision problem.

part two

Probability

5
Sets, Functions, and Combinatorial Analysis

This chapter will be devoted to a discussion of certain concepts which are a necessary preliminary to the material which follows.

5.1 SETS

A *set* is defined as any collection of objects having some describable similarity. All the cards in a deck of ordinary playing cards, all the people living in some particular town or city, all the integers between 1 and 1,000; all these are examples of sets.

We can describe or specify a set in two different ways. One way is to list all the objects included in the set. A second way is to devise a rule by which we can tell whether any specific object is included or excluded from the set under consideration. When a set is described by listing its elements, the individual elements of the set are separated by commas and enclosed in braces. For example, the set of all odd integers between zero and 10 would be listed as $S = \{1,3,5,7,9\}$.

A set that consists of some portion of the members of some other set is called a *subset* of the original set. For example, if set A is made up of all the members of a particular class in algebra, and if set B consists of those members of set A having brown hair, then set B is a subset of set A. More formally, set B is a subset of set A if and only if every element of set B is also an element of set A. It follows then that every set can be a subset of itself. Further, there is a subset of every set which contains zero elements and which is called the *empty set*. The empty set is generally designated with the symbol $\varnothing$.

It is possible to have many subsets of any given set. For example, we could designate a set C as consisting of all the male members of the set A described previously. Then set C is also a subset of set A.

In the fields of statistics and probability it is frequently convenient to call any process of observation an *experiment*. Therefore, a set which includes all the possible outcomes of an experiment is called the *sample space* of that experiment. Another term which is analogous to that of sample space is *possibility space*, or in some cases the term *universal set* is used. An outcome, or a group of outcomes, of an experiment can be called an *event*; therefore, the sample space of the experiment can also be called an *event space*. All these terms, *universal set*, *possibility space*, *sample space*, and *event space* mean the same thing.

Suppose we were to define our experiment as consisting of three tosses of a coin in order to observe the occurrence of a head, which would, in this case, be the event of interest. The sample space or event space of this experiment could be all the possible outcomes of the three coin tosses. In listing these possible outcomes, we shall let a 1 represent the occurrence of a head and let a zero represent the occurrence of a tail, which in this case is equivalent to the occurrence of a "no head." The outcomes of this experiment can be listed as follows:

Each outcome of the experiment can now be considered as a point in the sample space. Outcome 1 above is that event in which no head appears, outcome 2 is that event in which two tails appear followed by a head, and so

	1st toss	*2nd toss*	*3rd toss*
Outcome 1	0	0	0
Outcome 2	0	0	1
Outcome 3	0	1	0
Outcome 4	1	0	0
Outcome 5	0	1	1
Outcome 6	1	0	1
Outcome 7	1	1	0
Outcome 8	1	1	1

on down to outcome 8, which is that event in which all three tosses result in the appearance of heads.

Let us now define the term *event* as being some subset of the universal set or sample space, keeping in mind that an event can be a single outcome of the experiment, corresponding to a single point in the sample space, or a group of outcomes of the experiment corresponding to several points in the sample space, or even all the outcomes of the experiment corresponding to all the points in the universal set.

As an example, the event which corresponds to the occurrence of a single head includes outcomes numbered 2, 3, and 4 of the sample space of the experiment. The event corresponding to the occurrence of no heads would include only outcome number 1.

5.2 OPERATIONS ON SETS

Let us, for the sake of convenience, designate the possibility space or sample space as S. Some subset A of S can be shown as in Fig. 5.1.

In Fig. 5.1, the shaded area represents subset A, while the universal set S is represented by the total area enclosed within the rectangle. These diagrams which serve to illustrate the relationships between sets are called *Venn diagrams*.

Again referring to Fig. 5.1, since the shaded area represents subset A, all the *unshaded* area within the rectangle is called the *complement* of A or "not A" and can be designated by A'.

We can use the Venn diagram to depict more than a single subset of the universal set or sample space as shown in Fig. 5.2.

Here we have shown two subsets of S, subset A and subset B, and it can easily be seen from the diagram that since the subsets A and B intersect one another, there are certain points, or more precisely, a certain area, which is common to both A and B. This common area, which is doubly cross-hatched in the diagram, is called the *intersection* or the *logical product* of A and B and is designated $A \cap B$ in the notation of set theory and read A AND B.

On the other hand, that set of points, or in the diagram that area, which is contained either in set A or in set B or in both A and B is called the *union* or

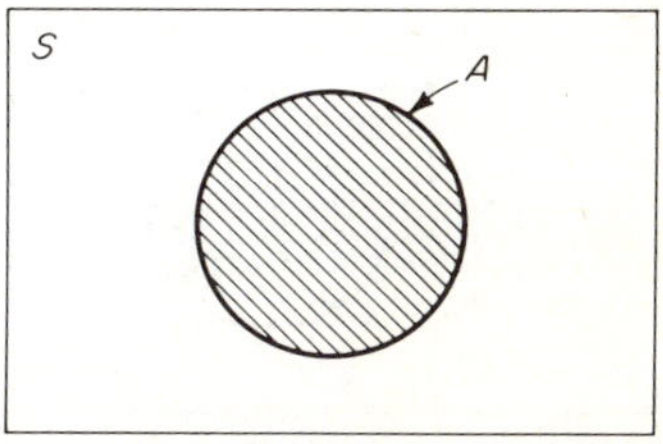

Fig. 5.1

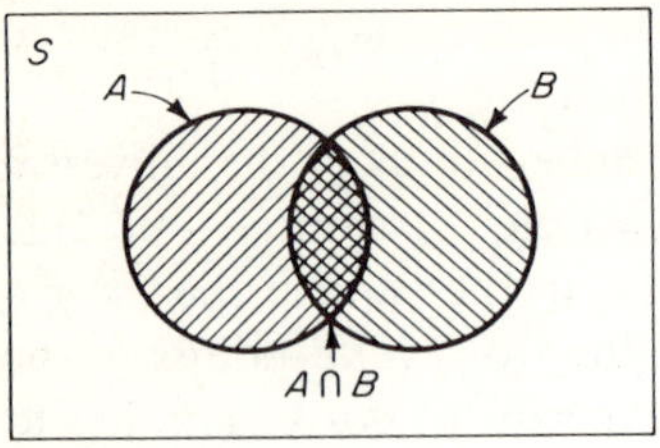

Fig. 5.2

the *logical sum* of A and B. The union of A and B is designated $A \cup B$ and is read A OR B. In Fig. 5.2, $A \cup B$ is the total shaded area contained in the rectangle.

Suppose, as an example, we consider that set S is an ordinary deck of playing cards. Let subset A be all the hearts in the deck and let subset B be all the picture cards in the deck.

There are a total of 13 hearts in the deck and 12 picture cards. Subset A contains all the 13 hearts, while subset B contains all the 12 picture cards as illustrated by Fig. 5.3. Subset $(A \cap B)$ is that subset which contains those cards which are both hearts and picture cards at the same time, that is, the intersection of A and B, and the specific cards that belong to $A \cap B$ are $\{J\heartsuit, Q\heartsuit, K\heartsuit\}$. Subset $(A \cup B)$ contains all cards that are either hearts or pictures or both, that is, all the cards which are listed in Fig. 5.3. There is also a set $A' \cap B'$ which includes all the other cards in the deck, that is, all the cards *not* specifically listed in Fig. 5.3. Since $A \cup B$ represents the cards listed in the figure, all the cards not listed and designated as belonging to the set $A' \cap B'$ must constitute the complement of $A \cup B$. Since the complement of $A \cup B$ can be written $(A \cup B)'$, then $(A \cup B)' = A' \cap B'$. This is indeed so and can be derived from the simple application of DeMorgan's laws, which were discussed previously. The set, or subset, $A' \cap B'$ consists of the Ace through 10 of spades, of clubs, and of diamonds.

Other sets which could be defined from this example are:

$A \cap B'$: Ace through 10 of hearts.
$A' \cap B$: Jack, Queen, and King of diamonds, spades, and clubs.

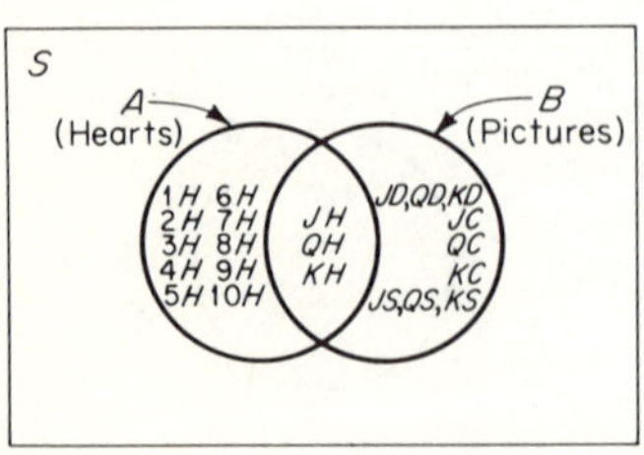

Fig. 5.3

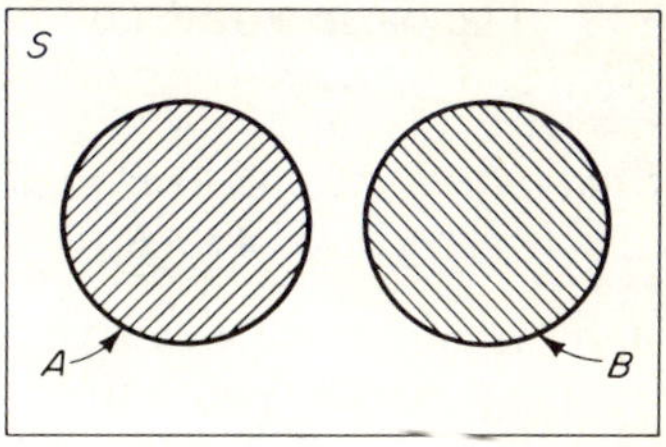

Fig. 5.4

$A \cup B'$: All cards except the Jack, Queen, and King of diamonds, spades, and clubs.
$A' \cup B$: All cards except the Ace through 10 of hearts.
$(A \cap B)$: All cards except the Jack, Queen, and King of hearts.

The intersection or logical product of sets can also be called their *conjunction.* Sets which have no points (or area) in common are said to be *disjoint* sets, that is, for two sets, $A \cap B = 0$. Figure 5.4 illustrates two disjoint sets.

5.3 ELEMENTARY SET ALGEBRA

The algebra of sets is the same as the boolean algebra discussed previously. Generally, and except for differences in notation, it can be easily seen that set theory, boolean algebra, and symbolic logic are essentially the same. This section on set algebra parallels the section on boolean algebra in the previous chapter. It is included, however, to provide some review and to accustom the reader to the slight differences in notation and to the application of the theory in a slightly different context.

Set A is equal to set B if and only if each and every member of set A is also a member of set B and each and every member of set B is also a member of set A. Now if S is the universal set and if, as established previously, A' means the complement of A, then

$$A \cup A' = S \tag{5.1}$$

$$A \cap A' = 0 \tag{5.2}$$

These are called the *complementation laws of sets.*

Equation 5.1 simply states that all the members of set A combined with all the members of the complement of set A are equal to the universal set. Equation 5.2 states that there are no members common to both set A and its complement, set A'. This must be true simply because of the definition of the complement of a set.

The basic axioms of set theory from which all theorems can be derived are listed below.

Commutation:	$A \cap B = B \cap A$ $A \cup B = B \cup A$
Association:	$(A \cap B) \cap C = A \cap (B \cap C)$ $(A \cup B) \cup C = A \cup (B \cup C)$
Distribution:	$A \cap (B \cup C) = (A \cap B) \cup (A \cap C)$ $A \cup (B \cap C) = (A \cup B) \cap (A \cup C)$
Identity:	$A \cup 0 = A$ $A \cap S = A$
Closure:	If $A \in S$, and $B \in S$, then $A \cap B \in S$ and $A \cup B \in S$

5.4 FUNCTIONS

Very generally, a function can be thought of as a rule that assigns an object to every member of a given set. It might, however, be a good idea to consider the nature of a function in a bit more detail at this point. In order to do this, several other terms require definitions and explanations.

When a set is specified by listing its elements, such as the set of odd numbers between zero and 10, $S = \{1,3,5,7,9\}$, nothing whatsoever is implied about the order in which the elements appear. The set just specified is identical with the set $\{9,5,1,3,7\}$. If it is desired to specify the order of the elements in a given set, the elements are enclosed by parentheses, rather than braces, and listed in the required order. Such a set is called an *ordered set* and would be written $S = (1,3,5,7,9)$.

If a set consists of two elements, say a and b, it is called a *pair* and would be written $S = \{a,b\}$. If the ordering of the elements is specified, say, for example, that a precedes b, or that a is the first element in the set and b is the second, we are specifying an ordered set of two elements or an *ordered pair*. An ordered pair would be written (a,b).

Suppose we have two sets, set A containing m elements and set B containing n elements. It would be possible to designate a set of all the ordered pairs which can be made by selecting the first element of the pair from set A and the second element of the pair from set B. Such a set of ordered pairs is called the *cartesian product* of the sets A and B and is designated $A \times B$. There would obviously be $m \cdot n$ elements to this cartesian product set of A and B.

For example, if $A = \{s,f\}$ and $B = \{1,2,3\}$, $A \times B = \{(s,1), (s,2), (s,3), (f,1), (f,2), (f,3)\}$. Since there were two elements in A and three elements in B, the cartesian product set $A \times B$ contained $2 \cdot 3 = 6$ elements or ordered pairs.

Since the elements of the cartesian product set are ordered pairs, it should be apparent that $A \times B \neq B \times A$. Considering the same sets A and B as before, we see that the cartesian product $B \times A = \{(1,s), (1,f)$ $(2,s), (2,f), (3,s), (3,f)\}$.

Since we have previously defined an ordered set as being a set in which the elements appear in a certain order, this obviously does not limit us to ordered pairs. For example, we can have ordered triplets which are ordered sets containing three elements or, for that matter, ordered n-tuples which are ordered sets containing n elements.

We can, therefore, see that the cartesian product of three sets would consists of a set of ordered triplets and the cartesian product of n sets would consist of a set of ordered n-tuples.

Since a cartesian product is itself a set of ordered n-tuples, any subset of a cartesian product is called a *relation*. If there are n elements (ordered pairs, triplets, etc.) in the cartesian product set, there are 2^n relations. In general, if there are n elements in any given set, the number of subsets of that set, including the null set and the universal set, is equal to 2^n.

Suppose $A = \{1,3\}$ and $B = \{2,4\}$. $A \times B = \{(1,2), (1,4), (3,2), (3,4)\}$. There are four elements (ordered pairs) in $A \times B$. The number of relations in $A \times B$ is $2^4 = 16$. We can list them as follows:

$\{\varnothing\}$
(1,2)
(1,4)
(3,2)
(3,4)
(1,2), (1,4)
(1,2), (3,2)
(1,2), (3,4)
(1,4), (3,2)
(1,4), (3,4)
(3,2), (3,4)
(1,2), (1,4), (3,2)
(1,2), (3,2), (3,4)
(1,2), (1,4), (3,4)
(1,4), (3,2), (3,4)
(1,2), (1,4), (3,2), (3,4)

We are generally interested in certain types of relations. For example, if x is the first number in an ordered pair and y is the second, find the relation such that $x > y$. Or symbolically, find $Z = \{(x,y) | x > y\}$. This consists of the single element (3,2).

If we were asked to find the relation in which $x < y$, that is, $Z = \{(x,y)|x < y\}$, the relation would be $Z = \{(1,2), (1,4), (3,4)\}$.

A *function* is a special case of a relation. More specifically, all the relations in a cartesian product constitute a set of relations. Certain of these relations are functions. Consequently, a function is a subset of the set of relations. Those relations are functions from A to B which assign to each and every element in A a uniquely specified element in B.

For example, out of the total set of 16 relations resulting from $A \times B$, the functions from A to B are the relations:

(1,2), (3,2)
(1,2), (3,4)
(1,4), (3,2)
(1,4), (3,4)

If the x_i are the members of set A and the y_i are the members of set B, note that for every function, each of the $x_i \in A$ appears once and only once, and for each x_i there is a unique y_i. Each function can then be written

$$y = f(x)$$

which reads y is a function of x and means that for every element $x \in A$, f specifies the set or the rule which assigns to this x an element $y \in B$.

For any function f of A into B or $y = f(x)$, the set A is called the *domain* of the function, while the set of all elements in B is called the *co-domain*.

The elements of set B which appear in the function are called the *range* of the function. For the four functions of A to B listed above, the range of the first one is simply $\{2\}$. The range of the second and third functions is $\{2,4\}$, and in these cases the range is identical with the co-domain. In the last function, the range is $\{4\}$.

There is a special class of functions in which all the elements in the range are numbers. This is the type of function that will most commonly be encountered in the area of probability and statistics and is called simply a *numerical function*.

Suppose, for example, it is stated that $y = x^2$. This means that y is that function of x resulting from the multiplication of x by itself. Suppose we designate the set of all the x_i as X and the set of all the y_i as Y. The set X is the domain of the function, and Y is its range. If $X = \{1,2,3\}$, $Y = \{1^2,2^2,3^2\} = \{1,4,9\}$. Or again suppose $y = f(x) = x - 1$. This means that y is now that function of x resulting from the subtraction of one unit from x. If $X = \{1,2,3\}$, for this function $Y = \{1 - 1, 2 - 1, 3 - 1\} = \{0,1,2\}$.

5.5 COMBINATORIAL ANALYSIS

Frequently when dealing with sets composed of discrete objects or with experiments involving specific outcomes, it is convenient and often necessary

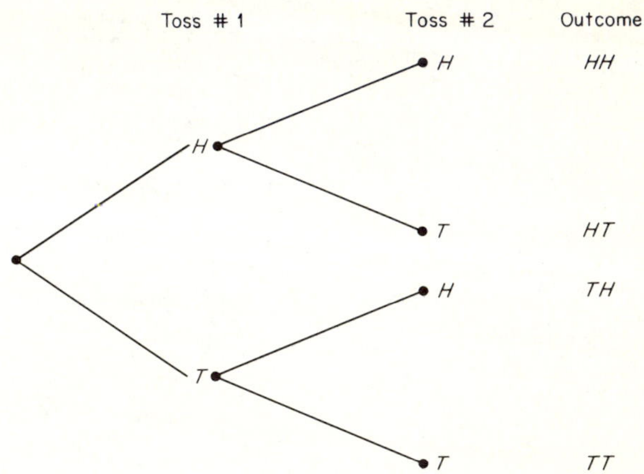

Fig. 5.5

to enumerate the number of elements in the event space of interest or to count the number of possible outcomes of an experiment. One very simple method for systematic counting is by the construction of a tree diagram.

Suppose, in a very simple case, we wished to enumerate the possible outcomes of a coin-tossing experiment in which we toss a fair coin twice. There are two steps in this experiment corresponding to each toss, and each step has two possible outcomes, heads or tails. The outcomes of this experiment can be diagrammed as shown in Fig. 5.5.

A tree diagram can be used to enumerate the number of ways in which any multistage operation can be performed. For example, suppose a consignment of goods is to be shipped from London, England to Los Angeles, California. The consignment can be shipped from London to New York City either by plane or by ship. However, it can go from New York to Los Angeles by plane, truck, or train. The two stages of the operation are London–New York and New York–Los Angeles, and the operation can be described by the transportation methods utilized to complete the shipment, that is, plane-truck, ship-plane, etc. The total number of ways in which the shipment can be made can be diagrammed as in Fig. 5.6.

The construction of a tree diagram is quite simple when the number of stages in the operation or experiment and the number of elements in each stage are small. However, when these elements or stages are large, the tree diagram becomes very cumbersome and impractical.

There are, however, more convenient methods for arriving at the number of outcomes without going through the tedious procedure of constructing tree diagrams. These methods can be generalized by the following theorems.

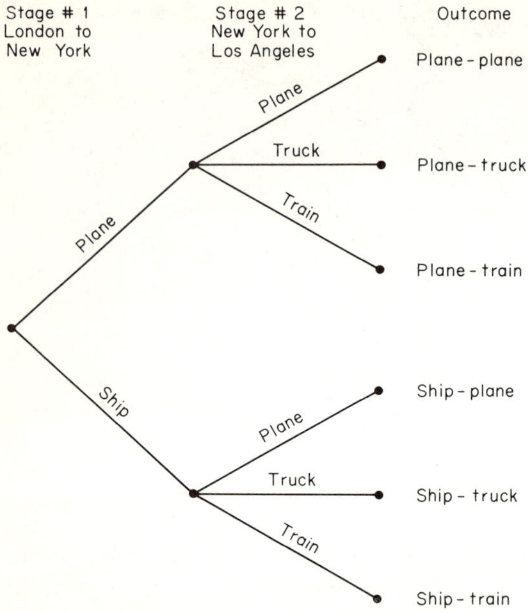

Fig. 5.6

Theorem 5.1 *If sets $A_1, A_2, \ldots, A_k$, respectively, contain $n_1, n_2, \ldots, n_k$ elements, then there are $n_1 \times n_2 \times \cdots \times n_3$ ways in which an element can be selected first from set A_1, second from $A_2, \ldots$, and finally from set A_k. This is the cartesian product of the sets A.*

This theorem can be restated to be more applicable to the performance of an operation or process as follows:

Theorem 5.2 *If an operation is performed in a series of k steps, such that step 1 can be performed in n_1 different ways, step 2 can be performed in n_2 different ways, . . . , and step k in n_k different ways, then the entire operation can be performed in $n_1 \times n_2 \times \cdots \times n_k$ different ways.*

Now, referring to the two previous examples, since the first experiment consisted of two coin tosses each having two possible outcomes, the total possible number of outcomes of the experiment is simply $2 \times 2 = 4$. In the second example, the operation consisted of two stages; the first (London–New York) could be accomplished in two ways, while the second (New York–Los Angeles) could be accomplished in three ways. Therefore, the total number of ways in which this operation could be completed is $2 \times 3 = 6$.

5.6 PERMUTATIONS

We are frequently faced with problems which involve the arrangement of the elements of some set in some specific order. That is, if a_1 and a_2 are elements of set A, the arrangement a_1a_2 is considered to be different from the arrangement a_2a_1. Such an ordering or arrangement of elements is called a *permutation.*

An example of a permutation problem might be to determine the number of different ways in which it is possible to seat three people in a row of three chairs. As a matter of simple reasoning we can see that it is possible to seat any one of the three people in the first chair. That is, there are three ways in which we can fill chair 1. However, having made the selection for the first chair, we now have only two people left unseated from which to fill the second chair, and, of course, the second chair having been filled, the third and last chair must be filled with the single person left unseated. Refer to Theorem 5.2; since chair 1 could be filled in three ways, chair 2 in two ways, and chair 3 in one way only, the total number of ways possible for seating three people in three chairs is $3 \times 2 \times 1 = 6$. Or in general, the number of permutations of any n things taken altogether is given by $n(n-1)(n-2)\cdots 3\cdot 2\cdot 1$. This last expression, commonly called n factorial, is written $n!$ and simply means the product of all terms beginning with n and decreasing by one unit down to the number 1.

Suppose, as another example, we wanted to find out how many ways it is possible to fill the same three chairs, but this time having five people to choose from. We would approach the problem in the same way, filling chair 1 first, chair 2 next, etc. However, in filling the first chair we would now have five people to choose from and would, therefore, be able to fill the first chair in five ways. After filling chair 1, we would have a choice of four people for chair 2, and finally after filling chairs 1 and 2, we would still have three choices for the third chair. Again from Theorem 5.2, since the first chair could be filled in five ways, the second in four ways, and the third in three ways, the total number of ways of seating five prople in three chairs is $5 \times 4 \times 3 = 60$. The theorem covering problems of this type is stated below.

Theorem 5.3 *The number of permutations of r objects selected from a set of n objects is*

$$n(n-1)(n-2)\cdots(n-r+1) = \frac{n!}{(n-r)!} \tag{5.3}$$

When $n = r$, the above expression reduces to

$$\frac{n!}{(n-n)!} = \frac{n!}{0!} = n!$$

In the factorial notation, $0! = 1$.

The second part of Eq. (5.3) is derived from the following reasoning. We wish to multiply all the numbers beginning with n and ending with the number $n - r + 1$. If we write $n!$, we have the product of all the numbers beginning with n down to and including the number 1. We wish to cancel from the series of numbers which constitute $n!$ all those numbers beginning with $n - r$ and continuing down to and including the number 1. This latter product can be written as $(n - r)!$. Therefore,

$$\frac{n!}{(n-r)!} = n(n-r) \cdots (n-r+1)$$

A generally accepted notation which stands for the number of permutations of n objects taken r at a time is

$${}_nP_r \qquad \text{or} \qquad P(n,r)$$

A special case of permutations arises when certain of the objects to be arranged are indistinguishable from one another. Recall that in discussing permutations previously we always discussed the permutation of distinct objects. However, suppose we wish to know the number of permutations possible in the arrangement of five books on a shelf when three of the books have red covers and two have blue covers. We shall specify that the books of the same color are indistinguishable from each other.

First let us begin by determining the number of possible permutations of the five books if they were all distinct from one another. The number of permutations of five objects taken five at a time would be $P(5,5) = 5!$.

The 5! permutations or orderings of the five books, assuming that they are all distinct, includes the number of permutations of the three red books, assuming that they are distinguishable, and the number of permutations of the two blue books, assuming that they are distinguishable from one another. Under these assumptions, the number of permutations of the red books is 3! and the number of permutations of the blue books is 2!. However, since neither the red books nor the blue books are distinguishable among themselves, and each group represents only a single ordering, the total 5! permutations which would be possible if all the individual books were distinct must be reduced or divided by the 3! and 2! permutations of the red and the blue books, respectively.

Therefore, the number of permutations of the three red books and the two blue ones taken together is arrived at by finding the total number of permutations of all the books *if* they had all been distinguishable from each other, and then dividing that number by the number of permutations of each distinguishable set of objects *if* they had been distinguishable from each other. The answer to the problem given would be

$$\frac{5!}{3!2!} = 10$$

The general theorem which applies to this type of problem follows.

Theorem 5.4 *The number of permutations of n objects of which r_1 are alike, r_2 are alike, . . . , r_k are alike, is given by*

$$\frac{n!}{r_1!r_2! \cdots r_n!} \tag{5.4}$$

Theorem 5.4 also leads us into a similar formula for determining the number of combinations of objects as discussed in the succeeding section.

5.7 COMBINATIONS

When we are interested only in the number of distinct subsets that we can make out of a set of objects, without regard to the order in which the individual objects are arranged, we are then concerned with *combinations*. Let us take as an example the number of committees of three members that we can select from a set of five people. Here we do not distinguish between the three people once they have been selected. A committee made up of persons A, B, and C is the same committee as C, B, and A. To emphasize this point further, ABC and CBA are two permutations but are only a single combination.

We are now dealing with two sets of objects (or people), the members of each, for our purpose, being indistinguishable from the other members of the same set. First, there is the set of people selected for the committee, and, second, there is the set of people *not* selected. The situation is identical with the illustration of the books given in the previous section, and the solution can be determined by Theorem 5.4. From a total of $n = 5$ people we want to determine the number of ways in which we can select a subset of $r_1 = 3$ members (all indistinguishable from each other) and a second subset of $r_2 = n - r_1 = 2$, also indistinguishable from each other. This is given by

$$\frac{n!}{r_1!r_2!} = \frac{n!}{r_1!(n - r_1)!} \tag{5.5}$$

which is the formula for the number of combinations of n things taken r (or r_1) at a time. The notation most commonly used for combinations is ${}_nC_r$ or $\binom{n}{r}$.

Comparing the formula for combinations with the one for permutations,

$$\binom{n}{r} = \frac{n!}{r!(n-r)!}$$

$$P(n,r) = \frac{n!}{(n-r)!}$$

we see that the number of combinations of n objects taken r at a time is the number of permutations of n objects taken r at a time divided by $r!$, or

$$\binom{n}{r} = \frac{P(n,r)}{r!}$$

To solve the committee problem discussed above, the number of committees of three members that can be selected from five people is

$$\binom{5}{3} = \frac{5!}{3!2!} = 10$$

5.8 BINOMIAL COEFFICIENTS

From the algebra we have learned how to expand an expression such as $(a + b)^2$ into its equivalent expression which is $1a^2 + 2ab + 1b^2$. We arrived at this result by multiplying $(a + b)$ by itself and in the process we get $(a \times a) + (a \times b) + (b \times a) + (b \times b)$.

It is evident that the expansion of $(a + b)^2$ gives us one set consisting of two a's, one set consisting of two b's, and two sets each containing a single a and a single b. The coefficients of the expansion given above indicate the number of ways of getting each *combination* of letters from combining the factors $(a + b)$ and $(a + b)$. The expansion of the expression $(a + b)^3$ comes from the multiplication of the factors $(a + b)(a + b)(a + b)$ and results in $1a^3 + 3a^2b + 3ab^2 + 1b^3$. The expansion indicates that from the factors of the expression $(a + b)^3$ there are:

One way to select 3 a's
One way to select 3 b's
Three ways to select 2 a's and 1 b, and
Three ways to select 1 a and 2 b's

In general, for $(a + b)^n$ the coefficient of the rth term of the expansion is given by the combinatorial formula $\binom{n}{r-1}$, and the coefficients of all the terms of the expansion are given by $\sum_{r=1}^{n} \binom{n}{r-1}$, where the symbol $\sum$ stands for "the sum of." In the expansion of $(a + b)^3$, the coefficient of the second term was simply $\binom{3}{1} = 3$.

The algebraic expansion of an expression of the form $(a + b)^n$ is called a *binomial expansion*, and the coefficients of the terms of the expansion are called the *binomial coefficients*.

Another simple method of determining the binomial coefficients is by the use of what is called Pascal's triangle, which begins as shown below and can be expanded for any number of terms.

$$\begin{array}{ccccccccccc} & & & & & 1 & & & & & \\ & & & & 1 & & 1 & & & & \\ & & & 1 & & 2 & & 1 & & & \\ & & 1 & & 3 & & 3 & & 1 & & \\ & 1 & & 4 & & 6 & & 4 & & 1 & \\ \cdot & & \cdot & & \cdot & & \cdot & & \cdot & & \cdot \end{array}$$

Starting with the third row corresponding to $n = 2$, the coefficients are always the sum of the two numbers in the preceding row on each side of the required number. For example, the coefficients for the expansion of the expression $(a + b)$ would be 1, 4, 6, 4, and 1; the expansion would be $a^4 + 4a^3b + 6a^2b^2 + 4ab^3 + b^4$.

5.9 SUMMARY

The material dealt with in this chapter is prerequisite for the understanding of much that will follow. For example, the elementary rules of probability theory are most easily explained in terms of sets and operations on sets. Permutations, combinations, and other devices for enumerating possibilities or outcomes are also necessary to an understanding of the probability functions which will be encountered later.

Also, an understanding of the relationship between sets, boolean algebra, and symbolic logic will allow us to use symbols and concepts from all three in the development and understanding of models and operations on models which will be discussed subsequently.

A brief explanation of functions and the functional notation as well as a discussion of the binomial expansion were encountered early in the book, since they will be used throughout.

PROBLEMS

5.1. Let $A = \{1,2,3,4,5,6\}$, $B = \{2,4,6,8,10\}$.

(*a*) What are the members of $A \cup B$?

(*b*) What are the members of $A \cap B$?

(*c*) What are the members of $A' \cap B$?
(*d*) What are the members of $A \cup B'$?

5.2. Let $S = \{1,2,3,4,5,6\}$, $A = \{1,2\}$, $B = \{2,4,6\}$, and $C = \{5,7,9\}$.
(*a*) Is A a subset of S?
(*b*) Is C a subset of S?
(*c*) What are the members of $C \cap S'$?
(*d*) What are the members of $A' \cap B' \cap C'$?
(*e*) What are the members of $S \cap A' \cap B'$?

5.3. Let $A = \{a,b,c\}$ and $B = \{1,2\}$.
(*a*) Write the set $A \times B$.
(*b*) Write the set $B \times A$.
(*c*) Does $A \times B = B \times A$?
(*d*) How many relations are there in $A \times B$?

5.4. Let $A = \{w,x\}$ and $B = \{y,z\}$.
(*a*) Form the cartesian $B \times A$.
(*b*) List the relations in the set $B \times A$.
(*c*) List the functions of B to A.

5.5. Let $A = \{a,b,c,d\}$ and $B = \{0,2,5\}$.
(*a*) Is the relation $\{(a,0), (b,0), (c,0), (d,0)\}$ a function of A to B?
(*b*) Is the relation $\{(a,0), (b,2), (c,5)\}$ a function of A to B?
(*c*) Is the relation $\{(a,5), (b,2), (b,0), (c,2)\}$ a function of A to B?
(*d*) Is the relation $\{(a,5), (b,2), (c,5), (d,2)\}$ a function of A to B?
(*e*) Is the relation $\{(a,5), (b,2), (d,0)\}$ a function of A to B?

5.6. (*a*) If we conduct an experiment in which we roll a die first and then toss a coin, construct a tree diagram showing all the possible outcomes, assuming that we record the number on the die and the occurrence of a head or a tail on the coin.

(*b*) Draw the tree diagram that would describe the experiment if we tossed the coin first and then rolled the die.

5.7. Find the value of
(*a*) $P(3,2)$
(*b*) $P(4,0)$
(*c*) $P(5,4)$
(*d*) $P(3,3)$
(*e*) $P(4,2)$

5.8. Find the value of
(*a*) $C(3,2)$
(*b*) $C(4,0)$
(*c*) $C(5,4)$
(*d*) $C(3,3)$
(*e*) $C(4,2)$

5.9. If the number of permutations of n things taken three at a time, $P(n,3)$, is equal to 60, how many combinations of the same n things taken three at a time are there?

5.10. From a club consisting of 15 members,

(*a*) How many different ways can a president, a vice-president, a secretary, and a treasurer be elected?

(*b*) From the same club, how many committees of four members can be elected?

(*c*) From the same club, how many committees consisting of a chairman, a vice-chairman, and two members can be selected?

5.11. A haberdashery stocks shirts by collar style, color, neck size, and sleeve length. In order to have four shirts of each kind in stock, how many shirts must they have if there are three colors, three collar styles, ten neck sizes, and eight sleeve lengths?

5.12. On an examination there are five problems on statistics and four on probability. Each student must select four statistics problems and two probability problems. How many different ways can a student choose the required problems?

5.13. If a manufacturer produces his product in lots of 25 and he inspects a sample of five items from each lot before he ships the lot to his customer, how many different samples could he possibly select from a single lot?

5.14. A market researcher wants to conduct interviews with four families from a block containing 15 single-family residences. How many different ways could he select the four families to be interviewed?

5.15. Suppose, in the previous problem, that of the 15 families on the block, 11 had children and 4 did not.

(*a*) If the market researcher wanted his sample of size 4 to contain exactly three families with children, how many ways could he select these three families from the families with children on the block?

(*b*) If three families out of his sample of four were to have children, then the remaining family would be one without children. How many ways could he select a family without children from the families having no children?

6

ɔbability

The concept of probability plays a major role in any type of problem-solving decision process which deals realistically with real-life situations. It is very seldom, outside of textbooks of course, that problems are encountered for which all the factors or variables are completely determined or determinable. There is always some element of uncertainty in everything we do, and that element of uncertainty is inherently a part of all real problem situations requiring solutions and decisions.

In analyzing a decision problem, that is, a complex situation requiring that a decision be made, we have discussed techniques for translating the conditions of the problem into a logical model of the problem situation. The logical model has provided a means for determining the state of the system (or primary-problem situation) in terms of the states of its component parts. This is certainly a valuable technique for the manager for, knowing the absolute states of all components bearing on his primary problem, he can make a decision with some assurance that it is a good one. However, seldom is the absolute state of anything known absolutely. There is always bound to be some uncertainty regarding the states of the components, and, consequently, regardless of how accurate the logical formulation of the system model turns out to be, there is bound to be some uncertainty about the state of the overall system. Therefore, even though the logical model provides the manager with a basis for making a decision, there remains some probability that the decision will be a bad one.

It is inevitable, then, that we insert the concept of probability into any decision situation. If the component states can be determined with their associated probabilities, then the probability of the system being in any particular state can also be determined. However, in order to deal with probabilistic situations, it is necessary that at least the basic concepts of probability theory be understood.

The word "probability," to most people, is generally associated with the idea of gambling and games of chance. This is a very natural association since the outcomes of gambling games and the betting odds established for these games are directly related to and based on the rules of probability. It is said that early research into probability theory was motivated by the desire of the then Duke of Burgundy to determine mathematically his chances of winning at the game of roulette. Thus, in the year 1654, the Duke commissioned a mathematician by the name of Blaise Pascal to provide an answer to this problem.

While Pascal is generally credited with providing a basis or framework for probability theory, his work was developed further by Pierre de Fermat and Christiaan Huygens. Fermat treated the gambling problem within a general theory of combinations. This theory was expanded by the Swiss mathematician Jacques Bernoulli, who is generally regarded as the founder of probability theory as a branch of mathematics.

Although the origins of probability theory are found in the field of gambling, today it has been applied to almost every field of human endeavor. For example, the decision as to whether a new product should be produced and marketed is highly dependent upon probabilities, favorable or unfavorable to the enterprise. The marketing manager wants to know the probability that the market for the product is at least as great as some predetermined value. The purchasing manager wants to know the probability that a vital raw material can be procured for less than some given price. An engineering manager wants to know the probability that the product will properly perform its intended function under certain types of conditions and circumstances. And of course the president or chief decision maker would certainly like to know the probability that his decision, to proceed with or to cancel the project, is a good one.

There have been long and lengthy discussions among mathematicians regarding the true meaning of probability. One division among mathematicians is between what we might call objectivists and subjectivists. The former, to sum up very briefly, consider probability to be a state of the universe, while the latter consider that probability is a state of belief. We shall not take sides in these philosophical arguments but shall use those concepts which are most useful to us in any particular context. In this chapter we shall adopt the objectivist view of probability. However, in later chapters we shall find it useful to utilize subjective probabilities in the decision process.

Even from the objectivist point of view, however, there are different definitions of probability. One, which might be called the "equally likely" definition, states that the probability of an event occurring is simply the ratio of the number of ways in which that event can occur to the total number of ways in which the event could either occur or fail to occur, provided that all ways are equally likely. As an example, consider a simple gambler's die. Since a die is a cube with exactly six faces, the probability of any particular face showing after the die is tossed is simply $1/6$. This derives from the consideration that there is only a single way in which a particular face could appear, and one plus five total ways in which the die could land. It should be apparent that the phrase "equally likely" is basic to this concept of probability.

Mathematically this definition could be written as follows: If an event A can occur in n different ways and fail to occur in m different ways such that $m + n = N$, the total number of ways in which event A can either occur or fail to occur, and if all N ways are equally likely, then

$$P(A) = \frac{n}{m + n} = \frac{n}{N} \tag{6.1}$$

where $P(A)$ represents the probability of event A occurring.

A second definition of probability frequently quoted is called the *relative-frequency definition.* This states that if event A occurs n times out of a total of N trials of an experiment that could lead to the occurrence of event A, then the probability of event A is the limit of the ratio of n/N as N, the number of trials, approaches infinity. Mathematically this can be stated as

$$P(A) = \lim_{N \to \infty} \frac{n}{N} \tag{6.2}$$

The distinctions between these definitions of probability are essentially philosophical and have little practical effect as far as their application is concerned. For our purposes we shall turn to the concept of sets and devise a definition which lends itself to the exposition to follow. It is essentially the equally likely definition but can be extended to include the relative-frequency definition also. We shall state it as follows: If the total number of points in the universal set are $n(S)$, and the number of points in S which correspond to event A are $n(A)$, then

$$P(A) = \frac{n(A)}{n(S)} \tag{6.3}$$

This definition pertains, of course, to finite sample spaces composed of discrete elements. It can, however, be extended to include infinite continuous sample spaces.

Probability deals with uncertainty, or more specifically, with phenomena which occur with uncertainty. However, there is a type of phenomenon for which, although its occurrence or nonoccurrence at any given time (or observation) is uncertain, exhibits a predictable regularity over a very long (possibly infinite) sequence of observations. These phenomena can be called *random phenomena*, and the event of their occurrence or nonoccurrence can be called a *random event*.

6.1 DEFINITIONS AND BASIC CONCEPTS

Several definitions pertinent to the discussion which follows will be stated here. Other definitions will follow as the discussion proceeds.

Definition 6.1. *Probability*: A measure of the likelihood of occurrence of a random event. (This definition of probability may be distinguished from those given and discussed in the previous section by referring to this one as a general definition while the previous ones were mathematical definitions.)

Definition 6.2. *Sample space:* The set of all possible outcomes of an experiment. Synonymous with *universal set*, *possibility space*, *event space*.

Definition 6.3. *Experiment:* Any well-defined action upon which an observation can be made or a measurement taken.

Definition 6.4. *Outcome:* Each possible result of an experiment.

Definition 6.5. *Event:* Any well-defined subset of the sample space.

Definition 6.6. *Function:* A rule that assigns a value to each element of a set.

Definition 6.7. *Probability function:* A function that assigns a probability value to each element of a sample space.

We shall use the notation of set theory in the discussion of probability which follows in order to clarify and illustrate the relationships between events for which we wish to determine probabilities. For example, if we have two events designated event A and event B, then $P(A \cap B)$ represents the probability of the occurrence of both event A AND event B. $P(A \cup B)$ represents the occurrence of A OR B which we interpret as meaning either A or B or both. Although the symbols used here come from set theory, the logical concepts of AND and OR are identical with those of symbolic logic and boolean algebra discussed previously.

The axioms of probability derive from the following statement: Let S be a sample space on which the probability function P is defined. Let event A and event B be any two subsets defined on S.

Axiom 1: $0 \leq P(A) \leq 1$. $0 \leq P(B) \leq 1$.
Axiom 2: $P(S) = 1$.
Axiom 3: $P(A \cup B) = P(A) + P(B)$, if events A and B are mutually exclusive, that is, if they are a disjoint subset of S.

Axiom 1 simply states that a probability measure must be a real nonnegative number not greater than 1. Axiom 2 states that the probability of a certain event is 1. Axiom 3 states that if A and B are mutually exclusive events, the probability of either A or B occurring is simply the sum of their individual probabilities. Axiom 3 is called the *special additive rule of probability*.

The term "mutually exclusive" requires defining at this point.

Definition 6.8. *Mutually exclusive:* If events A and B are two subsets of S, and if the occurrence of one absolutely precludes the occurrence of the other, then events A and B are said to be mutually exclusive.

In terms of sets, mutually exclusive implies that A and B are disjoint subsets of S. The Venn diagram in Fig. 6.1 will illustrate this condition.

Since A and B have no points (or area) in common, they are disjoint subsets and therefore mutually exclusive.

Certain theorems can now be derived from the basic axioms of probability.

Theorem 6.1 *If $\varnothing$ is an impossible event, $P(\varnothing) = 0$.*
We can prove this theorem by making use of the facts that S and $\varnothing$ are disjoint subsets of S, and from set theory, $S \cup \varnothing = S$. Then

$$P(S \cup \varnothing) = P(S)$$
$$P(S) + P(\varnothing) = P(S)$$
$$P(\varnothing) = 0$$

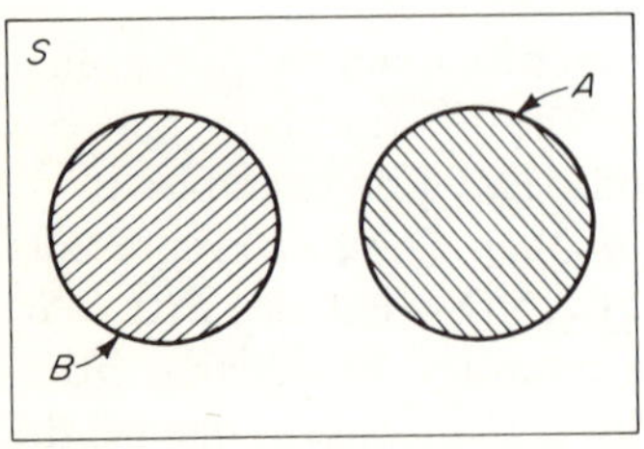

Fig. 6.1

Theorem 6.2 *If A' is the complement of A, $P(A') = 1 - P(A)$. Since A and its complement are disjoint subsets, and since $P(A \cup A') = 1$, then*

$$P(A) + P(A') = 1$$
$$P(A') = 1 - P(A)$$

Let us illustrate some of these basic concepts with reference to the rolling of dice. A single die, as is commonly known, has six faces numbered 1 to 6. We can define an experiment as a single roll of a die and the outcome of the experiment as the number on the face showing after the roll. Given a fair die, the likelihood of the occurrence of any face is equal to that of any other, and we shall assume a fair die. Therefore, all the outcomes of the experiment are equally likely.

The sample space of the experiment is the set $S = \{1,2,3,4,5,6\}$. If we want to determine the probability of a 2 showing on a single roll of the die, we would refer to our mathematical definition of probability. If there are $n(S)$ points, or possible outcomes in the sample space, and if $n(A)$ of these correspond to the event of interest, then $P(A) = n(A)/n(S)$.

The event of interest in this experiment is the outcome 2, and the probability of its occurrence is $P(2)$. Since there is only one way in which we can get a 2 on a single roll of the die, that is, there is only a single point in the sample space corresponding to the event 2, $n(2) = 1$. The total number of points or possible outcomes in the sample space is $n(S) = 6$. Therefore, $P(2) = 1/6$.

Since all the outcomes of this experiment are equally likely, $P(1) = P(2) = P(3) = P(4) = P(5) = P(6)$. $P(7) = 0$ since the outcome 7 is not a member of the sample space and is therefore impossible, illustrating Theorem 6.1.

The probability of rolling a 1 or a 2 on a single roll of the die can be written $P(1 \cup 2)$. The event of interest consists of two of the possible outcomes of the experiment. These outcomes are mutually exclusive since the rolling of any one number on any toss of the die absolutely precludes the rolling of any other number on the same toss. According to Axiom 3, this probability then is merely the sum of the probabilities of the individual outcomes, or

$$P(1 \cup 2) = P(1) + P(2) = 1/6 + 1/6 = 2/6 = 1/3$$

We would arrive at the same answer by the reasoning that since the event of interest can happen in two ways out of a total of six equally likely outcomes, $P(1 \cup 2) = 2/6 = 1/3$.

By extensions, the probability of a 1, a 2, or a 3 is

$$P(1 \cup 2 \cup 3) = P(1) + P(2) + P(3)$$
$$= 1/6 + 1/6 + 1/6 = 3/6 = 1/2$$

and the probability of a 1, a 2, a 3, a 4, a 5, or a 6, which outcomes constitute the entire sample space, is

$$\begin{aligned} P(S) &= P(1 \cup 2 \cup 3 \cup 4 \cup 5 \cup 6) \\ &= P(1) + P(2) + P(3) + P(4) + P(5) + P(6) \\ &= \tfrac{1}{6} + \tfrac{1}{6} + \tfrac{1}{6} + \tfrac{1}{6} + \tfrac{1}{6} + \tfrac{1}{6} = \tfrac{6}{6} = 1 \end{aligned}$$

If the event of interest is the rolling of a 1 on a single roll of the die, the event 1′ or the complement of the event 1 would be the rolling of any number except 1, that is, the rolling of a 2, a 3, a 4, a 5, or a 6. Therefore, $P(1') = P(2 \cup 3 \cup 4 \cup 5 \cup 6) = P(2) + P(3) + P(4) + P(5) + P(6) = \tfrac{1}{6} + \tfrac{1}{6} + \tfrac{1}{6} + \tfrac{1}{6} + \tfrac{1}{6} = \tfrac{5}{6} = 1 - P(1)$, which illustrates Theorem 6.2.

Since we shall not always be dealing with mutually exclusive events, the special additive rule of probability will not always be applicable. It is necessary to consider the situation in which the events of interest are not mutually exclusive and to establish a rule for determining their probabilities. As an illustration, let us define a new experiment as the tossing of two dice simultaneously, and the recording of the numbers which show after the toss. If we identify the dice as die 1 and die 2, then we can list all the possible outcomes of the experiment as in Table 6.1, where the first number in the parentheses represents the number showing on die 1 and the second number represents the number showing on die 2. It is evident that there are 36 possible outcomes for this experiment. We could also have arrived at the number of possible outcomes without listing them by applying Theorem 3.1 of Chap. 3.

Now let us determine the probability of rolling a 1 on any single toss of the two dice. Of the 36 possible outcomes there are six outcomes in which we get a 1 on die 1. These are listed horizontally in row 1 across the top of Table 6.1. There are also six outcomes in which we get a 1 on die 2. These are listed vertically in the first column of the table. We might then conclude that there are 12 ways of getting a 1 out of thc 36 possible outcomes and therefore,

$$P(1) = \tfrac{12}{36} = \tfrac{1}{3}$$

Table 6.1 Sample space of two-dice experiment

		2d die 1	2	3	4	5	6
	1	(1,1)	(1,2)	(1,3)	(1,4)	(1,5)	(1,6)
	2	(2,1)	(2,2)	(2,3)	(2,4)	(2,5)	(2,6)
1st	3	(3,1)	(3,2)	(3,3)	(3,4)	(3,5)	(3,6)
die	4	(4.1)	(4,2)	(4,3)	(4,4)	(4,5)	(4,6)
	5	(5,1)	(5,2)	(5,3)	(5,4)	(5,5)	(5,6)
	6	(6,1)	(6,2)	(6,3)	(6,4)	(6,5)	(6,6)

This conclusion is incorrect. It is incorrect because we have double-counted the outcome listed in the first row and first column, outcome (1,1). We counted outcome (1,1) when we determined the number of ways of getting a 1 on the first die, then we counted it again when we determined the number of ways of getting a 1 on the second die. Since we counted this outcome twice, we can correct our previous conclusion as to the number of ways of getting a 1. Instead of the 12 ways which we had concluded previously, we see now that there are actually only 11 *different* ways of getting a 1 in a single roll of the two dice. The probability of getting a 1 is, therefore, $P(1) = {}^{11}/_{36}$. It becomes obvious from Table 6.1 that the occurrence of a 1 on die 1 and the occurrence of a 1 on die 2 are not mutually exclusive events since it is possible to have a 1 on both dice at the same time.

To further illustrate the concept of events which are not mutually exclusive, let us consider the drawing of marbles from an urn or bowl. Suppose our bowl or urn contains four marbles and we differentiate between these elements as follows:

One big white marble
One little white marble
One big red marble
One little red marble

Let the experiment consist of reaching into the bowl and drawing out the first marble touched. What is the probability that a big marble will be selected on a single draw? Since two of the marbles out of the total of four marbles are big, the probability of selecting a big one is $P(B) = n(B)/n(S) = {}^2/_4 = {}^1/_2$. This assumes, of course, that the probability of selecting any single marble from the bowl is the same for all marbles.

The probability of selecting a red marble is also $P(R) = n(R)/n(S) = {}^2/_4 = {}^1/_2$.

By the special additive rule of probability, on the assumption that these were mutually exclusive events, the probability of selecting either a red marble or a big marble from the bowl would be

$$P(R \cup B) = P(R) + P(B) = {}^1/_2 + {}^1/_2 = 1$$

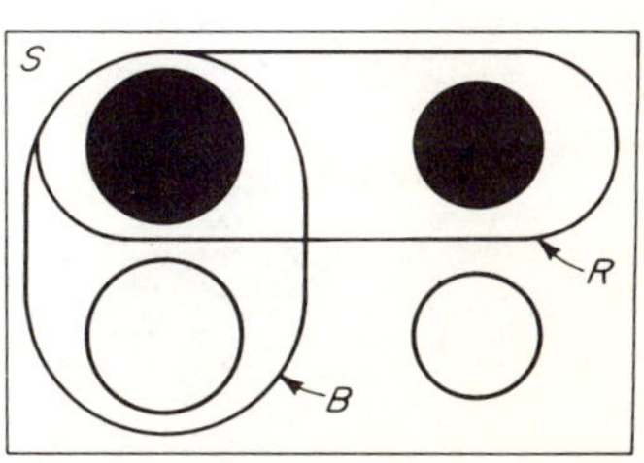

Fig. 6.2

This answer is, however, incorrect, and the reason for its being incorrect is evident from the illustration in Fig. 6.2.

The universal set S consists of all four marbles. Set R is that subset of S consisting of the big marbles. The number of marbles in set B is $n(B) = 2$. The number of marbles in set R is $n(R) = 2$. However, if we attempt to determine the number of marbles which are either in set B or in set R by simply adding $n(B) + n(R)$, we find that we have counted the big red marble twice since that single marble is a member of *both* sets. The number of marbles in either set R or set B which we designate by $n(R \cup B)$ is in fact three. We can enumerate the members of set $(R \cup B)$ as follows:

One little red marble
One big red marble
One big white marble

The true probability of selecting either a big marble or a red marble in one draw from the bowl is then $n(R \cup B)/n(S) = 3/4$.

What then is the rule which can be used to cover cases in which the events of interest are not mutually exclusive? In this example, as in the previous one, by using the special additive rule of probability, we have counted one of the elements twice. In this case, the big red marble was counted twice, once as a member of set R and once again as a member of set B. We would arrive at the correct answer for the number of members of set $(R \cup B)$ if we used the special rule and then subtracted from the answer we got that member which we counted twice. The big red marble represents the intersection or conjunction of sets R and B and is designated $R \cap B$. Therefore, for sets (or events) which are not mutually exclusive, we have the *general additive rule of probability* which is stated as follows:

$$P(R \cup B) = P(R) + P(B) - P(R \cap B) \tag{6.4}$$

This rule holds in any circumstance since, if sets R and B were mutually exclusive, $P(R \cap B) = 0$, and the rule reduces to the special case.

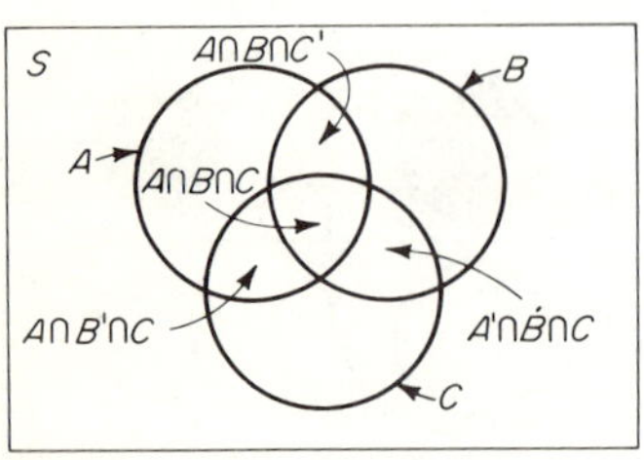

Fig. 6.3

If we had three sets A, B, and C, the rule becomes

$$P(A \cup B \cup C) = P(A) + P(B) + P(C) - P(A \cap B) - P(B \cap C) - P(A \cap C) + P(A \cap B \cap C)$$

The three-event case is illustrated in Fig. 6.3.
The extension to n sets or events is straightforward.

6.2 CONDITIONAL PROBABILITY

The probability of any event must always be considered wth reference to some specific sample space or event space. We have seen that if the total number of outcomes of an experiment (the sample space of the experiment) is $n(S)$ and if the number of outcomes which constitute event A is $n(A)$, then the probability of event A occurring when the experiment is performed is $P(A) = n(A)/n(S)$. Now event A has been defined on sample space S, and its probability $P(A)$ is only meaningful in that context. For that reason a more precise way of expressing the probability of the occurrence of event A with reference to the sample space S would be $P(A|S)$. This last symbol is read "the conditional probability of A given S." Since the probability of any event by itself and without reference to some sample space is meaningless, in the strict sense, all probabilities are conditional probabilities. However, it has become common practice to use the simpler symbol $P(A)$ instead of $P(A|S)$ whenever the sample space of the problem is apparent and no confusion is likely to result from the use of the simplified notation.

Suppose we have defined an event A and an event B on sample space S. $P(A|S)$ or simply $P(A) = n(A)/n(S)$ and $P(B) = n(B)/n(S)$. Suppose, further, that we are interested in determining the probability of event A based on the assumption that it is known that event B has already occurred; that is, we want to determine the probability of event A given that event B has already occurred. This probability is written $P(A|B)$. Figure 6.4 is a Venn diagram showing two subsets of S labeled A and B which correspond to the events A and B and which are not mutually exclusive. That is, there is an area in the diagram common to both A and B. This common area, as dis-

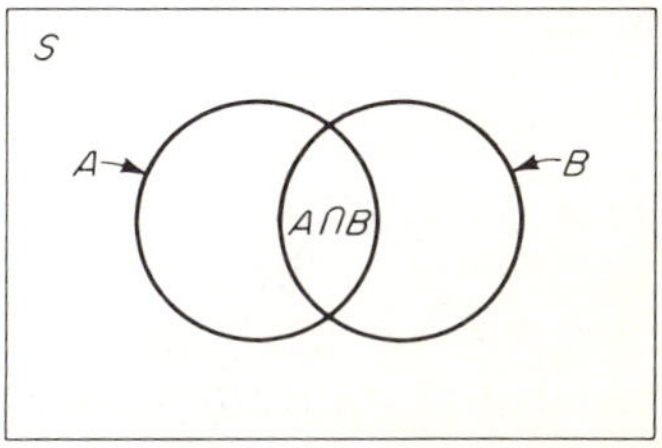

Fig. 6.4

cussed previously, is the *intersection* or *conjunction* of the two sets and is designated $A \cap B$ or, in an alternate notation, simply AB.

The probability of A given B in relation to Fig. 6.4 can be interpreted as the probability of being in the circle designated as set A given that you are also in the circle designated as set B. Now there is only one segment of the Venn diagram in which it is possible to be in circle A and circle B at one and the same time. This segment is the *intersection* of the two circles, or that area which has been labeled $A \cap B$. Therefore, the set which constitutes the event $A|B$ on the diagram must be represented by the area $A \cap B$. However, the sample space of concern with reference to the event $A|B$ is no longer set S because we have placed the restriction or condition that event B is known to have occurred. This condition reduces the total sample space to the space of event B only. Therefore, the probability of $A|B$ must mean, given that event B has occurred, the probability that event A has also occurred, and this is given by

$$P(A|B) = n(AB)/n(B) = P(AB)/P(B) \tag{6.5}$$

Equation 6.4 can be derived with reference to the total sample space S as follows. Since $P(AB) = n(AB)/n(S)$ and $P(B) = n(B)/n(S)$, then

$$\frac{P(AB)}{P(B)} = \frac{n(AB)/n(S)}{n(B)/n(S)} = \frac{n(AB)}{n(B)}$$

Since $P(A|B) = P(AB)/P(B)$, we can determine, by a simple algebraic manipulation, a formula for the probability of A AND B, that is, $P(AB)$. Multiplying both sides of the equation by $P(B)$, we get

$$P(AB) = P(B)P(A|B) \tag{6.6}$$

Furthermore, if $P(A|B) = P(AB)/P(B)$, then

$$P(B|A) = \frac{P(AB)}{P(A)}$$

and

$$P(AB) = P(A)P(B|A)$$

It then follows that $P(A)P(B|A) = P(B)P(A|B)$.

We have thus derived what is called the *general multiplicative rule of probability* which can be restated as

$$P(A \cap B) = P(A)P(B|A) = P(B)P(A|B) \tag{6.7}$$

In plain English, Eqs. (6.6) and (6.7) say that the probability of the *joint* occurrence of the events A AND B is equal to the probability of the occurrence of event A times the probability of the occurrence of event B, given that event A has already occurred. This is also equal to the probability of the occurrence of event B times the probability of the occurrence of event A, given that event B has already occurred.

In the previous chapter we described an experiment which consisted of the tossing of a fair coin three times, and we listed the outcomes which defined the sample space of the experiment as shown in Table 6.2, with the numeral 1 representing a head and zero representing a tail.

Let us define event A as the occurrence of exactly two heads in the three coin tosses. The outcomes of the experiment corresponding to event A are outcomes 5, 6, and 7. If we assume that all outcomes are equally likely, then by the definition of probability, $P(A) = 3/8$.

Let us also define event B as the occurrence of a head on the first toss of the coin. The outcomes corresponding to event B are outcomes 4, 6, 7, and 8; and $P(B) = 4/8 = 1/2$.

Now let us determine the probability of getting exactly two heads, given that the first toss of the coin resulted in a head. This probability can be expressed as $P(A|B)$. We are now limiting our sample space to event B which consists of only four outcomes of the experiment out of a total of eight possible outcomes. That is, $n(B) = 4$. Of these four outcomes corresponding to event B (outcomes 4, 6, 7, and 8), only outcomes 6 and 7 also belong to event A, that is, exactly two heads. Therefore,

$$P(A|B) = \frac{P(AB)}{P(B)} = \frac{2/8}{4/8} = 2/4 = 1/2$$

Now let us reverse the problem and determine the probability that a head occurred on the first toss, given that we observed exactly two heads on three tosses. This probability is $P(B|A)$. Now our sample space is limited to the event A which corresponds to outcomes 5, 6, and 7. Of these three outcomes only outcomes 6 and 7 also belong to event B (head on first toss). Therefore,

$$P(B|A) = \frac{P(AB)}{P(A)} = \frac{2/8}{3/8} = 2/3$$

Table 6.2 Outcomes of a three-coin toss experiment

	1st toss	*2d toss*	*3d toss*
Outcome 1	0	0	0
Outcome 2	0	0	1
Outcome 3	0	1	0
Outcome 4	1	0	0
Outcome 5	0	1	1
Outcome 6	1	0	1
Outcome 7	1	1	0
Outcome 8	1	1	1

Furthermore, $P(B|A)P(A)$ should equal $P(A|B)P(B)$. We find that this is indeed so by substituting the numerical values which we had previously determined into the equation thus,

$$(2/3)(3/8) = (1/2)(1/2)$$

$$(1/4) = (1/4)$$

Another example of conditional probability which might seem to relate to a more practical situation than that of a coin-tossing experiment is as follows. Suppose a machine shop turns out a particular part in batches of 100 on two different machines which we shall label machine A and machine B. In filling an order for 200 of these parts, we compile certain data regarding the output of good and defective parts from both machines which is given in Fig. 6.5. An arrangement of this type is sometimes called a *contingency table*. We shall consider these data to be representative of the output of these two machines and of the process as a whole. In the table, A stands for machine A, B for machine B, D stands for defective, and G for good. Our experiment now consists of the selection of a part from the 200 produced and an observation of the characteristic of that part which indicates the machine which produced it and whether it is good or defective. Since the experiment could result in the selection of any one of the 200 parts, the total number of elements in the sample space is equal to 200.

The total sample space S consists of 200 elements divided into subsets as shown in the figure. Subsets A and B each contain 100 elements as shown in the bottom margin of the figure. Subsets G and D contain 168 and 32 elements, respectively, as shown in the right-hand margin of the figure. The numbers within the boxes show the numbers of elements in the intersections of the subsets just mentioned, that is, $A \cap G$, $B \cap D$, etc. These intersections are, of course, also subsets.

From these data it is possible to compute certain probabilities. For example, the probability of selecting a defective part at random from the total of 200 parts is given by

$$P(D) = \frac{n(D)}{n(S)} = \frac{32}{200} = 0.16$$

	A	B	
G	80	88	168
D	20	12	32
	100	100	200

Fig. 6.5

This is simply the number of elements belonging to the set of defective parts divided by the number of elements in set S. The probability of selecting a good part at random is

$$P(G) = \frac{n(G)}{n(S)} = \frac{168}{200} = 0.84$$

$P(G)$ is also $1 - P(D)$.

We might also mention at this point that since the 200 parts for which these data have been compiled are considered to be representative of the total possible output of these machines or of this process, then these probabilities could also be said to apply to the probability of getting good or defective parts from the process.

Obviously, the probability of selecting a part that was produced on machine A would be 0.50, and the same probability applies to the selection of a part that came from machine B.

The probabilities which we have just computed could be called *unconditional probabilities*, although we have previously stated that in the strict sense, all probabilities are conditional since they must be expressed with reference to some sample space. In this case, that sample space S is the total output of the parts from the two machines. In order to avoid this contradiction in terminology, these probabilities are generally called *marginal probabilities*. It will be noted that in determining the marginal probabilities from Fig. 6.5, only the numbers from the margin of the table were used.

Now suppose that we want to determine the probability that a part is defective given that it was produced on machine A. Since this is a conditional probability we must now limit ourselves to considering only those parts produced on machine A rather than the total 200 parts. In other words, the sample space is now restricted to subset A where $n(A) = 100$. Then, since 20 of those 100 parts were defective,

$$P(D|A) = \frac{n(AD)}{n(A)} = \frac{20}{100} = 0.20, \text{ or}$$

$$P(D|A) = \frac{P(AD)}{P(A)} = \frac{0.1}{0.5} = 0.20$$

The probability of being in sets A and D simultaneously can be called the *joint* probability of A and D and, as is evident, is represented by the conjunction or intersection of the two sets, that is $A \cap D$ or simply AD. Since it is impossible for a part to be both good and defective at one and the same time, the sets G and D are mutually exclusive, and of course $P(G \cap D) = 0$. Similarly, $P(G|D) = 0$.

It is a simple matter to turn the previous problem around and ask for the probability that a part came from machine A, given that it is defective. This would be:

$$P(A|D) = \frac{P(AD)}{P(D)} = \frac{20/200}{32/200} = \frac{20}{32} = 0.625$$

Since $P(A|D) = 0.625$ and $P(D)$ was previously determined to be 0.16,

$$P(AD) = P(A|D)P(D) = (0.625)(0.16) = 0.10$$

This is easily verified from the table which shows that

$$P(AD) = 20/200 = 0.10$$

We shall consider one other illustration. Suppose our experiment is defined as drawing two cards in succession from an ordinary deck of playing cards. The first card is not replaced before the second card is drawn. We want to know the probability that the two cards drawn are both hearts. Let us designate the event "heart on first draw" as A, and "heart on second draw" as B. The problem now is to determine the joint probability of A and B, that is, $P(A \cap B)$. From the general multiplicative rule of probability, this is

$$P(A \cap B) = P(A)P(B|A)$$

This can also be considered as two repetitions of the experiment which consists of drawing a single card from the deck of playing cards. The sample space which applies to the first repetition of the experiment consists of 52 points or possible outcomes, and since there are 52 cards in the deck,

$$P(A) = 13/52$$

Given that a heart has been drawn on the first draw, the sample space for the second repetition of the experiment has been reduced by one point, or by one card, so that for the second draw there are only 51 possible outcomes, and since we specify that one heart has already been drawn, only 12 hearts are left in the deck. Therefore, the conditional probability of a heart on the second draw, given that a heart has already been drawn from the deck, is

$$P(B|A) = 12/51$$

Now $P(A \cap B) = P(A)P(B|A) = (13/52)(12/51) = 156/2652 = 1/17$

Let us now change the experiment slightly. We shall again draw two cards from the deck; however, we shall replace the first card before the second card is drawn. Event A is still "heart on first draw" and event B is still "heart on second draw." $P(A) = 13/52$ as in the previous experiment.

However, since the first card was returned to the deck prior to the second draw, the deck for the second draw, or the sample space for the second repetition of the experiment, is exactly the same as it was for the first repetition or draw. Therefore, $P(B|A) = {}^{13}\!/_{52}$. Also, $P(B|A')$, which is the probability of a heart on the second draw given that a heart was not drawn on the first, is also ${}^{13}\!/_{52}$. It is apparent then that $P(B) = {}^{13}\!/_{52}$ regardless of the result of the first draw. In this case, event B is said to be *independent* of event A, and in fact *statistical independence* is defined in this way. That is, event B is independent of any event A if

$$P(B|A) = P(B)$$

Therefore, for independent events,

$$P(A \cap B) = P(A)P(B)$$

This is called the *special multiplicative rule of probability.* For the last example given above, the probability of drawing two hearts in two draws when the first card is replaced before the second is drawn is

$$P(A \cap B) = P(A)P(B) = ({}^{13}\!/_{53})({}^{13}\!/_{52}) = {}^{1}\!/_{16}$$

6.3 BAYES' RULE

Let us refer to the Venn diagram given in Fig. 6.6.

We have two intersecting sets A and B. The set $A \cup B$ is, of course, represented by that area included in either or both of the two intersecting circles. $A \cup B$ can be partitioned or divided into three mutually exclusive subsets labeled $A \cap B'$, $A \cap B$, and $A' \cap B$ as shown in Fig. 6.6. It should be obvious that $A \cup B = A \cap B' + A \cap B + A' \cap B$.

Suppose, however, that we are interested only in event A for the time being. It can be seen from the diagram that $A = A \cap B' + A \cap B$, and therefore the probability of event A is

$$P(A) = P(A \cap B') + P(A \cap B) \tag{6.8}$$

From the previous material on conditional probability, we found that

$$P(A \cap B) = P(A|B)P(B) = P(B|A)P(A) \tag{6.7}$$

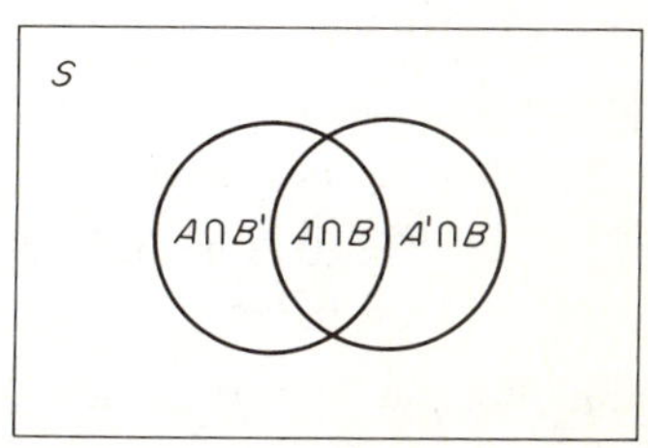

Fig. 6.6

and it follows that

$$P(A \cap B') = P(A|B')P(B') = P(B'|A)P(A)$$

Therefore, we can write

$$P(A) = P(A|B)P(B) + P(A|B')P(B') \tag{6.9}$$

More generally, if $B_1, B_2, \ldots, B_n$ constitute a partition of the event space containing A and represent a set of mutually exclusive events, none of which has a zero probability, then

$$P(A) = P(A|B_1)P(B_1) + P(A|B_2)P(B_2) + \cdots + P(A|B_n)P(B_n)$$
$$= \sum_{i=1}^{n} P(A|B_i)P(B_i)$$

The above rule is frequently called the *rule of elimination* and states that if event A is dependent upon the occurrence of any one of several mutually exclusive events one of which must occur, then the probability of the occurrence of event A equals the sum of the conditional probabilities of event A given B_i times the probability of B_i.

Let us consider an example. Suppose we plan an automobile trip to city A during the winter following a heavy snowstorm. We shall designate event A as our arrival at city A before dark on the day we leave home, and event A' as our failure to arrive at A before dark. There are three possible routes which can be taken, and we shall designate these routes as B_1, B_2, and B_3. These routes are of different lengths, and the probability of arriving at city A before dark depends upon the route taken. The recent snowstorm has closed all three routes, and we shall take the first one cleared and opened by the highway department. In the past, each one of these routes has been cleared first about an equal number of times, and we therefore assume that the probability of our taking any one of these routes, which is equal to the probability that it is the first onc cleared of snow, is

$$P(B_1) = P(B_2) = P(B_3) = \tfrac{1}{3}$$

That is, all routes are equally likely. Furthermore, from past experience we estimate that

$$P(A|B_1) = 0.70 \qquad \text{therefore } P(A'|B_1) = 0.30$$
$$P(A|B_2) = 0.85 \qquad \text{therefore } P(A'|B_2) = 0.15$$
$$P(A|B_3) = 0.75 \qquad \text{therefore } P(A'|B_3) = 0.25$$

From the rule of elimination, then,

$$P(A) = P(A|B_1)P(B_1) + P(A|B_2)P(B_2) + P(A|B_3)P(B_3)$$
$$= (0.70)(0.333) + (0.85)(0.333) + (0.75)(0.333)$$
$$= 0.766$$

and $P(A') = 1 - P(A) = 0.234$

This example can easily be visualized with the aid of the tree diagram in Fig. 6.7.

Each of the terms from which we calculated $P(A)$ is a path along the tree diagram leading to A. We could just as easily have computed $P(A')$ by the same formula, and we would then have terms corresponding to the paths leading to A'.

Now let us assume that we have reached our destination before sundown and have called home to report our safe and successful arrival to our families. We did not, however, tell them which route we took. After hanging up the phone, one of the family members, who happened to be a statistician, was curious as to whether we took route B_1, B_2, or B_3, and he decided to see if he could determine the probabilities. In other words, given A, what is the probability that we took B_1, B_2, or B_3? Mathematically he wants to determine the probabilities

$$P(B_1|A) \qquad P(B_2|A) \qquad P(B_3|A)$$

Starting with $P(B_1|A)$, we know from the discussion concerning conditional probability that $P(A \cap B_1) = P(A|B_1)P(B_1) = P(B_1|A)P(A)$. We can also solve the equation

$$P(A|B_1)P(B_1) = P(B_1|A)P(A)$$

for $P(B_1|A)$ and get

$$P(B_1|A) = \frac{P(A|B_1)P(B_1)}{P(A)}$$

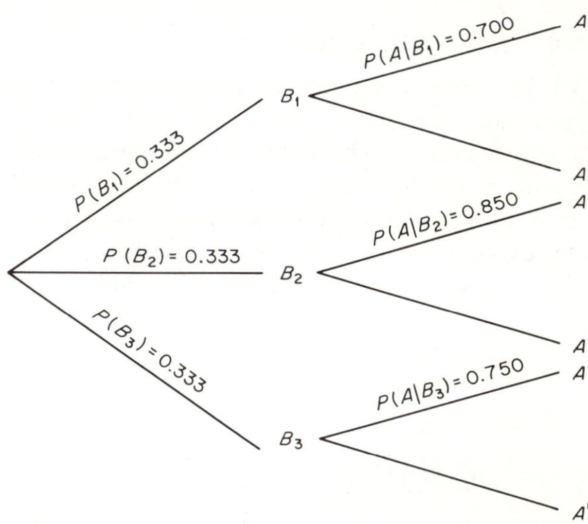

Fig. 6.7

But from the rule of elimination,

$$P(A) = P(A|B_1)P(B_1) + P(A|B_2)P(B_2) + P(A|B_3)P(B_3) \tag{6.10}$$

and therefore, by substitution,

$$P(B_1|A) = \frac{P(A|B_1)P(B_1)}{P(A|B_1)P(B_1) + P(A|B_2)P(B_2) + P(A|B_3)P(B_3)} \tag{6.11}$$

We have thus derived the rule of Bayes which we shall state as the following theorem:

Theorem 6.3 *If $B_1, B_2, \ldots, B_n$ constitute a partition of the event space A such that $P(B_i) \neq 0$, then*

$$P(B_i|A) = \frac{P(A|B_i)P(B_i)}{\sum_{i=1}^{n} P(A|B_i)P(B_i)}$$

To conclude the illustration begun above,

$$P(B_1|A) = \frac{(0.700)(0.333)}{0.766} \doteq 0.304$$

$$P(B_2|A) = \frac{(0.850)(0.333)}{0.766} \doteq 0.364$$

$$P(B_3|A) = \frac{(0.750)(0.333)}{0.766} \doteq 0.326$$

6.4 INDEPENDENCE

We have previously defined independence as being that property of events such that if $P(A|B) = P(A)$, then events A and B are said to be independent of one another. This definition can be extended beyond the concept of two events to include any number of events. We shall illustrate with three events, A, B, and C, defined on a sample space S. Let us write $P(C|AB)$ and call this expression the conditional probability of C given both A and B. From Fig. 6.8, the event corresponding to the occurrence of A and B is the total

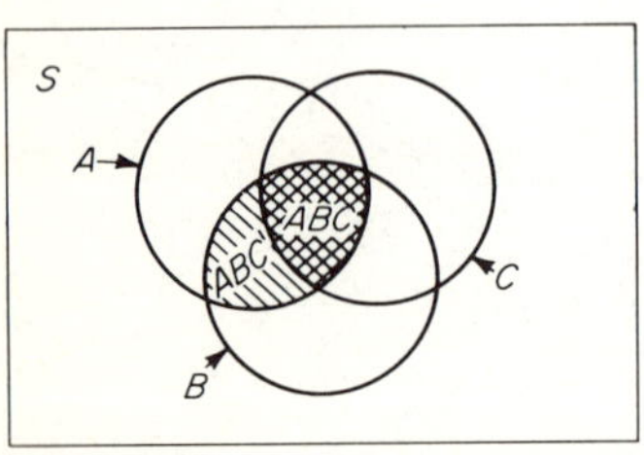

Fig. 6.8

crosshatched area representing the intersection of sets A and B. This subset $A \cap B$ becomes the reduced sample space for our probability statement since we have imposed the condition that both A and B must have occurred. Note that

$$A \cap B = A \cap B \cap C \cup A \cap B \cap C' \tag{6.12}$$

Now $C|AB$ means that subset of $A \cap B$ which is also in C. In Fig. 6.8 $C|AB$ is the doubly crosshatched area labeled ABC. Then the probability of C given A AND B is

$$P(C|AB) = \frac{P(ABC)}{P(AB)} \tag{6.13}$$

We can extend the above to a definition of the independence of the three events as follows:

Definition 6.9: Events A, B, and C, defined on the same sample space, are statistically independent if

$$P(AB) = P(A)P(B) \qquad P(AC) = P(A)P(C)$$
$$P(BC) = P(B)P(C) \qquad \text{and} \qquad P(ABC) = P(A)P(B)P(C)$$

The extension of this definition to four or more events is straightforward.

6.5 INDEPENDENT TRIALS

Let us define a *stochastic process* as a sequence of random phenomena or experiments that can be analyzed probabilistically. We can illustrate a stochastic process with a tree diagram such as the one shown in Fig. 6.9.

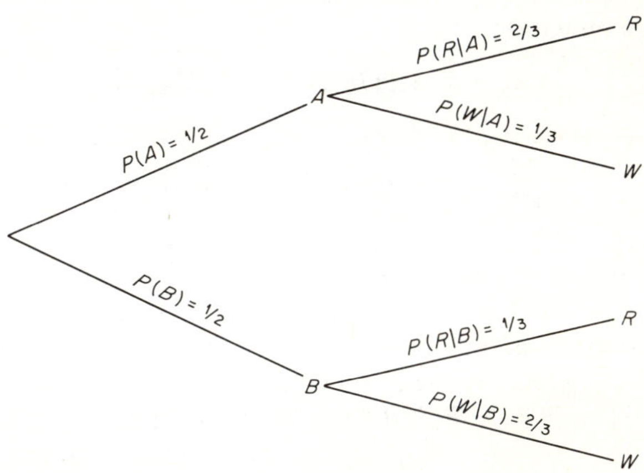

Fig. 6.9

Let us assume that we have two bowls designated A and B. In bowl A are two red marbles and one white marble. In bowl B are two white marbles and one red marble. The experiment sequence will be to select a bowl at random and then draw a marble at random from the bowl. There are four possible outcomes of this experiment as shown in Fig. 6.9 and enumerated below.

Outcome 1: A-Red, $P(1) = (\frac{1}{2})(\frac{2}{3}) = \frac{2}{6}$
Outcome 2: A-White, $P(2) = (\frac{1}{2})(\frac{1}{3}) = \frac{1}{6}$
Outcome 3: B-Red, $P(3) = (\frac{1}{2})(\frac{1}{3}) = \frac{1}{6}$
Outcome 4: B-White, $P(4) = (\frac{1}{2})(\frac{2}{3}) = \frac{2}{6}$

The sum of the probabilities of all possible outcomes is 1, as it should be.

The process we have just described occurred in two stages. The first stage was the selection of the bowl, and the second stage was the selection of a marble from the bowl. We now want to determine whether this is an *independent stochastic process.*

We know from the section on conditional probability and independence that any two events A and B are independent if and only if $P(A|B) = P(A)$ and $P(B|A) = P(B)$. A stochastic process is independent if the outcome of any stage of the process is independent of the outcome of any previous stage. For example, the probability that the outcome of stage 2 of the process just described results in a red marble should be independent of which bowl was selected in stage 1, if the process is independent.

First, let us determine the probability of getting a red marble as a result of the two-stage process. A red marble can result if bowl A is selected and a red marble drawn from bowl A, or if bowl B is selected and a red marble drawn from bowl B. Since the selection of bowl A precludes the selection of bowl B, A and B are mutually exclusive events, and by the rule of elimination

$$P(R) = P(A)P(R|A) + P(B)P(R|B)$$

Substituting the probabilities shown in Fig. 6.9, we get

$$P(R) = (\tfrac{1}{2})(\tfrac{2}{3}) + (\tfrac{1}{2})(\tfrac{1}{3}) = \tfrac{1}{2}$$

But $P(R|A) = \frac{2}{3}$, and $P(R|B) = \frac{1}{3}$; therefore, it is obvious that $P(R) \neq P(R|A) \neq P(R|B)$, and the process is *not* an independent process.

If, however, we change the experiment slightly by placing two red marbles and one white marble in bowl A and by placing two red marbles and one white marble in bowl B, the process looks like the diagram in Fig. 6.10. Now $P(R) = P(R|A)P(A) + P(R|B)P(B) = (\frac{2}{3})(\frac{1}{2}) + (\frac{2}{3})(\frac{1}{2}) = \frac{2}{3}$. Also, $P(R|A) = \frac{2}{3}$ and $P(R|B) = \frac{2}{3}$. Since $P(R) = P(R|A) = P(R|B)$ and it can be shown in the same way that $P(W) = P(W|A) = P(W|B)$, then all out-

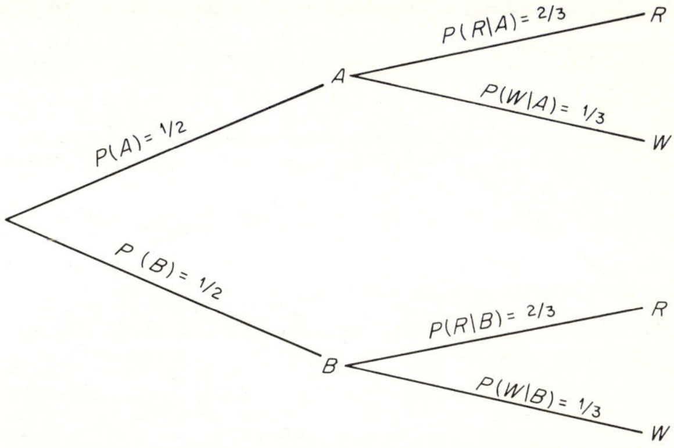

Fig. 6.10

comes of the second stage of the process are independent of the outcomes of the first stage, and this last experiment is an independent stochastic process.

We can generalize from the above into a definition of an independent process.

Definition 6.10: An *independent process* is one for which the probability that the outcome of the nth stage of the process is any particular element of the set of possible outcomes is completely independent of the outcome of the previous $n - 1$ stages.

If we let S_i = the ith stage of the process and if $P(S_i = a)$ means the probability that the outcome of the ith stage is outcome a, then for an independent process

$$P[(S_1 = a) \cap (S_2 = b) \cap \cdots \cap (S_n = k)] = P(S_1 = a)P(S_2 = b) \cdots P(S_n = k)$$

which is analogous to the definition for independent events.

If we look at the tree diagram of an independent process, we can see that the probabilities of the paths issuing from any branch point in a given stage of the process are identical with the probabilities issuing from all other branch points in that stage. However, at different stages, the probabilities can be different. An independent process is shown in Fig. 6.11.

A special type of independent process is called an *independent trials process*. An independent trials process is an independent process where not only are the path probabilities issuing from a branch point in a given stage the same as those issuing from every other branch point in that stage, but the path probabilities are also the same in every stage. This is illustrated in Fig. 6.12.

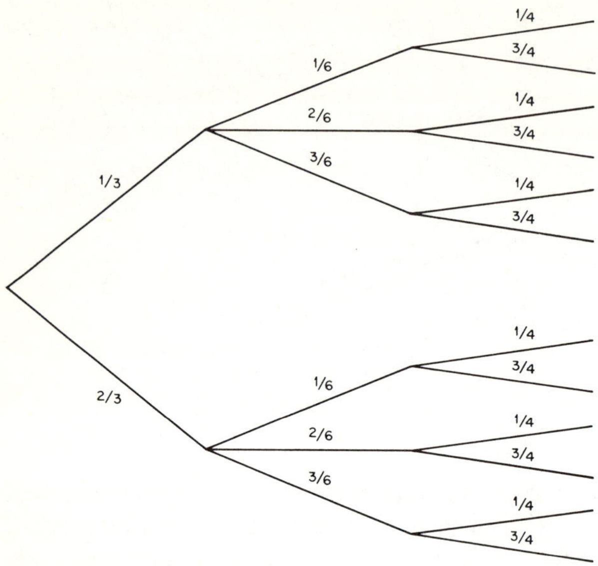

Fig. 6.11

An example of an independent trials process could be an experiment concerned with repeated tosses of a single die. The outcome of interest could be showing of a 1 or Ace, which we shall designate A, and $P(A) = \frac{1}{6}$; the showing of a 2 or a 3, which we shall designate event B and $P(B) = \frac{2}{6}$; and the showing of either a 4, a 5, or a 6, which we shall call event C and $P(C) = \frac{3}{6}$. At any stage of the experiment (any roll of the die) the outcomes are either A, B, or C, and the probabilities of A, B, or C are $\frac{1}{6}$, $\frac{2}{6}$, and $\frac{3}{6}$, respectively, regardless of the stage of the experiment. That is, $P(S_i = a) = P(S_j = a)$ for any i and j and for all outcomes a.

A very important type of independent trials process is called an *independent Bernoulli trials process* or simply *independent Bernoulli trials.* Independent Bernoulli trials are an independent trials process such that at each stage of the experiment there are only two possible outcomes. That is, there are only two paths leading from each branch point in the tree diagram.

Repeated independent Bernoulli trials result from an experiment for which at each stage there are only two possible outcomes, and the probability of each outcome remains constant from trial to trial or from stage to stage.

The previous experiment with the die could be transferred into an independent Bernoulli trials process if the outcomes of interest were limited to either the occurrence of a 1 on each toss which will still be designated event A, or the occurrence of any other number, that is 2, 3, 4, 5, or 6, which we shall call A'. $P(A) = \frac{1}{6}$. $P(A') = \frac{5}{6}$. These probabilities remain constant, no matter how many times the die is tossed.

The probability, then, of two successive 1s in two tosses of the die is simply, by the multiplicative rule of probability, $P(A)P(A)$ or $[P(A)]^2 = (\frac{1}{6})^2 = \frac{1}{36}$. The probability of two successive 1s followed by any other number in three rolls of the die would be $[P(A)]^2P(A') = (\frac{1}{6})^2(\frac{5}{6}) = \frac{5}{216}$.

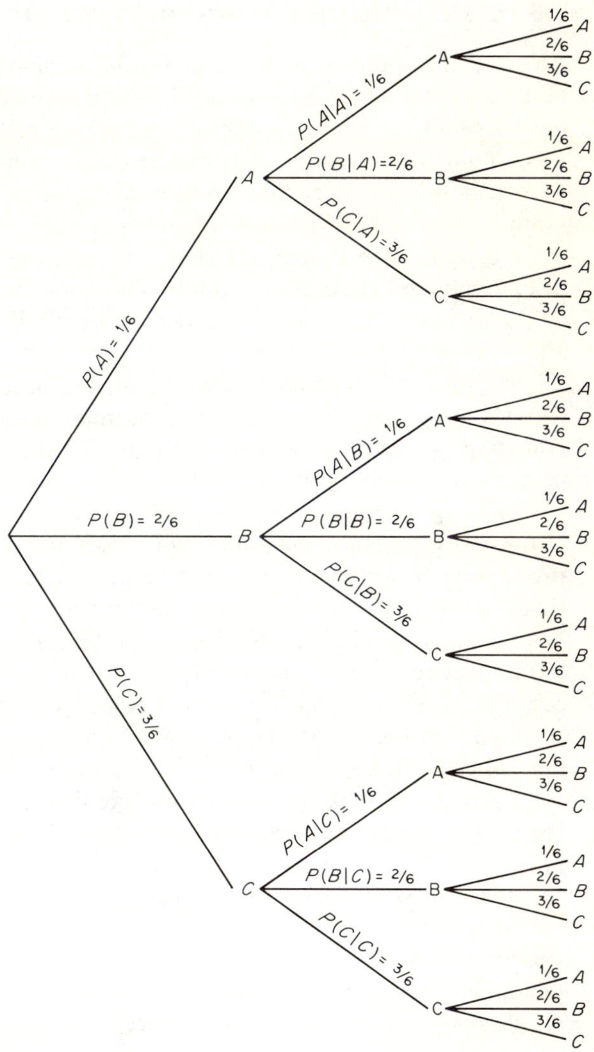

Fig. 6.12

Many probability problems are posed so that the outcomes of an independent Bernoulli trials process are simply labeled success or failure. Conventionally, the probability of success is denoted by p, while the probability of failure is $(1 - p) = q$. Then in n independent Bernoulli trials, the probability of x successive successes followed by $(n - x)$ successive failures would be given by $p^x q^{(n-x)}$.

6.6 CONTINUOUS PROBABILITY THEORY

Although the point was not specifically emphasized previously, the probability concepts which have been discussed assumed that the universal set, or the possibility space, with reference to which probabilities were determined, was a finite set consisting of discrete points. The subsets or events involved were also assumed to be discrete points or groups of discrete points within the sample space. This restriction is not necessary, and a possibility space can, in fact, be infinite though consisting of discrete points (sometimes called a discrete possibility space) or infinite and continuous.

An example of an infinite discrete possibility space would be the set of all integers. An experiment which results in a possibility space of this type might consist of repeated tosses of a coin in order to observe the number of tosses until a head appears. The sample space of this experiment would consist of an infinite number of points which would represent an infinite number of possible outcomes of the experiment of the form *H*, *TH*, *TTH*, *TTTH*, . . . , and so on, corresponding to the integers 0, 1, 2, 3, . . . , which in turn correspond to the number of tosses until the first head appears. The probability of any outcome can be calculated; for example, the probability that the first head will appear on the third toss given that the probability of a head on any toss is $\frac{1}{2}$, would be $(\frac{1}{2})(\frac{1}{2})(\frac{1}{2})$, or $(\frac{1}{2})^3$. This is simply the multiplicative rule of probability applied to the coin-tossing situation, assuming that the result of each toss is independent of the result of all others. In general, if the probability of a head on any toss is p, then the probability that a head will appear for the first time on the nth toss is $(1 - p)^{(n-1)}p$.

An example of an infinite and continuous possibility space might be the set of all real numbers in a given interval. An experiment which would illustrate a sample space of this type would generally involve measurements. Suppose we were to weigh all the men in a particular auditorium. The sample space would contain an infinite number of possible points corresponding to every possible weight within some interval. Our measurements would be limited by the accuracy of the measuring device, but the actual weights possible within the interval are infinite in number.

An infinite set can be represented by a line or by a plane area. Previously, the probability of an event A had been defined as the ratio of the total number of points or outcomes corresponding to A to the total number of points in the sample space. That is,

$$P(A) = \frac{n(A)}{n(S)}$$

For a continuous sample space, where $n(S) = \infty$, the probability of any single point, or of an event defined as a specific point or points in the sample space occurring, is always zero. Probabilities of events in a continuous sample space must therefore be considered as the probability of the occurrence of *any* point in some given interval. That is, the subset corresponding to the event of interest must be designated as an interval, as must the universal set.

For example, if the possibility space S is designated to be the interval of all real numbers between zero and 1, which we shall designate (0,1), and if we wish to determine the probability of the occurrence of some number in a subset which is itself the interval (a,b) such that $0 \leq a \leq b \leq 1$, then that probability is

$$P(a,b) = \frac{b-a}{1-0} = \frac{b-a}{1} = b - a$$

The probability then corresponds to the ratio of the intervals, or in this specific case the probability corresponds to the length of the interval which represents the event of interest.

Let us now define a function F which assigns to every element in set X a corresponding element in set Y such that $y = f(x)$. Let the set Y have the limits [0,1] which we shall call the range of F, and let set X be continuous between the limits x_1 and x_2, with $x_1 < x_2$. Then let $F(x_1) = 0$ and $F(x_2) = 1$. Since the set X is continuous, the number of points contained in any subset of X is infinite, and it is reasonable then to deal with intervals in X or with subsets of X defined by their limits.

For any interval (a,b) in X,

$$Y(a,b) = F(b) - F(a) = \int_a^b F'(x)\, dx$$

For the set X defined by the interval (x_1,x_2)

$$Y(x_1,x_2) = \int_{x_1}^{x_2} F'(x)\, dx = 1$$

The function F can be called the *cumulative distribution function* of X or the *cumulative density function* of X, and the function $F' = f$ is called the *density function* of X.

The set Y has the following properties:

1. $Y \geq 0$
2. $Y(x_1,x_2) = 1$
3. $Y(a,b) = \int_a^b F'(x)\,dx$

Y can be considered as a probability measure of X, and $F(x)$ and $F'(x)$ can therefore be called the *cumulative probability distribution* of X and the *probability density function* of X, respectively.

6.7 SUMMARY

Probability has achieved a role of great importance in practically all branches of human activity for the very simple reason that in most practical problems it is infrequent that all factors are completely determined or determinable.

The concepts of probability are most easily explained in terms of sets, subsets, and experiments. The totality of all possible outcomes of an experiment constitutes the universal set of sample space. An event is some subset of the universal set and corresponds to certain outcomes of the experiment. The probability of the occurrence of any event is defined as being the ratio of the number of points in the sample space corresponding to the event of interest to the total number of points in the sample space, or $P(A) = n(A)/n(S)$.

The probabilities of more than one event can be viewed as the probability of a compound event which is similar to the concept of a compound statement in symbolic logic or to operations on several variables in boolean algebra. For example, the compound event A AND B is simply the intersection or conjunction of events A and B, and the probability of its occurrence is $P(A \cap B)$, called the joint probability of A and B.

The compound event A or B is the symbolic logic compound statement A OR B, the two statements linked by the inclusive OR, and its probability is expressed $P(A \cup B)$.

The compounding of probabilities leads to the general and special additive and multiplicative rules of probability and to the concepts of mutually exclusive events, independent events, and conditional probabilities. The concept of independent events or independence in general leads to the consideration of processes which generate events. We have considered processes of this type which we have called stochastic processes, and in particular we have considered some special types of stochastic processes.

First we looked at a type of stochastic process which we called an independent process in which the outcomes at any stage of the process are completely independent of the outcome at any previous stage. We then considered the independent trials process which we defined as an independent process for which the probability of any outcome is the same at every stage of the experiment or process. Finally, a very important type of independent trials process was considered in which the number of events that could result at any stage of the process is limited to two. This latter was called an independent Bernoulli process.

Although the probability theory discussed in this chapter was approached from the standpoint of finite sets of discrete elements, we have shown that probability spaces need not be finite nor need they consist of discrete elements. When sample spaces are continuous, we have shown that the concept of the event corresponding to a single specific point in the sample space is meaningless, and that probability must be considered in terms of intervals.

PROBLEMS

6.1. A fair coin is tossed three times. What is the probability of getting:
(*a*) Three heads?
(*b*) One head followed by two tails?
(*c*) Two heads followed by a tail?
(*d*) Three tails?

6.2. A fair die is rolled once. What is the probability of getting:
(*a*) A 2?
(*b*) An odd number?
(*c*) A number less than 3?
(*d*) A number greater than 6?

6.3. A fair coin is tossed three times. Let A be the event "the first toss is a head." Let B be the event "two or more tails."
(*a*) What is $P(A)$?
(*b*) What is $P(B)$?
(*c*) What is $P(A \cap B)$?
(*d*) What is $P(A \cup B)$?
(*e*) What is $P(A|B)$?
(*f*) What is $P(B|A)$?

6.4. In the experiment described in Prob. 6.3, are A and B independent?

6.5. In the experiment described in Prob. 6.3, let C be the event "the second toss is a tail."
(*a*) Are A and C independent?
(*b*) Are B and C independent?

6.6. If a 5 or a 6 is considered a success on a single roll of a die, and if a number less than 5 is considered a failure, then on three rolls of the die what is the probability of:
(*a*) Two successes followed by a failure?
(*b*) Two failures followed by a success?
(*c*) The second roll being a failure?
(*d*) The second roll being a success?
(*e*) Three successes?
(*f*) Three failures?

6.7. If the probability of drawing a picture card from an ordinary deck of 52 playing cards is designated $P(P)$ and the probability of drawing a spade is designated $P(S)$, then on a single draw what is $P(P|S)$?

6.8. If the probability of drawing a red card from an ordinary deck of playing cards is designated $P(R)$ and the probability of drawing a Queen is designated $P(Q)$, then on a single draw what is $P(R \cap Q)$?

6.9. An experiment consists of drawing two cards from an ordinary deck of playing cards. The first card is not replaced before the second card is drawn. If the probability of getting a King on the first draw is $P(K_1)$ and the probability of getting an Ace on the second draw is $P(A_2)$, what are the following probabilities:

(*a*) $P(A_2|K_1)$?
(*b*) $P(K_1 \cap A_2)$?
(*c*) $P(K_1 \cup A_2)$?

6.10. Consider the following table which classifies students in a university according to their sex and according to their enrollment in either the School of Business or the School of Engineering. M refers to male; F refers to female; B refers to business; E refers to engineering.

	M	F	
B	350	250	600
E	350	50	400
	700	300	1,000

If a student is selected at random from the student body,

(*a*) What is $P(E)$?
(*b*) What is $P(B|F)$?
(*c*) What is $P(F|E)$?
(*d*) What is $P(M \cap E)$?
(*e*) What is $P(E \cap F)$?
(*f*) What is $P(F \cup E)$?

6.11. Are the events Female and Business School independent?

6.12. The first-string quarterback of State's football team was injured in their second-last game of the season. The coach estimates that if the quarterback recovers sufficiently to play in the final game against Tech, State's probability of winning is 0.75; otherwise it is only 0.25. The team doctor is consulted and says that there is about one chance in three that the quarterback will be able to play. What is the probability that State will defeat Tech?

6.13. I have two coins in my pocket, one of which is a fair coin, while the other is biased. The probability of a head $P(H)$ on the biased coin is 3/4. I reach into my pocket, select a coin at random, and toss it twice. If I observe two heads, what is the probability that I tossed the biased coin?

6.14. Prior to the election, both candidate A and candidate B promised that if elected they would reduce taxes. Candidate A has a record of keeping campaign promises about 20 percent of the time, while candidate B's record shows that he keeps campaign promises about 35 percent of the time. The latest poll taken on the eve of the election shows that the probability of *A* winning the election is 55 percent, while the probability that *B* will win is 45 percent. If the only information that you are able to obtain after the election is that taxes were actually reduced, what is the probability that *B* won the election?

6.15. Three boxes which are identical on the outside contain different amounts of money. Box *A* contains two $1 bills. Box *B* contains a $1 bill and a $20 bill. Box *C* contains two $20 bills.

(*a*) If a random process is used to select one of the boxes, what are the probabilities for each box being selected?

(*b*) If after a box is selected a single bill is drawn at random from that box and it turns out to be a $20 bill, what is the probability that the box selected was *A*? That it was *B*? That it was *C*?

(*c*) If after the $20 bill was drawn from the box, as discussed in *b* above, it was replaced and a second random selection was made from the same box, again resulting in a $20 bill, what new probabilities should you assign to the selection of each box?

7
Probability Functions

We have previously defined a function in a broad sense as a rule which assigns a value to every element of a set. We extended this definition and defined a probability function as a type of function which assigns a probability value to every element of a sample space. In the last section of the previous chapter we considered the general case of a continuous-event space and two types of probability functions which were called a cumulative probability distribution or density function and a probability density function.

In this chapter we shall consider certain specific probability functions. Before looking at these specific functions, however, it will be necessary to address ourselves to two related topics, random variables and the mathematical expectation of a random variable, and also to consider probability functions as models of real phenomena.

7.1 PROBABILITY FUNCTIONS AS MODELS OF REAL PHENOMENA

We have discussed the use of models as a means of representing some system under consideration in order to facilitate the process of arriving at optimum decisions regarding the system. Our discussion began with a general explanation of the types of models which can be developed, and some attention was paid to the progression from a simple graphical model through a logical model and on to a probability model. The latter was defined as being a model by means of which the probability of the occurrence of some specific system state or outcome could be determined.

The probability function as discussed in this chapter certainly qualifies as a model since it can be used as a mathematical representation of some real phenomenon. It is certainly a probability model since it determines or assigns probabilities to all points or outcomes in the sample space.

We can think of both the probability function and the probability distribution which it generates as models. The distinction between the function and the distribution is a fine one and would probably not even be made by most mathematicians. It is not an important distinction and is made here only to assist the reader in visualizing a process which assigns probabilities to points or outcomes.

For the decision maker, the system or process of interest is the occurrence or nonoccurrence of certain events or conditions which affect the state of the system. The probability of occurrence of these events, which are points or combinations of points in the event space, can be represented by a probability function. The function then, or the probability distribution which it generates, can be used as a model of the process of interest, providing that the model generates a reasonable approximation to the real-life process. The selection of a type of probability distribution to represent a given process is to some extent a matter of judgment, although one particular statistical method for assisting in this selection will be considered at a later time.

7.2 RANDOM VARIABLES

The observation or measurement of a random phenomenon is usually associated with a number. For example, in a coin-tossing experiment, the observation of interest might be the number of heads which occur after some specific number of coin tosses. In examining the output of some industrial process, the observation might be the number of defective parts in a production run of a certain size. Or, rather than merely counting the number of defectives in the production run, we might instead measure some critical dimension of each part as it emerges from the process or machine which produced it and record the measurement.

The number associated with some such particular observation or outcome is called a *random variable*. It is a variable since prior to the experiment its value is not fixed, although it may be limited to some particular range of values. It is random because it is associated with random phenomena or random outcomes.

Since the value of the random variable is a function of the experiment performed, we can define this term as follows:

Definition 7.1. *Random variable:* a numerically valued function defined on a sample space.

If the s_i are the elements of the set S, then $x = f(s_i)$ defines the random variable X as that function which assigns a value to every s_i in S. The set S is the domain of the function, while the set of values in X is the range of the random variable.

We shall adopt the convention of using capital letters to designate random variables and lowercase letters to represent specific values in the range of the variable. For example, $P(X = x)$ is read as "the probability that the random variable X equals some specific value x." The specific value of the random variable X can also be designated by a lowercase letter x with a subscript such as x_0, x_i, etc.

We shall encounter two types of random variables just as we have already encountered two types of sample spaces, namely *discrete* and *continuous.* A discrete random variable is one which can assume only a finite or denumerably infinite number of values. In the coin-tossing experiment, if the random variable represents the number of heads in three tosses of the coin, the only values which the variable can assume are 0, 1, 2, 3. If the experiment were to toss a coin and count the number of heads until the first tail appeared, the random variable could assume the values 0, 1, 2, 3, 4, . . . , etc. In the latter case the range of the random variable is infinite, but it can still only assume discrete values.

A continuous random variable, on the other hand, can assume a continuum of values. Experiments which give rise to a continuous random variable generally involve measurements of some sort. The measurement of the diameter of a part as it comes out of some production process produces a continuous random variable which can take on any value in some range of values. Although the accuracy of the measurement itself may be limited by the measuring instrument utilized, the true value of the variable is not limited within its range.

There is certainly a direct relationship between the sample space upon which the random variable X is defined and the nature of the variable itself. If the sample space is discrete, then X is discrete. If the sample space is continuous, X must be a continuous random variable.

Furthermore, the probability that a random variable assumes any value or set of values in its range is equal to the probability assigned to the associated element or set of elements in the sample space.

For example, if the experiment is the tossing of a coin three times, the probabilities associated with the events "no heads," "one head," "two heads," and "three heads," are, respectively, $\frac{1}{8}$, $\frac{3}{8}$, $\frac{3}{8}$, and $\frac{1}{8}$. If the random variable X is the number of heads observed, then the probabilities that $X = 0,1,2,3$ are also, respectively, $\frac{1}{8}$, $\frac{3}{8}$, $\frac{3}{8}$, and $\frac{1}{8}$.

Even though the random variable may be defined as a function, we are frequently concerned with functions of the random variable itself, specifically with a special type of function of the random variable which is a probability function. The probability function is that function of the random variable which assigns a probability that the variable X will assume some specific value in its range, if X is discrete, or that X will fall within some range of values, if it is continuous.

For a discrete random variable X we shall denote $P(X = x)$ by $f(x)$, which we shall call the *probability distribution function* of S or simply the *probability function* of X. For brevity we shall sometimes use the abbreviation PDF. The probability distribution function $f(x)$ of a discrete random variable X provides the probability that X equals some specific value within its range.

The probability $P(X \leq x)$ will be denoted $F(x)$, and for discrete random variables is the sum of the probabilities that $X = x_i$ for all $x_i \leq x$. That is,

$$F(x) = \sum_{x_i \leq x} f(x_i)$$

$F(x)$ will be called the *cumulative distribution function* for discrete random variables and will be abbreviated CDF.

If X is a continuous random variable, $f(x)$ will be called the *probability density function* of X, also abbreviated PDF, and $f(x) = dF(x)/dx$. Consequently,

$$F(x) = \int_{-\infty}^{x} f(x_i)\, dx_i$$

$F(x)$ will be called the *cumulative density function* for continuous random variables and can also be abbreviated CDF.

Statistical notation is not always consistent from author to author, and $F(x)$ is frequently called the *distribution function* of X whether X is discrete or continuous, and $f(x)$ is sometimes referred to as the *frequency function* of X when X is discrete. The terminology used is not of greatest importance, provided it is consistent in any single context, and provided also that there is no doubt as to the meaning when the meaning is pertinent.

In this book, the above terminology will be used, and, in addition, the terms *probability function* and *cumulative probability function* will refer to $f(x)$ and $F(x)$, respectively, when it is immaterial whether X is continuous or discrete.

We shall also make the distinction that a *probability distribution* can be either discrete or continuous and arises from the application of the probability function to all the elements in the set X. In other words, the distribution of probability values over the entire range of X is the probability distribution. The probability function actually performs the distribution of probability values as specific values are substituted for the random variable into the function. We might say that the function describes the distribution.

7.3 MATHEMATICAL EXPECTATION

In conducting an experiment or observing some random phenomenon, the variable of interest, whether discrete or continuous, can generally assume any one of a set of values within its range. There is a particular value within the range of the random variable X which is called the *mathematical expectation* or the *expected value* of X and is denoted by $E(X)$.*

If $f(x)$ is the probability function of the discrete random variable X, then

$$E(X) = \sum_i x_i f(x_i) \tag{7.1}$$

Equation (7.1) means simply that the expected value of the random variable X is the product of each specific value x_i in the set X and the probability that X will assume that value x_i, summed over all the values x_i in the set X.

For example, in the experiment which consists of two tosses of a coin, the random variable X, which equals the number of heads observed, can take on the values 0, 1, or 2. The probability of 0, 1, or 2 heads is, respectively, $f(0) = 1/4$, $f(1) = 1/2$, $f(2) = 1/4$. The mathematical expectation, or expected value of X, is therefore

$$E(X) = (0)(1/4) + (1)(1/2) + (2)(1/4) = 1$$

The expected number of heads resulting from two tosses of a coin is 1.

If we tossed the same coin three times, the random variable could take on the values 0, 1, 2, or 3. The probability associated with each value, corresponding to a point in the sample space, would be $f(0) = 1/8$, $f(1) = 3/8$, $f(2) = 3/8$, $f(3) = 1/8$, and the expected value of X would be

$$E(X) = (0)(1/8) + (1)(3/8) + (2)(3/8) + (3)(1/8) = 1\tfrac{1}{2}$$

It is, of course, impossible to ever actually get $1\frac{1}{2}$ heads on three, or for that matter, on any number of tosses of a coin, since the random variable, X = number of heads, is a discrete random variable and can only assume integral values. However, the expected value need not be one of the points in the discrete sample space. The expected value is, in fact, an average value, and we define the mean of a probability distribution in exactly the

* For a discrete random variable X, $E(X)$ need not be one of the points in the set X.

same way we define the mathematical expectation of a random variable. The expected value of a random variable is, therefore, equal to the mean of its probability distribution.

Since the mean of any probability distribution is generally denoted by the Greek letter μ (mu), we can write,

$$E(X) = \mu$$

For a continuous random variable X,

$$E(X) = \int_{-\infty}^{\infty} xf(x)\,dx = \mu$$

It is frequently of interest to determine the expected value, not only of the random variable itself, but also of certain functions of the random variable which are in themselves random variables. Suppose, for example, we are interested in some function of X, $g(x) = x^2$. Now the probability that $g(x) = g(x_i)$ is equal to the probability that $X = x_i$, which is $P(X = x_i) = f(x_i)$. Therefore,

$$E[g(x)] = \sum_i g(x_i)f(x_i)$$

if X is discrete, or

$$E[g(x)] = \int_{-\infty}^{\infty} g(x)f(x)\,dx$$

if X is continuous.

In the first coin-tossing experiment described above where a coin is tossed twice and the random variable X corresponds to the number of heads observed, that is 0, 1, or 2,

$$E[g(x)] = E(x^2) = \sum_{i=0}^{2} g(x_i)f(x_i) = \sum_{i=0}^{2} x_i^2 f(x_i)$$
$$= (0)^2(\tfrac{1}{4}) + (1)^2(\tfrac{1}{2}) + (2)^2(\tfrac{1}{4}) = 1\tfrac{1}{2}$$

There is a function of the random variable X that is of special interest in any discussion of probability distributions. This is the function $g(x) = (x - \mu)^2$. The expected value of this function of X is called the *variance* of X, or the variance of the probability distribution of X, and is designated σ^2, the Greek letter sigma, squared. Since $g(x) = (x - \mu)^2$, $\sigma^2 = E[g(x)] = E[(x - \mu)^2]$.

The variance of the distribution of a random variable is a commonly used measure of the variability or dispersion of a random variable about its mean. Again for the experiment consisting of two tosses of a coin,

$$\sigma^2 = (0 - 1)^2(\tfrac{1}{4}) + (1 - 1)^2(\tfrac{1}{2}) + (2 - 1)^2(\tfrac{1}{4})$$
$$\sigma^2 = \tfrac{1}{4} + 0 + \tfrac{1}{4} = \tfrac{1}{2}$$

The symbol E, used in the above context to mean expected value, is called an *operator*. It is essentially an instruction to take the expected value of the variable or function which follows in parentheses. There are certain rules for handling the operator E which can be summarized as follows:

Rule 1: The expected value of a constant C is the constant itself, that is, $E(C) = C$.

Rule 2: The expected value of a constant times a variable is the constant times the expected value of the variable, that is, $E(CX) = CE(X)$.

Rule 3: The expected value of a sum of random variables is equal to the sum of their expected values, that is, $E(X_1 + X_2 + \cdots + X_n) = E(X_1) + E(X_2) + \cdots + E(X_n)$.

7.4 DISCRETE PROBABILITY DISTRIBUTIONS

First, consideration will be given to probability functions of discrete random variables. The event space involved can be either finite or infinite, but the random variable itself can take on only discrete values.

THE BINOMIAL DISTRIBUTION

One of the most common discrete probability distributions encountered in statistics is the binomial distribution. It arises from an independent Bernoulli trials process in which the outcomes of each trial are usually, but not necessarily, labeled *success* or *failure*. As discussed previously, the probability of either outcome remains constant from trial to trial. If the two possible outcomes of each trial are labeled success or failure, we shall denote the probability of success on any single trial by the Greek letter θ (theta) and the probability of failure on any single trial by $1 - \theta$.

We had previously indicated that in an experiment consisting of n independent Bernoulli trials in which the probability of success on a single trial was θ, the probability of exactly x successes in a row followed by exactly $n - x$ failures in a row is given by $\theta^x(1 - \theta)^{n-x}$. As an example we considered the tossing of a single die three times. Success was defined as the appearance of a 1 after the toss, while failure was defined as the appearance of any other number. The probability of success on any single toss of the die would be $\frac{1}{6}$, and the probability of failure would be $1 - \frac{1}{6} = \frac{5}{6}$. Consequently, the probability of observing exactly two successes in a row followed by a failure in three tosses would be $(\frac{1}{6})^2(\frac{5}{6}) = \frac{5}{216}$. This probability, however, pertains to the occurrence of the two successes and one failure out of the three tosses in some very specific order. The order specified above was

success, success, failure

The other possible orderings of two successes and one failure would be

success, failure, success

and

failure, success, success

It should be apparent that there are a total of three ways in which we can get two successes and one failure in three trials of this experiment. Since each way has a probability of $5/216$ of occurring, the probability of the occurrence of two successes and one failure in any one of the three possible ways would, by the special additive rule of probability, be simply the sum of the individual probabilities. Since these individual probabilities are all equal, the total probability for the event is three times the probability of its occurrence in any one specific order, or $(3)(5/216) = 15/216$.

Recalling our previous discussion of combinations, we remember that there is a special designation and formula for determining the number of ways in which things can be selected from a group of n things, or, what is the same thing, the number of ways of getting exactly x successes out of n trials of an experiment. This happens to be the combinatorial formula which can be written

$$\binom{n}{x} = \frac{n!}{x!(n - x)!}$$

In the above example, where $n = 3$ and $x = 2$,

$$\binom{n}{x} = \frac{3!}{2!1!} = 3$$

In general, then, the probability of x successes out of n independent Bernoulli trials occurring in any order whatsoever, where θ is the probability of success on any one trial, is given by

$$\binom{n}{x} \theta^x(1 - \theta)^{n-x} \tag{7.2}$$

Expression (7.2) is called the *binomial distribution*. Its parameters are n, the number of trials, and θ, the probability of success on a single trial.

The probability of the occurrence of r or fewer successes in n trials is given by the cumulative distribution function which is

$$\sum_{X=0}^{r} \binom{n}{X} \theta^X(1 - \theta)^{n-X} \tag{7.3}$$

and if we sum (7.2) over all values of x from zero to n we would get

$$\sum_{X=0}^{n} \binom{n}{X} \theta^X(1 - \theta)^{n-X} = [\theta + (1 - \theta)]^n$$

which is the binomial expansion from which this distribution gets its name. The value of the previous sum is, of course, 1.

The mean of the binomial distribution is $n\theta$, and its variance is $n\theta(1 - \theta)$.

Since the mean of a probability distribution is simply the expected value of the random variable, we now have a shortcut for computing the expected value of the binomially distributed random variable X. $E(X) = n\theta$.

In the experiment which consisted of rolling a single die where the event of interest was the occurrence of a 1, we might wish to determine the expected number of 1s occurring in three rolls of the die when the probability of a 1 on any single roll is $\theta = 1/6$. This would be the same as the expected value of the random variable X in three trials of the experiment. By Eq. (7.1)

$$E(X) = \sum_i x_i f(x_i)$$

and in this experiment $n = 3$, the x_i are 0,1,2,3, and $f(x)$ is $\binom{n}{x} \theta^x(1 - \theta)^{n-x}$. $E(X)$ would then be determined from the evaluation of

$$E(X) = \sum_{i=0}^{3} x_i \binom{n}{x_i} \theta^{x_i}(1 - \theta)^{n-x_i}$$

as follows:

$$\begin{aligned} E(X) &= (0)\binom{3}{0}(1/6)^0(5/6)^3 + (1)\binom{3}{1}(1/6)^1(5/6)^2 + (2)\binom{3}{2}(1/6)^2(5/6)^1 \\ &\quad + (3)\binom{3}{3}(1/6)^3(5/6)^0 \\ &= 0 + (1)(3)(1/6)(25/36) + (2)(3)(1/36)(5/6) + (3)(1)(1/216)(1) \\ &= 0 + (75/216) + (30/216) + (3/216) \\ &= 108/216 \\ &= 1/2 \end{aligned}$$

By evaluating the formula, we have determined that the expected number of 1s resulting from three tosses of a single die is $1/2$. However, since we know that the variable X, which in this case represents the number of 1s occurring, has a binomial distribution, and since the expected value of a random variable is simply the mean of its distribution, we can arrive at the same result by using the formula for the mean of the binomial distribution. This would be

$$E(X) = n\theta = (3)(1/6) = 1/2$$

This is certainly much simpler than going through the rather lengthy calculation shown above.

Other illustrative experiments of the types described in the previous chapters which give rise to the binomial distribution are repeated drawings of cards from a deck or marbles from an urn, provided that the random variable is defined such that there are only two possible outcomes on each trial, and most important, that each element drawn is replaced before succeeding drawings are made. The replacement is necessary in order to meet the requirement that the probability must remain constant from trial to trial. If the element is not replaced before the next element is drawn, the sample space changes after every draw, and the probabilities also change. Replacement also ensures that the requirement of independence among trials is met.

In practical applications, the binomial distribution can be used to model situations involving sampling with replacement, sampling from a hypothetically infinite population, or sampling from a population of such magnitude with respect to the size of the sample that the binomial provides a convenient and reasonable approximation to the actual probabilities.

THE MULTINOMIAL DISTRIBUTION

A generalization of the binomial distribution results if our experiment is structured so as to allow for more than two possible outcomes on any trial. Suppose we revise the die-tossing experiment so as to allow the observation of three possible events on each trial. Event A will be the occurrence of a 1. Event B will be the occurrence of a 2 or a 3, and event C will be the occurrence of a 4, a 5, or a 6. The corresponding probabilities are, of course, $P(A) = 1/6$, $P(B) = 2/6$, $P(C) = 3/6$, and the sum of the probabilities of all possible outcomes is equal to 1. In order to be consistent with the notation of the previous section, we shall designate $P(A) = \theta_1$, $P(B) = \theta_2$, and $P(C) = \theta_3$.

Now in three rolls of the die, what is the probability that we get a 1 on the first roll, a 2 or a 3 on the second roll, and a 4, a 5, or a 6 on the third roll? In terms of the events A, B, and C, we are asking for the probability that event A occurs first, followed by event B, and that, in turn, followed by event C in three trials of the experiment.

This experiment is an independent-trials process since the outcome on any roll is independent of the result of any previous roll. Therefore, the probability of events A, B, and C in succession on three rolls of the die, by the special multiplicative rule of probability, would be $\theta_1\theta_2\theta_3 = (1/6)(2/6)(3/6) = 1/36$.

Suppose we rolled the die five times and wished to determine the probability of event A occurring twice followed by event B occurring twice followed by event C. This probability would be given by $\theta_1{}^2\theta_2{}^2\theta_3 = (1/6)^2(2/6)^2(3/6) = 1/648$.

In general, if we have a series of possible events or outcomes resulting from an independent trials process $A, B, C, \ldots, K$, with probabilities

$\theta_1, \theta_2, \theta_3, \ldots, \theta_K$, the probability that A will occur exactly x_1 times, B exactly x_2 times, C exactly x_3 times, . . . , K exactly x_k times, in some specific order in $n = x_1 + x_2 + x_3 + \cdots + x_k$ trials is

$$\theta_1^{x_1}\theta_2^{x_2}\theta_3^{x_3} \cdots \theta_k^{x_k} \tag{7.4}$$

However, if we are interested in the probability of x_1 outcomes of A, x_2 outcomes of B, . . . , x_k outcomes of K in any order whatsoever, then Expression (7.4) must be multiplied by the total number of ways in which the n trials can consist of the specified number of outcomes of each event. From Theorem 5.4 we recall that the number of permutations, or orderings, of n objects, or trials, of which x_1 are alike, x_2 are alike, . . . , x_k are alike, is given by

$$\frac{n!}{x_1!\,x_2! \cdots x_k}$$

This applies to outcomes as well as objects, and, therefore, the probability of x_1 outcomes of A, x_2 of B, . . . , x_k of K in any order whatsoever is given by

$$f(x_1,x_2, \ldots ,x_k) = \frac{n!}{x_1!x_2! \cdots x_k!}\,\theta_1^{x_1}\theta_2^{x_2} \cdots \theta_k^{x_k} \tag{7.5}$$

which is called the *multinomial distribution*, with parameters n and θ_1, $\theta_2, \ldots, \theta_k$. When $k = 2$, the multinomial reduces to the binomial distribution.

The multinomial distribution can be used to model independent trials processes under conditions similar to the binomial except that the number of outcomes on each trial is not limited to two.

THE NEGATIVE BINOMIAL DISTRIBUTION

The assumption of an independent Bernoulli process can result in another distribution which is closely related to the binomial, merely by defining the experiment and the random variable differently.

In the binomial, the number of trials was fixed in advance, and the random variable was specified as the number of occurrences of one of the possible outcomes during the n trials. The negative binomial specifies the number of occurrences in advance and lets the random variable become the number of trials required until that specified number of occurrences is observed.

The physical phenomenon being observed is the same as for the binomial distribution; however, the event of interest is different. Let the experiment again be the tossing of a coin. To use the binomial model, we specify the number of trials of the experiment which becomes one of the parameters of the distribution n, and the random variable observed is the number of heads observed in the n trials. To use the negative binomial model, we specify that the experiment will continue until a given number of heads are observed. Let this number of heads be designated c. The random variable of this experiment X will be the number of trials required to produce the c heads.

The probability of a head occurring, or in general that outcome which we call *success* in this type of experiment, is labeled θ and is a parameter of the negative binomial just as it was of the binomial distribution. The other parameter of the negative binomial distribution is c, the number of successes to be observed.

If c represents the number of successes to be observed and X is the number of trials until exactly c successes occur, then $X - c$ is the number of failures.

The negative binomial provides the distribution of the random variable X and is given by

$$f(X) = \binom{x-1}{c-1}\theta^c(1-\theta)^{x-c} \tag{7.6}$$

The probability that c successes occur in exactly x trials is equivalent to the probability that exactly $c - 1$ successes occur in $x - 1$ trials and the cth success occurs on the xth trial. The probability that, given c and θ, the cth success will occur on or before the rth trial is given by

$$P(X \leq r|c,\theta) = \sum_{X=c}^{r} \binom{X-1}{c-1}\theta^c(1-\theta)^{X-c} \tag{7.7}$$

Because of the relationship between the negative binomial and the binomial distributions, the probability that the cth success will occur on or before the rth trial is exactly equal to the binomial probability that the number of successes in r trials is greater than or equal to c. That is, if we designate x_r as the number of successes in r trials, Eq. (7.7) is exactly equal to

$$P(X_r \geq c|r,\theta) = \sum_{x_r=c}^{r} \binom{r}{x_r}\theta^{x_r}(1-\theta)^{r-x_r} \tag{7.8}$$

For example, suppose a company which produces a critical missile part tests each unit before shipping it to the customer. Suppose also that from past experience they estimate that the probability that any one of the parts produced is defective is equal to 0.2. What then is the probability that they will find the first defective part by the time they have tested 10 of the parts? In this example, success corresponds to a defective part, and $\theta = 0.2$.

The probability that the first defective will occur on or before the tenth test is given by

$$P(X \leq 10|1,0.2) = \sum_{X=1}^{10} \binom{X-1}{0}(0.2)^1(0.8)^{X-1}$$

This is exactly equal to the binomial probability that there will be one or more defectives in the first 10 parts tested, which is given by

$$P(X_r \geq 1|10,0.2) = \sum_{x_r=1}^{10} \binom{10}{x_r}(0.2)^{x_r}(0.8)^{10-x_r}$$

and the latter summation can be found in any set of binomial tables.

Since the evaluation of sums such as those given previously can become a very tedious operation, tables of the various distributions and cumulative distributions are extremely valuable as time-saving devices. Since the binomial is a widely tabulated distribution, it is helpful to realize that the negative binomial can be converted to an equivalent binomial distribution as shown above. Therefore, a set of binomial tables is all that is needed to evaluate the sum of a negative binomial distribution.

The mean and variance, respectively, of the negative binomial distribution are

$$\mu = \frac{c(1-\theta)}{\theta} \qquad \text{and} \qquad \sigma^2 = \frac{c(1-\theta)}{\theta^2}$$

THE POISSON DISTRIBUTION

The Poisson distribution is frequently used as a model in situations in which some event or change of state occurs randomly in time or over distances, areas, or volumes. It is particularly well suited to the description of the occurrence of events in the time domain where it is impossible to enumerate the number of nonoccurrences of the event.

For example, in a given period of time we can count the number of lightning flashes which have occurred, but we certainly cannot count the number of flashes that did not occur. It is certainly possible to determine the number of automobile accidents which have occurred on a particular stretch of highway during the past year, but it is not possible to determine the number of accidents which have not occurred.

The Poisson probability distribution can be derived from the expression

$$e^{\mu}e^{-\mu} = 1 \tag{7.9}$$

Since e^{μ} can be expanded into the following infinite series,

$$e = 1 + \mu + \frac{\mu^2}{2!} + \frac{\mu^3}{3!} + \cdots$$

Eq. (7.9) can be written

$$e^{-\mu}\left(1 + \mu + \frac{\mu^2}{2!} + \frac{\mu^3}{3!} + \cdots\right) = 1$$

or as

$$\sum_{i=0}^{\infty} e^{-\mu}\mu^{x_i}/x_i! = 1 \tag{7.10}$$

Equations (7.9) and (7.10) meet the requirement that the sum of a probability distribution over the entire range of the random variable be equal to 1.

If we now define μ as the average or mean number of occurrences of some event in a time T, then Eq. (7.10) takes on certain specific probability meanings. For example, $e^{-\mu}$ is the probability that the event will occur zero times in time T; that is, it will not occur. The term $\mu e^{-\mu}$ provides the probability that the event will occur once in time T; $\mu^2 e^{-\mu}/2!$ is the probability that the event will occur twice, etc. The expression

$$e^{-\mu}\mu^{x}/x! \tag{7.11}$$

is then the probability that the event will occur exactly x times in time T. This function (7.11) is the Poisson distribution, or probability distribution function, and provides the probability of any number of occurrences of an event providing only that the average number of occurrences in time T is known or can be estimated. The probability of r or fewer occurrences of the event is given by the Poisson CDF which is

$$\sum_{X=0}^{r} e^{-\mu}\mu^{X}/X! \tag{7.12}$$

The Poisson is a single-parameter distribution, the parameter being μ, which is the mean of the distribution. The variance is also equal to μ.

The assumptions necessary in order for the Poisson distribution to be applicable as a model for a given situation are these:

1. The occurrence of the event of interest during any interval of time (or over any interval of space) is independent of its occurrence during any other interval.
2. The probability of any given number of occurrences of the event in an interval is proportional to the width, or size, of the interval but is independent of the location of the interval.
3. An interval T can be divided into t subintervals of width ΔT such that the probability of more than one occurrence of the event in any ΔT is negligible.

4. There is a constant θ, such that the probability of the event occurring in any ΔT is equal to $\theta\,\Delta T$, that is,
   $P_0(\Delta T) = 1 - \theta\,\Delta T$
   $P_1(\Delta T) = \theta\,\Delta T$
   $P_2(\Delta T) = 0$
   where $P_i(\Delta T)$ stands for the probability of i occurrences of the event in ΔT.

Under these assumptions, the mean of the Poisson distribution $\mu = \theta T$.

Suppose the average number of requests for information received at the information desk of a bus terminal in a quarter of an hour is seven. What is the probability that in any given 15-min period, exactly three requests will be received? Three or fewer?

The answers are provided by the Poisson distribution with $\mu = 7$. Values of the Poisson distribution having different means have been extensively tabulated. The probability of receiving exactly three requests at the information desk during any 15-min period is given by

$$\frac{e^{-7}7^3}{3!} = 0.0521$$

The probability of three or fewer is given by

$$\sum_{i=0}^{3} e^{-7}7^{x_i}/x_i! = 0.0817$$

Under certain circumstances, the Poisson distribution can be used to approximate binomial probabilities. The approximation is good when the binomial n is large and θ is small. As a rule of thumb, the approximation is satisfactory when the binomial $n\theta$ or $n(1 - \theta) \leq 5$.

As an example, suppose that the probability of getting a defective part from some particular production process is estimated to be 0.02. What then is the probability that a given production run of 200 parts contains five or fewer defectives? The solution to this problem is the evaluation of the binomial

$$P(X \leq 5) = \sum_{i=0}^{5} \binom{200}{x_i} \theta^{x_i}(1 - \theta)^{200 - x_i} = 0.788$$

Since $n\theta = (200)(0.02) = 4$, and this is also the mean of the binomial distribution, the Poisson distribution with a mean equal to 4 can be used as an approximation. The approximate solution results from

$$\sum_{i=0}^{5} \frac{e^{-4}4^{x_i}}{x_i!} = 0.785$$

which is quite close to the solution resulting from the exact method.

Since the Poisson function can be written $(e^{-\mu})(\mu^x/x!)$, the function can be evaluated, although somewhat tediously, even if tables of the distribution are not available. All that is needed is a table of the exponential $e^{-\mu}$. The factor $\mu^x/x!$ can be calculated arithmetically and the product taken.

THE HYPERGEOMETRIC DISTRIBUTION

The binomial distribution was the proper model to use for the calculation of probabilities arising from an independent Bernoulli trials process. One of the main requirements for the binomial to be applicable was that the probability of the occurrence of the event of interest must remain constant from trial to trial. We have seen that, in selecting cards from a deck of cards or in sampling elements from a production run of a given size, this requirement is met only if we replace each element before the next one is selected. If we fail to replace, the complement of the deck of cards, the production run, or in general any finite population is changed every time an element is taken away from it. Consequently, the probability of selecting any element also changes.

In an experiment of the *sampling without replacement* type, which allows only two possible outcomes to each trial, the proper probability model is called the *hypergeometric distribution.*

Assume that we have a set of N elements, some of which possess some characteristic, called A, and some of which do not possess characteristic A. The probability of A, $P(A) = \theta$, and of course $P(A') = 1 - \theta$. If the number of elements having characteristic A is designated by $N(A)$, then $P(A) = N(A)/N = \theta$, and $N(A) = N\theta$. It follows that the number of elements which do not possess characteristic A is $N(1 - \theta)$.

Now suppose that we select n elements out of the total set of N elements without replacement and want to know the probability that x of these n elements has characteristic A. The random variable X represents the number of elements in our drawing or sample possessing the characteristic A.

We have defined the probability of an event as the ratio of the number of ways in which it can occur to the total number of ways in which it can either occur or fail to occur. This definition could also be rephrased to state that the probability of an event is the ratio of the number of outcomes or points in the sample space corresponding to that event, to the total number of points in the sample space. Now the probability of getting exactly x elements with characteristic A in a drawing or sample of n elements corresponds to the event:

Select x elements with A out of $N\theta$ elements with A

and

Select $n - x$ elements with A' out of $N(1 - \theta)$ elements with A'.

The number of ways in which we can select x of the A elements out of $N\theta$ of the A elements is $\binom{N\theta}{x}$. The number of ways we can select $n - x$ of the A' elements out of $N(1 - \theta)$ of the A' elements is $\binom{N(1-\theta)}{n-x}$. The number of ways in which we can do both is the product of the number of ways in which we can do either. Therefore, the product

$$\binom{N\theta}{x}\binom{N(1-\theta)}{n-x}$$

represents the total number of outcomes corresponding to the event of interest.

Now the number of points or outcomes in the sample space is simply the total number of ways in which it is possible to select a sample of n elements out of a total population of N elements, and this is $\binom{N}{n}$. Therefore, the function which gives us the probability of the occurrence of the event of interest is the hypergeometric probability distribution function, which is given by

$$f(x) = \frac{\binom{N\theta}{x}\binom{N(1-\theta)}{n-x}}{\binom{N}{n}} \tag{7.13}$$

The parameters of this distribution are N, n, and θ. Its mean is $n\theta$, and its variance is $n\theta(1 - \theta)(N - n)/N - 1$. It is apparent that the mean of the hypergeometric distribution is identical with the mean of the binomial. As N becomes large with respect to n, the variance of the distribution approaches the binomial variance.

A somewhat more convenient way of writing the hypergeometric function would be to denote the number of elements in the sample space which have characteristic A as $a = N\theta$. Then

$$f(x) = \frac{\binom{a}{x}\binom{N-a}{n-x}}{\binom{N}{n}} \tag{7.14}$$

As an example of the use of this distribution, suppose that a particular process turns out on the average 20 percent defectives. In each lot of say 10 parts we would expect to find two defective parts. Suppose that from a given lot of $N = 10$ we sample three parts at random and inspect them. What is the probability that, given two defectives in the lot, our sample contains exactly one defective?

In this example, $N = 10$, $n = 3$, and $a = 2$. $P(X = 1)$ is given by

$$f(1) = \frac{\binom{2}{1}\binom{8}{2}}{\binom{10}{3}} \doteq 0.466$$

If we had used the binomial to determine this probability, we would have evaluated

$$f(x) = \binom{n}{x}\theta^x(1 - \theta)^{n-x}$$

which would have resulted in $f(1) = \binom{3}{1}(0.2)(0.8)^2 = 0.684$, a rather substantial error. However, when N is very large relative to n, the hypergeometric and the binomial approximate each other rather well. The binomial approximation to the hypergeometric can be used when $n/N \leq 0.05$.

7.5 CONTINUOUS PROBABILITY DISTRIBUTIONS

Those functions of a random variable which are in themselves continuous random variables give rise to *density functions*. We have previously defined $F(x)$ as the cumulative distribution function or cumulative density function of S and stated that it represents the probability that X is equal to or less than some value x. In the continuous case, the probability that X assumes any specific value within its range is zero; thus

$$P(X \leq x) = P(X < x)$$

The probability that X assumes a value within the limits (a,b) where $a < b$ is given by

$$\int_a^b f(x)\,dx = F(b) - F(a)$$

Several of the more common and important probability density functions will be considered next.

THE UNIFORM DISTRIBUTION

Let us specify that the probability that $X < x$ is given by

$$F(x) = \begin{cases} 0 & \text{when } x \leq a \\ (x - a)/(b - a) & \text{when } a < x < b \\ 1 & \text{when } b \leq x \end{cases} \tag{7.15}$$

The graph of this function is shown in Fig. 7.1.

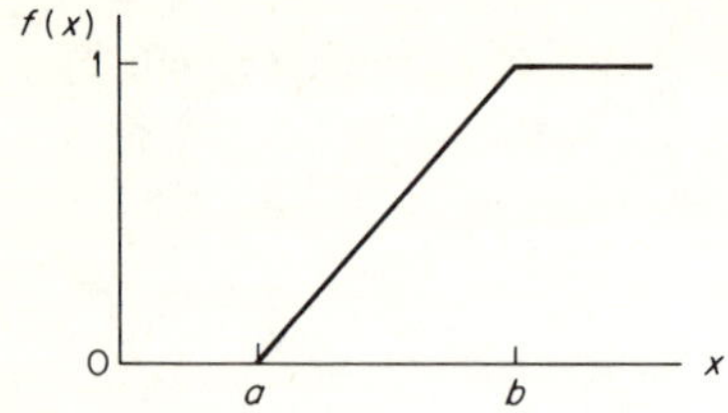

Fig. 7.1

Since $f(x) = dF(x)/dx$, we can obtain the density function by differentiation. Thus

$$f(x) = \begin{cases} 0 & \text{when } x \leq a \\ 1/(b-a) & \text{when } a < x < b \\ 0 & \text{when } b \leq x \end{cases} \tag{7.16}$$

and a graph of the density function is shown in Fig. 7.2.

First, let us verify that this is indeed a probability function by integrating $f(x)$ over the entire range of the random variable.

$$\int_a^b f(x)\,dx = \int_a^b \frac{1}{b-a}\,dx = \frac{x}{b-a}\bigg|_a^b = \frac{b-a}{b-a} = 1$$

Now, consider a specific uniform probability where $b = 3$ and $a = 1$. The graph of this function is shown in Fig. 7.3.

Let us evaluate the probability that X is less than 2.

$$P(X < 2) = \int_1^2 \frac{dx}{3-1} = \frac{x}{2}\bigg|_1^2 = 1 - \tfrac{1}{2} = \tfrac{1}{2}$$

or

$$F(2) - F(1) = 1 - \tfrac{1}{2} = \tfrac{1}{2}$$

The probability that X is between 1.5 and 2.5 is given by

$$P(1.5 < x < 2.5) = \int_{1.5}^{2.5} \frac{dx}{3-1} = \frac{x}{2}\bigg|_{1.5}^{2.5} = 1.25 - 0.75 = 0.5$$

or

$$F(2.5) - F(1.5) = 0.5$$

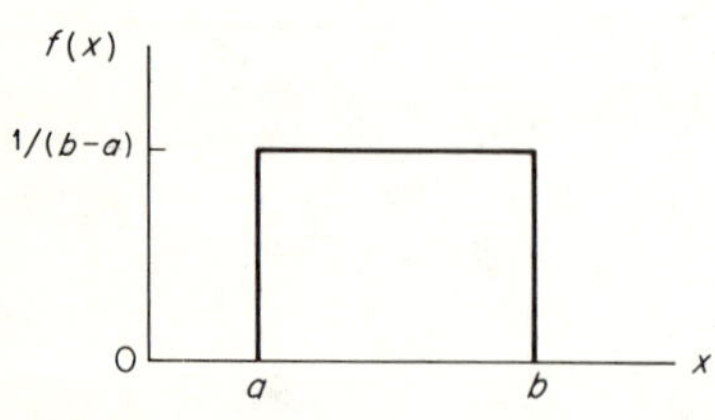

Fig. 7.2

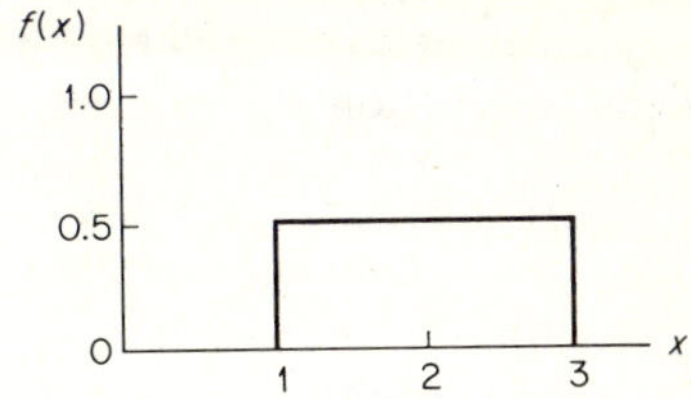

Fig. 7.3

And, in general, for the uniform density or any other density function, the probability that the random variable assumes any value within some range is found by integrating the density function over the specified range.

The uniform density function has limited application as a model for real phenomena, although some do exist. It is introduced here primarily to illustrate the method employed for finding probabilities given the density function, since it is the simplest of all the continuous distributions.

The mean of the uniform density function is $(a + b)/2$, and its variance is $(b - a)^2/12$.

THE NORMAL DISTRIBUTION

Probably the most important of all the continuous probability distributions is the normal or Gaussian distribution (see Fig. 7.4). The normal distribution can be represented by a bell-shaped curve and has the following properties:

1. It is a two-parameter distribution with parameters μ, the mean, and σ, called the standard deviation, which is simply the square root of the variance.
2. It is symmetrical about its mean.
3. It is infinite in extent, extending from $-\infty$ to $+\infty$.

The notation commonly used to designate a normal distribution with parameters μ and σ is $N(\mu,\sigma)$.

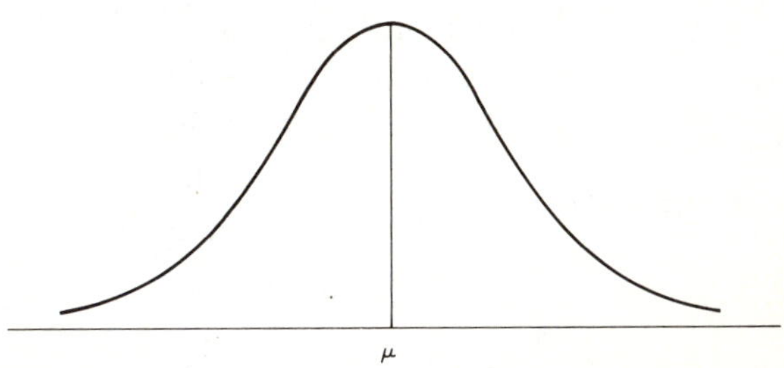

Fig. 7.4

The mathematical equation which describes the normal probability density function is

$$f(x) = \frac{1}{\sigma\sqrt{2\pi}} e^{-1/2[(x-\mu)/\sigma]^2} \tag{7.17}$$

The cumulative density function which provides the probability that the random variable $X < x$ is given by

$$F(x) = \frac{1}{\sigma\sqrt{2\pi}} \int_{-\infty}^{x} e^{-1/2[(x-\mu)/\sigma]^2}\, dx \tag{7.18}$$

and the probability that X assumes any value between the limits a,b is given by Eq. (7.18), with the integral evaluated from a to b.

The normal distribution is widely tabulated, making it unnecessary to evaluate Eq. (7.18) by performing the indicated integration. However, every combination of values μ and σ describes a different normal distribution, while in fact only one distribution, called the *standard normal*, is tabulated. The standard normal distribution is that one with parameters $\mu = 0$ and $\sigma = 1$, and is denoted $N(0,1)$. This presents no difficulty whatsoever, since it is a very simple matter to transform a random variable X which is distributed $N(\mu_x,\sigma_x)$ to another random variable Z which is $N(0,1)$, so that $P(X < x) = P(Z < z)$, and the latter probability can be found in the tables of the standard normal distribution. The transformation is simply to let $z = (x - \mu)/\sigma$.

The mathematical expression for the standard normal CDF can be derived from Eq. (7.18) by making the same substitution. If

$$z = \frac{x - \mu}{\sigma}$$

then

$$dx = \sigma\, dz$$

and

$$\frac{1}{\sigma\sqrt{2\pi}} \int e^{-1/2[(x-\mu)/\sigma]^2}\, dx = \frac{1}{\sqrt{2\pi}} \int e^{-1/2z^2}\, dz \tag{7.19}$$

The probability that the random variable X assumes a value within the interval $\pm k\sigma$ is then equivalent to the probability that the new random variable Z assumes a value within the interval $(-k,+k)$; that is,

$$\begin{aligned} P(\mu - k\sigma < x < \mu + k\sigma) &= \frac{1}{\sigma\sqrt{2\pi}} \int_{\mu-k\sigma}^{\mu+k\sigma} e^{-1/2[(x-\mu)/\sigma]^2}\, dx \\ &= P(-k < x < k) \\ &= \frac{1}{\sqrt{2\pi}} \int_{-k}^{+k} e^{-1/2z^2}\, dz \end{aligned} \tag{7.20}$$

or, because of the symmetry of the normal distribution, Eq. (7.20) is equal to

$$\frac{2}{\sqrt{2\pi}}\int_0^k e^{-1/2z^2}\,dz \tag{7.21}$$

For example, if X is a random variable having a normal distribution with mean equal to 10 and a standard deviation equal to 2, then the probability that $8 < x < 12$ can be found by evaluating the integral

$$\frac{1}{\sigma\sqrt{2\pi}}\int_8^{12} e^{-1/2[(x-10)/2]^2}\,dx \tag{7.22}$$

Or, we can make the substitution $z = (x - 10)/2$ so that for $x = 8$, $z = -1$, and for $x = 12$, $z = +1$. The evaluation of (7.22) is, therefore, equivalent to

$$\frac{1}{\sqrt{2\pi}}\int_{-1}^{1} e^{-1/2z^2}\,dz \tag{7.23}$$

We can, therefore, refer to tables of the standard normal distribution and find the probability that a standard normal variate Z takes on a value between -1 and $+1$. This probability happens to be approximately 0.68.

Many numerically valued random phenomena are distributed normally or approximately so, which makes the normal distribution extremely useful as a model. As an example, the normal distribution serves as a very good model for the observations of times until wearout of various types of mechanical devices. It has been determined that for certain types of devices, if observations are made of the times until wearout of large numbers of the same type of device, the times will tend to cluster about the mean value and tail off symmetrically in either direction.

Measurement errors also appear to have a normal distribution, and at one time the normal distribution was referred to as *the normal curve of errors.*

In addition to its value as a model of a wide range of random phenomena, the normal distribution is also used as an approximation to other probability distributions. It was earlier stated that the Poisson distribution was useful as an approximation to the binomial under certain conditions. It can be shown that the normal distribution also provides a good approximation to the binomial under certain other conditions. In order to use the Poisson as an approximation of the binomial distribution, it was necessary that the binomial parameter n be large while θ is small. In order to use the normal to approximate the binomial, n should also be large, but θ should not be small. A rule of thumb that is useful for determining when this approximation can be used is that $n\theta > 5$ when $\theta \leq 0.5$, and $n(1 - \theta) > 5$ when $\theta > 0.5$.

If we have a binomially distributed variable, it would be preferable to determine exact probabilities from the binomial distribution itself, rather than to use an approximation. However, the evaluation of the binomial for large values of n is extremely tedious, and if normal tables are available, their use represents a tremendous saving of time with very little loss in accuracy.

THE GAMMA DISTRIBUTION

A very important probability density function which will be considered next is the gamma density function. This distribution is extremely useful as a model for time-dependent phenomena. Just as the Poisson distribution could be used to provide the probability of the occurrence of some number x of events, knowing only the average number of event occurrences over some span of time, space, or volume, the gamma can provide the probability that it will take some magnitude of time t before r occurrences of the event are observed, given λ, the rate of occurrence of the event per unit time. The parameters of the gamma distribution are λ and r, and for certain values of these parameters, the gamma probability function reduces to other important probability distributions such as the chi-square (χ^2) and the exponential.

The PDF of the gamma distribution of the random variable T is given by

$$f(t) = \begin{cases} \dfrac{\lambda^r}{(r-1)!} t^{r-1} e^{-\lambda t} & \text{for } t > 0 \\ 0 & \text{for } t \le 0 \end{cases} \tag{7.24}$$

If λ is considered to be the rate of occurrence of an event per unit time, then $1/\lambda = \theta$ is the average amount of time between occurrences. If we let $\theta = 1/\lambda$ in Eq. (7.24), then the density function can be written for $t > 0$

$$f(t) = \frac{1}{\theta^r (r-1)!} t^{r-1} e^{-t/\theta} \tag{7.25}$$

and of course the cumulative probability density function or CDF is

$$F(t) = \int f(t)\, dt = \frac{1}{\theta^r (r-1)!} \int t^{r-1} e^{-t/\theta}\, dt \tag{7.26}$$

One of the valuable characteristics of these various probability models which we have been discussing is their generality. It is not necessary that the variable in the gamma distribution be labeled "time"; it is in fact a general random variable that can be given any appropriate meaning. If we make the substitution $x = t/\theta$, then Eq. (7.26) becomes a function of the random variable X, and

$$F(x) = \frac{1}{(r-1)!} \int x^{r-1} e^{-x}\, dx \tag{7.27}$$

The integral in Eq. (7.26) is called the *gamma function*, which is not the same as the gamma probability function given by Eq. (7.24) or the cumulative gamma probability function given by the total expression (7.26). The coefficient which precedes the gamma function in Eq. (7.26) is a constant selected such that the value of the total expression for $F(x)$ is equal to 1.

The gamma function of r, written $\Gamma(r)$, satisfies the recursion formula $\Gamma(r) = (r - 1)\Gamma(r - 1)$. When r is a positive integer, $\Gamma(r) = (r - 1)!$. The gamma function is also called the *factorial function.*

The gamma probability function of the random variable T can then be written

$$f(t) = \frac{1}{\theta^r \Gamma(r)} t^{r-1} e^{-t/\theta} \tag{7.28}$$

The mean and variance of the gamma distribution are $r\theta$ and $r\theta^2$, respectively.

In the absence of a table of gamma probabilities, the relationship between the gamma and Poisson distributions can be utilized.

$$P_\Gamma(t \geq T | \theta, r) = P_P(\tilde{r} < r | T/\theta) \tag{7.29}$$

where P_Γ and P_P represent gamma and Poisson probabilities, respectively, and the symbol $\tilde{r}$ is used to represent a random variable r where r had previously been a parameter of the other (gamma) distribution. This notation (the tilde over a letter to represent a random variable), will be used extensively in the decision theory part of this book.

THE EXPONENTIAL DISTRIBUTION

If in the gamma probability density function given in Eq. (7.24) we let $r = 1$, the function reduces to

$$f(t) = \begin{Bmatrix} \lambda e^{-\lambda t} & \text{for } t > 0 \\ 0 & \text{for } t < 0 \end{Bmatrix} \tag{7.30}$$

The exponential CDF is given by

$$\int \lambda e^{-\lambda t} = -e^{-\lambda t} \tag{7.31}$$

If we were to use the gamma CDF as the model for determining the probability that time $T = t$ until the rth occurrence of some event, then where $r = 1$, the resulting exponential CDF can be used as a model for determining the probability that time $T = t$ until the first occurrence of the event of interest. The probability that the random variable T is less than some specific value t is given by

$$P(T \leq t) = 1 - e^{-\lambda t} \tag{7.32}$$

where the parameter λ is the rate of occurrence of the event of interest per unit time.

This function takes on a special meaning if we let the event of interest be the failure of a piece of equipment. Then λ becomes the rate of failure of that equipment per unit time, and

$$F(t) = 1 - e^{-\lambda t}$$

provides the probability that the equipment will fail before time t. It is, however, of greater interest to estimate the probability that the equipment will *not* fail before some time t. This probability is simply $1 - F(t) = e^{-\lambda t}$. The function

$$e^{-\lambda t} \tag{7.33}$$

is frequently called the *reliability function* and is used to estimate the reliability or probability of nonfailure of certain types of equipment for which it has proved, through experience, to be a useful model. The equipment for which this function is suitable as a model must have a failure rate that is constant over time. Generally, random failures of electronic equipment follow the exponential PDF as do failures of complex, repairable systems.

As with any model, caution must be exercised in adopting it for any specific purpose. There are many types of equipment for which the exponential model is not suitable. Most mechanical devices, as an example, do not have an exponential failure distribution.

One very convenient feature of the reliability function is that if several equipments $E_1, E_2, \ldots, E_n$, each having an exponential failure distribution with failure rates $\lambda_1, \lambda_2, \ldots, \lambda_n$, are all required to operate without failure for a time t in order that some function or mission be completed successfully, then the reliability of the total system for that time is given by

$$R = \exp\left(-t_1 \sum_{i=1}^{n} \lambda_i\right)$$

and the failure rate of the total system is simply the sum of the failure rates of its individual components.

The reliability function can also be derived from consideration of the Poisson PDF. If we represent the occurrence of failures by the Poisson distribution with the parameter μ equal to the average number of failures in some time t, and if we let $\mu = \lambda t$, then the Poisson CDF can be written as follows:

$$P(X \leq x) = \sum (\lambda t)^x \exp(-\lambda t/x!) \tag{7.34}$$

where X is a random variable representing the number of failures occurring. If we write the first few terms of this summation letting X take on the values 0, 1, 2, . . . , n, thus

$$\frac{(\lambda t)^0 e^{-\lambda t}}{0!} + \frac{(\lambda t)^1 e^{-\lambda t}}{1!} + \frac{(\lambda t)^2 e^{-\lambda t}}{2!} + \cdots$$
$$= e^{-\lambda t} + \lambda e^{-\lambda t} + (\lambda t)^2 e^{-\lambda t}/2! + \cdots$$

then each term of the expression provides the probability that exactly 0, 1, 2, . . . failures will occur in time t. It should be apparent that the first term in the expansion for which $X = 0$ is the reliability function, providing the probability that zero failures will occur in time t.

The mean and variance of the exponential distribution are $1/\lambda$ and $(1/\lambda)^2$, respectively.

Since λ is the rate of occurrence per unit time, $1/\lambda = \theta$ is the average or mean time between occurrences, and the mean and variance of the distribution can also be written θ and θ^2.

When used as a failure model, θ is called the *mean time between failures.*

THE BETA DISTRIBUTION

The beta function of m and n, as distinguished from the beta probability function, is given by

$$\beta(m,n) = \int_0^1 x^{m-1}(1 - x)^{n-1}\,dx \tag{7.35}$$

The beta function is related to the gamma function by the equation

$$\beta(m,n) = \frac{\Gamma(m)\Gamma(n)}{\Gamma(m + n)} \tag{7.36}$$

The beta probability density function is

$$f(x) = \begin{cases} \dfrac{1}{\beta(m,n)}\,x^{m-1}(1 - x)^{n-1} & \text{for } 0 < x < 1 \\ 0 & \text{elsewhere} \end{cases} \tag{7.37}$$

Because of the relationship (7.35), the coefficient in Eq. (7.36) can be written

$$\frac{\Gamma(m + n)}{\Gamma(m)\Gamma(n)}$$

or simply as

$$\frac{(m + n - 1)!}{(m - 1)!(n - 1)!}$$

The beta cumulative probability density function is

$$F(x) = \frac{(m + n - 1)!}{(m - 1)!(n - 1)!} \int x^{m-1}(1 - x)^{n-1}\, dx \tag{7.38}$$

The parameters of this distribution are m and n, which are positive real numbers.

The mean of the beta distribution is $\mu = m/(m + n)$, and its variance is $\sigma^2 = mn/(m + n)^2(m + n + 1)$. The beta distribution has several applications as a model. It is widely used in PERT (Program Evaluation and Review Technique) as a model for the time duration of the various activities that constitute the program. Another important application of this distribution is as a model of the distribution of the estimator of the parameter of the binomial distribution. This will be discussed further in Chap. 12.

7.6 SUMMARY

In order to convert a logical model into a probability model, it is necessary to assign probability values to its components, or, more specifically, to the states of its components.

Probability distributions or functions assign probabilities to members of a set which in the context of the decision problem are outcomes, states, or conditions of the system components. Combining these individual probability values according to the model and the probability laws discussed then provides a probability value for the state of the total system.

Since probability functions are functions of a random variable, it was necessary to define and discuss the nature of numerical random variables which assign numerical values to the members of an event space, and to consider the two types of random variables, discrete and continuous.

The concept of the random variable leads logically to the discussion of functions of a random variable which assign probabilities to those specific values which the random variable itself can assume.

The expected value of a random variable turned out to be nothing more than the mean of its probability distribution, and could be determined by weighting each possible value of the variable by its probability of occurrence and summing over all possible values.

The assignment of probabilities to the system components involves the selection of a probability model suitable for describing the states of the components. Many of the most common probability distributions have been described, including both discrete and continuous distributions. The selection of the proper distribution as a model for the particular phenomenon of interest is to a great extent a matter of judgment, although a statistical procedure for determining the suitability of a specific model on the basis of empirical data will be discussed later.

PROBLEMS

7.1. A carnival concession features a wheel of fortune on which are marked numbers from 1 to 20. When the wheel is spun and allowed to come to rest, the person betting on the number under the pointer wins a prize. Assuming that all numbers are equally likely to win, what is the probability that a person betting on any single number will win?

7.2. If X represents the winning number on each spin of the wheel in Prob. 7.1, what is $E(X)$?

7.3. Suppose the rules of the game in the previous problems specify that a winning player will receive 15 times the amount he bets. What is the expected value of the payment to the player if he bets 50 cents on each play?

7.4. If the probability of producing a defective part on a particular production process is 0.2, and if a random sample of 10 parts is taken from that process, what is the probability that the sample contains exactly three defectives? At least three defectives? Fewer than three defectives? What is the appropriate distribution? What are its parameters?

7.5. An urn contains two white balls and three black ones. If two balls are selected at random from the urn in such a way that the first ball is returned to the urn before the second one is drawn, what is the probability that both balls selected were white? that both were black? that one was white and one was black? What is the appropriate distribution? What are its parameters?

7.6. Assume the same situation as in Prob. 7.5 except that the two balls were drawn from the urn without replacement. Answer the same questions.

7.7. In a draw poker hand of five cards, what is the probability that it contains two Aces? all hearts?

7.8. If a lot of 20 parts contains 5 percent defectives and a nonreplacement random sample of size 10 is drawn from the lot, what is the probability that the sample contains no defectives? less than two defectives? What is the appropriate distribution? What are its parameters?

7.9. If it is known that of all the adult males in the United States 40 percent use electric razors, 55 percent use safety razors, and 5 percent still use straight razors, and if a random sample of 10 men is selected, what is the probability that the sample will contain exactly four safety-razor users, four electric-razor users, and two straight-razor users? What is the appropriate distribution? What are its parameters?

7.10. If a marksman's probability of hitting the bull's-eye of his target on any shot is 0.2, what is the probability that he will get his second bull's-eye with his sixth shot? What is the probability that he will get his second bull's-eye on or before his sixth shot? What is the appropriate distribution? What are its parameters?

7.11. If a particular production process produces 10 percent defectives, what is the probability of finding a defective among the first five parts produced? What is the appropriate distribution? What are its parameters?

7.12. If the average number of defects observed in a bolt of cloth is 2.2 per square yard, what is the probability that any given square yard of the material will contain zero defects? exactly three defects? no more than one defect? What is the appropriate distribution?

7.13. Past experience indicates that a particular part of an oil well drilling rig will have on the average one breakdown every 200 hr of operation. What is the probability that more than two breakdowns will occur in 500 hr of operation? What is the probability that less than two breakdowns will occur in 300 hr of operation?

7.14. In the previous problem, if a breakdown means that the part must be replaced and if the rig is intended to operate at the drilling site continuously for 2,000 hr, how many spare parts should the drillers have on hand in order to have at least a 90 percent probability that the rig will not have to shut down due to the lack of this particular part?

7.15. Considering the data in Prob. 7.13, what is the average number of hours of operation until this part fails? What is the probability that the part will operate 300 hr without failing? 400 hr? What is the probability that the part will fail during the first 100 hr of operation? What is the appropriate distribution?

7.16. For the data in Prob. 7.13, what is the probability that the rig can be operated for 600 hr before the second breakdown occurs? What is the appropriate distribution? What are its parameters?

7.17. Measurement errors generally have a normal distribution with a mean of zero. If the standard deviation of the measurement error for a given procedure is 0.025, for any given measurement, what is the probability that the measurement, error will be

less than ± 0.053
greater than $+0.039$
less than -0.048
greater than ± 0.02

7.18. If a population has a mean $\mu = 175$ and a standard deviation $\sigma = 15$, and if a single element is randomly selected from the population, what is the probability that the element will have a value

less than 150
exactly 150
between 143 and 158
greater than 200

8
Probability Networks

The logical model and network discussed previously aided the decision maker by providing a method for determining system state from the states of its interrelated components. On the basis of the system state, either good or bad, a decision could be made.

In any physical system consisting of hardware elements to which we are comparing our decision system, it is *possible* to determine exactly the state of each component. The fact that it is possible does not mean that it is always practical to do so; nevertheless, it is conceivable that each component of a physical system could be inspected and/or tested to determine its true state. If this is indeed done, there need be no doubt about the state of the total system.

However, in many complex hardware systems and in a decision system composed of components that are not pieces of hardware, it is frequently impractical and sometimes impossible to determine the exact state of a component and, therefore, impossible to determine the exact state of the system. Under these circumstances, the value attached to the state of any component and to the system as a whole is only an estimate. Therefore, even though a component or system appears to be in the *good* state as a result of the evaluation of a logical model, there is some *probability* that it is, in fact, bad. Consequently, a decision based on this assessment could be *wrong* with some probability.

The decision maker forced to base his decision upon the evaluation of such a logical model should realize that the decision indicated may indeed be *wrong* or *bad*. Just what is meant by a wrong or a bad decision will be discussed later. At this point we shall use these terms without delving into their implications with respect to the decision environment.

The intelligent decision maker forced to act on this type of information should insist on having some indication of the chances he is taking when he acts according to the logical outcome of this model. In other words, he should want to know the probability that if he acts according to the outcome of the logical model, he will be making the right decision.

Since the system state is a function of the component states, the probability that the system is in a given state is also a function of the probabilities that the components are in their estimated states. If probability values can be assigned to the estimates of the component states, the system state can also be determined as a probability by means of the model. Given the state probabilities of all components, the system state probability results from the network evaluation. The assignment of probabilities to the components now transfers the logical network into a probability network. The method of so doing will now be considered.

8.1 COMPARISON OF LOGICAL OPERATIONS WITH OPERATIONS ON PROBABILITIES

In the logical model, a value was attached to each estimate of a component state. These values were limited to *zero* for an estimate of *bad* and 1 for an estimate of *good*. Logical operations were performed on these estimated values according to the rules of boolean algebra in order to determine the overall state of the system. These operations on boolean variables are analogous to operations on sets, as was also discussed previously.

Since the probability theory discussed previously was developed in relation to sets, at least as far as discrete sample spaces were concerned, operations on probabilities should be no different from the boolean operations of the logical network. This is indeed so.

For example, let $S = f(A,B)$, where $A = 0,1$ and $B = 0,1$. Let us compare S with $P(S)$, where $P(S) = fP(A,B)$, $P(A) = 0,1$, and $P(B) = 0,1$.

Suppose $S = A \cap B$; then

$$A = 1, B = 1, S = 1 \cap 1 = 1,$$
$$A = 1, B = 0, S = 1 \cap 0 = 0,$$
$$A = 0, B = 1, S = 0 \cap 1 = 0,$$
$$A = 0, B = 0, S = 0 \cap 0 = 0.$$

If $P(S) = P(A \cap B)$, where A and B are independent, then according to the special multiplicative rule of probability, $P(S) = P(A)P(B)$, and for

$$P(A) = 1, P(B) = 1, P(S) = 1.1 = 1,$$
$$P(A) = 1, P(B) = 0, P(S) = 1.0 = 0,$$
$$P(A) = 0, P(B) = 1, P(S) = 0.1 = 0,$$
$$P(A) = 0, P(B) = 0, P(S) = 0.0 = 0.$$

If $P(A)$ and $P(B)$ are not independent, then $P(S) = P(A|B)P(B) = P(B|A)P(A)$. The dependency relationship between $P(A)$ and $P(B)$ would be either:

1. If $P(A) = 1, P(B) = 1$, and if
   $P(A) = 0, P(B) = 0$, in which case, for
   $P(A) = 1, P(B|A) = 1, P(S) = 1.1 = 1,$
   $P(A) = 0, P(B|A) = 0, P(S) = 0.0 = 0.$

2. If $P(A) = 1, P(B) = 0$, and if
   $P(A) = 0, P(B) = 1$, in which case, for
   $P(A) = 1, P(B|A) = 0, P(S) = 1.0 = 0,$
   $P(A) = 0, P(B|A) = 1, P(S) = 0.1 = 0.$

If $S = A \vee B$, then for

$$A = 1, B = 1, S = 1 \vee 1 = 1,$$
$$A = 1, B = 0, S = 1 \vee 0 = 1,$$
$$A = 0, B = 1, S = 0 \vee 1 = 1,$$
$$A = 0, B = 0, S = 0 \vee 0 = 0.$$

Analogous to this is $P(S) = P(A \cup B)$, and by the general additive rule of probabilities

$$P(S) = P(A) + P(B) - P(AB), \text{ and for}$$
$$P(A) = 1, P(B) = 1, S = 1 + 1 - 1.1 = 1,$$
$$P(A) = 1, P(B) = 0, S = 1 + 0 - 0 = 1,$$
$$P(A) = 0, P(B) = 1, S = 0 + 1 - 0 = 1,$$
$$P(A) = 0, P(B) = 0, S = 0 + 0 - 0 = 0.$$

Finally, considering the negative operation,

$$A \wedge A' = 0, P(A)P(A') = 1.0 = 0,$$
$$A \vee A' = 1, P(A) + P(A') = 1 + 0 = 1.$$

Operations on probabilities are the same as the boolean operations used for the evaluation of the logical network, and, therefore, the same symbols and procedures can be used in evaluating the probability network. Since a probability value is a number between zero and 1, what is true for probabilities of zero and 1 is true for probabilities between zero and 1.

8.2 EXPECTED VALUE OF COMPONENT STATES

We have previously defined the concept of an expected value of a random variable as being equal to the mean of its probability distribution. We would determine this expected value of the random variable X by multiplying each of the possible values x_i, which the random variable can assume, by the probability associated with it and then taking the sum of all such possible products.

In the logical network the random variable X which corresponds to the component state can assume only the values zero or 1. If the component which we are considering is component A, the probability that A is in the good state is equal to $P(X = 1)$, while the probability that A is in the bad state is equal to $P(X = 0)$. The value that we shall assign to any component is then the expected value of the random variable corresponding to the state of the component.

If we have determined that the probability that A is good is equal to 0.5, then the probability that A is bad is also 0.5. Let X_A be the random variable corresponding to the state of component A. Then

$$P(X_A = 1) = 0.5$$
$$P(X_A = 0) = 0.5$$

and

$$E(X_A) = (1)(0.5) + (0)(0.5) = 0.5$$

If, on the other hand,

$$P(X_A = 1) = 0.7$$
$$P(X_A = 0) = 0.3$$

then

$$E(X_A) = (1)(0.7) + (0)(0.3) = 0.7$$

In a model allowing only two states to a component, the states being valued at zero and 1, the expected value of the state of the component is equal to the probability that the component is in the good state. That is,

$$E(X_A) = P(X_A = 1)$$

Therefore, in the probability network, we shall substitute for the values of the component state the expected value of the component state which, in the case of a two-state component with values zero and 1, is simply the probability that the component is good.

Let us clarify a possibly confusing notational device at this point. The capital letters A, B, C, etc., stand for a component of the system. As such, the notation $P(A)$, meaning probability of A, is meaningless. What we mean to imply in this context by the notation $P(A)$ is really the probability that component A is in the *good* state. Since the *good* state is equivalent, again in this context, to a value of 1, a better way of writing that probability would be $P(A = 1)$. However, in the interest of brevity, if it is understood that $P(A)$ means $P(A = 1)$, unless otherwise noted, no confusion should exist.

A probability statement equivalent to $P(A)$ or $P(A = 1)$ which was introduced in this section was $P(X_A = 1)$, where X_A is the random variable associated with component A.

For any component of a decision problem, the criteria for determining whether its state is good or bad must be specified. In the situation involving the development, manufacture, and marketing of a new product, for example, one of the major components of the problem would involve the state of the market. One of the components of the market state might be the state of the competition. In order to evaluate the state of the competition at the time the new product would be ready for the market, it might be specified that the presence of zero or one competitors at that time would be *good*, but that the presence in the market of two or more competitors would be *bad*.

Another component of the system might be the cost of certain raw materials at some future date. It might be determined that, for a particular critical material, a cost equal to or below some figure would be considered *good* while a cost above that figure would be *bad*. Regardless of the component considered, these criteria must be specified in advance of any attempt to evaluate the network.

8.3 ASSIGNMENT OF PROBABILITY VALUES TO NETWORK COMPONENTS

The process of assigning probability values to the state of the network components is, first, a matter of selecting a probability distribution as a model for the event or situation represented by the network component and, second, the estimation of the parameters of that distribution. It should be apparent that whether we deal with a logical model and assign values of zero and 1 to the components or deal with a probability model and assign probability values to the states, we are faced with the necessity of making an estimate.

In the case of the probability model, it is infrequent in a practical situation to determine the exact probability of a state or condition. We can, of course, state with reasonable certainty that the probability of a 4 showing after one roll of a die is $1/6$, or that the probability of a head occurring on one toss of a coin is $1/2$, simply by definition. But even these probabilities are based on the assumption of a fair coin or a fair die. In most practical situations, the parameters are unknown and must be estimated either as a matter of judgment or on the basis of experience, or possibly by a combination of both judgment and experience.

Parameter estimation will be discussed subsequently in Chap. 12, "Statistical Estimation." For the time being, probability values will be assigned to component states under the assumption that they have been derived in a reasonable manner and do represent the true probabilities of the component states to which they have been assigned.

The selection of the distribution to be used as the probability model for the event of interest, as has been stated, is based on a knowledge of the process to be evaluated and on familiarity with the type of distributions available, such as were discussed previously. A method for determining the fitness of any particular model from an analysis of empirical data will also be discussed subsequently.

8.4 EVALUATION OF A PROBABILITY NETWORK

Suppose the logical network for a given problem situation is constructed as shown in Fig. 8.1.

The logical equation for the system state is

$$S = [A \vee (B \wedge C)] \wedge [D \wedge (E \vee F)] \tag{8.1}$$

Recall that we are interested in the component states that make the system good. When we write an equation like (8.1), we imply that this is the relationship that is required to make the system *good*, that is, for which $S = 1$. Now if we change Eq. (8.1) into a probability statement about S, $P(S)$ represents the probability that the system is in a good state. A more precise way of writing that probability would be $P(S = 1)$. However, since we are discussing the probabilities of the system and/or its components being good, the abbreviated notation should not lead to any confusion.

In terms of probabilities, then, the probability that the system is good can be written

$$P(S) = P\{[A \cup (B \cap C)] \cap [D \cap (E \cup F)]\} \tag{8.2}$$

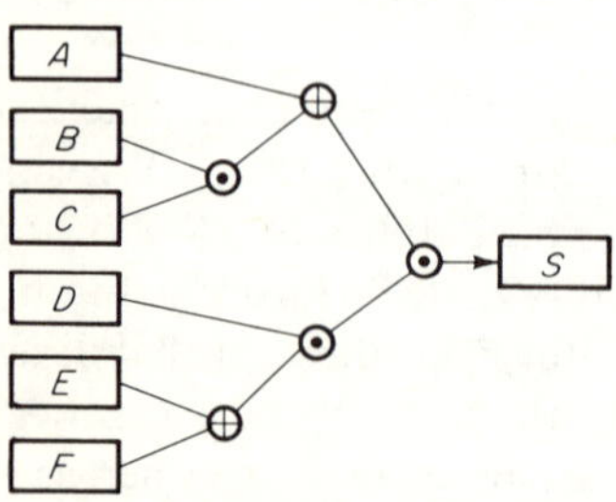

Fig. 8.1

Let us assume for the moment that the states of the components are independent of each other; then Eq. (8.2) can be simplified, by using the probability rules discussed previously, into the following:

$$P(S) = P[A \cup (B \cap C)]P[D \cap (E \cup F)]$$

by the special multiplicative rule;

$$P[A \cup (B \cap C)] = P(A) + P(BC) - P(ABC)$$

by the general rule of addition and the special multiplicative rule;

$$P[D \cap (E \cup F)] = P(DE) + P(DF) - P(DEF)$$

by the general rule of addition and the special multiplicative rule. Therefore,

$$P(S) = [P(A) + P(BC) - P(ABC)][P(DE) + P(DF) - P(DEF)]$$

Suppose the probabilities assigned to each of the components (probabilities of being in the good state) are as follows:

$$\begin{aligned} P(A) &= 0.90 \\ P(B) &= 0.95 \\ P(C) &= 0.90 \\ P(D) &= 0.85 \\ P(E) &= 0.70 \\ P(F) &= 0.75 \end{aligned}$$

Then

$$\begin{aligned} P[A \cup (B \cap C)] &= (0.90) + (0.95)(0.90) - (0.90)(0.95)(0.90) \\ &= (0.90) + (0.86) - (0.77) \\ &= 0.99 \end{aligned}$$

and

$$\begin{aligned} P[D \cap (E \cup F)] &= (0.85)(0.70) + (0.85)(0.75) - (0.85)(0.70)(0.75) \\ &= (0.60) + (0.64) - (0.45) \\ &= 0.79 \end{aligned}$$

Therefore

$$P[D \cap (B \cap C)]P[D \cap (E \cup F)] = (0.99)(0.79) = 0.77$$

and the probability that the system is in a good state, given the probabilities for each of its components being in the good state, as noted above, is

$$P(S) = 0.77$$

With this information the decision maker is in a somewhat better position for deciding his course of action. If this system had been evaluated strictly on the basis of the logical model with no probabilities attached, the evaluation would have led to $S = 1$, that is, the system in the good state. The logical decision would then have been to make the decision equated with an $S = 1$. However, given these probabilities, he now has an indication of the chances that the decision equated with $S = 1$ may be a wrong one. With $P(S) = 0.77$ and the decision made for $S = 1$, the odds are approximately 3 to 1 that the decision is a good one. However, there is one chance in four that the decision would be wrong. With no further information bearing on the decision problem, the decision maker must decide if the odds are sufficiently good for him to take whatever risks are involved in acting as though $S = 1$. We shall subsequently see how the economic consequences of a wrong decision as well as the risk of making a wrong decision can be incorporated into the decision model.

Suppose that in the previous example the logical model was evaluated prior to the assignment of any probabilities, and the states of all components were determined to be good, equivalent to a valuation of 1, with the exception of component D. That is, $D = 0$. Since D is essential to a good system state, on that basis $S = 0$, and the decision would be that which is equivalent to the system being in a bad state.

Now, however, suppose data are collected and analyzed and probability values assigned to the state of all components. Assume that the probabilities for A, B, and C are the same as those given in the previous example. Let us suppose that the probability that D is *bad* was determined to be 0.55, which is consistent with a valuation of $D = 0$ in the logical model. If $P(D = 0) = 0.55$, then $P(D = 1) = 0.45$. Let us suppose $P(E) = P(F) = 0.95$. Now let us evaluate the probability model with $P(D = 1) = 0.45$.

$$P[A \cup (B \cap C)] = 0.99$$

as determined previously.

$$P[D \cap (E \cup F)] = (0.45)(0.95) + (0.45)(0.95) - (0.45)(0.95) = 0.46$$

This indicates that with $P(D = 1) = 0.45$, the probability that the system is good is 0.46, or less than $\frac{1}{2}$, and is consistent with the decision resulting from an evaluation of the logical model without probabilities. However, the additional information regarding the odds favoring a right or wrong decision is still extremely valuable to the decision maker.

8.5 DEPENDENCIES AND CONDITIONAL PROBABILITIES

Conditional probabilities arise whenever a decision point appears in the probability network. Consider the situation illustrated previously in Fig. 3.16. Component A is evaluated, and following this evaluation appears decision α. Depending upon the state or value of component A, a choice is made between decision α_1, leading to B and consequently to the system state given that B has occurred, and α_2, leading to C and the system state given C.

If Fig. 3.6 represents a logical network, we base our decision on an estimate of the absolute state of component A either good or bad. If A is good, that is, $A = 1$, then since only one of the decisions α_i can be made, the system state is determined by B. That is, $S = (B|A = 1)$. However, if $A = 0$, then $S = (C|A = 0)$.

The system logical equation should state that the system is good if A is good and B is good, or if A is bad and C is good. Since A and A' are mutually exclusive, this equation could be written with either the inclusive or exclusive OR. That is,

$$S = (A \wedge B) \veebar (A' \wedge C) = (A \wedge B) \vee (A' \wedge C) \tag{8.3}$$

The *probability* of S would be equivalent to the probability of A and B occurring or the probability of A' and C occurring, but not both since A and A' are mutually exclusive. This could be written

$$P(S) = P(A \cap B) + P(A' \cap C) \tag{8.4}$$

or

$$P(S) = P(A)P(B|A) + P(A')P(C|A') \tag{8.5}$$

If it were possible to take both path α_1 and α_2 leading to both B and C then there would be no need for the decision α at this point in the network. The situation, under those conditions, could be represented with the inclusive OR, meaning B or C or both in conjunction with A. Then the logical equation would be

$$S = A \wedge (B \vee C)$$

and the network could appear either as Fig. 8.2 or 8.3.

However, given the network as shown in Fig. 3.16 with decision box α, let us determine the equation for the system state probability. Before continuing, let us emphasize once more that the notation $P(K)$, where K represents any box in the network, is equal to $P(K = 1)$. Also, $P(K = 0) = P(K' = 1)$.

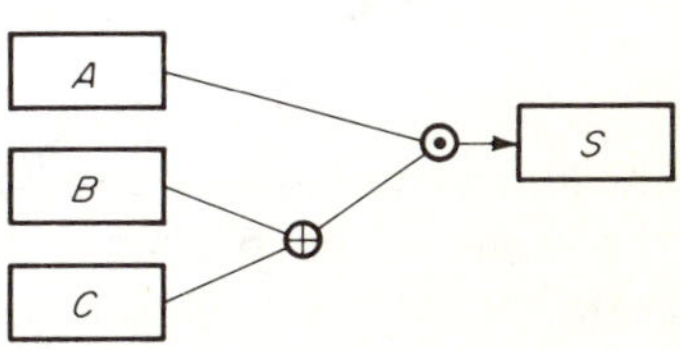

Fig. 8.2

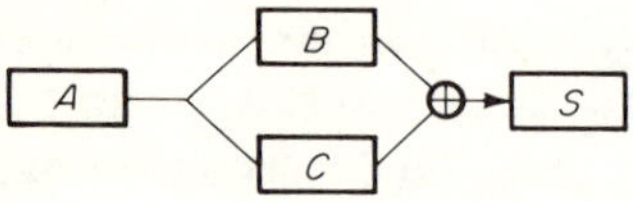

Fig. 8.3

The law of elimination, discussed previously, stated that if an event, call it A, is dependent upon the occurrence of any one of several other mutually exclusive events B_i, one of which must occur, then the probability of event A is equal to the sum of the conditional probabilities of A given B_i, times the probability of B_i.

In this instance the event $S = 1$ is dependent upon the state of A which can be $A = 1$ or $A = 0$ (in which case $A' = 1$). A and A' are, of course, mutually exclusive, and in this context one of these states must occur. Now before we know anything about the state of A,

$$P(S) = P(S|A)P(A) + P(S|A')P(A')$$

But the probability of S given A is equal to the probability of B; that is, $P(S|A) = P(B)$, and the probability of S given A' is equal to the probability of C; that is, $P(S|A') = P(C)$.

Therefore

$$P(S) = P(S|A)P(A) + P(S|A')P(A')$$

or

$$P(S) = P(B)P(A) + P(C)P(A') \tag{8.6}$$

Of course, after the fact, that is, when the state of A is known, one of the terms of Eq. (8.6) will become zero. If we evaluate A and find that its state is good, then $P(A) = 1$ and $P(A') = 0$, and $P(S) = P(B)$.

If, on the other hand, we find that A is bad, then $P(A) = 0$ and $P(A') = 1$, and $P(S) = P(C)$. Let us illustrate the foregoing. Suppose $P(A) = 0.80$ and $P(A') = 0.20$. Further, suppose $P(B) = 0.70$ (independent of A) and $P(C) = 0.40$ (also independent of A). Then

$$\begin{aligned} P(S) &= P(S|A)P(A) + P(S|A')P(A') \\ &= P(B)P(A) + P(C)P(A') \\ &= (0.70)(0.80) + (0.40)(0.20) \\ &= 0.56 + 0.08 \\ &= 0.64 \end{aligned}$$

The logical possibilities can best be illustrated by the tree diagram in Fig. 8.4. The sum of the probabilities $P(S|A) + P(S'|A) + P(S|A') + P(S'|A') = 1.00$.

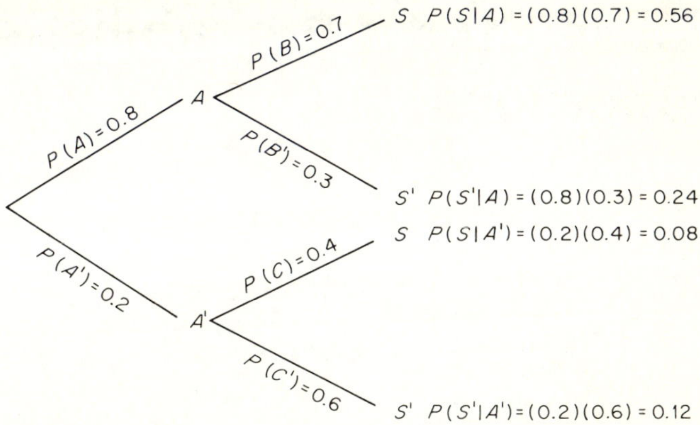

Fig. 8.4

8.6 SUMMARY

The process of converting the logical network to a probability network is simply a matter of assigning probability values to the states of the network components. Once these probability values are assigned, the evaluation of the system state proceeds in exactly the same manner as for the logical network, since operations with probabilities and boolean operations are essentially the same.

Sequential decisions and dependencies are covered by the use of conditional probabilities and the insertion of decision boxes into the network.

9
Case Study: Probabilistic Decisions

This case study represents a continuation of the previous case which illustrated a decision reached by logical analysis alone. Rather than devise a completely different decision problem and develop the solution through the stage of logical analysis, it would seem reasonable to pick up the previous case and utilize the same decision situation illustrating how a probabilistic analysis can be applied. Consequently, the following analysis will refer to the Pennwood Corporation problem first discussed in Chap. 4. New complications will, however, be introduced where they serve to illustrate a point.

9.1 THE CASE

The Pennwood Corporation considered three major factors in its decision to market a new lower-cost heat pump to the residential construction industry. These factors were:

1. The manufacturing cost of the unit which was, in turn, dependent upon labor negotiations in a basic materials industry.

2. The number of new housing starts in the $50,000-plus price range during the first year of marketing the new product.
3. The presence or absence of a competitive product.

A logical model of the decision problem was constructed which illustrated the logical relationships between these factors and the overall decision system or problem. The state of each component of the decision system was evaluated and determined to be either *good* or *bad* on the basis of criteria established by the decision maker. Having assigned values to each system component, the logical model provided the state value of the system which happened to be good. Consequently, a decision made at that point would be the selection of the act of manufacturing and marketing the heat pump.

Pennwood management realizes, however, that the assignment of state values to the various system components is subject to error. For example, although the factor of economic conditions, which affect the number of new houses which will be constructed in the proper price range, was assigned a value of 1, equivalent to the good state, there is some probability that this factor will in fact be bad. The same could be said of factor C relating to the competition. Although the logical analysis is capable only of assigning a state value of good or bad, zero or 1, to the overall system, it is necessary to realize that the final assignment of a state value to the system could be in error. The decision whether or not to market the heat pump would be based on more solid grounds if some expression were given to the probability of error, that is, the probability that the system is good or bad if the logical analysis indicated the opposite. This overall system probability of being good or bad is a function of the probabilities that the components are good or bad in much the same way that the system state is a function of the component states.

Management therefore decides to base its decision on a probabilistic analysis of the system rather than on the simple logical analysis which has just been concluded. Consequently, instead of assigning values of zero or 1 to the system components, assigning probability values to these components becomes necessary.

For example, in the previous logical analysis the component C was assigned the value 1, that is, $C = 1$. The values assigned in the probabilistic analysis would be values of the probability that $C = 1$, that is, $P(C = 1)$, or more simply stated, $P(C)$. Keep in mind that

$$P(C = 1) = P(C' = 0)$$

and

$$P(C' = 1) = P(C = 0)$$

Also, from the rules of probability and the previous relationships,

$$P(C = 1) = 1 - P(C' = 1)$$

9.2 ANALYSIS

Before the probabilistic analysis of the system was begun, the chief engineer of the Pennwood Corporation provided an item of information that had been overlooked previously. The success or failure of the project must be judged not solely on its contribution to profit during the first year, but also on the ability of the product to function effectively. If the heat pump breaks down in actual operation, causing excessive calls for repair as well as customer dissatisfaction, then even though first year's sales are large enough to return the company's investment, the effect on future sales of the heat pump, the company's reputation, and the future sales of other products of the company could be disastrous.

Now, all the physical components of the heat pump were tried and tested for years in other products and were considered to be highly reliable with a single exception. This exception was a special sensing-switching device which was necessary to switch the pump from its heating cycle to its cooling cycle and back. If the chief engineer had to assign a value *good* or *bad* to the factor "reliability of the product," he would first have to adopt some criterion of goodness or badness. The criterion which he suggested was that not more than 1 percent of the number of heat pumps produced during the first year should fail to perform properly during a 1-year period due to the sensor switch. Since the exact number of heat pumps which would be produced could not be known, the chief engineer assumed the maximum number, which was 1,200. One percent of 1,200 is 12, and the criterion adopted was that not more than 12 should fail for this reason. This factor, reliability of the product, will be designated with the letter D.

The new logical model of the decision system is now given in Fig. 9.1.

Another way of drawing the system might be to create another level component and designate it E pertaining to the marketability of the product and have the A, B, C components feeding into E, with D and E ANDed together as shown in Fig. 9.2.

For the logical model given in Fig. 9.1, the logical equation is

$$S = [C + ABC']D \tag{9.1}$$

If the model in Fig. 9.2 is used, the logical equation is

$$\begin{aligned} S &= DE \\ E &= C + ABC' \end{aligned} \tag{9.2}$$

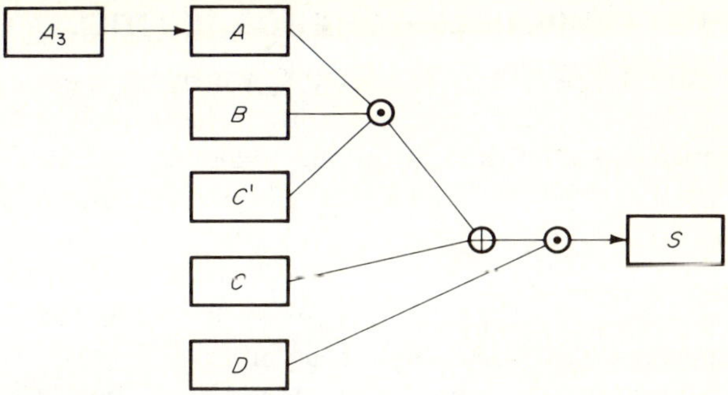

Fig. 9.1

In a probabilistic analysis the expression or equation which we need is $P(S = 1)$, or simply $P(S)$. Starting with Eqs. (9.2) and using the symbols $\cap$ for AND and $\cup$ for OR, we get

$$P(S) = P(D \cap E) = P(D)P(E)^{*}$$

Since $E = C + ABC'$,

$$P(E) = P[C \cup (A \cap B \cap C')] = P(C) + P(A)P(B)P(C')^{\dagger}$$
$$P(C') = 1 - P(C). \quad \text{Therefore}$$
$$P(E) = P(C) + P(A)P(B)[1 - P(C)]$$

and, by substitution,

$$\begin{aligned} P(S) &= P(D)\{P(C) + P(A)P(B)[1 - P(C)]\} \\ &= P(D)P(C) + P(A)P(B)P(D)[1 - P(C)] \end{aligned} \tag{9.3}$$

The probability value of the system, that is, $P(S = 1)$, can be determined from Eq. (9.3), once probability values have been assigned to each component.

* Independence is assumed.
† The set C and its complement C' are mutually exclusive; therefore C and $A \cap B \cap C'$ must also be mutually exclusive.

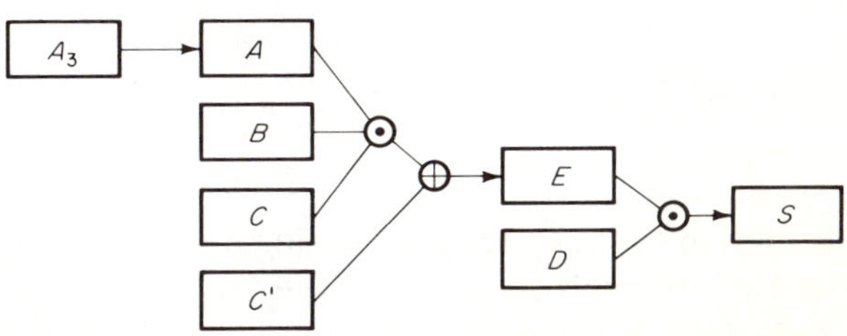

Fig. 9.2

9.3 ASSIGNMENT OF PROBABILITIES

Consider system component D which represents the reliability of the heat pump, or, more specifically, the reliability of the sensor switch, which is a critical part of the heat pump. The term "reliability" as used here refers to the probability that this device will operate successfully for 1 year. The criterion for component D to be judged *good* is that not more than 12 out of 1,200 heat pumps will fail in operation (due to the sensor switch) within 12 months. This probability must be estimated in two stages. First, the probability of any single heat pump failing because of the sensor switch in 12 months must be determined. Then, given this probability, the probability that not more than 12 out of 1,200 will fail must be determined. Consider the first probability.

In typical operation, it is estimated that the heat pump will cycle from heating to cooling or cooling to heating approximately 10 times per year on the average. For the heat pump to survive 12 months without failure implies that the sensor switch must survive 10 cyclings without failure. A probability model which is frequently applicable to a situation of this type is the exponential model, which provides that the probability of survival is given by the expression $e^{-\lambda x} = P(H)$, where x represents a measure of the operating time of the device and $P(H)$ is the probability that the heat pump will survive the specified time period. Since time in this particular case is measured in equivalent switching cycles, the previous equation can be written for a single heat pump as

$$P(H) = e^{-\lambda c} \tag{9.4}$$

c represents the number of cycles per year, which in this case is equal to 10. λ represents the rate of failure of the device for some convenient unit of time, or, in this case, of cycles.

The unknown parameter in Eq. (9.4) is λ, the failure rate. Pennwood's engineering department acquired a number of the sensor switches and subjected them to a total of 10,000 cyclings as part of a reliability testing program. The number of failures which were observed in 10,000 cycles of operation was 7. The department's estimate of the failure rate of the device based on these tests was $\lambda = 7/10{,}000 = 0.0007$ failures per cycle.

Computing $P(H)$ from Eq. (9.4), we get

$$P(H) = e^{-\lambda c} = e^{-(0.0007)(10)} = e^{-0.007}$$
$$= 0.993$$

This means that the probability that a heat pump will survive 1 year of operation without failure is estimated from the test to be 0.993. Conversely, the probability that it will fail is $1 - 0.993 = 0.007$.

This, however, is only part of the probability that is required. If the probability of a single heat pump not failing in 12 months is 0.993, what is

$P(D)$, the probability that no more than 12 will fail out of 1,200 in the same time period? This latter probability would appear to be binomial, and its exact expression would be

$$P(D) = \sum_{r=0}^{12} \binom{1{,}200}{r} (1 - p)^r p^{1{,}200-r}$$

where r represents the number of failures and $p = 0.993$, the probability of no failure for a single unit.

Without a digital computer this expression is impractical to evaluate. However, for n as great as 1,200, the normal approximation to the binomial probability should be adequate. We shall use a normal distribution with mean and standard deviation equal to the binomial mean and standard deviation, and shall consider the random variable to be r = the number of failures.

For the binomial,

$$E(r) = n(1 - p) = (1{,}200)(0.007) = 8.4$$

The standard deviation

$$\sigma_r = \sqrt{np(1 - p)} \doteq 2.9$$

The approximating normal distribution has the parameters $\mu = 8.4$, $\sigma = 2.9$, and we wish to know the probability that r is less than or equal to 12. The appropriate normal distribution is shown in Fig. 9.3.

$$P(D) = P(r \leq 12) = P\left(z \leq \frac{r - \mu}{\sigma}\right)$$

$$= P\left(z \leq \frac{12 - 8.4}{2.9}\right) = P(z \leq 1.24)$$

$$= 0.8925 \doteq 0.9$$

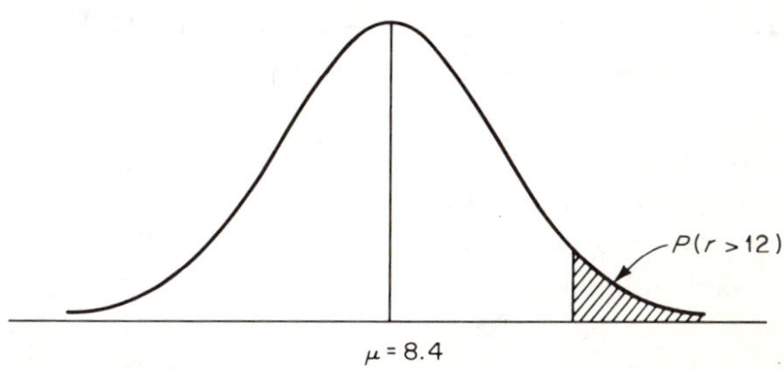

Fig. 9.3

The probability value for system component D, then, was determined by the application of two probability models, the exponential and the binomial, to factors relating to the criterion established for this particular decision component.

The application of specific probability models to other decision system components may not be as straightforward as the above. Consider component A, the manufacturing cost of the heat pump, which is dependent upon a favorable settlement (from Pennwood's point of view) of labor negotiations in a basic materials industry. If forced to assign a value of zero or 1 to this component, Pennwood would assign zero, since a settlement without a substantial wage increase appears unlikely. However, "unlikely" does not mean "impossible." Consequently, there is some probability that $A = 1$, and this probability must be estimated.

The estimate at this point can be a subjective one since it might be difficult to obtain quantitative data capable of providing a valid objective estimate. The subjective estimate would not be a simple hunch or guess, but would probably be a reasoned evaluation of the situation based on all available information and reflecting the opinion of labor economists familiar with the negotiations.

It is possible that, in an attempt to bring more objective or at least quantitative data to bear on the problem, the history of past negotiations under similar circumstances might be compiled. Even here, however, the selection of cases which are deemed to be *similar* and the elimination of others which are considered to be *not similar* must contain a subjective element.

Suppose, however, that in 15 previous negotiations that were considered to be similar to the one in process, only three were settled without an immediate substantial wage increase, nine were settled with substantial wage increases, and three resulted in strikes. Using relative frequency as an estimate of probability, the probability that A_3 is good and consequently that A is good would be $^3/_{15}$, or 0.20.

Regardless of how Pennwood arrived at its estimate, $P(A_3)$ was assigned 0.2, leading to $P(A) = 0.2$.

The probability that economic conditions would be good during the coming year leading to construction of 60,000 new homes in the \$50,000 and up price range was estimated to be 0.90, that is, $P(B) = 0.90$.

The competitive situation was more difficult to assess. One major competitor was known through marketing intelligence to be working on the heat pump principle. Whether they were far enough along to introduce a competitive product soon enough to influence Pennwood's first year's sales was problematical. Although in the simpler logical analysis this component was assumed to be good, when forced to assign a probability to the good component state, management reflected its uncertainty about the competition by assigning the value 0.75.

By use of Eq. (9.3), the probability that the system is in the *good* state is determined as follows:

$$
\begin{aligned}
P(A) &= 0.20 \\
P(B) &= 0.90 \\
P(C) &= 0.75 \\
P(D) &= 0.90 \\
P(S) &= P(D)P(C) + P(A)P(B)P(D)[1 - P(C)] \\
&= (0.90)(0.75) + (0.20)(0.90)(0.90)(0.25) \\
&= 0.675 + 0.0405 \\
&= 0.7155 \doteq 0.72
\end{aligned}
$$

The probability that the decision system is in the *good* state and that the project will be successful according to the criterion established is approximately 0.72. Obviously, this indicates that there is about one chance in four that the project will be unsuccessful. Considering only the logical analysis by itself, management should undertake the project. However, the probabilistic analysis now indicates that although the odds are almost 3 to 1 that the project will be successful, there is still a significant chance that it will fail. Management must now decide whether a 0.72 probability of success is sufficiently high for it to undertake the project. Once again the element of subjectivity enters the decision picture. Only management can determine the odds at which it is willing to bet, that is, to invest in the project.

Of course, in determining acceptable odds, management should and does consider the possible gains and losses inherent in the decision. In making a decision on the basis of the probability model, these economic consequences are considered outside of the decision model. Management decides whether a 0.72 probability of success is high enough for it to take the risk, considering the economic consequences of its decision. If so, the decision should be to market the heat pump; if not, the project should be canceled.

We might also consider what management's decision would be if $P(S) < 0.5$. Logically the decision would be to cancel the project. However, if the rewards for success were sufficiently large, management might be inclined to take the risk. Once again it becomes apparent that the economic consequences should not be separated from the decision procedure.

On examining the logical model it seemed apparent that the most critical factor bearing on the state of the system was component C, the state of competition. This evaluation is borne out by the probabilistic analysis. $P(S)$, the probability that the system is in the good state, is almost identical with $P(C)$. It will not necessarily always occur that the probability that the system state is good will depend so heavily on a single component or even on a few components. However, there are frequently one or two major components that have the principal effect on the state of the system. Frequently these are difficult to identify without going through the analysis presented here. This analysis does tend to identify the important factors and allows many of the unimportant ones to be eliminated.

In this case, if the decision analysis is continued, the state of nature or state of the system could be identified with component C, the state of the competition, and all attention now directed to this single state of nature.

9.4 SUMMARY

The probability model goes one step beyond the logical model in that it considers that the state conditions assigned to the various components of nature or the decision system are, at least from the standpoint of the decision maker, uncertain. Consequently, probability values should be used to describe this uncertain character of the states. By application of the rules of probability to the model, a probability value is obtained for the total decision system; that is, the probability that the system or nature is in a good or favorable state. At this point the decision maker must determine for himself whether this probability is good enough to warrant the risk involved in his decision.

It becomes obvious that in order to make his decision, these risks must be considered. In the probability analysis only the probability values are used explicitly for the decision making. However, the risk or consequences resulting are considered by the decision maker outside of the actual structure of the model.

part three

Statistics

10
Statistical Treatment of Data

Our primary concern up to this point has been to develop models for the general decision problem facing the decision maker and to evaluate those models so as to reach a conclusion as to the state of the system which bears on the decision to be made. It should be apparent that whether we base our decision on the evaluation of a logical model or a probability model, we are faced with the problem of assigning *values* to the state of the components of the system. In the case of the logical model, these values are either zero or 1 corresponding to the states *good* and *bad*. For the probability model, these values correspond to the probability that a component is in the *good* state and therefore may vary between zero and 1.

In the examples used to illustrate the evaluation of the logical and probability models or networks, the values were arbitrarily assigned to each component. In a real decision problem these values must be estimates of the true states or state probabilities and should generally be based on some empirical evidence.

Fortunately, in most decision situations, there is evidence in abundance. In those infrequent cases where such empirical evidence does not exist, there are procedures for inserting subjective estimates of the states or state probabilities into the model, and these procedures will be considered later.

The empirical evidence, or data, upon which most of the estimates will be based exists in many different forms. It may already be collected and compiled, or it may require collection and/or compilation. As an example of useful data that may already exist and be at the disposal of the decision maker, there is historical data regarding prices of raw materials, wage rates by labor classification, percentage defectives from some production process, distribution costs, etc. Data that may have to be acquired could include information about various market characteristics for which a market survey may have to be initiated. In any case, once the data are collected and placed at the disposal of the decision maker, they must be organized and treated in some way so that intelligence can be derived from them and their pertinent characteristics can become evident. In the final analysis, the purpose of collecting, compiling, and analyzing data is simply to determine or to estimate the characteristics of parameters of the population from which they were taken and which they represent.

When data collection or compilation becomes a goal for its own sake, the effect on any practical decision situation can be disastrous. The collection of large masses of unnecessary data can lead to excessive expense and create confusion that serves only to obscure the real requirements of the decision problem. For this reason, data which already exists should be compiled, and new data collected and complied, only when there is a definite requirement for that specific data for the estimation of component states or state probabilities in the decision system. In order to avoid complications, it is necessary that the formulation of the logical model precede any data collection or compilation activity whatsoever. Once the logical model is constructed, then the data requirements for the problem at hand become obvious.

This chapter, and several which follow, will be devoted to the statistical methods for analyzing data and arriving at conclusions about the population from which they were derived.

10.1 POPULATIONS AND SAMPLES

A *population* is any collection or set of objects or elements which have some common characteristic. In this sense, a population is a *set* as defined previously. The term "population" may be used to refer to the individual elements themselves or to observations taken on those elements. Consequently, any given set of elements can produce more than one population. For example, if the set of elements to be observed is a specific group of persons, and if we make observations of their weights and of their heights, then the resulting set of weights is one population, while the set of heights is another. Sometimes the term "universe" is used to refer to the elements themselves, while "population" refers to the measurements or observations.

A population may be finite or it may be infinite. The number of people living in a particular geographical area, the number of students in a university, the number of parts produced on one particular machine last Thursday are all examples of finite populations.

On the other hand, all the points on a straight line, the set of all integers, all possible tosses of a particular coin, or all the parts that might possibly be produced on the machine mentioned in the previous paragraph are examples of infinite populations.

An observable characteristic or property of a population is called a *parameter*. The parameter of a population is essentially the same as the parameter of a probability distribution as discussed previously, since probability distributions also represent theoretical populations. In fact, the value of a probability distribution as a model of some real phenomenon lies in its ability to represent some real population with a reasonable degree of accuracy. Parameters, whether of real populations or of theoretical probability distributions, will generally but not always be represented by Greek letters. The size of a finite population is simply the number of elements contained in it. We shall use the capital letter N to represent the size of a population.

If the population of interest is finite and small, it is conceivable that we can find out all that we wish to know about it by observing every one of its members. However, situations like this are exceedingly rare. The usual case is that the population of interest is so large that it is impractical, if not impossible, to observe all its members. In this case, we attempt to acquire information about the population by observing some portion or subset of the total population. This portion or subset of a population is called a *sample*.

It is possible that the same set of elements can be both a population and a sample. For example, the output of the machine mentioned above on some particular day could constitute a population about which certain information is required. At the same time, this same output could be considered as a sample of the output of that machine considered over a longer period of time, say a week, a month, or a year. As another example, the members of a particular class in statistics at a university could be a population in itself or they could be considered as a sample of students from the population of students in the entire university.

Since samples are used for the purpose of making inferences about the population from which they are drawn, sample characteristics are used to estimate population characteristics. A value computed from a sample for the purpose of estimating a population parameter is called a *statistic*. A sample statistic will be represented by an English letter.

The size of a sample is the number of elements contained in it. We shall use the letter n to represent the size of a sample.

10.2 TYPES OF DATA

Statistical data can be classified according to the type of observation taken on the element. If the observation consists of a measurement on the elements of the set under consideration, the data are of the *quantitative* type and the characteristic is called a *variate*. Another term used for quantitative data is *variables data*. Variables data can be classified into two types, *discrete* and *continuous*. The distinction between discrete and continuous data was made previously with respect to sets and probability distributions. We shall, however, make the distinction again. Discrete data are such that they can take on certain values only. These values are generally, but not necessarily, the integers. For example, the measurement of family size in a given population produces discrete, quantitative data. The variable can take on values corresponding only to the positive whole numbers. A family may consist of two members, three members, four members, etc.; it cannot consist of $2\frac{1}{2}$ members or $3\frac{1}{4}$ members.

Continuous data are such that they can take on an infinity of values. Measurements of heights, weights, distances, etc. are limited only by the precision of the measuring instruments used, and the variable can assume any one of an infinite number of values. In measuring the diameters of a part, we might obtain a value of 2.54 in. With a more precise measuring instrument we might obtain a value for the same part of 2.543 in. Further refinements in the measuring instrument could result in more precise readings such as 2.54372, etc. It should be noted that continuous distributions really exist only in theory. In practice, all measurements are discrete. However, continuous theoretical distributions are frequently used as models for discrete data distributions.

When the observations consist of noting the absence or presence of some property or characteristic, the data are referred to as *qualitative* and the property observed is called an *attribute*. Frequently the term *attributes data* is used for data of this type.

In a particular bridge hand, data regarding the number of cards in the hand of each suit would be qualitative data. The attributes of the cards observed are spades, hearts, diamonds, and clubs. In testing parts produced from a machine, the observations of good and defective parts represent qualitative data where the observed attributes are *good* and *defective*.

In treating qualitative data, we categorize the members of the set being observed according to the presence or absence of the attributes of interest and observe the numbers in each category. In the coin-tossing experiment referred to so frequently in previous chapters, the attributes of interest would be *heads* and *tails*, and our observations would record the number of each which occurred in some number of tosses.

10.3 FREQUENCY DISTRIBUTIONS

When faced with a large quantity of data relating to some population of interest, it is necessary to organize the data in some way so as to make them intelligible, amenable to analysis, and productive of information bearing on the decision problem at hand. One of the first steps in the statistical treatment of data is to organize them into a *frequency distribution.*

A frequency distribution is simply a tabular arrangement of the data into classes and a tally of the number of observations which fall into each class. Tables 10.1 and 10.2 are examples of two kinds of frequency distributions. Table 10.1 illustrates a quantitative or numerical distribution, while Table 10.2 illustrates a qualitative or categorical distribution.

Frequency distributions are constructed from empirical data by grouping observations into classes and counting the number of observations in each class. The first step, then, in constructing a frequency distribution is to determine the number of classes in which the data are to be grouped and to define the classes such that there can be no uncertainty regarding the class to which each and every observation belongs. This last is accomplished by making certain that the classes include *all* the data and that the individual classes are *mutually exclusive.* In practice, a frequency distribution *usually* has at least six classes and at most about 15. A rough guide to the number of classes is given by the formula

$$k = 1 + 3.22 \log N$$

where k represents the number of classes and N is the number of elements in the set of data.

Table 10.1 Frequency distribution, diameters of parts produced on machine A (week of April 3, 1970)

Diameter, in.	*Number of parts*
2.05 to 2.14	3
2.15 to 2.24	39
2.25 to 2.34	70
2.35 to 2.44	205
2.45 to 2.54	378
2.55 to 2.64	191
2.65 to 2.74	66
2.75 to 2.84	41
2.85 to 2.94	7

Table 10.2 Frequency distribution, classification of diameters of parts produced on machine A (week of April 3, 1970)

Classification	*Number of parts*
Undersize	112
Within tolerance	774
Oversize	114

The distribution in Table 10.2 violates this rule since it has only three classes. It is a good example of why too few classes make the distribution of limited use. In determining the characteristics of the output of machine *A* during the week of April 3, 1970, it should be apparent that the distribution in Table 10.1 is a great deal more descriptive and informative than that of Table 10.2. Table 10.2, with only three classes, obscures most of the information about the distribution of the part diameters which is contained in Table 10.1. It is conceivable, however, that for some decision problems Table 10.2 provides all the information that is required.

Too many classes also tend to obscure information about the distribution. In the extreme case there would be a class for every observation, and the characteristics of the distribution would be obscured by the extreme detail.

Each class into which the data are grouped is defined by the *class limits*. The class limits are the largest and smallest values that can go into any given class. In Table 10.1, the *lower class limits* are 2.05, 2.15, 2.25, 2.35, 2.45, 2.55, 2.65, etc. The *upper class limits* are 2.14, 2.24, 2.34, 2.44, 2.54, 2.64, etc. The class limits are specified to the same precision that the measurements are made. That is, if measurements are made to two decimal places, the class limits are specified to two decimal places also. It is apparent that the classes are defined so that no two classes overlap, and therefore there can be no question as to the class in which a particular observation belongs.

For data which are inherently continuous, however, it is necessary that there be no gaps between the classes. For this reason the class with the *limits* 2.15 and 2.24 actually includes all observations with values between 2.145 and 2.245. The class with *limits* 2.25 and 2.34 includes all observations with values 2.245 to 2.345. These latter values are called the *class boundaries.*

The term *class mark* refers to the midpoint of the class and is simply the average of the two class limits. The class mark of the class with the limits 2.45 and 2.54 is 2.495.

The *class interval* is the length of the class. It can be obtained by determining the difference between any two successive class marks, any two

Table 10.3 Cumulative frequency distribution, diameters of parts produced on machine A (week of April 3, 1970)

Diameter, in.	*Number of parts*
2.04 or less	0
2.14 or less	3
2.24 or less	42
2.34 or less	112
2.44 or less	317
2.54 or less	695
2.64 or less	886
2.74 or less	952
2.84 or less	993
2.94 or less	1,000

successive lower or upper class limits, or the two class boundaries of the same class.

A *cumulative frequency distribution* provides information regarding the number of observations which are less than or equal to some value. We could convert Table 10.1 into a cumulative frequency distribution by successively adding the frequencies in each class as shown in Table 10.3.

Suppose, instead of the absolute frequency of occurrences in each class, we are more interested in the relative frequency or percentage of occurrences in each class. We can convert any frequency distribution into a relative frequency distribution by simply dividing each frequency or the number of observations in each class by the total number of observations taken. Table 10.4 shows the relative frequency distribution of the data given in Table 10.1.

Table 10.4 Relative frequency distribution, diameters of parts produced on machine A (week of April 3, 1970)

Diameter, in.	*Absolute frequency*	*Relative frequency*
2.05 to 2.14	3	3/1,000 = 0.003
2.15 to 2.24	39	39/1,000 = 0.039
2.25 to 2.34	70	70/1,000 = 0.070
2.35 to 2.44	205	205/1,000 = 0.205
2.45 to 2.54	378	378/1,000 = 0.378
2.55 to 2.64	191	191/1,000 = 0.191
2.65 to 2.74	66	66/1,000 = 0.066
2.75 to 2.84	41	41/1,000 = 0.041
2.85 to 2.94	7	7/1,000 = 0.007
Totals	1,000	1,000/1,000 = 1.000

Table 10.5 Cumulative relative frequency distribution, diameters of parts produced on machine A (week of April 3, 1970)

Diameter, in.	*Cumulative relative frequency*
2.04 or less	0.000
2.14 or less	0.003
2.24 or less	0.042
2.34 or less	0.112
2.44 or less	0.317
2.54 or less	0.695
2.64 or less	0.886
2.74 or less	0.952
2.84 or less	0.993
2.94 or less	1.000

The relative frequency distribution of Table 10.4 can be converted to a *cumulative relative frequency distribution* in the same way that any ordinary frequency distribution is converted to a cumulative distribution, simply by adding each successive class to the preceding class or classes. This is shown in Table 10.5.

The relationship between a relative frequency distribution and a probability distribution should be noted here. The relative frequency definition of probability states that if an event occurs n times out of a total of N trials of an experiment which could lead to the occurrence of that event, then the probability of the event occurring is the limit of the ratio n/N as N approaches infinity. An estimate of the probability of the event of interest is given by n/N.

If the occurrence of a measurement of the diameter of one of the parts falling in some one of the specified classes is the event of interest, then an estimate of its probability is the relative frequency of its occurrence in the trials observed. Consequently the relative frequency distribution derived from a sample of data is an estimate of the underlying probability distribution of the population. If the data include the entire population of interest, then their relative frequency distribution is the probability distribution of the population.

10.4 HISTOGRAMS

It is frequently desirable to draw a picture of a frequency distribution in order to visualize its characteristics more clearly. The most common graphical representation of a frequency distribution is called a *histogram*. A histogram is constructed by letting the horizontal scale or *abscissa* represent the observed measurements and the vertical scale or *ordinate* represent the frequencies or relative frequencies. The abscissa is divided into sections, each one representing one of the class intervals of the distribution and constituting the base of a rectangle. The class intervals and, therefore, the bases of the rectangles should be equal. The height of each rectangle is drawn proportionate to the frequency of the observations in the class which it represents. Since the rectangles are adjacent to one another, the vertical edges of each rectangle correspond to the class limits or, more precisely, to the class boundaries. The horizontal scale can be labeled either with class boundaries or class marks. The histogram corresponding to the data of the frequency distribution shown in Table 10.1 is given in Fig. 10.1.

As long as the class intervals of all the classes are equal, then the area of each bar as well as its height is proportional to the frequency in the class which it represents. In order to approximate frequency distributions with theoretical continuous probability distributions, an approximation procedure which we shall find very useful and convenient, it will be necessary to relate frequencies to areas. Consequently, in constructing histograms which provide accurate pictures of frequency distributions, care should be taken to see that the bases of the rectangles are all equal. If, for example, we were to combine two of the classes in the histogram of Fig. 10.1 and to represent their total frequency by the height of the bar against the scale on the ordinate, the picture would be misleading since the area of the bar would no longer be proportional to the frequency.

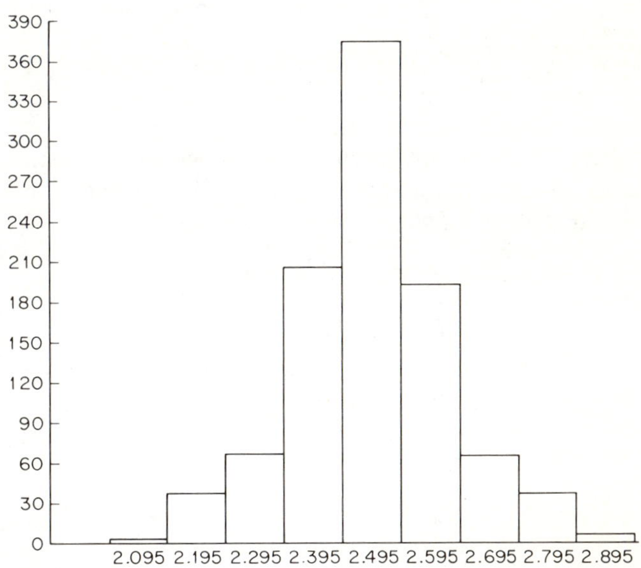

Fig. 10.1

10.5 DESCRIPTIVE MEASURES: LOCATION

In order to comprehend more easily the nature or characteristics of a large mass of data or of the population from which it has been derived, we have organized the data into a frequency distribution and then represented it pictorially by means of a histogram. Even this device may, however, fail to tell us all that we should like to know about the data or the population, and other types of descriptions are necessary. One type of descriptive measure is an indication of the location of the data on the scale of values assigned to the observations. Let us note here that we are primarily referring to quantitative data. However, attributes or qualitative data can be treated quantitatively when it is desirable to do so.

Most frequently, but not always, we are concerned with the location of the center or midpoint of a collection of data. Measures which indicate the location of the "center" of a distribution are generally called *measures of central tendency*. The most common of these is the *arithmetic mean*, or simply, the *mean*.

The arithmetic mean is the measure that is commonly referred to when the term *average* is used. There are, however, other means, such as the *geometric mean* and the *harmonic mean*. When the term *mean* is used in this book, without any modifying adjective, let it be understood that it is the arithmetic mean that is referred to.

The mean of a set of N values is simply the sum of the individual values divided by N. If the set of values, let us call them X, represents a finite population in its entirety, then the population mean is designated by the Greek letter μ, and

$$\mu = \frac{\sum x}{N} \tag{10.1}$$

where N is the population size as previously indicated. If the X values are only a sample from some larger population, then the mean of the sample is designated by $\bar{x}$ (x bar), and

$$\bar{x} = \frac{\sum x}{n} \tag{10.2}$$

where n is the sample size.

For a small amount of data, the mean can be computed directly by Eqs. (10.1) and (10.2). For large amounts of data grouped into a frequency distribution, the comparable formulas for μ and $\bar{x}$ are

$$\mu = \frac{\sum_i x_i f(x_i)}{N} \tag{10.3}$$

$$\bar{x} = \frac{\sum_i x_i f(x_i)}{n} \tag{10.4}$$

where $f(x_i)$ represents the frequency of the occurrence of each of the individual x_i. The x_i can be each individual value x which occurs or, with little loss in accuracy, it can be the class mark of each of the i classes into which the data are grouped, in which case $f(x_i)$ represents the number of values in the ith class.

Equations (10.3) and (10.4) should be compared with Eq. (7.1) for the expected value of a random variable X. These formulas are almost identical since the expected value of a random variable, the mean of a probability distribution, and the mean of a frequency distribution all represent the same measure. The $f(x_i)$ in Eq. (7.1) represents the probability function of the random variable which is equivalent to $f(x_i)/N$ in Eq. (10.3) and $f(x_i)/n$ in Eq. (10.4), since the frequency distribution can be converted to a relative frequency distribution by dividing the frequencies in each class by the total number of observations in the set which is in turn a method for approximating a probability distribution.

The mean is an extremely useful measure for describing a set of data for several reasons. First, it is quite easy to compute. Second, it can always be calculated for any set of numerical data. Third, it utilizes all the data. One of its deficiencies in describing a set of data is that one or two extreme values in the set can affect the value of the mean to such an extent that it may not be truly representative of the entire mass of data. Consequently, other measures of central tendency are available, and the analyst can select that one which appears to best represent the specific set of data under consideration.

One of these alternate measures is called the *median*. For ungrouped data the median is simply the *value* of the middle item of any set of data containing an odd number of items or observations. For example, if the data consisted of the values 2, 7, 9, 19, 30, and 39, the median would be 19. If there are an even number of observations, the median is the mean of the two middle values. For the data consisting of the values 2, 7, 9, 19, 30, and 39, the median is found by adding the two middle items and dividing by 2. Thus $\tilde{x} = (9 + 19)/2 = 14$, where $\tilde{x}$ designates the median of the x's from a sample. We shall let $\tilde{\mu}$ represent the population median.

For sample data grouped into a frequency distribution, we first must determine the class into which the median falls by dividing the total number of observations by 2. The class in which the $n/2$ item falls contains the median. Since in a frequency distribution the values of the individual items within a class are lost, and only the number of items in each class are given, we find the median value as follows. Add to the lower class *boundary* of the median class the difference between $n/2$ and the number of items contained in all the classes below the median class combined. Divide this difference by the number of items in the median class and multiply the result by the class interval. This procedure may sound complicated, but it is really very simple. As an example, consider the frequency distribution given in Table 10.6.

Since $n = 50$, $n/2 = 25$, and the median class is the class containing the twenty-fifth observation, in this case the class with the limits 30 to 39. The lower class boundary of this class, designated L, is halfway between its lower class limit and the upper class limit of the next lower class, that is, 29.5. Let m represent the number of items or observations contained in all the classes below the median class. In this case $m = 23$. The number of items in the median class is $f = 16$. The class interval is 10. Then the median is given by

$$\breve{x} = 29.5 + \left(\frac{25 - 23}{16}\right)10$$

$$\breve{x} = 29.5 + \left(\frac{2}{16}\right)10$$

$$\breve{x} = 29.50 + 1.25$$
$$\breve{x} = 30.75$$

The general formula for the median of a set of grouped observations is

$$\breve{x} = L + \left[\frac{(n/2) - m}{f}\right]C \qquad (10.5)$$

where

L = lower boundary of median class
n = total number of observations
m = number of observations in all classes below median class
f = number of observations in median class
C = class interval

The median is also called the fiftieth percentile because it is the point which divides the data in half. That is, one-half of the observations are

Table 10.6 Frequency distribution

Class	*Frequency*	*Cumulative frequency*
0–9	3	3
10–19	8	11
20–29	12	23
30–39	16	39
40–49	9	48
50–59	2	50

below the median value and one-half lie above it. In a continuous probability distribution, the median divides the area under the curve into two equal parts.

It should be apparent that the median and the mean of the same set of data need not be the same value. For example, the median of the frequency distribution given in Table 10.6 was calculated to be 30.75. The mean of that distribution is 29.7. When the mean and the median do coincide, as is the case with the normal distribution discussed previously, the distribution is symmetrical.

Just as the median divides a set of data into two equal parts, other points can be determined in a similar manner which divide the distribution into other proportions. For example, the data can be divided into *quartiles* by the points Q_1, Q_2, and Q_3 such that 25 percent of the values fall in the first quartile, that is, below Q_1, 25 percent fall in the second quartile, which is between points Q_1 and Q_2, 25 percent fall in the third quartile, and 25 percent in the fourth quartile.

Deciles divide the data into 10 equal parts, and *percentiles* divide them into 100 equal parts. The ninth decile and the ninetieth percentile, for instance, are identical and define a point such that 90 percent of the values lie below that point and 10 percent lie above it. Quartiles, deciles, and percentiles, while measures of location, are not measures of central tendency. They may, however, be even more useful to the decision maker than the mean or median, in certain circumstances.

As an example, an importer and distributor of expensive foreign automobiles might want to know the level in income exceeded by the most affluent 10 percent of the residents of some particular community. A social service agency might want to know the level of income which provides the upper bounds of earnings for the 10 percent of the population of the community at the lowest extreme of the earnings scale.

Still another measure of central tendency is called the *mode*. The mode is that value from a set of data that occurs with the greatest frequency. It is possible that in some set of data two values might have the same frequency of occurrence which is greater than that of any other single value in the set. In that case, both values are modes, and the distribution is said to be *bimodal*. For grouped data, the mode is the class mark of the class having the greatest frequency. If two adjacent classes have the same frequency which is greater than that of any other class, the mode is their common class boundary.

One final measure of central tendency which we shall consider here is called the *midrange*. This is simply the mean of the highest and lowest values contained in the set. For grouped data, it can be computed by averaging the lower class boundary of the lowest class with the upper class boundary of the highest. Even more simply, if there is an odd number of classes, the midrange is the class mark of the middle class. For an even number of classes, it is the common class boundary of the two middle classes. The usefulness of the midrange lies only in its ease of computation.

10.6 DESCRIPTIVE MEASURES: VARIATION

In order to achieve a useful description of a set of data, at least two measures are generally necessary. An indication of the location of the midpoint of the set of data, whether it be the mean, the median, or the mode, says nothing about the dispersion of the data over the scale of values which constitute the observations. The fact that a set of data can be organized into a frequency distribution indicates that the individual observations are not all the same, and that they are, in fact, distributed over some range or scale of values.

Measures of location or, more specifically, measures of central tendency describe one of the two most important properties of a set of data. However, they indicate nothing at all about the second important property. It is therefore necessary to devise an indication of the extent to which the data are dispersed.

As an illustration, let us consider three different sets of data containing the following values:

Set A: 1, 2, 3, 3, 4, 5
Set B: 0, 1, 3, 3, 5, 6
Set C: 3, 3, 3, 3, 3, 3

The mean, the median, and the mode of all three sets are exactly the same, and all are equal to the value 3. Yet it is apparent that the amount of variation in the data differs from set to set.

One of the simplest measures of variation or dispersion is called the *range*. The range is simply the difference between the largest and the smallest values in the set. If we let R designate the range of a set of values, L represent the largest member of the set, and S represent the value of the smallest member, then

$$R = L - S$$

For the three sets given as examples above, the ranges are as follows:

$$R_A = 5 - 1 = 4$$
$$R_B = 6 - 0 = 6$$
$$R_C = 3 - 3 = 0$$

The major advantage and disadvantage of the range as a measure of dispersion are the same as the advantage and disadvantage of the midrange as a measure of central tendency. The advantage lies in its ease of computation, while the disadvantage lies in the fact that this measure utilizes only the extreme values of the set and therefore can be misleading since it completely ignores all the other members.

It would seem logical to expect that a useful measure of variation should utilize the data in its entirety and should have a large value if the members of the set of data are widely dispersed and a small value if the members are closely bunched together. In order to define such a measure, it becomes necessary to select some reference point. The most obvious reference point from which to measure the dispersion of a set of data would seem to be the mean of the set of data. If the set is considered to be a population with mean μ and the individual values of the set designated by x_i, then a measure called the *variance* is defined as the mean of the squared deviations of the individual values from their own mean. The variance is designated by the symbol σ^2, which is the Greek letter sigma squared. That is,

$$\sigma^2 = \frac{\sum_{i=1}^{N} (x_i - \mu)^2}{N} \tag{10.6}$$

One might ask, why must the deviations be squared? It can be shown that the sum of the deviations of the individual values about their own mean is always equal to zero, since the positive and negative deviations will exactly cancel each other. However, by squaring the deviations, negative values are eliminated, and the variance is always a positive number.

The positive square root of the variance is called the *standard deviation*, and for a population is given by

$$\sigma = \sqrt{\frac{\sum_{i=1}^{N} (x_i - \mu)^2}{N}} \tag{10.7}$$

The standard deviation is generally a more convenient measure of variation since it is always in the same units of measurement as the original data, whereas the variance is not.

In general, the variance and standard deviation of any set of data are defined according to Eqs. (10.6) and (10.7). However, if the set of data is considered to be a sample from some larger population, its variance is designated by s^2 and its standard deviation simply by s. The formulas for the sample variance and the sample standard deviation are the same as those given in Eqs. (10.6) and (10.7), with the exceptions that the divisor is taken as 1 less than the sample size, that is $(n - 1)$, and the deviations are measured from the sample mean which is designated $\bar{x}$. The formulas for the sample variance and sample standard deviation are

$$s^2 = \frac{\sum_{i=1}^{n} (x_i - \bar{x})^2}{n - 1} \tag{10.8}$$

$$s = \sqrt{\frac{\sum_{i=1}^{n} (x_i - \bar{x})^2}{n - 1}} \tag{10.9}$$

The reason for dividing by $n - 1$ instead of n when computing the sample variance or standard deviation has to do with a property of an estimator called *bias*. Properties of estimators will be considered at greater length in Chap. 12, "Statistical Estimation." Let it suffice to say here that s^2 as an estimator of σ^2 would be, on the average, too small if n was used as the divisor. This bias is corrected by the use of $n - 1$.

If we were to consider set A, given above, as a population, we could compute its mean, variance, and standard deviation in the following way:

	x_i	$x_i - \mu$	$(x_i - \mu)^2$
	1	$1 - 3 = -2$	4
	2	$2 - 3 = -1$	1
	3	$3 - 3 = 0$	0
	3	$3 - 3 = 0$	0
	4	$4 - 3 = 1$	1
	5	$5 - 3 = 2$	4
Sums	18	0	10

$$\mu = \frac{\sum_i x_i}{N} = \frac{18}{6} = 3$$

$$\sigma^2 = \frac{\sum_i (x_i - \mu)^2}{N} = \frac{10}{6} = 1\tfrac{2}{3}$$

$$\sigma = \sqrt{1\tfrac{2}{3}}$$

If set A happened to be a sample selected from some population and its variance and standard deviation were to be used as estimators of the population variance and standard deviation, then we would compute the mean, variance, and standard deviation as follows:

	x_i	$x_i - \bar{x}$	$(x_i - \bar{x})^2$
	1	$1 - 3 = -2$	4
	2	$2 - 3 = -1$	1
	3	$3 - 3 = 0$	0
	3	$3 - 3 = 0$	0
	4	$4 - 3 = 1$	1
	5	$5 - 3 = 2$	4
Sums	18	0	10

$$\bar{x} = \frac{18}{6} = 3$$

$$s^2 = \frac{\sum_{i=1}^{n} (x_i - \bar{x})^2}{n - 1} = \frac{10}{5} = 2$$

$$s = \sqrt{2}$$

Although this method of computing the variance and standard deviation is very simple for a small set of numbers, it can become very cumbersome when the set becomes large. There is another formula for the variance and the standard deviation that is easier to use, particularly when the number of data elements is large, and is particularly well suited to calculating on a desk calculator. These alternate formulas, for populations and samples, respectively, are

$$\sigma^2 = \frac{\sum_i x_i^2 - N\mu^2}{N} \tag{10.10}$$

$$s^2 = \frac{\sum_i x_i^2 - (\sum_i x_i)^2/n}{n - 1} \tag{10.11}$$

and of course σ and s are simply the positive square roots of σ^2 and s^2.

To illustrate the use of Eq. (10.11), we could compute s^2 and s for the same set of data as follows:

	x_i	x_i^2
	1	1
	2	4
	3	9
	3	9
	4	16
	5	25
Sums	18	64

$$\bar{x} = \frac{18}{6} = 3$$

$$\sum_{i=1}^{n} (x_i^2) = 64$$

$$\left(\sum_{i=1}^{n} x_i\right)^2 = (18)^2 = 324$$

$$s^2 = \frac{64 - (324/6)}{6 - 1} = \frac{64 - 54}{5} = 2$$

$$s = \sqrt{2}$$

For the other two sets, B and C, the variances are, respectively, 5.2 and 0. The variance of zero for set C should be intuitively satisfying since all the values in the set are exactly the same, and since there is in fact no variability or dispersion of the data.

For grouped data from a sample, the standard and short-cut formulas for the variance are as follows:

$$s^2 = \frac{\sum_{i=1}^{n} (x_i - \bar{x})^2 f_i}{n - 1} \tag{10.12}$$

$$s^2 = \frac{\sum_{i=1}^{n} x_i^2 f_i - \left(\sum_{i=1}^{n} x_i f_i\right)^2 / n}{n - 1} \tag{10.13}$$

where x_i is the class mark and f_i is the frequency of the ith class.

For populations, the appropriate formulas are:

$$\sigma^2 = \frac{\sum_i (x_i - \mu)^2 f_i}{N} \tag{10.14}$$

$$\sigma^2 = \frac{\sum_i x_i^2 f_i - N\mu^2}{N} \tag{10.15}$$

10.7 CHEBYSHEV'S INEQUALITY

Given the mean and the standard deviation for any set of data, there is a theorem known as Chebyshev's inequality that allows us to make a probability statement about the distribution of the set of data even though no further information is available to us. The inequality is as follows:

$$P(|x - \mu| < k\sigma) \geq 1 - \frac{1}{k^2} \tag{10.16}$$

The inequality (10.16) stated simply means that for any type of distribution whatsoever, the probability that any element lies within the limits defined by the mean plus k standard deviations and the mean minus k standard deviations is always greater than $1 - 1/k^2$. This can also be interpreted to mean that $1 - 1/k^2$ is the proportion of the elements of the set which lies within those same limits.

For example, given a distribution with a mean of 30 and a standard deviation of 3, we can be assured that at least

$$1 - 1/2^2 = 1 - 1/4 = 3/4$$

of the data elements lie between the values 24 and 36, which are two standard deviations on either side of the mean. We can go further and say that within three standard deviations of the mean, that is, between the limits 21 and 39, will lie at least

$$1 - 1/3^2 = 1/9 = 8/9$$

of the data elements. The inequality does not hold, however, for $k \leq 1$.

Now, given the two characteristics of a set of data, the mean and the standard deviation, it is possible to make statements about the proportions of the data which can be expected to fall between or outside of specified limits. Inequality (10.16) can be transformed so as to provide the probability that an element will fall further than k standard deviations from the mean, or to provide the proportion of elements which will fall further than k standard deviations from the mean, as follows:

$$P(|x - \mu| > k\sigma) < \frac{1}{k^2} \tag{10.17}$$

As has been mentioned, Chebyshev's inequality holds for any set of data, regardless of its distribution. If further information is known or can be assumed about the distribution of the data, then more precise statements can be made.

For example, if the distribution is *unimodal*, that is, has a single mode, and if it is also symmetrical, then

$$P(|x - \mu| < k\sigma) > 1 - \left(\frac{2}{3k}\right)^2 \tag{10.18}$$

Equation (10.18) is known as the Camp-Meidel inequality.

Given this information in addition to the mean of 30 and the standard deviation of 3, then the proportion of the data elements lying between the values 24 and 36 will be at least

$$1 - \left(\frac{2}{3.2}\right)^2 = 1 - \left(\frac{2}{6}\right)^2 = 1 - \frac{1}{9} = \frac{8}{9}$$

With the further information that the distribution is normal, the statement could be made that 95 percent of the data lies within the mean and $\pm$ two standard deviations. The last statement is derived from the characteristics of the normal distribution.

As an example of the application of these theorems to a practical situation, suppose we have estimated the mean and standard deviation of the distribution of a critical part dimension resulting from some production process. Even though we know nothing about the shape of the distribution, using Chebyshev's inequality we can estimate the maximum proportion of parts for which the critical dimension will exceed those specific limits which constitute a defective part. Of course, the more we know about the distribution of these measurements, the more precise we can be in our estimate of the proportion of defectives.

10.8 COEFFICIENT OF VARIATION

It is frequently desirable to compare the variation among one set of data with that of another set in order to determine which set exhibits the greatest variability. The most commonly used measure of variation, as previously mentioned, is the variance or its square root, which is the standard deviation.

The standard deviation of a set of data is given in the units by which the original data elements were measured, which is as it should be. However, in comparing two different sets of data which appear in different units of measurement, the standard deviation in itself is not sufficient for the determination of which set is the more variable. For example, if one set consists of the heights of a group of men and has a standard deviation of 2.2 in., while the second set of data consists of the weights of the same group of men and has a standard deviation of 11 lb, it is not possible on the basis of this information alone to say whether the distribution of heights or the distribution of weights exhibits the greater variability.

Even for two sets of measurements given in the same units of measurement, it is not always obvious which set is the more variable. It is apparent, in most instances, that sets whose elements are small values vary numerically less than sets whose elements are large values. If in the above example, instead of a set of heights and a set of weights taken from the same group of individuals, we had two sets of weights, one of which was taken from a group of boys aged 7 years and having a standard deviation of 3.7 lb, while the second was the set of adult weights given above, we would still be unable to ascertain from the standard deviations alone which set had the greater variability.

For this reason, a measure of relative variation called the *coefficient of variation* has been devised and is defined as

$$V = \frac{s}{\bar{x}}$$

and is simply the ratio of the standard deviation of the data to its mean.

For the first example given, if the mean height was 69 in. with a standard deviation of 2.2 in. and if the mean weight was 162 lb with a standard deviation of 11 lb, then the coefficient of variation of the heights is $V_1 = 2.2/69 \doteq 0.032$. For the set of weights, $V_2 = 11/162 \doteq 0.068$. It is now apparent that the set of weights is more than twice as variable as the set of heights.

For the second illustration, if the mean weight of the 7-year-old boys was 55 lb with a standard deviation of 3.7 lb, while the mean weight of the men was 162 lb with a standard deviation of 11 lb, then

$$V_1 = \frac{3.7}{55} \doteq 0.068$$

$$V_2 = \frac{11}{162} \doteq 0.068$$

10.9 SUMMARY

The purpose of collecting data is that some estimate can be made about the parameters of the population from which the data were derived. It is assumed that these parameters are those which bear on the valuation of the system or component state necessary to the solution of the decision problem. In order to make these estimates, it is necessary to evaluate and analyze the data. The first step in the evaluation of the data requires that they be organized and, once organized, they can then be described in some manner.

We have discussed the organization of data into frequency distributions and the description of the data by means of certain measures of location and variation. We have also discussed Chebyshev's theorem, which allows us to make certain other assumptions about the data based only on a knowledge of its mean and standard deviation.

As we continue, we shall delve more deeply into the statistical analysis of data in order to estimate or to test assumptions about its pertinent characteristics. First, however, it is necessary to take up the subject of sampling, since practically all the data with which it will be practical to deal in any given decision situation will represent samples taken from some larger population.

PROBLEMS

10.1. Fredericks Department Store was interested in performing an analysis of its accounts receivable. One of the factors of interest to the store's management was charge account balances. A random sample of 50 charge accounts was selected, and the balance owed to the store on each one was noted as follows:

\$77.97	\$ 3.07	\$ 32.67	\$142.11	\$ 12.98	\$ 17.64	\$398.17	\$ 47.13	\$ 69.94	\$ 21.20
34.40	487.67	114.84	79.61	89.19	51.69	354.26	20.64	11.10	641.01
208.89	13.02	185.41	96.90	145.51	38.74	292.03	962.40	81.59	99.08
93.91	124.89	32.54	207.54	218.01	166.72	419.84	182.88	17.97	226.76
60.94	78.56	147.34	243.87	90.99	12.18	68.13	316.49	288.25	43.66

(*a*) Arrange the data into a frequency distribution.
(*b*) Construct a histogram of the distribution.

10.2. A chain of shoe stores was interested in collecting data about their customers. The following frequency distribution was constructed from data regarding age:

Age of customer	*Frequency*
16 to 20	22
21 to 25	94
26 to 30	101
31 to 35	49
36 to 40	18
41 to 45	11
46 to 50	3
51 to 55	1
56 to 60	1
	300

(*a*) What is the lower class limit of the second class?
(*b*) What is the upper class limit of the fifth class?
(*c*) What is the upper class boundary of the seventh class?

(*d*) What is the lower class boundary of the eighth class?
(*e*) What is the class interval?
(*f*) What is the class mark of the third class?

10.3. For the frequency distribution in Prob. 10.2,
(*a*) What is the mode?
(*b*) What is the median?
(*c*) What is the mean?
(*d*) What is the midrange?

10.4. For the frequency distribution in Prob. 10.2,
(*a*) Find the range of the data.
(*b*) Find the standard deviation, assuming that the data represent a sample.
(*c*) Find the standard deviation, assuming that the data represent a total population of customers.

10.5. For the frequency distribution in Prob. 10.2,
(*a*) Convert it to a cumulative frequency distribution.
(*b*) Draw a histogram of the cumulative distribution.
(*c*) How many of the customers are 25 years old or younger?
(*d*) How many of the customers are 45 years old or younger?
(*e*) How many of the customers are *at least* 36 years old?

10.6. For the frequency distribution of Prob. 10.2,
(*a*) Convert it to a relative frequency distribution.
(*b*) What proportion of the customers were in the age group 26 to 30?
(*c*) What proportion of the customers were at least 21 and not over 40?
(*d*) What is the sum of the relative frequencies?

10.7. Over a long period of time, Mr. Brown carefully recorded the time it took him to get from his home to his office. He found that the mean time was 35 min and the standard deviation was 4 min. Having no other information about the distribution of times,

(*a*) On any given day, what is the probability that it will take him between 25 and 45 min to get to the office?

(*b*) If work starts at 9:00 A.M., at what time should Mr. Brown leave his home in order to have a probability of 0.75 that he will be on time?

10.8. If we knew that the distribution of times in Prob. 10.7 had a single mode and was symmetrical, answer the same two questions.

10.9. A manufacturer of a component of a satellite system found it necessary to control two critical characteristics, the weight and length. On the last lot of parts produced, he found that the average weight was 1.41 oz with a standard deviation of 0.03 oz, while the average length was 9.15 in. with a standard deviation of 0.12 in. Which characteristic exhibits the greater relative variation?

11
Sampling and Sampling Distributions

Data are collected and analyzed in order to learn, either by direct observations or by inference, something about the population from which they were drawn. In the decision context, the populations of interest are components of the decision system, and an evaluation of the states of those components involves a determination or estimation of the values of their unknown parameters.

Whenever it is impossible or impractical to observe every element of the population of interest, it becomes necessary to estimate the parameters of that population from a sample of elements taken from that population. In nearly every practical decision situation, the data referred to will be sample data drawn from the larger population of interest.

The process of selecting a sample or samples from some population is called *sampling*. A value computed entirely from the sample data is called a *statistic* as defined previously. A statistic is a random variable and as such has a distribution of its own. In order to use a statistic as an estimator of a population parameter or to make some inference about the population, something should be known about the distribution of that statistic. The distribution of a statistic is called a *sampling distribution*. Several of the more important sampling distributions will be discussed in this chapter after a brief discussion of the elements of the sampling process.

11.1 RANDOM SAMPLING

In order to use a sample to make valid inferences about a population, it is necessary that the sample be truly representative of the population from which it is drawn. In sampling terminology, the sample must be free from *bias*. The concept of bias with respect to statistics or estimators will be discussed at greater length in Sec. 11.2. Let us use the term at present to denote an undesirable characteristic of a sample. Bias in a sample usually results when certain elements in the population are more likely to be chosen as part of the sample than are other elements. The sampling procedure should ensure that every population element has an equal chance of being selected. When this criterion is met, the sampling procedure is said to be random. The definition, then, for a *random sample* is as follows:

Definition 11.1: A *random sample* is a sample selected in such a way that every element of the population from which the sample is drawn has an equal chance of being included in the sample and each selection is independent of all other selections.

Random sampling procedures are used for another reason in addition to avoiding bias. If the sample is a random sample, it is possible to obtain a measure of the representativeness of the sample from the sample data, and this is a very important factor in the inferential process.

It should probably be mentioned that the definition given above is in reality a definition of *simple random sampling*. There are other methods of sampling, most of which employ some element of randomness in the selection of elements. For example, stratified random sampling divides the population into sections, or *strata*, and specified numbers of elements are selected from each stratum. The sampling within each stratum is random. Cluster sampling selects clusters, or groups, of elements from the population at random but, having selected a cluster, the required observation is taken on every element in the cluster.

In this discussion, however, all sampling will be considered to be random or simple random sampling, and other sample designs or sampling procedures will be ignored.

In drawing a random sample from a finite population, we might proceed in the following manner. Suppose the population consists of five distinguishable elements, $N = 5$, and we desired a sample of size 2, $n = 2$. We shall first determine exactly how many different samples of size 2 we could select from a population of five elements by applying the combinatorial formula given previously as Eq. (5.5).

This formula applies only when the sampled items are not replaced after each selection. The number of combinations of N things taken n at a time is the same as the number of different samples of size n that can be taken from a population of size N and is

$$\frac{n!}{n!(N-n)!}$$

For $N = 5$ and $n = 2$ we find that it is possible to select 10 different samples. If we were to list the elements in each of the 10 different samples and number the samples 1 through 10, we could easily select a random sample by numbering 10 slips of paper, from 1 to 10, mixing them thoroughly, and then selecting one slip from a hat or bowl. In this way each sample would have a probability of $1/10$ of being selected, and all elements would have an equal probability of being included in the sample.

If the population is finite but large it would be impractical to list every possible sample that could be drawn. It might, however, be possible to number every element in the population, writing each number on a slip of paper and drawing the slips at random. In order for each selection to be independent of all other selections, each slip should be replaced before the next one is drawn. However, when the population is large with respect to the size of the sample, the effect of nonreplacement on the randomness of the selection is negligible. In actual practice, sampled elements are not usually replaced. Another method of selection which would eliminate the numbering and drawing of slips of paper could be to utilize a table of random numbers.

In sampling from a hypothetically infinite population, the question of replacement or nonreplacement is irrelevant. The criteria governing the randomness of the sampling process are that the selection of each element must be independent of every other selection and that all selections must have the same probability of occurrence.

11.2 SAMPLING DISTRIBUTIONS

We have previously defined a *statistic* as being some value computed from a sample. Statistics are generally used to estimate the value of an unknown population parameter.

It is usually possible to draw or select many different samples from any given population. If a particular statistic were computed from several different samples of a given size drawn from the same population, the value of the statistic would vary from sample to sample. If we constructed a frequency table of the values assumed by the statistic and its frequency of occurrence, we would then have a distribution of values or a *sampling distribution* of the statistic of interest. As mentioned previously, since the statistic is capable of assuming different values, it is a random variable in its own right and, as such, has its own distribution.

Suppose, for example, we computed the means, designated $\bar{x}$, of all possible samples of size n drawn from a population of size N. We would then have a sampling distribution of means. This sampling distribution would have a mean which would be the average value of all the sample $\bar{x}$'s and would be designated $\mu_{\bar{x}}$. It is interesting to note that in random sampling, the mean of the distribution of $\bar{x}$'s is the same as the population mean; that is, $\mu_{\bar{x}} = \mu$. The sampling distribution of the mean also has a variance designated $\sigma_{\bar{x}}{}^2$, and the square root of the variance of a sampling distribution is called the *standard error*, as distinguished from the standard deviation of a population.

The same procedure could be followed in computing the variance or any other statistic from all possible samples of a given size taken from some population, and we would then have a sampling distribution of the variance, etc., with its own mean, variance, and standard error. By examining the sampling distribution of a statistic, it is possible to make statements regarding the probability that the statistic of interest will take on some value within some given interval of values.

The distinction between the concept of a sampling distribution and the various probability distributions discussed previously should be emphasized at this point. Probability distributions such as the normal, the binomial, the gamma, etc., are essentially mathematical models which are used as convenient representations for various phenomena. As such they can be used as models for some theoretical or real population of values or as models of the distribution of statistics computed from some sampling process. When we say that some population has a normal distribution, we imply that the mathematical model $(1/\sigma\sqrt{2\pi}) \exp[-\frac{1}{2}(x - \mu/\sigma)^2]$ provides a useful approximate description of the manner in which the population values are distributed. When we say that the means of samples of a given size taken from an unknown population are distributed normally, we are implying that this same model is also useful for describing this sampling distribution of means.

Some probability distributions, such as the normal, are useful as models both for population distributions and for sampling distributions. Others, such as Student's t, are primarily used as models for the sampling distribution of some statistic. This is not to say that one of the many probability distributions discussed here might not be a suitable model for some unknown population which may be encountered in practice. How well any given model fits some particular problem situation can frequently be determined by statistical techniques which will not be discussed at this time. In certain circumstances, the selection of an appropriate model can be a function of the decision maker's judgment.

Some special sampling distributions will be considered subsequently.

11.3 BIAS

We have previously disposed of the concept of bias with the remark that it is an undesirable characteristic of a sample and that it usually occurs when the sampling process is not random. Since the purpose of sampling is to allow inferences to be made about a population on the basis of observations on less than the total population, the concept of bias refers to the estimates derived from the sampling procedure as well as to the sampling procedure itself.

Bias in sampling can be described in the following way. Let us compare the process of parameter estimation to the act of shooting a gun at a target. If several shots are fired at the target, the accuracy of the gun, or the error in the volley, has two components; first, the dispersion of the bullets about their own center (or mean), and second, the relationship of the center of the volley to the bull's-eye of the target. If all the bullets hit the target grouped closely together in one small area, the gun is very *precise*. However, if the center of the volley is displaced from the center of the target, the gun has *bias*. On the other hand, if the center of the volley is in the target's bull's-eye, the gun is unbiased. However, the dispersion of the individual shots may be very great, showing that the gun lacks precision. In order for the gun to be accurate, it must be free of bias, that is, center on the bull's-eye, and it must also be precise, that is, place all shots close together.

In estimation, accuracy is sometimes measured by the *mean square error* (MSE) in the estimate. For a statistic r and a parameter ρ,

$$\text{MSE}(r) = E(r - \rho)^2 \tag{11.1}$$

The mean square error in an estimate has two components, the variance and the bias. This can be shown as follows:

$$\begin{aligned}\text{MSE}(r) &= E(r - \rho)^2 \\ &= E[r - E(r) + E(r) - \rho]^2 \\ &= E[r - E(r)]^2 + E(r - \rho)^2 \\ &= \text{var}\,(r) + (\text{bias})^2\end{aligned}$$

For an estimator such as r, if the mean of the sampling distribution of r is equal to the parameter which r is to estimate, then the statistic r is an *unbiased* estimator of the parameter ρ and the mean square error is simply the variance of r.

The mere fact that a statistic is biased does not mean that it is useless as an estimator. If the bias in the estimator is known, it can be corrected.

Frequently an estimator with a known bias and high precision (that is, small variance) is preferable to an unbiased estimator with a large variance.

As we shall see in the next section, a sample variance S^2 derived from random, nonreplacement sampling from a finite population is a biased estimator of the population variance σ^2. However, the amount of bias in the estimate is known to be $n/(n-1)$ and, therefore, by applying a correction factor to S^2, we can estimate σ^2. That is, $[n/(n-1)]S^2 = \sigma^2$.

11.4 SAMPLING FROM A FINITE POPULATION

There are two basically different methods of sampling from a finite population. The first method we shall call *replacement* sampling. This means that each element selected from the population is returned to the population before the next element is selected. Consequently, it is possible that a single element will appear more than once in any given sample.

The second basic type of sampling procedure is called *nonreplacement* sampling. This means that the individual elements are *not* returned to the population after having been selected as part of the sample. In nonreplacement sampling, it is impossible for the same element to appear more than one time in any sample.

For both replacement and nonreplacement sampling, it is of interest to know how many possible samples can be drawn from a finite population of a given size. This raises the problem of whether we shall count each permutation of elements as a different sample or whether the same elements constitute only a single sample regardless of the order in which they are drawn. Rather than propose an answer to this problem, we shall treat all cases and show that this question is really immaterial.

Let us take a population of only three elements, a, b, and c, and select samples of size 2. We shall specify four different cases as follows:

Case 1: Random replacement sampling in which each permutation is counted as a different sample. The number of possible samples of this type is

$R_R = N^n$

Case 2: Random nonreplacement sampling in which the selected elements constitute a single sample regardless of the order in which they are selected. The number of possible samples of this type is

$$R_{NR} = \frac{N!}{n!(N-n)!}$$

which should be recognized as being the combinatorial formula.

Case 3: Random nonreplacement sampling in which each permutation is counted as a different sample. The number of possible samples of this type is

$$R_{NRX} = \frac{N!}{(N-n)!}$$

which is simply the formula for permutations.

Case 4: Random replacement sampling in which ordering is not considered. The number of possible samples of this type is given by

$$R_{RX} = \frac{(N+n-1)!}{n!(N-1)!}$$

For the population of $N = 3$ and $n = 2$, the number and listing of possible samples for each case specified are as follows:

Case 1: $R_R = 3^2 = 9$, and the possible samples are

Sample 1 a, b
Sample 2 a, c
Sample 3 b, c
Sample 4 b, a
Sample 5 c, a
Sample 6 c, b
Sample 7 a, a
Sample 8 b, b
Sample 9 c, c

Case 2: $R_{NR} = 3!/2!1! = 3$, and the possible samples are

Sample 1 a, b
Sample 2 a, c
Sample 3 b, c

Case 3: $R_{NRX} = 3!/1! = 6$, and the possible samples are

Sample 1 a, b
Sample 2 a, c
Sample 3 b, c
Sample 4 b, a
Sample 5 c, a
Sample 6 c, b

Case 4: $R_{RX} = 4!/2!2! = 6$, and the possible samples are

Sample 1 a, b
Sample 2 a, c
Sample 3 b, c
Sample 7 a, a
Sample 8 b, b
Sample 9 c, c

Regardless of which one of these sampling methods is selected, it should be apparent that every element of the population has an equal chance of being included in a sample. Suppose that observations or measurements on the population elements produce these results:

$$a = 1 \qquad b = 2 \qquad c = 3$$

The mean of the population is then

$$\mu = \frac{1 + 2 + 3}{3} = 2$$

and the population variance is

$$\sigma^2 = \frac{(1 - 2)^2 + (2 - 2)^2 + (3 - 2)^2}{3} = \tfrac{2}{3}$$

For each method of sampling let us compute the mean and variance for every sample and then find the mean or average value of the sample means and variances. Recall that in computing a sample variance, the divisor is $n - 1$, in order to make it an unbiased estimate of the population variance.

Case 1: Nine samples

Sample no.	*Elements*	*Values*	*Sample mean,* $\bar{x}$	*Sample variance,* s^2
1	*a, b*	1, 2	1.5	0.5
2	*a, c*	1, 3	2.0	2.0
3	*b, c*	2, 3	2.5	0.5
4	*b, a*	2, 1	1.5	0.5
5	*c, a*	3, 1	2.0	2.0
6	*c, b*	3, 2	2.5	0.5
7	*a, a*	1, 1	1.0	0
8	*b, b*	2, 2	2.0	0
9	*c, c*	3, 3	3.0	0
			18.0	6.0

$\sum \bar{x} = 18$, $\sum s^2 = 6.0$, $\sum \bar{x}/n = \mu_{\bar{x}} = 2$, $\sum s^2/n = 2/3$

Note that we designate the average of the means of all the samples as $\mu_{\bar{x}}$. Note also that $\mu_{\bar{x}} = \mu$; that is, the mean of the $\bar{x}$'s from all the samples is exactly equal to the population mean, and the average of the sample variances from all the samples under this type of random replacement sampling is exactly equal to the population variance.

Having computed the mean or $\bar{x}$ from all possible samples, we now have a population of $\bar{x}$ where mean $\mu_{\bar{x}} = \mu$. Let us now compute the variance of the $\bar{x}$'s, that is, $\sum (\bar{x}_i - \mu)^2/N$, where N represents the population of $\bar{x}$'s. The variance of $\bar{x}$, $\sigma_{\bar{x}}^2 = 1/3$. The ratio $\sigma^2/\sigma_{\bar{x}}^2 = (2/3)/(1/3) = 2$, which is the sample size. Therefore, $\sigma_{\bar{x}}^2 = \sigma^2/2$ or, in general,

$$\sigma_{\bar{x}}^2 = \sigma^2/n \tag{11.2}$$

We can conclude from this that the variance of the distribution of sample means from a given population is smaller than the variance of the population and, in fact, is smaller by the factor $1/n$, where n is the size of the sample from which the means were computed.

Since the average $\bar{x}$ and the average s^2 for this type of random replacement sampling are exactly equal to the population mean and variance, we can say that this type of sampling provides *unbiased* estimates of the population mean and variance.

Case 2: Three samples

Sample no.	*Elements*	*Values*	*Sample mean,* $\bar{x}$	*Sample variance,* s^2
1	*a, b*	1, 2	1.5	0.5
2	*a, c*	1, 3	2.0	2.0
3	*b, c*	2, 3	2.5	0.5
			6.0	3.0

$\sum \bar{x} = 6.0$, $\sum s^2 = 3.0$, $\sum \bar{x}/n = \mu_{\bar{x}} = 2$, $\sum s^2/n = 1$

Again $\mu_{\bar{x}} = \mu$, and random nonreplacement sampling also provides an *unbiased* estimate of the population mean. However, the average of the sample variances, denoted by s^2, is *not* equal to the population variance and is, in fact, too large. That is, it is biased by a factor $N/(N-1)$. In order to remove this bias, we can multiply the mean s^2 by $(N-1)/N$. Thus

$$\frac{N-1}{N}\bar{s}^2 = \left(\frac{2}{3}\right)(1) = \frac{2}{3} = \sigma^2$$

We can then state that when sampling without replacement from a small finite population, an unbiased estimate of σ^2 is given by $\hat{\sigma}^2 = [(N-1)/(N)]s^2$. This correction factor is seldom used, and obviously, when N is large, the ratio of $N:N-1$ is so close to 1 that it can be ignored.

The variance of the sample means can also be computed from the data above from the formula

$$\sigma_{\bar{x}}^2 = \frac{\sum (\bar{x} - \mu_x)^2}{N}$$

and is equal to $\frac{1}{6}$. However, we are used to thinking of $\sigma_{\bar{x}}^2 = \sigma^2/n$, and obviously for $\sigma^2 = \frac{2}{3}$ as previously given, $\sigma^2/n = \frac{2}{3} \div 2 = \frac{1}{3} \neq \frac{1}{6}$. The fact that σ^2/n does not equal $\sigma_{\bar{x}}^2$ is due to the fact that in this case we are sampling without replacement from a small finite population. If we were to multiply σ^2/n by the factor $(N - n)/(N - 1)$, we would get

$$\left(\frac{3-2}{3-1}\right)\left(\frac{1}{3}\right) = \left(\frac{1}{2}\right)\left(\frac{1}{3}\right) = \frac{1}{6} = \sigma_{\bar{x}}^2$$

This factor $(N - n)/(N - 1)$ is called the *finite population correction* or the FPC, and for random nonreplacement sampling the variance of the sample mean is equal to the population variance divided by n and multiplied by the FPC, that is,

$$\sigma_{\bar{x}}^2 = \left(\frac{N-n}{N-1}\right)\frac{\sigma^2}{n} \tag{11.3}$$

When the population is large with respect to the sample, as a rule of thumb when $n/N < 0.05$, the FPC is very close to 1 and, in most practical instances, can be ignored. However, when $n/N \geq 0.05$, the finite population correction should be used.

Case 3: Six samples

Sample no.	*Elements*	*Values*	*Sample mean,* $\bar{x}$	*Sample variance,* s^2
1	*a, b*	1, 2	1.5	0.5
2	*a, c*	1, 3	2.0	2.0
3	*b, c*	2, 3	2.5	0.5
4	*b, a*	2, 1	1.5	0.5
5	*c, a*	3, 1	2.0	2.0
6	*c, b*	3, 2	2.5	0.5
			12.0	6.0

$\sum \bar{x} = 12$, $\sum s^2 = 6.0$, $\sum \bar{x}/n = \mu_x = 2$, $\sum s^2/n = 1$

It is apparent that the results here are identical with the results of case 2. Both are nonreplacement sampling methods, but here we have essentially counted each sample from the previous method twice. This has no effect on the mean of the $\bar{x}$'s or the mean of the sample variances.

Case 4: Six samples

Sample no.	*Elements*	*Values*	*Sample mean,* $\bar{x}$	*Sample variance,* s^2
1	a, b	1, 2	1.5	0.5
2	a, c	1, 3	2.0	2.0
3	b, c	2, 3	2.5	0.5
7	a, a	1, 1	1.0	0
8	b, b	2, 2	2.0	0
9	c, c	3, 3	3.0	0
			12.0	3.0

$\sum \bar{x} = 12.0, \sum s^2 = 3.0, \sum \bar{x}/n = \mu_{\bar{x}} = 2, \sum s^2/n = \frac{1}{2}$

Again, $\mu_{\bar{x}} = \mu$. The variance of the mean is $\frac{5}{12}$, which is not equal to $\sigma^2/n = \frac{2}{3} \times \frac{1}{2} = \frac{1}{3}$. The variance of the mean from these samples is too large by a factor of $(N + n)/(N + 1)$. If we multiply $\frac{5}{12}$ by $(N + n)/(N + 1)$, we get the following result: $\frac{5}{12} \times \frac{4}{5} = \frac{1}{3} = \sigma^2/n$. Consequently,

$$\sigma_{\bar{x}}^2 = \left(\frac{N + n}{N + 1}\right) \frac{\sigma^2}{n} = \left(\frac{5}{4}\right)\left(\frac{1}{3}\right) = \frac{5}{12}$$

Also, the mean of the sample variances is $\frac{1}{2} \neq \frac{2}{3} = \sigma^2$. The mean s^2 is too small by a factor of $N/(N + 1)$; therefore,

$$\frac{N + 1}{N} \frac{\sum s^2}{n} = \left(\frac{4}{3}\right)\left(\frac{1}{2}\right) = \frac{2}{3} = \sigma^2$$

and

$$\frac{N}{N + 1} \sigma^2 = \left(\frac{3}{4}\right)\left(\frac{2}{3}\right) = \frac{1}{2} = \frac{\sum s^2}{n}$$

This latter method of sampling provides an unbiased estimate of μ, as did the others, but provides biased estimates of σ^2 and $\sigma_{\bar{x}}^2$. However, since the bias is known, it can be corrected.

11.5 ANALYSIS OF THE SAMPLING METHODS

The sampling-with-replacement method described as case 1 essentially simulates an infinite population. It provides unbiased estimates of the population mean and variance, and also of the variance of the sample means. It is unusual and, in many cases, impossible to sample with replacement. One instance where replacement sampling is impossible is when the sampled items are subject to destructive testing. Consequently, the nonreplacement sampling procedure is much more common. Once again, estimates of the population variance and the variance of the sample means are biased. The extent of the bias being known, however, it can be corrected, and for non-replacement sampling

$$\sigma^2 = \frac{N-1}{N} s^2$$

and

$$\sigma_{\bar{x}}^2 = \frac{N-n}{N-1}\frac{\sigma^2}{n}$$

and it follows that

$$\sigma_{\bar{x}}^2 = \frac{N-n}{N-1}\frac{N-1}{N} s^2$$

where $(N - n)/(N - 1)$ is the finite population corrector.

The replacement sampling method discussed as case 4 is never encountered and was used simply as an added illustration to indicate how bias can be removed from an estimate.

11.6 THE USE OF SAMPLING DISTRIBUTIONS IN PARAMETER ESTIMATION

An unbiased statistic (or estimator) has the property that its expected value, which is the mean of its sampling distribution, is equal to the parameter which it estimates. If r is the statistic and ρ the parameter, then $E(r) = \rho$ if r is an unbiased estimator of ρ.

If we have a value of r computed from a sample, and if we know the characteristics of the sampling distribution of r, we are then able to make probability statements about the closeness of r to the parameter ρ. For this reason, it becomes necessary to study the characteristics of the sampling distributions of some of the commonly used estimators. Before considering specific sampling distributions, we shall consider two very important statistical laws relating to this problem.

11.7 THE LAW OF LARGE NUMBERS

We have previously discussed Chebyshev's inequality, which states that

$$P(|x - \mu| > k\sigma) < \frac{1}{k^2} \tag{11.4}$$

that is, the probability that any element of a distribution lies further from its mean than k standard deviations is less than $1/k^2$. Since this applies to any distribution, it also applies to the distribution of $\bar{x}$'s. Therefore,

Chebyshev's inequality, as it applies to the distribution of sample means, can be written

$$P(|\bar{x} - \mu| > k\sigma_{\bar{x}}) < \frac{1}{k^2} \tag{11.5}$$

or

$$P\left(|\bar{x} - \mu| > \frac{k\sigma}{\sqrt{n}}\right) < \frac{1}{k^2} \tag{11.6}$$

If we let $e = k\sigma/\sqrt{n}$, then

$$k = \frac{e\sqrt{n}}{\sigma}$$

and

$$\frac{1}{k^2} = \frac{\sigma^2}{ne^2}$$

and (11.6) can be written

$$P(|\bar{x} - \mu| > e) < \frac{\sigma^2}{ne^2} \tag{11.7}$$

Now it should be apparent that as n gets larger, the right side of the inequality (11.7) approaches zero. Therefore (11.7) tells us that the probability that a sample mean will fall further away from the population mean than some arbitrarily small number e as it approaches zero as the sample size is increased. We can infer from this fact that in estimating a population mean from a sample mean, we can make the error in the estimate arbitrarily small by making the sample large enough. This result is called the *law of large numbers.*

It is possible to use this result to determine the sample size necessary to ensure that the error in the estimate of the mean will not exceed some given amount e with a probability α.

For example, suppose we wish to be sure that the error in our estimate will not exceed $\sigma/10$ with a probability of 95 percent. That is,

$$P\left(|\bar{x} - \mu| > \frac{\sigma}{10}\right) < 0.05$$

Then setting 0.05 equal to σ^2/ne^2, we would get

$$0.05 = \frac{\sigma^2}{n(\sigma/10)^2}$$

since e is equal to $\sigma/10$. Solving for n produces

$$0.05n = \frac{\sigma^2}{\sigma^2/100} = 100$$

$$n = 2{,}000$$

If the problem was stated that the population variance $\sigma^2 = 1$, and the maximum allowable error in the estimate was 0.1 with probability 95 percent, then the solution would be

$$0.05 = \frac{1}{n(0.1)^2}$$

$$0.05n = \frac{1}{0.01} = 100$$

$$n = 2{,}000$$

11.8 THE CENTRAL-LIMIT THEOREM

One of the most important theorems in statistics is the *central-limit theorem.* It can be stated as follows:

Theorem 11.1 *For any population whatsoever having a mean μ and a variance σ^2, the distribution of the sample mean approaches a normal distribution with mean μ and variance σ^2/n as n, the sample size, approaches infinity.*

In actual practice, the distribution of $\bar{x}$ approaches a normal distribution very rapidly so that for a sample size as small as 30, the approximation is very good and for $n > 50$ the form of the parent population has little effect on the distribution of $\bar{x}$.

For large samples, size 30 or greater, then, the central-limit theorem allows us to estimate the error in an estimate of the population mean simply by referring to tables of the normal distribution. Suppose we plan to take a sample of size $n = 81$ from an infinite or very large population, with a known variance of $\sigma^2 = 9$. We know from the central-limit theorem that $\bar{x}$ is approximately normally distributed and that $\sigma_{\bar{x}}{}^2 = \sigma^2/n$ and $\sigma_{\bar{x}} = \sigma/\sqrt{n} = \frac{1}{3}$. We are then able to make the following probability statements by referring to tables of the normal distribution. The probability that the sample mean differs from the population mean by less than one standard error, that is, by *less than* $\frac{1}{3}$, is equal to 0.682. The probability that the sample mean differs from the population mean by *more than* two standard errors, that is, by more than $\frac{2}{3}$, is equal to 0.046. The probability that the population mean is included in the interval defined by $\bar{x} \pm 1$ is equal to 0.998.

11.9 SAMPLING DISTRIBUTION OF THE MEAN

The sampling distribution of the mean for large samples from an infinite population is normal with $\mu_{\bar{x}} = \mu$ and $\sigma_{\bar{x}}{}^2 = \sigma^2/n$. If the population from which the sample is taken is known to be normal, then the above holds true regardless of the size of the sample. Furthermore, the statistic

$$z = \frac{(\bar{x} - \mu)}{\sigma/\sqrt{n}} = \frac{(\bar{x} - \mu)\sqrt{n}}{\sigma} \tag{11.8}$$

is distributed according to the standard normal distribution with $\mu_z = 0$ and $\sigma_z = 1$. For finite populations, when the ratio $n/N \geq 5$ percent, a finite population correction must be applied to the variance of the sample means so that

$$\sigma_{\bar{x}}{}^2 = \frac{N - n}{N - 1}\frac{\sigma^2}{n} \tag{11.9}$$

11.10 DISTRIBUTION OF THE DIFFERENCE BETWEEN SAMPLE MEANS

Occasions frequently arise in statistical investigations when the difference between two sample means is the statistic of interest rather than the individual means by themselves. Suppose a random sample of size n_1 has been taken from a population having a mean μ_1 and a variance $\sigma_1{}^2$, while another random sample of size n_2 was taken from a population with mean μ_2 and variance $\sigma_2{}^2$. We can consider a statistic

$$\Delta\bar{x} = \bar{x}_1 - \bar{x}_2$$

and its distribution where $\bar{x}_1$ is the mean of the first sample and $\bar{x}_2$ is the mean of the second.

The mean of the difference between the sample means is given by

$$\mu_{\bar{x}_1 - \bar{x}_2} = \mu_{\bar{x}_1} - \mu_{\bar{x}_2} = \mu_1 - \mu_2 \tag{11.10}$$

and the variance of the difference between the sample means is given by

$$\sigma^2_{\bar{x}_1 - \bar{x}_2} = \sigma_{\bar{x}_1}{}^2 + \sigma_{\bar{x}_2}{}^2 = \frac{\sigma_1{}^2}{n_1} + \frac{\sigma_2{}^2}{n_2} \tag{11.11}$$

Furthermore, the statistic

$$z = \frac{(\bar{x}_1 - \bar{x}_2) - (\mu_1 - \mu_2)}{\sqrt{(\sigma_1{}^2/n_1) + (\sigma_2{}^2/n_2)}} \tag{11.12}$$

is a normally distributed variate with a mean of zero and a standard deviation equal to 1.

11.11 CHI-SQUARE DISTRIBUTION

There is a distribution which appears frequently in statistical work called the chi-square distribution and represented by the Greek letter χ^2. The derivation of this distribution will not be presented here, but its density function is given by

$$f(x) = \frac{x^{(\nu/2)-1}e^{-x^2/2}}{2^{(\nu/2)}\Gamma(\nu/2)} \tag{11.13}$$

This is a continuous distribution with a single parameter ν (the Greek letter nu), which is called the *degrees of freedom*. Tables of the cumulative χ^2 distribution can be found in most standard statistical texts.

If α is the probability that x in Eq. (11.13) exceeds some particular value, say $\chi_{\nu,\alpha}$, the tables of chi-square provide values of the integral

$$\int_{\chi^2_{\nu,\alpha}}^{\infty} f(x)\,dx = \alpha$$

The curve of a chi-square distribution appears as shown in Fig. 11.1. There is, of course, a different χ^2 distribution for every value of the parameter ν.

The χ^2 distribution approaches a normal distribution with $\mu = \nu$ and $\sigma^2 = 2\nu$ as ν gets large. For $\chi^2 \geq 60$, the approximation is reasonable.

In our discussion of the normal distribution we noted that if x is a normally distributed random variable with mean μ and standard deviation σ, that is, x is $N(\mu,\sigma)$, then the variable $z = (x - \mu)\sigma$ is $N(0,1)$.

It is also true that the variable

$$z^2 = \frac{(x-\mu)^2}{\sigma^2} \tag{11.14}$$

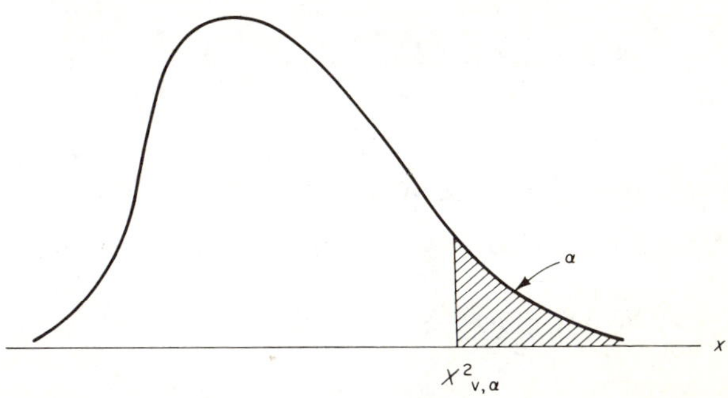

Fig. 11.1

has a chi-square distribution with 1 degree of freedom, and if a random sample of size n is taken from a normal population with mean μ and standard deviation σ, then

$$z^2 = \sum_{i=1}^{n} \frac{(x_i - \mu)^2}{\sigma^2} \tag{11.15}$$

has a chi-square distribution with n degrees of freedom. That is, $\nu = n$. Furthermore, since

$$z' = \frac{(\bar{x} - \mu)\sqrt{n}}{\sigma} \tag{11.16}$$

is also a normal variate with zero mean and unit variance, z'^2 has a chi-square distribution with 1 degree of freedom.

Another interesting property of chi-square variates is that if z_1^2, $z_2^2, \ldots, z_n^2$ are all independent random variables each having a chi-square distribution with $\nu_1, \nu_2, \ldots, \nu_n$ degrees of freedom, respectively, the new variable

$$w = \sum_{i=1}^{n} z_1^2$$

has a chi-square distribution with $\nu = \sum_{i=1}^{n} \nu_i$ degrees of freedom.

11.12 DISTRIBUTION OF THE SAMPLE VARIANCE FROM NORMAL POPULATIONS

If x is a normally distributed random variable, its variance is given by

$$\sigma^2 = \frac{\sum (x_i - \mu)^2}{N}$$

If a random sample of size n is taken from the population, the sample variance is given by

$$s^2 = \frac{\sum (x_i - \bar{x})^2}{n - 1}$$

and

$$(n - 1)s^2 = \sum (x_i - \bar{x})^2 \tag{11.17}$$

From what has been shown in the previous section.

$$\sum_{i=1}^{n} \frac{(x_i - \mu)^2}{\sigma^2}$$

has a chi-square distribution with n degrees of freedom.

From Eq. (11.17) we see that

$$(n-1)s^2 = \sum_{i=1}^{n} (x_i - \bar{x})^2$$

and therefore

$$\frac{(n-1)s^2}{\sigma^2} = \frac{1}{\sigma^2}\sum_{i=1}^{n} (x_i - \bar{x})^2$$

It can be shown from the above relationship that

$$\sum_{i=1}^{n} \frac{(x_i - \mu)^2}{\sigma^2} = \frac{(\bar{x} - \mu)\sqrt{n}}{\sigma} + \frac{(n-1)s^2}{\sigma^2} \tag{11.18}$$

Since the left-hand side of Eq. (11.18) is distributed as chi-square with n degrees of freedom, and from Eq. (11.16) we know that the first term on the right-hand side of Eq. (11.18) is distributed as chi-square with 1 degree of freedom, it follows that

$$\frac{(n-1)s^2}{\sigma^2}$$

is distributed as chi-square with $n - 1$ degrees of freedom.

11.13 STUDENT'S *t* DISTRIBUTION

We have seen that the sampling distribution of $(\bar{x} - \mu)\sqrt{n}/\sigma$ from normal population is normal with mean zero and standard deviation 1. A difficulty that arises in practical problems is that σ, the true population standard deviation, is generally unknown, and all that is available with which to estimate σ is s, the sample standard deviation. However, if we substitute s for σ, the statistic

$$t = \frac{(\bar{x} - \mu)\sqrt{n}}{s}$$

has a *t distribution* with $\nu = n - 1$ degrees of freedom. The t distribution is a symmetrical, unimodal distribution with a mean of zero, closely resembling the normal. Its density function is

$$f(t) = \frac{\Gamma[(\nu + 1)/2][1 + (t^2/\nu)]^{-(\nu+1)/2}}{\Gamma(\nu/2)} \tag{11.19}$$

The exact shape of the distribution is determined by its single parameter ν, the degrees of freedom which is always 1 less than the sample size.

As ν gets large, the t distribution gets closer and closer to the normal distribution until at $\nu > 30$, the normal provides a very good approximation. However, for small samples, $n \leq 30$, use of the normal distribution would give probabilities that are consistently too small.

Again, if α is the probability that a random variable t exceeds some specific value, say $t_{\nu,\alpha}$, the tables provide the value of the integral

$$\int_{t_{\nu,\alpha}}^{\infty} f(t)\, dt = \alpha$$

11.14 THE *F* DISTRIBUTION

The F distribution is a two-parameter distribution whose parameters are ν_1 and ν_2. The density function of F is quite complicated and will not be reproduced here. If samples of size n_1 and n_2 are taken from two normal populations with variances $\sigma_1{}^2$ and $\sigma_2{}^2$, and the sample variances $s_1{}^2$ and $s_2{}^2$ are computed, the variable $(s_1{}^2/\sigma_1{}^2)/(s_2{}^2/\sigma_2{}^2)$ has an F distribution with parameters $\nu_1 = n_1 - 1$ and $\nu_2 = n_2 - 1$. Under the assumption that $\sigma_1{}^2 = \sigma_2{}^2$, the variable $s_1{}^2/s_2{}^2$ is distributed as F with $\nu_1 = n_1 - 1$ and $\nu_2 = n_2 - 1$.

One of the major applications of the F distribution is in determining whether the variances of two normal populations are equal.

Tables of F generally provide values of the integral

$$\int_{F_{\nu_1,\nu_2,\alpha}}^{\infty} f(F)\, dF = \alpha$$

11.15 SUMMARY

In most practical situations, data utilized in decision problems will consist of samples taken from populations which are too large to be observed in their entirety. In these situations, sample data must be used to estimate or test hypotheses about the parameters of the population from which the samples are taken.

In order for estimates, derived from sample data, to be useful, the samples must truly represent the population from which they are taken. In order to ensure this, the sampling procedure must be *random*; that is, all population elements must have an equal probability of being included in the sample. When a sample is not truly representative of the population from which it is taken, the sample is considered to be *biased*.

A *statistic* is a value computed from a sample generally for the purpose of estimating some population parameter. A statistic may also be biased. However, if the bias in the statistic is known and can be corrected, the statistic may still be a useful estimator. A statistic is *biased* if its expected value does *not* equal the parameter which it will be used to estimate.

Since the same statistics computed from different samples taken from a population can take on different values, the statistic is itself a random variable and, as such, has a distribution. The distribution of a statistic is called a sampling distribution. Various sampling distributions have been considered here; however, a discussion of their application has been deferred to later chapters.

PROBLEMS

11.1. Given a population consisting of eight elements,

(*a*) How many different random replacement samples of size 3 can be obtained?

(*b*) How many different random nonreplacement samples can be obtained?

11.2. From a population of 10 elements a random nonreplacement sample of size 4 is drawn. The sample standard deviation was computed to have a value of 6.5.

(*a*) Compute an unbiased estimate of σ.

(*b*) Compute an unbiased estimate of $\sigma_{\bar{x}}$.

11.3. How large a sample must be taken in order to estimate a population mean such that there is a probability of at least 0.95 that the error in the estimate will *not* exceed two units? Assume $\sigma = 4$.

11.4. How large a sample must be taken in order to estimate a population mean such that there is a probability of at least 0.95 that the error in the estimate will *not* exceed 5 percent of the population σ?

11.5. If X is normally distributed with $\mu = 27$ and $\sigma = 8$, what is the probability that the statistic $\bar{x}$ computed from a sample of size 36 taken from X will have a value:

(*a*) Greater than 29?

(*b*) Between 29 and 30?

(*c*) Between 25 and 26.5?

11.6. If X_1 is normally distributed with $\mu_1 = 115$ and $\sigma_1 = 20$, and X_2 is normally distributed with $\mu_2 = 150$ and $\sigma_2 = 15$, find the probability that the statistic $\Delta\bar{x} = \bar{x}_2 - \bar{x}_1$ computed from samples of $n_1 = 100$ and $n_2 = 50$, respectively, will have a value:

(*a*) Between 34 and 36?

(*b*) Greater than 33?

(*c*) Between 37 and 40?

11.7. Assume that the statistic u has a χ^2 distribution with 20 degrees of freedom. Find a value of u, call it u_0, such that the following probability statements are true:

(*a*) $P(u > u_0) = 0.100$

(*b*) $P(u > u_0) = 0.950$

(*c*) $P(u < u_0) = 0.025$

11.8. If u has a χ^2 distribution with 30 degrees of freedom, what are the probabilities corresponding to the following statements?

(*a*) $P(u > 20.6)$

(*b*) $P(u < 14.95)$

(*c*) $P(u < 43.77)$

(*d*) $P(u > 53.67)$

11.9. If a statistic t has a Student's t distribution with 15 degrees of freedom, what are the probabilities corresponding to the following statements?

(*a*) $P(-1.753 < t < +1.753)$
(*b*) $P(-0.866 < t < +0.866)$
(*c*) $P(t < +2.947)$
(*d*) $P(t < -1.074)$
(*e*) $P(t > +0.691)$

11.10. If a statistic t has a Student's t distribution with 5 degrees of freedom, find a value of t, call it t_0, such that the following probability statements are true:

(*a*) $P(-t_0 < t < +t_0) = 0.60$
(*b*) $P(-t_0 < t) = 0.70$
(*c*) $P(t_0 < t) = 0.025$
(*d*) $P(t < -t_0) = 0.025$

11.11. If a statistic v has an F distribution with $\nu_1 = 10$ and $\nu_2 = 9$, find a value of the statistic, call it v_0, such that the following probability statements are true:

(*a*) $P(v > v_0) = 0.05$
(*b*) $P(v < v_0) = 0.99$

12
Statistical Estimation

The state of a decision system is a function of the states of its individual components. After constructing the system model, a decision maker is faced with the problem of evaluating the state, good or bad, of each system component. It is generally assumed that the evaluation of the state of each component is based on some process of observation or on the analysis of data resulting from a process of observation, although it is quite conceivable that the evaluation of any given component state could be based solely on the judgment of the decision maker.

Since the evaluation of a logical model provides the decision maker with no information as to the probability that a decision based on the evaluation of that model will be good or bad, the assignment of probability values to the component states is the next step in the decision process. Again it is conceivable that the decision maker might assign probabilities to the component states purely on the basis of his personal, subjective feelings. It is more likely, however, that some empirical data will be utilized in the evaluation of the state probabilities either by themselves or in conjunction with the decision maker's subjective judgments.

We might think of the state or condition of any decision component as being some function of an unknown parameter of a population which this particular component represents. For example, a decision to develop and market a new type of transmitter might partially depend upon the expected lifetime of a particular kind of traveling wave tube. If the average or mean-time-to-failure of this tube is 5,000 hr or greater, then the state of this decision component is good. If, however, the mean-time-to-failure of this tube is less than 5,000 hr, the component state is bad. For this decision component, a good or bad state depends upon an unknown parameter, mean-time-to-failure, which must be estimated.

A decision to open a department store in a planned shopping center might partially depend upon the income level of the residents of that particular trading area. This might involve an estimate of the average income of the population, in which case a good state might coincide with the average income equal to or greater than $8,000 per year and the bad state equivalent to an average income less than $8,000 per year.

Instead of estimating average income, this same component might be evaluated by estimating the proportion of people with incomes greater than or equal to $8,000 per year. System state might be considered good if that proportion is greater than 45 percent and bad if that proportion is less than or equal to 45 percent.

In the first case above, the population which the decision component represents is a population of tube lifetimes. In the second case, the population is that of incomes. In either case, the component is in a good state if the parameter exceeds some critical value and in a bad state if it fails to exceed that value. The probability, then, of a component being in either state depends upon an estimate of the unknown parameter, and the estimate must be such that probabilities can be assigned to each state. This leads the discussion into the area of statistical estimation. The problem of estimation then is this: Provide an estimate of the parameter that determines whether the state of a decision component is good or bad and specify a confidence value or probability that the critical parameter is within the estimation interval.

12.1 THE ESTIMATION PROBLEM

Statistical estimation involves an inference about some characteristic or parameter of an unknown population. The key word in the previous sentence is the word "unknown." If the population of interest were completely known, it would be unnecessary to infer or to estimate. For completely known populations, parameter determination is simply a process of observation or measurement.

For large, finite populations, it might be theoretically possible to observe or measure all the population members. However, the cost in time or money involved in such a procedure could be, and generally is, prohibitive. For infinite populations, such a procedure is obviously impossible.

Even for small, finite populations, it is frequently impractical to attempt to observe or measure every element. For example, suppose an estimate is needed of the mean burst pressure of a particular type of vessel or tank. The population of interest is the population of burst pressures of a small lot of similar vessels. However, the only way to measure burst pressure is to apply increasing pressure until the vessel breaks. This procedure obviously results in the destruction of the vessel. It would be impossible to measure the entire population of burst pressures since to do so would result in the total destruction of the physical population from which the measurements were derived.

For these and similar reasons, it is seldom possible to observe an entire population and determine the value of the parameter of interest. Consequently, sampling techniques are utilized in order to draw inferences about the population on the basis of some segment or subset of the population called a *sample*.

There are several steps to any process of estimation. These steps are as follows:

Step 1: Select a statistic which will be used to estimate the parameter of interest. This statistic will be called an *estimator*.
Step 2: Draw a sample from the population.
Step 3: Compute the value of the estimator from the sample.
Step 4: Use the computed value of the estimator to make an inference about the value of the population parameter.

12.2 ESTIMATORS AND THEIR PROPERTIES

We can define an estimator as follows:

Estimator: Some function of a sample which is used to provide an estimate of an unknown population parameter.

An estimator, then, is simply a statistic. However, for any specific problem of parameter estimation, there are frequently several statistics that *might* be used as estimators for a given parameter.

For example, in estimating the mean of a population, we might choose between three different statistics which could be derived from the same sample, the arithmetic mean, the median, and the mode. In estimating the variability of the same population, we might want to consider either the sample range or the sample standard deviation. Because we are generally faced with several alternative estimators in any given situation, there should be some criteria which would enable us to select the best estimator from those available. The principle criteria for selecting what might be called a good estimator are as follows:

1. Consistency
2. Unbiasedness
3. Efficiency or relative efficiency
4. Sufficiency

CONSISTENCY

If a statistic is used as an estimator of some population parameter which we shall designate θ, it should be apparent that the value of the statistic will not always be exactly equal to θ, and most likely will differ from θ by some amount. The difference between the value of the estimator and the parameter which it is supposed to estimate is called the *sampling error* and is given by $|\hat{\theta} - \theta|$.

One desirable characteristic of an estimator $\hat{\theta}$ is that the sampling error resulting from the use of $\hat{\theta}$ as an estimate of θ should decrease as the sample size gets larger. If, for example, we were attempting to estimate the parameter θ of a finite population, it should be apparent that as the sample size n approaches the size of the population N, the estimate $\hat{\theta}$ should also approach the parameter θ. When $n = N$, that is, when the sample consists of the entire population, there should be no sampling error in the estimate at all.

In mathematical terms, we would describe the property as follows:

$$|\hat{\theta} - \theta| \to 0 \qquad \text{as } n \to \infty$$

or

$$\hat{\theta} \to \theta \qquad \text{as } n \to \infty$$

This property is called *consistency*, and an estimator which has this property is called a *consistent estimator.*

UNBIASEDNESS

Because of the variability of the sampling distribution of any statistic, the concept of sampling error is inherent in any process of statistical estimation. However, in determining whether or not a given statistic is a "good" estimator of the unknown population parameter, we would like to feel that in the long run, that is, in repeated samples from the population, the estimator will tend to be equal to the parameter. To be more precise, if we took all the possible samples of a given size from the population and computed the value of the estimator for each sample, the mean or average value of the estimator should equal the population parameter.

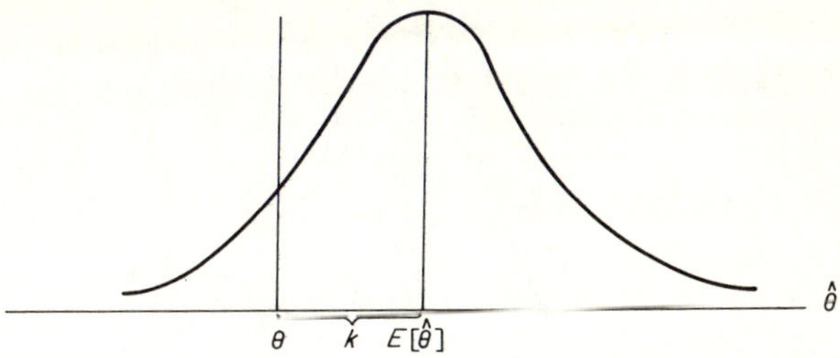

Fig. 12.1

In the chapter on sampling and sampling distributions, we found that the mean of the sampling distribution of $\bar{X}$ was equal to μ and concluded that $\bar{X}$ was therefore an unbiased estimator of the population mean.

Since the mean of the distribution of any variable is its *expected value*, we can state that an estimator is unbiased if its expected value is equal to the parameter which it is intended to estimate. Mathematically we can state that $\hat{\theta}$ is an unbiased estimator of θ if

$$E(\hat{\theta}) = \theta$$

Conversely, $\hat{\theta}$ is a biased estimator of θ if

$$E(\hat{\theta}) \neq \theta$$

Suppose, as in Fig. 12.1, that the mean of the sampling distribution of $\hat{\theta}$ is at some value of $\theta + k$. Then we can see that on the average, $\hat{\theta}$ will give an estimate of θ that is too large by the factor k. That is, on the average, $\hat{\theta}$ will estimate θ as $\theta + k$ since $\hat{\theta}$ is biased by the amount k.

If we know the bias in an estimator $\hat{\theta}$, it is possible to correct for it. For example, if $\hat{\theta}$ has other desirable properties as an estimator, we might still use it to estimate θ and correct for the bias. In that case we would estimate θ by $\hat{\theta} - k$.

However, a desirable property of a good estimator is that it be unbiased.

EFFICIENCY, RELATIVE EFFICIENCY, AND PRECISION

In choosing between two different estimators of the parameter θ, let us say $\hat{\theta}_1$ and $\hat{\theta}_2$, both of which are equally desirable in terms of other criteria of goodness, we would prefer to use that estimator having a sampling distribution which was most concentrated about the unknown population parameter. Consider the sampling distribution of $\hat{\theta}_1$ and $\hat{\theta}_2$ in Fig. 12.2. The means of both sampling distributions are at θ, the population parameter, indicating that both estimators are unbiased. However, $\hat{\theta}_1$ has a sampling distribution

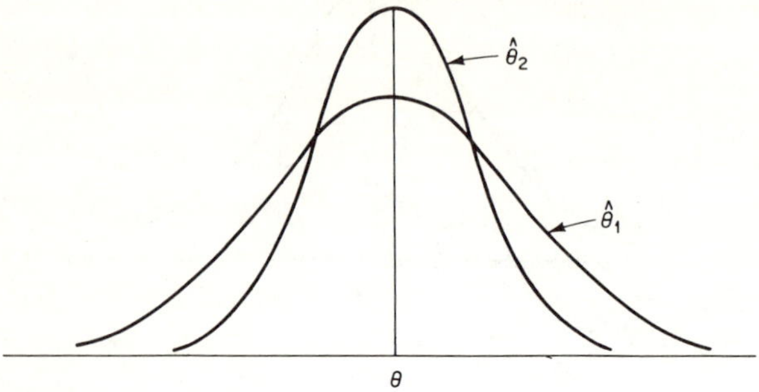

Fig. 12.2

which is much more widely spread out about its mean than is $\hat{\theta}_2$. This would indicate that values of $\hat{\theta}_1$ are more likely to deviate from θ than are values of $\hat{\theta}_2$. The spread or variability of a distribution is measured by its variance. In Fig. 12.2, the variance of $\hat{\theta}_2$ is smaller than that of $\hat{\theta}_1$, and therefore $\hat{\theta}_2$ is considered to be relatively more *efficient* as an estimator of θ than is $\hat{\theta}_1$.

In comparing estimators, then, $\hat{\theta}_2$ is said to be relatively more efficient than $\hat{\theta}_1$ if var $(\hat{\theta}_2)$ is less than var $(\hat{\theta}_1)$. Since the more efficient estimator has the smaller variance, it would seem desirable to define a measure for which the better estimator has a greater value. Such a measure is called *precision* and is defined as the reciprocal of the variance. That is, the precision of $\hat{\theta}_2$ is given by

$$P(\hat{\theta}_2) = \frac{1}{\text{var}\,(\hat{\theta}_2)}$$

and

$$P(\hat{\theta}_1) = \frac{1}{\text{var}\,(\hat{\theta}_1)}$$

Then the relative precision of $\hat{\theta}_2$ with respect to $\hat{\theta}_1$ is given by the ratio

$$\frac{P(\hat{\theta}_2)}{P(\hat{\theta}_1)} = \frac{\text{var}\,(\hat{\theta}_1)}{\text{var}\,(\hat{\theta}_2)}$$

which can also be called the *relative efficiency*.

An estimator having the greatest precision or, what is the same thing, the smallest variance, is called the *minimum variance estimator* and is sometimes referred to as the *best estimator*.

SUFFICIENCY

A fourth property of a good estimator is that it be a *sufficient* estimator. A sufficient estimator is one that utilizes all the information contained in a sample relevant to the estimation of the parameter. In simple terms, $\hat{\theta}$ is a sufficient estimator of θ if $\hat{\theta} = f(x_i)$, and given the value of $\hat{\theta}$, then the individual x_i's can contribute no additional information about the parameter θ.

MEAN SQUARE ERROR

The *accuracy* of an estimator is sometimes measured by the mean square error which is defined as

$$\text{MSE}(\hat{\theta}) = E(\hat{\theta} - \theta)^2$$

that is, the expected value of the square of the total error in the estimate of θ resulting from the use of $\hat{\theta}$ as the estimator. The mean square error consists of two error components, one of which is the variability of the sampling distribution of $\hat{\theta}$ and the second being the bias, if any, in $\hat{\theta}$ as an estimator of θ.

The variability of $\hat{\theta}$ is simply its variance which is given by

$$E[\hat{\theta} - E(\hat{\theta})]^2$$

The bias in $\hat{\theta}$ as an estimator of θ is simple $E(\hat{\theta}) - \theta$. Therefore

$$\begin{aligned}
\text{MSE}(\hat{\theta}) &= E(\hat{\theta} - \theta)^2 \\
&= E[\hat{\theta} - E(\hat{\theta}) + E(\hat{\theta}) - \theta]^2 \\
&= E\{[\hat{\theta} - E(\hat{\theta})] + [E(\hat{\theta}) - \theta]\}^2 \\
&= E\{[\hat{\theta} - E(\hat{\theta})]^2 + [E(\hat{\theta}) - \theta]^2 + 2[E(\hat{\theta}) - \theta][\hat{\theta} - E(\hat{\theta})]\} \\
&= E[\hat{\theta} - E(\hat{\theta})]^2 + [E(\hat{\theta}) - \theta]^2 + 2[E(\hat{\theta}) - \theta]E[\hat{\theta} - E(\hat{\theta})] \\
&= \text{var}(\hat{\theta}) + [\text{bias}(\hat{\theta})]^2
\end{aligned}$$

with the cross-product term equal to zero, since $E[\hat{\theta} - E(\hat{\theta})] = 0$.

Obviously, when $\hat{\theta}$ is an unbiased estimate of θ, bias $(\hat{\theta}) = 0$, and $\text{MSE}(\hat{\theta}) = \text{var}(\hat{\theta})$.

12.3 MAXIMUM LIKELIHOOD ESTIMATION

Although we have listed various desirable properties of good estimators, we have not so far indicated any procedure for obtaining estimators which have these properties. Several methods are available for obtaining "good" estimators. These are:

1. The method of moments
2. The method of least squares
3. The minimum chi-square method
4. The method of maximum likelihood

The method of maximum likelihood, attributed to R. A. Fisher, is a method which is frequently used and which generally yields estimators having the desirable properties discussed previously.

The method of maximum likelihood is based on the following reasoning. A sample is taken from an unknown population for the purpose of estimating a parameter of that population. If the sample is drawn properly, that is, if it is a random sample, it is more likely that the sample will resemble the population from which it was taken than that its characteristics will deviate markedly from those of the population. On the basis of the sample, therefore, select that population which has the greatest likelihood of having produced the given sample. Since the population is characterized by its parameter (or parameters), select the population parameter which characterizes the most likely population. Or, more to the point, select that function of the population random variable sampled which maximizes the likelihood of the occurrence of that sample.

Suppose $f(x,\theta)$ is the probability density function of the random variable X taken from a population with the unknown parameter θ. A random sample of size n is taken from the population resulting in n values of the random variable $x_1, x_2, \ldots, x_n$. The probability of each of the x_i's being selected in the sample is given by $f(x_i,\theta)$, and since in a random sample each observation is considered an independent event, the probability that the given set of x_i's was obtained in the specific order of their occurrence is given by

$$L(x_i,\theta) = f(x_1,\theta)f(x_2,\theta) \cdots f(x_n,\theta) = \prod_{i=1}^{n} f(x_i,\theta)$$

which has been called the *likelihood function*. Now, any estimate based on a sample is a function of the sample values. Once the sample is taken, however, the x_i's are fixed and the likelihood function becomes a function of θ only. Therefore, the problem of finding a maximum likelihood estimator of θ is simply one of finding some value of θ in terms of the sample values which maximize the likelihood function. This can be achieved with the use of calculus by differentiating the likelihood function with respect to the unknown parameter θ, setting the derivative equal to zero, and solving for θ. The procedure generally yields an absolute maximum.

Suppose the x_i are a random sample from a population for which the exponential probability density function is assumed. That is, $f(x,\theta) = (1/\theta)e^{-x/\theta}$. This density function would be assumed as a model for determining the mean-time-to-failure of the traveling wave tubes mentioned previously in this chapter. A random sample is taken resulting in n values of the x_i, $x_1, x_2, \ldots, x_n$ which are the individual times to failure of the tubes sampled. The parameter to be estimated is θ. The likelihood function is

$$L(x,\theta) = \prod_{i=1}^{n} f(x,\theta) = \left(\frac{1}{\theta}\right)^n \exp - \left(\frac{1}{\theta}\right) \sum_{i=1}^{n} x_i$$

Differentiating with respect to θ, we get

$$\frac{dL}{d\theta} = \frac{e^{-\Sigma x_i/\theta}}{\theta n + 1} \left(\frac{\sum x_i}{\theta} - n\right)$$

Setting $dL/d\theta = 0$ and solving for θ, we find it apparent that one of the factors must be equal to zero. If the first factor is equal to zero, then there is no value of θ which will satisfy the equation, and there is no probability density function. Therefore, the solution must be obtained by letting the second factor equal zero, resulting in

$$\frac{\sum x_i}{\theta} = n$$

and

$$\theta = \frac{\sum x_i}{n}$$

which is the maximum likelihood estimator of the parameter θ in this function.

In some instances it is more convenient to differentiate the logarithm of the likelihood function, in which case

$$\frac{d \log L}{d\theta} = 0$$

is solved for θ. The result is the same.

We have demonstrated that the maximum likelihood estimator of the parameter of an exponential probability density function is

$$\bar{x} = \frac{\sum x_i}{n} = \hat{\theta}$$

Some other commonly used maximum likelihood estimators are:

1. For the binomial probability density function with the parameter θ, $\hat{\theta} = x/n$ is the maximum likelihood estimator of θ.
2. For the Poisson probability density function with parameter μ, $\bar{x} = \sum x_i/n$ is the maximum likelihood estimator of μ.
3. For the normal probability density function with parameters μ and σ^2, $\bar{x} = \sum x_i/n$ and $S^2 = \sum (x - \bar{x})^2/n$ are maximum likelihood estimators of μ and σ^2, respectively.

However, S^2 is a biased estimator of σ^2 since $E(S^2) = (n - 1/n)\sigma^2 = \sigma^2 - (\sigma^2/n)$ where $-\sigma^2/n$ is the amount of the bias. A simple correction for the bias will result in $E[n/(n - 1)\, S^2] = \sigma^2$, or, directly, $s^2 = \sum (x - \bar{x})^2/(n - 1)$ provides an unbiased estimate of σ^2.

12.4 POINT AND INTERVAL ESTIMATES

The previous discussion has been entirely concerned with a process of estimation called *point estimation.* In estimating a parameter θ with a point estimate, the four-step procedure given in Sec. 12.1 of this chapter is utilized. This procedure involved the following:

1. Selecting an estimator
2. Drawing a sample from the population
3. Computing the value of the estimator
4. Using the computed value of the estimator as an estimate of the unknown parameter

Since the value of an estimator computed from a sample is a single value or point, this procedure results in a *point estimate.*

However, it should be apparent that although the point estimate may indeed be quite close to the unknown parameter, it is extremely unlikely that it will equal the unknown parameter exactly. In fact, if another sample of exactly the same size is taken from the population in exactly the same way and the same statistic is computed, it is very likely that its value will differ from that of the statistic computed from the previous sample. It is this variation from sample to sample which provides the sampling distribution of a statistic.

Consequently, any point estimate of a parameter is subject to sampling error, and it would be desirable to be able to make some statement about the size of the error in the estimate and the probability that an error of that size will occur. Point estimates, by definition, consist of a single number with no indication of error size or probability. In order to make a more meaningful statement about the estimate, it is useful to define an interval such that a statement can be made as to the probability that the given interval does contain the parameter to be estimated.

For example, in using $\hat{\theta}$ to estimate θ, the value of $\hat{\theta}$ computed from the sample would be a point estimate. It is possible to define an interval about $\hat{\theta}$ of the type $\hat{\theta} \pm k$ such that we could make a statement about the probability that θ lies in that interval. To be more precise, since the parameter θ is a constant, it is not correct to speak of the probability that θ lies within a given interval. It is more usual to state that there is some probability that any given interval will include the parameter θ since it is the intervals which are variable. This probability is referred to as *confidence*, and an interval of this type is called a *confidence interval*.

For example, an interval defined in such a way that there is a probability of 95 percent that the given interval contains the parameter is called a 95 percent confidence interval. In general, if the probability that an interval contains the desired population parameter is γ, then the interval is referred to as a 100γ percent confidence interval.

The idea of a confidence interval can be interpreted in the following manner. If several samples were drawn from the unknown population, each sample would probably result in a different value of $\hat{\theta}$. Consequently, each $\hat{\theta}_i$ would produce a different interval $\hat{\theta}_i \pm k$.

If, let us say, 100 samples were taken and 100 values of $\hat{\theta}$ were computed, there could be 100 different interval estimates. If 95 percent confidence intervals were specified, then on the average we could expect that 95 of the 100 intervals would include the parameter θ while 5 would miss it entirely.

Figure 12.3 illustrates this concept of a confidence interval. The solid horizontal line represents the parameter θ which has a constant value. The vertical lines with upper and lower limits represent the 100γ percent confidence intervals. Some of these intervals include the parameter θ; that is, the vertical line crosses the horizontal line. A few of the intervals do not cross the horizontal line. These few do not include θ. If these are 100γ percent intervals, then 100γ percent of them will include the parameter θ.

In estimating some parameter θ with a statistic $\hat{\theta}$ computed from sample values of a random variable from the population with parameter θ, it is necessary to select as an estimator some statistic $\hat{\theta}$ whose distribution does not depend upon the unknown parameter. After drawing the sample and

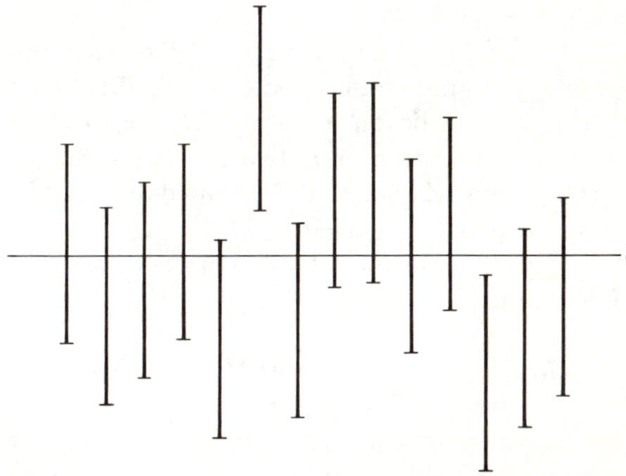

Fig. 12.3

computing a value of $\hat{\theta}$, the difference $|\hat{\theta} - \theta|$ is the sampling error. Let us designate the sampling error

$$|\hat{\theta} - \theta| = \varepsilon \tag{12.1}$$

or

$$\hat{\theta} - \theta = |\varepsilon| \tag{12.2}$$

The absolute value signs indicate that although the estimate can deviate in either a positive or negative direction from the parameter, the sampling error is always expressed as a positive number which can assume some range of values in the same scale of units as that of the random variable.

Since the sampling distribution of a statistic can provide a measure of the probability that the specified statistic computed from a random sample will have a value which falls between certain limits, these limits can be used to define an interval within which the statistic will fall with a given probability.

Suppose we use some statistic $T = \hat{\theta}$ to estimate θ, which is, for the sake of simplicity, taken to be the single parameter in the density function of the population $f(x,\theta)$. The estimator T is computed from a random sample of observations drawn from the population and is, therefore, a function of the sample values $T = g(x) = g[f(x,\theta)]$.

The estimator T has a sampling distribution which is known, and therefore for any given value of the parameter θ it is possible to determine the probability that T will fall between any two specific values, say t_1 and t_2.

Let us assume that there are many different possible populations of the form $f(x,\theta)$ and the problem in estimating θ is one of selecting the specific population from which the sample was drawn. That is, on the basis of a value T computed from a random sample, select from among N populations, each having a parameter $\theta_1, \theta_2, \ldots, \theta_N$, the particular parameter θ_j for which $T = g(x,\theta_j)$.

Figure 12.4 shows a graph of T plotted against various parameters θ. For any given population parameter θ_j, the possible values of T drawn from that population lie on a horizontal line through the value θ_j. From the sampling distribution of T, two points on this horizontal line can be determined, t_{j_1} and t_{j_2}, such that the probability that T will fall between these two points is equal to γ. That is, $P(t_{j_1} < T < t_{j_2}) = \gamma$.

If $G(T|\theta_j)$ is the cumulative distribution function for T given some value θ_j, then

$$G(t_1|\theta_j) = \frac{1-\gamma}{2} \qquad G(t_2|\theta_j) = \frac{1+\gamma}{2}$$

Since the ordinate scale in Fig. 12.4 represents a range of values for θ from many possible hypothetical populations, for every possible value of θ in this range, two points, t_1 and t_2, can be located such that $P(t_1 < t < t_2) = \gamma$.

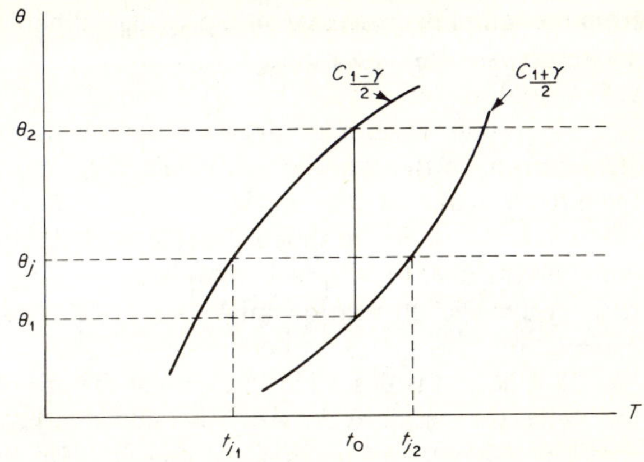

Fig. 12.4

If all such points t_1 and t_2 were plotted over the range of θ, these points would lie on curves similar to those labeled $C_{½(1-\gamma)}$ and $C_{½(1+\gamma)}$ in Fig. 12.4. The region bounded by these two curves can be constructed from the sampling distribution of $T|\theta$.

In estimating θ, a single random sample is drawn from the population, and a specific value of $T = t_0$ is obtained. If an ordinate is drawn at t_0 cutting the curves $C_{½(1+\gamma)}$ and $C_{½(1-\gamma)}$ at $\theta = \theta_1$ and $\theta = \theta_2$, respectively, then all points on these ordinates between θ_1 and θ_2 lie within the confidence belt and

$$P(T < t_0|\theta = \theta_1) = ½(1 + \gamma)$$

or

$$G(t_0,\theta_1) = ½(1 + \gamma)$$

and

$$P(T < t_0|\theta = \theta_2) = ½(1 - \gamma)$$

or

$$G(t_0,\theta_2) = ½(1 - \gamma)$$

We can therefore state, on the basis of the sample value t_0, that we are 100γ percent confident that the population from which the sample was drawn has a parameter θ with a value between θ_1 and θ_2. In this case, γ is the confidence coefficient, and θ_1 and θ_2 are the lower and upper confidence limits on θ based on the sample drawn.

Any ordinate drawn within the confidence belt constitutes a confidence interval of θ. For any given value of θ, say θ_j, a random sample drawn from that population could result in a value of $T = t$. Each value of t resulting from the sampling process would provide a different confidence interval for θ. Therefore, since T is a random variable, a confidence interval based on t is also a random variable.

In repeated samples drawn from the population for which $\theta = \theta_j$, 100γ percent of the samples will result in $t_{j_1} \leq T \leq t_{j_2}$, and 100γ percent of the intervals calculated from these values of T will include the parameter θ_j. Consequently, it can be stated that the probability that a confidence interval computed from $T|\theta_j$ will include θ_j is γ.

A specific illustration might be useful in understanding the previous explanation.

Suppose it is desirable to estimate the unknown mean of a population for which the standard deviation is known to be $\sigma = 25$. The estimator of μ will be $\bar{x}$ from a sample of size $n = 100$. The sample mean will be used to construct an interval which should include the true population with a probability of 0.96, that is, a 96 percent confidence interval.

The sample is drawn, and the sample mean is computed to be $\bar{x} = 100$. The data on which the 96 percent confidence interval will be based is summarized as follows:

$$n = 100 \qquad \bar{x} = 100 \qquad \sigma = 25 \qquad \sigma_{\bar{x}} = \frac{25}{\sqrt{100}} = 2.5$$

As discussed previously, the sampling distribution of $\bar{x}$ is normal, for sample sizes as large as $n = 100$, with a mean of μ; therefore the confidence interval on μ can be constructed assuming a normal sampling distribution for the estimator.

The mean of the distribution of $\bar{x}$, $\mu_{\bar{x}} = \mu$, plus and minus some $k_{0.96}$ multiples of $\sigma_{\bar{x}}$ will include the desired area under the curve of the sampling distribution which in this case is 96 percent of the area. The probability that any $\bar{x}$ computed from a random sample of $n = 100$ from this population will fall within the interval $\mu \pm k_{0.96}\sigma_{\bar{x}}$ is 0.96. This can be written

$$P(\mu - k\sigma_{\bar{x}} < \bar{x} < \mu + k\sigma_{\bar{x}}) = 0.96 \tag{12.3}$$

The following steps result from simple algebraic manipulation:

$$P(-k\sigma_{\bar{x}} < \bar{x} - \mu < +k\sigma_{\bar{x}}) = 0.96$$
$$P(-\bar{x} - k\sigma_{\bar{x}} < -\mu < -\bar{x} + k\sigma_{\bar{x}}) = 0.96$$
$$P(\bar{x} + k\sigma_{\bar{x}} > \mu > \bar{x} - k\sigma_{\bar{x}}) = 0.96$$
$$P(\bar{x} - k\sigma_{\bar{x}} < \mu < \bar{x} + k\sigma_{\bar{x}}) = 0.96 \tag{12.4}$$

Equations (12.3) and (12.4) show that a confidence interval on an unknown parameter can be based on a sample $\bar{x}$.

For the specific example, $k_{0.96} = 1.88$, and the interval

$$\bar{x} \pm k_{0.96}\sigma_{\bar{x}} = 100 \pm (1.88)(2.5) = 100 \pm 4.7$$

which provides the limits 95.3 and 104.7. This is a single interval based on $\bar{x} = 100$. If the sample $\bar{x}$ had been some other value, a different interval would have resulted.

Suppose the true mean of the population actually had been $\mu = 100$. Then a 96 percent confidence interval on $\bar{x}$ would have resulted in exactly the same limits, that is,

$$\mu \pm k\sigma_{\bar{x}} = 100 \pm 4.7$$

providing the limits 95.3 and 104.7.

Suppose, however, that $\mu = 102$. A 96 percent interval on $\bar{x}$ would then result in 102 ± 4.7, giving the limits 97.3 and 106.7.

Considering several hypothetical populations with different means, we could set up a table of confidence limits on $\bar{x}$ given various possible values of μ. This is shown in Table 12.1.

Figure 12.5 provides a graph of $\bar{x}$ versus various values of the parameter μ. The slanted lines represent the 96 percent confidence belt, and the ordinate constructed at $\bar{x} = 100$ which cuts the belt at $\mu = 95.3$ and $\mu = 104.7$ represents the confidence interval constructed from the sample $\bar{x} = 100$. For any sample value of $\bar{x}$, an ordinate constructed at that sample value will cut the confidence belt at two points corresponding to two values which we can label μ_L and μ_U.

We can then state that on the basis of the sample value $\bar{x}$ we are 96 percent confident that the population from which the sample was taken has a parameter $\mu_L < \mu < \mu_U$, where the values μ_L and μ_U constitute the lower and upper confidence limits. In this case for $\bar{x} = 100$, $\mu_L = 95.3$ and $\mu_U = 104.7$.

Table 12.1 Confidence intervals on $\bar{x}$ for alternative values of μ

	96% confidence interval on $\bar{x}$	
μ	*Lower limit*	*Upper limit*
94	89.3	98.7
96	91.3	100.7
98	93.3	102.7
100	95.3	104.7
102	97.3	106.7
104	99.3	108.7
106	101.3	110.7

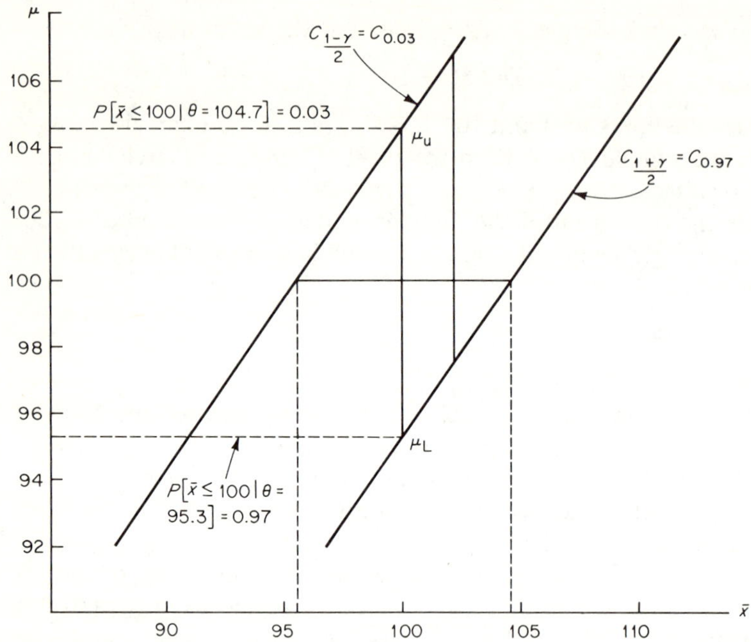

Fig. 12.5

If a sample value $\bar{x} = 102$ had resulted, the ordinate constructed at $\bar{x} = 102$ would have represented the confidence interval, and the limits would have been $\mu_L = 97.3$ and $\mu_U = 106.7$. For any sample value of $\bar{x}$ from the population with a given value of μ, an interval can be constructed which will include the true value of the parameter with a probability of 0.96.

12.5 ONE-SIDED AND TWO-SIDED CONFIDENCE INTERVALS

The previous discussion on confidence intervals involved the determination of two limits, an upper and lower, between which the true value of the unknown parameter was expected to lie with some degree of confidence.

Frequently situations arise in which a decision maker is interested in determining only an upper or a lower bound on the parameter, but not both. For example, suppose a decision must be made by an East Coast producer of a perishable commodity whether to market his product on the West Coast. His decision may be based on the time it takes to ship the product from his East Coast base of operations to a West Coast distributor. In this case he wants to estimate the average shipping time. A single value for this average time will not suffice since he knows that estimates are subject to error and a point estimate will provide no information on the probability that the true value of the average shipping time will differ from the estimate by some specified amount. An interval estimate is therefore required.

A two-sided interval will specify, with a given confidence, that the true average shipping time is greater than some minimum and less than some maximum value. However, the shipper may not be concerned with the minimum; he is concerned only with the maximum because if the maximum is exceeded there is a likelihood that his product will spoil in transit. In this case, he is interested only in a confidence interval with an upper bound. To be more specific, he would like a statement to the effect that the average shipping time is less than some value with a specified probability or confidence level.

A manufacturer interested in marketing a system component subject to wear-out might be concerned only that its mean life is greater than some minimum amount. In this case the confidence interval which he should insist upon need have only a lower bound.

Intervals of these types are one-sided confidence intervals. A 100γ percent confidence interval is constructed from the sampling distribution of a statistic in much the same way that a two-sided interval is constructed. The difference between the two is that for a two-sided interval, two limits are determined which include 100γ percent of the area under the curve of the sampling distribution between them. A one-sided interval is constructed by determining a single limit such that 100γ percent of the area is either above or below that limit. (See Fig. 12.6.)

12.6 ESTIMATION OF MEANS

NORMAL POPULATION, σ KNOWN

In estimating the mean of a population on the basis of a sample mean, it is not likely that the population standard deviation is known. It might be conceivable that long experience with similar populations has produced an estimate of the population standard deviation which can be assumed to be a known σ and which would make it unnecessary to estimate σ from the proposed sample. However, even though the assumption of a known σ is uncommon, we shall make this assumption in order to provide a procedure to cover this eventuality.

The maximum likelihood estimator of μ is $\sum x_i/n = \bar{x}$ from the sample. The sampling distribution of $\bar{x}$ drawn from a normal population is also normal with a mean $\mu_{\bar{x}} = \mu$ and standard deviation $\sigma_{\bar{x}} = \sigma/\sqrt{n}$.

A two-sided 100γ percent confidence interval on the mean is given by $\bar{x} \pm z_\gamma \sigma_{\bar{x}}$ where z_γ represents the number of standard deviations of a normally distributed variate which when added to and subtracted from the mean includes 100 percent of the distribution.

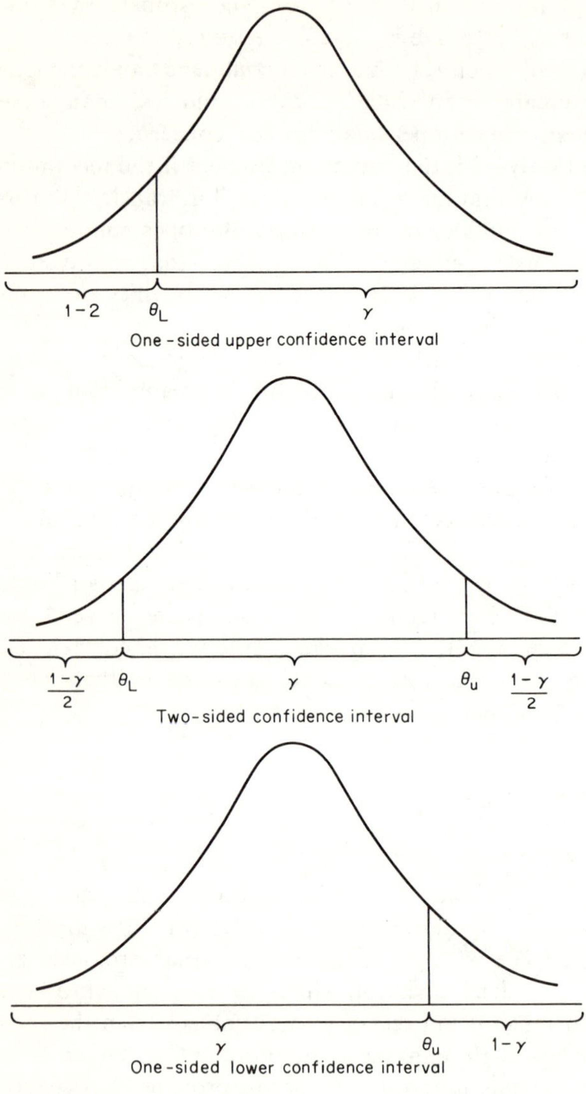

Fig. 12.6

The z_γ of this formula is related to the random variable Z, which is the standard normal variate. z_γ is the specific numerical value of the random variable Z corresponding to the desired confidence coefficient.

Example 12.1 A decision regarding the establishment of a retail outlet in a new shopping center is to be based upon an estimate of the mean or average family income in the vicinity of the shopping center. A random sample of 100 families

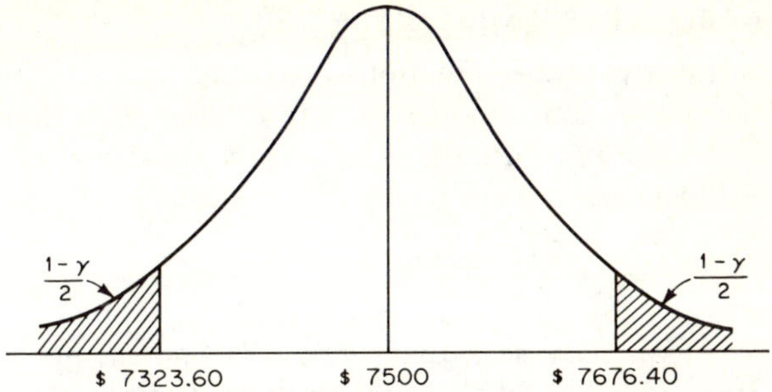

Fig. 12.7

is to be taken, and the average income will be estimated from the sample mean. It is specified that the estimate should be in the form of an interval such that there is a probability of 0.95 that the interval contains the true mean. From previous experience it is known that although average income levels in various neighborhoods differ, the variability within neighborhoods tends to be constant at a σ of \$900.

After the sample is taken, the sample mean is computed, and $\bar{x}$ = \$7,500. A two-sided interval is computed from $\bar{x} + z_\gamma \sigma_{\bar{x}}$ where $z_{0.95} = 1.96$, and $\sigma_{\bar{x}} = \sigma/\sqrt{n}$ = \$900/10 = \$90. Consequently, the upper confidence limit is

$$\$7{,}500 + (1.96)(\$90) = \$7{,}676.40$$

and the lower confidence limit is

$$\$7{,}500 - (1.96)(\$90) = \$7{,}323.60$$

The confidence interval is illustrated in Fig. 12.7.

If, instead of requiring a two-sided-interval estimate of the mean, it was decided that a lower one-sided confidence limit on the mean was more appropriate, the procedure would be similar. In this case, the estimate would take the form of a value such that it could be stated with 95 percent confidence that the true population mean is greater than the stated value.

The lower one-sided confidence limit would be computed from $\bar{x} - z_\gamma \sigma_{\bar{x}}$ where in this case $z_{0.95} = 1.645$ and the lower limit would be

$$\$7{,}500 - (1.645)(\$90) = \$7{,}351.95$$

The lower one-sided confidence interval on the mean is shown in Fig. 12.8.

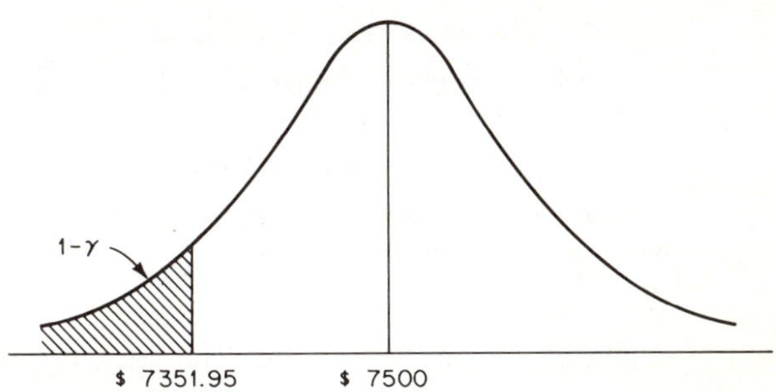

Fig. 12.8

NORMAL POPULATION, UNKNOWN σ

In most practical situations involving the estimation of a population mean, the population standard deviation will not be known, and in its place it will be necessary to use the sample standard deviation which we have previously defined as

$$s = \sqrt{\frac{\sum (x_i - \bar{x})^2}{n - 1}}$$

We have seen that when σ is known, our estimate of the population mean is based on the sampling distribution of the variable

$$z = \frac{\bar{x} - \mu}{\sigma/\sqrt{n}}$$

which is the standard normal variate as discussed in the chapter on sampling distributions.

When σ is unknown, it is necessary to determine a new variable $t = (\bar{x} - \mu)(s/\sqrt{n})$, which has Student's t distribution.

Confidence intervals on the mean are given by $\bar{x} \pm t_\gamma s_{\bar{x}}$ where $s_{\bar{x}} = s/\sqrt{n}$, and t_γ represents the number of standard deviations of the variate t which, when added to and subtracted from the mean, include 100γ percent of the distribution.

Example 12.2 Suppose in the previous example regarding the establishment of a retail outlet in a new shopping center, the population σ was unknown. However, the standard deviation of the sample of size 100 was $s =$ \$900. The sample mean as before was $\bar{x} =$ \$7,500.

A two-sided confidence interval is computed from $\bar{x} + t_\gamma s_{\bar{x}}$ where $t_{0.95,\,99} =$ 1.98.

$$s_{\bar{x}} = \frac{s}{\sqrt{n}} = \frac{\$900}{10} = \$90$$

The upper limit is

$$\$7{,}500 + (1.98)(\$90) = \$7{,}678.20$$

and the lower limit is

$$\$7{,}500 - (1.98)(\$90) = \$7{,}321.80$$

An upper one-sided interval would be bounded by the limit $\bar{x} - t_\gamma s_{\bar{x}}$ where $t_{0.95,\,99} =$ 1.66, and the lower limit would be

$$\$7{,}500 - (1.66)(\$90) = \$7{,}350.60$$

It should be apparent that the difference in the interval computed from a known σ and z and that computed from s and t is extremely small for a sample size of 100.

In general, when $n > 30$, the z statistic can be used as an approximation for t with little loss of accuracy. However, for a sample of $n \leq 30$, the t distribution should be used.

ESTIMATION OF MEANS FROM NONNORMAL POPULATIONS

When the distribution of the population is unknown, or known not to be normal, a new problem arises. Fortunately, if the sample size is large, the central limit theorem indicates that sample means will be approximately normally distributed regardless of the shape of the parent population. This allows us to apply the normal theory without much loss of accuracy.

If the sample sizes are so small that the error introduced by the approximate procedure is not acceptable, then it is necessary to use the exact methods related to the particular distribution involved. The basic approach to confidence interval estimation was discussed in Sec. 12.4.

12.7 ESTIMATION OF THE DIFFERENCE BETWEEN TWO MEANS

Frequently problems arise where an estimate of the difference between the means of two populations is desired rather than separate estimates of the two means. These estimation procedures will assume normal populations. When the populations are not normal, the previous remarks regarding nonnormal populations will apply.

The statistic used as an estimator of the difference between two means is $\bar{x}_1 - \bar{x}_2 = \Delta\bar{x}$. In order to draw inferences about a population from an estimator, it is necessary that the sampling distribution of the estimator be known. If $\bar{x}$ is normally distributed with mean μ and standard deviation $\sigma_{\bar{x}}$, then the difference between two means $\bar{x}_1 - \bar{x}_2 = \Delta\bar{x}$ is normally distributed with mean $\mu_1 - \mu_2 = \Delta\mu$. The standard error of the difference, which we shall designate $\sigma_{\Delta x}$, is determined by the following relationship between variances:

The variance of a difference is equal to the sum of the variances.

If independent random samples are drawn from two normal populations with variances of ${\sigma_1}^2$, and ${\sigma_2}^2$, respectively, and if the observations are paired and the statistic $x_1 - x_2 = \Delta x$ is computed, then the variance of the sampling distribution of Δx is ${\sigma_{\Delta x}}^2 = {\sigma_1}^2 + {\sigma_2}^2$.

If the samples are drawn from populations having equal variances, that is, ${\sigma_1}^2 = {\sigma_2}^2 = \sigma^2$, then ${\sigma_{\Delta x}}^2 = 2\sigma^2$.

It follows that if two samples of size n_1 and n_2 are drawn from populations having variances ${\sigma_1}^2$ and ${\sigma_2}^2$, and the sample means are computed, then the sampling distribution of $\bar{x}_1$ will have a variance of ${\sigma_{\bar{x}_1}}^2 = {\sigma_1}^2/n_1$, while the sampling distribution of $\bar{x}_2$ will have a variance of ${\sigma_{\bar{x}_2}}^2 = {\sigma_2}^2/n_2$. The statistic $\bar{x}_1 - \bar{x}_2 = \Delta\bar{x}$ will have a variance of

$$ {\sigma_{\Delta\bar{x}}}^2 = \sigma^2_{\bar{x}_1 - \bar{x}_2} = \frac{{\sigma_1}^2}{n_1} + \frac{{\sigma_2}^2}{n_2} $$

and

$$\sigma_{\Delta\bar{x}} = \sqrt{\frac{{\sigma_1}^2}{n_1} + \frac{{\sigma_2}^2}{n_2}} \tag{12.5}$$

If

$${\sigma_1}^2 = {\sigma_2}^2$$

then

$$\sigma_{\Delta x} = \sqrt{\frac{\sigma^2}{n_1} + \frac{\sigma^2}{n_2}} \tag{12.6}$$

We shall consider several different situations below.

STANDARD DEVIATION KNOWN AND $\sigma_1 = \sigma_2$

When $\sigma_1 = \sigma_2 = \sigma$ and σ is known, then the sampling distribution of $\bar{x}_1 - \bar{x}_2 = \Delta\bar{x}$ is normal with mean $\mu_1 - \mu_2$ and

$$\sigma_{\Delta x} = \sqrt{\frac{\sigma^2}{n_1} + \frac{\sigma^2}{n_2}}$$

A 100 percent confidence interval on $\Delta\bar{x}$ is given by $\Delta\bar{x} \pm z_\gamma \sigma_{\Delta\bar{x}}$.

Example 12.3 A manufacturer hires workers for a production process requiring a particular technical skill. His general hiring practice has been to advertise in the local paper and to hire applicants with no previous experience at a basic labor rate. The applicants receive on-the-job training and get pay raises as their proficiency improves.

The head of a technical training school in the city informed the manufacturer that he conducts a training course in the particular skill required and could supply already-trained people to the manufacturer. Since they have had training, they would expect to be hired at a wage rate higher than that offered to completely untrained personnel.

The manufacturer agrees that it would be worthwhile to hire the trained people at a higher rate, but the exact starting wage would have to be determined by some measure of their increased proficiency resulting from the training program. In short, he wishes to measure the difference in proficiency between the graduates of the training school and the inexperienced employees he is accustomed to hiring.

Consequently, a proficiency test is devised and administered to 50 inexperienced employees hired on the basis of the latest newspaper advertisement and 50 of the latest technical school graduates.

We shall designate the technical school graduates as group 1 and the inexperienced employees group 2.

The test results were averaged for each group with $\bar{x}_1$ from group 1 equal to 91 points out of a possible 100, and $\bar{x}_2 = 86$. In similar proficiency tests of this type conducted in the past, the standard deviation of test scores was relatively constant at $\sigma = 6$ points.

The manufacturer wishes to estimate the true difference in proficiency between the two populations at a confidence level of 95 percent so that he can make a decision regarding the wage differential.

The test statistic to be used is, of course, $\bar{x}_1 - \bar{x}_2 = \Delta\bar{x}$. The standard error of $\Delta\bar{x}$ from Eq. (12.6) is given by

$$\sigma_{\Delta\bar{x}} = \sqrt{\frac{\sigma^2}{n_1} + \frac{\sigma^2}{n_2}} = \sqrt{\frac{36}{50} + \frac{36}{50}} = \sqrt{\frac{72}{50}} = \sqrt{1.44} = 1.2$$

The 95 percent confidence interval on the difference between the two population means is given by

$$\Delta\bar{x} \pm z_{0.95}\sigma_{\Delta\bar{x}} \qquad \text{where } z_{0.95} = 1.96$$

and

$$\Delta\bar{x} = \bar{x}_1 - \bar{x}_2 = 91 - 86 = 5$$

By substitution we get

$$5 \pm (1.96)(1.2)$$

and the upper and lower 95 percent confidence limits on the difference between the two population means are 7.35 and 2.65, respectively.

STANDARD DEVIATION KNOWN BUT $\sigma_1 \neq \sigma_2$

When $\sigma_1 \neq \sigma_2$, the standard error of $\Delta\bar{x}$ from Eq. (12.5) is given by

$$\sigma_{\Delta\bar{x}} = \sqrt{\frac{{\sigma_1}^2}{n_1} + \frac{{\sigma_2}^2}{n_2}}$$

Otherwise the estimation procedure is identical with the previous case.

UNKNOWN BUT EQUAL STANDARD DEVIATIONS

In most estimation problems involving means, it is most unlikely that the population standard deviations will be known. It may, however, be reasonable to assume that even though unknown, the standard deviations of the two populations are equal to one another. When this assumption can be made, an estimate of $\sigma_{\Delta\bar{x}}$ must be based on an estimate of the common population σ derived from the two sample standard deviations. Since two sample standard deviations are now available, both should be used to estimate σ. A pooled estimate of the common population standard deviation is obtained from

$$\hat{\sigma} = \sqrt{\frac{(n_1 - 1){s_1}^2 + (n_2 - 1){s_2}^2}{n_1 + n_2 - 2}} \tag{12.7}$$

where ${s_1}^2$ and ${s_2}^2$ are the variances of the first and second samples, respectively.

An estimate of the standard error of the difference between two means is then given by

$$\hat{\sigma}_{\Delta\bar{x}} = \sqrt{\frac{\hat{\sigma}^2}{n_1} + \frac{\hat{\sigma}^2}{n_2}} \tag{12.8}$$

The statistic

$$\frac{\Delta\bar{x} - \Delta\mu}{\hat{\sigma}_{\Delta\bar{x}}} = t$$

has a Student's t distribution with $n_1 + n_2 - 2$ degrees of freedom.

A 100γ percent confidence interval on $\Delta\mu$ is given by $\Delta\bar{x} \pm t_{\gamma,\nu}\hat{\sigma}_{\Delta\bar{x}}$.

Example 12.4 In the previous example, suppose that the data were exactly the same except that σ was unknown. It was assumed, however, that the standard deviations of both populations were the same and could be estimated from the sample standard deviations which were, for groups 1 and 2, respectively, $s_1 = 5$ and $s_2 = 7$.

The pooled estimate of the common population standard deviation was obtained from Eq. (12.7) as follows:

$$\hat{\sigma} = \sqrt{\frac{(49)(25) + (49)(49)}{98}} \doteq 6$$

The standard error of the difference using Eq. (12.8) is

$$\hat{\sigma}_{\Delta x} = \sqrt{\frac{\hat{\sigma}^2}{n_1} + \frac{\hat{\sigma}^2}{n_2}} = \sqrt{\frac{36}{50} + \frac{36}{50}} = 1.2$$

The 95 percent confidence interval on the difference between the two population means is given by

$$\Delta\bar{x} \pm t_{\gamma,\nu}\hat{\sigma}_{\Delta\bar{x}} \qquad \text{where } t_{0.95,98} = 1.98$$

By substitution we get

$$5 \pm (1.98)(1.2)$$

and the upper and lower confidence limits on the difference are now 7.38 and 2.62, respectively.

The difference in the interval resulting from a known σ and the normal variate and that of the estimated $\hat{\sigma}$ and the t variate is very small for a combined sample of size 100.

As in the problem of estimating a single mean, when the sample or the combined samples result in a variate with more than 30 degrees of freedom, the normal approximation can be used with little loss of accuracy. When $\nu \leq 30$, it is necessary to refer to the t distribution.

STANDARD DEVIATIONS UNKNOWN AND NOT NECESSARILY EQUAL

When the population standard deviations are not known and when the assumption of equal standard deviations is not warranted, the preceding procedure is not valid. An approximate procedure which produces generally satisfactory results makes the assumption that $s_1 \doteq \sigma_1$ and $s_2 \doteq \sigma_2$.

$\sigma_{\Delta\bar{x}}$ is then approximated by $\hat{\sigma}_{\Delta\bar{x}} = \sqrt{s_1^2/n_1 + s_2^2/n_2}$, and the procedure described in the previous example is then used.

12.8 ESTIMATION OF PROPORTIONS

When the population of interest is a population of attributes, that is, characteristics that are observed only as to their presence or absence, the estimation procedure is one of estimating the proportion of the population which possesses one or more of these attributes. Commonly, a population of this type can be modeled by the binomial distribution since the population can be divided into elements which possess the attribute of interest and those elements which do not. For simplicity, we might label the occurrence or observation of an element having the desired attribute a success, while the occurrence or observation of an element lacking that attribute is labeled a failure.

As discussed previously in Chap. 7, the binomial probability distribution generates the probability of x successes in any n trials or observations for a given θ, which is the true population proportion.

$$P(x) = \binom{n}{x} \theta x (1 - \theta)^{n-x}$$

The mean of this distribution is $n\theta$, and its standard deviation is $\sqrt{n\theta(1 - \theta)}$.

If the variable of interest is x/n, the proportion of successes in n trials rather than the absolute number of successes occurring, the sampling distribution of the proportion is also binomial and

$$P(x/n) = \binom{n}{x} \theta^x (1 - \theta)^{n-x}$$

However, the mean or expected value of x/n is $n\theta/n = \theta$, and its standard deviation is $\sqrt{\theta(1 - \theta)/n}$.

If we wish to estimate θ, the true population proportion, the best point estimate is $p = x/n$, where x is the number of successes observed in a sample of size n. In order to construct a 100γ percent confidence interval on the true population parameter θ, the exact procedure involves the simultaneous solution of the two binomial probabilities which follow for the value p.

$$\sum_{X=0}^{x} (X^n) p^X (1 - p)^{n-X} = \frac{1 - \gamma}{2} \tag{12.9}$$

$$\sum_{X=x}^{n} (X^n) p^X (1 - p)^{n-X} = \frac{1 - \gamma}{2} \tag{12.10}$$

The solution of Eq. (12.9) provides the upper limit on θ, while that of Eq. (12.10) provides the lower limit.

As an example, for $n = 10$, $x = 1$, the upper and lower 90 percent confidence limits on θ are approximately 0.49 and 0.99, respectively.

The evaluation of equations such as (12.9) and (12.10) can most easily be accomplished by using tables of the cumulative binomial distribution. When such tables are not available or when the available tables do not include values for the sample size of interest, some approximation procedure is necessary.

THE NORMAL APPROXIMATION

As discussed previously, the normal distribution provides a reasonably good approximation to binomial probabilities when n is large and the true proportion is close to 0.5. A convenient rule of thumb states that the normal approximation may be used when $np < 5$ for $p > 0.5$ and $n(1 - p) > 5$ when $p > 0.5$.

In this case an approximate 100γ percent confidence interval on the population proportion is given by $p \pm z_\gamma \sigma_p$, where $\sigma_p = \sqrt{p(1 - p)/n}$ and z_γ is the number of standard deviations about the mean which includes 100γ percent of the area under the approximating normal curve.

A confidence interval resulting from this approximating procedure will be symmetrical about p, the sample proportion. When $\theta \neq 0.5$, the precise confidence interval on the proportion based on the exact procedure should be asymmetrical. However, this approximation is generally close enough to the exact interval to be useful and is very simple to construct.

THE POISSON APPROXIMATION

To approximate binomial probabilities for circumstances where $np < 5$ and $p < 0.5$, or $n(1 - p) < 5$ and $p > 0.5$, the Poisson distribution is often used. The Poisson is a single-parameter distribution which provides $P(x) = e^{-\mu}\mu^x/x!$ where μ is the parameter. In using the Poisson approximation to the binomial, np is substituted for the Poisson parameter μ.

For the 100γ percent confidence interval on θ, instead of evaluating Eqs. (12.9) and (12.10), we could approximate the interval by evaluating

$$\frac{\sum_{X=0}^{x} e^{-np}(np)^X}{X!} = \frac{1-\gamma}{2} \tag{12.11}$$

and

$$\frac{\sum_{X=x}^{n} e^{-np}(np)^X}{X!} = \frac{1-\gamma}{2} \tag{12.12}$$

These equations can be easily solved for p by using tables of the cumulative Poisson distribution.

As an example for the data given previously, $n = 10$, $x = 1$, and $\gamma = 0.9$, we must refer to tables of the cumulative Poisson distribution and find a value for U such that

$$P\left(x \leq \frac{2}{\mu_U}\right) = 0.05$$

and

$$P\left(x \geq \frac{2}{\mu_L}\right) = 0.05$$

From the table we would find $\mu_U = 6.30$ and $\mu_L = 0.35$. Since $\mu = n\theta$, $\theta = \mu/n$ and $\theta_U = 6.30/10 = 0.630$, $\theta_L = 0.350/10 = 0.035$.

12.9 ESTIMATION OF THE DIFFERENCE BETWEEN PROPORTIONS

As in the case of population means, it is sometimes desirable to estimate the difference between the proportions of two different populations which possess some attribute of interest. If $x_1/n_1 = p_1$ is a sample statistic used to estimate θ_1, the true proportion from the first population, and if $x_2/n_2 = p_2$ is used to estimate θ_2 of the second population, then $p_1 - p_2 = \Delta p$ will be used as an estimator of $\theta_1 - \theta_2 = \Delta\theta$. Assuming that the two samples are independent and large, then the sampling distribution of Δp is approximately normal with a mean

$$\mu_{\Delta p} = \Delta\mu$$

and

$$\sigma_{\Delta p} = \sqrt{\frac{\theta_1(1 - \theta_1)}{n_1} + \frac{\theta_2(1 - \theta_2)}{n_2}}$$

Since θ_1 and θ_2 are unknown, the sample values can be used as an approximation, and

$$\hat{\sigma}_{\Delta p} = \sqrt{\frac{p_1(1 - p_1)}{n_1} + \frac{p_2(1 - p_2)}{n_2}} \qquad (12.13)$$

A 100γ percent two-sided confidence interval on $\Delta\mu$ is given by

$$\Delta p + z_\gamma \sigma_{\Delta p} \qquad (12.14)$$

Example 12.5 A public opinion poll is taken in a particular state to determine the difference between the proportions of registered Democrats and registered Republicans who favor a state income tax. Six hundred Democrats were polled and four hundred Republicans. A total of 240 Democrats favored the income tax as opposed to 100 Republicans. The sample proportion of Democrats favoring the tax is $x_D/n_D = 240/600 = 0.40 = p_D$. For the Republicans, $x_R/n_R = 100/400 = 0.25 = p_R$.

From Eq. (12.13),

$$\hat{\sigma}_{\Delta\bar{x}} = \sqrt{\frac{(0.40)(0.60)}{600} + \frac{(0.25)(0.75)}{400}} = 0.0295$$

A 95 percent confidence interval on the true difference using Eq. (12.14) is

$$(0.40 - 0.25) \pm (1.96)(0.0295)$$

The upper limit is then 0.199, and the lower limit is 0.101.

12.10 ESTIMATION OF VARIANCES

We have seen previously that a sample variance defined as $s^2 = \sum (x - \bar{x})^2/(n - 1)$ is an unbiased estimator of the population variance. From our definition of bias, the statement that s^2 is an unbiased estimator of σ^2 simply means that the mean of the sampling distribution of s^2 is equal to σ^2.

Although s^2 from a sample provides a point estimate of the population variance, it would be desirable, as it was for other parameters, to construct a confidence interval based on s^2 which will include σ^2 with some stated level of confidence.

In order to construct such a confidence interval on σ^2 then, it is necessary to find a statistic which involves σ^2 and s^2, and whose sampling distribution is known and does not depend upon any other unknown parameter. Such a statistic is $(n - 1)s^2/\sigma^2$, which, when computed from a random sample from a normal population, is known to have a chi-square distribution with $\nu = n - 1$ degrees of freedom.

For a two-sided 100γ percent confidence interval on σ^2, it is necessary to find two points on the sampling distribution of the statistic such that the probability that the statistic will have a value between these two points is equal to γ.

In order to arrive at the desired confidence interval, we should start with the following inequality:

$$P\left[\chi^2_{(1-\gamma)/2,\nu} < \frac{(n-1)s^2}{\sigma^2} < \chi^2_{(1+\gamma)/2,\nu}\right] = \gamma \tag{12.15}$$

Since we are looking for a confidence interval on σ^2, a few simple algebraic manipulations will serve to leave σ^2 standing by itself between the inequality signs, resulting in the following interval:

$$P\left[\frac{(n-1)s^2}{\chi^2_{(1+\gamma)/2,\nu}} < \sigma^2 < \frac{(n-1)s^2}{\chi^2_{(1-\gamma)/2,\nu}}\right] = \gamma \tag{12.16}$$

The intermediate steps will be omitted and left as an exercise for the reader.

If a confidence interval on σ is required rather than σ^2, an approximate 100γ percent interval on σ will result from taking the square roots of the limits on σ^2.

One-sided 100γ percent confidence intervals on the variance would be defined as:

Upper one-sided limit:

$$P\left[\sigma^2 < \frac{(x-1)s^2}{\chi^2_{1-\gamma,\nu}}\right] = \gamma \tag{12.17}$$

Lower one-sided limit:

$$P\left[\sigma^2 > \frac{(x-1)s^2}{\chi^2_{\gamma,\nu}}\right] = \gamma \tag{12.18}$$

Example 12.6 The variability of the burst pressure of a tank made from a new metallic alloy must be estimated. A sample of 50 tanks was randomly selected and subjected to a destructive test. Pressure was applied to each tank until it burst. From the sample of 50, s^2 was computed to be 400 pounds per square inch. A 99 percent confidence interval on the true σ^2 was required. This was computed from

$$P\left[\frac{(49)(400)}{\chi^2_{0.995,\,49}} < \sigma^2 < \frac{(49)(400)}{\chi^2_{0.005,\,49}}\right] = 0.99$$

where

$$\chi^2_{0.995,\,49} = 78.2 \qquad \text{and} \qquad \chi^2_{0.005,\,49} = 27.2$$

The confidence interval was computed to be

$$P\left(\frac{19{,}600}{78.2} < \sigma^2 < \frac{19{,}600}{27.2}\right) = 0.99$$

$$P(249.3 < \sigma^2 < 720.6) = 0.99$$

If the same confidence interval estimate has been required on σ, it would be approximated from

$$P(\sqrt{249.3} < \sigma < \sqrt{720.6}) \doteq 0.99$$

$$P(15.8 < \sigma < 26.8) \doteq 0.99$$

Upper one-sided 99 percent confidence intervals on σ^2 and σ would be

$$P\left[\sigma^2 < \frac{(n-1)s^2}{\chi^2_{0.01,\,49}}\right] = P\left[\sigma^2 < \frac{19{,}600}{31.6}\right] = P(\sigma^2 < 620.2) = 0.99$$

and

$$P(\sigma < \sqrt{620.2}) = P(\sigma < 24.9) \doteq 0.99$$

12.11 DETERMINATION OF SAMPLE SIZE

MEANS

It is frequently desirable to estimate the approximate size of the sample necessary in order to estimate some unknown parameter at a given level of confidence for some acceptable error. If the size of the error and the confidence level are specified, a relationship between error, confidence level, and the estimate can be established which also involves n, the sample size. This relationship can then be solved for n.

For example, in estimating the mean of a population, the estimator would be $\bar{x}$, the sample mean, which has a standard error of $\sigma/\sqrt{n}$. The error in the estimate would be $|\bar{x} - \mu|$, and if the confidence level is specified as γ, the error can be stated in terms of standard errors of $\bar{x}$.

That is, if we wish the maximum error to be equal to $k_\gamma \sigma_{\bar{x}}$, then

$$|\bar{x} - \mu| = k_\gamma \sigma_{\bar{x}} \tag{12.19}$$

Since $\sigma_{\bar{x}} = \sigma/\sqrt{n}$, Eq. (12.19) can be written as

$$|\bar{x} - \mu| = \frac{k_\gamma \sigma_{\bar{x}}}{\sqrt{n}} \tag{12.20}$$

For a known σ, k_γ is simply the number of standard deviations about the mean of a normally distributed variate that will include 100γ percent of the area under the curve of the sampling distribution.

Equation (12.18) can be solved for n; thus

$$n = \left(\frac{k_\gamma \sigma}{\bar{x} - \mu}\right)^2 \tag{12.21}$$

and since $|\bar{x} - \mu|$ is simply the error, we can designate $\bar{x} - \mu = E$ and write Eq. (12.19) as follows:

$$n = \left(\frac{k_\gamma \sigma}{E}\right)^2 \tag{12.22}$$

Since σ is generally unknown, it must be estimated either subjectively or on the basis of collateral information.

Example 12.7 In establishing an incentive system for manufacturing employees, a company operations manager wants to estimate the average amount of time it takes for a particular manufacturing operation. He wishes to have the operation performed experimentally n times (essentially a sample of n performances) such that he can be 95 percent confident that the error in the estimate of the average time is less than 3 min. From data acquired in the performance of similar operations, he assumes that the standard deviation of the time will be 12 min. How large a sample should be taken? As we saw above,

$$n = \left(\frac{k_\gamma \sigma}{E}\right)^2$$

where $k_{0.95} = 1.96$

$\sigma = 12$

maximum error $E = 3$

Therefore

$$n = \left[\frac{(1.96)(12)}{3}\right]^2 = 61.46$$

and we can conclude that a sample of size $n = 62$ will be satisfactory.

PROPORTIONS

The same procedure can be followed to estimate the approximate sample size required in order to estimate a population proportion with a specified maximum error at a given confidence level. Although $x/n = p$ is a binomially distributed variable, we shall assume that the normal approximation will provide a satisfactory approximation.

For a given error $|p - \theta| = E$ we shall establish $E = k_\gamma \sigma_p$ where k_γ has the same meaning discussed in the previous section, and

$$\sigma_p = \sqrt{\theta(1 - \theta)/n}$$

Since θ is unknown, we can make use of the knowledge that σ_p is a maximum when $\theta = 0.5$. For a conservative estimate, therefore, we would be safe in substituting 0.5 for θ in the formula and solving

$$E = k_\gamma \sqrt{(0.5) \times (0.5)/n}$$

for n, resulting in

$$n = \frac{k_\gamma^2}{4E^2} \tag{12.23}$$

Example 12.8 The personnel department of a large company wants to determine the proportion of employees that would approve of a new medical insurance program being considered. The new program would require an additional payroll deduction; therefore, they want to estimate the true proportion such that the error is no greater than 3 percent with a confidence of 99 percent.

In this case, $E = |p - \theta| = 0.3$, and $k_\gamma = 2.33$. The required sample size is $n = (2.33)^2/4(0.03)^2 = 1{,}508$.

12.12 SUMMARY

Various techniques have been discussed for the estimation of unknown population parameters. These techniques involve the use of sample data in computing estimates having certain desirable properties. These estimators are then used for the purpose of making inferences about the true value of the population parameters of interest.

In order for any estimate to be useful in a decision context, the decision maker must have an estimate which is coupled with a statement regarding the probability of error in the estimate. This can be accomplished by the construction of confidence intervals, such that a statement can be made that a particular interval includes the unknown parameter with some specified probability.

A confidence interval estimate then provides the decision maker with information regarding the probability that a decision based on the estimate will be in error.

PROBLEMS

12.1. Show algebraically that $\sum (x - \bar{x})^2/n = S^2$ is a biased estimator of σ^2.

12.2. The standard errors of the sampling distributions of two different estimators of a population parameter θ are $\sigma_{\theta_1}{}^2 = 7.2$ and $\sigma_{\theta_2}{}^2 = 6.3$.

(*a*) Which estimator, θ_1 or θ_2, is more efficient?

(*b*) What is the relative efficiency of θ_1 with respect to θ_2?

(*c*) What is the relative efficiency of θ_2 with respect to θ_1?

12.3. Show that x/n is a maximum likelihood estimator of the binomial parameter θ.

12.4. A chain of supermarkets hired a market research company to estimate the average weekly expenditures for food made by families in a particular area in which management was contemplating opening a new market. The researchers took a random sample of 200 families and found the sample average to be \$58. From previous surveys of this type of information, they knew that $\sigma = \$7.50$.

(*a*) Construct a 95 percent two-sided confidence interval on the population average.

(*b*) Construct a 98 percent two-sided confidence interval on the population average.

(*c*) Suppose the sample size had been 400 instead of 200. What would the 98 percent confidence interval have been?

(*d*) What size sample would be required if we wanted to use a 99 percent two-sided confidence interval with the same sampling error obtained with the 95 percent two-sided confidence interval constructed in part (*a*)?

12.5. Suppose in Prob. 12.4 that σ had not been known and had to be estimated from the sample standard deviation $s = \$7.50$. How would the answers have changed?

12.6. Suppose in Prob. 12.4 that the sample size was 25 and σ was unknown. The sample standard deviation was $s = \$8.50$. Construct (*a*) 95 percent and (*b*) 98 percent two-sided confidence intervals on the population mean.

12.7. Suppose in Prob. 12.4 that the president of the supermarket chain was interested only in a lower limit on the average expenditures. Construct (*a*) 95 percent and (*b*) 98 percent appropriate one-sided confidence intervals on the population mean.

12.8. The supermarket chain in the previous problem had recently conducted a similar market survey in a nearby area. The sample average resulting from that survey based on a sample of 100 families was \$64.50. The population σ was also assumed to be \$7.50. The chain subsequently opened a supermarket in that area which turned out to be very successful. Since the means from the two samples (this one and the one in Prob. 12.4) differed, the company statistician was asked to construct a 99 percent two-sided confidence interval on the difference between the two population means. You do the same.

12.9. A manufacturer produces large quantities of a particular part by a highly automatic process. The automatic equipment must be properly adjusted and set periodically to avoid the production of an undesirably large proportion of defective parts. The production manager periodically takes samples from recent production and inspects the parts to estimate the true proportion of defective parts being produced for that period. If the estimate of θ, the true proportion defective, is too large, production must be stopped and the equipment adjusted. From the last sample of 150 parts inspected, 10 were found to be defective. Using the appropriate approximation procedure:

(*a*) Construct a 99 percent two-sided confidence interval on θ, the true proportion defective.

(*b*) Find the 99 percent upper *one-sided* confidence limit on the true proportion defective.

12.10. Suppose, in the previous problem, only one defective was discovered in the sample of 150. Using the appropriate approximation procedure:

(*a*) Construct a 99 percent two-sided confidence interval on the true proportion defective.

(*b*) Find the 99 percent upper one-sided confidence limit on the true proportion defective.

12.11. A plant operating two shifts each day selected a random sample of 100 items from each shift's output and inspected each item in the sample. At the end of 1 week 21 defectives were observed from the day shift's production and 15 from that of the night shift. Construct (*a*) a 99 percent and (*b*) a 95 percent two-sided confidence interval on the true difference in the proportion defective produced by each shift.

12.12. The variance of a sample of twenty-five 1-lb boxes of candy was 0.82 oz.

(*a*) Construct a 99 percent two-sided confidence interval on the population variance.

(*b*) Construct a 95 percent two-sided confidence interval on the population standard deviation.

(*c*) Provide the lower limit of a one-sided 95 percent confidence interval on the population variance.

(*d*) Provide the upper limit of a one-sided 99 percent confidence interval on the population standard deviation.

12.13. How large a sample would be required to estimate a population mean with 90 percent confidence that the error in the estimate is less than 5? Assume that $\sigma = 7.5$.

12.14. In Prob. 12.13 how large a sample would be required if the confidence was increased to 99 percent?

12.15. How large a sample would be required to estimate a population proportion with a confidence of 96 percent that the error in the estimate is less than 0.04?

(*a*) Assume no information whatsoever about the true population proportion.

(*b*) Assume that a preliminary sample indicated that the true value of the proportion is no greater than 0.02.

13
Statistical Tests of Hypotheses

In any decision situation, an evaluation of the states of each component of the decision system is required in order for a determination of system state to be accomplished. The previous discussion assumed that in the absence of any information about the state of any specific system the proper procedure would be to collect data and to estimate the values of the pertinent parameter on the basis of the data.

There is, however, another approach to the state determination problem. If some assumption can be made about the value of the pertinent parameter, this assumption can be tested by what is known as a statistical hypothesis test. For example, if the state of the particular decision component depends on the value of the mean-time-to-failure of a traveling wave tube, and if the critical value is 5,000 hr, we can test the hypothesis that the true mean-time-to-failure of the tube is greater than or equal to 5,000 hr against an alternate hypothesis that it is less than 5,000 hr. This procedure or test would substitute for an attempt to estimate the actual mean-time-to-failure of the tube.

In the example in which the parameter pertinent to the decision problem was the average income of some particular population, rather than attempt to estimate that average income, it would be proper to test the hypothesis that the average income is greater than \$8,000 against the alternate hypothesis that it is less than or equal to \$8,000. Sample data would be collected and a statistic computed from the sample would be used to test this hypothesis about the average income. If the value of the statistic tends to verify the hypothesis that the population mean is greater than \$8,000, the component would then be assumed to be in the good state. If the value computed from the sample tends to discredit this hypothesis, the assumption would be that the component state is bad. The criterion for accepting or rejecting any hypothesis is called the *decision rule*, and the procedure for selecting decision rules will be discussed subsequently.

13.1 THE RATIONALE FOR HYPOTHESIS TESTING

If a random sample taken from a population is representative of that population, it is a reasonable assumption that the sample will resemble the population. It is on the basis of this assumption that estimates can be made of population parameters using sample statistics that have certain desirable properties as estimators.

If an assumption is made about the value of a population parameter, it is also reasonable to expect that a statistic computed from a random sample drawn from that population should have a value close to the population parameter. This is assuming, of course, that the sample statistic computed has those properties which make it a good estimator of the pertinent parameter.

As discussed previously, every statistic has a sampling distribution which exhibits the property of variability. Consequently, it is not necessary that the statistic be exactly equal to the assumed value of the parameter in order to accept the hypothesis that the parameter does indeed have that value. However, if the value of the statistic deviates significantly from the assumed parameter value, our faith or confidence in the assumption that the assumed or hypothesized value is correct should be reduced. The greater the deviation between the hypothesized value and the sample value, the lower our confidence in the assumption that the hypothesis is correct.

It is not sufficient, however, to speak in generalities about small or large deviations from some assumed value. It is necessary to specify in quantitative terms exactly what constitutes a significant deviation from the hypothesized value. It is proper to measure the significance of a deviation in terms of its probability of occurrence assuming that the hypothesis is true. That is, knowing the properties of the sampling distribution of the statistic which will be used to test the hypothesis, we can determine the probability of a deviation of any size from the hypothesized value. It is only necessary, then, for the statistician to decide on the probability level which to him constitutes significance under the circumstances of the test.

The statistician may decide that a deviation which could occur by chance 10 percent of the time is not significant. On the other hand, a deviation that could occur by chance only 5 percent of the time might be significant. That deviation which occurs by chance with a probability that the statistician concludes is significant is called the *significance level* of the test. If, after the sample is taken and the value of the statistic is computed and compared with the hypothesized parameter value, the resulting deviation is such that it could occur with a probability less than or equal to the significance level selected for the test, the hypothesis is rejected.

13.2 THE NULL HYPOTHESIS

The assumed value or values of the population parameter which will be accepted or rejected on the basis of the test constitutes the *null hypothesis*, generally referred to as H_0. Rejection of the null hypothesis is equivalent to acceptance of the alternate hypothesis that H_0 is not true, that is, $H_0' = H_a$.

The null hypothesis with respect to an unknown parameter θ can be established with θ equal to some value, less than some value, or greater than some value. In the first case if it is desirable to test the assumption that θ is equal to some constant k, the null hypothesis would be written

$$H_0\colon \theta = k$$

The alternate hypothesis implied by this statement of H_0 is simply

$$H_a\colon \theta \neq k$$

If the assumption to be tested is that θ is greater than k, the hypothesis would be stated

$$H_0\colon \theta > k$$

$$H_a\colon \theta \leq k$$

For the assumption that θ is less than k, the inequality signs in H_0 and H_a would simply be reversed.

It is common practice to establish the null hypothesis in such a way that acceptance maintains the status quo, whereas rejection leads to some positive act. For example, if a decision involves the opening of a service station in some particular location, the decision maker might be influenced in his decision by the average number of cars which pass the location on a typical business day. If the mean number of cars is greater than or equal to some particular number k, he would make the decision to open the station;

otherwise, he would not act. The null hypothesis in this situation would most likely be

$$H_0: \mu < k$$

while the alternate hypothesis would be

$$H_a: \mu \geq k$$

In this case, if the null hypothesis is accepted, the service station would not be opened. What is done in setting up the null hypothesis in this manner is to assume that the *bad* state exists and then see whether or not the sample evidence tends to contradict this assumption.

Another example which illustrates why the *bad* state is generally assumed for the null hypothesis concerns the marketing of a new drug by a manufacturer. The decision as to whether or not to market the new drug (aside from its efficacy in treating disease) must be based on whether it may be dangerous to the patient. If the evidence indicates that the drug may be dangerous, it will not be marketed. On the other hand, if the evidence indicates that it is safe, it will be placed on the market. In other words, *safe* implies action; *not safe* implies no action.

In considering the establishment of the null hypothesis, the reader should bear in mind that the hypothesis can never be proved on the basis of sample evidence. All that can be done is to reason that the null hypothesis either appears to be consistent with the sample evidence or it does not. Whichever conclusion is reached, there is always some probability of error. That is, there is some probability of making a wrong decision based on the sample evidence.

In the drug situation, the null hypothesis could be either

H_0 (the drug is safe)

or

H_0 (the drug is not safe)

In the first case, if we accept the null hypothesis and it is not true, a dangerous drug will be marketed. On the other hand, if we reject the null hypothesis even though it is true, we have also erred, but no physical harm to a population of potential patients will occur.

In the second case, if we accept the null hypothesis when it is false, no harm will occur, but rejecting it when it is true implies that we shall market the dangerous drug.

The error which occurs when we reject a true null hypothesis is relatively easy to control. However, it is more difficult to control the error resulting from accepting a false null hypothesis. Since we can control the probability of rejecting a true null hypothesis, we can minimize any adverse consequence of an error by establishing the hypothesis that the drug is not safe and marketing the drug only if the sample evidence tends to disprove this.

We shall consider then two different types of errors which can occur in hypothesis testing in the next section.

13.3 TWO TYPES OF ERRORS

Having established a null hypothesis to be tested, it is desirable that the testing procedure should always lead to acceptance of the null hypothesis when it is true and rejection when it is false. However, as long as the decision to accept or reject is based on sample data, no testing procedure will *always* lead to the correct decision. Since the probability of error is inherent in a procedure of this type, it is necessary to consider the two types of error which are possible.

If the null hypothesis is true, the decision to reject it constitutes an error. Statisticians call any error of this type a type-1 error or an error of the first kind.

If the null hypothesis is false, the decision to accept it would also constitute an error. This type of error is called a type-2 error or an error of the second kind.

A convenient illustration of the meaning of the two types of errors is given in Fig. 13.1.

The null hypothesis constitutes an assumption about an unknown state of nature or, in the statistical context, an assumption about the value of an unknown population parameter. Depending upon the actual though un-

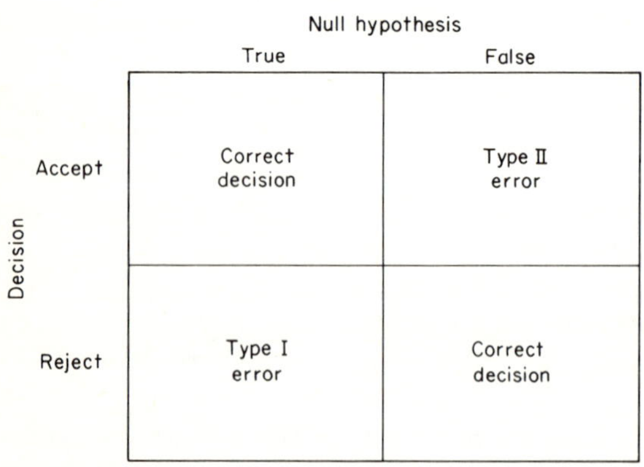

Fig. 13.1

known value of the parameter, the null hypothesis is either true or false. The decision maker has his choice of two acts. He can either accept the null hypothesis or he can reject it. To accept the null hypothesis when it is true is a correct decision. Rejecting the null hypothesis when it is false is also a correct decision. However, rejecting the null hypothesis when it is true constitutes a type-1 error. Similarly, accepting the null hypothesis when it is false constitutes a type-2 error. Statisticians measure the size of each of these types of errors by their probability of occurrence under a given decision or testing procedure and a specific set of circumstances. The size of a type-1 error is always referred to as α, while the size of a type-2 error is called β.

Definition 13.1

Type-1 Error: The decision to reject the null hypothesis when it is true is called a type-1 error. The size of a type-1 error, called α, corresponds to its probability of occurrence.

Type-2 Error: The decision to accept the null hypothesis when it is false is called a type-2 error. The size of a type-2 error, called β, corresponds to its probability of occurrence.

13.4 DECISION RULES

In hypothesis testing, a decision rule specifies the action to be taken with regard to the null hypothesis for every possible outcome in the sample space. In testing an assumption about a population parameter which is stated as the null hypothesis, the actions available to the decision maker are simply to accept the null hypothesis or reject it. Consequently, the decision rule is simply a method for partitioning the sample space into an acceptance region and a rejection or critical region.

Since statistical assumptions about population parameters are basically assumptions about numerical values, and since the sample statistics used for testing these assumptions will assume numerical values, the decision rule is essentially a partitioning of some subset of the set of real numbers into acceptance and rejection regions. The decision rule then becomes a rule for associating each and every element of the sample space with a decision, either to accept the null hypothesis or to reject it. For any test of a hypothesis it is possible to select among various decision rules. It would be desirable to select that decision rule, from among alternate decision rules, for which the probability of error is the smallest.

In selecting a decision rule, a statistician must decide in advance what risks of error would be acceptable to him. Obviously, it is impossible to select a decision rule for which there is absolutely no probability of error. For any specified sample size, the probability of making a type-1 error and the probability of making a type-2 error have an inverse relationship. That is, an attempt to decrease α increases β, and vice versa. In practice, it is common for a statistician to fix the acceptable α risk for a given sample size and then select a decision rule for which β is the smallest. If for a given α and n, all admissible decision rules provide a β risk which is unacceptable, the statistician has no alternative but to increase the sample size. Both α and β can be reduced simultaneously if the size of the sample is increased. The value selected for α, the probability of making a type-1 error, is the significance level of the test.

In practical decision situations, there is cost associated with sampling. Obviously, as the sample gets larger, the cost of sampling also increases. It should follow that the statistician should weigh in advance the relative costs of making either type of error with the cost of sampling. In classical statistical hypothesis testing, the statistician is generally not concerned with the costs or consequences of error, but simply with the probabilities associated with each type of error.

13.5 PROCEDURE FOR HYPOTHESIS TESTING

The procedure for a classical test of a statistical hypothesis can be reduced to the following steps:

1. Establish the null and alternate hypotheses.
2. Select the test statistic. The selection of the test statistic implies knowledge regarding the nature and characteristics of the sampling distribution of the statistic.
3. Select the decision rule. The selection of the decision rule implies specifying the significance level of the test, the sample size, and the nature and the location of the critical or rejection region.
4. Draw a random sample of size n from the population of interest.
5. Compute the value of the test statistic from the sample.
6. Accept or reject the null hypothesis according to the value of the test statistic and the decision rule.

13.6 ONE-TAILED AND TWO-TAILED TESTS

The specification of a null hypothesis H_0 automatically specifies an alternate hypothesis which we shall designate H_a. In testing a hypothesis about the value of an unknown parameter, we might be interested in testing that the parameter is exactly equal to some constant, in which case the null and alternate hypotheses would be

$$H_0 : \theta = k$$
$$H_a : \theta \neq k$$

On the other hand, we might wish to test that θ is less than or equal to k, in which case the null and alternate hypotheses would be

$$H_0: \theta \leq k$$
$$H_a: \theta > k$$

Or the hypotheses might be that θ is greater than or equal to k, and

$$H_0: \theta \geq k$$
$$H_a: \theta < k$$

The selection of acceptance-rejection criteria (or the decision rule) depends upon the nature of the hypothesis to be tested.

Suppose we are testing the hypothesis $H_0: \theta = k$ against the alternate $H_a: \theta \neq k$. A sample will be taken and the value of the test statistic will be determined. If this value is reasonably close to the hypothesized value k, we would accept H_0. However, if the statistic deviates significantly from k in *either* direction, we would reject H_0. A significant deviation in either direction results in rejection of H_0 because the null hypothesis states that θ is exactly equal to k. A statistic that is significantly greater than k or significantly less than k would tend to discredit that null hypothesis; consequently, it would be rejected.

In order to reject H_0 when the statistic deviates significantly in either direction, we must provide for a rejection or critical region in both tails of the sampling distribution of the test statistic. This is what is meant by a two-tailed test.

If the significance level for the test is α, we should select the critical region such that $\frac{1}{2}\alpha$ is placed in each tail. This is illustrated in Fig. 13.2.

Now suppose we wish to test the hypotheses $H_0: \theta \geq k$ versus $H_a: \theta < k$. Again we sample and compute the value of the test statistic. Now, however, if that value is greater than k, the null hypothesis is reinforced.

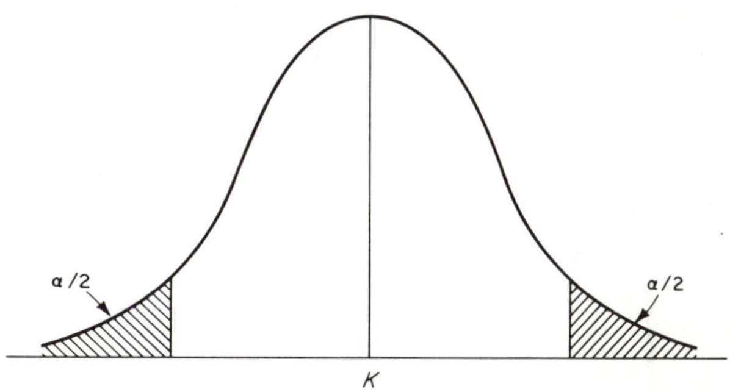

Fig. 13.2

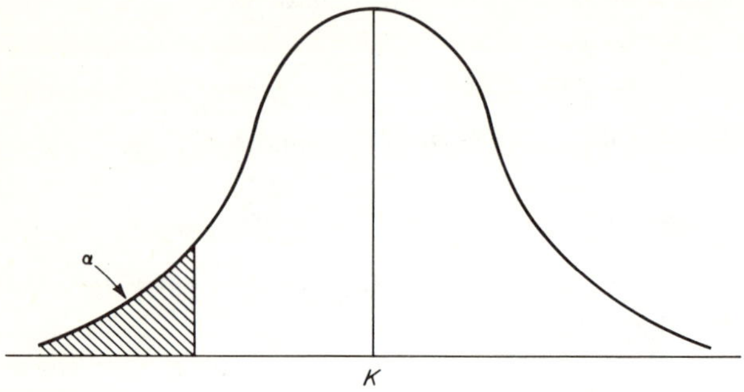

Fig. 13.3

The larger the value of the test statistic, the more the null hypothesis is reinforced. Therefore, we would not want to reject H_0 for values of the test statistic which are greater than k, and consequently there should be no rejection region in the right-hand tail of the sampling distribution. We would, however, want to reject H_0 for values of the test statistic which are less than k, since such small values would tend to discredit the null hypothesis. Consequently, we would want the entire rejection region to be in the left-hand tail of the curve as in Fig. 13.3.

Finally, suppose $H_0\colon \theta \le k$ is to be tested against $H_a\colon \theta > k$. The previous argument operates in reverse. Small values of the test statistic now tend to reinforce H_0, while large values greater than k tend to discredit H_0. In this case we would want the entire critical region in the right tail of the curve as shown in Fig. 13.4.

These last two tests would be one-tailed tests of the hypotheses.

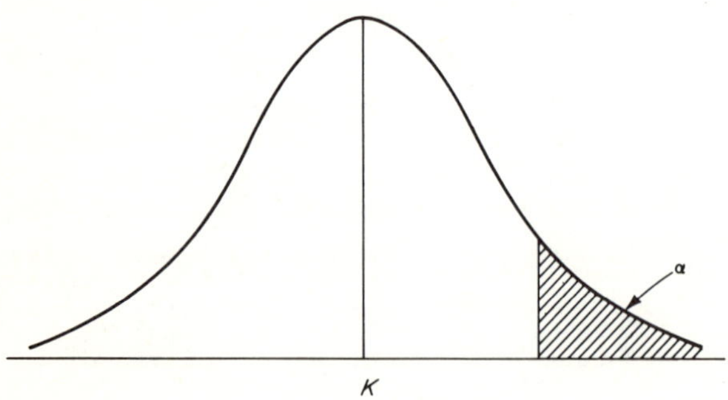

Fig. 13.4

13.7 SELECTING A DECISION RULE

For a classical test of a statistical hypothesis α, an acceptable probability of making a type-1 error is specified and a decision rule is selected which will minimize β, the probability of a type-2 error. In order to determine which of two possible decision rules has the smaller β risk, it is necessary to plot an operating characteristic curve for each rule.

THE OPERATING CHARACTERISTIC CURVE

Suppose it is desired to test a hypothesis about the mean of an unknown population. Specifically, $H_0:\mu = 30$ versus $H_a:\mu \neq 30$. This is, of course, a two-tailed test since we would want to reject H_0 if the sample statistic deviated significantly from the hypothesized mean in either direction.

The statistic used to test a hypothesis about a population mean would be the sample mean $\bar{x}$. It is known that the sampling distribution of $\bar{x}$ is normal with a mean equal to the population mean and a standard error of $\sigma/\sqrt{n}$.

Let us assume a sample size of $n = 100$ and a known $\sigma = 15$. Let us also suppose that a probability of 0.05 is considered an acceptable risk of rejecting H_0 if it is true; that is, $\alpha = 0.05$.

If the null hypothesis is true, then the sampling distribution of $\bar{x}$ will have a mean of 30. The critical region must be determined such that $\frac{1}{2}\alpha = 0.025$ of the area is in each tail of the distribution. Since $\bar{x}$ is distributed normally, $\bar{x} \pm 1.96\sigma_{\bar{x}}$ will include $1 - \alpha = 0.95$ of the area under the curve with 0.025 in each tail. This is shown in Fig. 13.5.

That is, the critical region is defined by $30 \pm (1.96)^{15}/_{10} = 30 \pm 2.94$, and becomes that area bounded on the right by 27.06 and on the left by 32.94. The decision rule then states that if the sample value of the statistic is less than or equal to 27.06 or greater than or equal to 32.94, reject H_0; otherwise

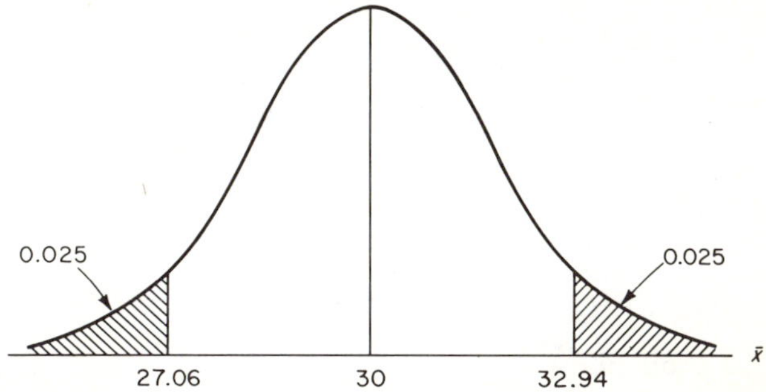

Fig. 13.5

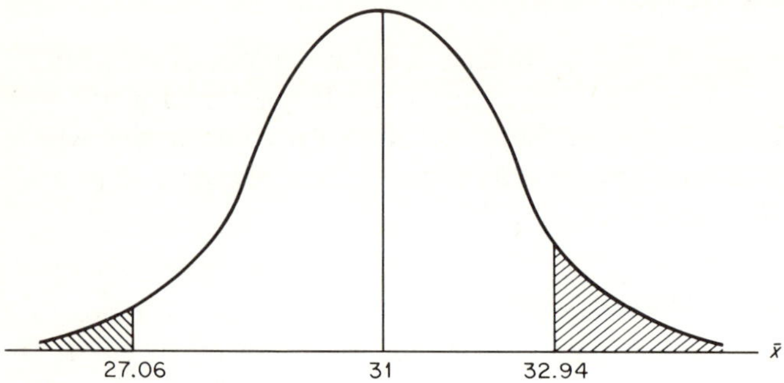

Fig. 13.6

accept. Under this decision rule, find β, the probability of making a type-2 error. We shall designate this decision rule δ_1.

The probability of making a type-2 error is defined as the probability of accepting H_0 when it is false. Although, under this particular null hypothesis, there is only one value, $\mu = 30$, for which the null hypothesis is true, the null hypothesis is false for any value other than 30. Consequently, for any other value of the true population mean, there is a unique probability of accepting H_0 under decision rule δ_1.

Suppose, for example, the true mean was actually 31. Then the sampling distribution of $\bar{x}$ would have a mean of 31, and the distribution with the critical regions defined under the specified decision rule would appear as shown in Fig. 13.6. Now the act of accepting the null hypotheses constitutes a type-2 error, and its probability is equal to the probability that $27.06 < \bar{x} < 32.94$. We can determine this probability from the table of the standard normal probability distribution by converting both critical points into values of Z, the standard normal variate, and finding the probability that a statistic Z computed from the sample will fall between these two values. Since

$$z = \frac{\bar{x} - \mu}{\sigma_x}$$

$$z_1 = \frac{27.06 - 31}{1.5} = -2.63$$

$$z_2 = \frac{32.94 - 31}{1.5} = 1.30$$

The probability

$$P(27.06 < \bar{x} < 32.94) = P(-2.63 < z < 1.30) = 0.8989$$

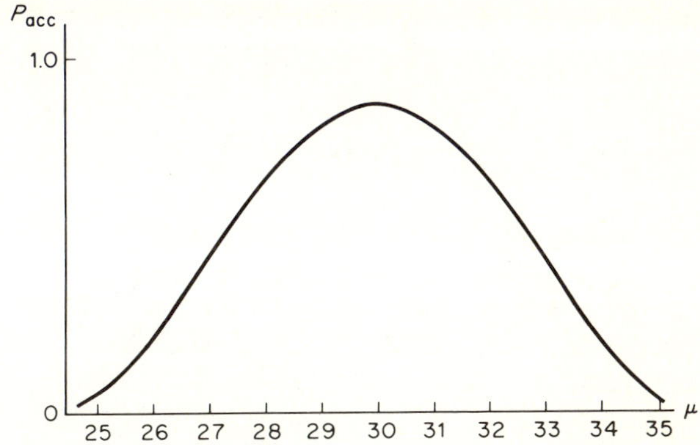

Fig. 13.7 *OC* curve for δ_1.

In the same manner, probabilities of accepting H_0 under the given decision rule for various alternate values of μ can be computed. These are given in Table 13.1. Note that the second column of Table 13.1 provides the probability of accepting H_0 under the given decision rule for various alternate values of the mean. When the mean is equal to 30, the probability of accepting H_0, $P_{acc} = 0.9500$, which is exactly $1 - \alpha$. This probability, $1 - \alpha$, is *not* the probability of a type-2 error since accepting H_0 when $\mu = 30$ is a correct decision. It is only when $\mu \neq 30$ that accepting H_0 is an error.

If these probabilities of accepting H_0 for alternate values of μ are plotted on a chart as in Fig. 13.7, we have the operating characteristic curve of the decision rule, sometimes referred to as the *OC* curve.

Now let us suppose that we wish to compare the previous decision rule δ_1 with an alternate rule having the same α risk but different critical regions.

Table 13.1

Alternate values of μ	*Probability of accepting* H_0 *under* δ_1
25	0.0853
26	0.2389
27	0.4840
28	0.7352
29	0.8989
30	0.9500
31	0.8989
32	0.7352
33	0.4840
34	0.2389
35	0.0853

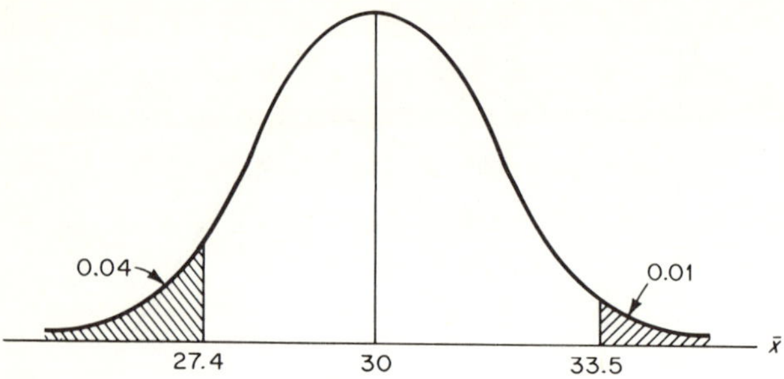

Fig. 13.8

The sample size and the α risk will be identical with the previous decision rule; however, the second decision rule, which we shall call δ_2, provides that a sample size of 100 will be taken, $\bar{x}$ computed, and H_0 will be accepted if $27.4 < \bar{x} < 33.5$.

The sampling distribution of $\bar{x}$ under δ_2, if the null hypothesis is true, is illustrated in Fig. 13.8. Under δ_2, the probability of rejecting H_0 when it is true is still 0.05, but this probability is not equally divided between the two tails of the distribution.

Since $\alpha = 0.05$ for both decision rules, we would wish to select that decision rule for which the β risk is lower. It is therefore necessary to determine the probability of accepting H_0 under δ_2 for alternate values of μ. These probabilities are given in Table 13.2.

Let us now plot the *OC* curve for δ_2 on the same graph as the *OC* curve for P_{acc}. This is done in Fig. 13.9.

It should be apparent from Fig. 13.9 that β, the probability of accepting the null hypothesis when it is false, is greater for δ_2 than for δ_1 when the true

Table 13.2

Alternate values of μ	*Probability of accepting* H_0 *under* δ_2
25	0.0548
26	0.1762
27	0.3936
28	0.6553
29	0.8563
30	0.9500
31	0.9443
32	0.8402
33	0.6292
34	0.3707
35	0.1588

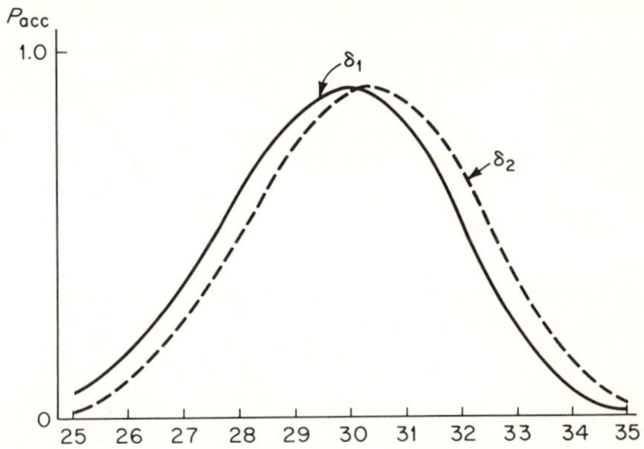

Fig. 13.9

parameter value is greater than 30. When the true parameter value is less than 30, then δ_2 provides the smaller β. How then should we select between the decision rules? If there is reason to believe that if μ is not equal to 30 it is greater than 30, then δ_1 would provide the smaller β. On the other hand, if there was reason to believe that μ was less than 30 if not equal to 30, then δ_2 would be preferable.

If, as is generally assumed in classical statistics, when a two-tailed test is used, it is equally likely that μ is greater than or less than 30, then the decision rule is selected for which the expected value of β is the least.

In this case, δ_1, which places equal areas in each tail, has the smallest expected value of β; and in general for a hypothesis of this type and a statistic whose sampling distribution is symmetrical about its mean, equal areas in each tail would provide the optimum decision rule. This conclusion can be reached by use of the likelihood ratio test which is described by Hoel.*

POWER CURVES

The operating characteristic curve of a test provides a graph of the probability of *accepting* a specified null hypothesis for various possible values of the unknown parameter. This probability of acceptance is the probability that the test statistic will fall in the acceptance or noncritical region. Frequently, it is more convenient to relate to the critical or rejection region and to construct a curve of the probability of *rejecting* the null hypothesis for various possible values of the unknown parameter. A curve of this type has been called the *power curve* of the test since it represents the power of a given test to reject a false null hypothesis. Since the probability of rejection is simply

* An extensive discussion of methods for determining best tests is given by Paul G. Hoel, "Introduction to Mathematical Statistics," Wiley, New York, 1954.

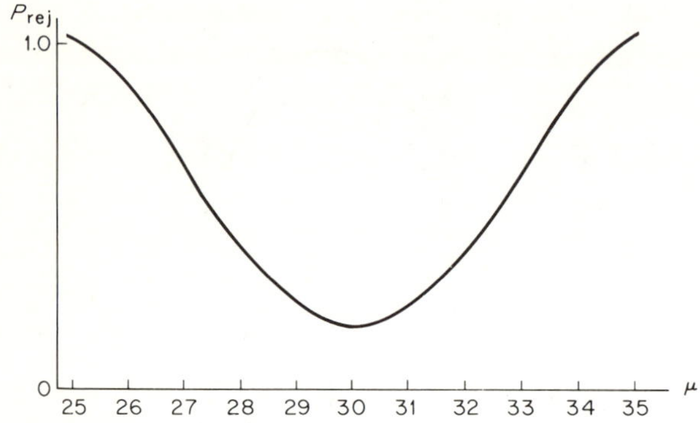

Fig. 13.10

one minus the probability of acceptance for a given test, the power curve for the test discussed above with the *OC* curve given in Fig. 13.7 is illustrated in Fig. 13.10.

It should be apparent that as the probability of rejecting H_0 under a given test increases the further removed the true value of the parameter is from the value specified under the null hypothesis.

For all values of the parameter other than that specified under the null hypothesis, the probability of accepting H_0 is β. Therefore, the probability of rejecting H_0 for those same values is $1 - \beta$, which equals the *power* of the test.

13.8 BALANCING THE PROBABILITIES OF ERROR

In classical statistical methods, as mentioned previously, the size of the type-1 error is generally specified, and a decision rule which minimizes the probability of a type-2 error is adopted. The sample size for the test is generally determined by economic considerations, i.e., the cost of sampling.

Let us suppose that a manufacturer of men's shaving accessories and toiletries wanted to test a hypothesis about the average age of the purchasers of one of his products. Conceivably, the average age of this population would influence his advertising campaign. Specifically, he wanted to test the hypothesis that the average age of purchasers was 30 against a single alternate hypothesis that the average age was 35. In this instance, the two hypotheses would be stated:

$$H_0 : \mu = 30$$
$$H_a : \mu = 35$$

Let us assume that data collected from previous studies lead to the conclusion that populations of this type are normally distributed and that the standard deviation is reasonably constant and is equal to 6 years.

A decision rule is adopted specifying that a random sample of 16 purchasers will be taken and the mean computed. If the sample mean $\bar{x} < 33.5$, H_0 will be accepted. If $\bar{x} \geq 33.5$, H_0 will be rejected, and the alternate hypothesis will be accepted.

This decision rule has certain error characteristics. Specifically, we can determine the probability of making a type-1 error under the decision rule, and since we are considering only a single alternate hypothesis, we can also determine the probability of making a type-2 error.

If the null hypothesis is true, that is, $\mu = 30$, then a picture of the sampling distribution of $\bar{x}$ would resemble Fig. 13.11*a*. The probability of making a type-1 error, α, would be proportional to the area under the curve of the sampling distribution of $\bar{x}$ to the right of $\bar{x} = 33.5$, which determines the *critical* or *rejection* region. This probability is easily determined to be $\alpha = 0.01$. That is, the probability of rejecting H_0 under this decision rule, even though it is true, is approximately 0.01.

On the other hand, suppose H_0 is false and the true population mean $\mu = 35$. Then the sampling distribution of $\bar{x}$ would look like that of Fig. 13.11*b*. Since under this decision rule any $\bar{x} \geq 33.5$ would lead to rejection of H_0 and the acceptance of H_a, the probability of accepting H_0 when the true value of the mean is 35 is equal to the probability that $\bar{x} < 33.5$, given $\mu = 35$. This probability is also easily determined to be $\beta = 0.16$.

Suppose that after analyzing the decision rule and considering the nature of the decision which will be based upon the results of this test, it is concluded that β is too large and should be reduced to a maximum value of 0.025. We would determine the critical region under the new test by assuming that H_0 is false and therefore the true mean is 35. Consequently, the acceptance region under this assumption must be equal to 0.025. Since the Z value corresponding to this area in the left-hand tail of the distribution is -1.96, Eq. (13.1) can be solved for the critical $\bar{x}$. Thus

$$-1.96 = \frac{\bar{x} - 35}{1.5} \qquad (13.1)$$

$$\bar{x} \doteq 32$$

The new decision rule states that H_0 will be accepted if $\bar{x} < 32$; otherwise it will be rejected, and for this decision rule, $\beta \doteq 0.025$. Now if H_0 is false and $\mu = 35$, the sampling distribution of $\bar{x}$ would look like Fig. 13.12*b*.

If the null hypothesis is true, however, then the sampling distribution of $\bar{x}$ would look like Fig. 13.12*a*. Since the new decision rule was based upon a specified value of β, it is now necessary to determine α. α is the

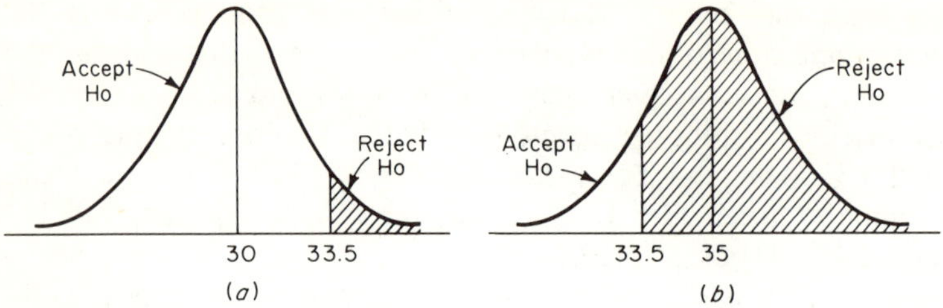

Fig. 13.11

probability that $\bar{x} \geq 32$, given $\mu = 30$. This probability can be determined to be approximately 0.09. It is apparent that in attempting to reduce β we have increased α, and that the opposite would also be true.

It would appear that this particular businessman is willing to accept a risk of making a type-1 error of $\alpha = 0.01$. He is also willing to accept a risk of making a type-2 error of $\beta = 0.025$. However, for the decision rules specified, these two values are not consistent with each other. Is there any way by which both α and β can be controlled? There is one other controllable factor in this type of problem. That factor is the sample size. We previously specified that the sample size is generally determined on the basis of economic considerations. If the sample size is fixed and cannot be changed, then this manufacturer must accept the fact that one of the two types of error will be larger than he would wish. If this is the case, then generally it is the value of α that is specified. However, if the sample size can be increased, it is possible to hold both α and β at a fixed value.

In order to hold $\alpha = 0.010$ when $\mu = 30$ and $\beta = 0.025$ when $\mu = 35$, the following relationships must hold:

$$P(\bar{x} \geq \mu_0 + z_\alpha \sigma_{\bar{x}}) = 0.01$$
$$P(\bar{x} < \mu_a - z_\beta \sigma_{\bar{x}}) = 0.025$$

z_α and z_β can be determined to be 2.33 and 1.96, respectively, from a table of the standard normal distribution.

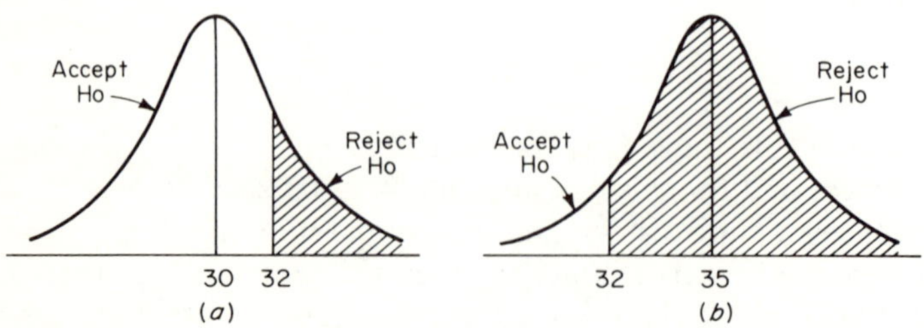

Fig. 13.12

In order for the two previous equations to hold for a given decision rule, the following relationship must also be true:

$$\mu_0 + z_\alpha \sigma_{\bar{x}} = \mu_a - z_\beta \sigma_{\bar{x}} \qquad (13.2)$$

Since $\sigma_{\bar{x}} = \sigma/\sqrt{n}$, Eq. (13.2) can be written

$$\mu_0 + \frac{z_\alpha \sigma}{\sqrt{n}} = \mu_a - \frac{z_\beta \sigma}{\sqrt{n}} \qquad (13.3)$$

Since the only unknown in this equation is n, the solution will provide the size of the sample required in order that the specified α and β risks can be achieved. By substitution, Eq. (13.3) becomes

$$30 + \frac{(2.33)(6)}{\sqrt{n}} = 35 \frac{(1.96)(6)}{\sqrt{n}}$$

and $n = 26.52$, or 27 to the next larger whole number.

Consequently, if the decision maker can afford to increase the size of his sample from 16 to 27, he can adopt a decision rule specifying that the mean will be computed from a sample of size 27 and the null hypothesis will be accepted if $\bar{x} < 32.7$; otherwise the null hypothesis will be rejected, and the alternate will be accepted. The α and β risks under this new decision rule can easily be determined to be 0.01 and 0.025, respectively.

13.9 HYPOTHESES ABOUT MEANS

NORMAL POPULATION, KNOWN σ

If the hypothesis to be tested involves the population mean, and if the population σ is known, then either the sample $\bar{x}$ or $z = (\bar{x} - \mu)/\sigma_{\bar{x}}$ can be used as the test statistic.

In the first case the critical point or points which define the rejection region in the distribution of $\bar{x}$ are computed for a given significance level. The sample $\bar{x}$ is then determined. If $\bar{x}$ falls within the acceptance region, H_0 is accepted. Otherwise H_0 is rejected.

The critical points for a two-tailed test are derived from $\mu_0 \pm z_{\frac{1}{2}\alpha}\sigma_{\bar{x}}$ where μ_0 is the value of the mean to be tested under the null hypothesis, and z_α is the number of standard deviations of the standard normal variate which will place 100α percent of the area in the proper tail or tails.

For one-tailed tests the critical points result from $\mu_0 + z_\alpha \sigma_{\bar{x}}$ or $\mu_0 - z_\alpha \sigma_{\bar{x}}$, depending upon the tail used for the critical region. The value μ_0 in this case is simply the limiting value of μ specified under H_0.

Example 13.1 A decision regarding the establishment of a retail outlet in a new shopping center will be based upon the average income level of the population in the

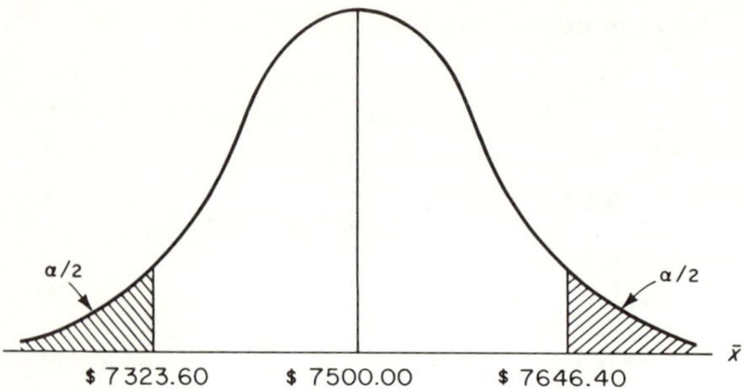

Fig. 13.13

area. (See the example in Sec. 12.6.) Instead of estimating the population mean, it has been decided to test the hypothesis that the average income is \$7,500. If this hypothesis is accepted the retail outlet will be opened. Otherwise it will not.

A random sample of 100 families will be drawn from the population, and the sample mean computed and used to test the hypothesis. It has been decided that a 5 percent probability of making a type-1 error is acceptable. The test can be summarized as follows:

$H_0{:}\mu = \$7{,}500$
$H_a{:}\mu \neq \$7{,}500$

$$n = 100 \qquad \sigma = \$900 \qquad \sigma_{\bar{x}} = \frac{\$900}{10} = \$90 \qquad \alpha = 0.05$$

If the null hypothesis is true, the sampling distribution of $\bar{x}$ will be normal with $\mu_{\bar{x}} = \$7{,}500$ and $\sigma_{\bar{x}} = \$90$. For a two-tailed test with $\alpha = 0.05$, the critical region will be defined by the points $\mu_0 \pm z_{\frac{1}{2}\alpha}\sigma_{\bar{x}} = \$7{,}500 \pm (1.96)(\$90)$, providing critical points of \$7,323.60 and \$7,676.40.

The critical or rejection region is shown in Fig. 13.13. Observe that the critical points for the test of the hypothesis arc identical with the confidence limits on the interval estimate as illustrated in Sec. 12.6, when $\alpha = 1 - \gamma$.

The critical region for this test as illustrated in Fig. 13.13 was defined on the sampling distribution of $\bar{x}$. $\bar{x}$ can be converted to z by the simple transformation:

$$z = \frac{\bar{x} - \mu}{\sigma_{\bar{x}}}$$

Critical regions can also be found on the standard normal distribution as shown in Fig. 13.14.

Since z is the standard normal variate with $\mu_z = 0$ and $\sigma_z = 1$, the critical points are ± 1.96 for this example, where $\alpha = 0.05$.

Once the decision rule has been established, the sample is taken, and either $\bar{x}$ or z is computed and compared with the critical points on the appropriate distribution. In this example, $\bar{x}$ from the sample was computed to be \$7,689.52. Since this falls in the critical region in the right tail of the distribution of $\bar{x}$, the

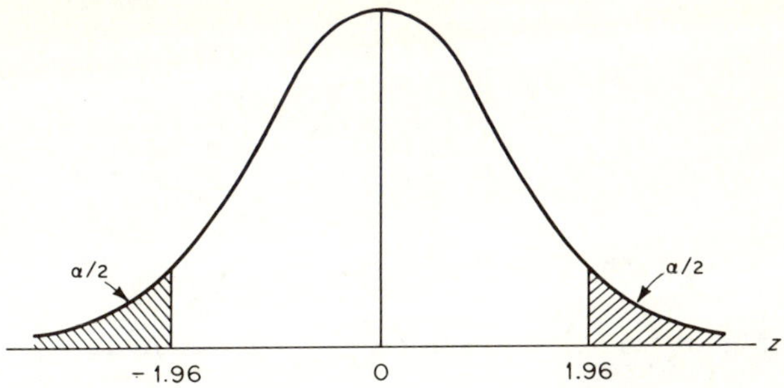

Fig. 13.14

null hypothesis is rejected. The same conclusion would be reached if $\bar{x}$ is converted to a z value. Thus

$$z = \frac{\bar{x} - \mu}{\sigma_{\bar{x}}} = \frac{7{,}689.52 - 7{,}500}{90} = 2.2$$

Instead of testing the hypothesis that the average was equal to \$7,500, suppose it was decided that it would be better to test the hypothesis that it was greater than or equal to \$7,500. The null hypothesis would then be stated

$H_0{:}\mu \geq \$7{,}500$
$H_a{:}\mu < \$7{,}500$

$$n = 100 \qquad \sigma = \$900 \qquad \sigma_{\bar{x}} = \frac{\$900}{10} = \$90 \qquad \alpha = 0.05$$

The procedure would be the same except that the test would be one-tailed. The critical point defining the rejection region on the sampling distribution of $\bar{x}$ would be given by

$$\mu_x - z_\alpha \sigma_{\bar{x}} = \$7{,}500 - (1.645)(\$90) = \$7{,}351.95$$

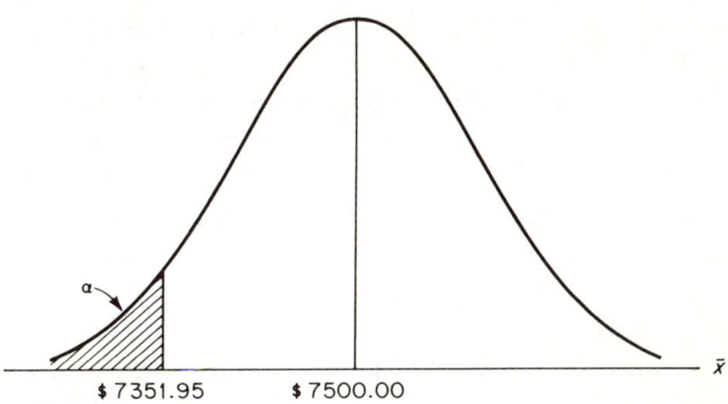

Fig. 13.15

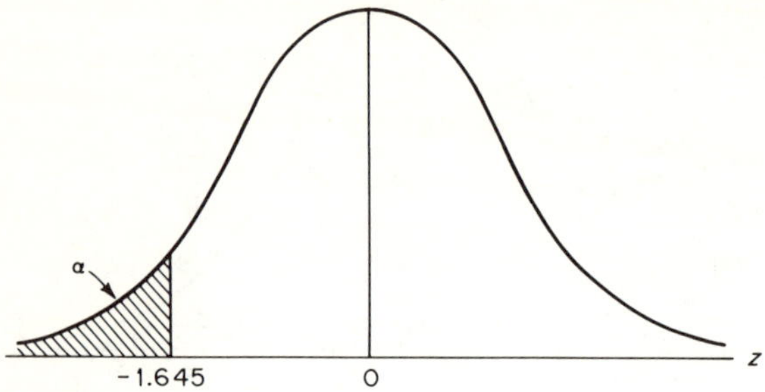

Fig. 13.16

as shown in Fig. 13.15. Once again it should be noted that the critical point for the test is the same as the lower, one-sided confidence limit on the mean as given in Sec. 12.6.

The equivalent critical region in the distribution of z is shown in Fig. 13.16.

The sample value of $\bar{x}$ = \$7,689.52 would in this case result in the acceptance of the null hypothesis, as would the equivalent sample value of z.

$$z = \frac{\$7{,}689.52 - \$7{,}500}{\$90} = 2.2$$

NORMAL POPULATION, UNKNOWN σ

Where it is necessary to test a hypothesis about an unknown population mean and σ is unknown and must be estimated, the estimator will be

$$\hat{\sigma} = s = \sqrt{\frac{\sum (x - \bar{x})^2}{n - 1}}$$

Consequently, $\sigma_{\bar{x}}$ must also be estimated by the statistic $s/\sqrt{n}$. As mentioned previously, the statistic $t = (\bar{x} - \mu)/(s/\sqrt{n})$ has Student's t distribution, and this distribution must be used for determining the critical sample values. If the critical regions are to be determined on the sampling distribution of $\bar{x}$, the fact that $\sigma_{\bar{x}}$ is unknown must be taken into consideration. To establish a critical region of size α on the sampling distribution of $\bar{x}$ which is $N:(\mu_{\bar{x}},\sigma_{\bar{x}})$, both $\mu_{\bar{x}}$ and $\sigma_{\bar{x}}$ must be known. The mean of this distribution is established by the value to be tested under the null hypothesis. However, $s/\sqrt{n}$ from the sample is a biased estimator of $\sigma_{\bar{x}}$. Therefore, in order to be assured that the critical region does not contain a greater area than that implied by the selection of α, it is necessary to select a critical point or points further from the mean than would be necessary if $\sigma_{\bar{x}}$ was known. Consequently, the critical points for a two-tailed test which define the rejection region on the sampling distribution of $\bar{x}$ are given by $\mu_0 \pm t_{\frac{1}{2}\alpha,(n-1)}s/\sqrt{n}$, where the value of t is determined from tables of Student's t distribution for the appropriate significance level and degrees of freedom. For one-tailed tests the critical points result from $\mu_0 + t_{\alpha,(n-1)}s/\sqrt{n}$, or $\mu_0 - t_{\alpha,(n-1)}s/\sqrt{n}$.

Example 13.2 In the previous example, suppose σ was unknown and had to be estimated from the sample. If the sample standard deviation $s = \$900$ and the sample size was $n = 100$, then $\hat{\sigma}_{\bar{x}} = s_{\bar{x}} = s/\sqrt{n} = \$900/10 = \$90$. For a significance level of $\alpha = 0.05$, the corresponding t value with 99 degrees of freedom would be

$$t_{0.025,\,99} = 1.98$$

The null hypothesis to be tested is exactly the same as in the previous example, that is,

$$H_0{:}\mu = \$7{,}500$$
$$H_a{:}\mu \neq \$7{,}500$$

The critical points on the sampling distribution of $\bar{x}$ would be determined from

$$\mu_x \pm t_{½\alpha,99}s_{\bar{x}} = \$7{,}500 \pm (1.98)(\$90)$$

resulting in the points \$7,321.80 and \$7,678.20.

Once again observe that the critical points for this test of the hypothesis are the same as the confidence limits of the interval estimate of the mean as determined in Sec. 12.6 when $\alpha = 1 - \gamma$.

The critical points for this test could just have easily been defined on the sampling distribution of the statistic

$$t = \frac{x - \mu}{s_x}$$

which has the Student's t distribution with the parameter $\nu = n - 1$.

The critical points on the t distribution are given by $0 \pm t_{½\alpha,(n-1)}$, or, specifically for this example, by 0 ± 1.98. Assuming that $\bar{x}$ from the sample is computed to be $\bar{x} = \$7{,}689.52$, then on comparing this value with the critical points on the distribution of $\bar{x}$, we would reject H_0. The same conclusion would be reached if we made the transformation

$$t = \frac{\bar{x} - \mu}{s_{\bar{x}}} = \frac{\$7{,}689.52 - \$7{,}500}{\$90} = 2.1$$

and compared this value with the critical points on the t distribution.

The procedure for one-tailed tests is identical with that described in the preceding section, except that the t statistic and distribution is used instead of z and the normal distribution. It should be apparent that for samples as large as $n = 100$, the critical regions determined by *estimating* $\sigma_{\bar{x}}$ and using the t statistic are almost identical with those found when $\sigma_{\bar{x}}$ was known. Consequently, for large samples, that is, $n > 30$, the z statistic and the normal distribution can be used with little loss of accuracy. For $n \leq 30$, however, the exact method should be used.

13.10 HYPOTHESES ABOUT THE DIFFERENCE BETWEEN TWO MEANS

Hypotheses regarding the difference between two means can take the following forms:

1. $H_0: \mu_1 = \mu_2$
   $H_a: \mu_1 \neq \mu_2$
2. $H_0: \mu_1 \geq \mu_2$
   $H_a: \mu_1 < \mu_2$
3. $H_0: \mu_1 \leq \mu_2$
   $H_a: \mu_1 > \mu_2$

Since case 2 and case 3 are identical except for the direction of the inequalities, we shall not illustrate case 3.

The statistic used to test these hypotheses will be $\Delta\bar{x} = \bar{x}_1 - \bar{x}_2$. In order to use $\Delta\bar{x}$ as the test statistic, it is necessary that the characteristics of the sampling distribution of $\Delta\bar{x}$ be known.

If the sample means $\bar{x}_1$ and $\bar{x}_2$ are normally distributed, then $\Delta\bar{x} = \bar{x}_1 - \bar{x}_2$ also has a normal distribution with $\mu_{\Delta\bar{x}} = \mu_1 - \mu_2$. Furthermore,

$$\sigma_{\Delta\bar{x}} = \sqrt{\frac{{\sigma_1}^2}{n_1} + \frac{{\sigma_2}^2}{n_2}}$$

STANDARD DEVIATION KNOWN AND $\sigma_1 = \sigma_2$

To test $H_0: \mu_1 = \mu_2$ versus $H_a: \mu_1 \neq \mu_2$ when $\sigma_1 = \sigma_2 = \sigma$, $\sigma_{\Delta\bar{x}}$ is computed from $\sigma_{\Delta\bar{x}} = \sqrt{({\sigma_1}^2/n_1) + ({\sigma_2}^2/n_2)}$. Since $\Delta\bar{x}$ is normally distributed with $\mu_{\Delta\bar{x}} = \mu_1 = \mu_2$, under the null hypothesis $\mu_0 = 0$. The critical points on the sampling distribution of $\Delta\bar{x}$ would be determined from $\mu_{\Delta\bar{x}} \pm z_{\frac{1}{2}\alpha}\sigma_{\Delta\bar{x}}$.

In order to test $H_0: \mu_1 \geq \mu_2$ versus $H_a: \mu_1 < \mu_2$ under the same conditions, a single point on the distribution of $\Delta\bar{x}$ is given by

$$\mu_{\Delta\bar{x}} - z_\alpha \sigma_{\Delta\bar{x}}$$

Example 13.3 In the previous chapter an example was considered in which the difference in the test scores of two differently trained groups of individuals was estimated. Group 1 consisted of 50 graduates of a technical school, while group 2 consisted of 50 new employees with no previous technical training. If the group 1 personnel could be shown to achieve significantly higher scores on a proficiency test, then the technical school graduates would be hired at a higher initial rate of pay than would totally inexperienced new hires.

To establish test criteria in this situation, it would not be sufficient to test whether there was a significant difference in test scores since a significant difference could result if the group 2 scores were better than the group 1 scores, leading to an inconsistent result in terms of the action to be taken. For the technical school graduates to be hired at a higher starting rate of pay than the inexperienced hires, group 1 scores must be greater than group 2 scores.

We could establish a null hypothesis $H_0:\mu_1 > \mu_2$, $(\Delta\mu > 0)$ versus $H_a:\mu_1 \leq \mu_2$, $(\Delta\mu \leq 0)$ and test using $\Delta\bar{x} = \bar{x}_1 - \bar{x}_2$ as the test statistic. However, if this is the hypothesis to be tested, acceptance implies only that the sample evidence tends to indicate that the average group 1 score is greater than the group 2 average or that the difference is greater than zero without implying anything about the magnitude of the difference.

If the hypotheses were tested as stated above, the test statistic $\Delta\bar{x}$ would, if the null hypothesis were true, have a mean $\mu_{\Delta\bar{x}} = \Delta\mu_0$. Since the null hypothesis simply states that $\Delta\mu > 0$, in computing critical regions on the sampling distribution of $\Delta\bar{x}$, $\mu_{\Delta\bar{x}}$ would be assumed to be equal to zero. The critical region would be in the left-hand tail of the sampling distribution and would be determined from $0 - z_\alpha\sigma_{\Delta\bar{x}}$ as shown in Fig. 13.17. The decision rule used to test the null hypothesis would provide that H_0 would be accepted if $\Delta\bar{x} > -z_\alpha\sigma_{\Delta\bar{x}}$; otherwise it would be rejected.

It is conceivable and even quite probable that H_0, which states that $\mu_1 > \mu_2$, could be accepted even though the sample value of $\Delta\bar{x}$ was negative; that is, $\bar{x}_2 > \bar{x}_1$ since the acceptance region of the test includes negative values of $\Delta\bar{x}$.

It might be better if the manufacturer decided that the pay increment would be given to the technical school graduates if and only if their average test scores were at least five points higher than the untrained employees. This new null hypothesis to be tested would then be

$$H_0:\mu_1 > \mu_2 + 5$$

versus

$$H_a:\mu_1 \leq \mu_2 + 5$$

Now the statistic $\Delta\bar{x}$ under the null hypothesis would have a sampling distribution which is normal, and with a mean no less than

$$\mu_{\Delta\bar{x}} = \mu_1 - \mu_2 = 5$$

and a standard deviation based upon an assumption that $\sigma = 6$,

$$\sigma_{\Delta\bar{x}} = \sqrt{\frac{36}{50} + \frac{36}{50}} = 1.2$$

The critical region on the distribution of $\Delta\bar{x}$ at $\alpha = 0.05$ results from

$$\mu_0 - z_\alpha\sigma_{\Delta\bar{x}} = 5 - (1.645)(1.2) = 3.03$$

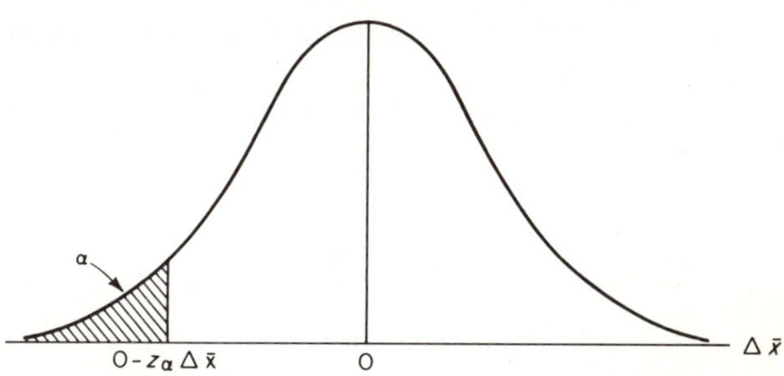

Fig. 13.17

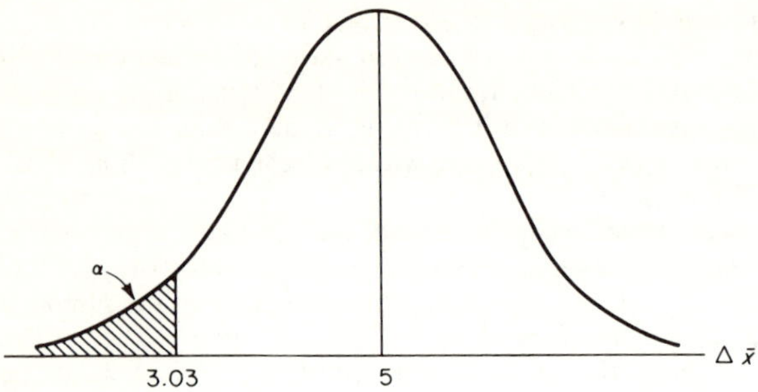

Fig. 13.18

and the decision rule would specify that if $\Delta\bar{x} = \bar{x}_1 - \bar{x}_2 > 3.03$, accept H_0; otherwise reject it. The sampling distribution and critical region under this test are given in Fig. 13.18. There are no negative values of $\Delta\bar{x}$ in the acceptance region of this decision rule.

After the test was given to each group of 50 and the average scores computed, $\bar{x}_1 = 92$, $\bar{x}_2 = 88$, $\Delta\bar{x} = 92 - 88 = 4 > 3.03$, and the null hypothesis is accepted.

A decision rule relating to the sampling distribution of the statistic Z could have been obtained as follows:

$$\mu_Z - z_\alpha \sigma_z$$

resulting in $0 - (1.645)(1) = -1.645$.

In this case the sample value $\Delta\bar{x} = \bar{x}_1 - \bar{x}_2$ would be converted to

$$z = \frac{\Delta\bar{x} - \Delta\mu_0}{\sigma_{\Delta\bar{x}}}$$

$$= \frac{4 - 5}{1.2} = -0.833 > -1.645$$

and H_0 is accepted.

UNKNOWN BUT EQUAL STANDARD DEVIATIONS

Where it can be assumed that $\sigma_1 = \sigma_2$ even though σ is itself unknown, $\sigma_{\Delta\bar{x}}$ must be estimated on the basis of the two sample standard deviations as explained in Sec. 12.7.

A pooled estimate of the common population variance is obtained from

$$\hat{\sigma}^2 = s^2 = \frac{(n_1 - 1)s_1^2 + (n_2 - 1)s_2^2}{n_1 + n_2 - 2}$$

and

$$\hat{\sigma}_{\Delta\bar{x}} = s_{\Delta\bar{x}} = \sqrt{\frac{s^2}{n_1} + \frac{s^2}{n_2}}$$

The variate

$$\frac{(\bar{x}_1 - \bar{x}_2) - (\mu_1 - \mu_2)}{s_{\Delta\bar{x}}}$$

has a t distribution with $n_1 + n_2 - 2$ degrees of freedom, and critical points on the sampling distribution of the test statistics must now be determined with reference to Student's t distribution rather than to the normal distribution.

Example 13.4 In the previous example assume the same data except that the population standard deviation was unknown. Instead, the sample standard deviation of the test scores of each group are available, and are $s_1 = 5$ and $s_2 = 7$.

The pooled estimate of the common population standard deviation would be

$$s = \sqrt{\frac{(49)(25) + (49)(44)}{98}} \doteq 6$$

The null hypothesis is still $H_0\!:\mu_1 > \mu_2 + 5$ versus $H_a\!:\mu_1 \leq \mu_2 + 5$. $\alpha = 0.05$ and

$$\hat{\sigma}_{\Delta\bar{x}} = s_{\Delta\bar{x}} = \sqrt{\frac{36}{50} + \frac{36}{50}} = 1.2$$

Critical points on the sampling distribution of $\Delta\bar{x}$ must now be obtained with reference to Student's t from

$$\begin{aligned} \mu_{\Delta\bar{x}} - t_{\alpha,(n_1+n_2)-2}\, s_{\Delta\bar{x}} &= 5 - t_{0.05,\,98}(1.2) \\ &= 5 - (1.664)(1.2) \\ &= 5 - 2 \\ &= 3 \end{aligned}$$

The decision rule now specifies that if $\Delta\bar{x} = \bar{x}_1 - \bar{x}_2 > 3$, accept H_0; otherwise reject H_0.

For combined samples as large as 100 it is apparent that the approximation of the critical points on the sampling distribution with the normal variate instead of using Student's t would make little if any difference. Consequently, for combined samples greater than 30 the normal can be used as an approximation with little loss in accuracy.

The corresponding critical point on the distribution of $t = \Delta\bar{x}(\mu_1 - \mu_2)/s_{\Delta x}$ would be -1.664.

13.11 TESTS OF HYPOTHESES ABOUT PROPORTIONS

Hypotheses regarding proportions generally involve a test of the true value of θ from a binomial population, that is, a population of attributes in which the true proportion of the population which possesses the attribute of interest is constant.

As discussed previously, the binomial provides the probabilities associated with a random variable X defined as the number of successes in some number of trials as well as the probabilities associated with the random variable X/n, the proportion of successes in n trials.

The mean and standard error of X are $n\theta$ and $\sqrt{n\theta(1 - \theta)}$, respectively, while the mean and standard error of $X/n = p$ are θ and $\sqrt{\theta(1 - \theta)/n}$. A test of a hypothesis about θ can be performed using either X or p as the test statistic.

Binomial probabilities can be determined either by evaluating the probability function directly, by referring to tables, or by using an appropriate approximation (Poisson or normal) as discussed in the previous chapter. The test procedure itself is identical with that used in other tests of hypotheses.

Example 13.5 Suppose we wish to test the hypothesis that we own a fair coin. A fair coin is obviously one for which the probability of a head appearing on a single toss is exactly equal to the probability of a tail appearing and both probabilities are equal to 0.5. Let us assume that we shall toss the coin 10 times, observe either the number or the proportion of heads occurring, and then accept or reject the hypothesis that the coin is fair on the basis of the result of the sample or experiment. If θ represents the probability of a head, then

$$H_0: \theta = 0.5$$
$$H_a: \theta \neq 0.5$$

We have decided that $n = 10$ and the significance level of the test $\alpha = 0.05$.

Under the null hypothesis the sampling distribution of p, the proportion of heads, would be binomial with a mean equal to θ and a $\sigma_p = \sqrt{\theta(1 - \theta)/n}$. We must now find the critical points on the distribution of p such that given that H_0 is true, that is, $\theta = 0.5$, then the probability that the sample value of p falls within the critical or rejection region is equal to α or, in this case, 0.05.

At this point we shall introduce a new notational device to distinguish between a general random variable and a specific value of that random variable. Previously we have used the capital letter, such as X, to represent the general random variable, and the lower-case letter x to represent some specific value of x. The notation $P(X = x)$ means simply the probability that the random variable X is equal to some value x.

We shall now adopt another notation to represent a general random variable. We shall use a tilde ($\tilde{}$) over a letter to mean a general random variable and the letter itself to represent the specific value. Then the notation $P(\tilde{x} = x)$ means exactly the same thing as $P(X = x)$.

This new device is introduced here because we are dealing with a statistic p which is the sample proportion. Rather than use the capital P in the sense of $P(P = p)$, we prefer to use $P(\tilde{p} = p)$. This notation is common in statistical decision theory and will be used extensively in the portion of this book related to that topic. Used here, it avoids confusion between P as a random variable and P representing probability.

The sampling distribution of $\tilde{p}$, the proportion of heads in 10 coin tosses given that $\theta = 0.5$, is given in Table 13.3.

Table 13.3

$\tilde{p}$	$P(\tilde{p})$
0.0	0.0010
0.1	0.0098
0.2	0.0439
0.3	0.1172
0.4	0.2051
0.5	0.2461
0.6	0.2051
0.7	0.1172
0.8	0.0439
0.9	0.0098
1.0	0.0010

Since this is a two-tailed test, we would want to reject the null hypothesis if a sample proportion occurs which is either considerably smaller or considerably larger than 0.5 such that the difference would occur by chance less than 5 percent of the time. This involves selecting critical points in both tails of the sampling distribution of $\tilde{p}$ which cut off critical regions in each tail containing 2½ percent of the total area.

Because the binomial is a discrete distribution, it is not possible, in this case, to find critical points which correspond exactly to the desired 5 percent significance level. If the critical points selected are 0.1 and 0.9, the decision rule would then state that the null hypothesis would be rejected if either 0, 1, 9, or 10 heads occur in the sample. The probability of this occurring would be $0.0010 + 0.0098 + 0.0098 + 0.0010 = 0.0216$, which is less than the 5 percent desired.

On the other hand, if the critical points were 0.2 and 0.8, implying rejection if 0, 1, 2, 8, 9, or 10 heads occur, the probability of this occurrence would be 0.1094, which is considerably more than the 5 percent desired. Consequently, the hypothesis can be tested only at the 0.0216 or the 0.1094 level of significance. However, if it is desired in establishing the test that the null hypothesis be rejected when true *not more than* 5 percent of the time, then the critical points 0.1 and 0.9 would be selected.

For large values of n, the calculation of exact probabilities from the binomial probability function becomes tedious. If tables of these probabilities are not available, then some approximation to the exact binomial probabilities must be used.

The normal and Poisson probability distributions provide reasonably accurate approximations to binomial probabilities under certain circumstances. When the hypothetical value of θ is close to 0.5 and n is large enough such that both $n\theta$ and $n(1 - \theta)$ are greater than 5, the normal approximation is appropriate.

When θ is small and n is large, the Poisson approximation is appropriate. As a rule of thumb we might specify that for the Poisson to be used,

$\theta < 0.1$ and $n > 50$. See Sec. 12.8. When the Poisson distribution is used, the mean of the Poisson is $\mu = n\theta$. When the normal approximation is used, $\mu = n\theta$ and $\sigma = \sqrt{\theta(1 - \theta)/n}$.

A further caution in the use of the normal approximation to the binomial requires the use of a continuity correction. This correction applies whenever a discrete distribution is approximated by a continuous distribution. Probabilities for a discrete random variable correspond to specific points 1, 2, etc. Probabilities for a continuous random variable correspond to areas under the curve of the probability function between two points. Figure 13.19 illustrates the approximation of a discrete random variable with a continuous function.

To find the exact probability that the discrete random variable X is equal to 1, 2, or 3, the probabilities at $X = 1$, $X = 2$, and $X = 3$ are summed. The bars of the histogram in Fig. 13.19 represent the probabilities, and the area of each bar is proportional to the probability that X is equal to that discrete value.

When a smooth curve is superimposed over the histogram, the probability is represented by an area. It becomes necessary to determine what specific area under the smooth curve should be used to represent the discrete probabilities which are represented by the histogram.

The probability that $X = 2$, for example, is represented by the bar of the histogram centered at the value 2. To be precise, this probability could be shown as a single vertical line at $X = 2$, its height being proportional to the probability. Other vertical lines at 1, 3, etc., would represent the probability that X takes on those values. Since this is a discrete random variable, there is zero probability that X takes on any value between 1 and 2, 2 and 3, and

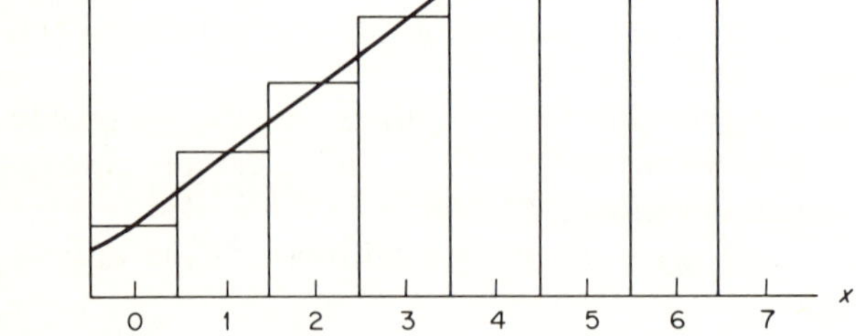

Fig. 13.19

so on. However, to approximate $P(X = 2)$ with the smooth curve, an area between two points is required. These points should lie halfway between the discrete value or values desired and the adjacent value or values.

To approximate $P(X = 2)$ with the smooth curve, the area is required between corresponding values of $X = 1.5$ and $X = 2.5$, in other words, the space occupied by the bar centered at $X = 2$. To approximate the probability that X equals 1, 2, or 3, the approximating area under the smooth curve should run from $X = 0.5$ to $X = 3.5$, corresponding to the area occupied by the three bars on the histogram centered at 1, 2, and 3. This half-unit correction factor is called a *continuity correction* and is required when discrete probabilities are approximated with a continuous curve.

If we can consider the discrete probability distribution as a form of a frequency distribution, then each discrete value is comparable to a class mark, while the class boundaries lie halfway between successive class marks. The discrete probabilities are approximated by areas under a continuous curve between the lower class *boundary* of the lower discrete value up to the upper class *boundary* of the higher discrete value.

When n is greater than or equal to 100, the continuity correction can be ignored with little loss in accuracy.

Example 13.6 A manufacturer of household detergents is presented with a new detergent which is supposedly better than those already on the market. The manufacturer consults with his marketing manager and they decide on a test. Two hundred packages of the new detergent will be distributed to a random sample of housewives in a certain marketing area. After a trial period each housewife will be asked whether she prefers the new detergent to the one she was using previously. The marketing manager believes that more than 30 percent of the housewives who try the new detergent will prefer it. The manufacturer decided that if this proportion is correct, he will market the new detergent. The null hypothesis is established in such a way that to accept H_0 is to maintain the status quo. Therefore

$H_0: \theta \leq 0.30$
$H_a: \theta > 0.30$

It was decided that the significance level of the test should be 1 percent; therefore, the probability of marketing the new detergent if the true proportion of housewives which really preferred the new detergent was less than or equal to 30 percent would only be 0.01.

The results of the sample showed that of the 200 women who tried the new detergent, 74 said they preferred it. This constituted a sample $p = {}^{74}\!/_{200} = 37$ percent. Since the sample size was 200 and the hypothesized value of θ was large enough such that both $n\theta$ and $n(1 - \theta)$ were greater than 5, the normal approximation is appropriate.

The distribution of the sample proportion under the null hypothesis would have a mean of $p = 0.03$ and a standard deviation of

$$\sigma_p = \sqrt{\frac{\theta_0(1 - \theta_0)}{n}} = \sqrt{\frac{(0.03)(0.7)}{200}} = 0.032$$

Therefore the approximating normal distribution should have the parameters $\mu = 0.3$, $\sigma = 0.032$.

In order to determine the probability that 37 percent of the housewives in the sample would prefer the new detergent if the true percentage were actually 30 or less, a comparable value must be defined for the standard normal variate Z. This is

$$z = \frac{p - \theta}{\sigma_p} = \frac{0.37 - 0.30}{0.032} = 2.18$$

Therefore

$$P(p \geq 0.37 | \theta = 0.30) = P(z \geq 2.18) = 0.015$$

Since $0.015 > 0.01$, the significance level of the test, the null hypothesis is accepted and the new detergent is *not* marketed.

13.12 TEST OF THE DIFFERENCE BETWEEN TWO PROPORTIONS

The problem of testing whether there is a significant difference between two sample proportions is similar to that of testing the difference between two means. As with the means, these can be either two-tailed or one-tailed tests. The most usual null hypothesis is, however, the one which states that there is no difference between the proportions or, what is the same thing, that the difference is zero. If we were to test that $H_0: \theta_1 = \theta_2$ versus $H_a: \theta_1 \neq \theta_2$, we would have two sample proportions p_1 and p_2.

If the null hypothesis were true, $\Delta p = p_1 - p_2$ would have a sampling distribution $N(0, \sigma_{\Delta p})$.

Since σ is dependent upon θ, it would first be necessary to estimate the population θ under the assumption that the null hypothesis is true. This is done by taking a weighted average of the sample proportions. Thus

$$\hat{\theta} = \frac{n_1 p_1 + n_2 p_2}{n_1 + n_2}$$

and

$$\sigma_{\Delta p} = \sqrt{\frac{\hat{\theta}(1 - \hat{\theta})}{n_1} + \frac{\hat{\theta}(1 - \hat{\theta})}{n_2}} = \sqrt{\hat{\theta}(1 - \hat{\theta}) + \frac{n_1 + n_2}{n_1 n_2}}$$

Example 13.7 Two large shipments of parts were received by a manufacturer on successive days from the same vendor. Receiving inspection followed a sampling plan that involved sampling 200 parts at random from a shipment and accepting the shipment if there were 10 or fewer defectives in the sample. Otherwise the shipment was rejected and returned to the vendor.*

When shipment 1 was sampled, eight defectives were found constituting a fraction defective $p_1 = x_1/n_1 = 0.04$. Subsequently, a sample drawn from shipment 2 resulted in 12 defectives or $p_2 = x_2/n_2 = 0.06$.

* Single sampling plan (200,10) from Mil-Std-105D. Code letter L, normal inspection.

Since both shipments were received within such a short time and the inspection procedure indicated that one shipment should be rejected and the other accepted, the quality control manager questioned whether the difference in the fraction defective from the two shipments indicated that they came from two different populations of parts each having a different population fraction defective. Consequently, he determined to test whether the difference between p_1 and p_2 was significant at the 5 percent level.

He first established a null hypothesis that there was no significant difference. Thus

$$H_0: \theta_1 = \theta_2$$
$$H_a: \theta_1 \neq \theta_2$$

The sample sizes were both $n = 200$. In order to find $\sigma_{\Delta p}$, the standard error of the difference, it was necessary to estimate the population θ from the two samples.

$$\hat{\theta} = \frac{n_1 p_1 + n_2 p_2}{n_1 + n_2} = \frac{8 + 12}{400} = \frac{20}{400} = 0.5$$

$$\sigma_{\Delta p} = \sqrt{\frac{\hat{\theta}(1 - \hat{\theta})(n_1 + n_2)}{n_1 n_2}} = \sqrt{\frac{(0.05)(0.95)(400)}{40{,}000}}$$

$$= \sqrt{\frac{19}{40{,}000}} = \sqrt{0.00475} = 0.0218$$

The statistic z can be computed from

$$z = \frac{(p_1 - p_2) - (\theta_1 - \theta_2)}{\sigma_{\Delta p}} = \frac{(0.04 - 0.06) - 0}{0.0218}$$

$$= -0.917$$

and the probability that the sample difference could be as great as $\Delta p = p_1 - p_2$ if the null hypothesis were true is equal to

$$P(Z < -0.917) = 0.179$$

Since $0.179 > \alpha = 0.05$, or, what is the same thing,

$$|z| < \frac{z_\alpha}{2}$$

H_0 would be accepted, leading to the conclusion that both shipments came from the same population of parts, and that the difference was due to sampling error.

The critical points on the distribution of Z would be ± 1.96, to which the $Z = -0.917$ obtained from the sample could be compared. Since $-1.96 < -0.917 < +1.96$, the null hypothesis is accepted.

13.13 TESTS OF VARIANCES

The techniques which allow us to test the validity of predetermined or hypothetical values of a mean or proportion can also be applied to variances and standard deviations.

TESTS OF A SINGLE VARIANCE

As noted in the previous chapter, the statistic $(n - 1)s^2/\sigma^2$ computed from random samples taken from a normal population has a χ^2 (chi-square) distribution with $n - 1$ degrees of freedom. Suppose we wish to test the hypothesis

$$H_0 : \sigma^2 = k$$

versus

$$H_a : \sigma^2 \neq k$$

at the α significance level.

A sample of size n is drawn from the population, and $s^2 = \sum (x_i - \bar{x})/(n - 1)$ is computed. The ratio $(n - 1)s^2/\sigma_0{}^2$, which is simply the sum of the squared deviations about the sample mean divided by the value of the variance being tested under the null hypothesis, is found. Two values of χ^2 having the appropriate number of degrees of freedom are determined such that $100(1 - \alpha)\%$ of the area under the curve lies between these two points, designated

$$\chi^2_{\alpha/2,n-1} \qquad \text{and} \qquad \chi^2_{(1-\alpha)/2,n-1}$$

The null hypothesis is accepted if

$$\chi^2_{\alpha/2,n-1} < \frac{(n-1)s^2}{\sigma_0{}^2} < \chi^2_{(1-\alpha)/2,n-1}$$

otherwise it is rejected.

It is usually more common to test the hypothesis that the true variance of a population is less than or equal to some value. In this case the critical point for a significance level of α would be $\chi^2_{(1-\alpha)/2,n-1}$, and the null hypothesis would be accepted if

$$\frac{(n-1)s^2}{\sigma_0{}^2} < \chi^2_{1-\alpha,n-1}$$

Assuming that the null hypothesis to be tested was that the population variance is greater than or equal to some specified value, the acceptance region would correspond to

$$\frac{(n-1)s^2}{\sigma_0{}^2} > \chi^2_{\alpha,n-1}$$

Example 13.8 In Example 12.3 a situation was discussed in which a manufacturer desired to determine the difference in proficiency between graduates of a technical training school and totally inexperienced new hires by means of a proficiency test. It was stated that experience from tests administered previously led to the conclusion that the standard deviation of test scores was fairly constant and equal to 6. This, of course, implies that the population variance is 36.

The personnel manager, who administers the test, had reached this conclusion simply by observing the results of several such tests given previously, but he had never applied a statistical hypothesis test to his assumption. Before making any decision regarding starting wage rates for the two groups of new employees, he decided to test this hypothesis: that is,

$H_0\!:\sigma^2 = 36$

versus

$H_a\!:\sigma^2 \neq 36$

at the $\alpha = 0.05$ significance level. He took a random sample of 25 tests from his files and computed the sample variance, $s^2 = 42$.

In order to define his acceptance and rejection region, he needed the two points $\chi^2_{(0.025)(24)} = 12.4$ and $\chi^2_{(0.975)(24)} = 39.4$. He then computed the statistic

$$\frac{(n-1)s^2}{\sigma^2} = \frac{(24)(42)}{36} = 28$$

Since $12.4 < 28 < 39.4$, he accepts the null hypothesis.

As an alternative, the personnel manager might have wished simply to test the hypothesis that the variance was less than or equal to 36; that is

$H_0\!:\sigma^2 \leq 36$

versus

$H_a\!:\sigma^2 > 36$

In that case, the single critical point would be $\chi^2_{(0.95)(24)} = 36.4$. Since $(n-1)s^2/\sigma^2 = 28 < 36.4$, this hypothesis would be accepted.

TEST OF TWO VARIANCES

There are many cases in statistical inference where an assumption is made that two normal populations have equal variances. This characteristic is called *homoscedasticity*. The homogeneity of two population variances is tested by the F ratio and reference to the F distribution.

The hypotheses to be tested would be

$H_0\!:\sigma_1^2 = \sigma_2^2$

versus

$H_a\!:\sigma_1^2 \neq \sigma_2^2$

and the significance level of the test is α.

The statistic $F = s_1^2/s_2^2$, which is the ratio of the sample variances, is used as the test statistic. If the two normal populations do indeed have equal variances, we would expect the F ratio to be close to 1. If this ratio is larger or smaller than would be expected by chance $100(1-\alpha)\%$ of the time, we would reject the null hypothesis. Otherwise it would be accepted.

Generally, the larger sample variance is put in the numerator of the ratio so that the computed value of F is always greater than or equal to 1. Under these circumstances, the equality hypothesis can always be tested by a one-tailed test as long as it can be assumed that if the null hypothesis is not true, then the larger sample variance will always come from the population having the larger variance.

The F distribution has two parameters, ν_1 and ν_2, corresponding to the number of degrees of freedom associated with each estimate of σ^2, that is, $n_1 - 1$ and $n_2 - 1$. Critical points on the distribution of F corresponding to given significance levels and the appropriate degrees of freedom can be determined from the tables of the F distribution in the same way as for χ^2, t, etc., except that now two parameters must be found.

With the larger sample variance in the numerator, only the upper or right tail of the distribution is required; that is, the rejection region will always be in the right tail. Most tables of F provide only the upper percentage points.

If F is computed with the smaller s^2 in the numerator, and if the available tables provide only the upper percentage points, the corresponding lower percentage point for the given α can be obtained from the reciprocal of F with ν_1 and ν_2 interchanged.

For the test

$$H_0: \sigma_1^2 = \sigma_2^2$$
$$H_a: \sigma_1^2 \neq \sigma_2^2$$

a single critical point would be found corresponding to the desired level of significance, and the decision rule would indicate acceptance of the null hypothesis if

$$F = \frac{s_1^2}{s_2^2} < F_{(1-\alpha)(n_1-1)(n_2-1)}$$

If the previous assumption cannot be made and a two-tailed test is required to test

$$H_0: \sigma_1^2 = \sigma_2^2$$
$$H_a: \sigma_1^2 \neq \sigma_2^2$$

then both upper and lower critical points would be required, and the null hypothesis would be accepted if

$$F_{(\alpha/2)(n_1-1, n_2-1)} < F = \frac{s_1^2}{s_2^2} < F_{(1-\alpha/2)(n_1-1, n_2-1)}$$

Example 13.9 The personnel manager of the previous example has now administered his proficiency test to two groups of new employees, those who had received no previous training and those who were graduates of a technical training school. In addition to the average test score from each group of 25, he also obtained the sample variances which were $s_1^2 = 25$ and $s_2^2 = 49$. In those cases where the true population variances are not known and must be estimated from the sample variances, it is convenient to be able to make the assumption that although σ_1^2 and σ_2^2 are unknown, they are, at least, equal.

He will then test the hypothesis that both sample variances come from populations having equal variances versus the alternative that if the population variances are not equal, $\sigma_2^2 > \sigma_1^2$ since $s_2^2 > s_1^2$. The hypotheses would be

$H_0: \sigma_1^2 = \sigma_2^2$
$H_a: \sigma_1^2 < \sigma_2^2$

This would be an upper-tail test, and the critical value of F would be $F_{\alpha=0.05, \nu_1=24, \nu_2=24}$. From the tables, the critical value is 1.98.

The ratio $s_2^2/s_1^2 = 49/25 = 1.96$ is then computed. Since $1.96 < 1.98$, the null hypothesis would be accepted at the 5 percent level.

13.14 TEST OF GOODNESS OF FIT

Quite frequently a particular statistical technique or mathematical relationship is appropriate only when the random variable of interest has some specific distribution. Most of the tests described in this chapter are based on populations which are normally distributed. Some are based on variables which have a binomial distribution.

In many other instances theoretical probability distributions will be adopted to represent real phenomena which are relevant to a decision process. There should be some method for defining how good such an assumption regarding a distribution really is. One such procedure is the chi-square test for goodness of fit.

The statistic

$$\sum_{i=1}^{m} \frac{(o_i - e_i)^2}{e_i} = \chi^2$$

has an approximate chi-square distribution with $m - 1 - k$ degrees of freedom, where m is the number of groups of observations or cells for which an expected frequency is calculated, k is the number of parameters of the theoretical distribution which had to be estimated, o is the observed frequency in each group or cell (of which there should be at least five), and e is the expected frequency in each group or cell under the assumption that the theoretical distribution applies.

Example 13.10 The field service department of a manufacturer of a widely used industrial product kept accurate records of product failures due to various causes as reported to field offices. The breakage of one particular component part appeared to be the most common cause of failure.

A company statistician decided to test whether the breakage of this particular part could be modeled with a Poisson distribution. He first took a sample from failure reports for the previous 200 days and computed the average number of daily failures of the part to be $\mu = 3$. He then counted the frequency of daily occurrences of 0, 1, 2, 3, . . . failures of the part and listed them as shown in Table 13.4.

Table 13.4

Number of days with X failures	*Observed frequency of X failures*		*Expected frequency of X failures*	
0	6		9.96	
1	32		29.88	
2	48		44.80	
3	52		44.80	
4	25		33.60	
5	14		20.16	
6	9		10.08	
7	4	} 14	4.32	} 6.70
8	3		1.62	
9	4		0.54	
10	3		0.22	

The expected frequencies were computed from Poisson probabilities with an assumed $\mu = 3, 0, 1, 2, 3, \ldots$ failures, multiplying each probability by 200, the sample size. Since the statistic $\chi^2 = \sum (o - e)^2/e$, a very small value of the expected frequency would lead to very large values of chi square, not because of the departure of the observed values from the expected values, but simply because of the smallness of the expected frequency. Consequently, the expected frequency in any cell should not be less than 5. When smaller expected frequencies are encountered, cells should be combined, as in Table 13.5, which also shows the calculations of χ^2.

The difference between the observed and the expected frequencies are computed in column 4, squared in column 5, and divided by the expected frequencies in column 6. The sum of these entries in column 6 is the statistic $\chi^2 =$ 15.26.

This value of χ^2 computed from the data is compared with an appropriate percentage point on the chi-square distribution. If we want to reject the hypothesis of a Poisson distribution such that $\alpha = 0.01$, we would look up the chi-

Table 13.5

(1) X	(2) o_i	(3) e_i	(4) $o_i - e_i$	(5) $(o_i - e_i)^2$	(6) $(o_i - e_i)^2/e_i$
0	6	9.96	−3.96	15.68	1.57
1	32	29.88	2.12	4.49	0.15
2	48	44.80	3.20	10.24	0.23
3	52	44.80	7.20	51.84	1.16
4	25	33.60	−.60	73.96	2.20
5	14	20.16	−6.16	37.95	1.88
6	9	10.06	−1.08	1.17	0.12
7 or more	14	6.70	7.30	53.29	7.95
					15.26

Table 13.6

(1) X	(2) o_i	(3) e_i	(4) $o_i - e_i$	(5) $(o_i - e_i)^2$	(6) $(o_i - e_i)^2/e_i$
0	6	9.0	−3.0	9.00	1.00
1	32	28.0	4.0	16.00	0.57
2	48	43.2	4.8	23.04	0.53
3	52	44.8	7.2	51.84	1.16
4	25	34.6	−9.6	92.16	2.66
5	14	21.4	−7.4	54.76	2.56
6	9	11.2	−2.2	4.84	0.43
7 or more	14	7.8	6.2	38.44	4.92
					13.83

square value corresponding to $1 - \alpha = \gamma = 0.99$. The degrees of freedom would be $m - 1 - k$, or, since there are seven cells and one parameter was estimated from the data, we have $7 - 1 - 1 = 5$ degrees of freedom. $\chi^2_{0.01,5} = 15.1$; therefore, we reject the hypothesis of a Poisson distribution since $15.26 > 15.10$.

Suppose, however, the statistician discovered a great deal of additional data on breakage of that particular part which indicated that the true average number of part breakages per day was 3.1 instead of 3.0. If this could be assumed to be a known parameter, since it is based on a large amount of data, then the expected frequencies would be somewhat different.

The statistician computed a new chi-square value based on the same data but using a mean of 3.1 as the true population parameter and derived the data given in Table 13.6.

The new value of the chi-square statistic from the data is $\chi^2 = 13.83$. Degrees of freedom would now be simply $7 - 1 - 0 = 6$, since *no* parameters were estimated from the data leading to the chi-square value. The critical value $\chi^2_{0.01,6} = 16.80$. Since $13.83 < 16.80$, we would accept the hypothesis that the breakage frequency has a Poisson distribution.

13.15 STATISTICAL ESTIMATION VERSUS HYPOTHESIS TESTING IN DECISION SITUATIONS

In the decision context the decision maker is concerned about the state of the various components which bear upon the state of the overall decision model. Whether the component state is good or bad in turn is dependent upon the value or values of some pertinent parameter or parameters of that component. Evidence relating to the value of the pertinent parameter can be obtained through a process of sampling from the population to which the decision component relates. This process of sampling and of obtaining information about an unknown population can be called *experimentation.*

Every decision component has a parameter or parameters which are pertinent to the decision process. Although at the outset the parameter value is unknown, there is some range of values such that if the parameter is included within this range the component state can be considered to be *good*. If the parameter is not included in this range, then the component state is considered to be *bad*.

In references to some previous examples it was suggested that pertinent parameters of components of two different decision systems might be, in one case, the mean lifetime of a traveling wave tube and, in the second case, the average income of residents of a particular marketing area.

The population to which the mean lifetime of the traveling wave tube relates would be the population of all traveling wave tubes of that type which either exist or might be manufactured. In that sense we are referring to an infinite population. The mean income parameter relates to the population of individuals or families residing in some particular geographical area. This latter population is certainly finite, although it could be quite large.

Information about the state of the decision component can be obtained at some cost, by experimentation or by sampling. Information obtained by this manner will enable the decision maker to reach some conclusion about the component state. However, sampling information is never perfect. Unless the sample includes the entire population (an impossibility for infinite populations), there is always some error inherent in sampling information. Even for 100 percent samples, there is generally some amount of measurement or observational error included in the results. So, although an experiment is conducted and conclusions are reached as a result, there is some probability that a good component will be called bad or that a bad component will be called good.

In probability models of decision systems an attempt is made to avoid calling a component good or bad. It is preferable to recognize that such an evaluation is less useful than an estimate of the probability that the component is in a good state or a bad state. In the logical model, components were assessed as either good or bad, and the overall system state was determined to be good or bad as a consequence. In the probability model *each component* is evaluated as to its probability of being in a good state, and the probability that *the system* is in a good state can then be determined.

In evaluating state probabilities, we are led to the acquisition of information about parameter values through sampling or experimentation. In this and the previous chapter we have considered two procedures for utilizing this information, the first being statistical estimation and the second being hypothesis testing. Which, if either, method is preferable in any given decision situation?

In hypothesis testing we partition the sample space of the experiment into an acceptance region and a rejection region. The acceptance region of the test is determined by finding a portion of the sample space defined by a critical point or points such that if the component is in the good state, that is, the pertinent parameter lies within an acceptable range of values, then the probability that the sample statistic will fall within the acceptance region is $\gamma = 1 - \alpha$, where α is the significance level of the test.

For example, suppose that the pertinent parameter was the mean of a normally distributed variable. The good state has been defined as that set of values $x_i \geq x_0$ such that if $\mu \geq x_0$, the component state is good; otherwise it is bad.

We would set up a hypothesis

$$H_0\!:\mu \geq x_0$$

versus

$$H_a\!:\mu < x_0$$

and test it with the statistic $\bar{x}$ from a sample of size n. We would decide in advance the significance level of the test designated α, which is also the probability of making a type-1 error. We would later partition the sample space of the experiment such that

$$P(\bar{x} < x_0 - k_\alpha \sigma_{\bar{x}} | \mu \geq x_0) \leq \alpha$$

where

$$x_0 - k_\alpha \sigma_{\bar{x}} = x_c$$

Note that this is a one-tailed test and the critical point is determined beforehand by the value x_0.

The hypothesis testing procedure has certain desirable qualities. First, it enables us to specify in advance of the test a parameter value or a range of parameter values which corresponds to the good state. Second, it allows us to establish, again in advance, the acceptable magnitude of the risk of either one or even both types of errors. Finally, having made these specifications, it provides the decision maker with his exact decision, that is, to accept the hypothesis that the state is good or reject.

The values α and β are the conditional probabilities of, in the first case, calling the component state bad when it is good, and, in the second case, calling the component state good when it is bad. What is not provided by this procedure, although it is easy to obtain, is the probability, based on the sample evidence, that the component state is indeed good or bad.

The alternate procedure is that of estimating the value of the parameter directly from the sample values. Suppose we want a probability equal to γ that some interval x_L, ∞ includes μ. We would take a sample of size n, compute the statistic $\bar{x}$, and define an interval based on the value of $\bar{x}$ such that

$$P(\bar{x} - k\sigma_{\bar{x}} < \mu) \geq \gamma$$

where

$$x_L = \bar{x} - k\sigma_{\bar{x}}$$

Now what is the relationship between x_c, μ, $\bar{x}$, x_0, and x_L? If we assume in this instance that the good state of the decision component corresponds to a parameter value greater than x_0 (in other situations, the good state could correspond to a parameter value less than x_0 or even between two values x_0 and x_1), then x_0 corresponds to the limit on parameter values in the good state. For hypothesis testing, $\mu_0 = x_0$. $\bar{x}$ is a random variable resulting from the sampling process. Since it is a random variable, it can take on any value, but the probability that $\bar{x}$ is equal to any value or falls within some range of values depends upon the true but unknown value of μ.

x_c is a critical point on the sample space of the experiment computed from the value x_0. That is, $x_c = x_0 - k_\alpha\sigma_{\bar{x}}$. x_L is the lower confidence limit on μ corresponding to $\gamma = 1 - \alpha$, computed from $\bar{x}$. That is, $x_L = \bar{x} - k_\alpha\sigma_{\bar{x}}$. Now if $\bar{x}$ happens to equal x_0, then $x_L = x_c$. However, it is not likely that $\bar{x} = x_0$. Suppose $\bar{x} < x_0$. The relationship between these various qualities is shown in Fig. 13.20.

The lower one-sided 100γ percent confidence limit on μ is x_L. We would infer from the sample value $\bar{x}$ that $P(x_L < \mu|\bar{x}) = \gamma$. In other words, we have confidence equal to γ that the population parameter is greater than the value x_L. However, this is not what we want. In order for the component to be in the state *good*, it is necessary that the mean be greater than or equal to x_0, not x_L. The confidence interval based on $\bar{x}$ does not provide the necessary information, that is, the probability that the state of the component is indeed good, which is $P(x_0 \leq \mu|\bar{x})$. However, it is quite simple to determine this probability.

Obviously, then, neither the traditional test of hypothesis nor the estimation procedure automatically provides the information desired, which is the probability that the decision component is in the good state. How-

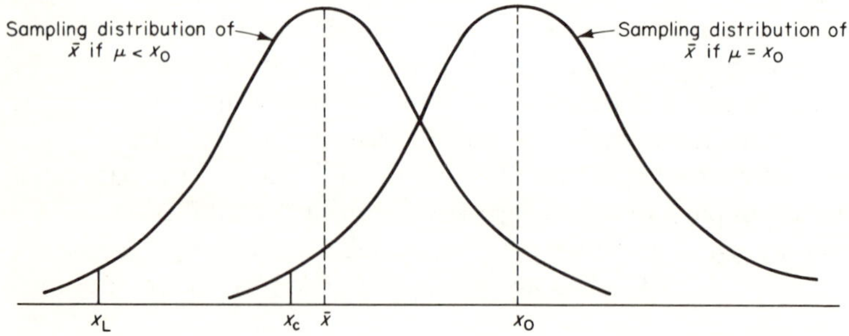

Fig. 13.20

ever, for any value of $\bar{x}$ computed from a sample of size n, this probability can be determined since

$$P(x_0 \leq \mu|\bar{x}) = P(\bar{x} \leq x_0 - k\sigma_{\bar{x}}|\mu = x_0) = P\left(\left|\frac{\bar{x} - \mu}{\sigma_{\bar{x}}}\right| \leq k|\mu = x_0\right)$$

13.16 SUMMARY

Various techniques for testing hypotheses about the value of population parameters have been discussed. In general, the procedure of hypothesis testing is similar to the process of confidence interval estimation. Both techniques involve sampling, the selection of a statistic either for use as an estimator or as a test value, some knowledge about the sampling distribution of the statistic, and the computation of certain limiting values or critical points. The confidence coefficient γ in interval estimation is related to the significance level of the test called α such that $\alpha = 1 - \gamma$.

Whereas a confidence interval estimate is computed directly from the sample statistic, the acceptance and critical areas of the test are based on the hypothetical value of the pertinent parameter.

The classical hypothesis testing procedure is frequently referred to as statistical decision making, since the result of such a test leads to a decision either to accept or to reject the null hypothesis. A decision rule is formulated, and it then becomes possible to determine the risk of making an error of either the first or a second kind. These risks and the magnitude of the risk referred to as α and β are important factors in choosing a decision rule.

The classical hypothesis testing procedure does not, however, directly provide a measure of the probability that a given decision component or the parameter of that component is in the good state. This probability, which is necessary in order to evaluate the probability decision model can, however, be determined from the sample result.

In addition to tests about parameters, a test for goodness of fit was also described. This provides a method for determining whether an assumed probability distribution is a suitable model for the particular phenomenon of interest.

PROBLEMS

13.1. On the basis of extensive testing, the Bright Light Bulb Company believes that the life of its bulbs has a normal distribution with a mean life of 400 hr. The standard deviation of the population is 40 hr. In a recent life test of a sample of 100 light bulbs, the average life was computed to be 390 hr.

(*a*) Is this result consistent with the assumption that the population from which the sample was drawn has a mean of 400 hr at $\alpha = 0.05$?

(*b*) Is this result consistent with the assumption that the population from which the sample was drawn has a mean of 400 hr at $\alpha = 0.01$?

(c) Is this result consistent with the assumption that the population from which the sample was drawn has a mean greater than 400 hr at $\alpha = 0.05$?

(d) Is this result consistent with the assumption that the population from which the sample was drawn has a mean greater than 400 hr at $\alpha = 0.01$? Explain your answers.

13.2. Answer the same questions in Prob. 13.1 using the same data except that the size of the sample is now 16 instead of 100.

13.3. Suppose in Prob. 13.2 that the population standard deviation was not known but that the sample standard deviation was 40 hr. Answer the same questions.

13.4. A manufacturer buys a particular part from a vendor in very large lots. There is a critical diameter which must be controlled in order for the part to fit another assembly. A sample of size 25 is taken, and the diameters are measured. The sample average is $\bar{x} = 3.518$ in. The sample standard deviation is $s = 0.035$ in. The manufacturer wants to test the hypothesis that the true average diameter of the population of parts is exactly 3.5 in. at a significance level of 5 percent.

(a) What is the null hypothesis?
(b) What is the alternate hypothesis?
(c) What are the critical values of $\bar{x}$?
(d) State the decision rule for this test.

13.5. For the data of Prob. 13.4 what is the size of β, the type-2 error, if

(a) The population mean $\mu = 3.510$ in.
(b) The population mean $\mu = 3.504$ in.?
(c) The population mean $\mu = 3.3498$ in.?

13.6. Suppose the manufacturer in Prob. 13.4 takes an additional sample of 100 units. The mean of the second sample $\bar{x} = 3.504$ in. and the standard deviation $s = 0.032$ in. Using the results of sample 2 only, he tests the same hypothesis at $\alpha = 0.01$.

(a) What are the critical values of $\bar{x}$?
(b) State the decision rule for this test.
(c) Is the null hypothesis accepted or rejected?

13.7. Considering the data in Probs. 13.4 and 13.6, the manufacturer now wants to test whether the two sample means obtained could have come from the same population.

(a) State the null hypothesis.
(b) What test statistic is used?
(c) The standard error of the test statistic has what value?
(d) State the decision rule for this test.
(e) Is the null hypothesis accepted or rejected?

13.8. In testing a hypothesis about the unknown mean of a normal population with a known standard deviation of $\sigma = 30$, a sample of size 25 is to be taken. The null hypothesis states that $\mu = 115$. The alternate hypothesis states that $\mu = 100$. The decision rule for this test states

Accept H_0 if $\bar{x} \geq 108$
Reject H_0 if $\bar{x} < 108$

(a) What is α, the probability of a type-1 error under this decision rule?
(b) What is β, the probability of a type-2 error under this decision rule?
(c) What size sample would be required to test this hypothesis if it were specified that $\alpha = 0.02$ and $\beta = 0.04$?

13.9. In testing the hypothesis at $\alpha = 0.02$ that the true proportion defective produced by a particular continuous manufacturing process is less than 10 percent, a random sample of 225 units was inspected resulting in 32 defective parts.

(a) State the null and alternate hypotheses for this test.

(*b*) State the decision rule for this test.
(*c*) What is the critical value of p, the sample proportion?
(*d*) Is the null hypothesis accepted or rejected?

13.10. In order to test the effectiveness of an advertising campaign, the Roadway Tire Company had its market research department take random samples of licensed drivers prior to the campaign and asked them to name the best-known brand of tires that they could think of. Out of the first sample of size 80, 12 people mentioned Roadway. After the campaign a second sample of 120 was taken and Roadway was mentioned by 24 persons. Did the advertising campaign have any effect on consumer recognition of the Roadway brand name?
(*a*) at the 5 percent significance level?
(*b*) at the 1 percent significance level?
(*c*) How should the null and alternate hypotheses have been stated?

13.11. Referring to Prob. 13.3, test the hypothesis that the population variance is equal to 40 hr at the 5 percent level of significance.

13.12. Referring to Prob. 13.3, test the hypothesis that the population variance is less than 40 hr at the 1 percent level of significance.

13.13. Suppose in Prob. 13.4 that the sample standard deviation $s = 0.035$ in. had come from a sample of size 25, while in Prob. 13.6 the sample standard deviation $s = 0.032$ in. had come from a sample of size 30. Test the hypothesis that both samples came from populations having the same variance at both the 1 and 5 percent significance levels.

13.14. To determine whether the number of mistakes made by a typist per page of material follows a Poisson distribution, a random sample of 100 typewritten pages was selected from the output of a typing pool. The number of mistakes per page and the number of pages with that number of mistakes were:

No. of mistakes	*No. of pages*
0	7
1	14
2	36
3	24
4	12
5	7
	100

The average number of mistakes per page was estimated from the data. The significance level of the test is $\alpha = 0.05$.
(*a*) State the null hypothesis.
(*b*) What are the expected frequencies?
(*c*) What is the value of χ^2 from the data?
(*d*) How many degrees of freedom does this χ^2 have?
(*e*) What is the critical value of χ^2 for this test?
(*f*) Is the null hypothesis accepted or rejected?

14
Correlation and Regression

We have been considering statistical techniques for analyzing data and for evaluating the probability state of the components of the decision system. Inferences regarding the states of these components based on sample information have been made either by utilizing an estimation procedure or by testing a hypothesis about the state of the component, or more precisely, about the value of the pertinent parameter of that component.

In order to use either of these two techniques, it must be possible to observe directly some elements of the population which the decision components represent. There are, however, instances where it is either not possible or not practical to observe elements of the population of interest at the time the data are required. When this situation occurs, it becomes necessary to find some method of predicting this component state which does not involve direct observation of the population of interest.

In all aspects of business and industry there are numerous cases of relationships between factors or variables. The price of a product and the demand for that product are one example. Most marketers know that, within certain limits and under certain circumstances, the higher the price of the product, the smaller the demand. Under conditions which are applicable, it is possible to draw a curve showing this relationship such that for a specified price, the demand in units can be predicted. In industry, before spending money on training a new employee for a particular job, the new employee is usually given an aptitude test under the assumption that there will be a relationship between his test performance and his ability to do the job satisfactorily.

The analytical technique which attempts to determine and describe the relationship between two or more variables is called *regression analysis.* However, before a relationship can be described, it is necessary that a relationship exist. Those techniques used to determine whether or not a relationship exists between two or more variables is called *correlation analysis.*

Correlation and regression analyses are called *simple* correlation and regression if only two variables are involved. If more than two variables are involved, then the analysis is referred to as *multiple* correlation and/or regression. Furthermore, if the relationship between the variables can be described by a straight line, then it is called a *linear* regression. If the relationship can be described only by a curve other than a straight line, it is called *curvilinear* regression.

We shall consider both simple and multiple correlation and regression but will limit ourselves to linear regression analysis.

14.1 SIMPLE CORRELATION

SCATTER DIAGRAMS

Correlation deals with the problem of measuring the closeness of the relationship between two variables. In beginning any correlation analysis, a simple method of estimating whether or not a relationship exists is to construct a chart called a scatter diagram.

A *scatter diagram* is simply a chart in which all pairs of values of the two variables are plotted. For example, let us consider two variables which we shall simply label variable X and variable Y. Every paired X and Y value can be plotted on a chart on which the horizontal axis represents the X values and the vertical axis represents the Y values. Suppose we have the following 10 pairs of X, Y values:

Pair no.	1	2	3	4	5	6	7	8	9	10
X	8	7	9	1	11	1	4	8	2	6
Y	4	4	10	0	9	2	4	9	6	5

Each pair is represented by a point on Fig. 14.1.

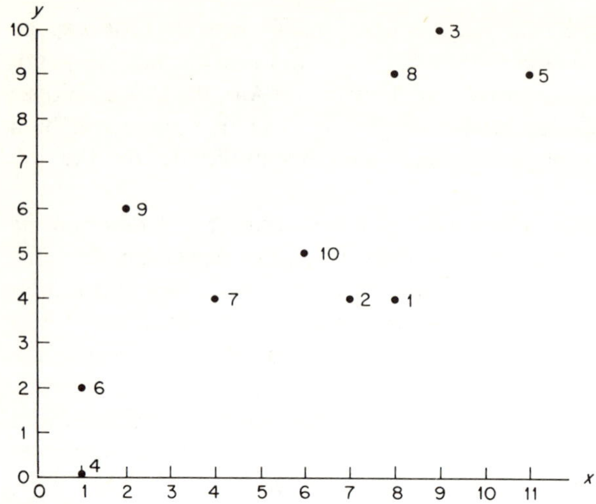

Fig. 14.1

It would appear from the diagram that there is some relationship between the X and the Y values. At least in the diagram in Fig. 14.1, large values of X generally appear to be associated with large values of Y, and small values of X appear to be associated with small values of Y. If this relationship could be represented by a straight line, that line would slope upward from the lower left-hand corner of the chart to the upper right. When a relationship exists such that large values of one variable are associated with large values of the other and vice versa, then they are said to be *positively* correlated.

Now consider another set of X, Y pairs.

Pair no.	1	2	3	4	5	6	7	8	9	10
X	7	10	6	9	4	5	0	1	1	3
Y	0	3	7	1	8	6	9	8	10	7

These values are plotted in Fig. 14.2.

Once again a relationship between X and Y seems apparent. However, from the scatter diagram in Fig. 14.2, it appears that large values of X are associated with small values of Y, and large values of Y with small values of X. This type of relationship is called *negative* correlation. It would also appear from Fig. 14.2 that the relationship between X and Y in this case is *linear*, that is, it could be approximated by a straight line.

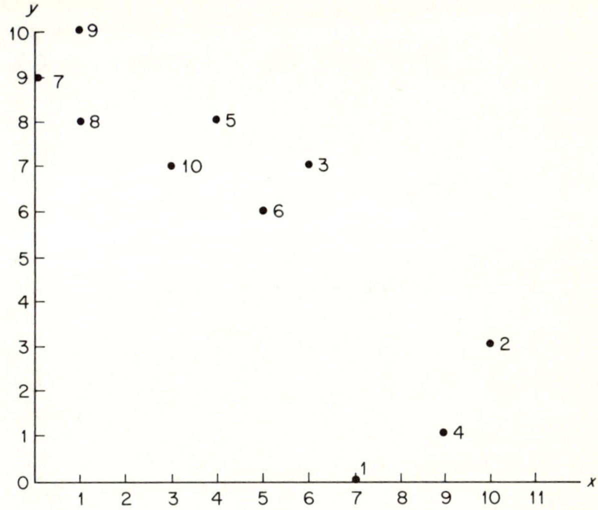

Fig. 14.2

Consider still another set of X and Y values.

Pair no.	1	2	3	4	5	6	7	8	9	10
X	4	3	0	8	1	10	4	9	7	6
Y	1	7	9	9	10	2	4	5	3	9

This third set of values is plotted in Fig. 14.3.

This set of points appears to be scattered fairly randomly across the chart. Although scatter diagrams alone are not conclusive evidence of the existence or nonexistence of a relationship between two variables, a pattern such as displayed in Fig. 14.3 would tend to indicate the absence of any relationship between the variables X and Y, and certainly would indicate the lack of a linear relationship.

Let us consider one last case. The points below are plotted in Fig. 14.4.

Pair no.	1	2	3	4	5	6	7	8	9
X	-4	-4	-2	-1	0	1	2	3	4
Y	16	9	4	1	0	1	4	9	16

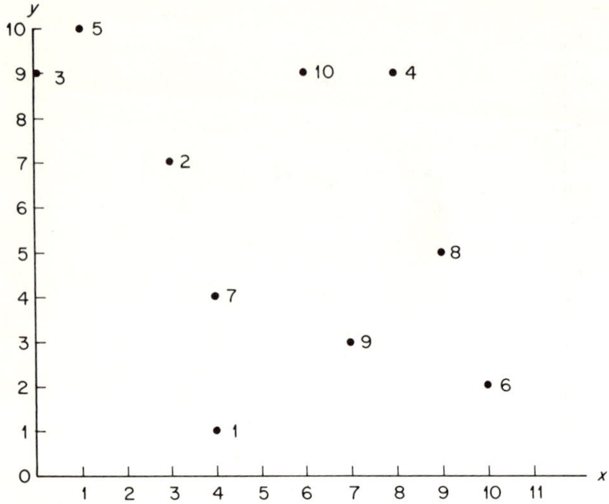

Fig. 14.3

Although the relationship between these two variables X and Y is obviously not linear, a relationship does indeed exist. In fact, this scatter diagram shows that the two variables are perfectly correlated. The relationship is, however, curvilinear, and can be represented by the equation $Y = X^2$.

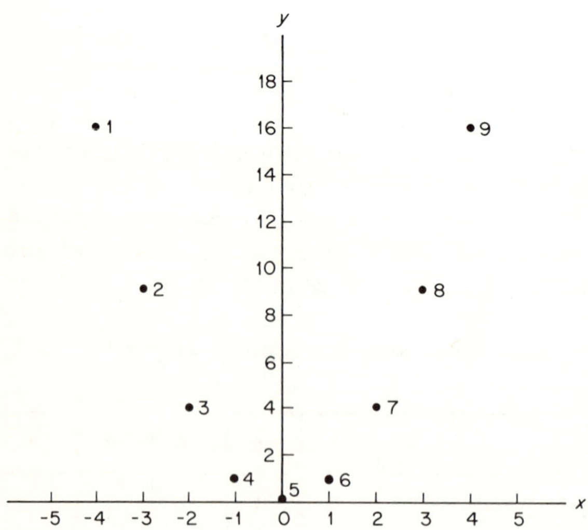

Fig. 14.4

THE CORRELATION COEFFICIENT

A measure of the strength of the relationship between two variables is called the *correlation coefficient*. Theoretically, there is a true correlation coefficient between any population of X values and any population of Y values. If all members of each population could be observed and paired, this true coefficient of correlation, designated ρ, could be determined.

The linear correlation coefficient can be defined in terms of a value which is called the *covariance* and is equal to

$$\frac{\sum_i (x_i - \mu_X)(y_i - \mu_Y)}{N}$$

where μ_X and μ_Y represent the means of the X and Y populations, respectively.

The linear correlation coefficient is simply the covariance divided by $\sigma_X\sigma_Y$, or

$$\rho = \frac{\text{cov}}{\sigma_X\sigma_Y} = \frac{\sum_i (x_i - \mu_X)(y_i - \mu_Y)}{N\sigma_X\sigma_Y}$$

Since

$$\sigma_X = \sqrt{\frac{\sum (x - \mu_X)^2}{N}}$$

and

$$\sigma_Y = \sqrt{\frac{\sum (y - \mu_Y)^2}{N}}$$

then

$$\rho = \frac{\sum (x_i - \mu_X)(y_i - \mu_Y)}{\sqrt{[\sum (x - \mu_X)^2][\sum (y - \mu_Y)^2]}} \tag{14.1}$$

Since the decision maker seldom deals with total populations of anything, estimates of the population must be made from sample data. If paired X and Y values are drawn from the X and Y populations, the sample coefficient of linear correlation can be obtained from

$$r = \frac{\sum (x_i - \bar{x})(y_i - \bar{y})}{\sqrt{[\sum (x - \bar{x})^2][\sum (y - \bar{y})^2]}} \tag{14.2}$$

A more convenient form for calculating the value of r from sample data is

$$r = \frac{n \sum xy - \sum x \sum y}{\sqrt{[n \sum x^2 - (\sum x)^2][n \sum y^2 - (\sum y)^2]}} \tag{14.3}$$

It can easily be seen that the coefficient of correlation must have a value between $+1$ and -1; that is, $-1 \leq r \leq +1$, where -1 represents a

Table 14.1

X	Y	XY	X^2	Y^2
7	0	0	49	0
10	3	30	100	9
6	7	42	36	49
9	1	9	81	1
4	8	32	36	64
5	6	30	25	36
0	9	0	0	81
1	8	8	1	64
1	10	10	1	100
3	7	21	9	49
$\sum x = 46$	$\sum y = 59$	$\sum xy = 182$	$\sum x^2 = 338$	$\sum y^2 = 453$

perfect negative linear relationship and $+1$ represents a perfect positive linear relationship. A value of $r = 0$ indicates that there is no linear relationship between the two variables.

Example 14.1 Let us refer to the set of XY values which we plotted in Fig. 14.2. The individual X and Y values will be reproduced in the first two columns of Table 14.1, while the additional columns will record other values required to evaluate the correlation coefficient.

Substituting these values in Eq. (14.2), we get

$$r = \frac{(10)(182) - (46)(59)}{\sqrt{[(10)(338) - (46)^2][(10)(453) - (59)^2]}}$$

$$= \frac{-894}{\sqrt{(1{,}264)(1{,}049)}} = -\frac{894}{1{,}151.5}$$

$$= -0.766$$

The sign on r is negative, which is appropriate since in the set of data given, high values of X were associated with low values of Y, and vice versa.

Since r is computed from sample data, inferences about the true value of ρ, the population correlation, must be made with caution. Inferences about ρ will be discussed in the following section.

14.2 STATISTICAL INFERENCE ABOUT THE CORRELATION COEFFICIENT

Hypotheses about the value of ρ can be tested utilizing r, the value of the correlation coefficient computed from the sample data. The procedure is similar to all other hypothesis tests discussed in the previous chapter.

In order to test any hypothesis, the sampling distribution of the test statistic must be used. In this case the test statistic r does not follow any of the commonly known and tabulated distributions. There are, however, simple transformations which result in statistics which do have common sampling distributions.

THE t TRANSFORMATION

To test the hypothesis $H_0: \rho = 0$ versus $H_a: \rho \neq 0$, the following transformation is used:

$$t = \frac{r\sqrt{n-2}}{\sqrt{1-r^2}}$$

The statistic t has the Student's t distribution with $n - 2$ degrees of freedom. The significant values of t can be determined from tables of Student's t distribution, and H_0 is rejected if $t \geq t_{(\alpha, n-2)}$ or if $t \leq -t_{(\alpha, n-2)}$.

Example 14.2 In the previous example 10 pairs of sample values of the variables of X and Y were subjected to a correlation analysis resulting in $r = -0.766$. It is desired to test whether a value of r that deviates from zero by that amount could have occurred by chance with a probability greater than 0.05 if the true population correlation coefficient were equal to zero. Specifically, test

$H_0: \rho = 0$

versus

$H_a: \rho \neq 0$

at $\alpha = 0.05$.

$$t = \frac{r\sqrt{n-2}}{\sqrt{1-r^2}} = \frac{(-0.776)(2.83)}{0.63} = -3.48$$

The significant values of t for $\alpha = 0.05$ and $n - 2 = 8$ degrees of freedom are -2.306 and $+2.306$; therefore, the null hypothesis is rejected, and a significant relationship between the variables X and Y is implied at $\alpha = 0.05$.

THE z TRANSFORMATION

In testing the hypothesis $H_0: \rho = \rho_0$ versus $H_a: \rho \neq \rho_0$ where $\rho_0 \neq 0$, the previous test is not valid since $(r\sqrt{n-2})/(\sqrt{1-r^2})$ does not have the Student's t distribution *unless* $\rho_0 = 0$.

There is another transformation available which converts r into a value z from the relationship

$$z_r = \tfrac{1}{2} \ln \frac{1+r}{1-r} \tag{14.4}$$

Tables are available which present

$z_r = f(r)$

and eliminate the need for evaluating Eq. (14.4).

z_r is approximately normally distributed with mean z_{ρ_0}, that is, with a mean equal to the z value corresponding to the value of ρ under the null hypothesis, and with a variance $\sigma_z = 1/(\sqrt{n-3})$.

For testing the hypothesis about ρ, we convert r to z_r and compute the value of the standard normal variate from $z = (z_r - z_{\rho_0})/\sigma_z$.

Critical points corresponding to a significance level of α can be found for the standard normal distribution, and the null hypothesis is rejected if $Z \geq z_{\alpha/2}$ or if $Z \leq -z_{\alpha/2}$.

Example 14.3 In the previous example we found that a coefficient of linear correlation $r = -0.776$ was significant at the 5 percent level when derived from a sample of size 10. Suppose that we now want to test whether the true value of the linear coefficient of correlation is less than or equal to -0.5. Specifically, we shall test:

$H_0: \rho \leq -0.5$

versus

$H_a: \rho > -0.5$

at $\alpha = 0.05$.

Since $\rho_0 \neq 0$, the t transformation cannot be used. Instead we shall use the z transformation. For $r = -0.776$, $z_r = -1.035$.

Now z_r is approximately normally distributed with a mean, if H_0 is true, of $z_{\rho_0} = z_{(-0.5)} = -0.549$, and $\sigma_z = 1/\sqrt{n-3} = 1/2.65 = 0.377$.

The standard normal variate

$$z = \frac{z_r - z_{\rho_0}}{\sigma_z} = \frac{-1.035 + 0.549}{0.377} = \frac{-0.486}{0.377}$$

$$= -1.29$$

The significant value of z for $\alpha = 0.05$ is 1.645. Since $z = -1.29 < 1.645$, we would accept the null hypothesis that $\rho \leq -0.5$.

14.3 SIMPLE LINEAR REGRESSION

Suppose we have a large basket full of envelopes, each envelope containing a slip of paper with a number on it. We shall consider this entire set of numbered slips as a population of Y values. Let us further suppose that we have agreed to play a game with an opponent in which the opponent will reach into the basket and select an envelope at random. We shall be asked to predict the value of the number inside that envelope and shall be rewarded in proportion to the closeness of our prediction to the actual value.

In order to help us in this prediction, we shall be allowed to select 10 envelopes at random from the basket prior to the one on which we must make the prediction and observe their values.

Since our required prediction will be of a single value of Y, it will constitute a point estimate. The parameter which we shall attempt to estimate is the expected value of a random draw. From what we know of expected values, $E(Y) = \mu_Y$, and the best point estimate of μ_Y would be $\bar{y}$

from a sample. Since we are allowed to take a sample from the population before making our prediction, the logical procedure would be to compute $\bar{y}$ from the sample and use this as our estimate or prediction of $E(Y)$. How good this prediction or point estimate will turn out to be will depend upon the variability of the population which can be represented by

$$\sigma_Y = \sqrt{\frac{\sum (y - \mu_Y)^2}{N}}$$

For example, if there was zero variability in the population, that is, all the Y values were exactly the same, then the prediction based on $\bar{y}$ would always be exactly right. If all the Y values were either 1, 2, or 3, then the prediction could never be in error by more than two units. On the other hand, if the Y values varied greatly, the expected error would depend upon the magnitude of the variability in the Y population.

Now suppose that on the back of every envelope a second number was written. The entire set of numbers marked on the envelopes will constitute a population of X values. In taking our sample from the Y population, we shall also be allowed to observe the corresponding values of X. Furthermore, when our opponent selects the envelope for which we must predict the Y value, we shall be allowed to see the X value on the envelope before making our prediction.

Now if there is some relationship between X values on the envelopes and the Y values inside the envelopes, and if we could determine the nature of that relationship, then our observation of the X values marked on the envelope selected by our opponent in the game would help us in predicting the Y value inside. If there were absolutely no relationship whatsoever, then our "best" estimate of the Y value would simply be $\bar{y}$ from the sample.

Since we are allowed to take a random sample of 10 envelopes from the basket prior to making our prediction, we can use the sample values to determine whether a relationship exists and, if so, to define that relationship. Let us assume that the pairs of values resulting from this sample were the ones plotted in Fig. 14.2 and used in the previous example. The scatter diagram tended to indicate a linear relationship between the two variables, and the sample correlation coefficient was computed to be $r = -0.776$. We have also tested and rejected the hypothesis that a value of $r = -0.776$ from a sample of size 10 could have come from a population for which $\rho = 0$. Having established to our own satisfaction that a relationship exists, our next step is to define the relationship between the two variables, that is, to determine the *regression equation.*

DEPENDENT AND INDEPENDENT VARIABLES

In estimating the degree of the relationship between two variables in correlation analysis, no inferences can be made regarding causation. That is, although two variables appear to be related, no conclusion can be drawn which establishes whether one of the variables actually causes the values observed on the second variable. Correlation simply measures the apparent degree of association between the two variables and does not imply that a cause-and-effect relationship exists. Furthermore, in a simple correlation analysis, neither variable can be labeled as being the dependent variable or the independent variable.

In regression analysis, however, the purpose is to predict the value of one variable on the basis of its relationship to the second variable. In regression, therefore, the variable to be predicted is called the *dependent* variable, while the variable upon which the prediction is based is called the *independent* variable.

The same caution, however, must again be specified. Even the predictive procedure of regression analysis does not imply causation.

In simple regression analysis we shall generally label the dependent variable Y and the independent variable X.

THE REGRESSION LINE

Let us continue to use as an example the data plotted in the scatter diagram shown in Fig. 14.2. In order to predict a value of X, the relationship between the two variables must be established. Since we are limiting ourselves to cases of linear regression only, a linear relationship can be described by using the equation of the line, that is, $Y = a + bX$, where the constant a represents the value of Y when X is equal to zero, called the Y intercept, and the coefficient b represents the change in Y for a unit change in X which is the slope of the line. From the scatter diagram in Fig. 14.2, it would appear that such an equation should describe the relationship between the X and Y values adequately.

It should be apparent, however, that an entire family of lines could be drawn to fit the points on the scatter diagram. Frequently a line could be plotted to the points simply by visual examination of the diagram, and the equation of the line obtained directly from the graph. The drawback to this procedure is that probably no two individuals would fit the same line to the same set of data. In order to have an objective procedure which will result in the same line from a given set of data regardless of who does the analysis, a criterion has been adopted for determining the equation of the "best" line to fit any set of data. This line is called the *least-squares line*.

THE LEAST-SQUARES REGRESSION LINE

The least-squares line has the property that it minimizes the sum of the squared vertical distances between the observed values and the line. If we let y be the observed value of the dependent random variable for a given value of the independent random variable and y_c be the point on the regression line corresponding to the same value of the independent variable, then for the least-squares line $\sum (y - y_c)^2$ = minimum.

From a given set of data the least-squares line can be obtained from the simultaneous solution of two equations called the normal equations. These normal equations are determined by methods of calculus. For the two-variable case, the normal equations are

$$\sum y = na + b \sum x \tag{14.5}$$

$$\sum xy = a \sum x + b \sum x^2 \tag{14.6}$$

Some simple algebraic manipulation will convert these normal equations into the following equations which provide a simpler computational procedure:

$$a = \bar{y} - b\bar{x} \tag{14.7}$$

$$b = \frac{\sum xy - n\bar{x}\bar{y}}{\sum x^2 - n\bar{x}^2} \tag{14.8}$$

From the data given in Table 14.1, we can compute the regression line as follows:

$$\bar{x} = \frac{\sum x}{n} = \frac{46}{10} = 4.6$$

$$\bar{y} = \frac{\sum y}{n} = \frac{59}{10} = 5.9$$

$$\bar{x}\bar{y} = (4.6)(5.9) = 27.1$$

$$\bar{x}^2 = (4.6)^2 = 21.2$$

Consequently,

$$b = \frac{\sum xy - n\bar{x}\bar{y}}{\sum \bar{x}^2 - n\bar{x}^2} = \frac{182 - 271}{338 - 212} = \frac{-89}{126} = -0.71$$

and

$$a = \bar{y} - b\bar{x} = 5.9 - (-0.71)(4.6) = 9.2$$

The least-squares regression equation for these data is

$$y_c = 9.2 - 0.17x$$

The data and the regression line are plotted in Fig. 14.5.

Referring to the game of prediction which was hypothesized as an example previously, we now have a basis on which to predict the next Y

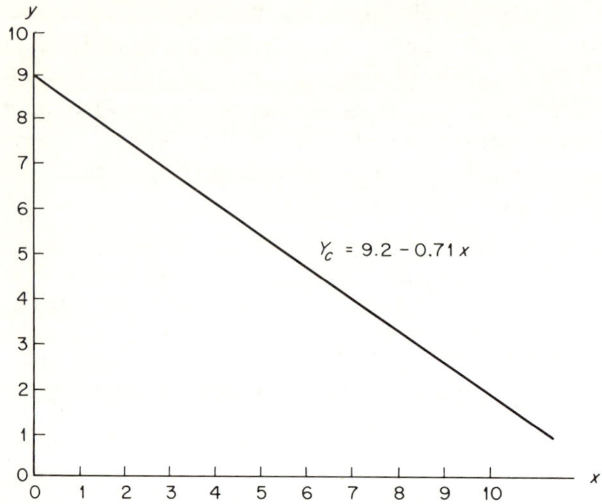

Fig. 14.5

value drawn at random from the basket. On the basis of our sample of size 10, we have estimated the regression relationship between the X and Y values to be $y = 9.2 - 0.71x$.

Now suppose our opponent selects a new envelope containing a Y value. We are allowed to observe the X number written on the envelope, which turns out to be 8. The predicted value for Y based on the regression equation would then be $y = 9.2 = 0.71(8) = 3.5$.

Let us digress briefly to be sure that the implications of regression analysis are clear. Assume first that there is a perfect and exact fixed linear relationship between two variables X and Y such that for any value of X there is a single actual value of Y which we shall designate y_a. Since this relationship is linear, it can be represented by the equation $y_a = \alpha + \beta X$, where α and β are the parameters of the regression equation. If it were possible to obtain exact measurements of y_a for given values of X, two such measurements would be sufficient to determine α and β. Having found α and β under these assumptions, given a value of X, the value of y_a could be determined with no error whatsoever.

However, both X and Y are random variables. Even though they are related, it is unusual for them to relate perfectly. Since they are both random variables, each has a probability distribution, and because of their relationship, they have a *joint distribution* which provides the probability that Y will take on some particular value y when X takes on some particular value x. The distribution of Y for some specific value of X is called the conditional distribution of Y given $X = x$, or $f(y|x)$. This means that in the population, for any fixed value of X there is a distribution of Y values. For regression analysis the assumption is made that this distribution of Y is normal, and that σ_Y^2 is the same for all values of X. This last condition is called *homoscedasticity*.

Consequently, for the known population values of α and β which describe the relationship between Y and X, any value $y_c = \alpha + \beta x$ may deviate from an actual observed value y since, for less than a perfect relationship, not all the Y values will fall on the regression line.

Furthermore, assume for the moment that the values of Y for given values of X must be read from some measuring instrument. These observed values Y are subject to error and are therefore inexact. The measurement error could be due to lack of precision in the measuring instrument, calibration error in the instrument, human error in reading the measurements, or any combination of these possibilities. Therefore, the observed values $y = y_a + e = \alpha + \beta x + e$, where e represents the error.

If we can assume that e is normally distributed with a mean of 0, which is a reasonable assumption for errors in measurement, we can also assume that Y is also normally distributed with $\bar{y} = \alpha + \beta x$. That is, if $E(e) = 0$, then $E(Y) = E(\alpha + \beta x + e) = \alpha + \beta x + 0$, for a fixed value of X. Furthermore, if $e{:}N(0,\sigma)$, this applies to any fixed value of X, and therefore $Y{:}N(\bar{y},\sigma)$ for all values of X.

In order to estimate the true regression line, a sample of values is taken, and these sample values are used to determine the equation $y_c = a + bx$, where y_c is the computed value of Y for a given value of X, and a and b are estimates of α and β, respectively.

THE STANDARD ERROR OF THE ESTIMATE

In the absence of any relationship between X and Y, we stated previously that the best estimate or prediction of the expected value of a Y value selected at random from the population would be the population mean, if known. If we use the mean as the estimate of some random value for the population, its worth as an estimator can be represented by the size of the expected error or, more accurately, by the magnitude of the expected squared error which is $E(y - \mu_Y)^2 = \sigma_Y^2$, or the population variance.

Since in our example we shall estimate the expected value of the Y's using a sample mean, that is, $\bar{y} = \hat{\mu}_Y$, the population variance must also be estimated from the sample; that is, $s^2 = \hat{\sigma}^2$. It would seem logical to estimate $E(Y - \mu_Y)^2$ with the sample values and $E(Y - \bar{y}^2)$, or to use the formula and estimate $\sum (y - \mu_Y)^2/N$ with $\sum (y - \bar{y})^2/n$.

However, the latter expression provides a biased estimate of σ^2, and, in fact, $E(Y - \bar{y})^2 = [(n - 1)/n]\sigma^2$.

In order to get an unbiased estimate of the population, the estimate must be modified by the factor $n/(n - 1)$, and therefore

$$\hat{\sigma}^2 = s^2 = \frac{\sum (y - \bar{Y})^2}{n - 1}$$

This explanation was given previously in Chap. 12, Statistical Estimation.

If there is a relationship between the X and the Y variables as assumed in our example, then knowledge of the X values should assist us in predicting a Y value. That is, instead of using the mean of all the Y values, or an estimate of that mean in predicting an expected Y value, we shall use the mean or its estimate of the Y value corresponding to a specific value of X.

The error in the estimate based on the X values is a function of the variability of the Y's about their mean value for a given X, that is, the variability about $Y_c = \mu_{Y/X} = \alpha + \beta X$, which is the value on the regression line. This variability is measured in a similar manner to the variance and is designated

$$\sigma^2_{Y \cdot X} = \frac{\sum (y - y_c)^2}{N}$$

The square root of this value is $\sigma_{Y \cdot X}$, and is called the *standard error of the estimate*.

Once more, however, the estimating equation or regression line from which we compute our predicted Y values is based on sample data from the population. That is, $y_c = a + bx$ where a and b are estimates of α and β. Consequently, our estimate of the variability of the population about the estimated regression line is $s^2_{Y \cdot X} = \sum (y - y_c)^2/(n - 2)$, and the square root of this value $s_{Y \cdot X}$ is called the *sample standard error of the estimate*. The factor $1/(n - 2)$ is used to provide an unbiased estimate of $\sigma^2_{Y \cdot X}$.

Just as there are more convenient computational formulas for the population and sample variances and standard deviations, there is also a computational formula for $s^2_{Y \cdot X}$. This is

$$s^2_{Y \cdot X} = \frac{\sum y^2 - a \sum y - b \sum xy}{n - 2} \tag{14.9}$$

and of course $s_{Y \cdot X}$ is simply the square root of Eq. (14.9).

Figure 14.6 will help to illustrate the measures of error in the prediction.

If the mean $\bar{y}$ was used to predict the value of Y corresponding to x_0 and the observed value y_0, the error would have been $y_0 - \bar{y}$. However, given a relationship between Y and X described by the line $y_c = a + bx$, for a known value of $X = x_0$, the value y_c would have been used as the prediction resulting in an error of $y_0 - y_c < y_0 - \bar{y}$. The closer the relationship between the two variables, the greater the difference in the error between the two predictors $\bar{y}$ and y_c.

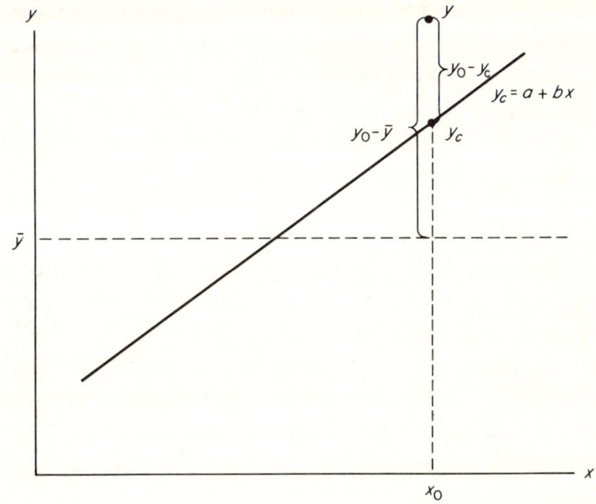

Fig. 14.6

For the data in the example,

$$s_{Y\cdot X} = \sqrt{\frac{453 - (9.2)(59) - (-0.71)(182)}{10 - 2}}$$

$$= \sqrt{\frac{40}{8}} = \sqrt{5} = 2.24$$

which is the standard error of the estimate computed from the sample and, to repeat, is a measure of the variability of the observed values about the regression line.

Compare $s_{Y\cdot X}$ with s_Y, which is simply the standard deviation of the Y values about their mean computed from the sample.

$$s_Y = \sqrt{\frac{\sum y^2 - n\bar{y}^2}{n - 1}} = \sqrt{\frac{453 - 348}{9}} = \sqrt{11.7} = 3.42$$

In a comparison of $s_{Y\cdot X}$ with s_Y, it is apparent that the variability of the Y values about the regression line is considerably less than the variability of the Y values about their own mean. This might have been expected from the value computed for $r = -0.776$ which indicates a reasonably strong relationship between the variables.

THE COEFFICIENT OF DETERMINATION

A useful measurement in regression analysis would be one which indicates how much we can improve our prediction of the Y value by using the regression relationships over our prediction based simply on $\bar{y}$ from the sample.

If there was absolutely no relationship between the two variables, then information about X would be of no use in predicting Y. Our best prediction of any Y value would simply be $\bar{y}$ from the sample, and our measure of the variability of the Y values about $\bar{y}$ is given by s_Y or by $s_y{}^2$, the variance of Y.

On the other hand, if a relationship does exist between Y and X, then our prediction should be based on the value computed from the regression line y_c. A measure of the variability about the regression line is given by $s_{Y \cdot X}$ or $s^2_{Y \cdot X}$. Now, if the relationship between Y and X was perfect, every Y value would fall on the regression line, and the difference $y - y_c$ would be zero for all Y, and $s^2_{Y \cdot X}$ consequently would equal zero. Therefore, for a perfect regression relationship between Y and X, $s^2_{Y \cdot X} = 0$.

If, however, there is no relationship between the two variables whatsoever, in which case our best value for prediction would be $\bar{y}$, then $s^2_{Y \cdot X} = s_Y{}^2$.

Since, for any regression analysis, $0 \leq s^2_{Y \cdot X} \leq s_Y{}^2$, we might compare $s^2_{Y \cdot X}$ with $s_Y{}^2$ in order to determine how much we improve our estimate of Y, that is, how much we reduce the possible error in our estimate by using X as a predictor. One way to compare these two values would be to use the ratio of one to the other, that is, $s^2_{Y \cdot X}/s_Y{}^2$.

If $s^2_{Y \cdot X} = s_Y{}^2$, then $s^2_{Y \cdot X}/s_Y{}^2 = 1$, representing a condition of *no* relationship.

If $s^2_{Y \cdot X} = 0$, then $s^2_{Y \cdot X}/s_Y{}^2 = 0$, representing a perfect relationship.

This would seem to be a reasonable measure of the value of X in predicting Y; however, rather than use a value of zero to represent a perfect relationship, and a value of 1 for no relationship at all, it would seem to be preferable if zero represented the absence of any relationship and 1 meant a perfect relationship. This can be accomplished simply by subtracting the ratio $s^2_{Y \cdot X}/s_Y{}^2$, from 1, that is, $1 - s^2_{Y \cdot X}/s_Y{}^2$, so that when there is no relationship whatsoever, the value $1 - s^2_{Y \cdot X}/s_Y{}^2 = 1 - 1 = 0$, and when there is perfect relationship, $1 - s^2_{Y \cdot X}/s_Y{}^2 = 1 - 0 = 1$.

One other modification to this procedure is necessary, particularly when the sample is small. Both $s^2_{Y \cdot X}$ and $s_Y{}^2$ are estimates of the population values $\sigma^2_{Y \cdot X}$ and $\sigma_Y{}^2$, respectively. In order that these estimates be unbiased, the sum of the squared deviations about the reference points $\bar{y}$ and y_c are divided by $n - 1$ and $n - 2$, respectively. The difference between $n - 1$ and $n - 2$ degrees of freedom in the calculation can alter the value of the ratio appreciably for small samples. Therefore, instead of using $s^2_{Y \cdot X}$ and $s_Y{}^2$ in the above ratio, we shall use simply the sum of squares about each reference point. That is, instead of $s^2_{Y \cdot X}$ we shall use $\sum (Y - Y_c)^2 = (n - 2)s^2_{Y \cdot X}$, and instead of $s_Y{}^2$ we shall use $\sum (Y - \bar{Y})^2 = (n - 1)s_Y{}^2$.

These values are referred to simply as the *sum of squares about the mean* and the *sum of squares about the regression line*, and can be designated ss_Y and $ss_{Y \cdot X}$. These values can be substituted for $s^2_{Y \cdot X}$ and $s_Y{}^2$ to form the ratio $ss_{Y \cdot X}/ss_Y$.

The expression

$$1 - \frac{ss_{Y \cdot X}}{ss_Y} = r^2 \qquad (14.10)$$

is called the *coefficient of determination*, and is a measure of the proportion of the variability in the dependent variable Y which is accounted for by its relationship to the independent variable X.

If we consider $ss_Y = \sum (y - \bar{y})^2$ as representing the total variability in the Y variable, and $ss_{Y \cdot X} = \sum (y - y_c)^2$ as representing the amount of variability remaining after utilizing the regression relationship with X, then the ratio $ss_{Y \cdot X}/ss_Y$ represents the proportion of the total variability still *unaccounted for* after utilizing the regression relationship.

Since a proportion can vary only between zero and 1, subtracting the proportion of variation that is unaccounted for from 1 produces the proportion of the variability that *is accounted for*. Therefore, the coefficient of determination indicates the proportion of the variability in Y that *is accounted for* by X.

For the previous example,

$$s_{Y \cdot X}^2 = 5 \quad \therefore \; ss_{Y \cdot X} = (n - 2)(5) = 40$$

$$s_Y{}^2 = 11.7 \quad \therefore \; ss_Y = (n - 1)(11.7) = 105$$

and the coefficient of determination is given by

$$r^2 = 1 - \frac{40}{105} = 1 - 0.381 = 0.619$$

A coefficient of determination of 0.619 can be interpreted to mean that approximately 61.9 percent of the variation in the Y values can be accounted for by the variation in the X values. Obviously, if 61.9 percent of the variation is accounted for, then 100 minus 61.9 or 38.1 percent of the variation is unaccounted for by the regression relationship.

The square root of the coefficient of determination is simply the coefficient of correlation which we had computed previously for the same data using Eq. (14.3). Given $r^2 = 0.619$, $r = \sqrt{0.619} \doteq 0.776$, and the minus sign must be affixed to agree with the sign of b in the regression equation.

The approximate coefficient of correlation can also be obtained from the following relationship:

$$r = \frac{bs_X}{s_Y} \qquad (14.11)$$

After computation of s_X from $\sqrt{(\sum x^2 - n\bar{x}^2)/(n - 1)} \doteq 3.74$, $r = (-0.71)(3.74)/3.42 \doteq -0.77$.

Example 14.4 A group of manufacturing employees was to be selected to be trained as inspectors. The basis for their selection was to be their scores on an aptitude

Table 14.2

X	Y	XY	X^2	Y^2
80	70	5,600	6,400	4,900
80	60	4,800	6,400	3,600
45	24	1,080	2,025	576
70	38	2,660	4,900	1,444
95	45	4,275	9,025	2,025
20	30	600	400	900
50	35	1,750	2,500	1,225
90	50	4,500	8,100	2,500
25	25	625	625	625
50	20	1,000	2,500	400
605	397	26,890	42,875	18,195

test to be administered. In order to determine the relationship between test scores and their success on the job, 10 workers were chosen at random and given the test. They were then trained and put to work as inspectors. After a week, their proficiency in the job was measured by their output per shift. Table 14.2 shows the test score X and a measure of the average output per shift Y for each of the 10 employees. The other columns provide the necessary data for computing the following:

1. Coefficient of correlation
2. Regression line
3. Standard error of the estimate
4. Coefficient of determination

From the data, $\bar{x} = 605/10 = 60.5$ and $\bar{y} = 397/10 = 39.7$. The coefficient of correlation is, from Eq. (14.3),

$$r = \frac{n \sum xy - \sum xy}{\sqrt{[n \sum x^2 - (\sum x)^2][n \sum y^2 - (\sum y)^2]}}$$

$$= \frac{(10)(26{,}890) - (605)(397)}{\sqrt{[(10)(42{,}875) - (605)^2][(10)(18{,}195) - (397)^2]}}$$

$$= \frac{28{,}715}{\sqrt{(62{,}725)(24{,}341)}}$$

$$= \frac{28{,}715}{39{,}000}$$

$$\doteq 0.74$$

The regression coefficients are obtained from

$$b = \frac{\sum xy - n\bar{x}\bar{y}}{\sum x^2 - n\bar{x}^2} = \frac{26{,}890 - 24{,}018}{42{,}875 - 36{,}603} = 0.46$$

$a = \bar{y} - b\bar{x} = 39.7 - (0.46)(60.5) = 11.9$, and the equation of the regression line is $y = 11.9 + 0.46x$.

The standard error of the estimate is found from the sample values by

$$s_{Y \cdot X} = \sqrt{\frac{\sum y - a\sum y - b\sum xy}{n - 2}}$$

$$= \sqrt{\frac{18{,}195 - (11.9)(397) - (0.46)(26{,}890)}{10 - 2}}$$

$$= \sqrt{\frac{1{,}111}{8}}$$

$$= \sqrt{138}$$

$$= 11.7$$

The sum of squares about the regression line is simply $ss_{Y \cdot X} = 1{,}111$.

In order to compute the coefficient of determination, we must find the sum of squares about the mean value of Y; that is,

$$ss_Y = \sum y^2 - n\bar{y}^2 = 2{,}434$$

The coefficient of determination is simply $r^2 = 1 - 1{,}111/2{,}434 = 1 - 0.46 = 0.54$, which indicates that approximately 54 percent of the variability in output seems to be accounted for by the aptitude as measured in the test.

The coefficient of correlation $r = \sqrt{r^2} = \sqrt{0.54} \doteq 0.74$, as computed previously.

14.4 MULTIPLE REGRESSION

Up to this point we have been attempting to predict the value of one dependent variable which we have labeled Y on the basis of a single independent variable X. Referring to the previous example, Y was some measure of job performance, and X was the score on an aptitude test. After completing the simple regression analysis, we found that the coefficient of determination $r^2 = 0.54$. By definition, the coefficient of determination indicates the proportion of the variation in the dependent variable that is accounted for by the regression relationship. In this case we would conclude that only 54 percent of the variation in performance was accounted for by the variable measured by the aptitude test. If we wanted to improve our predictive capabilities, we might look for some other variable or variables which would help to account for the remaining 46 percent of the variability in Y.

When a dependent variable Y is related in a regression equation to two or more independent variables, we are then performing a multiple regression analysis. We shall limit ourselves to situations in which the relationship between the variables is linear; consequently, the equation can be written

$$y_c = a + b_1x_1 + b_2x_2 + \cdots + b_nx_n$$

We shall continue to use Y or y_c as the designation for the dependent variable. X_i will designate the ith independent variable, b_i is the regression coefficient corresponding to the X_i, and a is the Y intercept of the line, or, more simply, the value of y_c when all $X_i = 0$.

Most of the concepts introduced in multiple regression are simple extensions of those studied in simple regression. For example, in a three-variable multiple regression, we shall find

$s_{Y\cdot 12}$ = standard error of the regression of Y on variables 1 and 2

$R^2_{Y\cdot 12}$ = coefficient of multiple determination

$R_{Y\cdot 12}$ = coefficient of multiple correlation

In addition, however, we shall also find

$r^2_{Y1\cdot 2}$ = coefficient of partial determination between Y and X_1 with X_2 held constant

$r^2_{Y2\cdot 1}$ = coefficient of partial determination between Y and X_2 with X_1 held constant

The corresponding coefficients of partial correlation are $r_{Y1\cdot 2}$ and $r_{Y2\cdot 1}$.

For illustration, let us continue the last example used for simple regression. Y is still the measure of on-the-job performance in terms of output per shift. X in that example is designated X_1 and represents scores on an aptitude test given before training on a new job. In an attempt to account for some of the variability in Y not accounted for by the simple regression relationship, a third variable X_2 will be considered which represents years of previous experience. The data acquired for the multiple regression analysis are presented in Table 14.3.

Before going into a complicated multiple regression analysis, it would behoove the analyst to determine whether there is any relationship at all between Y and the new variable X_2. The first step would be to draw a scatter diagram for these two variables and, if a linear relationship is indi-

Table 14.3

Y	X_1	X_2	Y^2	X_1^2	X_2^2	X_1Y	X_2Y	X_1X_2
70	80	5	4,900	6,400	25	5,600	350	400
60	80	9	3,600	6,400	81	4,800	540	720
24	45	1	576	2,025	1	1,080	24	45
38	70	0	1,444	4,900	0	2,660	0	0
45	95	4	2,025	9,025	16	4,275	180	380
30	20	2	900	400	4	600	60	40
35	50	3	1,225	2,500	9	1,750	105	150
50	90	6	2,500	8,100	36	4,500	300	540
25	25	2	625	625	4	625	50	50
20	50	2	400	2,500	4	1,000	40	100
397	605	34	18,195	42,875	180	26,890	1,649	2,425

cated, to compute the simple correlation coefficient between Y and X_2. This would be

$$r_{Y \cdot X_2} = \frac{n \sum x_2 y - \sum x_2 \sum y}{\sqrt{[n \sum x_2^2 - (\sum x_2)^2][n \sum y^2 - (\sum y)^2]}}$$

For the new data given,

$$r_{Y \cdot X_2} = \frac{(10)(1{,}649) - (34)(397)}{\sqrt{[10(180) - (34)^2][10(18{,}195) - (397)^2]}}$$

$$= \frac{16{,}490 - 13{,}498}{\sqrt{(644)(24{,}341)}}$$

$$= \frac{2{,}992}{3{,}960}$$

$$\doteq 0.76$$

The previous coefficient of correlation between Y and what is now designated X_1 was $r_{Y \cdot X_2} \doteq 0.74$.

It is apparent from the sample that X_2 is even more closely related to Y than is X_1, and that using them together in a regression equation should provide a better prediction of Y than could be obtained by using either one by itself. We would therefore proceed with the multiple regression analysis.

THE MULTIPLE REGRESSION EQUATION

The multiple regression equation is the least-squares line fitted to the observed Y values. Consequently, the sum of the squares of the vertical distances from the point to the line, $\sum (y - y_c)^2$, is minimized. The regression coefficients of the line are obtained from a set of three normal equations where three variables are involved. The normal equations for the three-variables case are:

$$\sum y = na + b_1 \sum x_1 + b_2 \sum x_2$$

$$\sum x_1 y = a \sum x_1 + b_1 \sum x_1^2 + b_2 \sum x_1 x_2$$

$$\sum x_2 y = a \sum x_2 + b_1 \sum x_1 x_2 + b_2 \sum x_2^2$$

There are several methods for solving sets of simultaneous equations. For three equations in three unknowns, an algebraic solution by hand is relatively simple. For larger sets of equations it is best to resort to the use of a computer.

For the data given in Table 14.3, the normal equations become, after substitution,

$$397 = 10a + 605b_1 + 34b_2$$
$$26{,}890 = 605a + 42{,}875b_2$$
$$1{,}649 = 34a + 245b_1 + 180b_2$$

Step 1: Eliminate a from the three equations.

Multiply the first equation by 17 and the third equation by 5, resulting in

$$8{,}245 = 170a + 12{,}125b_1 + 900b_2$$
$$6{,}749 = 170a + 10{,}285b_1 + 578b_2$$

Subtracting the bottom equation from the top one, we get

$$1{,}496 = 1{,}840b_1 + 322b_2$$

Multiplying the first equation by 121 and the second equation by 2 results in

$$48{,}037 = 1{,}210a + 73{,}205b_1 + 4{,}114b_2$$
$$53{,}780 = 1{,}210a + 85{,}750b_1 + 4{,}850b_2$$

Subtracting the top equation from the bottom one, we get

$$5{,}743 = 12{,}545b_1 + 736b_2$$

Step 2: Eliminate b_2 from the two resulting equations:

$$5{,}743 = 12{,}545b_1 + 736b_2$$
$$1{,}496 = 1{,}840b_1 + 322b_2$$

Multiply the first equation by 14 and the second equation by 32, resulting in

$$80{,}402 = 175{,}630b_1 + 10{,}304b_2$$
$$47{,}872 = 58{,}880b_1 + 10{,}304b_2$$

Subtracting the bottom equation from the top one, we get

$$32{,}530 = 116{,}750\,b_1$$

or

$$b_1 = \frac{32{,}530}{116{,}750} \doteq 0.278$$

Step 3: Substitute the value for b_1 into one of the equations in b_1 and b_2 and solve for b_2.

$$1{,}496 = 1{,}840b_1 + 322b_2$$
$$1{,}496 = 1{,}840(0.278) + 322b_2$$
$$1{,}496 = 511.52 + 322b_2$$
$$322b_2 = 984.48$$
$$b_2 = 3.057$$

Step 4: Substitute the values for b_1 and b_2 into one of the equations in a, b_1, and b_2, and solve for a.

$$397 = 10a + 605b_1 + 34b_2$$
$$397 = 10a + 605(0.278) + 34(3.057)$$
$$10a = 397 - 168.19 - 103.938$$
$$10a = 124.872$$
$$a = 12.487$$

Step 5: Substitute the values for a, b_1, and b_2 into the regression equation.

$$y_c = 12.487 + 0.28x_1 + 3.057x_2$$

THE STANDARD ERROR OF THE ESTIMATE—MULTIPLE REGRESSION

The standard error of the estimate in multiple regression measures the variability of the observed Y values about the regression line just as in the case of simple regression. If we could compute the regression line from the entire population of values, the regression equation would provide $y_c = \alpha + \beta_1 X_1 + \beta_2 X_2$, and the standard error of the estimate would be

$$\sigma_{Y\cdot 12} = \sqrt{\frac{\sum (y_i - y_c)^2}{N}}$$

Just as in the case of simple regression, however, the estimating equation was based on a sample from the population, and instead of having values for α, β_1, and β_2, estimates of these parameters, a, b_1, and b_2, were computed from the sample data. Consequently, the sample standard error of the estimate is defined as

$$s_{Y\cdot 12} = \sqrt{\frac{(y_i - y_c)^2}{n - 3}}$$

where 1 degree of freedom is subtracted from the sample size n in the denominator for each parameter estimated from the sample values.

A more convenient computational form for the standard error of the estimate is

$$s_{Y\cdot 12} = \sqrt{\frac{\sum y^2 - a\sum y - b_1\sum x_1y - b_2\sum x_2y}{n - 3}}$$

For the example

$$s_{Y\cdot 12} = \sqrt{\frac{18{,}195 - (12.487)(397) - (0.278)(26{,}890) - (3.057)(1{,}649)}{7}}$$

$$= \sqrt{\frac{18{,}195 - 4{,}957.330 - 7{,}475.42 - 5{,}040.993}{7}}$$

$$= \sqrt{\frac{721.248}{7}}$$

$$= \sqrt{103.035}$$

$$= 10.15$$

We can now compare the standard error of the multiple regression with the standard error of the simple regression which was computed previously:

$$s_{Y\cdot 12} = 10.15 < 11.70 = s_{Y\cdot X_1}$$

It is apparent that by introducing the second independent variable, the variability in the observed Y values has been reduced. This is even more obvious when we compare the sums of the squared deviations in the Y values about $\bar{y}$, about the simple regression line, and about the multiple regression line. The actual variability of the output can best be expressed in terms of the sum of squares, as follows:

$$ss_Y = 2{,}434$$

$$ss_{Y\cdot X_1} = 1{,}111$$

$$ss_{Y\cdot 12} = 721$$

where ss_Y is the sum of squares about the mean Y value or $\bar{y}$, $ss_{Y\cdot X_1}$ is the sum of squares about the simple regression line, and $ss_{Y\cdot 12}$ is the sum of squares about the multiple regression line where X_1 and X_2 were the independent random variables.

It is quite apparent that the variability, as represented by the sum of squares, is much less about the simple regression line than it is about $\bar{y}$. There is even less variability about the multiple regression line than about the simple regression of Y on X_1. As for the simple regression case, it is desirable to have some measure of the variability in the dependent random variable which is explained by the regression relationship. This is provided by the coefficient of multiple determination.

THE COEFFICIENTS OF MULTIPLE DETERMINATION AND MULTIPLE CORRELATION

The *coefficient of multiple determination* is similar to the coefficient of determination in simple regression in that it measures the proportion of the variability in Y which is accounted for by the regression equation.

The sum of squares about the mean of Y, ss_Y, still represents the total variability in Y. The sum of squares about the regression line, $ss_{Y \cdot 12}$, represents the variability still unaccounted for after utilizing the regression relationship. The ratio $ss_{Y \cdot 12}/ss_Y$ is therefore the *proportion* of unaccounted-for variability, and

$$R^2 = 1 - \frac{ss_{Y \cdot 12}}{ss_Y} \tag{14.12}$$

is the *coefficient of multiple determination*, which is the proportion of the variability in Y that *is accounted for* by the regression relationship.

The square root of the coefficient of multiple determination is the *coefficient of multiple correlation.* Thus

$$R = \sqrt{1 - \frac{ss_{Y \cdot 12}}{ss_Y}}$$

For the previous example, $R^2 = 1 - 721/2{,}434 = 0.704$, indicating that 70.4 percent of the variability in Y has been accounted for by the relationship between Y and X_1 and X_2 taken together in the regression equation. This should be compared with the coefficient of simple determination between Y and X_1 computed previously, which was $r^2 = 0.540$.

This indicates that a considerable amount of the variability in Y which was still *unaccounted for* after the simple regression relationship was established between Y and X_1 has now been explained. Even now, however, only 70.4 percent of the variability in Y has been explained, which leaves 29.6 percent of the variability still unaccounted for. This might lead us to look for a third independent variable which is related to Y. We shall not, however, undertake that exercise here.

The coefficient of multiple correlation for the example is simply

$$\mathrm{R} = \sqrt{R^2} = \sqrt{0.704} = 0.84$$

THE COEFFICIENTS OF PARTIAL DETERMINATION AND PARTIAL CORRELATION

In simple regression analysis the dependent variable and a *single* independent variable are the only variables considered. Although there may be other independent variables which are related to the dependent variable and which would help to account for some of its variability, they are ignored. Consequently, the coefficients of simple determination and regression measure the relationship between the dependent variable and the single independent variable, ignoring all other possible related variables.

In the multiple regression utilizing two independent variables, a second factor or independent variable was identified as being related to Y, the dependent variable, and a new regression equation was determined relating Y to both X_1 and X_2. The coefficients of multiple determination and correlation then measured the relationship between Y and X_1 and X_2 simultaneously, when taken together in the specified regression equation. Any other possibly related independent variables not included in the regression equation were ignored.

It is frequently of interest to measure the strength of the relationship between the dependent variable and one of the independent variables in a multiple regression under the condition that all other independent variables included in the regression are held constant. This is done by the coefficients of *partial* determination and regression.

The standard error of the estimate for the multiple regression $s_{Y \cdot 12}$ is a measure of the *unaccounted for* variation in Y after both X_1 and X_2 were included in the regression. If a simple regression analysis were done separately between Y and X_1 on the one hand, and between Y and X_2 on the other, we would then have two standard errors of the estimate, one for each simple regression analysis performed. These would be $s_{Y \cdot 1}$ between Y and X_1 and $S_{Y \cdot 2}$ between Y and X_2. The standard error $S_{Y \cdot 1}$ represents the unexplained variability in Y still remaining after X_1 was used in a simple regression which ignored X_2. The standard error $s_{Y \cdot 2}$ represents the unexplained variability in Y still remaining after X_2 was used in a simple regression which ignored X_1.

Since we have been using the sum of squares to represent the variability in Y, consider $ss_{Y \cdot 12}$, $ss_{Y \cdot 1}$, and $ss_{Y \cdot 2}$ as representing the unexplained variability, instead of the standard errors of estimate mentioned previously.

Now if $ss_{Y \cdot 12}$ is the unexplained variability after using both X_1 and X_2, and if $ss_{Y \cdot 1}$ is the unexplained variability after using X_1 but before using X_2, then $ss_{Y \cdot 12} \leq ss_{Y \cdot 1}$, since each time we introduce an additional related independent variable into the analysis we reduce the amount of unexplained variability, and the difference $ss_{Y \cdot 1} - ss_{Y \cdot 12}$ represents the amount of that variability in Y that has been accounted for by introducing X_1 after X_2 has already been used.

Also, the ratio

$$\frac{ss_{Y \cdot 1} - ss_{Y \cdot 12}}{ss_{Y \cdot 1}} = 1 - \frac{ss_{Y \cdot 12}}{ss_{Y \cdot 1}} = r^2_{Y2 \cdot 1}$$

is the proportion of the variability in Y accounted for by the use of X_2 after X_1 has been used, and is called the *coefficient of partial determination* between Y and X_2 with X_1 held constant.

The square root of the coefficient of partial determination is the *coefficient of partial correlation.*

Continuing the previous example, from the simple analysis between Y_1, units of output per shift, and X_1, scores on an aptitude test, $ss_{Y\cdot 1}$ was found to be 1,111. The sum of squares about the multiple regression line $ss_{Y\cdot 12}$ was 721. The coefficient of partial determination between Y and X_2 with X_1 held constant is therefore

$$r_{Y2\cdot 1}^2 = 1 - \frac{ss_{Y\cdot 12}}{ss_{Y\cdot 1}} = 1 - \frac{721}{1{,}111} = 0.351$$

which can be interpreted to mean that the addition of variable X_2 to the regression analysis with the effects of X_1 held constant accounts for 35.1 percent of the variability in Y.

The coefficient of partial correlation between Y and X_2 is given by

$$r_{Y2\cdot 1} = \sqrt{0.351} = 0.592$$

It is left as an exercise for the reader to compute the coefficients of partial determination and partial correlation between Y and X_1, given that X_2 is held constant.

14.5 SUMMARY

Correlation and regression analysis is a method by which estimates or predictions can be made about the value of some random variable based upon the knowledge of the value of some one or more other random variables which are related to it. Correlation analysis determines whether a linear relationship does exist between two variables and provides a measure of the strength of the relationship. Regression analysis is a method of defining that relationship and estimating its parameters.

It is possible, by using techniques of correlation and regression analysis, to predict values of a decision component state in situations where it is impossible or impractical to observe elements of the population which that decision component represents.

PROBLEMS

14.1. For the set of X, Y values plotted in Fig. 14.1, find
- (*a*) The correlation coefficient.
- (*b*) The regression equation of Y on X.
- (*c*) The predicted value of Y when $X = 5$.

14.2. For the data in Prob. 14.1, test the hypothesis that $\rho = 0$,
- (*a*) Using the t transformation.
- (*b*) Using the z transformation.

14.3. A sample of 30 X, Y pairs yields a correlation coefficient of 0.720. Test the hypotheses that

(*a*) $\rho \geq 0.9$ at $\alpha = 0.05$.
(*b*) $\rho < 0.5$ at $\alpha = 0.01$.

14.4. In studying the relationship between the number of tractors sold in a particular rural area and the number of farms in that area, a manufacturer obtained the following data for *eight* rural counties. Let Y represent the number of tractors sold and X the number of farms.

$$\sum x = 160 \qquad \sum x^2 = 3{,}600$$
$$\sum y = 104 \qquad \sum y^2 = 1{,}800$$
$$\sum xy = 2{,}400$$

(*a*) Compute the correlation coefficient between X and Y.
(*b*) Determine the regression equation of Y on X.
(*c*) Find the standard error of the estimate $s_{y \cdot x}$.
(*d*) If this area is assumed to be typical of all the rural counties in the state, what is the predicted number of tractors which would be sold in an area having 97 farms?

14.5. For the data in Prob. 14.4, what percentage of the variability in the number of tractors sold is accounted for by the relationship with the number of farms?

14.6. An experiment was conducted to determine the effect of varying amounts of rainfall and the yield of a certain strain of wheat. The X values represent equivalent rainfall in inches. The Y values represent the yield from a plot of a given size in ounces. The data for 10 X, Y pairs are as follows:

X	Y
5	1.2
10	1.9
15	2.8
20	2.9
25	3.4

X	Y
30	4.4
35	4.9
40	5.1
45	5.7
50	5.8

(*a*) Find the regression equation of Y on X.
(*b*) Find $s_{Y \cdot X}$.
(*c*) Find the coefficient of determination $r^2_{Y \cdot X}$.
(*d*) Find the coefficient of correlation $r_{Y \cdot X}$.

14.7. A multiple regression analysis was performed on a sample of $n = 10$ relating the dependent random variable Y to two independent variables X_1 and X_2. A regression equation was obtained as well as the following measures:

$$s_{Y \cdot 12} = 5.4$$
$$s_Y = 20.0$$

(*a*) Find the coefficient of multiple correlation.
(*b*) The percent of the variability in Y which has been accounted for by the regression relationship with X_1 and X_2 is what?

14.8. For the multiple regression

$$y_c = 3 - 1.54x_1 + 4x_2$$

(*a*) What is the value of y_c when $X_1 = -9$ and $X_2 = 14$?
(*b*) If the variable X_1 is held constant, how much does y_c change for every unit change in X_2?

14.9. A company manufacturing and marketing a widely used consumer item desires to improve their sales forecasts. It has been suggested that sales in any particular area should be related to the population in that area and to the amount spent by the company in advertising the product in that area. The following data were compiled for six "typical" marketing areas for the previous year:

Area	*Sales in millions of dollars*	*Population in millions*	*Advertising expenditures in thousands of dollars*
1	34	5.0	50
2	29	4.2	45
3	43	8.5	100
4	12	1.4	25
5	35	3.6	50
6	27	1.3	30

Letting $Y =$ sales, $X_1 =$ population, and $X_2 =$ advertising expenditures,

(*a*) Find the regression equation of Y on X_1 and X_2.

(*b*) Find the standard error $s_{y \cdot 12}$.

(*c*) Find the coefficient of multiple determination $R^2_{y \cdot 12}$.

(*d*) Find the coefficient of partial correlation of Y on X_1 with X_2 constant, $r_{y1 \cdot 2}$.

(*e*) Find the coefficient of partial correlation of Y on X_2 with X_1 constant, $r_{y2 \cdot 1}$.

part four

Decision Theory

15
Risk and Uncertainty in Decision Making

The process of decision making involves the selection of an act or course of action from among alternative acts or courses of action. The rational decision maker desires to select that act which will produce optimum results under some criterion of optimization. In the usual decision situation, the consequence of any act is dependent upon certain factors beyond the control of the decision maker. In referring to a complex decision situation as a decision system consisting of various components, the uncontrollable factors in the system were the states of the decision components.

When considering a decision based on either the simple logical model or the probability model, the only component states considered were *good* or *bad*, and the available actions were also limited to two alternatives. In most practical situations, the states of the decision system components, or, to use the terminology of decision theory, *the states of nature*, are not limited to *good* and *bad*. In fact, to be realistic, the terms *good* and *bad* relate rather to the consequences of the decision process rather than to the state of nature. Good and bad are applied to the states of nature only to associate their observable or measurable characteristics with the consequences of a given decision. Consequently, the assigning of values, good or bad, to a state of nature is simply a method of evaluating the consequences of a decision if a particular state should occur. This means that rational decision making is based on the evaluation of consequences to the decision maker whether this fact is explicitly stated as part of the decision procedure or not.

In most situations, the two states good and bad do not sufficiently describe the consequences, and to be realistic, the decision maker should concern himself with the degree of goodness or badness involved. Furthermore, the number of acts available to the decision maker are not necessarily limited to two. Therefore, in order to be useful, a decision procedure should accommodate multiple states and multiple acts.

Even in the simple case, where it is reasonable to assume only two states of nature and where there are only two acts available to the decision maker, an evaluation of the consequences of each act for each state of nature should enable the decision maker to make a better or more optimal selection between the acts than would occur from consideration of probabilities alone.

This and subsequent chapters will continue to develop the decision procedure such that the dimension of consequences is added to the decision system which previously considered only logical relationships and probabilities.

15.1 CERTAINTY, RISK, AND UNCERTAINTY

Since the consequences of any act are dependent upon the state of nature, knowledge about the state of nature is certainly beneficial to the decision maker. In certain circumstances, all the facts regarding the state of nature are known. The decision process, under these circumstances, becomes simply the selection of a single act from among the acts available which will prove to be optimal for the known state of nature.

The utilization of the logical model for the selection of an act is an example of decision making under certainty. Here, even though the decision system may be quite complex, the state of the system as a whole is completely determined by the known states of its components, and with the state of the system known, the decision maker simply selects the act leading to the most favorable consequences under the known state of the system.

Risk and uncertainty traditionally refer to different degrees of lack of knowledge regarding the state of nature. When the state of nature is unknown, but objective or empirical evidence exists which would allow the decision maker to assign probabilities to the various states possible, the process of doing so in order to arrive at the decision is called decision making under *risk*. When the states of nature are unknown and no objective information regarding their probabilities of occurrence is available, then the decision process is called decision making under *uncertainty*.

However, even under uncertainty a decision maker may, according to statisticians belonging to the bayesian school, assign subjective probabilities to the states of nature to help him in arriving at a decision. Once probabilities are assigned to the state of nature, then the decision procedure is the same regardless of whether the probabilities resulted from empirical data or were purely subjective. Consequently, for practical purposes, risk and uncertainty are the same thing, and decision making under both circumstances will be referred to here as decision making under uncertainty.

15.2 STATES OF NATURE AND COMPETITOR'S ACTS

It has been stated previously that the consequences of any act on the part of the decision maker are dependent upon certain factors beyond the control of the decision maker. These factors are generally called the *states of nature*. The term state of nature does not refer to nature in the usual sense of the word but is a general term used to include all factors beyond the control of the decision maker. In addition to actual states of nature such as rainfall, drought, fire, storm, famine, etc., the term includes prices of raw materials, wage rates for labor, and availability of capital, as well as the conscious acts of competitors.

Since for most decisions the total number of combinations of all possible factors which might affect the consequences of an act could be so large as to be unmanageable, it becomes necessary to consider only those factors whose effect would be considered to be significant. A single state of nature then becomes a single combination of the joint occurrence of factors considered to have a significant effect upon the outcome or consequence of any act.

For example, suppose the decision must be made between the acts "market product *A*" or "do not market product *A*." The significant uncontrollable factors affecting the consequence of either act are the size of the market which can be categorized by large or small, and the act of a single competitor either to market a similar product or not to market a similar product. These two factors result in four states of nature. Thus we have the following:

State 1: small market and no competition
State 2: small market and competition
State 3: large market and no competition
State 4: large market and competition

As far as the decision maker is concerned, whether the state of nature is a true natural phenomenon, a condition occasioned by the nondirected activities of a large segment of the population, or the calculated activity of a competitor is of no consequence. Since these are all factors beyond the control of the decision maker, they are treated identically in the decision context.

15.3 MEASUREMENT OF CONSEQUENCES: PAYOFF

The selection of an act from among alternative acts should be based upon the consequences to the decision maker resulting from that act. These consequences, as has been pointed out, depend in turn upon the prevailing state of nature. That is, for any act selected there is a specific consequence or outcome which is dependent on the state of nature. The outcome of an act given a specific state of nature is called the *conditional outcome* of the act. In order to evaluate this conditional outcome, its value must be expressed in terms of some quantitative measure, and for many business situations the most appropriate quantitative measure of value would be dollars.

A matrix which relates the conditional outcomes of the available acts to the possible states of nature is called a *payoff table*. To show how such a payoff table might be constructed, consider the following example.

An independent television repairman has an opportunity to purchase a stock of discontinued television receivers from a small manufacturer who is going out of business. There is a total of five identical sets of good quality but bearing a virtually unknown label. The sets were originally designed to sell at retail for \$200 each. The repairman is offered all five for \$300, which makes his cost \$60 for each. If he can sell them at all, he believes that he should be able to get \$150 for each of them, providing himself with a profit of \$90 per set sold. Should he purchase the sets or not?

There are obviously only two acts in this problem, either "purchase" or "do not purchase." The state of nature, in this case, is simply the demand for the television sets which could be anywhere between zero and 5. If we designate the states of nature as the S_i where $i = 0, 1, 2, 3, 4, 5$, we can construct a payoff table which indicates the conditional value of the outcome of each act for every state of nature. This payoff table, in terms of dollars of profit, would appear as shown in Table 15.1.

Payoff tables reflect actual in-pocket profit or out-of-pocket losses. In this case, the payoff associated with a_2 is zero regardless of the state of nature.

Table 15.1

	S_0	S_1	S_2	S_3	S_4	S_5
a_1	− \$300	− \$150	0	+ \$150	+ \$300	+ \$450
a_2	0	0	0	0	0	0

That is, if the repairman selects the act "do not purchase," he will neither make nor lose any money, regardless of what the demand for the sets happens to be. The conditional values or payoffs for a_1, on the other hand, vary from a loss of \$300 to a profit of \$450, depending upon the demand.

These conditional values of the payoff for each act can be obtained from an equation called the *payoff function.* There is an equation for each act. In this specific case, the payoff functions are linear. That is, the payoff resulting from the selection of each act can be expressed as the equation of a straight line of the form $Q = b + mx$. The payoff function for a_2 in this case results from the fact that the profit or payoff is zero for all states of nature. Therefore,

$$Q_2 = 0$$

For act a_1, there is an initial investment or cost of \$300, while income is \$150 times the number of sets sold. If costs or losses are considered to be negative quantities and profits or income is positive, then

$$Q_1 = -\$300 + \$150x$$

where x is the number sold or demanded. By letting x vary from zero to 5 in the equation for Q_1, we obtain all the conditional values for a_1 in the payoff table.

A payoff table can also be constructed in terms of out-of-pocket losses to the decision maker. When the conditional values in the table are losses, they are represented as positive values, while any profits realized can be looked upon as negative losses.

It is apparent from Table 15.1 that under the assumption that a rational decision maker will attempt to maximize his profits or minimize his losses, neither act is best for all the possible states of nature. For states S_0 and S_1, act a_2 would be preferred to a_1. For states S_3, S_4, and S_5, a_1 would be preferred to a_2. For state S_2, the decision maker would be indifferent since the consequences are the same for both acts.

This point in a two-action problem at which the payoffs are equal is called the *break-even point*. It can be obtained simply by equating Q_1 and Q_2 and solving for the variable x. In this example, if we designate the *break-even* value of x as x_k, then

$$-\$300 + \$150x_k = 0$$

$$x_k = 2$$

15.4 MEASUREMENT OF CONSEQUENCES: REGRET

It has become common to consider the consequences of an act for any given state of nature in terms of opportunity loss or regret. *Opportunity loss* or *regret* is simply the absolute value of the difference between the payoff

Table 15.2

	S_0	S_1	S_2	S_3	S_4	S_5
a_1	\$300	\$150	0	0	0	0
a_2	0	0	0	\$150	\$300	\$450

actually realized under the act selected and the payoff which could have been obtained had the best or optimum act been selected. Obviously, then, the regret associated with the optimum act for a given state of nature would be zero. For any act other than the optimum, the regret will be some *positive* number.

Consider Table 15.1. This payoff table can be converted to a regret table in the following manner. For each state of nature find the optimum act, that is, the act with the maximum payoff. The regret for that act and the given state of nature is zero. For all other acts and the given state, the regret is simply the absolute difference between the conditional value of that act and the conditional value of the optimum act. The regret table corresponding to Table 15.1 is given in Table 15.2.

In comparing the regret table with the payoff table in terms of profit, it becomes apparent that for a given state of nature the better act is the one with the *smaller* regret. For the profit or payoff table, the better act was the act having the greater profit. This is reasonable, since regret is an opportunity loss or cost, and it is always desirable to minimize losses. The difference between a regret table and a payoff table in which the consequences are specified in terms of loss or cost is that a regret is never negative; that is, regret can never be smaller than zero. As was mentioned previously, in an ordinary loss table there can be negative losses.

15.5 DECISION FUNCTIONS

In order to clarify the preceding material, a mathematical formulation will be given to several of the concepts described.

In brief, the decision problem consists of a situation in which a choice must be made among alternative acts. The consequence of any act depends upon the factors beyond the control of the decision maker, which are called the "states of nature."

We shall designate the set of all possible acts $\{a_0,a_1, \ldots ,a_n\} = A$, the action space. The possible states of nature bearing on the decision problem can be designated $\{\theta_0,\theta_1, \ldots ,\theta_n\} = S$.

As discussed previously, every act has a consequence which depends upon the true, but unknown, state of nature. We can define a function

$\pi(\theta,a)$, which we shall call a payoff function, which assigns a value to every combination of θ and a. This value is a conditional value; that is, it is the consequence of the act *given* that the specified state of nature occurs.

Payoffs can be specified in terms of either profit or loss. If payoffs are specified as profits, then any loss incurred by selecting an act under a given state of nature is represented by a negative quantity. If, on the other hand, payoffs are specified as costs or losses, then a gain or profit is indicated by a negative loss.

It is convenient to represent the conditional consequences of any act by means of a function for which all the resulting values are positive. Such a function is called a *regret function* and can be designated $R(\theta,a)$. Any payoff function can be converted to a regret function by subtracting from each conditional consequence or payoff the optimum consequences possible for the given state of nature. That is,

$$R(\theta,a) = Q(\theta,a) - \min_a Q(\theta,a)$$

where payoffs are given in terms of losses, and

$$R(\theta,a) = \max_a Q(\theta,a) - Q(\theta,a)$$

where payoffs are given in terms of profits.

For decision making under certainty, the state of nature is known. Under this circumstance, the decision maker must select a single act from the set of acts which is in some way best under the known state of nature. A rational decision would be the selection of the act for which the regret would be minimized.

For decision making under circumstances other than certainty, there are several criteria for selecting a "best" act which will be discussed later. One reasonable approach, however, would be to attempt to determine the expected value of each act. In order to do so, however, it is necessary to make some assumption about the probability of occurrence of each state of nature. This assumption can take the form of a probability distribution on the state of nature which assigns a probability value to each possible state. It is well to mention at this point that the assignment of equal probabilities to each possible state of nature is as much of an assumption as the assignment of different probabilities to each state. How these probabilities should be assigned will also be discussed subsequently.

Since the expected value of an act, in terms of regret, is simply the sum over all possible states of nature of the conditional values of the act multiplied by their probability of occurrence, we can write

$$E(a) = \sum_\theta R(\theta,a)P(\theta) \tag{15.1}$$

If it is desirable to obtain information about the true state of nature before selecting an act, the process of obtaining such information will be called *experimentation.* The possible outcomes of an experiment will be designated $z_1, z_2, \ldots, z_n$, and the experiment or sample space is $Z = \{z\}$.

Suppose instead of selecting an act directly, we decide to select the act on the basis of the experimental result. That is, we establish a rule such that for each and every possible result of the experiment, the rule specifies the act that should be selected. Such a rule is called a *decision function* and is designated $\delta(z)$. Since for every z in Z, $\delta(z) = a$, the regret function can be written

$$R[\theta,\delta(z)] \tag{15.2}$$

The problem of selecting an act has now become one of selecting a decision function. In order to do so, it is necessary to know the expected consequences, given θ, of selecting decision function $\delta(z)$. This expected consequence is the expected regret of using $\delta(z)$ for some given state of nature which is the sum over all possible outcomes of the experiment of the conditional consequences, multiplied by the probability that the decision rule would result in those consequences, given a specific state of nature. This can be written

$$\begin{aligned} E\{R[\theta,\delta(z)]\} &= \sum_{Z} R(\theta,a)P[\delta(z)|\theta] \\ &= \rho[\theta,\delta(z)] \end{aligned} \tag{15.3}$$

and is called the *risk function* of the decision rule.

The experiment or sample space Z is such that the value of z resulting from the experiment should provide some information about the true value of θ. Z is a statistic and has a sampling distribution, and it is from the specific value or values of Z resulting from the experiment and some knowledge about the distribution of Z that one is able to determine the probabilities that the decision rule $\delta(z)$ will result in act a for a given θ.

For example, suppose an experiment consists of drawing a sample and estimating θ on the basis of a statistic computed from the sample; that is, $z = \hat{\theta}$. Suppose the decision rule $\delta(z)$ says select a_1 if $z > k$, and select a_2 if $z \leq k$. Then

$$P(a_1) = P(z > k|\theta)$$

and

$$P(a_2) = P(z \leq k|\theta)$$

The regret table for the two acts, two states of nature, and the rule $\delta(z)$ is shown in Table 15.3.

Table 15.3

	θ_1	θ_2
$z_1 = z > k \rightarrow a_1$	$R(a_1,\theta_1)$	$R(a_1,\theta_2)$
$z_2 = z \leq k \rightarrow a_2$	$R(a_2,\theta_1)$	$R(a_2,\theta_2)$

The risk function of the decision rule $\delta(z)$ for state of nature θ_1 would be

$$\rho[\theta_1,\delta(z)] = R(a_1,\theta_1)P(z > k|\theta_1) + R(a_2,\theta_1)P(z \leq k|\theta_1)$$
$$= \sum_{z} R(a,\theta_1)P[\delta(z)|\theta_1]$$

The risk function of the decision rule for state of nature θ_2 would be

$$\rho[\theta_2,\delta(z)] = R(a_1,\theta_2)P(z > k|\theta_2) + R(a_2,\theta_2)P(z \leq k|\theta_2)$$
$$= \sum_{z} R(a,\theta_2)P[\delta(z)|\theta_2]$$

The probability $P(z|\theta)$ depends upon the true but unknown value of θ, and therefore the risk function of a decision rule must be computed for all possible values of θ or for those values considered to be critical to the decision problem at hand.

It has also been stated that the problem of selecting an act has now become one of selecting a decision rule, of which there could be many. Having evaluated the expected regret or risk for each decision rule and for each possible value of θ, it becomes necessary to pick that decision rule which is "best." Just as in selecting an act from among the possible acts, there is not necessarily a decision rule which is best for all values of θ.

Without making assumptions about the probability of the occurrence of any specific state of nature, there are certain criteria which can be used in selecting among decision rules. These are similar to criteria for selecting between acts.

One method of selecting an act from among the set of acts was to compute the expected value of each act using some assumption about the probability of the occurrence of the various states of nature. The same procedure can be used in selecting a decision rule from among a set of alternate decision rules.

The expected value of a risk function with respect to an assumed probability distribution on the state of nature we shall call the *Bayes' risk* and define as

$$\sum_{\theta} \rho[\theta,\delta(z)]P(\theta) \tag{15.4}$$

The computation of the Bayes' risk for the decision rule specified in Table 15.3 would result from the following procedure:

$$\sum_{\theta}\sum_{z} R(a,\theta)P(z|\theta)P(\theta) \tag{15.5}$$

There is a criterion for selecting among decision rules known as the *Bayes' criterion*, which states that the decision rule should be selected for which the Bayes' risk is a minimum.

15.6 UTILITY

In considering any decision situation, it is necessary that the decision maker evaluate the consequences of each possible act under every state of nature affecting the problem. In most examples, the payoffs, costs, or regrets are expressed in terms of dollars. The dollar, or some other monetary unit, appears to be a reasonable measure of economic consequences, particularly in the management situations with which we are primarily concerned.

However, monetary value is adequate as a measure of economic consequences only so long as every dollar has exactly the same value as every other dollar. Although this may be true at a given point in time when considering the value of a dollar in terms of the goods and services it can purchase, it may not be true with respect to the individual decision maker.

Consider, for example, the value of a dollar to an individual in terms of the task he may be required to perform in order to obtain it. Suppose our hypothetical individual is offered a dollar if he will perform a task which is extremely distasteful to him. For the sake of illustration, assume the task is to clean out a stable. If the individual has no job and no money at all he may be inclined to accept the job. On the other hand, if he already has a steady job and is carrying \$100 in his pocket, it is quite likely that he would refuse. Depending upon his circumstances, the value of a dollar to him varies.

From the viewpoint of an organization which the decision maker represents, the same type of situation may exist. It would seem to be obvious that any profit-oriented company would prefer a profit of \$100,000 to a profit of \$50,000, and the latter to a loss of, say, \$10,000. But suppose the decision to be made involved the selection between two acts, one of which would result in a profit of \$50,000 with absolute certainty, the other in either a \$100,000 profit or a \$10,000 loss, each with the probability of one-half. Which act should the decision maker select? We might calculate the expected monetary value (abbreviated EMV) of each act and select that act for which this value was the highest. Under this set of circumstances, EMV for the two acts would be \$50,000 and \$45,000, respectively, leading to the selection of the $50,000 certain act. Suppose, however, that this particular decision maker is the proprietor of a small business in dire financial straits. He requires $100,000 in order to avoid bankruptcy. In his case, a profit of $50,000 is little better than a loss of $10,000, but a profit of $100,000 will allow him to remain in business.

Or suppose the probabilities of the outcomes were $50,000 with certainty on the one hand and either $100,000 with probability 0.6 and a loss of $10,000 with probability 0.4 on the other. The expected monetary values are now $50,000 for the first act and $56,000 for the second. Also, suppose that the decision maker needs only $50,000 to avoid bankruptcy. Now which act would he prefer?

To answer this question involves the consideration of a theory of utility in an attempt to measure a decision maker's preference for consequences which are not satisfactorily represented by monetary values.

THE VON NEUMAN-MORGENSTERN METHOD

John von Neuman and Oskar Morgenstern developed a method for measuring utility.* This method is known as the *standard gamble technique* and involves the conversion of the betting odds which a rational individual would insist upon before accepting some risk into a curve of the utility of money to the individual.

Suppose you are attempting to determine the utility curve of a particular decision maker. You might begin by asking the decision maker to express his preferences between a gamble in which he has a 50/50 chance of winning either $10,000 or nothing and a certain gift of, say, $5,000. If he expresses a preference for the $5,000 certain, you would lower the amount of the "certain" value until a point is reached at which the decision maker is indifferent as to the gamble and the gift. This point is called the *certainty monetary equivalent* of the gamble, or simply the CME. Suppose, in this example, the decision maker is indifferent between the gamble and a gift of $3,000. This particular individual's certainty monetary equivalent to the gamble offered is then $3,000.

The first step in constructing the utility curve is to assign a utility number to two values in the gamble. This assignment of utility numbers or *utils* can be arbitrary, subject to the restriction that the utility of $10,000 must be greater than the utility of $0. Suppose we assign a utility of 10 to $10,000 and a utility of zero to $0. Since the decision maker has expressed his indifference between the stated gamble and the certain gift of $3,000, then the utility of the gamble is equal to $3,000. This can be expressed in words as "the utility of $10,000 with a probability of 0.5 plus the utility of $0 with a

* John von Neuman and Oskar Morgenstern, "Theory of Games and Economic Behavior," 2d ed., Princeton University Press, Princeton, N.J., 1947.

probability of 0.5 is equal to the utility of \$3,000 with a probability of 1.0." Expressed as an equation, this would be

$$\tfrac{1}{2}U(\$10{,}000) + \tfrac{1}{2}U(\$0) = U(\$3{,}000)$$

Substituting the assigned utility numbers we get

$$\tfrac{1}{2}(10) + \tfrac{1}{2}(0) = U(\$3{,}000)$$
$$5 + 0 = U(\$3{,}000)$$

or \$3,000 has a utility of 5 utils.

We now have three values for the utility curve; they are \$10,000 = $10U$, \$3,000 = $5U$, and \$0 = $0U$. In order to get additional points on the curve, the same procedure is repeated, but other gambling odds are specified. For example, the decision maker might be asked to specify his certainty equivalent for a gamble in which he has a probability of $\tfrac{3}{4}$ of winning \$10,000 and a probability of $\tfrac{1}{4}$ of winning \$0. Suppose the certain value which is equivalent to this gamble is \$8,000. The utility of \$8,000 is calculated in the same manner as previously, using the new probabilities as follows:

$$\tfrac{3}{4}U(\$10{,}000) + \tfrac{1}{4}U(\$0) = U(\$8{,}000)$$
$$\tfrac{3}{4}(10) + \tfrac{1}{4}(0) = U(\$8{,}000)$$
$$7.5 = U(\$8{,}000)$$

that is, the utility of \$8,000 is equal to 7.5 utils.

A slightly different approach in the questioning can be used in which the decision maker is asked to specify the odds or probabilities of the gamble which will make him indifferent between the gamble and a certain gift of a specified amount. For example, we might offer him a choice between a gamble having a probability of p of winning \$50,000, and a probability of $(1 - p)$ of winning \$0 and a certain gift of \$10,000. The decision maker might indicate that he would be indifferent between the two if $p = \tfrac{4}{10}$. His utility for \$50,000 could then be determined from:

$$\tfrac{4}{10}U(\$50{,}000) + \tfrac{6}{10}U(\$0) = U(\$10{,}000)$$

By substitution we get:

$$\tfrac{4}{10}U(\$50{,}000) + \tfrac{6}{10}0 = 10$$
$$U(\$50{,}000) = 25$$

Additional utility equivalents could be obtained by the same procedure. With several of these numbers available it becomes possible to plot the decision maker's utility curve for money. The curve in Fig. 15.1 is based on the same values obtained above. In plotting any utility curve for use in assessing consequences in a decision problem, it would be desirable to find more than four points on the curve.

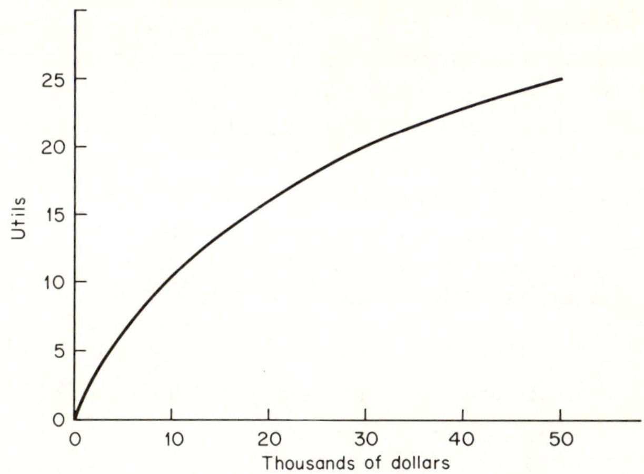

Fig. 15.1

Caution must be exercised in interpreting utility values: these utility numbers represent the utility of money for a particular decision maker. Since the utility index is personal and subjective, it is not possible to compare the utility function of one person with that of another.

This standard lottery technique is not limited to finding an individual's utility curve for money. It works equally well in assigning utility values to any outcome, even those that can be evaluated only in a qualitative sense. In the latter instance the decision maker would simply express his preferences between outcomes which would occur or not occur with specific probabilities and outcomes certain to occur.

As an example, let us obtain utilities for a specific manager's possible career objectives. Let us suppose that this specific individual is at present the assistant sales manager for chemical products for the Monroe Corporation. His ultimate career objective is to be promoted to marketing vice-president for the corporation. Let us arbitrarily assign a utility value of 10 to this occurrence. At the moment, the worst that he can imagine happening to him would be to be fired. We can assign a utility of zero to this occurrence. Let us proceed to obtain a scale of utilities for other possible occurrences such as:

1. Promotion to sales manager for chemical products
2. Transfer to assistant sales manager for pharmaceutical products
3. Appointment to a staff department as market research manager

We might ask this individual to make a choice between a lottery in which the outcomes are immediate promotion to marketing vice-president with a probability of p or loss of his job with a probability of $(1 - p)$, and a certain promotion to sales manager for chemical products. His choice would of course depend upon the value of p, and we would ask him to specify the value of p at which he would be indifferent between the two choices.

If the individual had difficulty in selecting a probability value, the questioner could assist by making suggestions. We might find that for $p = 0.5$ he would select the certain promotion. At $p = 0.8$, he would take the gamble. We shall finally arrive at $p = 0.75$ as the indifference point. The utility of the promotion to sales manager would then be:

$$U(\text{sales mgr. chem.}) = 0.75U(\text{vice-pres.}) + 0.25U(\text{fired})$$

$$U(\text{sales mgr. chem}) = (0.75)(10) + (0.25)(0)$$

$$U(\text{sales mgr. chem}) = 7.5$$

Next, evaluate the utility of a transfer to assistant sales manager for pharmaceuticals. His indifference point between the two choices in the case might be 0.6, and the utility would be 6.

By the same procedure we might determine that the utility of promotion to market research manager is 7 and that the utility of his present job is 5.

We might continue the questioning in an attempt to assign a utility value to promotion to the position of corporation president with probability p, firing with probability $(1 - p)$, or certain promotion to marketing vice-president. He might indicate that he would take the marketing vice-presidency with certainty unless p in this case was 0.98. The utility of the corporation presidency to him would be determined from:

$$0.98U(\text{corp. pres.}) + 0.02U(\text{firing}) = U(\text{vice-pres.})$$

$$0.98U(\text{corp. pres.}) + 0 = 10$$

$$U(\text{corp. pres.}) = 10.2$$

It is apparent that the utility which this individual assigns to the office of corporation president is very little greater than that which he assigns to the position of marketing vice-president.

A LOGARITHMIC UTILITY FUNCTION

The personal utility function derived from the standard gamble technique is pictured in Fig. 15.1. It has been emphasized that utility functions are personal and subjective, and differ between individuals and even differ for the same individual under different circumstances. However, there appear to be certain characteristics which are common to most individual utility functions. First, it would seem logical to assume that the function be an increasing one, although possibly asymptotically so. This implies that a greater amount of money never has less utility than a lesser amount. Second, the rate of increase in utility should decrease. This implies that as an individual acquires more and more money, the incremental utility of each additional dollar acquired decreases. The utility function plotted in Fig. 15.1 has these characteristics.

A function which has these characteristics is the logarithmic function. The logarithm of a number is the exponent to which a base number must be raised in order to equal the number. When we state that a number b raised to the xth power is equal to y, then x is the logarithm of y to the base b. This is written

$$\log_b Y = X$$

There are two systems of logarithms in common usage, a system of *common logarithms* in which the base number used is 10, and a system of *natural logarithms* in which the base used is the special number $e = 2.718\ldots$. Any dollar value can be converted into utilities, if we accept the premise that the utility of money is logarithmic, by simply letting

$$\log X = U\$X \tag{15.6}$$

that is, letting the logarithm of X equal the utility of X dollars. The logarithmic system chosen is inconsequential.

One problem encountered in Eq. (15.6) is that the logarithm of 1 is zero and the logarithm of zero is minus infinity. This situation can be corrected by letting

$$\log (X + 1) = U\$X \tag{15.7}$$

that is, the logarithm of $X + 1$ equals the utility of X dollars.

Because of what has been said about the subjectivity of an individual's utility function, it should be apparent that a general function will not represent anyone's utility function exactly. However, when it is not possible to evaluate a specific decision maker's personal utility function for money under a given situation, it may provide a better approximation to that function than the more generally used assumption that the utility for money is linear.

WHEN THE UTILITY FUNCTION OF MONEY IS LINEAR

It has been pointed out that there are many instances in which the utility of every dollar is not the same as the utility of every other dollar and in these cases, monetary value is not a valid guide to action in a decision situation. There are, however, circumstances in which monetary value is a perfectly legitimate measure of consequences.

Individuals and businessmen both act on the basis of monetary value when the amount of money at stake is not too large. We could say that within a certain range of values, the utility for money is approximately linear.

Under these circumstances, the utility associated with each outcome is simply the number of dollars of payoff or regret resulting from the selection of the act for a given state of nature.

It is probably fairly safe to state that monetary value is a valid guide to action in the majority of business decision situations. However, before making this assumption, it is possible to determine by means of a simple test whether it is indeed valid. This test, as described by Schlaiffer,* provides that expected monetary value is a valid guide to action in any decision problem if the decision maker would use it as his criterion in choosing between an act which is *certain* to result in the receipt or payment of a definite amount of cash and an act which will result in either the best or the worst of all the possible consequences of the real decision problem.

As an illustration let us designate $\$W$ as being the monetary value of the worst possible consequence of a decision situation and let $\$B$ represent the monetary value of the best. If the decision maker is offered a choice between a_1, an act which leads to $\$C$ with certainty, and a_2, an act which leads to $\$B$ with probability p and $\$W$ with probability $(1 - p)$, and if he always selects a_1 when

$$\$C > (p)\$B + (1 - p)\$W$$

and selects a_2 when

$$\$C < (p)\$B + (1 - p)\$W$$

and is indifferent between a_1 and a_2 when

$$\$C = (p)\$B + (1 - p)\$W$$

then we can conclude that this decision maker values the consequences of the decision situation at their expected monetary valucs. And for him, the utility of every consequence between the two reference consequences, that is, the worst and the best, is numerically equal to its monetary value.

To state this conclusion in another way, under the above circumstances the decision maker's utility curve for money is linear in the range W, B.

15.7 SUMMARY

All business decision situations involve a selection between alternative acts, each of which leads to some economic consequence the value of which depends upon certain factors, called states of nature, beyond the control of the decision maker. When the state of nature is known, the decision problem is called decision making under certainty. Those situations in

* Robert Schlaiffer, "Introduction to Statistics for Business Decisions," p. 29, McGraw-Hill, New York, 1961.

which the state of nature is unknown or uncertain lead to decision making under uncertainty.

In order to make rational decisions under uncertainty, it becomes necessary to specify the consequences or conditional values of every act for each state of nature. One method of so doing is by means of a payoff table. It has become common, however, to convert payoffs to regrets by taking the positive difference between the best consequence possible for a particular state of nature and all other consequences for that state of nature. The procedure is repeated for all possible states of nature. It is possible to specify rules or functions which provide the conditional values of each outcome. These rules are called payoff functions or regret functions.

Although in many business decision situations the conditional consequences of any act can be stated in monetary value, there are circumstances where monetary value is not a valid representation or guide to action. Under these circumstances the concept of utility is used to express the relative value of decision outcomes. The utility of any outcome for an individual decision maker can be determined from a procedure known as the standard gamble technique. Other approximations for an individual utility curve for money are that it is logarithmic or that it is linear over a certain range. When the latter is true, the number of dollars of gain or loss as a consequence of an act is proportional to the utility of the consequence.

PROBLEMS

15.1. Mr. Jones owns 20 acres of land very close to the route of a proposed expressway. If the expressway route is approved, he believes that he can sell the land for $500,000. If the route is not approved and an alternate route is selected, he would have to subdivide the land and sell 1-acre building sites at $10,000 per lot. Costs associated with subdividing and selling amount to $1,000 per lot. He has received an offer of $300,000 for the land from a large development company and must make a decision on their offer within 48 hr.

(*a*) What is the set of acts?

(*b*) What is the set of states of nature?

(*c*) Set up a payoff table showing the conditional consequences of Mr. Jones' available acts for each state of nature.

(*d*) Convert the payoff table to a regret table.

15.2. A variety store manager is offered a lot of 500 ball-point pens, "as is," for $64. He can sell each good pen for 39 cents, but defective pens represent a total loss. From past experience he has learned to classify lots into three categories, good, fair, and poor. Good lots contain on the average 20 percent defective items, fair lots 50 percent, and poor lots 70 percent defective items.

(*a*) What are the acts available?

(*b*) What are the states of nature?

(*c*) What are the payoff functions for each act?

(*d*) Set up a payoff table.

(*e*) Set up a regret table.

15.3. Given the following payoff function for acts a_1 and a_2:

$$Q_{a_1} = -30 + 50X$$
$$Q_{a_2} = -90 + 20X$$

(*a*) What is the break-even value of X?
(*b*) If $X = 10$, which is the better act?
(*c*) If $X = 10$, what is the regret of the poorer act?
(*d*) If $X = -5$, which is the better act?
(*e*) If $X = -5$, what is the regret of the poorer act?

15.4. The Royal Order of Gophers is planning a Fourth of July picnic to raise money for their treasury. The cost of printing tickets, prizes for the raffle, and renting space at a local park amounts to \$390. Tickets will be sold for \$1.50 each, which entitles each ticket holder to entry to the grounds, a chance at the prizes to be raffled off, and one free beer and hot dog. Each beer and hot dog given away costs the lodge 20 cents.

(*a*) What is the payoff function for the act of holding a picnic?
(*b*) How many tickets must they sell to break even?
(*c*) The goal is to raise \$1,000 for the treasury. How many tickets must they sell to achieve their goal?

15.5. An alternate suggestion for fund raising for the Gopher treasury is to sell chances on a new automobile. One of the Gophers, being a dealer, can provide the car at a cost of \$2,000 to the Gophers. Tickets would be sold at \$2 each. Those in favor of the car raffle point out that if it rains on the day of the picnic the ticket money would have to be refunded and the lodge's investment would be lost.

(*a*) What is the payoff function for the act "raffle the car"?
(*b*) How many tickets must be sold in order to make \$1,000 for the lodge?

15.6. One of the members of the lodge is a professional fund raiser. Based on his experience with picnics, raffles, etc., he estimates that the lodge will sell 1,250 tickets on the automobile and can sell 1,100 tickets to the picnic. However, it is apparent that the weather would have no effect on the auto raffle, while a rainy day would wash out the picnic entirely.

(*a*) Considering rain and no rain on the Fourth of July as the two states of nature, construct a payoff table for the two fund-raising proposals.
(*b*) Construct a regret table.
(*c*) Suppose the lodge decides on the picnic and it rains. What would their regret be with respect to the auto raffle?
(*d*) Suppose the lodge decides on the auto raffle and the Fourth of July is a warm sunny day. What would their regret be?
(*e*) In order for the lodge to make a rational decision between the two proposals, what additional information is required?

15.7. Suppose a businessman arbitrarily assigns a utility of 25 utils to the amount \$100,000 and zero utils to zero dollars. Further, suppose by questioning it has been determined that his certainty monetary equivalent to a gamble in which he can win \$100,000 with a probability of 0.40 or win nothing with a probability of 0.60 is \$30,000. What is his utility for \$30,000?

15.8. Suppose that in the previous problem when the utility of \$100,000 was 25 utils and the utility of zero dollars was zero utils, the businessman was asked to specify the probability of winning a prize of \$100,000 or nothing such that he would be indifferent between the gamble and a certain gift of \$25,000. Suppose he specified that the probability of winning \$100,000 would have to be 0.50. What is his utility for \$25,000?

15.9. Assume a utility equation for dollars was

$$\log \$(X + 1) = U\$X$$

Use logarithms to the base 10 and find:

(*a*) The utility of $15.
(*b*) The utility of $500.
(*c*) The utility of $2,000.
(*d*) The utility of $80,000.

15.10. Assign utility values of your own to various career objectives which you might consider. Show how you arrived at each value.

16
Decision Making under Uncertainty without Sampling

Decision making involves the selection of a course of action from among alternate courses of action under circumstances in which the consequences of each act are dependent upon the unknown state of nature. Although the specific state of nature is unknown, the states which are possible can be enumerated, and the decision maker can make an estimate of the likelihood of occurrence of each state belonging to the set of states. The decision maker's estimate may be based on empirical data which are available to him or may be based entirely upon his own subjective judgment.

Under these circumstances, it should be apparent that some additional information bearing on the state of nature would be helpful to the decision maker. In this chapter, however, we shall consider only those situations in which a decision must be made without recourse to any experimentation or other investigation designed to obtain additional information about the state of nature.

16.1 DECISION CRITERIA BASED SOLELY ON ECONOMIC CONSEQUENCES

Frequently decisions are made without reference to or consideration of the likelihood that any particular state of nature will occur. Hundreds of thousands of tickets are sold monthly in the New York State lottery, for example. The probability that any individual ticket holder will win a prize depends upon the total number of tickets sold. Yet most purchasers of tickets have no idea of the probability associated with the drawing of their individual tickets. No odds are published for them to refer to. Most individuals buy these tickets simply on the basis of a comparison of economic consequences. A single ticket costs only $1. Prizes can be worth thousands of dollars. Those who buy these tickets weigh the relative consequences of the acts "buy" and "don't buy" and make their decision. They rationalize their decision to buy by expressing the hope that maybe this time they will be lucky.

A businessman sometimes purchases large quantities of distressed merchandise from a competitor who is forced to go out of business. If the price is low enough, he will decide to make the purchase on the assumption that if he can sell it he stands to make a large profit while his potential losses are relatively small. It is quite likely that this businessman subjectively assesses the probabilities of gain or loss, and in this sense the concept of probability enters the decision process. However, these probabilities are seldom quantified or even articulated.

It is possible to establish decision criteria which are based upon economic consequences and which should, at the very least, inject some element of consistency into decision making under the given set of circumstances or attitudes which are held by the decision maker. Let us examine some of these criteria with respect to a decision situation similar to the example given in the previous chapter. In that example a television repairman had the opportunity to purchase a stock of discontinued television receivers from a manufacturer who was going out of business. There were a total of five sets having a retail price of $200 each. In that example, the repairman had the option of buying all five for a total of $300 or of declining to buy. In this example we shall provide him with the option of buying any number of the sets from zero to five inclusive.

The cost per set is $60. He plans to sell them at $150 each. The states of nature are, as in the previous example, the demand for the sets, that is, $S{:}\{s_0,s_1,s_2,s_3,s_4,s_5\}$, where s_i represents the demand for i sets. The actions available to the repairman are $A{:}\{a_1,a_2,a_3,a_4,a_5\}$, where a_i represents his act of purchasing i sets.

We can set up a payoff table relating the economic consequences resulting from the selection of any act and the occurrence of each state of nature. If Q represents the quantity purchased and D represents the number

Table 16.1

States (*Demand D*)	a_0	a_1	a_2	a_3	a_4	a_5
	Acts (purchase Q)					
s_0	0	−60	−120	−180	−240	−300
s_1	0	90	30	−30	−90	−150
s_2	0	90	180	120	60	0
s_3	0	90	180	270	210	150
s_4	0	90	180	270	360	300
s_5	0	90	180	270	360	400

demanded by customers, then the payoff for each combination of D and Q can be determined. Since each set costs him \$60 and he receives \$150 for each one he sells, his payoff can be determined from the following payoff functions:

$$\text{For } D \geq Q, P = (\$150 - \$60)Q = \$90Q$$
$$\text{For } D \leq Q, P = \$150D - \$60Q$$

The payoff table for this problem is given in Table 16.1.

Assuming that the decision must be made entirely on the basis of the information provided in Table 16.1, how should the rational decision maker act? There are several criteria which might be used to select an act which is optimum in some sense. It should be pointed out, however, that what is optimum to one decision maker under some given set of circumstances may not be optimum to a different decision maker under the same set of circumstances or even to the same decision maker should the circumstances change.

THE CRITERION OF PESSIMISM, MAXIMIN

The maximin criterion assumes that a decision maker should maximize his payoff under the assumption that the worst possible state of nature will prevail. In using the maximin criterion, the decision maker should refer to his payoff table and for each act find the worst possible consequence, that is, the minimum payoff. From Table 16.1 the minimum payoff for each act can be determined to be as follows:

a_0	a_1	a_2	a_3	a_4	a_5
0	−60	−120	−180	−240	−300

The decision maker would then select that act for which the minimum payoff is the maximum. In this example, a_0 with a minimum payoff of zero would be selected, indicating that the repairman should not purchase any of the sets.

In a decision situation of this type where the worst state of nature is "no demand" for a product, the maximin criterion directs the decision maker not to purchase. By not investing in the product he will suffer no out-of-pocket loss should the worst state of nature prevail. However, the decision not to purchase also precludes any profit should some other state of nature occur. The businessman who always uses the maximin criterion for making decisions would soon go out of business.

THE CRITERION OF OPTIMISM, MAXIMAX

If the decision maker were optimistic about his situation, he might want to use a criterion for selecting an act which would maximize his payoff under the best of the possible states of nature. Under this criterion, the decision maker would refer to his payoff table and list for each act the highest payoff as follows:

a_0	a_1	a_2	a_3	a_4	a_5
0	90	180	270	360	450

He would then select that act for which the maximum payoff is the greatest. In this case a_5 would be selected, and the repairman would purchase all five sets.

Although these criteria lead to the selection of an act without resorting to information regarding the likelihood of the occurrence of any state of nature, the selection of a criterion based on optimism or pessimism is inherently a function of some judgment on the part of the decision maker as to which of the states he feels is more likely to occur.

In a sense, the decision maker who chooses the criterion of optimism is assigning a probability of 1 to the best possible state of nature and a probability of zero to the others. Obviously the selection of the maximin criterion would be an irrational choice if the decision maker actually believed that the most favorable state of nature would indeed occur. Since probabilities of zero and 1 are theoretically no different from any other value of probability it is really not true that the selection of one of these criteria is made without any assessment of probabilities on the possible states of nature.

THE CRITERION OF RATIONALITY, LAPLACE

When there is no information available about the likelihood of occurrence of each state of nature, and when there is no reason to believe that any one state is more or less likely to occur than any other, then, according to this criterion, a set of equal weights should be applied to the payoffs under each state of nature, and the sum of the weighted payoffs should be computed for each act. The act with the highest value of this sum should then be selected.

For the payoff table in Table 16.1, there are six possible states of nature. If it is assumed that all states are equally likely to occur, then an equal weight should be applied to each state. The numerical value of the weight in this case is unimportant. Each state could be assigned a weight of $\frac{1}{6}$, but for the sake of simplicity we could assign a weight of 1 to each state. The value of each act is obtained by multiplying the payoff for each state of nature by the weight assigned to that state of nature and summing these products over all possible states. Since all states are weighted equally with the weight 1, the value of the act is simply the sum of all the payoffs over all the states of nature. For the example, these values would be as follows:

a_0	a_1	a_2	a_3	a_4	a_5
0	390	810	720	660	450

The act having the greatest value under this criterion would be a_2, that is, purchase two sets. It is necessary to comment at this point that assigning equal weights to the states of nature is just as much of an assumption on the part of the decision maker as the utilization of any other weighting scheme.

THE MINIMAX CRITERION

As discussed in the previous chapter, a payoff table can just as easily be constructed in terms of costs or losses as in terms of profits. If the entries in the table are losses, then profits or gains are shown simply as negative losses. For the example, the data in terms of losses would appear as in Table 16.2.

The minimax criterion applied to a loss table selects that act which minimizes the maximum loss. For Table 16.2 the maximum loss for each act is as follows:

a_0	a_1	a_2	a_3	a_4	a_5
0	60	120	180	240	300

The act for which the maximum loss is a minimum is a_0.

Table 16.2

States	*Acts (purchase Q)*					
(Demand D)	a_0	a_1	a_2	a_3	a_4	a_5
s_0	0	60	120	180	240	300
s_1	0	−90	−30	30	90	150
s_2	0	−90	−180	−120	−60	0
s_3	0	−90	−180	−270	−210	−150
s_4	0	−90	−180	−270	−360	−300
s_5	0	−90	−180	−270	−360	−400

16.2 PROBABILITIES AND DECISION MAKING

The criteria discussed in the previous section utilized only economic considerations in determining a course of action. However, the decision maker, in selecting a criterion to apply to the situation, either consciously or subconsciously referred to his own subjective evaluation of the likelihood of occurrence of the possible states of nature. In choosing between maximin, maximax, and the LaPlace criteria, he either weighted the worst state most heavily, the best state most heavily, or all states equally. Since a weighting of the states of nature is an inherent part of the selection of an act, or in the selection of the criterion which leads to the selection of an act, it seems reasonable to adopt some explicit weighting system for the states of nature in a given decision situation.

In decision making we are concerned with the so-called states of nature which affect the consequences of a decision. In a somewhat narrower sense, we are concerned with the state of a particular decision component which is a function of some unknown parameter. If we knew the value of this particular parameter, we would know the corresponding state of nature, and our decision would no longer be made under conditions of uncertainty. It is this uncertainty about the states of nature or the value of the unknown parameter which we are attempting to express in terms of a weighting system. Since we are primarily concerned with the relative likelihood of the occurrence of each possible state of nature, a logical weighting system to adopt would be one which uses probability values as weights. Having determined the weights to use, we would then have something which would be very similar to a probability distribution on the states of nature or, what is essentially the same thing, on the unknown parameter.

Most statisticians are aware that in the strict sense, a parameter cannot have a probability distribution. Probability distributions apply to quantities which are variable, not to quantities which have a fixed value. Estimates of a parameter derived from samples do have distributions, and statisticians have adopted various conventions as means for making probability statements about estimates of a parameter. One statement of this type refers to the probability that a given interval contains the parameter. In other instances the terms *likelihood*, *confidence*, and *fiducial probability* have all been used in order to avoid the implication of variability to a parameter. Regardless of the words used, however, statements regarding the uncertainty in any estimate of an unknown parameter are expressed, or at least interpreted, in terms of probability. As Lindgren states,

> . . . not knowing the actual state of nature, one must take into account somehow the various possible states of nature. A distribution on the state of nature weights the possible states according to one's pleasure—or more accurately, according to one's past experience or information.

> There may be situations, of course, in which it is not unreasonable to think of the state of nature as random in that the state came to pass by a random process and, though now fixed, is still unknown (as in the toss of a coin: after the coin has fallen, the result is not really random, but not knowing the outcome, one is forced to behave as though it were random).*

If we assume the validity of a weighting system for the possible states of nature which we shall refer to as probabilities, the question arises as to how these probabilities are determined.

16.3 OBJECTIVE PRIOR PROBABILITY DISTRIBUTIONS

The weighting system or probability distribution which is used at the inception of the decision analysis is generally referred to as the *prior distribution.* In many instances it is possible to develop the prior distribution from empirical information or data that is already available. For example, historical data on the number of sales or requests for a particular item of merchandise each day for a period of 100 days would provide a frequency distribution from which probabilities could be estimated. The number of defectives per lot produced over some period of time could provide information from which a probability distribution on the fraction defective could be based. In some instances it might be reasonable to assume that the phenomenon of interest follows a particular theoretical distribution and that the parameters of that distribution can be estimated from available data.

In all cases similar to those mentioned, where there is some objective basis for assigning prior probabilities to the states of nature, this prior distribution is considered to be an objective prior distribution.

16.4 SUBJECTIVE PRIOR PROBABILITY DISTRIBUTIONS

When no empirical information is available, the prior distribution must be determined subjectively. The subjective estimates leading to the prior distribution should not simply be guesses. They should result from a careful analysis of the situation and an assessment by the decision maker of the probabilities or odds that a particular state of nature will prevail. It is quite likely that a decision maker has either in his possession or at his disposal considerable expertise and experience relating to the given decision situation which could be utilized. The fact that this information does not exist in some objective, quantitative form does not mean that it should be discarded as useless.

* B. W. Lindgren, "Statistical Theory," p. 182, Macmillan, New York, 1960.

Consider the following simplified situation. The president of a large corporation plans to build a new plant. The time at which construction must begin is flexible. He could begin to build immediately or defer the project for 6 months. However, because of the demand for his product and his future delivery commitments, it is necessary that he expand his capacity sometime in the near future. Therefore, the decision with which he is faced is not one of whether or not to build but simply one of when to build.

The planned expansion is to be financed by a loan. The critical parameter is the prevailing interest rate. There is some opinion that the rate of interest may go down within the next 6 months. If this should occur, it would be to the company's advantage to wait. On the other hand, if interest rates remain at the same level or rise, it would be advantageous to obtain the loan and begin construction immediately. His selection between the acts "build now" and "build in six months" could be based simply on an assessment of the economic consequences of each act, e.g., maximin, maximax, etc. However, if he were able to assign probabilities to the possible states of nature, he might be able to arrive at a better decision.

The decision maker, having been in business for many years, has had considerable experience in assessing economic conditions. He might be inclined to refer to his assessments as hunches or intuition, but over the years his observations of the reactions of the economy and of interest rates to various conditions and stimuli have enabled him to make reasonably accurate judgments or predictions about conditions in the near future. However, not satisfied to rely solely on his own store of knowledge, he consults with his banker, the company economist, the market research department, and possibly with his stockbroker. On the basis of all the information and advice which he could acquire, he assigns probabilities to the two pertinent states of nature.

1. Interest rates will fall.
2. Interest rates will stay the same or rise.

He may have arrived at the specific probabilities by asking himself the question "Would I be willing to accept a bet at 2-to-1 odds that interest rates will go down?"

If he would accept this bet, then he believes that there are two chances in three that the interest rate will fall and one chance in three that it will not. In this case his subjective estimate of the probability that interest rates will fall is $\frac{2}{3}$ versus a probability of $\frac{1}{3}$ that the interest rates will not fall. If he would reject such a bet at 2-to-1 odds but accept it at even money, then his subjective probabilities of the two states are $\frac{1}{2}$ and $\frac{1}{2}$.

These subjective probabilities reflect the uncertainty in the mind of the decision maker about the unknown states of nature bearing on his problem.

They need not be supported by empirical evidence, and it is quite likely that two different decision makers confronted by identical situations would assess the probabilities differently. However, once these prior probabilities are determined for a given situation, they are treated just like any other probability values, and all the classical rules of probability apply.

16.5 DECISION CRITERIA BASED SOLELY ON PROBABILITIES

Consider the ubiquitous newsboy. He buys his papers for a nickel and sells them for a dime. From experience he has learned that he profits most when he buys the exact number of papers that he is able to sell on a given day. If he buys more papers than he can sell, he loses the 5 cents which he paid for each paper that is left over. There is no market for old newspapers. If he buys too few papers, he will turn customers away and consequently will lose the 5 cents which he could have made on the sale.

If the demand for papers were constant from day to day, the newsboy would have no problem. He would know exactly how many papers to buy. However, the demand varies from day to day, and on some days he buys too few and on others he buys too many. It is the rare occasion which finds him with the exact number of papers necessary to satisfy the demand.

Suppose, in an attempt to estimate the probability that the demand will be any specific number of papers on a given day, the newsboy keeps a record of the actual number of papers demanded on each of 50 successive days. Arranged in a frequency distribution, his record appears as shown in Table 16.3.

Table 16.3

Number of papers demanded X	*Number of days, frequency* f	*Relative frequency* $f/\Sigma f$
Less than 14	0	
14	4	0.08
15	11	0.22
16	10	0.20
17	7	0.14
18	7	0.14
19	6	0.12
20	5	0.10
More than 20	0	
	50	1.00

Assuming that the relative frequencies based on a sample of 50 days adequately represent the probabilities of any number of papers being demanded on any day, the newsboy might attempt to decide on his optimal order quantity based entirely on this data.

The mode of this frequency distribution of demand is 15, that is, the quantity most frequently demanded. The mean or expected value is 17. Since 14 papers were the fewest ever demanded, this number would ensure the newsboy that he would never have any papers left over. On the other hand, since there has never been a demand for more than 20 papers, if he ordered that number he could be quite sure that he would never have to turn a customer away. Even with the data compiled as in Table 16.3, he might still be unable to decide if 14, 15, 17, 20, or some other number might represent an optimal number of papers for him to buy each day.

Without considering the costs or consequences associated with a decision to buy any number of papers, it would be difficult to make a decision or determine a decision rule which would consistently lead to beneficial results for the newsboy. We shall therefore turn to a criterion that utilizes both probabilities and economic consequences in selecting a decision rule.

16.6 EXPECTED VALUE AS A DECISION CRITERION: A BAYES' CRITERION

Let us consider the function $f(a,\theta) = Q$, which we call a *payoff function.* The payoff function provides a measure of the economic consequences of selecting act a_i for each possible state of nature. $Q_{ij} = f(a_i,\theta_j)$ is the payoff corresponding to the selection of act a_i if θ_j is the prevailing state of nature. We can call Q_{ij} the conditional payoff of a_i given θ_j or $Q(a_i|\theta_j)$.

Given a probability distribution on θ, the product $Q(a_i|\theta_j)P(\theta_j)$ can be called *the conditional expected* value of $a_i|\theta_j$, that is, the conditional value of a_i given θ_j times the probability that $\theta = \theta_j$. Summing the conditional expected values over all θ_j results in the expected value or expected payoff of the act a_i. This can be expressed as follows:

$$E[Q(a_i)] = \sum_j Q(a_i|\theta_j)P(\theta_j) \tag{16.1}$$

Let us refer to the newsboy problem discussed in the previous section. The payoff function for his problem would be

$$Q(a_i|\theta_j) = 5a_i¢ \qquad \text{for } a_i \leq \theta_j$$
$$Q(a_i|\theta_j) = 10\theta_j¢ - 5a_i¢ \qquad \text{for } a_i < \theta_j$$

The a_i represent the i acts available to the newsboy, where $i = 1, 2, \ldots, 7$, and where a_i represents the purchase of 14 papers, a_2 the purchase of 15 papers, and so on. The θ_j, where $j = 1, 2, \ldots, 7$, represent the demand for papers on any day such that θ_1 represents a demand for 14 papers, θ_2 a demand for 15 papers, and so on.

A payoff table can be constructed and is shown in Table 16.4 together with the probability distribution on θ based on the relative frequencies given in Table 16.3. The expected values of payoffs for each act are given at the base of each column. The highest expected payoffs are realized if either 16 or 17 papers are purchased by the newsboy. To illustrate the computation, the expected payoff for the act "purchase 16 papers" is given by:

$$
\begin{aligned}
E[Q(a_3)] &= \sum_j Q(a_3|\theta_j)P(Q_j) \\
&= (60¢)(0.08) + (70¢)(0.22) + (80¢)(0.20) + (80¢)(0.14) \\
&\quad + (80¢)(0.14) + (80¢)(0.12) + (80¢)(0.10) \\
&= 76.2¢
\end{aligned}
$$

We can arrive at the same conclusion by working with opportunity loss or regret rather than payoff. Since regret represents a loss, we should select that act for which $E(R)$ is the least.

The regret function for this problem would be

$$
\begin{aligned}
R(a_i,\theta_j) &= 5¢(a_i - \theta_j) \qquad \text{for } a_i \geq \theta_j \\
R(a_i,\theta_j) &= 5¢(\theta_j - a_i) \qquad \text{for } a_i \leq \theta_j
\end{aligned}
$$

Regret is obviously zero for $\theta_j = a_i$. When $a_i > \theta_j$, the newsboy will lose 5 cents for each paper he has left over. When $\theta_j > a_i$ he will lose 5 cents for each sale he must pass up because he is out of papers. The regret table corresponding to the payoffs in Table 16.4 can be found in Table 16.5.

Table 16.4

States: number of papers demanded			*Acts: number of papers ordered*						
$P(\theta)$	θ		a_1 (14)	a_2 (15)	a_3 (16)	a_4 (17)	a_5 (18)	a_6 (19)	a_7 (20)
0.08	14		70¢	65¢	60¢	55¢	50¢	45¢	40¢
0.22	15		70¢	75¢	70¢	65¢	60¢	55¢	50¢
0.20	16		70¢	75¢	80¢	75¢	70¢	65¢	60¢
0.14	17		70¢	75¢	80¢	85¢	80¢	75¢	70¢
0.14	18		70¢	75¢	80¢	85¢	90¢	85¢	80¢
0.12	19		70¢	75¢	80¢	85¢	90¢	95¢	90¢
0.10	20		70¢	75¢	80¢	85¢	90¢	95¢	100¢
1.00		$E(Q)$	70¢	74.2¢	76.2¢	76.2¢	74.8¢	72¢	68¢

Table 16.5

States: number of papers demanded			*Acts: number of papers ordered*						
$P(\theta)$	θ		a_1 (14)	a_2 (15)	a_3 (16)	a_4 (17)	a_5 (18)	a_6 (19)	a_7 (20)
0.08	14		0	5	10	15	20	25	30
0.22	15		5	0	5	10	15	20	25
0.20	16		10	5	0	5	10	15	20
0.14	17		15	10	5	0	5	10	15
0.14	18		20	15	10	5	0	5	10
0.12	19		25	20	15	10	5	0	5
0.10	20		30	25	30	15	10	5	0
1.00		$E(R)$	14	9.8	7.8	7.8	9.2	12.0	16.0

Expected regret is obtained in exactly the same way as expected payoff. For the act "purchase 16 papers"

$$\begin{aligned} E[R(a_3)] &= \sum_j R(a_3|\theta_j)P(\theta_j) \\ &= (10)(0.08) + (5)(0.22) + (0)(0.20) + (5)(0.14) \\ &\quad + (10)(0.14) + (15)(0.12) + (20)(0.10) \\ &= 7.8 \end{aligned}$$

Just as it was for payoff or profits, the act with the least expected regret is either a_3 or a_4, that is, purchase either 16 or 17 papers.

16.7 TWO-ACTION PROBLEMS WITH LINEAR PAYOFF FUNCTIONS

For two-action problems there is a value of θ which is called the *break-even value* and is designated θ_k. The break-even point for acts a_1 and a_2 occurs when the payoffs for both acts are equal, that is, when $Q(a_1) = Q(a_2)$.

If $Q(a_1) = b_1 + m_1\theta$ and $Q(a_2) = b_2 + m_2\theta$, then θ_k results from the solution of $b_1 + m_1\theta = b_2 + m_2\theta$ for θ, which results in

$$\theta = \frac{b_2 - b_1}{m_1 - m_2} = \theta_k \tag{16.2}$$

Figure 16.1 illustrates graphically the break-even point in a two-action problem with linear payoff functions.

It should be apparent from Fig. 16.1 that for all values of $\tilde{\theta} < \theta_k$, act a_2 provides the higher payoff since the line representing $Q(a_2)$ is above the line

$Q(a_1)$ for this portion of the graph. For values of $\tilde{\theta} > \theta_k$, act a_1 provides the higher payoff. All that is necessary in a problem of this type then is to compare $E(\tilde{\theta})$ with θ_k. If $E(\tilde{\theta}) > \theta_k$, select a_1. If $E(\tilde{\theta}) < \theta_k$, select a_2.

Example 16.1 Let us consider the following problem. A manufacturer ships his product in lots of 1,000 units to his customers. The proportion of defective pieces in each lot varies from lot to lot but is generally either 0.05, 0.10, or 0.15. From past experience he estimates the probability that a lot contains a proportion defective equal to θ as follows:

θ	$P_0(\theta)$
0.05	0.60
0.10	0.30
0.15	0.10

The manufacturer has a choice to make between two possible courses of action. He could inspect each lot in its entirety before shipping and thereby eliminate all defective items from the lot. The cost of inspection is 10 cents per article inspected, and therefore the cost of inspecting an entire lot would be \$100. Let the act "inspect 100 percent" be designated a_1.

The manufacturer's alternative course of action a_2 is to ship each lot without inspecting. However, each defective found by the customer must be replaced at a cost of \$1.25 per defective item. Obviously, the number of defectives in any lot, and therefore the cost to the manufacturer, of each act is a function of θ. Let the act "ship as is" be designated a_2.

The payoff function for each act in terms of cost is linear. For act a_1, inspect all items, it would be

$$Q(a_1) = \$100^*$$

* $Q(a_1) = b_1 + m_1\theta$ where $b_1 = \$100$ and $m_1 = 0$

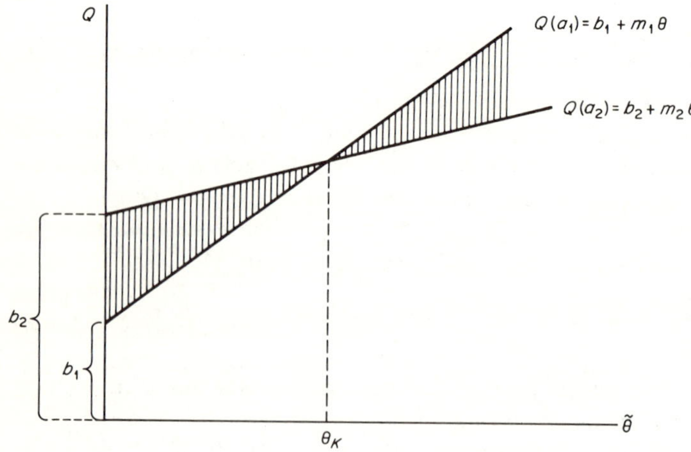

Fig. 16.1

Table 16.6

Prior probability $P_0(\theta)$	State of nature θ	Payoff table (costs) a_1	a_2	Regret table (opportunity loss) a_1	a_2
0.60	0.05	100	62.50	37.50	0
0.30	0.10	100	125.00	0	25.00
0.10	0.15	100	187.50	0	87.00
Expected value	0.075	100	93.75	22.50	16.25

For act a_2,

$Q(a_2) = (\$1.25)(1{,}000)\theta = \$1{,}250\theta$*

Using the longer method of solution, we would set up the payoff or regret table and find the expected value of each act using the prior probability distribution on θ which has been given above. This is done in Table 16.6.

Using the expected value or Bayes' criterion, the expected payoff of a_1 is $E[Q(a_1)] = \$100$. The expected payoff of a_2 is $E[Q(a_2)] = \$93.75$. Therefore, the optimum or best act is a_2, "ship as is." The same conclusion is reached by referring to the last two columns in the table, which provide the expected regrets of each act. Here the act having the smaller expected regret is optimum.

The expected value of $E(\theta) = 0.075$. Substituting this in the payoff function for each act, we would obtain

$$E[Q(a_1)] = \$100 + (0)(0.075) = \$100$$
$$E[Q(a_2)] = 0 + (\$1{,}250)(0.75) = \$93.75$$

which provides exactly the same results as the longer method. The break-even value of θ, θ_k, is obtained from the solution to

$$\$100 = \$1{,}250\theta_k$$

$$\theta_k = \frac{100}{1{,}250}$$

$$\theta_k = 0.08$$

Since $\theta_k = 0.08 > 0.075 = E(\theta)$, we would select a_2.

16.8 REGRET FUNCTIONS

For two-action problems having linear payoff functions the regret for each action is represented by the crosshatched area between the lines of Fig. 16.1. Since regret represents the difference between the payoff resulting from the optimum action and the payoff from the alternate act, it is apparent from the figure that for act a_1, regret is positive to the left of the break-even point and becomes zero at θ_k. For a_2, regret is positive to the right of θ_k and is zero otherwise. This figure shows that the regret function for each act has two parts, depending upon whether $\theta > \theta_k$ or $\theta < \theta_k$.

* $Q(a_2) = b_2 + m_2\theta$ where $b_2 = 0$ and $m_2 = \$1{,}250$

For the previous example the regret functions for the two acts are as follows:

$$R(a_1,\theta):\begin{cases}\$1{,}250(\theta_k - \theta) & \text{for } \theta < \theta_k\\ 0 & \text{for } \theta \geq \theta_k\end{cases}$$

$$R(a_2,\theta):\begin{cases}0 & \text{for } \theta \leq \theta_k\\ \$1{,}250(\theta - \theta_k) & \text{for } \theta > \theta_k\end{cases}$$

Because these regret functions are represented by two broken straight lines, if plotted on a graph versus values of θ rather than by a single straight line as is the case with the payoff function, the expected regret cannot be obtained from the regret function simply by inserting $E(\theta)$. Except in certain special situations which will be discussed later, expected regret must be obtained by the longer method utilizing the regret table.

16.9 MULTIACTION PROBLEMS WITH LINEAR PAYOFF FUNCTIONS

For a two-action problem we found that a payoff function had to be determined for each act. When more than two acts are available to the decision maker, there is a very broad class of decision problems for which two payoff functions are sufficient for all acts available. This type of problem includes decisions involving order quantities, stock levels, expenditure levels, etc. Refer back to the newsboy problem and the problem facing the television repairman. There, the acts available were the decision to stock or buy a certain quantity of an article. The state of nature was the demand for that article. In these cases, a single payoff function was sufficient for all acts in which the number of units stocked was less than the demand (the state of nature was underestimated), and another single payoff function was utilized for all acts in which the units stocked were greater than the demand (state of nature overestimated).

For the newsboy problem, these payoff functions, in terms of profit, were

$$Q(a_i,\theta_j) = 5a¢ \qquad \text{for } a_i \leq 0$$
$$Q(a_i,\theta_j) = 10\theta_j¢ - 5a_i¢ \qquad \text{for } a_i > \theta_j$$

where θ represented the demand for papers and the act a_i represented the act of stocking a number of papers corresponding to i by the newsboy.

The regret function can also be expressed for only two conditions, that is, $a_i \leq \theta_j$ and $a_i > \theta_j$, and as shown previously these are

$$R(a_i,\theta) = 5¢(a_i - \theta_j) \qquad \text{for } a_i \geq \theta_j$$
$$R(a_i,\theta) = 5¢(\theta_j - a_i) \qquad \text{for } a_i \leq \theta_j$$

When $|a_i - \theta_j| = 1$, we have the regret experienced which is due to overestimating or underestimating by a single unit. For any $a_i - \theta_j = 1$, the regret can be referred to as the regret due to overstocking or overestimating θ and is represented by k_o. For any $\theta_j - a_i = 1$, the regret experienced is regret due to understocking or underestimating, and is represented by k_u. There is a value called the critical ratio* which is given by

$$k = \frac{k_u}{k_u + k_o} \tag{16.3}$$

The optimum act in a multiact problem with linear payoff functions is that act a_i such that

$$P(\theta < \theta_i) < k$$

For the newsboy, it happens that $k_u = k_o = 5¢$, and

$$k = \frac{5¢}{5¢ + 5¢} = 0.5$$

The optimum act is therefore that act a_i such that $P(\theta < \theta_i) < k$. From the probability distribution assigned to the demand for papers, we can see that the highest value of i such that $P(\theta < \theta_i) < 0.5$ is 16. Therefore, the optimum act is "stock 16 papers." The act "stock 17 papers" in this case also produces the same expected payoff for the newsboy; however, the critical-ratio analysis leads to the lowest stock level with the optimum consequences. Hence, stock 16 papers.

16.10 SUMMARY

In this chapter we have considered various criteria for reaching a decision, that is, selecting between alternative courses of action under conditions of uncertainty. Previously the distinction was made between conditions of "risk" and "uncertainty" based upon the nature of the information available to the decision maker regarding the state of nature. The distinction was based primarily upon the relative objectivity or, conversely, the degree of subjectivity exercised by the decision maker in assessing this information. Once a weighting system of probabilities is applied to the possible states of nature, the analysis proceeds in exactly the same way regardless of how those weights were derived.

After examining decision criteria based solely on an evaluation of economic consequences or solely on a consideration of probabilities, we have concluded that in order to produce consistently effective results based on a reasonable decision maker's expectations, both consequences and probabilities should be utilized in the decision process. A criterion which does just

* See Sasaki, "Statistics for Modern Business Decision Making," Wadsworth, 1968.

this is based upon expected values and can be called an expected value or Bayes' criterion.

The Bayes' criterion consists of determining the expected value or regret of each act and selecting that act for which this expected value is optimal as compared with the alternatives.

For two-action problems involving linear payoff functions, a shortcut is available since the expected payoff of each act can be determined simply by substituting the expected value of the state of nature into each payoff function. For multiaction problems with linear payoff functions, a method called critical-ratio analysis leads to the optimum act. For problems in which the payoff is nonlinear, the longer method must be used.

PROBLEMS

16.1. Most motorists in purchasing automobile insurance can choose among a $100-deductible plan, a $50-deductible plan, and a no-deductible plan, or may choose not to buy any collision insurance. (The amount deductible is the amount paid by the car owner in the event of a loss. The balance of the loss is paid by the insurance company.) Mr. Allen finds that the costs of the three plans for his new car for the coming year are $45, $75, and $95, respectively. Insurance statistics show that the average claim against collision policies is $300, and that the probability that an individual driver has an accident resulting in such a claim during 1 year of driving is 0.05.

(*a*) What acts are available to Mr. Allen?

(*b*) What are the specific states of nature affecting the consequences of the act?

(*c*) Set up a payoff table in terms of losses.

(*d*) Set up a regret table.

16.2. For the previous problem, select the best act under:

(*a*) The criterion of pessimism (maximin).

(*b*) The criterion of optimism (maximax).

(*c*) The criterion of rationality.

16.3. For the data in Prob. 16.1, select the best act by the Bayes' criterion and specify both the expected loss and expected regret of that act.

16.4. In order to raise money for their summer camp, the scouts of Troop 39 were considering setting up a car wash for one day. A local gas station agreed to let them use a part of the station on the coming Saturday for a flat fee of $5. Their investment in chamois and drying cloths would amount to an additional $10. They realized that the cost of soap and detergent would depend upon the number of cars washed, and they estimated the cost at 10 cents per car. Having decided to charge $1.10 for each car wash, the only decision left for them to make was whether or not to proceed with the project.

(*a*) What is the payoff function for each act?

(*b*) What is the regret function for each act?

(*c*) What does the random variable of the function represent?

16.5. The boys in the previous problem estimate that they can wash one car every 15 min. Since they will be allowed to work on the gas station's property for 8 hr, they will be able to wash a maximum of 32 cars. How many cars *must* they wash in order to break even?

16.6. The father of one of the Boy Scouts in the previous problem operates a car wash and estimated the probability of their getting any number of customers from 0 to 32. His estimates in the form of a probability distribution were as follows:

Number of customers	*Probability*
less than 10	0
11	0.01
12	0.04
13	0.10
14	0.15
15	0.16
16	0.16
17	0.14
18	0.11
19	0.08
20	0.03
21	0.01
22	0.01
more than 22	0
	1.00

(*a*) What is the expected number of customers?
(*b*) What is the expected value of each act?
(*c*) Which is the optimal act under a Bayes' criterion?

16.7. For the data in Prob. 15.1,

(*a*) Suppose Mr. Jones estimates that the probability that the expressway route is approved to be 0.75. Which act should he select?

(*b*) Suppose Mr. Jones estimates that the probability that the expressway route is approved is 0.35. Which act should he select?

16.8. For the data in Prob. 15.2, the following additional information is available to the store manager. During several years of doing business with the manufacturer of the pens offered for sale, he calculates that he has received good lots 35 percent of the time, fair lots 45 percent of the time, and poor lots 20 percent of the time.

(*a*) What is the expected value of the proportion of defective pens in this lot?
(*b*) What is the expected payoff of each act?
(*c*) What is the expected regret of each act?
(*d*) What act should be selected?

16.9. For the data given in Probs. 15.4 to 15.6, suppose that weather bureau records show that the probability of rain on the Fourth of July is 40 percent.

(*a*) Should the lodge plan on the picnic or raffle the car?
(*b*) If the probability of rain is 60 percent, what should they do?
(*c*) For what probability of rain would it make no difference?

16.10. Every December, Boy Scout Troop 39 sets up a stand to sell Christmas trees. The trees are purchased from a supplier at \$2 each and are sold to customers for \$5. Any trees not sold by Christmas Eve are a total loss. Based on past experience and information received from other sales of Christmas trees, the following probabilities were assigned to the demand for trees:

Demand for trees	*Probability*
less than 19	0
20	0.03
21	0.05
22	0.07
23	0.10
24	0.13
25	0.15
26	0.18
27	0.15
28	0.08
29	0.04
30	0.02
more than 31	0
	1.00

Using critical-ratio analysis, determine the optimum number of trees that the Boy Scouts should buy.

16.11. A university student association is considering inviting a Shakespearean troupe to perform on campus. Tickets would be sold only to students for $3 per ticket. The fee for hiring the troupe is $3,600. In order to estimate attendance, the association studied attendance records for similar events and compiled the following data:

Attendance	*Relative frequency*
750	0.04
900	0.06
1,050	0.20
1,200	0.40
1,350	0.22
1,500	0.08

The total student body numbers 3,000.

(*a*) Set up a payoff table.

(*b*) Set up a regret table.

(*c*) Find EOL for the best act. (EOL stands for *expected opportunity loss*, which is the same as expected regret.)

16.12. A manufacturer's representative has been offered a new product line by a manufacturer. If he accepts the new line, he can handle it in one of two ways. The best way, according to the manufacturer, would be to set up a separate sales office and sales force to handle the new line exclusively. This would involve an initial investment of $100,000 in the office, equipment, and the hiring and training of salesmen. On the other hand, if the new line could be handled by the existing sales force using existing facilities, the initial investment would be only $30,000, principally for the training of his present salesmen.

The new product sells for $250. The representative normally receives 20 percent of the sales price on each unit sold, of which 10 percent is paid as commission to the salesman. In order to encourage the manufacturer's representative to set up a separate sales organization to handle the new product, the manufacturer offers to pay 30 percent of the sales price of each unit sold to the representative if the representative sets up a separate sales organization. Otherwise the normal 20 percent will be paid. In either case the salesman gets a 10 percent commission.

Based on the size of his territory and experience with other products, the representative estimates the following probabilities for annual sales of the new product:

Sales in units	*Probability*
1,000	0.10
2,000	0.15
3,000	0.40
4,000	0.30
5,000	0.05

(*a*) Set up a regret table.
(*b*) Find the expected regret of each act.
(*c*) Which act should be selected?
(*d*) Which act would have been best under the maximin criterion?

16.13. Do Prob. 16.12 using the following probability distribution on sales:

Sales in units	*Probability*
1,000	0.05
2,000	0.25
3,000	0.45
4,000	0.20
5,000	0.05

16.14. A manufacturer receives plans for a new product from his research department. He must decide whether to proceed with its development and market the product or whether to drop it entirely. So far, $50,000 has been spent on the research. It would cost an additional $150,000 to complete the development and bring the new product onto the market.

The manufacturer estimates that each unit of the product sold will contribute $8.50 to profit. His market research department has presented him with the following estimates of sales. If the product reaches the market before any competitor markets a similar product, the sales should be:

15,000 units with probability 0.10
20,000 units with probability 0.20
25,000 units with probability 0.45
30,000 units with probability 0.25

If a competitive product is marketed first, the sales estimates become:

15,000 units with probability 0.25
20,000 units with probability 0.30
25,000 units with probability 0.35
30,000 units with probability 0.10

The market research department further estimates that the probability of a competitive product reaching the market first is 0.30.

(*a*) Prepare a probability distribution on the units sold.
(*b*) What is the expected number of units sold?
(*c*) What is the break-even point?
(*d*) Prepare a regret table.
(*e*) Compute the expected regret of each act.

17
Decision Making under Uncertainty with Sampling

In the previous chapter we considered decision situations in which the consequence of an act was dependent upon some unknown state of nature. Although unknown, the probability that nature would assume each of its possible states could be assessed either objectively on the basis of information already at the disposal of the decision maker or subjectively by the decision maker. On the basis of the information available about the states of nature and the conditional consequences of each act for each possible state of nature, the decision maker was forced to make a selection of one of the acts available to him. We have not so far considered the possibility that the decision maker could defer his decision and secure additional information about the state of nature. This additional information is obtained through the process of sampling. The sample outcome will provide additional information about the state of nature, and, therefore, instead of selecting an act directly, we shall allow the sample outcome to select the act.

However, it becomes necessary to select a decision rule which specifies, for any possible sample outcome, the act to be selected. If the value resulting from the sampling process is some random variable X, then the function which relates each possible sample outcome to a specific act is called a *decision rule* and can be denoted by δ or $a = \delta(X)$.

In decision theory with sampling, then, the problem of selecting an act becomes a problem of selecting a decision rule which is optimum under some criterion. Since the decision rule is a function of a random variable, for any decision rule there is always some error probability, that is, some probability that the decision rule will lead to a wrong decision. Consequently, there is some risk associated with every decision rule. A desirable characteristic of any decision rule would be that the risk under that decision rule be less than under any other decision rule. The evaluation of decision rules will be our immediate concern.

We shall also consider the problem of determining when it is desirable to obtain additional information about the state of nature as opposed to making an immediate decision based on information already available.

17.1 THE VALUE OF INFORMATION

A decision maker in a typical decision situation is faced with the problem of making a choice between two or more alternate acts. We are, of course, referring to decisions under uncertainty where the consequences of a decision depend upon the state of nature, which is not known. However, before actually selecting his course of action with respect to the specific decision problem, the decision maker typically has another decision to make. This decision is whether to make the decision immediately, utilizing only the information already available to him, or to postpone this decision until he can obtain additional information about the state of nature.

The process of obtaining additional information has a cost associated with it. The decision maker should be concerned with the cost of the additional information and with its potential value to him in this particular decision situation. It is poor business practice to spend more for anything, including information, than it can possibly be worth. Consequently, the decision maker should have some way of determining the value of any additional information about the state of nature.

In a subsequent section of this book we shall concern ourselves with the determination of the potential value of information from any sampling experiment which might be decided upon. For the time being, we shall attempt to find an upper bound on this value, in other words, the maximum value that any amount of additional information about the state of nature could have with reference to some particular decision situation. The maximum value of additional information is sure to be obtained if we could obtain perfect knowledge about the state of nature. We could not possibly do better than gain perfect information or absolute certainty about the state of nature. In an attempt to evaluate the worth of perfect information, we shall arrive at a measure which we shall call the *expected value of perfect information* or, abbreviating, simply EVPI.

If the decision maker had perfect information about the state of nature, then his decision would always be the best or optimum decision under the circumstances. The difference between his payoff with perfect information, or under certainty, and the expected payoff under uncertainty represents the cost of the uncertainty. We have already derived a measure of this cost of uncertainty, and this measure is the expected regret of the optimal act under the Bayes' criterion. Since regret would be zero with perfect information (because under those conditions the right decision would always be made), the expected regret of the best act under uncertainty represents the amount by which the decision maker could improve the consequences of his decision making if he had perfect information. We can then define EVPI as being exactly equal to the expected regret of the *best* act (by the Bayes' criterion) under uncertainty.

EVPI can also be defined as being the absolute difference between expected payoff under certainty and the expected payoff of the best act under uncertainty. Either way it represents the maximum improvement that could be expected given perfect information. Since it is never possible to obtain perfect information through sampling, the value of additional information obtained by the decision maker by sampling must always be less than EVPI. This then provides a guide for the decision maker as to the maximum amount of expenditure which he should make in order to obtain additional information about the state of nature. His maximum expenditure for this purpose should always be *less* than EVPI.

Example 17.1 Consider the manufacturer's problem in Example 16.1. The decision facing him was to choose between the acts "inspect each lot 100 percent" or "ship each lot as is." This cost or payoff is dependent upon the state of nature which, in this case, was the true proportion of defectives in each lot. Based on his prior distribution on this parameter, the expected regret was computed for each act. For act a_1, "inspect 100 percent," $E[R(a_1)] = \$22.50$. For act a_2, "ship as is," $E[R(a_2)] = \$16.25$.

Based simply on his prior information, the manufacturer should select act a_2, which in the long run and in the absence of perfect information will incur an average opportunity loss for each lot shipped of only \$16.25 as opposed to \$22.50 for the alternative act. If the exact proportion of defectives in each lot was known before shipping, the manufacturer could *always* select the better act, and his opportunity loss or regret for each lot shipped would be zero. The amount \$16.25 is therefore the maximum improvement he could expect per lot if he had perfect information about each lot.

Since information about the state of nature is obtained from sampling, for which there is a cost, and since *perfect* information can never be obtained from a sample since there is always the factor of sampling error, then the value of perfect information should never be spent in obtaining information from a sample. In this case, the manufacturer should never spend as much as \$16.25 to sample from a lot before shipment.

Let us assume that sampling from each lot involves a fixed cost of \$5 plus 10 cents per sampled article. Then a sample of size 100 would cost \$5 plus \$10 = \$15, which is less than EVPI. A sample of 112 would cost \$16.20, still less than EVPI. However, a sample of 113 would cost \$16.30, which is greater than EVPI. Since the expenditure for sampling information should never equal EVPI, a sample of $n < 113$ is the maximum that should be taken if there is to be any sampling at all. Discussion of the concept of optimum sample size will be deferred until later in this chapter.

17.2 BAYES' THEOREM AND THE REVISION OF PROBABILITIES

Assuming for the time being that, having been faced with making a choice between alternate acts, the decision maker concludes that it would be worthwhile to defer this choice until additional information can be obtained, it then becomes necessary to specify a method by which the original and the new information can be combined and utilized in making the required decision. We shall refer to all information about the state of nature prior to sampling as being *prior* information. The information obtained through the sampling process is simply referred to as the *sampling* information. The procedure which we shall soon discuss will combine the prior information with the sampling information into the *posterior* information.

Since the information of concern to the decision maker is information about the state of nature, or to be more specific, information regarding the likelihood of occurrence of each of the possible states of nature, this prior information takes the form of a probability distribution or weighting system, and we have previously called this the *prior distribution.* We can designate the prior distribution as $P(\tilde{\theta} = \theta_i)$, or simply $P(\tilde{\theta})$.

In taking a sample, we shall observe some phenomenon relating to the decision problem and compute some value, called a statistic, from the sample. This is the same procedure we used previously in making inferences about an unknown population parameter in the chapters on estimation and hypothesis testing. We should recall from the previous chapters that a statistic computed from samples has a distribution which is called the *sampling distribution.* It is knowledge about the sampling distribution of a statistic that allows the statistician to make confidence statements or probability statements about the population parameter. Let us refer to this statistic computed from the sample values in general as X, and the sampling distribution of X provides $P(X = x|\theta)$. We can designate the sampling distribution simply as $P(X|\theta)$. When x is the result of a particular sampling process, the probability of having obtained that particular result for a given value of θ is often called the *likelihood.*

The purpose of combining the sampling information with the prior information is to obtain an estimate of the likelihood of occurrence of each possible state of nature that utilizes *all* the data available to the decision maker after or *posterior* to the sampling process. Consequently, the combination of the prior information and sampling information results in a new probability distribution or weighting system on the states of nature which is called the *posterior distribution.* Essentially the process involves the revision of the prior distribution in the light of the sampling information. The revised distribution is the posterior distribution. Since the posterior distribution now provides the probability that θ takes on a particular value or state given the sampling results, this probability can be expressed as $P(\tilde{\theta} = \theta_i | X)$, or simply as $P(\tilde{\theta} | X)$.

The method for combining the prior and sampling information into a new posterior distribution is provided by Bayes' theorem, which states

$$P(\tilde{\theta}_i | X) = \frac{P(X | \theta_i)P(\tilde{\theta}_i)}{\sum_i P(X | \theta_i)P(\tilde{\theta}_i)} \tag{17.1}$$

Bayes' theorem was discussed previously in Chap. 6 and presented with slightly different notation as Eq. (6.6*a*).

To illustrate this process of revising prior probabilities, consider the following situation. Assume that there are two identical urns, θ_1 and θ_2. In urn θ_1 there are 100 red balls; θ_2 contains 100 white balls. This information about the contents of each urn is made known to you, and, although the urns are labeled, the labels are hidden from your sight.

Someone, out of your sight, will toss a fair coin and select an urn in accordance with the rule:

Head: θ_1
Tail: θ_2

The coin is tossed, an urn is selected, and you are asked to guess which urn was selected. Your decision in this case would be purely a guess. However, since the choice of an urn was based on the toss of a fair coin, you would be able to assign probabilities to the choice of either urn. The reasonable probabilities to assign would be:

$$P(\theta_1) = 0.5$$

and

$$P(\theta_2) = 0.5$$

Now let us change the rules of the game slightly. After tossing the coin and selecting the urn, the coin tosser will reach into the urn which he selected and randomly draw out one of the balls. You will be allowed to see the ball drawn before making your guess. Will this additional information improve your score in guessing the urn chosen? It should. Since θ_1 contains all red balls and θ_2 contains all white balls, you should be able to specify the correct urn with no doubt whatsoever. If the ball is red, it had to come from θ_1 since θ_2 contains no red balls, and thereby we can see that $P(\theta_1|\text{red}) = 1$ and $P(\theta_2|\text{red}) = 0$. If the ball selected was white, it had to come from θ_2, and therefore $P(\theta_2|\text{white}) = 1$ and $P(\theta_1|\text{red}) = 0$.

By observing a single ball drawn from one of the urns, it has now become possible to revise the prior estimate of the probabilities associated with the selection of each urn. This could be done using Bayes' theorem as follows.

If a white ball was drawn,

$$P(\theta_1|W) = \frac{P(W|\theta_1)P(\theta_1)}{P(W|\theta_1)P(\theta_1) + P(W|\theta_2)P(\theta_2)}$$

$$= \frac{(0)(0.5)}{(0)(0.5) + (1)(0.5)} = 0$$

$$P(\theta_2|W) = \frac{P(W|\theta_2)P(\theta_2)}{P(W|\theta_1)P(\theta_1) + P(W|\theta_2)P(\theta_2)}$$

$$= \frac{(1)(0.5)}{(0)(0.5) + (1)(0.5)} = 1$$

It should be unnecessary to repeat this process to illustrate the case of the red ball being drawn.

Suppose, however, that instead of having 100 red balls in θ_1 and 100 white balls in θ_2, θ_1 contained 80 red balls and 20 white balls, and θ_2 contained 70 white balls and 30 red ones. Now the drawing of a red ball or a white ball is not conclusive evidence that the urn selected was either θ_1 or θ_2. However, knowing the contents of each urn, we recognize that a red ball is more likely to have come from θ_1 than from θ_2 and a white ball is more likely to have come from θ_2 than from θ_1. Having observed, let us say, a white ball, it is possible to revise the prior probabilities assigned to each urn by using Bayes' theorem.

The prior probability distribution is still

$$P(\theta_1) = 0.5$$

and

$$P(\theta_2) = 0.5$$

since the urn is selected by the toss of a fair coin. The conditional probabilities or likelihoods of the sample result "a white ball is drawn" are as follows:

$$P(W|\theta_1) = 0.2$$
$$P(W|\theta_2) = 0.7$$

The posterior probabilities of each urn, given that a white ball was drawn, are

$$P(\theta_1|W) = \frac{P(W|\theta_1)P(\theta_1)}{P(W|\theta_1)P(\theta_1) + P(W|\theta_2)P(\theta_2)}$$

$$= \frac{(0.2)(0.5)}{(0.2)(0.5) + (0.7)(0.5)} = \frac{0.10}{0.10 + 0.35}$$

$$= \frac{0.10}{0.45} = 0.222$$

$$P(\theta_2|W) = \frac{P(W|\theta_2)P(\theta_2)}{P(W|\theta_1)P(\theta_1) + P(W|\theta_2)P(\theta_2)}$$

$$= \frac{(0.7)(0.5)}{(0.2)(0.5) + (0.7)(0.5)} = \frac{0.35}{0.45}$$

$$= 0.778$$

Therefore, having observed a white ball under these circumstances, a reasonable observer should conclude that urn θ_2 was much more likely than urn θ_1. In terms of betting odds, the odds favor θ_2 by approximately 3.5 to 1.

The sampling experiment in this illustration consisted of drawing a single ball from the urn selected. Obviously, it would have been possible to draw two, three, or more balls from the urn before revising the prior probabilities. Suppose, for example, under the circumstances described, two balls were drawn from the urn selected, the first being replaced before the second was drawn. Suppose also that both balls were white. What would the revised probabilities be for each urn?

The prior probabilities for each urn have not changed. The likelihoods or conditional probabilities of the sampling result are different, however. If we designate the outcome of the replacement sample as being WW and assume that each drawing was independent of the other, then $P(WW) = P(W)P(W)$. But $P(W)$ depends, of course, upon the urn from which the drawing was made. Therefore

$$P(WW|\theta_1) = P(W|\theta_1)P(W|\theta_1) = (0.2)(0.2) = 0.4$$
$$P(WW|\theta_2) = P(W|\theta_2)P(W|\theta_2) = (0.7)(0.7) = 0.49$$

The posterior probabilities are obtained from

$$P(\theta_1|WW) = \frac{P(WW|\theta_1)P(\theta_1)}{P(WW|\theta_1)P(\theta_1) + P(WW|\theta_2)P(\theta_2)}$$

$$= \frac{(0.04)(0.5)}{(0.04)(0.5) + (0.49)(0.5)} = \frac{0.020}{0.265}$$

$$= 0.075$$

and

$$P(\theta_2|WW) = 1 - P(\theta_1|WW)$$
$$= 1.000 - 0.075$$
$$= 0.925$$

Now having seen two white balls drawn in succession from the selected urn, a reasonable observer should become even more certain about the identity of the urn selected. In terms of betting odds, the odds should now be greater than 9 to 1 that the urn from which the sample was taken was urn θ_2.

A different sample result would, of course, result in different posterior probabilities. After the sample was taken, we could compute the posterior probabilities for the observed sample outcome. However, it should be apparent that, having decided to take a sample of size 2 from the urn, it would be possible to compute posterior probabilities for each of the possible sample outcomes even before the sample was taken.

The other sample outcomes which could possibly result from this experiment and the corresponding posterior probabilities associated with each urn would be

Outcome RR	$P(\theta_1|RR) = 0.876$	$P(\theta_2|RR) = 0.124$
Outcome RW	$P(\theta_1|RW) = 0.432$	$P(\theta_2|RW) = 0.568$
Outcome WR	$P(\theta_1|WR) = 0.432$	$P(\theta_2|WR) = 0.568$

Since the sampling was random with replacement, the order of the occurrence of the red and white ball had no effect on the posterior probabilities. Also, the occurrence of one red and one white ball favors θ_2 as the urn from which the drawing was made. The explanation for this is left to the reader to provide in answering Prob. 17.12 at the end of this chapter.

Let us now return to the example of the manufacturer who must decide between the acts "inspect each lot 100 percent" or "ship each lot as is." The payoff function for each act was given as

$$Q(a_1) = \$100$$
$$Q(a_2) = \$1{,}250\theta$$

The unknown state of nature or parameter θ is the proportion defective in each lot. From past experience, the manufacturer assigned the following probabilities to the three values of θ which he considered to be possible.

θ	$P(\theta)$
0.05	0.60
0.10	0.30
0.15	0.10

Using these prior probabilities, the manufacturer computed the expected regret of each act resulting in

$$E[R(a_1)] = \$22.50$$
$$E[R(a_2)] = \$16.25$$

leading to a decision to ship each lot as is.

EVPI, the expected value of perfect information, being equal to the expected regret of the better act, was \$16.25. The manufacturer could afford to spend something less than \$16.25 to obtain additional information about the proportion defective in each lot. Since obtaining information involves sampling and the cost of sampling is \$5 plus 10 cents per sampled article, the manufacturer could conceivably take a sample of up to 112 items at a cost ranging up to \$16.20 for the sample of $n = 112$. Let us suppose he decided that some additional information would be beneficial and that he would take a sample of 20 items and observe the number of defectives. A sample is taken from the next lot ready to be shipped, and no defectives are found in the sample. How should this affect the manufacturer's decision?

The reasoning in this problem is the same as that which applied in the urn problem. A sample containing no defectives is more likely to have come from a popu'ation (or urn) with a small proportion of defectives than from one containing a large proportion of defectives. Consequently, more weight should be given to a small value of θ than to larger ones. Exactly what these weights should be are determined by the Bayes' rule. But first the conditional probabilities of likelihoods must be determined. In order to determine these likelihoods, something must be known about the sampling distribution of the statistic obtained.

When sampling from a large, dichotomous population and observing the number of elements possessing or failing to possess some attribute (in this case the attribute is "defective"), the sampling distribution of the "number of defectives" is binomial with parameters n and θ. For any specific n and θ, the probability of obtaining exactly x defectives is easily determined.

For this example, the probability of getting zero defectives out of a sample of 20 for each possible value of θ is

$$P(X = 0|\theta = 0.05) = 0.358$$
$$P(X = 0|\theta = 0.10) = 0.122$$
$$P(X = 0|\theta = 0.15) = 0.039$$

Now, using Bayes' theorem and given that $X = 0$ and $n = 20$,

$$P(\theta = 0.05|X = 0)$$
$$= \frac{P(X=0|\theta=0.05)P(\theta=0.05)}{P(X=0|\theta=0.05)P(\theta=0.05)+P(X=0|\theta=0.1)P(\theta=0.1)+P(X=0|\theta=0.15)P(\theta=0.15)}$$
$$= \frac{(0.358)(0.6)}{(0.358)(0.6) + (0.122)(0.3) + (0.039)(0.1)}$$
$$= \frac{0.2148}{0.2553}$$
$$= 0.841$$
$$P(\theta = 0.10|X = 0) = \frac{0.0366}{0.2553} = 0.143$$
$$P(\theta = 0.85|X = 0) = \frac{0.0070}{0.2234} = 0.016$$

The posterior probabilities computed by combining the prior information with the sample evidence are now 0.841, 0.143, and 0.016. We can designate the posterior probabilities as $P_1(\theta)$ as opposed to $P_0(\theta)$ for the prior.

Now, using the posterior probabilities, the decision maker can perform the same analysis that he did before when he used the prior probabilities.

Payoff table				*Regret table*	
$P_1(\theta)$	θ	a_1	a_2	a_1	a_2
0.841	0.05	100	62.50	37.50	0
0.143	0.10	100	125.00	0	25.00
0.016	0.15	100	187.50	0	87.50
	Expected values	100	73.45	31.53	4.98

Using the Bayes' criterion after sampling, we find that a_2, "ship as is," has the lower expected cost and the lower expected regret. The expected regret of the better act a_2 in this case is $4.98, which is EVPI after sampling. Although the conclusion is the same as that reached in the previous analysis, it is apparent that we have succeeded in reducing the cost of uncertainty by sampling.

The revision of probabilities can be accomplished even more simply by arranging the data in tabular form as shown in Table 17.1.

Table 17.1

State of nature θ (1)	*Prior probability* $P_0(\theta)$ (2)	*Cond. prob. likelihood* $P(X\mid\theta)$ (3)	*Joint probability* $P(X \cap \theta)$ (4)	*Posterior probability* $P_1(\theta)$ (5)
0.05	0.60	0.358	0.2148	$\frac{0.2148}{0.2553} = 0.841$
0.10	0.30	0.122	0.0366	$\frac{0.0366}{0.2553} = 0.143$
0.15	0.10	0.039	0.0039	$\frac{0.0039}{0.2553} = 0.016$
	1.00		0.2553	1.000

Column 1 simply lists the states of nature. The prior probabilities of each state are given in column 2. The conditional probabilities of the sample outcome, given each possible state of nature, appear in column 3. These particular probabilities are taken directly from the binomial tables for $n = 20$, $X = 0$, and θ (or p) $= 0.05$, 0.10, and 0.15. Column 4, the joint probabilities, is obtained by multiplying the entries in column 3 by the entries in column 2. The sum of the joint probabilities in column 4 is the marginal probability of the event "zero defectives."

The posterior probabilities in column 5 result from the division of each joint probability in column 4 by the marginal probability or sum of column 4. Both the prior and posterior probabilities add up to 1.

17.3 PREPOSTERIOR ANALYSIS: ANALYSIS IN THE EXTENSIVE FORM

We have previously indicated that in going from decision making without sampling to decision making with sampling, the problem of selecting an act becomes one of selecting a decision rule. This is true prior to the actual sampling process. Once the sample has been taken and the sample result is known, then sample evidence is combined with the prior information by way of Bayes' theorem, and the posterior distribution is used to select the optimum act by Bayes' criterion.

However, *before* the sample is taken, the decision maker may wish to specify the decision rule to use for selecting his action on the basis of the sample outcome. The optimum decision rule can be obtained by so-called preposterior analysis in which all possible sample outcomes, for a given sample size, are evaluated before the sample is taken and the optimum act is specified for each possible outcome.

Table 17.2

State of nature θ	*Prior* $P_0(\theta)$	*Likelihood* $P(X = 0\|\theta)$	*Joint probability* $P(X \cap \theta)$	*Posterior* $P_1(\theta)$	*Cost table* a_1	a_2	*Regret table* a_1	a_2
0.05	0.6	0.902	0.5412	0.632	100	62.50	37.50	0
0.10	0.3	0.810	0.2430	0.284	100	125.00	0	25.00
0.15	0.1	0.722	0.0722	0.084	100	187.50	0	87.50
	1.0		0.8564	1.000				
				Expected values	100	90.75	23.70	14.45

To continue with the previous example, suppose the manufacturer had decided to take a sample of $n = 2$ in order to gain additional information about the proportion defective in some particular lot. Before taking the sample, he wishes to decide upon the decision rule which will select the optimum act. The decision rule is some function of a random variable, say X, and, therefore, $a = \delta(X)$ means that for every X resulting from the sample, $\delta(X)$ will specify a, the optimum act.

The random variable to be observed as a result of the sampling process is X = the number of defectives. For this experiment in which $n = 2$, X can assume only the values 0, 1, 2; that is, $\{0,1,2\}$ is the set of all possible outcomes to this experiment. Before actually taking the sample, the decision maker will perform the following analysis.

Suppose the sample is taken and zero defectives are observed; that is, $X = 0$. The posterior probabilities and posterior expected regret for each act are computed in Table 17.2.

Since $E[R(a_1)] = \$23.70 > \$14.45 = E[R(a_2)]$, the optimum act for zero defectives would be a_2. We can write $\delta(0) = a_2$.

Suppose the sample is taken and a single defective is observed; that is, $X = 1$. The posterior probabilities and expected regret for each act are computed in Table 17.3. Since $E[R(a_1)] = \$15.68 < \$26.18 = E[R(a_2)]$, the optimum act after observing one defective is a_1; that is, $\delta(1) = a_1$.

Table 17.3

State of nature θ	*Prior* $P_0(\theta)$	*Likelihood* $P(X = 1\|\theta)$	*Joint probability* $P(X \cap 0)$	*Posterior* $P_1(\theta)$	*Cost table* a_1	a_2	*Regret table* a_1	a_2
0.05	0.6	0.095	0.0570	0.418	100	62.50	37.50	0
0.10	0.3	0.180	0.0540	0.396	100	125.00	0	25.00
0.15	0.1	0.255	0.0255	0.186	100	187.50	0	87.50
	1.0		0.1365	1.000				
				Expected values	100	110.50	15.68	26.18

Table 17.4

State of nature θ	*Prior* $P_0(\theta)$	*Likelihood* $P(X = 2 \mid \theta)$	*Joint probability* $P(X \cap 0)$	*Posterior* $P_1(\theta)$	*Cost table* a_1	a_2	*Regret table* a_1	a_2
0.05	0.6	0.002	0.0012	0.194	100	62.50	37.50	0
0.10	0.3	0.010	0.0030	0.490	100	125.00	0	25.00
0.15	0.1	0.022	0.0022	0.316	100	187.50	0	87.00
	1.0		0.0062	1.000				
				Expected values	100	132.62	7.27	39.90

Finally, suppose that the sample is taken and two defectives are observed; that is, $X = 2$. Table 17.4 gives the posterior probabilities and expected regrets for this case. Since $E[R(a_1)] = \$7.27 < \$39.90 = E[R(a_2)]$, the optimum act after observing two defectives is also a_1, and $\delta(2) = a_1$. It is obvious that for this problem and assuming a sample of size 2, act a_1, "inspect 100 percent," is optimum when 1 or 2 defectives are found in a sample of size 2, while a_2 is optimum if no defectives are found.

The optimum decision rule then specifies:

X	$\delta(X) \rightarrow a$
0	a_2
1	a_1
2	a_1

17.4 EXPECTED VALUE OF SAMPLE INFORMATION

We have previously considered the maximum value of information to the decision maker as being equal to the cost he incurs due to his uncertainty or lack of knowledge about the state of nature. The maximum value of information was called EVPI, and it equals the difference between the economic consequences which the decision maker would realize under conditions of certainty and the consequences which he would incur under the conditions of uncertainty which exist at the time the decision is made.

Since the decision maker can never do better than he could under conditions of certainty, that is, with perfect information, the expected value of perfect information, or EVPI, represents the maximum that should ever be spent for obtaining information about the state of nature. However, as long as information about the state of nature must be obtained through a process of sampling, perfect information is never possible to achieve. Therefore, an amount equal to EVPI should never be spent on the information-gathering process. The amount spent to acquire information should always be less than EVPI, but at the same time, the information obtained from the sample should at least be worth more than the cost of obtaining it. It then becomes necessary to determine the value of information which can be obtained from a sample of a given size before actually taking the sample. Since this value is estimated before taking the sample, it is an expected value and is referred to as the *expected value of sample information* or simply EVSI.

One measure of the value of the information obtained from a sample would be to compare the expected consequence of making a decision without sampling with the expected consequence after a sample of a given size was taken. Obviously, the expected consequence of a decision without sampling and a decision after taking a sample of a given size must be compared before the actual sampling is accomplished, since the reason for making this comparison is to determine whether it would be worthwhile to take the sample.

The measure of the expected consequence of making the decision without sampling is simply the expected payoff or regret of the best act prior to sampling. This would be called the *prior expected payoff* (either profit or cost) or if regrets are used, the *prior expected regret*. Keep in mind that the latter is equal to EVPI.

If a sample of size n were to be taken, we could compute a *posterior expected payoff* or *posterior expected regret* for each possible sample outcome. This has already been done for the example given in the section on preposterior analysis. The posterior expected payoff or regret is the expected payoff or regret of the best act available given a specific sample outcome. This value will differ depending upon the sample outcome, and since prior to sampling we do not know what the outcome will be, the question arises as to how to compute a single posterior payoff or regret.

Although we may not know which sample outcome will result from the experiment we may conduct, we do know the probability of each possible sample outcome. The probability of any sample outcome occurring is simply the marginal probability resulting from the preposterior analysis which is the sum of the joint probabilities of the sample result and θ. This can be written as

$$P(X = x) = \sum_{\theta} P(x \cap \theta) = \sum_{\theta} P(X|\theta)P(\theta) \tag{17.2}$$

We can, therefore, find the *expected value of expected posterior payoff* by taking the posterior payoff of the best act for each sample outcome, weighting each by the probability of that sample outcome occurring, and summing these weighted values over all possible outcomes. This is also called the *expected risk of the decision rule* or, alternately, the *Bayes' risk of the decision rule*. The expected value of sample information or EVSI is

Table 17.5

θ	$P_0(\theta)$	*Payoff (cost)* a_1	a_2	*Regret* a_1	a_2
0.05	0.6	100	62.50	37.50	0
0.10	0.3	100	125.00	0	25.00
0.15	0.1	100	187.50	0	87.50
Expected values		100	93.75	22.50	16.25

simply the difference between the expected prior payoff (or regret) and the expected value of the expected posterior payoff (or regret). If payoff is expressed in terms of profit, then EVSI equals expected posterior expected profit minus prior expected profit. If payoff is expressed in terms of cost, or if regret is used, then EVSI equals prior expected cost (or regret) minus expected posterior expected cost (or regret).

To illustrate the computation of EVSI, we shall continue the example of the manufacturer who must make the decision either to inspect each lot 100 percent before shipping or to ship each lot without inspecting. These acts are designated a_1 and a_2, respectively.

The possible values of θ, the proportion defective, the prior distribution on θ, and the payoff cost and regret tables of this example are given in Table 17.5.

On the basis of the prior information, the decision by the Bayes' criterion would be a_2, ship as is.

The prior expected payoff (cost) of this decision would be the expected payoff (cost) of the better act, or \$93.75. The prior expected regret would be the expected regret of the better act, or \$16.25.

Suppose the manufacturer could postpone his decision until additional information could be acquired by sampling. Since EVPI = \$16.25, he would want to spend less than this amount on sampling since sampling would never provide perfect information. Assume that he decides that if he samples at all, he will take a sample of size 2. The question that must be answered

Table 17.6 Sample outcome $X = 0$

$P_0(\theta)$	θ	$P_1(\theta)$	*Payoffs (costs)* a_1	a_2	*Regret* a_1	a_2
0.6	0.05	0.632	100	62.50	37.50	0
0.3	0.10	0.284	100	125.00	0	25.00
0.1	0.15	0.084	100	187.50	0	87.00
	Expected values		100	90.75	23.70	14.45

Table 17.7 Sample outcome $X = 1$

			Payoffs (costs)		*Regret*	
$P_0(\theta)$	θ	$P_1(\theta)$	a_1	a_2	a_1	a_2
0.6	0.05	0.418	100	62.50	37.50	0
0.3	0.10	0.396	100	125.00	0	25.00
0.1	0.15	0.186	100	187.50	0	87.50
	Expected values		100	110.50	15.68	26.18

is "What is the expected value of a sample of size 2 in this decision problem?"

From the previous preposterior analysis, we have the posterior distributions on θ that would result from each of the three possible sample outcomes. We also have the expected payoffs (costs) and regrets computed for each sample outcome and posterior distribution. These are recapitulated in Tables 17.6 to 17.8.

Table 17.9 shows the data entering into the computation of expected posterior expected payoff (cost) and expected posterior expected regret.

The columns in Table 17.9 are numbered for reference. Column 1 simply lists the possible outcomes resulting from a sample of size 2 where, in this case, the random variable X represents the number of defectives. The marginal probabilities in column 2 come from the sums of the columns labeled "joint probabilities" in Tables 17.2 to 17.4. The last marginal probability for $X = 2$ was altered slightly to make the sum of these probabilities equal 1.

Column 3 simply lists the optimal act for each sample outcome, while columns 4 and 6 provide the expected cost and regrets, respectively, for the specified optimal act. Columns 5 and 7 are the result of multiplying each value in columns 4 and 6 by the corresponding probability in column 2. Columns 5 and 7 were then summed to provide the expected posterior expected cost and expected posterior expected regret, respectively.

Table 17.8 Sample outcome $X = 2$

			Payoffs (costs)		*Regret*	
$P_0(\theta)$	θ	$P_1(\theta)$	a_1	a_2	a_1	a_2
0.6	0.05	0.194	100	62.50	37.50	0
0.3	0.10	0.490	100	125.00	0	25.00
0.1	0.15	0.316	100	187.50	0	87.50
	Expected values		100	132.62	7.28	39.90

Table 17.9

(1) Sample outcome	(2) Marg. prob. of sample outcome	(3) Optimal act	(4) Expected cost	(5) Conditional expected cost (col. 2 × col. 4)	(6) Expected regret	(7) Conditional expected regret (col. 2 × col. 6)
$X = 0$	0.856	a_2	90.75	77.68	14.45	12.37
$X = 1$	0.137	a_1	100.0	13.70	15.68	2.15
$X = 2$	0.007	a_1	100.0	0.70	7.28	0.06
	1.000		*Expected values*	92.08		14.58

EVSI can be obtained either by using expected costs or expected regrets.

$$\begin{aligned} \text{Prior Expected Cost } (a_2) &= \$93.75 \\ -\text{Expected Value of Posterior Expected Cost} &= 92.08 \\ \text{EVSI} &= \$\ 1.67 \end{aligned}$$

$$\begin{aligned} \text{Prior Expected Regret } (a_2) &= \$16.25 \\ -\text{Expected Value of Posterior Expected Regret} &= 14.58 \\ \text{EVSI} &= \$\ 1.67 \end{aligned}$$

The expected value of the information to be obtained from a sample of size 2 in this decision situation is \$1.67.

17.5 EXPECTED NET GAIN FROM SAMPLING

Having computed the expected value of the information which could be obtained from a sample of size 2 in the decision situation of the previous example, the question of whether or not a sample of that size should be taken still has not been answered. If sampling or information gathering could be accomplished with no cost, then it would always pay to gather additional information. However, there is always some cost associated with a sampling experiment, and it should be obvious that no more should be spent for additional information than the value or expected value of that information.

In the decision problem under consideration, the expected value of the information from a sample of size 2 was computed to be \$1.67. Sampling involved a fixed cost of \$5 plus a variable cost of 10 cents per item sampled. A sample of size 2 would, therefore, cost \$5 plus 20 cents, or a total of \$5.20. It certainly would not be worthwhile to spend \$5.20 in order to obtain information worth \$1.67. In this case, then, the sample of size 2 should not be taken.

The expected net gain from sampling, abbreviated ENGS, is simply EVSI minus the cost of sampling. If ENGS is zero or a negative quantity as it is in this example, the sample is not justified.

The question of whether a sample of size 2 should be taken is a part of a much broader question. The question the decision maker should ask is how large a sample should be taken. This question includes the possibility of a sample of size $n = 0$, or no sampling at all.

Since the expected value of sample information and the cost of sampling varies with the sample size, the expected net gain from sampling also varies. The selection of the optimal sample size will be considered next.

17.6 OPTIMUM SAMPLE SIZE

We have found that for a given sample of size n it was possible by preposterior analysis to determine the optimum decision rule and the expected risk or expected posterior expected regret for the rule. We could also determine the expected value of sampling information by finding the difference between the expected regret without sampling and the expected value of posterior expected regret. Since there is a cost associated with the sampling or information-gathering process, the expected net gain from a sample of size n, ENGS (n) is simply EVSI $-$ C(n) where $C(n)$ represents the cost of taking a sample of size n.

If ENGS (n) > 0, it would be worthwhile to take a sample of that size. If ENGS (n) ≤ 0, no advantage accrues to the decision maker from a sample of that size, and, therefore, the sample should not be taken. This conclusion is reached, however, only for the specific value of n for which the preposterior analysis was conducted. ENGS ≤ 0 for that particular n does not preclude the possibility that a sample of some other size might provide a positive net gain. Even if ENGS > 0, this does not mean that this particular n is optimum.

The problem is to find that particular value of n for which ENGS is a maximum. Let us designate the optimum sample size for a given problem as n^*. Let us designate the optimum decision rule as determined by preposterior analysis for a given $n = n_i$ as $\delta^*(n_i)$.

The cost of any sample of size n can generally be expressed as

$$C(n) = C_f + nC_v$$

That is, the total cost of a sample of size n is equal to the sum of the fixed cost of sampling and the variable cost per sampled unit times the number of units sampled.

The selection of an optimum sample size involves the computation of ENGS for various-size samples and the determination of that value of n for which ENGS is a maximum, provided that ENGS > 0. We can limit the number of values of n which should be considered since we have previously indicated the maximum *cost* of sampling should never equal EVPI. Therefore, the upper bound on n must be that n is such that

$$C(n_{max}) < \text{EVPI}$$

If we had to graph the cost of sampling and EVSI versus n, we would get curves similar to those shown in Fig. 17.1*a* and *b*.

Depending upon the nature of the decision problem and the parameter of the prior distribution, the value of sampling information may behave as shown in either Fig. 17.1*a* or *b*. In either case, whether the value of information increases rapidly with small samples or otherwise, the *rate* of increase eventually decreases as the value approaches a maximum. ENGS represents the difference between the cost and value curves. There is no guarantee that ENGS will ever be positive; that is, cost could exceed EVSI for all values of n. In that case, the optimum sample size is $n = 0$.

Determination of the optimum sample size in the general case involves the following steps for all sample sizes from $n = 0$ to $n = n_{max}$ where $C(n_{max}) <$ EVPI:

1. By preposterior analysis, define $\delta^*(n_i)$.
2. Compute expected value of posterior expected regret for $\delta^*(n_i)$.
3. Compute EVSI for $\delta^*(n_i)$ by subtracting the expected value of posterior expected regret from the prior expected regret of the best act.
4. Compute ENGS for $\delta^*(n_i)$ by subtracting $C(n_i)$ from EVSI.
5. The optimum sample size is that value of n for which ENGS of $\delta^*(n_i)$ is a maximum.

The computation of the values for a large set of n would be very tedious if done by hand. These calculations could, however, be done by computer in a fraction of the time. When a computer is not available, some approxi-

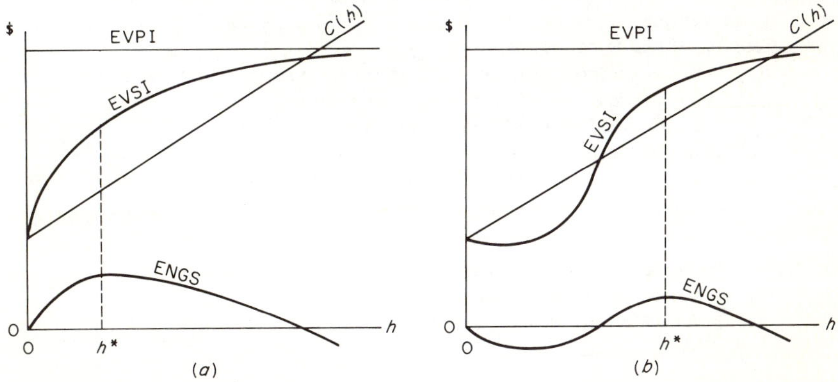

Fig. 17.1

mation method could be used. Schlaiffer has shown that a moderate error in sample size is of no practical importance.* A sample which deviates from the optimum by 10 percent cannot increase total expected cost by as much as 0.6 percent, while a sample which deviates as much as 20 percent from the optimum would increase total cost by less than 2.5 percent.

One approximation method would be a graphic solution. A sufficient number of values of ENGS should be computed over a sufficient range of values of n in order to allow a smooth curve to be drawn through the points. The approximate maximum and corresponding n can then be determined by visual inspection.

17.7 SUMMARY

Decision making under uncertainty with the possibility of sampling involves problems of selecting an optimum decision rule rather than selecting an optimum act, and also of determining an optimum sample size.

The optimum decision rule for a given sample size is determined by extensive form or preposterior analysis in which, prior to sampling, all possible sample outcomes are evaluated and the best act is determined for each possible sample outcome. The set of "best" acts for each possible sample outcome comprises the decision rule.

The expected value of information derived from a sample of any given size can also be determined prior to sampling. This value is designated EVSI. When the cost of sampling is deducted from EVSI, the expected net gain from sampling or ENGS is obtained. Optimum sample size is that size sample for which ENGS is a maximum.

PROBLEMS

17.1. Refer to Prob. 15.2 and Prob. 16.8. Suppose the store manager is allowed to take a random sample of five pens from the lot and determine the number of defective pens in the sample before making his decision. The manager draws a sample of size 5 and discovers three defective pens.

(*a*) What is the posterior distribution on the proportion of defectives?
(*b*) What is the expected value of $\tilde{p}$, the proportion defective?
(*c*) After taking the sample, which act should the manager select?
(*d*) Prior to taking the sample, what was EVPI?
(*e*) After taking the sample, what is EVPI?

17.2. Suppose in the previous problem that the manager was allowed to take a sample of 10 instead of 5 and found 4 defective.

(*a*) What is the posterior distribution on the proportion defective?
(*b*) What is the expected value of $\tilde{p}$, the proportion defective?
(*c*) Now which act should the manager select?
(*d*) What is the new EVPI?

* Robert Schlaiffer, "Probability and Statistics for Business Decisions," pp. 546–547, McGraw-Hill, New York, 1959.

17.3. Consider Probs. 17.1 and 2 as if the two samples were taken sequentially. That is, first the sample of 5 was taken, and $P_1(\tilde{p})$ was determined. Then the sample of size 10 was taken.

(*a*) What is $P_2(p)$?
(*b*) What is the expected value of p?
(*c*) Which act should the manager choose?
(*d*) What is EVPI?

17.4. In the previous problems, suppose the supplier of the pens, rather than offering to let the store manager take a sample of some specified size at no cost, offers to let the manager take a sample of any size he chooses, provided that he will pay \$2 for each pen sampled. What is the largest sample that the manager should consider taking?

17.5. If the store manager in the previous problem decided to take a sample of 5 pens, what should his decision rule be prior to any sample? Determine by extensive form analysis.

17.6. For the data in the previous problems,

(*a*) Find EVSI for a sample of size 5.
(*b*) Find ENGS for a sample of size 5.
(*c*) Find EVSI for a sample of size 7.
(*d*) Find ENGS for a sample of size 7.

17.7. For the data in the previous problem, find ENGS for enough additional possible sample sizes to be able to plot a curve of ENGS versus n. Determine an approximate optimal sample size.

17.8. For the data in Prob. 16.11, suppose that before making a decision as to whether to invite the Shakespearean troupe, it was decided that a random sample of students should be asked if they would buy tickets to the performance if the troupe was invited.

(*a*) Using the relative frequencies given in Prob. 16.11, set up the prior distribution on the proportion of the student body that would attend the performance.
(*b*) What is the expected attendance?
(*c*) What is the expected prior regret of each act?
(*d*) What is EVPI?
(*e*) What is the expected value of a sample of size 3?
(*f*) What is ENGS from a sample of size 3 if the cost of taking the sample was \$3?

17.9. Suppose in the previous problem that one of three students sampled indicated that he would attend.

(*a*) Find the posterior distribution on the proportion who would attend the performance.
(*b*) What is the expected regret of each act?
(*c*) What is EVPI after the sample of size 3?

17.10. For the same data used for Prob. 17.8, assume that a sample of 25 students was taken, of which five students said that they would buy tickets.

(*a*) Based on these sample results, find the posterior distribution on the proportion.
(*b*) What is the expected attendance based on the posterior distribution?
(*c*) What is the expected regret of each act?
(*d*) What is EVPI after this sample?

17.11. Do the previous problem assuming that only one of the sample of size 25 indicated that he would attend the performance.

17.12. For the urn example of Sec. 17.2 where two balls are sampled with replacement from the urn selected, explain why the drawing of one red ball and one white ball results in a higher posterior probability for urn θ_2.

18
Probability Distributions in Decision Analysis: The Beta Distribution

18.1 THEORETICAL DISTRIBUTIONS IN DECISION THEORY

In examples up to this point certain simplifying assumptions have been made about the state of nature. The first of these assumptions was that the state of nature could assume a limited number of discrete values. Now this assumption about the discreteness of the state of nature is relatively valid for all practical purposes although the limited number of discrete values which are generally considered is frequently unrealistic.

With respect to the assumption of discreteness, there are many characteristics which are inherently continuous. Dimensions, weight, and in general, any characteristic resulting from a process of measurement are continuous. However, to view the problem realistically, values of these characteristics can be obtained only by reading some sort of measuring device, and the readings from such a device are reported in terms of discrete measurement units. Therefore, even for an inherently continuous characteristic for which values are obtained by the process of reading an instrument, the actual values used in a decision problem can be represented by a set of discrete numbers. However, the number of distinct values which most characteristics could assume in the context of a given decision situation is generally very large. Therefore, to attempt to establish a prior distribution by assigning probability values to each one of these possible values and then to revise each of these prior probabilities utilizing the Bayes' theorem would constitute a tedious, if not, in some circumstances, an impossible, task. An alternative to listing a large number of discrete values and assigning individual probabilities to each is to select a continuous probability distribution to represent the prior probabilities for all possible states of values of nature. The problem here is to select a distribution which closely resembles the decision maker's own prior distribution on the state of nature.

We have spoken previously about the use of theoretical probability distributions as models of real phenomena. We shall soon see how certain theoretical distributions can be used to model or represent uncertainties about the state of nature and how theoretical and sampling distributions are used together to revise prior probabilities.

18.2 CONJUGATE DISTRIBUTIONS

Prior and posterior distributions on a state of nature or on a parameter provide a measure of probability that the value of the parameter lies within some interval. Rather than assign probability values to specific discrete values which the parameter might assume, it is frequently much more convenient to adopt a theoretical probability distribution as a model. Having selected a type of distribution as the appropriate model, it then remains only to estimate the parameters of the theoretical prior distribution. As with any prior distribution consisting simply of discrete values and probabilities, the estimate of the parameters of the prior distribution may be subjective or based on empirical data. Once the type of prior distribution is specified and its parameters estimated, these parameters can be modified or revised on the basis of additional empirical evidence resulting in a posterior distribution of the same type but with new parameter values.

The selection of the type of probability distribution to use for the state of nature presents a problem. There is, however, a theory of *conjugate distributions* which assists in selecting the type of distribution to be used for the prior. A prior distribution is conjugate to an experiment when the prior distribution is so related to the conditional distribution of the basic random variable of the experiment that the posterior distribution resulting is of the same type as the prior.

For example, if the sampling distribution of the experiment $f(x)$ is binomial, then $f(\theta)$ has a beta distribution. If $f(x)$ is assumed to be normal, then $f(\theta)$ is also normal. If $f(x)$ is Poisson, $f(\theta)$ is gamma. We shall consider binomial, normal, and Poisson sampling in subsequent sections.

These three sets of conjugate distributions should cover most decision situations likely to be encountered.

In selecting a family of distributions to represent the decision maker's prior belief about the state of nature, Raiffa and Schlaiffer suggest that such a family should meet the following requirements:

1. The family or type of distribution selected should be such that it is reasonably easy to determine the posterior distribution resulting from the given prior and the given sample, and, of course, the posterior should belong to the same family as the prior.
2. The family selected should be rich in the sense that there will exist a member of the family which adequately expresses the decision maker's prior information and beliefs.
3. The family should be parametrizable in a manner which can be easily interpreted in terms of the decision maker's prior judgment about the state of nature.*

Frequently this last requirement is the most difficult to obtain as we shall see with respect to some of the distributions to be discussed in this and in the following chapter.

18.3 THE DISTRIBUTIONS IN THE DECISION PROBLEM

There are four distinct distributions involved in a decision analysis, and it is important to be able to distinguish among them. First there is the distribution of the population or process having the unknown characteristic or parameter of interest which has been called the state of nature. It is the value of this parameter which is important to the decision maker. In order to gain information about the value of the parameter or the state of nature, an experiment is conducted which involves a process of sampling from this parent population. Some statistic is subsequently obtained from the sample which provides information about the state of nature. As has been discussed previously, there is a theoretical distribution of the statistic which is called a sampling distribution. The parameter or parameters of the sampling distribution have some relationship to the unknown population which allows estimates of the population parameter to be made from the sample information and confidence statements attached to these estimates.

The sampling distribution for a given parameter value can be called the *conditional distribution* and produces a value called the *likelihood* of the sample result for a given parameter value. This sampling or conditional distribution is the second of the four distributions encountered.

* Howard Raiffa and Robert Schlaiffer, "Applied Statistical Decision Theory," Harvard, Cambridge, Mass., 1961.

Having adopted the convention of referring to a weighting scheme regarding our uncertainty about the true value of the *population* parameter as a probability distribution on this parameter, the third distribution involved is the initial probability distribution on the unknown *population parameter.* It is called the *prior* distribution since it is assumed prior to the sampling process.

The fourth distribution is also a probability distribution on the unknown parameter. It results from the combination of the prior distribution with the sampling or conditional distribution and is called the *posterior* distribution. Keep in mind that if more than one sample is taken the distribution which is posterior to sample 1 is the prior distribution for sample 2, and so on.

18.4 BINOMIAL SAMPLING AND THE BETA DISTRIBUTION

When conditions are generated by a Bernoulli process, the sampling is binomial. That is, the sampling or conditional distribution is binomial. The distribution which is conjugate to the binomial sampling distribution is the beta distribution.

The binomial distribution provides the probabilities of obtaining r successes in n trials given θ, or more commonly, p. Since θ or p is the unknown population parameter, the distribution of $\tilde{p}$ is given by the beta distribution with parameters r and n.

We shall designate the binomial distribution function and probability by $f_b(\tilde{r}|n,p)$ and $P_b(\tilde{r}|n,p)$, respectively.

The correspondence beta density function and probability are $f_\beta(\tilde{p}|n,r)$ and $P_\beta(\tilde{p}|n,r)$. The beta density function is

$$f_\beta(\tilde{p}|n,r) = \frac{(n-1)!}{(r-1)!(n-r-1)!}\tilde{p}^{r-1}(1-\tilde{p})^{n-r-1} \tag{18.1}$$

Since $\tilde{p}$ is a continuous random variable ($0 \leq p \leq 1$), the cumulative probability density function or CDF must be used to determine a probability. That is, as discussed previously, probability is proportional to the area under the curve or density function. Since a point has no dimension, the probability at any single point is zero. We must find the area corresponding to the probability between two points.

Therefore

$$P_\beta(a \leq p \leq b|n,r) = \frac{(n-1)!}{(r-1)!(n-r-1)!}\int_b^a \tilde{p}^{r-1}(1-\tilde{p})^{n-r-1}\,d\tilde{p} \tag{18.2}$$

For any given beta distribution, the PDF provides the height of the ordinate for a given value of the variable $\tilde{p}$. Although p is continuous, in real situations it is necessary to measure the value of $\tilde{p}$ to some degree of accuracy. Suppose, for example, $\tilde{p}$ will be observed or measured only to the nearest tenth. In that case the interval between any two adjacent values of $\tilde{p}$ designated Δp will simply be $\frac{1}{10}$.

The probability that $\tilde{p} \doteq 0.10$ is proportional to the area under the curve between 0.05 and 0.15. This area can be approximated by multiplying Δp times the ordinate at $\tilde{p} \doteq 0.10$, since the area of a rectangle is simply its height times its width. To get the probability that $\tilde{p}$ lies between any two specific values a and b, $P_\beta(a \leq \tilde{p} \leq b)$, it would only be necessary to sum the areas of all the rectangles of width Δp between a and b. We shall let the value of the ordinate at p be designated by $P'(p)$.

Consider $f(p|10,3)$. Find the ordinate when $p = 0.6$.

$$\begin{aligned} P'(0.6) = f(0.6|10,3) &= \frac{(10-1)!}{(3-1)!(10-3-1)!} \\ &\quad \times (0.6)^{(3-1)}(1-0.6)^{(10-3-1)} \\ &= \frac{9!}{2!6!}(0.6)^2(0.4)^6 \\ &= (252)(0.36)(0.004096) \\ &= (252)(0.00147) \\ &= 0.371 \end{aligned}$$

Since $\Delta p = 0.10$, the rectangle with its center at $p = 0.60$ extends from $p = 0.55$ to $p = 0.65$. The area of this rectangle is

$$\begin{aligned} \Delta p P'(p) &= (0.10)(0.371) \\ &= 0.0371 \doteq P(p = 0.6) \end{aligned}$$

Let us evaluate $f(p|10,3)$ and find the ordinates for all values of p from zero to 1 in increments of 0.1, and estimate the probability distribution on $\tilde{p}$. This is done in Table 18.1.

The sum of all the individual probabilities should be equal to 1. The slight discrepancy is due to rounding errors and the approximate nature of this procedure. Figure 18.1 shows the distribution calculated above.

Since p in Table 18.1 is described as a discrete random variable, in approximating probabilities in this way the continuity correction must be used. This is due to the fact that for the continuous variable $\tilde{p}$, $P(\tilde{p} \geq p) = P(\tilde{p} > p)$, but for an approximation with a discrete distribution, $P(\tilde{p} \geq p) \neq P(\tilde{p} > p)$.

It is not necessary to compute the individual probabilities for the beta distribution if tables of the cumulative binomial distribution are available.

Table 18.1

p	$P'(p)$	$P(\tilde{p} = p)$
0	0	0
0.1	1.338	0.1338
0.2	2.641	0.2641
0.3	2.666	0.2666
0.4	1.880	0.1880
0.5	0.983	0.0983
0.6	0.371	0.0371
0.7	0.091	0.0091
0.8	0.010	0.0010
0.9	0	0
1.0	0	0
		$0.9980 \doteq 1$

The beta probabilities are related to binomial probabilities as follows:

$$\begin{aligned} P_\beta(\tilde{p} \le p|r,n) &= P_b(\tilde{r} \ge r|n-1,p) && \text{for } p \le 0.5 \\ P_\beta(\tilde{p} \le p|r,n) &= 1 - P_b(\tilde{r} \ge n-r|n-1,1-p) && \text{for } p \ge 0.5 \end{aligned} \tag{18.3}$$

$$\begin{aligned} P_\beta(\tilde{p} \ge p|r,n) &= P_b(\tilde{r} < r|n-1,p) && \text{for } p \le 0.5 \\ P_\beta(\tilde{p} \ge p|r,n) &= 1 - P_b(\tilde{r} < r|n-1,p) && \text{for } p \ge 0.5 \end{aligned} \tag{18.4}$$

The use of Eqs. (18.3) and (18.4) depends upon the way the binomial probabilities are tabulated.

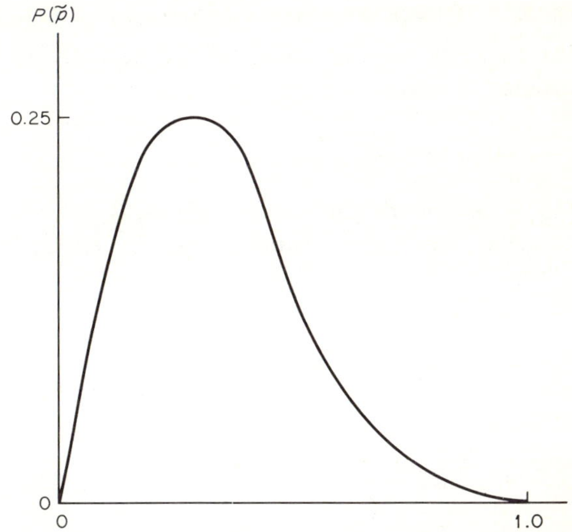

Fig. 18.1

As an example, given the beta distribution with $n = 10$ and $r = 3$, let us find the probability that p is less than or equal to 0.4.

For binomial tables which provide $P_b(\tilde{r} \geq r|n,p)$ using the first expression in (18.3), we get

$$\begin{aligned} P_\beta(\tilde{p} \leq 0.4|10,3) &= P_b(\tilde{r} \geq 3|9,0.4) \\ &= 0.7682 \end{aligned}$$

For the tables in the Appendix which provide $P_b(\tilde{r} \leq r|n,p)$, and using the first expression in Eq. (18.4), we get

$$\begin{aligned} P_\beta(\tilde{p} \leq 0.4|10,3) &= 1 - P_b(r < 3|9,0.4) \\ &= 1 - 0.2318 \\ &= 0.7682 \end{aligned}$$

To find the probability that p is greater than or equal to 0.7, and for tables of $P_b(\tilde{r} \geq r|n,p)$, we would get

$$\begin{aligned} P_\beta(\tilde{p} \geq 0.7|10,3) &= P_b(\tilde{r} \geq 10 - 3|10 - 1,1 - 0.7) \\ &= P_b(\tilde{r} \geq 7|9,0.3) \\ &= 0.0043 \end{aligned}$$

For the binomial tables in the Appendix,

$$\begin{aligned} P_\beta(\tilde{p} \geq 0.7|10,3) &= 1 - P_b(\tilde{r} < 10 - 3|10 - 1,1 - 0.7) \\ &= 1 - P_b(\tilde{r} < 7|9,0.3) \\ &= 1 - 0.9957 \\ &= 0.0043 \end{aligned}$$

MEAN, VARIANCE, AND MODE OF THE BETA DISTRIBUTION

The mean or expected value of the beta distribution is $E(\tilde{p}) = r/n$. The variance is

$$\text{var}(\tilde{p}) = \frac{r(n - r)}{r^2(n + 1)}$$

The mode is mode $(\tilde{p}) = (r - 1)/(n - 2)$.

For the beta distribution of the example with parameter $n = 10$, $r = 3$,

$$E(\tilde{p}) = 3/10 = 0.3$$

$$\text{var}(\tilde{p}) = \frac{3(10 - 3)}{10^2(100 + 1)} = \frac{(3)(7)}{(100)(101)}$$

$$= \frac{21}{10{,}100} = 0.0021$$

$$\text{mode}(\tilde{p}) = \frac{3 - 1}{10 - 2} = \frac{2}{8} = 0.25$$

PARAMETERS OF THE POSTERIOR BETA DISTRIBUTION

From Bayes' theorem it can be seen that the posterior probability is proportional to the product of the conditional probability or likelihood and the prior probability. Since sampling is taken to be binomial in this instance, the probability of getting exactly r occurrences of an event given n and p is

$$f_b = \binom{n}{r} p^r(1 - p)^{n-r}$$

It can be seen that f_b is proportional to $p^r(1 - p)^{n-r}$. Similarly, if we assume that the prior distribution is beta, then

$$P_0(\tilde{p}) = f_\beta(p|n_0,r_0) = \frac{(n_0 - 1)!}{(r_0 - 1)!(n_0 - r_0 - 1)!} p^{r_0 - 1}(1 - p)^{(n_0 - r_0 - 1)}$$

and f_β is proportional to

$$p^{r_0 - 1}(1 - p)^{(n_0 - r_0 - 1)} \tag{18.5}$$

Since the posterior probability is proportional to the product of the conditional and prior probabilities, then

$$\begin{aligned} P_1(\tilde{p}) &\propto p^r(1 - p)^{n-r}p^{(r_0 - 1)}(1 - p)^{(n_0 - r_0 - 1)} \\ &= p^{r + r_0 - 1}(1 - p)^{n + n_0 - r - r_0 - 1} \end{aligned}$$

or by grouping terms in the exponents

$$P_1(\tilde{p}) \propto p^{(r + r_0) - 1}(1 - p)^{(n + n_0) - (r + r_0) - 1} \tag{18.6}$$

The form of the posterior distribution is identical with the form of the prior distribution as given in (18.5). It follows that the posterior distribution of $\tilde{p}$ is also a beta distribution with parameters $n_1 = n + n_0$ and $r_1 = r + r_0$.

The mean and variance of the posterior distributions are

$$E_1(\tilde{p}) = \frac{r_1}{n_1} = \frac{r + r_0}{n + n_0}$$

$$\text{var}_1(\tilde{p}) = \frac{r_1(n_1 - r_1)}{n_1^2(n_1 + 1)} = \frac{(r + r_0)(n + n_0 - r - r_0)}{(n + n_0)^2(n + n_0 + 1)}$$

and the probability per unit width is

$$P'(\tilde{p}) = \frac{(n_1 - 1)!}{(r_1 - 1)!(n_1 - r_1 - 1)!} p^{r_1 - 1}(1 - p)^{(n_1 - r_1 - 1)}$$

18.5 ESTIMATING THE PARAMETERS OF THE PRIOR BETA DISTRIBUTION

It has been mentioned previously that the prior distribution can be based on empirical data, that is, quantifiable experience, or it can be purely subjective and based upon the decision maker's feelings about the pertinent parameter. Even in the latter case the subjective estimates of the prior probabilities, unless the decision maker claims no knowledge whatsoever, are generally based on some previous experience even though this experience is not in a quantitative form. The problem rests in converting this qualitative body of experience into quantitative form.

When empirical data do exist and consist of a tabulation of the occurrences of an event together with the number of observations, that is, r occurrences out of n observations, then the estimated parameters of the prior beta distribution are inherent in the data.

When no quantitative data exist, however, the decision maker must quantify his subjective feelings. His first step is to estimate the mean or expected value of $\tilde{p}$, that is, $E(\tilde{p})$. Suppose he feels that $E_0(\tilde{p}) = 0.4$. What are the parameters of his prior distribution?

Since $E_0(\tilde{p}) = 0.4$ and since $E_0(\tilde{p}) = r_0/n_0$, the decision maker must select r_0 and n_0 such that $r_0/n_0 = 0.4$. This requirement is satisfied for an infinite number of r,n pairs, some of which are

r	n
2	5
4	10
6	15
⋮	⋮
20	50
⋮	⋮
40	100
⋮	⋮

Each set of parameters defines a beta distribution with the same mean but with different variances. For example, for

$f_\beta(\tilde{p}\|5,2)$	$E(\tilde{p}) = 0.4$	$\text{var}(\tilde{p}) = 0.040$
$f_\beta(\tilde{p}\|10,4)$	$E(\tilde{p}) = 0.4$	$\text{var}(\tilde{p}) = 0.0218$
$f_\beta(\tilde{p}\|20,8)$	$E(\tilde{p}) = 0.4$	$\text{var}(\tilde{p}) = 0.0114$
$f_\beta(\tilde{p}\|25,10)$	$E(\tilde{p}) = 0.4$	$\text{var}(\tilde{p}) = 0.0092$

As the parameter n increases for a given value of r/n, the variance decreases, and the shape of the distribution becomes more peaked.

Figure 18.2 shows two beta distributions for which $E(p) = 0.4$.

The areas or probability densities for the two beta distributions shown in Fig. 18.2 are distributed differently. The probability densities for $\beta(10,4)$

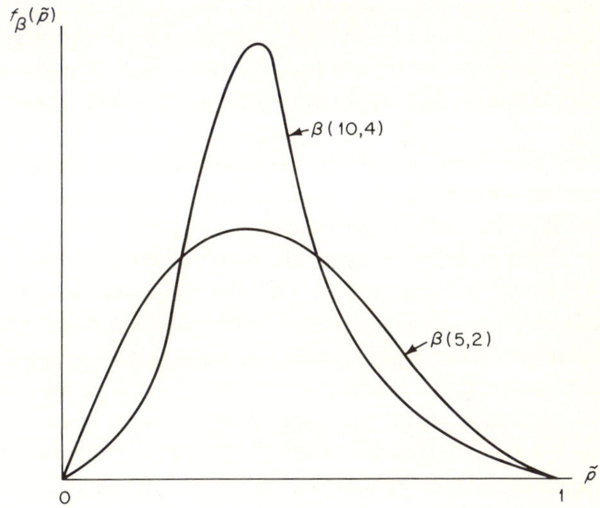

Fig. 18.2

are concentrated more closely about a central value than are the densities for $\beta(5,2)$. The decision maker who selects $\beta(10,4)$ for his prior distribution probably feels stronger about the location of $E(\tilde{p})$ than does the decision maker who selected $\beta(5,2)$. The former might equate his degree of knowledge about p to the information he would have at his disposal had he observed an experiment which had produced four occurrences of the event of interest out of 10 trials. The latter, on the other hand, might equate his degree of knowledge about p to the information that he would have after having observed two occurrences of the event out of only five trials of an experiment.

The process of selecting a value for the parameter n then becomes a process of evaluating the strength of the decision maker's feeling about his estimate of $E(\tilde{p})$. In order to assist the decision maker in arriving at this value, one might ask him the following question: If an experiment was conducted n times resulting in r occurrences such that $r/n \neq E_0(\tilde{p})$, which is your subjective estimate, what would n have to be in order that you would consider the experimental value as being equal in weight in the decision problem as your estimate?

If the decision maker were to answer that 25 repetitions of the experiment would make the experimental results equal to his subjective estimate, then n_0 for his prior distribution would be 25, and r_0 would be $(0.4)(25) = 10$.

On the other hand, if the decision maker stated that in order to be weighted equally with his prior estimate, the sample value would have to result from 100 observations, since he feels very strongly that his estimate is very close to the true value of p, then n_0 for his prior distribution should be 100, and $r_0 = 40$. Obviously, if the decision maker was not very certain that his estimate $E_0(\tilde{p}) = 0.4$ was close to the true value of p, he might be willing to assign equal weight to an experimental value resulting from as few as 10 sample observations. In that case, the parameters of his prior distribution would be $n_0 = 10$ and $r_0 = 4$.

Criticism can and has been directed at any attempt to let n and n_0 represent the amount of information contained in the sample and in the prior estimate, respectively. One major flaw in this procedure is that it is quite probable that the value of n which the decision maker would specify as being required in order for a sample or experimental value to be given a weight equal to his estimate would depend upon the size of the discrepancy specified between r/n and $E_0(\tilde{p})$. For example, if the decision maker's estimate was $E_0(\tilde{p}) = 0.4$ and he was asked that question with respect to a sample resulting in $r/n = 0.5$, he might be willing to assign an equal weight to the sample result for a sample as small as $n = 10$. On the other hand, for the same degree of certainty about his estimate, he might require a sample as large as $n = 100$ to give it equal weight had the sample result been $r/n = 0.8$.

There is no easy solution to the problem of eliciting parameters of prior distributions from decision makers. The previous approach with its obvious weaknesses might still be most practical, particularly when the decision maker has little knowledge of probability and statistics. Other methods for specifying the parameters of a prior beta distribution will be discussed subsequently.

Example 18.1 A job shop manufacturer is approached by an inventor with a new product. The manufacturer generally manufactures to order but would like to develop a line of proprietory products which he could distribute through various channels utilizing manufacturers' representatives, mail-order houses, etc.

The new product would lend itself to mail-order sales. The inventor will sell all rights to the product for \$5,000. The manufacturer contacts a mail-order distributor who will handle the advertising and the mailing to its (the distributor's) own mailing list of 100,000 names. The mail-order house will mail advertising literature to its mailing list for a flat fee of \$11,000 plus 5 percent of the retail price of each unit sold by mail. The mail-order house will receive all orders and process them. This includes storing up to 5,000 units of the product in its own warehouse.

The manufacturer's analysis indicates that the cost to manufacture the product involves an initial investment in equipment of \$15,000 and a variable production cost of \$1.10 per unit. Other variable costs total 15 cents per unit.

The manufacturer estimates that the highest price which he can charge for the product is \$3.

The manufacturer's decision is between the acts:

a_1 (manufacture the product)

a_2 (reject the product)

Needless to say, this is an expendable product, and reorders are expected. A summary of costs connected with the project are as follows:

Purchase of rights to the product	\$5,000	
Fixed distribution costs	11,000	
Fixed production costs	15,000	
Variable production costs		1.10/unit
Other variable costs		0.15/unit

The payoff functions for the acts are as follows:

$$\begin{aligned} Q_{a_1} &= -\$31{,}000 + (\$3 - \$1.40)(100{,}000)p \\ &= -\$31{,}000 + (\$1.60)(100{,}000)p \\ &= -\$31{,}000 + \$160{,}000p \\ Q_{a_2} &= 0 \end{aligned}$$

The break-even value of p is

$$p_k \simeq 0.193$$

That is, if the proportion of individuals on the mailing list that order the product is greater than 18 percent, the manufacturer will realize a profit. If $p \leq 18$ percent, the manufacturer will suffer a loss or no profit.

For a linear payoff function and no sampling, we can arrive at a decision by determining the expected value of each act from the following relationship:

$$EV(a) = b + mE(\tilde{p}) \tag{18.7}$$

In order to evaluate an expression of this type, the decision maker must supply an estimate of $E_0(\tilde{p})$. Suppose the manager estimates that 20 percent of the customers on the mailing list will order the product. In that case, $E_0(\tilde{p}) = 0.20$, by substitution and in Eq. (18.7),

$$\begin{aligned} EV(a_1) &= -\$31{,}000 + (\$160{,}000)(0.20) = \$1{,}000 \\ EV(a_2) &= 0 \end{aligned}$$

and, therefore, the manufacturer should accept the new product.

The same result could have been obtained more simply by observing that $E_0(\tilde{p}) = 0.20$ was greater than the breakdown value of $p_k = 0.193$, and, therefore, a_1 would be the more profitable act.

If the manufacturer does not wish to make a decision based solely on his own subjective estimate of the value of $\tilde{p}$, but instead wishes to obtain additional information about the proportion of individuals who will purchase the product, he must be more specific about defining his prior distribution. Since he intends to draw a sample from a very large dichotomous population, the sampling will be binomial. According to the theory of conjugate distribution, both his prior and posterior distributions should be beta.

The parameters of the beta distribution are n and r. So instead of simply specifying the expected value of $\tilde{p}$, the decision maker should estimate r and n in the ratio $r/n = E(\tilde{p})$. By his selection of n and r in the ratio r/n he is indicating how strongly he feels that $E(\tilde{p})$ is equal to 0.20. In order to do this, he must specify the size of an equivalent sample that he feels corresponds to the weight he will give to his prior estimate.

Let us consider two possible beta distributions, $\beta(n_0 = 5, r_0 = 1)$ and $\beta(n_0 = 200, r_0 = 40)$. The manufacturer decided to select a random sample of $n = 40$ from the distributor's mailing list and send out an advertising leaflet describing the product. As a result, he receives seven orders; that is, as a result of his sample, he obtains additional information resulting in $n = 40$, $r = 7$. The posterior distribution is, therefore, beta with parameter $n_1 = n_0 + n$ and $r_1 = r_0 + r$.

If his prior distribution had been $\beta(5,1)$, his posterior distribution would be $\beta(45,8)$ and $E_1(\tilde{p}) \doteq 0.177$. If his prior distribution had been $\beta(200,40)$, his posterior distribution would be $\beta(240,47)$ and $E_1(\tilde{p}) = 0.196$. In the first case he would have rejected the proposition, while in the second case he would have accepted the proposition and manufactured the product.

This result should caution the practitioner about assigning too much weight to his subjective distribution if unsupported by any empirical evidence.

BETA DISTRIBUTION—HIGHEST DENSITY REGIONS

For the beta distribution which is unimodal but generally not symmetrical, we can specify a region containing a given proportion and highest concentration of the area (probability) by specifying lower and upper limits. In confidence interval estimation, given the sampling distribution of an estimator, we could specify two limits such that the probability that the interval so determined contained the parameter to be estimated was fixed. So for any distribution, we can specify two limits which contain a given proportion of the area under the curve. In order to be meaningful in specifying a specific distribution, this interval should be the shortest possible interval or, more pertinent, that interval having the highest probability density.

The value of the highest density regions in specifying a particular beta distribution is this. A decision maker may find it difficult to specify the expected value of his prior distribution and fix an n_0 consistent with his willingness or reluctance to revise his opinion in the light of sample evidence. He may, however, be willing to quote betting odds that the true value of $\tilde{p}$ lies between two points. Or even more likely, he may be willing to specify the two limits on $\tilde{p}$ that he feels represent an even-money bet as to whether or not the true value of p is included between these two limits. He is actually specifying a particular beta distribution by selecting two points which contain between them 50 percent of the highest probability density.

For example, without being able to specify his exact estimate of p, the decision maker may state that he feels that it is an even-money bet as to whether or not p is between approximately 0.10 and 0.20. By referring to the table of highest-density regions for 50 percent probability found in the Appendix, we find that the $\beta(p|4,25)$ is a distribution with the highest density 50 percent between $p_l = 0.102$ and $p_u = 0.204$, which fits his prior estimate quite well. $E(\tilde{p})$ for this prior would be 0.16.

If, on the other hand, he specified the limits 0.15 and 0.25, $\beta(p|5,25)$ provides the limit on the highest density region for 50 percent probability as $p_l = 0.412$ and $p_u = 0.250$, again a reasonable approximation.

18.6 THE RECTANGULAR DISTRIBUTION

A beta distribution with parameters $n = 2$, $r = 1$ is the rectangular distribution. Recall that previously the rectangular distribution was defined as

$$f(x) = \frac{1}{b - a} \qquad \text{for } a < x < b$$

when

$$a = 0$$
$$b = 1$$
$$f(x) = 1$$

The expected value of the rectangular distribution

$$E(x) = \frac{a + b}{2} = \tfrac{1}{2}$$

and

$$\text{var}\,(x) = \frac{(b - a)^2}{12} = \tfrac{1}{12}$$

The beta distribution with $n = 2$, $r = 1$ reduces to the rectangular distribution with $a = 0$, $b = 1$. Consider a beta distribution with the random variable X substituted for $\tilde{p}$.

$$f_\beta(x|n,r) = \frac{(n - 1)!}{(r - 1)!(n - r - 1)!}\, x^{r-1}(1 - x)^{n-r-1}$$

Substituting $n = 2$ and $r = 1$, we get

$$f_\beta(x|2,1) = \frac{1!}{0!0!}\, x^0(1 - x)^0 = 1$$

$$E(X) = \tfrac{1}{2} \qquad \text{and} \qquad \text{var}\,(X) = \tfrac{1}{12}$$

The rectangular distribution is frequently used as the prior distribution when the decision maker professes to no knowledge whatsoever about the value of the parameter p. In this case one assumption to be made is that all values of p are equally likely, and this case is represented by the rectangular distribution with parameters $a = 0$ and $b = 1$, or the beta distribution with $r = 1$ and $n = 2$. This distribution is illustrated in Fig. 18.3.

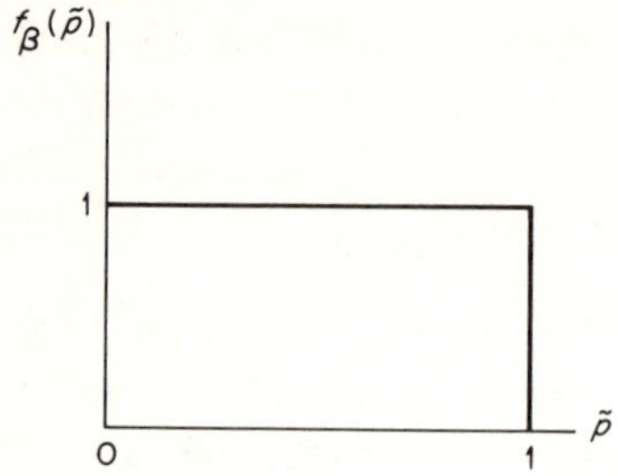

Fig. 18.3

Suppose, in the example in Sec. 18.5, the manufacturer was so uncertain about his estimate of the proportion of individuals on the mailing list who would purchase his product that he was reluctant to assume that any value of p was more likely than any other. An appropriate prior distribution in this case would be the beta with $n = 2$ and $r = 1$, which is the uniform or rectangular distribution.

He now takes his sample by sending a brochure to 40 individuals selected at random from the mailing list. As a result he receives 7 orders. His posterior distribution is beta with $n_1 = 2 + 40 = 42$ and $r_1 = 1 + 7 = 8$. $E_1(\tilde{p}) = {}^8\!/_{42} = 0.19$. Since $0.19 > 0.18 = p$, a_1 should be selected.

18.7 TABLES OF THE INCOMPLETE BETA FUNCTION

For integer values of r and n, cumulative beta probabilities can be obtained from binomial tables according to Eqs. (18.3) and (18.4). The incomplete beta function has been extensively tabulated by Pearson for both integer and noninteger values of r and n. It is not likely that a decision maker in a practical situation would find it necessary to adopt a prior beta distribution with noninteger parameters. However, a brief discussion on the use of these tables may be in order.

The tables provide the following probability:

$$P_\beta(X \leq x|p,q)$$

Using our notation, we let $X = \tilde{p}$ and $p + q = n$; then the following probability can be read from the tables:

$$P_\beta(\tilde{p} \leq p|r,n)$$

For example, for the rectangular distribution where $r = 1$ and $n = 2$, we would look up the parameter $q = 1$ in the tables. The probability that $\tilde{p} \leq p$ corresponds to the probability that $X \leq x$ given in the tables from $x = 0.01$ to $x = 1.00$ in increments of 0.01.

Consider $\beta(15,4)$, that is, $n = 15$ and $r = 4$. The probabilities are given under $q = 4$ and $p = 11$. That is, in the context of observing a

Bernoulli process, we have observed 4 occurrences of an event and 11 non-occurrences from a total of 15 observations.

In specifying the parameters of the prior beta distribution, the decision maker need not be restricted to integer values. A beta distribution with a mean of $r/n = 0.5$ could be represented by a rectangular distribution where $r = 1$ and $n = 2$; but it could also be represented by a beta distribution with the parameters $p = 0.5$ and $q = 0.5$, which, in our notation, would be $\beta(0.5,1.0)$. If the decision maker believes that the mean or expected value of his prior beta distribution is 0.4, he could use a distribution having the parameters n and r equal to (5,2), (10,4), (2.5,1), or as given in the tables, the parameters p and q equal to (3,2), (6,4), (1.5,1).

18.8 SUMMARY

When the possible states of nature on the critical parameter can assume more than a few values, it becomes convenient to represent the pertinent probabilities by a probability distribution rather than by assigning discrete probabilities to discrete values. The problem of assigning specific probability values to discrete points now becomes one of selecting an appropriate theoretical distribution and then specifying the value of its parameters. The theory of conjugate distributions leads to the proper prior distribution when the sampling distribution of the experiment is given. For typical binomial sampling, the prior distribution is the beta distribution, with parameters n and r.

The beta distribution with $n = 2$ and $r = 1$ becomes the rectangular distribution which is frequently used as a prior when the decision maker professes no knowledge about the states of nature or assumes that all possible states are equally likely.

PROBLEMS

18.1. Using binomial tables, find the following beta probabilities:

(*a*) $P_\beta(0.1 \leq \tilde{p} | 16,3)$
(*b*) $P_\beta(\tilde{p} < 0.7 | 20,7)$
(*c*) $P_\beta(0.1 \leq \tilde{p} \leq 0.7 | 10,6)$
(*d*) $P_\beta(0.8 \leq \tilde{p} | 12,7)$
(*e*) $P_\beta(0.4 \leq \tilde{p} \leq 0.6 | 25,12)$

18.2. Find $P'(\tilde{p}) = f(p|n,r)$, the ordinate of the beta distribution, for the following values of p, n, and r:

(*a*) $f(0.4|20,7)$
(*b*) $f(0.8|10,3)$
(*c*) $f(0.15|20,2)$
(*d*) $f(0.6|25,13)$
(*e*) $f(0.9|25,13)$

18.3. Using the table of highest density regions for 50 percent probability given in the Appendix, specify the parameters of the beta distribution which most nearly approximates the following prior estimates of the parameter p:

(*a*) There is a probability of 0.5 that p lies in the interval 0.45 to 0.75.
(*b*) There is a probability of 0.5 that p lies in the interval 0.45 to 0.60.
(*c*) There is a probability of 0.5 that p lies in the interval 0.35 to 0.65.
(*d*) There is a probability of 0.5 that p lies in the interval 0.05 to 0.15.
(*e*) There is a probability of 0.5 that p lies in the interval 0.5 to 0.7.

18.4. A decision maker selects as his prior distribution a beta with parameters $n_0 = 10$ and $r_0 = 2$. A sampling experiment is then conducted consisting of a total of 50 observations, resulting in 12 occurrences of the event of interest, that is, $r = 12$.

(*a*) What are the parameters of the decision maker's posterior distribution?

(*b*) What are the mean, mode, and variance of the decision maker's posterior distribution?

18.5. In Prob. 18.4, suppose the experiment resulted in $n = 30$, $r = 12$.

(*a*) What are the parameters of the decision maker's posterior distribution?

(*b*) What are the mean, mode, and variance of the decision maker's posterior distribution?

18.6. A manufacturer of household detergents has been presented with a new advertising campaign by his advertising agency. The campaign is to feature a one-eyed giant with magical housecleaning powers. Concerned with the image of his company, the president of the company wants to find out if most housewives would approve of this advertising approach. A sample advertisement is to be presented to a random sample of housewives who would be asked if they liked or disliked the ad. The company president, having recently completed a class in statistical decision theory, estimated that his prior distribution on the proportion of housewives who would approve of the new advertising approach had a beta distribution with parameters $n_0 = 10$ and $r_0 = 4$. In order to proceed with the campaign, the president specified that the sample results must be such that when combined with his prior the resulting posterior must have an expected value of 0.5 or greater.

(*a*) If a sample of $n = 60$ is taken, what proportion of the housewives in that sample must approve if the campaign is to proceed?

(*b*) If his prior had been $\beta(15,5)$, what proportion of the sample of 60 would have had to approve the campaign in order for it to proceed?

(*c*) Answer part *b* if the proposed sample size was 75.

(*d*) Answer part *a* if the president's prior distribution was rectangular.

18.7. If a decision maker's prior distribution has the following means and variances, specify the parameters of each prior distribution to the nearest whole number.

(*a*) $E(\tilde{p}) = 0.43$, $\text{var}\,(\tilde{p}) = 0.167$
(*b*) $E(\tilde{p}) = 0.25$, $\text{var}\,(\tilde{p}) = 0.600$
(*c*) $E(\tilde{p}) = 0.33$, $\text{var}\,(\tilde{p}) = 0.500$
(*d*) $E(\tilde{p}) = 0.67$, $\text{var}\,(\tilde{p}) = 0.187$
(*e*) $E(\tilde{p}) = 0.60$, $\text{var}\,(\tilde{p}) = 0.060$
(*f*) $E(\tilde{p}) = 0.60$, $\text{var}\,(\tilde{p}) = 0.032$

18.8. Suppose in Prob. 18.6 the only statement that the company president could make about his prior distribution was that he believed that there was a probability of 0.50 that the true proportion was between 0.37 and 0.53. Answer parts (*a*), (*b*), and (*c*).

18.9. The Welbilt Company manufactures a component designated part no. 17702 in lots of 1,000 units. The quality of this particular part has been difficult to control. The problem was caused by the extremely close tolerances required and the fact that the machine settings tend to drift. If the machines are readjusted prior to the production of each lot the percent of defective parts produced can be held at 2 percent. However, the readjustment of the machines costs $400 because of the technician's time required, loss of production time, etc. Without a readjustment the percent defective has varied. On questioning, information is elicited from the production manager that his prior distribution on the proportion defective without readjustment of the machines is beta with $n_0 = 10$ and $r_0 = 1$. Having received some very large orders for part no. 17702, management must decide whether to readjust the equipment for each lot produced or to continue production without the periodic adjustment. The cost of replacing defective parts is $5 per part. If a decision must be made immediately, what should Welbilt do?

18.10. Suppose in the previous problem it was decided that a sample of size 25 should be taken at the start of the production of each lot. The sample would consist of the first 25 items produced. The sample would be inspected, and the number of defectives observed. At the beginning of the next production run, the sample was taken and was found to contain one defective.

(*a*) Should the machinery be readjusted?

(*b*) Suppose the sample had contained five defectives. Should the machinery be readjusted?

19
Probability Distributions in Decision Analysis: The Normal Distribution

19.1 THE NORMAL DISTRIBUTION IN DECISION THEORY

In sampling from a Bernoulli process or a binomial population, the state of nature was represented by the unknown binomial parameter p. The prior distribution which lends itself to a representation of a distribution on p was the beta distribution.

There are many decision situations in which the state of nature is the unknown mean or average value of a population which we designate μ. In order to obtain information about the value of μ we can take a sample from the population and compute a statistic $\bar{x}$ which is the mean of the sample. We have mentioned previously that $\bar{x}$ is a maximum likelihood estimator of μ and that it has certain desirable properties as an estimator. We also know that the sampling distribution of $\bar{x}$ tends to become normal regardless of the shape of the parent population. The distribution conjugate to a normal sampling distribution is also normal, making the normal distribution a logical choice as a prior distribution in this type of decision situation.

19.2 DETERMINING THE PARAMETERS OF THE NORMAL PRIOR DISTRIBUTION

Since any normal distribution is completely determined by its mean and standard deviation, it is necessary only to specify these two values in order to specify the normal prior distribution. The decision maker may be in the position of having some data from which he can make an estimate relating to these parameters, or if no such data exist, his estimate would of necessity be purely subjective.

In the former case, for example, suppose in a production situation it is necessary to make a decision which is dependent upon a particular process average. Suppose this particular process will produce a part with a critical dimension that must meet certain specified tolerance limits. Assume that 10 lots have been produced and the mean of each lot's critical dimension resulted in 10 values of μ. In order to specify a prior distribution on $\tilde{\mu}$ which requires the two parameters $E(\tilde{\mu})$ and $\sigma(\tilde{\mu})$, the decision maker would simply use the available data in the same way he would for estimating any population parameter, that is,

$$E(\tilde{\mu}) = \frac{1}{n}\sum \tilde{\mu}_i \tag{19.1}$$

and

$$\sigma(\tilde{\mu}) = \left\{\frac{1}{n-1}\left[\sum \mu_i - E(\tilde{\mu})\right]^2\right\}^{1/2} \tag{19.2}$$

What does the decision maker do, however, if he has no empirical data upon which to base his estimate of the parameters of the prior distribution? In that case these parameters must be estimated subjectively. Since the normal distribution is perfectly symmetrical, the mean divides the distribution, or the area under the curve, into two equal parts corresponding to probabilities. Therefore, in specifying the mean of his distribution on $\tilde{\mu}$, the decision maker would be asked to pick a value of μ as an estimate such that he believes that there is the same chance of his estimate being too high as there is of its being too low. A slightly different way of stating this would be to ask the decision maker to select his estimate in such a way that if he had to make an even-money bet, either that the true value of the parameter was greater than his estimate or that it was less than his estimate, he would be completely indifferent as to which side to take. The value which he selects then would be his estimate of $E(\tilde{\mu})$ or the mean of his prior distribution on μ.

In order to specify the second parameter of the prior distribution, the decision maker would be asked to select two points, one on each side of the mean and equally distant from it, such that he believed that the probability of the true value of μ being between these two points was exactly equal to the probability that it was not between these two points. Or, in gambling terminology, the odds were exactly even as to whether these two points contained the true mean or not.

The two points specified are, then, in units of standard deviations from the mean, $E(\tilde{\mu}) + k\sigma(\tilde{\mu})$ and $E(\tilde{\mu}) - k\sigma(\tilde{\mu})$. Fifty percent of the area under the curve lies between these two points, and since the normal distribution is symmetrical, the area under the curve between $E(\tilde{\mu})$ and $E(\tilde{\mu}) + k\sigma(\tilde{\mu})$ is equal to 25 percent of the total area. Let us specify that the distance $E(\tilde{\mu}) + k\sigma(\tilde{\mu}) - E(\tilde{\mu}) = k\sigma(\tilde{\mu}) = d$. Since for a normal distribution the area between the mean and 0.675 standard deviation from the mean is 25 percent of the total area under the curve, $k\sigma(\tilde{\mu}) = d = 0.675\sigma(\tilde{\mu})$. Since the decision maker has already specified d, we can find his estimate of σ by solving $d = 0.675\sigma(\tilde{\mu})$ for $\sigma(\tilde{\mu})$, that is, $\sigma(\tilde{\mu}) = d/0.675$. See Fig. 19.1.

Example 19.1 The Ego Cosmetics Company is considering a change in the package of one of its products for men. The change would be relatively costly and would be worthwhile only if the result was a substantial increase in the sales of the product. In order to make a decision, the president of the company consulted a statistician and asked for help. As a first step the statistician attempted to elicit from the company president the parameters of his prior distribution on the probability that the *average change in sales per retail outlet* would take on any value whatsoever.

Consider this situation as one in which the proposed package change could ultimately have different effects on the buyers or potential buyers of the product. These effects could range from a large increase in average sales to a decrease in average sales or anything in between. After the package change, only one of these possible effects will prevail; however, prior to the package change, the uncertainty of the decision maker makes any one of these effects possible. It is up to the decision maker to express his uncertainty about the effect of the package change in terms of a probability distribution. Since the variable which is critical to his decision is $\tilde{\mu}$, the average change in sales per retail outlet, he must estimate

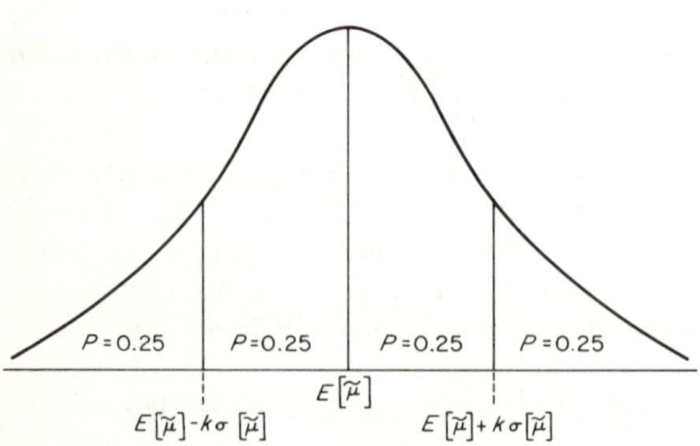

Fig. 19.1

the expected value of $\tilde{\mu}$ and also specify his feeling about the variability of $\tilde{\mu}$, which in effect reflects the strength of his feeling about the value $E(\tilde{\mu})$.

Suppose the president states that he feels that the odds are even that the average change in sales per retail outlet resulting from the package change will be plus 50 units of the product per week. That is, he believes that the probability that the average change will be less than plus 50 is equal to the probability that it will be greater than plus 50.

He also states that he believes that there is a probability of 0.5 that the average change in store sales will be between plus 35 and plus 65 units, that is, 50 ± 15. Fifteen units represents a deviation from the mean such that 50 percent of the area under the curve is between 50 ± 15, and due to symmetry, 25 percent of the area under the curve lies between the mean and a 15-unit deviation from the mean. Therefore, $d = 15$ represents $0.675\sigma(\tilde{\mu})$. Solving for $\sigma(\tilde{\mu})$, we get

$$\sigma(\tilde{\mu}) = \frac{15}{0.671} \doteq 22$$

Figure 19.2 shows the distribution specified by the company president. This distribution indicates that although he believes that a 50-unit increase in sales per store is most likely, he does not totally preclude the possibility that the change might result in a decrease in sales. The probability assigned to that occurrence is

$$P(\tilde{\mu} < 0) = P\left(Z < \frac{0 - 50}{22} = -2.27\right)$$
$$= 0.0116$$

In getting the decision maker to specify the parameters of his prior normal distribution, it is helpful to talk to him in terms of betting odds. In specifying the standard deviation, he could be asked to pick two points on opposite sides of and equidistant from his estimated mean such that he believes the odds are 2 to 1 that the true value of μ lies between these two points. That is, the mean plus or minus $d = k\sigma(\tilde{\mu})$ contains $^2/_3$ of the area under the normal curve. The value of k is therefore 1. This can be determined from tables of the standard normal distribution, and

$$\sigma(\tilde{\mu}) = \frac{d}{1} = d$$

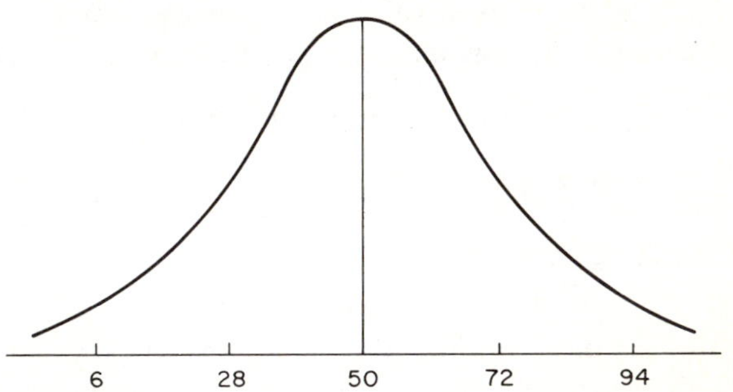

Fig. 19.2

For the previous example, having specified that $E(\tilde{\mu}) = 50$, the company president might have stated that he believes the odds were 2 to 1 that the actual effect of the package change or average sales per retail outlet would be between an increase of 28 units and an increase of 72 units, that is, the mean plus or minus 22 units. Then

$$\sigma(\tilde{\mu}) = \frac{22}{1} = 22$$

19.3 DECISIONS BASED ON A NORMAL PRIOR WITHOUT SAMPLING

In considering a two-action problem where the payoff of each act can be expressed as a linear function of the state of nature, that is,

$$Q = b + m\theta$$

the expected payoff can be expressed as

$$E(Q) = b + mE(\theta) \tag{19.3}$$

The normal distribution is used as a model for a state of nature that is basically continuous and most practically is some average value or mean. Consequently, Eq. (19.3) can be expressed as

$$E(Q) = b + mE(\tilde{\mu}) \tag{19.4}$$

If the expected payoff of act a_1 is given by

$$E(Q_1) = b_1 + m_1E(\tilde{\mu})$$

and the expected payoff of a_2 is given by

$$E(Q_2) = b_2 + m_2E(\tilde{\mu})$$

then a_1 is preferred to a_2 when $E(Q_1) > E(Q_2)$, and a_2 is preferred to a_1 when $E(Q_2) > E(Q_1)$, so long as the payoffs Q are in terms of profits. If Q is a cost, loss, or opportunity loss, these inequalities are reversed.

The break-even value of μ which we shall designate μ_k is that value of μ for which the payoffs of the two acts are equal, that is

$$Q_1 = b_1 + m_1\mu = b_2 + m_2\mu = Q_2$$

Solving for μ, we get

$$\mu_k = \frac{b_1 - b_2}{m_2 - m_1}$$

Let us continue the Ego Cosmetics example. Ego distributes its product in 1,000 retail outlets around the country. Each unit sold contributes \$1.50 to company profit. This is the price of the product less the variable cost. The cost of the package change would be \$60,000; therefore, the payoff function for act a_1 (change the package) is

$$\begin{aligned} Q_1 &= -\$60{,}000 + \$1.50(1{,}000)\mu \\ &= -\$60{,}000 + \$1{,}500\mu \end{aligned}$$

For act a_2, which involves no change,

$$Q_2 = 0 + 0\mu = 0$$

and

$$\mu_k = \frac{-\$60{,}000 - 0}{-\$1{,}500 - 0} = 40$$

The expected payoff of each act can be determined by simply substituting $E(\mu)$ from the decision maker's prior distribution into each payoff function.

$$\begin{aligned} E(Q_1) &= -\$60{,}000 + \$1{,}500(50) = \$15{,}000 \\ E(Q_2) &= 0 \end{aligned}$$

and obviously a_1 should be selected as the better act since $E(Q_1) > E(Q_2)$.

The same conclusion could be reached even more quickly by observing that since $E(\mu) = 50 > 40$ is obviously the better act.

The opportunity loss or regret functions for the two acts could also be determined as follows:

$$\begin{aligned} R_1 &= 0 && \text{if } \tilde{\mu} \geq \$40 = \mu_k \\ R_1 &= (\$1.50)(40 - \mu) && \text{if } \tilde{\mu} < \$40 = \mu_k \\ R_2 &= (\$1.50)(\mu - 40) && \text{if } \tilde{\mu} > \$40 = \mu_k \\ R_2 &= 0 && \text{if } \tilde{\mu} \leq \$40 = \mu_k \end{aligned}$$

A decision can be made with respect to the regret function of the two acts very simply by relating $E(\tilde{\mu})$ to μ_k. If $E(\tilde{\mu}) > \mu_k$, $R_1 = 0$, and, therefore, a_1 is the better act. If $E(\tilde{\mu}) < \mu_k$, $R_2 = 0$, and a_2 is the better act. If $E(\tilde{\mu}) = \mu_k$, the decision maker would be indifferent but would probably select a_2, which maintains the status quo; that is, it requires no specific action. In this example, $E(\tilde{\mu}) = 50 > 40 = \mu_k$ and, therefore, a_1 should be selected.

EXPECTED VALUE OF PERFECT INFORMATION

In all cases of decision making without sampling, the decision or the selection of a single act from among the available acts is based on a Bayes' or expected value criterion. If the decision maker has the option of deferring his decision until additional information can be obtained, we have seen previously that a measure of the maximum amount that should be spent in obtaining additional information is the expected value of perfect information or EVPI. Furthermore, we have indicated that EVPI is simply the expected opportunity loss or expected regret for the optimum act.

If the prior distribution on the states of nature was discrete, the expected regret for each act was obtained by simply multiplying each conditional regret of the act for a given state of nature by the probability of the occurrence of that particular state and then summing these products. When the prior distribution is continuous, this procedure does not apply. An approximation could be obtained if we were to divide the longitudinal axis of the distribution of $\tilde{\mu}$ into many small discrete intervals of width $\Delta\mu$ and consider the center of each such interval as a specific value of μ.

We could then proceed as in the discrete case by finding the area under the curve or the probability corresponding to each interval $\Delta\mu$ and multiplying that probability by the conditional loss of the act given the value of μ (the state of nature) at the midpoint of the interval. The products would, of course, be added in order to get the expected value. As we make these intervals narrower and narrower, the results approach the true expected value.

For the normal distribution, however, there is a simpler procedure. The expected value of perfect information is given by

$$\text{EVPI} = t\sigma_0(\tilde{\mu})L_N(D_0)$$

where

$$t = |m_1 - m_2| = \text{per unit opportunity loss}$$

$$\sigma_0(\mu) = \text{standard deviation of the prior distribution on } \tilde{\mu}$$

$$L_N(D) = \text{unit normal loss function, a table of which can be found in the Appendix}$$

$$D = \frac{|\mu_k - E_0[\tilde{\mu}]|}{\sigma_0(\tilde{\mu})}$$

For the Ego Cosmetic Company example,

$$t = |m_1 - m_2| = \$1{,}500 - 0 = \$1{,}500$$

$$\sigma_0(\tilde{\mu}) = 22$$

$$\mu_k = 40{,}000 \textit{ total} \text{ units}$$

However, to put the break-even value into the same units as the prior distribution, we must get break-even in terms of each retail unit. Since there are 1,000 retail units,

$$\mu_k = \frac{40{,}000}{1{,}000} = 40$$

$$D = \frac{|40 - 50|}{22} = 0.454$$

$$L_N(0.454) = 0.2124$$

and

$$\text{EVPI} = (\$1{,}500)(22)(0.2124) = \$7{,}009$$

19.4 MULTIACTION PROBLEMS WITH LINEAR PAYOFF FUNCTIONS

Suppose in the newsboy problem which was used as an example in Chap. 16, instead of specifying discrete probabilities for each state of nature corresponding to a demand for certain specific quantities of newspapers, we instead specified the parameters of a normal probability distribution. Let us assume that the probability distribution on the demand for papers can be represented by a normal distribution with $E_0(\tilde{\theta}) = 17$ and standard deviation $\sigma_0(\tilde{\theta}) = 1.8$.

Since the probabilities that we need are $P(\theta < \theta_i)$, we can determine these from the tables of the standard normal distribution after making the usual conversion to Z, the standard normal variate. Figure 19.3 shows the prior distribution on the demand as specified.

Since we are using a normal distribution to approximate a discrete random variable (obviously the demand for newspapers must be discrete), we must make a continuity correction before determining the probabilities. For example, the probability that $\tilde{\theta} < 14$ is represented by the area to the left of $\tilde{\theta} = 13.5$, and these probabilities can be calculated as follows:

$$P(\theta < 14) = P\left(Z < \frac{13.5 - 17}{1.8} = -1.94\right) = 0.0260$$

$$P(\theta < 15) = P\left(Z < \frac{14.5 - 17}{1.8} = -1.39\right) = 0.0823$$

and so on. The probabilities for all states of nature are summarized in Table 19.1.

The optimum act, then, is that act a_i such that $P(\theta < \theta_i) < 0.5$, since k for this problem was 0.5. Since $P(\theta < 17) = 0.488 < 0.5$ and $P(\theta < 18) = 0.512 > 0.5$, the optimum act is purchase 17 papers, not the same conclusion reached in the earlier example, but very close to it considering that a different probability distribution was used.

Fig. 19.3

Table 19.1

Demand θ	$P(\theta < \theta_i)$
14	0.0260
15	0.0820
16	0.2030
17	0.4880
18	0.5120
19	0.7970
20	0.9177

19.5 PARAMETERS OF THE POSTERIOR NORMAL DISTRIBUTION

Assuming that it is possible for the decision maker to defer his decision until additional information is obtained regarding the state of nature, we must now face the problem of combining sample data with prior information and the parameters of the posterior distribution. For normal sampling, that is, sampling from a normal population, the prior and posterior distributions are both normal. Schlaiffer provides the following results.*

Where (a) the prior distribution of the parameter $\tilde{\mu}$ is normal with parameters $E_0(\tilde{\mu})$ and $\sigma_0(\tilde{\mu})$, (b) the sampling distribution of $\bar{x}$ is normal with parameters μ and $\sigma_{\bar{x}}$, and (c) the value of $\sigma_{\bar{x}}$ is known (or can be estimated from the sample), then the posterior distribution of $\tilde{\mu}$ is normal with

$$E_1(\tilde{\mu}) = \frac{[E_0(\tilde{\mu})/\sigma_0^2(\tilde{\mu})] + \bar{x}/\sigma_{\bar{x}}^2}{[1/\sigma_0^2(\tilde{\mu})] + 1/\sigma_{\bar{x}}^2} \tag{19.5}$$

$$\sigma_1^2(\tilde{\mu}) = \frac{\sigma_0^2(\tilde{\mu})\sigma_{\bar{x}}^2}{\sigma_0^2(\tilde{\mu}) + \sigma_{\bar{x}}^2} \tag{19.6}$$

$$\frac{1}{\sigma_1^2(\tilde{\mu})} = \frac{1}{\sigma_0^2(\tilde{\mu})} + \frac{1}{\sigma_{\bar{x}}^2} \tag{19.7}$$

The reciprocal of the variance of a normally distributed variable is often considered to be a measure of the information content of that variable as an estimator. That is,

$$I_0 = \frac{1}{\sigma_0^2(\tilde{\mu})} = \text{quantity of information in } E_0(\tilde{\mu})$$

$$I_{\bar{x}} = \frac{1}{\sigma_{\bar{x}}^2} = \text{quantity of information in } \bar{x}\text{, the sample mean}$$

* Robert Schlaiffer, "Probability and Statistics for Business Decisions," p. 441, McGraw-Hill, New York, 1959.

and

$$I_1 = \frac{1}{\sigma_1^2(\tilde{\mu})} = \text{quantity of information in } E_1(\tilde{\mu}_1)$$

and Eq. (19.7) becomes

$$I_1 = I_0 + I_{\bar{x}} \tag{19.8}$$

which simply states that the information content of the posterior estimate $E_1(\tilde{\mu})$ is the sum of the information content of the prior estimate and the sample mean.

All the formulas stated above use the variable $\tilde{\mu}$, the unknown mean of a normal distribution. For $\tilde{\mu}$ could be substituted $\tilde{\theta}$, a more general designation of an unknown parameter or state of nature.

Example 19.2 George Jitney is the sole owner of a small shuttle bus firm in Funtown. He operates his service on several routes in the city between bus terminals, railway stations, and airports as well as in various commercial and shopping areas. He is considering establishing a new route and must decide whether it would be a wise decision to do so.

The fixed cost for city licenses and the overhaul of necessary equipment would come to about \$20,000 per year. The fare charged the customers is 25 cents, of which about 5 cents goes for the variable cost of operation. Each fare, then, contributes about 20 cents to profit. The payoff function, assuming that Mr. Jitney decides to open the new route, an act which we shall label a_1, would be:

$$\begin{aligned} Q_1 &= -\$20{,}000 + (\$0.20)(365)\tilde{\mu} \\ &= -\$20{,}000 + 73\tilde{\mu} \end{aligned}$$

where $\tilde{\mu}$ represents the average number of passengers per day. The alternate act a_2 represents taking no action, and $Q_2 = 0 + 0\tilde{\mu} = 0$.

Since the value of $\tilde{\mu}$ is the critical unknown for this analysis, Jitney must use his experience and ingenuity in arriving at some estimate. Based on other routes similar in nature to the one proposed, he estimates that the daily average number of passengers can be represented by a normal distribution and that the mean of this distribution is $E_0(\tilde{\mu}) = 250$.

Jitney realizes, of course, that although he considers this number to be the most likely, it is quite probable that the actual value will deviate from his estimate in either direction. He would, however, accept a bet at odds of 2 to 1 that the true mean, or daily average number of passengers, is within 100 units of the mean. His prior distribution looks like the one shown in Fig. 19.4.

The parameters of this prior distribution are

$$\begin{aligned} E_0(\tilde{\mu}) &= 250 \\ \sigma_0(\tilde{\mu}) &= 100 \end{aligned}$$

If Mr. Jitney had to make an immediate decision, he would compute the expected payoff of each act and select that act for which the expected payoff is the greater.

$$\begin{aligned} E(Q_1) &= -\$20{,}000 + \$73E(\tilde{\mu}) \\ &= -\$20{,}000 + \$18{,}250 \\ &= -\$1{,}750 \\ E(Q_2) &= \$0 - \$0E(\mu) \\ &= 0 \end{aligned}$$

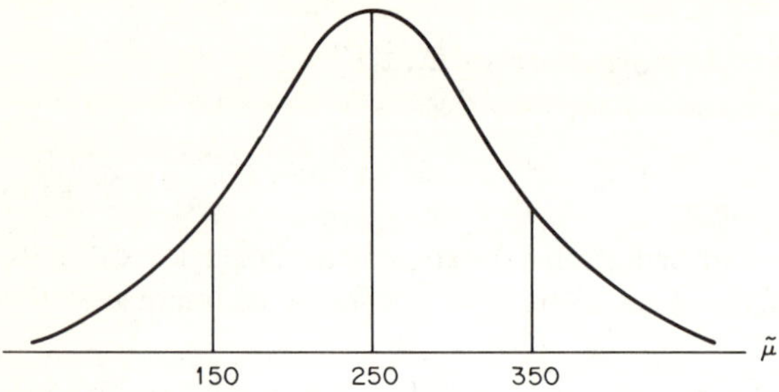

Fig. 19.4

Since a_1 results in a loss of \$1,750 while a_2 results in zero payoff, Jitney should select act a_2, that is, do not inaugurate the new route.

The same result could have been achieved if Jitney had first computed the break-even value of μ, thus:

$$\begin{aligned} -\$20{,}000 + \$73\mu &= 0 \\ \$73\mu &= \$20{,}000 \\ \mu_n &= 274 \end{aligned}$$

and observing that since $E_0(\tilde{\mu}) = 250 < 274 = \mu_k$, act a_2 should be chosen.

Although the decision based on Jitney's prior information was quite apparent, he began to wonder if it might be advantageous to acquire some additional information about the market for the new transportation service. First, he wondered how much perfect information might be worth to him.

The formula for EVPI using a normal prior is

$$\text{EVPI} = t\sigma_0 L_N(D_0)$$

where $t = m_1 - m_2 = \$73 - 0 = \$73$

$$D = \frac{\mu_k - E_0(\tilde{\mu})}{\sigma_0(\tilde{\mu})} = \frac{274 - 250}{100} = 0.24$$

$$L_N(D_0) = 0.2904$$

Therefore, EVPI = (\$73)(100)(0.2904) = \$2,119.92

Although Jitney realizes that no sampling plan will produce perfect information, he believes that since EVPI is over \$2,000, it would be wise for him to acquire some additional information by sampling, so long as his sampling cost does not equal EVPI.

He would, moreover, like to have a better idea of exactly what sampling information might be worth to him, and consequently he should look into the expected value of sampling information or EVSI. But first let us assume that he has already decided to acquire additional information by sampling and, furthermore, has decided on a trial operation on the new run for 1 week or 7 days. After this sample of size 7, the following results were obtained:

$$\bar{x} = 300$$
$$s = 50$$

Now for computing the parameters of the posterior distribution, it is assumed that σ, the standard deviation of the individual members of the population, is known. Schlaiffer says that even though σ is not known, we can treat an estimate s derived from a sample of size 25 or greater as though it were the true value of σ.* However, in this example our sample size is only 7, far less than 25. What do we do now? Schlaiffer also suggests that there are frequent situations in which σ can be treated as if it were known even when μ cannot.† Other experiments conducted under similar circumstances may have shown that the standard deviation of this or some similar population is relatively constant at some fixed value even though the mean varies. In a problem such as this, we might assume that Jitney, the decision maker, had his own prior estimates of σ which coincided rather closely with the $s = 50$ resulting from the sample. The agreement was close enough that he was willing to accept $\hat{\sigma} = 50$ as a reasonable estimate of the population standard deviation even though it was only based on a sample of size 7.

Consequently,

$$\hat{\sigma}_{\bar{x}} \simeq \frac{50}{\sqrt{7}} = 18.8$$

$$\hat{\sigma}_{\bar{x}}^2 \simeq 357$$

The posterior distribution of $\tilde{\mu}$, the average number of daily passengers, is, therefore,

$$\begin{aligned} E_1(\tilde{\mu}) &= \frac{E_0(\tilde{\mu})[1/\sigma_0^2(\tilde{\mu})] + \bar{x}(1/\sigma_{\bar{x}}^2)}{1/\sigma_0^2(\tilde{\mu}) + 1/\sigma_{\bar{x}}^2} \\ &= \frac{(250)(1/10{,}000) + (300)(1/357)}{(1/10{,}000) + (1/357)} \\ &= \frac{0.0250 + 0.8403}{0.0001 + 0.0028} \\ &= \frac{0.8653}{0.0029} \\ &= 298.4 \end{aligned}$$

$$\begin{aligned} \sigma_1^2(\tilde{\mu}) &= \frac{\sigma_0^2(\tilde{\mu})\sigma_{\bar{x}}^2}{\sigma_0^2(\tilde{\mu}) + \sigma_{\bar{x}}^2} \\ &= \frac{(10{,}000)(357)}{10{,}000 + 357} \\ &= \frac{3{,}570{,}000}{10{,}357} \\ &= 344.7 \end{aligned}$$

The quantity or amount of information in the prior, sampling, and posterior distributions is

$$I_0 + I_{\bar{x}} = I_1$$

$$0.0001 + 0.0028 = 0.00029$$

* *ibid.* Schlaiffer, p. 303.

† *Ibid.*

and

$$\sigma_1^2(\tilde{\mu}) = \frac{1}{I_1} = 344.7$$

On the basis of the combined prior and sample information, then

$$\begin{aligned} E(Q_1) &= -\$20{,}000 + (\$73)E_1(\tilde{\mu}) \\ &= -\$20{,}000 + (\$73)(298.4) \\ &= -\$20{,}000 + \$20{,}783 \\ &= \$783 \end{aligned}$$

$$E(Q_2) = 0$$

and a_1 now appears to be the better act.

We can now compute EVPI after or posterior to the sample using the same formulas as before except that now the posterior values of $E(\tilde{\mu})$ and $\sigma(\tilde{\mu})$ are used.

$$D_1 = \left|\frac{\mu_k - E_1(\tilde{\mu})}{\sigma_1(\tilde{\mu})}\right| = \left|\frac{274 - 298.4}{18.89}\right| = 1.29$$

and

$$\begin{aligned} \text{EVPI} &= t\sigma_1 L_N D_1 \\ &= (\$73)(18.89)(0.0465) \\ &= \$64.12 \end{aligned}$$

It appears that the result of taking a sample of size 7 was not only to lead to a different decision but also to reduce the *cost of uncertainty* (EVPI) from \$2,119.92 to \$64.12. However, as was pointed out previously, information is usually not obtained without cost. There are costs involved in any sampling experiment. The net gain which accrued to Mr. Jitney from the sample of 7 days operation was the reduction in the cost of uncertainty or EVPI less the cost of taking the sample.

Suppose the cost of running this sampling experiment (trial operation of the new bus route) was \$180 per day. This cost results from the diversion and utilization of equipment less the fares paid by the passengers which in this short period does not cover the costs. Then the 7-day sample cost which we shall designate $C(n = 7)$ was (7)(\$180) = \$1,260. The net gain from this sample was, therefore,

Prior cost of uncertainty (prior EVPI)	\$2,119.92
Less posterior cost of uncertainty (posterior EVPI)	−64.12
Value of sampling information	2,055.80
Less cost of sampling	−1,260.00
Net gain from sampling	\$795.80

Obviously, the sampling experiment was worthwhile since the net gain to Jitney was \$795.80. In a practical decision situation, however, it seems reasonable that some estimate of the value of the sample information should be available to the decision maker before he commits himself to taking the sample. Furthermore, he should be able to estimate the value of information from samples of various sizes so that he can select the optimum size for his sampling experiment. In line with the bayesian approach to decision making, these estimates will be expected values and will lead to EVSI, the *expected* value of sampling information, and to ENGS, the *expected* net gain from sampling. These concepts were discussed with respect to discrete prior distributions in the previous chapter.

19.6 PREPOSTERIOR ANALYSIS AND EVSI

In the example above, we computed the value of information from a given sample after the sample was taken and the result was known. After the sample result was known, the mean of the posterior distribution could be computed, and this, together with the posterior standard deviation, led to posterior EVPI. Before the sample is taken, however, the specific result is unknown, and since the posterior mean $E_1(\tilde{\mu})$ depends upon the same result, $E_1(\tilde{\mu})$ is a random variable. The probability distribution $E_1(\tilde{\mu})$ or, for the sake of brevity, $\tilde{E}_1$, is called the *preposterior distribution.* If both the prior distribution of μ and the sampling distribution are normal, then the preposterior distribution is also normal with parameters

$$E(\tilde{E}_1) = E_0(\tilde{\mu}) \tag{19.9}$$

and

$$\sigma^2(\tilde{E}_1) = \frac{[\sigma_0{}^2(\tilde{\mu})]^2}{\sigma_0{}^2(\tilde{\mu}) + \sigma_{\bar{x}}{}^2} \tag{19.10}$$

The parameters of the preposterior distribution are used to compute the *expected* value of sampling information or EVSI.

$\sigma^2(\tilde{E}_1)$, the variance of the preposterior distribution for a given sample, can be thought of as an estimate of the reduction in the variance or in the decision maker's uncertainty which would result if the sample were taken. Consequently, since

$$\sigma_1{}^2(\tilde{\mu}) = \frac{\sigma_0{}^2(\tilde{\mu})\sigma_{\bar{x}}{}^2}{\sigma_0{}^2(\tilde{\mu}) + \sigma_{\bar{x}}{}^2} \tag{19.11}$$

the preposterior variance can also be obtained from

$$\sigma^2(\tilde{E}_1) = \sigma_0{}^2(\tilde{\mu}) - \sigma_1{}^2(\tilde{\mu}) \tag{19.12}$$

Whether Eq. (19.10) or (19.12) is used, σ, the population standard deviation, must be known or estimated.

Keep in mind that the value of information from any given sample, after the sample is taken, is simply the difference between the cost of uncertainty prior to the sample and the cost of uncertainty after the sample has been taken. Since it is desirable to estimate the value of sampling information from any sample before actually taking the sample, this estimate takes the form of an expected value and is called the expected value of sampling information.

The prior cost of uncertainty or prior EVPI is still the same. However, for any proposed sample, the posterior cost of sampling or posterior EVPI depends upon the sample outcome, which, before the sample is taken, is a random variable.

In the case of a discrete prior distribution, we determined an *expected* value of posterior expected regret or cost by multiplying the expected consequences of the best act for a given sample outcome by the marginal probability that that outcome would occur and summed these values over all possible outcomes. Thus, the expected value of posterior expected regret (or cost) equals

$$\sum_{\mathscr{O}_1} E[R(a_{\text{opt}}|\mathscr{O})]P(\mathscr{O}) \tag{19.13}$$

where

$$\mathscr{O} = \text{sample outcome}$$
$$a_{\text{opt}} = \text{optimum act given } \mathscr{O}$$
$$E[R(a|\mathscr{O})] = \sum_{\theta} P(a|\theta)P_1(\theta)$$

In preposterior analysis with a normal prior and normal sampling distribution, EVSI can be determined by formula, utilizing the parameters of the preposterior distribution as follows:

$$\text{EVSI} = t\sigma(\tilde{E}_1)L_N(D_E)$$

where

$$D_E = \left|\frac{\mu_k - E(\tilde{E}_1)}{\sigma(\tilde{E}_1)}\right|$$

and, as before,

$$t = |m_1 - m_2|$$

In determining $\sigma^2(\tilde{E}_1)$, it is necessary that the population σ either be known or that some estimate be available. The estimate might come from data already available from previous studies or might result from a preliminary sample or pilot study of the phenomenon.

For the Jitney Bus Company example, suppose that prior to taking the sample of $n = 7$, Mr. Jitney wanted to estimate the value of the sample to him, that is, EVSI.

$$\text{EVSI} = t\sigma(\tilde{E}_1)L_N(D_E)$$

t is, as before, the difference between the slopes of the payoff functions, or $t = \$73$.

$$\sigma^2(\tilde{E}_1) = \frac{[\sigma_0{}^2(\tilde{\mu})]^2}{\sigma_0{}^2(\tilde{\mu}) + \sigma_{\bar{x}}{}^2} = \frac{(100^2)^2}{100^2 + [(50)^2/7]}$$

since $\sigma_{\bar{x}}^2 = \sigma^2/n$, and Jitney had previously estimated $\hat{\sigma} = 50$. Therefore

$$\sigma^2(\tilde{E}_1) = 9{,}655$$
$$\sigma(\tilde{E}_1) = \sqrt{9{,}655} \doteq 98.2$$

$$D_E = \left|\frac{\mu_k - E(\tilde{E}_1)}{\sigma(\tilde{E}_1)}\right| = \left|\frac{274 - 250}{98.2}\right| = 0.263$$

and

$$\text{EVSI} = \$73(98.2)(0.2811) = \$2{,}014.38$$

The *expected* value of a sample of size 7 to Jitney *prior* to actually taking the sample is \$2,014.38. Contrast this with EVPI before taking the sample of \$2,119.92 and with the actual value of sampling information from a sample of size 7 computed *after* taking the sample and obtaining the result $\bar{x} = 300$, which was \$2,055.80. EVSI is obviously less than EVPI since perfect information can never be obtained from a sampling experiment. EVSI could be either less than or greater than the actual value of sampling information after the sample is taken, depending upon the actual sample outcome. In this case, EVSI = \$2,014.38 < \$2,055.80 = actual value of sampling information.

To find the *expected* net gain from sampling, we must subtract the cost of sampling from EVSI. Thus,

$$\begin{aligned} \text{EVSI} &= \ \ \$2{,}014.38 \\ \text{less } C(n = 7) &= -1{,}260.00 \\ \hline \text{ENGS} &= \ \ \$\ \ 754.38 \end{aligned}$$

The expected net gain from sampling for a sample of size 7 in this decision situation is, therefore, \$754.38. It would appear worthwhile from the decision maker's point of view to take the sample.

19.7 OPTIMUM SAMPLE SIZE

Although the decision maker, Jitney, could conclude from the preposterior analysis that it would be worthwhile to take a sample of size 7 before making his decision, he still cannot be sure that $n = 7$ is the optimum size sample. In order to select the optimum sample size, he should compute ENGS for all sample sizes from $n = 0$ to $n = n_{\max}$, where $n_{\max}$ is that n such that

$$C(n_{\max}) < \text{EVPI}$$

He would then select that value of n for which ENGS is a maximum. Review Chap. 17 for a more detailed discussion of this procedure.

19.8 SUMMARY

When the sampling distribution of the experiment is normal, then both the prior and posterior distributions in the decision problem should also be normal. This situation arises when the pertinent parameter of the decision problem is an unknown population mean.

In situations such as this, the decision maker specifies his prior distribution on the unknown parameter by specifying the mean and standard deviation of a normal distribution that represents his subjective estimates. When the distribution on the unknown parameter is normal, the expected value of perfect information in a two-action situation can be determined from a formula which depends upon the standard deviation of the prior distribution, the per-unit regret, and the distance of the break-even value from the prior mean.

The value of the information obtained and the net gain from sampling after the sample has been taken can be determined as the difference between the cost of uncertainty before the sample and the cost of uncertainty after the sample. This, less the sampling cost, provides the net gain from the sample.

By preposterior analysis, an *expected* value of sampling information and an *expected* net gain from a sample of a given size can be determined before any sample is taken.

PROBLEMS

19.1. Specify the parameters of the prior distribution on μ, a population mean, if the decision maker assumes that his prior is normal and provides the following information:

(*a*) The true population mean is just as likely to be greater than 70 as it is to be less than 70. Furthermore, it is just as likely to be between 55 and 85 as it is to be either greater than 85 or less than 55.

(*b*) The true population mean is just as likely to be greater than 70 as it is to be less than 70. However, it is twice as likely to be between 55 and 85 than it is to be greater than 85 or less than 55.

(*c*) The true population mean is just as likely to be greater than 70 as it is to be less than 70. However, it is twice as likely to be either less than 55 or greater than 85 than it is to be between 55 and 85.

(*d*) The true population mean is just as likely to be greater than 70 as it is to be less than 70. However, it is three times as likely to be between 55 and 85 than it is to be greater than 85 or less than 55.

19.2. For the prior distribution determined in Prob. 19.1(*a*) and the following payoff functions:

$$Q_1 = -500$$
$$Q_2 = -1{,}625 + 15\mu$$

find EVPI.

19.3. For the prior distribution determined in Prob. 19.1(*b*) and the following payoff functions:

$$Q_1 = -2{,}000 + 50\mu$$
$$Q_2 = -140 + 20\mu$$

find EVPI.

19.4. For the prior distribution of Prob. 19.1(*b*) and the payoff function of Prob. 19.3 a sample of size $n = 100$ is taken, resulting in $\bar{x} = 75$, $\hat{\sigma}_{\bar{x}} = 11$.

(*a*) What are the parameters of the posterior distribution on μ?

(*b*) What is EVPI after the sample?

(*c*) What was the value of the information from the sample?

19.5. For the prior distribution of Prob. 19.1(*a*) and the payoff functions of Prob. 19.2, a sample of $n = 100$ is taken, resulting in $\bar{x} = 65$, $\hat{\sigma}_{\bar{x}} = 10$.

(*a*) What are the parameters of the posterior distribution on μ?

(*b*) What is EVPI after the sample?

(*c*) What was the value of the information from the sample?

19.6. For the following parameter values of normal prior distributions and the accompanying sample results, find the parameters of the posterior distributions.

(*a*) $E_0(\tilde{\mu}) = 75$, $\sigma_0(\tilde{\mu}) = 25$; $\bar{x} = 80$, $s = 75$, $n = 225$

(*b*) $E_0(\tilde{\mu}) = 160$, $\sigma_0(\tilde{\mu}) = 15$; $\bar{x} = 200$, $s = 110$, $n = 100$

(*c*) $E_0(\tilde{\mu}) = 35$, $\sigma_0(\tilde{\mu}) = 5$; $\bar{x} = 25$, $s = 10$, $n = 50$

(*d*) $E_0(\tilde{\mu}) = 35$, $\sigma_0(\tilde{\mu}) = 8$; $\bar{x} = 50$, $s = 20$, $n = 100$

(*e*) $E_0(\tilde{\mu}) = 500$, $\sigma_0(\tilde{\mu}) = 45$; $\bar{x} = 575$, $s = 100$, $n = 225$

19.7. If the prior distribution on $\tilde{\mu}$ is $N[E_0(\tilde{\mu}) = 100, \sigma_0(\tilde{\mu}) = 25]$, and if σ of the population to be sampled is 96, how large a sample must be taken so that $\sigma_1(\tilde{\mu}) \doteq 6$?

19.8. Mr. Baker, a business manager for several motion picture and television celebrities, was looking for a profitable short-term investment for one of his wealthy clients. He received a tip on an over-the-counter stock which could be purchased for $1 per share. The stock was supposed to double in value in 30 days. Mr. Baker considered buying 50,000 shares for his client and selling in 30 days. Commissions and other expenses connected with the transaction would cost the client $2,500.

Before making a decision regarding the advisability of buying the stock, Mr. Baker assessed his prior distribution on the probable increase in the value of the stock. Drawing upon his past experience and evaluating the source of the information about the stock, he estimated that the chances were about even as to whether the stock would increase more than 75 cents per share or less than 75 cents per share. He also felt that the odds were about even that the *increase* in the value of the stock would be between $1.10 and 40 cents per share as that it would be either less than 40 cents per share or greater than $1.10 per share. Considering the acts available to Mr. Baker, the payoff functions of the act, and his prior distribution,

(*a*) Which is the better act?

(*b*) What is the expected payoff of the better act?

(*c*) What is EVPI?

(*d*) Considering Mr. Baker's prior distribution, what is the probability that the stock will decline in value?

19.9. Considering the value of EVPI in the previous problem, Mr. Baker decided to defer his decision until he could obtain additional information. He selects a sample of 100 stocks which he considers similar in most respects to the stock under consideration. He then analyzes their performances under circumstances similar to the present situation.

The average increase per share of the 100 stocks was 25 cents. The standard deviation was 15 cents.

(*a*) What are the parameters of Mr. Baker's posterior distribution?
(*b*) Which is the better act after the sample?
(*c*) What is the expected payoff of the better act?
(*d*) What is the probability that the stock will decline in value?

19.10. For the previous problem,

(*a*) What was EVPI after the sample?
(*b*) What was the value of the sampling information to Mr. Baker?
(*c*) Assuming that it cost Mr. Baker \$250 to obtain the information, what was the net gain from sampling?

20
Probability Distributions in Decision Analysis: The Gamma Distribution

Consider a situation in which an event occurs in the time domain.* That is, in some given period of time, an event can fail to occur at all, can occur once, twice, or any number of times. The Poisson distribution, previously discussed, provides the probability that this particular event will occur any number of times in a specified time period given only that the mean or average number of occurrences for that time period is known or can be estimated.

The single parameter of the Poisson distribution is simply the average number of occurrences per unit of time (or space), and can be designated with the Greek letter μ. If we were to let λ represent the rate of occurrences of the event per unit of time and if t is expressed in terms of those units of time, then $\mu = \lambda t$ for any t.

The probability that the event will occur exactly r times in some time t is then given by

* As discussed in Sec. 7.4, the Poisson distribution is not restricted to events occurring in the time domain but is just as applicable to events observed on spatial units.

$$P(\tilde{r}) = \frac{e^{-\lambda t}(\lambda t)^r}{r!} \tag{20.1}$$

The Poisson is a discrete distribution, and r is a discrete random variable. If, however, we allowed t to become the random variable, the gamma distribution would provide the probability that some period of time t would pass before r occurrences of the event are observed. The gamma density function of the random variable t is given in Eq. (7.25) and is repeated below as Eq. (20.2)

$$f(t) = \frac{\lambda^r}{(r-1)!} t^{r-1}e^{-\lambda t} \tag{20.2}$$

Suppose, however, we are interested in a probability distribution on λ (or μ), the parameter of the Poisson process, instead of on t. The gamma distribution can, after a minor transformation, be written with λ as the random variable and with r and t as parameters as follows:

$$f(\lambda) = \frac{te^{-\lambda t}(\lambda t)^{r-1}}{(r-1)!} \tag{20.3}$$

We can now state that if the sampling distribution associated with the decision problem is Poisson, the decision maker's prior distribution should be gamma in which the probability that $a \leq \lambda \leq b$ is given by:

$$P(a \leq \lambda \leq b) = \int_b^a \frac{te^{-\lambda t}(\lambda t)^{r-1}\, dt}{(r-1)!} \tag{20.4}$$

The mean and variance of the gamma distribution are

$$E(\tilde{\lambda}) = \frac{r}{t} \tag{20.5}$$

$$\text{var}\ (\tilde{\lambda}) = \frac{r}{t^2} \tag{20.6}$$

20.1 THE PARAMETERS OF THE POSTERIOR GAMMA DISTRIBUTION

We have previously determined that the posterior distribution is proportional to the product of the prior distribution and the likelihood or conditional distribution. That is, $P_1(\tilde{\lambda}|r) \propto P(r|\lambda)P_0(\tilde{\lambda})$, where $P(r|\lambda)$ is Poisson and $P_0(\tilde{\lambda})$ is gamma.

The posterior distribution of $\tilde{\lambda}$ will be of the same form as the prior with $t_1 = t_0 + t$ and $r_1 = r_0 + r$. That is,

$$P_1(\tilde{\lambda}) = \frac{t_1 e^{-\lambda t_1}(\lambda t)^{r-1}}{(r-1)!} \tag{20.7}$$

The mean and variance of the posterior gamma distribution are

$$E_1(\tilde{\lambda}) = \frac{r_1}{t_1} \tag{20.8}$$

$$\text{var}\,(\tilde{\lambda}) = \frac{r_1}{t_1^{\,2}} \tag{20.9}$$

20.2 SPECIFYING PARAMETERS OF THE PRIOR GAMMA DISTRIBUTION

Obtaining the parameters r and t of the decision maker's subjective prior gamma distribution raises the same problems as those encountered when the beta distribution was discussed. The expected value or mean of the prior distribution consists of a ratio of two values, that is, r_0/t_0. Although various pairs of values for r_0 and t_0 can result in the same value of $E(\tilde{\lambda})$, each pair describes a different gamma distribution. Different approaches to the specification of parameters for the prior distribution were considered with respect to the beta distribution, and that discussion generally applies to the gamma as well. One of the simplest methods of obtaining the decision maker's proper prior gamma distribution, and the one that shall be recommended at this point, is to have the decision maker specify the parameters of an approximating normal distribution in the manner suggested for normal priors. Then a gamma distribution is selected which has the same mean and variance as the approximating normal distribution. Specific values for r_0 and t_0 can be obtained by equating the gamma mean and variance formulas to the specified normal mean and variance, respectively, and then solving simultaneously for r_0 and t_0. This and other important points will be illustrated in a subsequent example.

20.3 RELATIONSHIP BETWEEN GAMMA AND POISSON PROBABILITIES

Gamma probabilities can be obtained directly from Pearson's tables if they happen to be available.* However, because of the relationship between the gamma and Poisson distributions, the gamma probabilities can also be obtained from any set of Poisson tables by utilizing the following relationship:

$$P_\gamma(\tilde{\lambda} < \lambda | r,t) = P_p(\tilde{r} \geq r | \mu) \tag{20.10}$$

where P_γ is the gamma probability, P_p is the Poisson probability, and $\mu = \lambda t$.

* K. Pearson, "Tables of the Incomplete Gamma Function," Cambridge, London, 1922.

20.4 THE GAMMA DISTRIBUTION IN DECISION THEORY: AN EXAMPLE

An American oil company plans to send an expedition to a remote area in the Arctic next summer to drill for oil. Several exploratory wells will be drilled at the site, and all equipment must be flown in by air. A particular part of the drilling equipment is subject to breakage, and the frequency of breakage is a function of the composition of the terrain in which the drilling takes place. Each of these parts costs \$100. If shipped with the original expedition, the cost of shipping each part is \$75. However, if the expedition runs out of its supply of this part, then a replacement or replacements must be shipped from the United States at a cost of \$750 each. The problem becomes one of determining the optimum number of these parts to ship as spares with the expedition.

Let r be the number of spares needed and let k be the number shipped with the original expedition. Then the cost function will be:

$$C = \$75k \qquad \text{for } r \leq k$$

$$C = \$750r - \$675k \qquad \text{for } r > k$$

Assume that the maximum number of spares which can be accommodated with the original expedition is four. Therefore, the number of acts to be considered involves the shipping of from zero to four spares. The payoff table for this problem in terms of cost is given in Table 20.1.

The drilling expedition was scheduled to stay at the site for a period of 3 months. The drill would operate 24 hr a day for the entire period. In terms of hours of operation, the drill would operate for a total of 2,184 hr. From past experience based on drilling in various types of terrain, the company's engineers estimated that the critical part lasted, on the average, about 2,000 hr. This value, 2,000 hr, could be called the estimated mean-time-to-failure. In terms of rate of part breakage or failure rate, this would be one failure per 2,000 hr or $\lambda = 0.5$ failures per 1,000 hr. Let us emphasize here that these part failures were random events and not due to wear-out

Table 20.1

States: number of spares needed	$a_0{:}k = 0$	$a_1{:}k = 1$	$a_2{:}k = 2$	$a_3{:}k = 3$	$a_4{:}k = 4$
$S_0{:}r = 0$	0	75	150	225	300
$S_1{:}r = 1$	750	75	150	225	300
$S_2{:}r = 2$	1,500	825	150	225	300
$S_3{:}r = 3$	2,250	1,575	900	225	300
$S_4{:}r = 4$	3,000	2,325	1,650	975	300
$S_5{:}r = 5$	3,750	3,075	2,400	1,725	1,050

Table 20.2 Poisson probabilities for $\mu = 1.1$

$P(r = 0 \mid \mu = 1.1) = 0.333$
$P(r = 1 \mid \mu = 1.1) = 0.366$
$P(r = 2 \mid \mu = 1.1) = 0.201$
$P(r = 3 \mid \mu = 1.1) = 0.074$
$P(r = 4 \mid \mu = 1.1) = 0.020$
$P(r = 5 \mid \mu = 1.1) = 0.004$

of the part. In order to ensure the randomness of the part breakages, since the wear-out characteristics of the part were known, it was standard practice to replace the critical part before wear-out became a factor.

Although the engineers could estimate the average time to failure or, conversely, the rate of failure in terms of hours of operation, they were unable to estimate directly the probability of no failure, one failure, two failures, etc., for the period of operation. This latter consideration, however, turns out to be of little importance since, given the average rate of failure, they knew that they could determine the probability of any number of failures occurring simply by using the Poisson distribution with the appropriate mean as a model for the process.

For $\lambda = 0.5$ and t (in units of 1,000 hr) $= 2.184$, $\lambda t = \mu = 1.092$ or approximately 1.1. The probability that $\tilde{r} = r$ is given by the Poisson tables, and the appropriate probabilities are listed below in Table 20.2. The probability that $r \geq 6$ is considered to be negligible.

If a decision had to be made at this point, the decision maker should calculate the expected cost of each act utilizing Tables 20.1 and 20.2 and select that act (ship the corresponding number of spares) for which the expected cost is a minimum. Without showing all the calculations, the prior expected costs for each of the available acts are given in Table 20.3.

The optimum act, if an immediate decision is required, would be a_2, which is to ship two spares with the expedition at an expected cost of $247.96.

Table 20.3 Prior expected costs

Act	*Expected cost*
a_0	$826.50
a_1	$398.93
a_2	$247.96
a_3	$248.35
a_4	$304.50

Table 20.4

States: number of spares needed	Regret acts (ship Q with expectation) a_0 $Q = 0$	a_1 $Q = 1$	a_2 $Q = 2$	a_3 $Q = 3$	a_4 $Q = 4$
$S_0, r = 0$	0	75	150	225	300
$S_1, r = 1$	675	0	75	150	225
$S_2, r = 2$	1,350	675	0	75	150
$S_3, r = 3$	2,025	1,350	675	0	75
$S_4, r = 4$	2,700	2,025	1,350	675	0
$S_5, r = 5$	2,700	2,025	1,350	675	0

In terms of regret, refer to the regret table, which appears as Table 20.4, and the table of expected regrets for each act, which appears as Table 20.5. The expected regret of the best act is \$161.89, which is the *cost of uncertainty*, also EVPI, and corresponds to act a_2.

Since we have a multiaction problem with linear payoff functions, we could apply critical ratio analysis to the problem in order to arrive at a solution which involves somewhat less computation. The critical ratio is

$$k = \frac{k_u}{k_u + k_o}$$

where k_u is the regret due to underestimating the requirements by a single unit and k_o is the regret due to overestimating by one unit.

In this example, $k_o = \$75$ and $k_u = \$675$. The critical ratio therefore becomes

$$k = \frac{675}{675 + 75} = \frac{675}{750} = 0.90$$

Table 20.5 Prior expected regrets

Act	*Expected regret*
a_0	\$737.10
a_1	\$312.53
a_2	\$161.89
a_3	\$162.28
a_4	\$217.80

Table 20.6 Individual and cumulative Poisson probabilities for $\mu = 1.1$

r	$P(\tilde{r} = r)$	$P(\tilde{r} < r)$
0	0.333	0.000
1	0.366	0.333
2	0.201	0.699
3	0.074	0.900
4	0.020	0.974
5 or more	0.006	0.994

The optimum act is therefore that act a_i such that $P(\tilde{r} < r_i) < 0.90$. Referring to Table 20.6, which provides the individual and cumulative Poisson probabilities for $\mu = 1.1$, we see that the best act is the act a_i having the highest value of i such that the previous inequality holds. That act is a_2 since the act "ship two spares" involves the largest number of spares such that $P(\tilde{r} < 2) = 0.699 < 0.900$.

λ AS THE UNKNOWN PARAMETER

It should be obvious that the prior probabilities on the exact number of parts failing in time t is dependent upon λ. Once λ is specified, the probability of any number of parts breaking is also completely specified. The underlying states of nature whose probabilities must be estimated by the decision maker is therefore the parameter λ or μ rather than the individual probabilities that $\tilde{r} = r$. The decision to select act a_2, that is, "ship two spares with the expedition," is based on an estimate that $\lambda = 0.5$ and $\mu = 1.1$. If μ has any other value, the individual probabilities that $\tilde{r} = r$ would be entirely different, and the optimum act might also be some act other than a_2.

If λ, the rate of part breakage or failure under the conditions which were to be encountered, were *known* to be 0.5 failure per 1,000 hr, then the decision to select act a_2 based upon the expected costs of Table 20.3 or the expected regrets of Table 20.5 would be optimal under a Bayes' procedure. However, since λ is not known, these expected values are actually conditional expected values of cost and regret. They are conditional upon the true but unknown value of λ. Since $\lambda t = \mu$ and t is fixed, the previous discussion also applies to μ.

Let us suppose that the engineers in charge of the drilling operation cannot be certain about the exact value of λ, the failure rate, but are sure that it is one of only three possible values; 0.1 failure per 1,000 hr, 0.5 failure per 1,000 hr, or 1.0 failure per 1,000 hr. For $t = 2.184$ hr, the corresponding values of $\lambda t = \mu$ would be $\mu \doteq 0.2$, $\mu \doteq 1.1$, and $\mu \doteq 2.2$. Assume also

Table 20.7 Poisson probabilities

r	$P(\tilde{r} = r)$ *when* $\lambda = 0.1, \mu = 0.2$	$P(\tilde{r} = r)$ *when* $\lambda = 0.5, \mu = 1.1$	$P(\tilde{r} = r)$ *when* $\lambda = 1.0, \mu = 2.2$
0	0.819	0.333	0.111
1	0.164	0.366	0.244
2	0.016	0.201	0.268
3	0.001	0.074	0.197
4	0	0.020	0.108
5 or more	0	0.006	0.072

that the engineers' prior estimate of the probability that λ and consequently μ is indeed any one of these values is as follows:

λ	μ	$P(\lambda)$
0.1/1,000 hr	0.2	0.25
0.5/1,000 hr	1.1	0.50
1.0/1,000 hr	2.2	0.25
		1.00

These data represent the prior distribution on λ or μ. Now, in order to compare the consequences of each possible act with every other possible act, it is necessary to compute the *unconditional expected regret* of each act. The unconditional expected regret of an act a_i would be:

$$\sum_j \{E[R(a_i)]|\lambda_j\}P(\lambda_j) \tag{20.11}$$

In order to arrive at an optimal decision even without sampling, it would be necessary to go through the same procedure for all the possible values of λ (or μ) as was done previously for the single value of $\lambda = 0.5$.

Table 20.8 Conditional expected regrets

Acts	$\lambda = 0.1, \mu = 0.2$, *dollars*	$\lambda = 0.5, \mu = 1.1$, *dollars*	$\lambda = 1.0, \mu = 2.2$, *dollars*
a_0	134.33	737.10	1,422.50
a_1	73.58	312.53	822.73
a_2	135.83	161.89	412.35
a_3	209.88	162.28	203.18
a_4	285.08	217.80	143.18

Table 20.9 Unconditional expected regret of act a_0

λ	$P_0(\lambda)$	$E(R)\|\lambda$	$[E(R)\|\lambda]P_8(\lambda)$
0.1	0.25	$ 134.33	$ 33.58
0.5	0.50	737.10	368.55
1.0	0.25	1,422.50	355.62
		Unconditional expected regret	$757.75

The probability that $\tilde{r} = r$ would be different in each case, and these probabilities are given in Table 20.7. The conditional expected regrets of each act for each of the three possible values of λ are given in Table 20.8.

From Table 20.8, it can be seen that if $\lambda = 0.1$, the best act would be a_1. If $\lambda = 0.5$, on the other hand, the best act would be a_2. And if $\lambda = 1.0$, the best act would be a_4. Since the value of λ is not known and the information about this value takes a form of a probability distribution on the various possible values, the *unconditional* expected regret for each act must be determined by taking into consideration the expected regret of the act for each possible value of λ as well as the probability distribution on λ. The unconditional expected regret for act a_0 is computed in Table 20.9. Since the method of computation is the same for all acts, only the results are given for all five possible acts in Table 20.10.

Selecting that act for which the unconditional expected regret is the least leads to act a_3, "ship three spares with the expedition."

REVISING THE PRIOR DISTRIBUTION ON λ

Let us now suppose that the engineers working for the oil company decide to defer their decision regarding the number of spare parts to ship with the expedition until they can obtain additional information regarding the true value of λ, the part failure rate under the drilling conditions that will be encountered in the Arctic. They will obtain this additional information by

Table 20.10

Act	*Unconditional expected regret, dollars*
a_0	757.75
a_1	380.35
a_2	218.00
a_3	184.40
a_4	215.96

conducting a sampling experiment. For this example, the cost of the experiment will be ignored, and this oversight will be justified on the basis that the information from this experiment will have considerable value to the company aside from its value to this particular decision situation.

The experiment conducted was as follows. It was desirable to obtain as many hours of operation on the critical part under conditions similar to those encountered at the drilling site as possible. Since part failure was considered to be a random phenomenon, operating hours could be accumulated on several identical parts simultaneously. It was, therefore, decided to put five of the parts on test for 500 hr each under conditions deemed similar to those at the drilling site. If a breakage occurred on any part in less than the 500 hr, then, of course, testing on that particular part terminated. The total test time on the five parts would be accumulated, and the number of breakages noted. This data would be used to estimate the failure rate of the part under the specified conditions.

The time accumulated on the ith part is designated t_i. When the experiment was completed, the following data had been accumulated:

$$
\begin{aligned}
t_1 &= 500 \text{ hr} \\
t_2 &= 500 \text{ hr} \\
t_3 &= 350 \text{ hr} \\
t_4 &= 500 \text{ hr} \\
t_5 &= 450 \text{ hr} \\
\hline
\sum t_i &= 2{,}300 \text{ hr}
\end{aligned}
$$

There were a total of $r = 2$ failures in the 2,300 test hours, since part 3 broke after 350 hr and part 5 failed in 450 hr. On the basis of these data it would be possible to estimate λ. Two failures in 2,300 hr would lead to an estimate of $\lambda = 0.87$ failure per 1,000 hr. However, since the amount of test time was not very great and since the prior distribution on λ was based on a considerable amount of data accumulated from other drilling sites, the engineers decided to combine the sampling information with the prior distribution in order to take all the available data into account. Consequently, the prior distribution on λ was revised in exactly the same way as prior distributions have been revised in previous chapters after binomial sampling. The likelihood, or the conditional probability of the sample outcome, is provided by the Poisson distribution with $\mu = \lambda t$. Since t in the experiment was 2,300 hr, or 2.3 thousands of hours,

$$\text{When } \lambda = 0.1,\ \lambda t = (0.1)(2.3) = 0.23 = \mu$$

$$\text{When } \lambda = 0.5,\ \lambda t = (0.5)(2.3) = 1.15 = \mu$$

$$\text{When } \lambda = 1.0,\ \lambda t = (1.0)(2.3) = 2.30 = \mu$$

Table 20.11 Revision of prior probabilities on λ

λ	$P_0(\lambda)$	$\lambda t = \mu$	$P(r \mid \lambda t = \mu)$	$P(r \cap \mu)$	$P_1(\lambda)$
0.1	0.25	0.23	0.0215	0.0054	0.03
0.5	0.50	1.15	0.2091	0.1046	0.59
1.0	0.25	2.30	0.2656	0.0664	0.38
	1.00			0.1764	1.00

The likelihood $P(r \mid \mu)$ is found in the Poisson tables. The revision of the prior probabilities for the data of the experiment is summarized in Table 20.11.

After the sampling experiment the *unconditional expected regret* is computed in exactly the same way as before the experiment except that now the posterior probabilities are used in the calculations instead of the prior probabilities. The new unconditional expected regrets are given in Table 20.12.

The optimum act after sampling in this case is also a_3.

THE GAMMA DISTRIBUTION AS THE PRIOR

It is unreasonable to suppose that in a practical situation any decision maker would assume that the breakage or failure rate of some particular piece of equipment could assume only three discrete values to the exclusion of all others, and that he would then be able to assign probabilities to these values as was done with λ in this example.

To assume that λ could be only 0.1, 0.5, or 1.0 failure per thousand hours is a rather unlikely assumption. It is much more likely that λ could, in the opinion of the decision maker, take on a continuum of values between some limits, say between 0.1 and 1.0. However, any continuous variable must be measured or observed in discrete units. It is reasonable to *say* that a measured length can take on any value between, let us say, 1 and 2 in. But if the measuring instrument used for the purpose of determining that

Table 20.12

Act	*Unconditional expected regret after sampling, dollars*
a_0	979.47
a_1	499.24
a_2	256.28
a_3	179.26
a_4	191.46

length is capable of measuring only to the tenth of an inch, then the only values that could possibly be observed would be 1.0 in., 1.1 in., 1.2 in., . . . , 2.0 in., which values are, of course, discrete.

In the case of the parameter λ, a failure rate, it is conceivable that its true value for this particular part might actually be 0.00001 failure per 1,000 hr. However, in order to observe this as an actual occurrence, it would be necessary to have data relating to 100 million operating hours on the part. This amount of data might be difficult to obtain, particularly in a testing program. On the other hand, if data of this magnitude were available, there would probably be little uncertainty for the decision maker to deal with. Consequently, in a decision problem of this type, it is likely that the decision maker would consider more than three discrete possible values for λ. He would probably consider the interval that appears most likely to contain the parameter and divide it into several equal increments, letting the midpoint of each increment represent the entire increment. It is not too likely that the decision maker would divide the interval into so many increments as to make his solution arithmetically tedious; however, with the aid of computers or even a desk calculator the arithmetic of a solution can be considerably reduced.

Suppose that in this example the decision maker believed that λ did indeed lie in the interval 0.1 to 1.3. Further, suppose that he divided that interval into seven smaller intervals of equal length, letting the seven midpoints represent each interval in terms of a discrete value for the parameter. The task of assigning subjective probabilities to even seven points or possible parameter values now becomes more difficult than when only three discrete values were allowed. This task can, however, be simplified by using a continuous distribution to provide these probabilities. In this case, where the unknown state of nature is the value of the parameter of a Poisson process, the appropriate distribution to use is the gamma distribution.

Assume that a decision maker, in assessing his uncertainties about the value of λ, decided to let a gamma distribution represent his subjective probability distribution. Using a normal approximating procedure for specifying the parameters of his subjective prior distribution, he arrives at an estimate of the mean $E(\tilde{\lambda}) = 0.4$ and the variance var $(\tilde{\lambda}) = 0.08$. The gamma distribution that best fits would be the gamma with parameters $r = 2.0$ and $t = 5.0$. These values were determined by setting $E(\tilde{\lambda}) = r/t = 0.4$ and var $(\tilde{\lambda}) = r/t^2 = 0.08$ and solving simultaneously for r and t.

Using a regret table which provides values of regret for each act and each value of $r|\lambda$, it would now be necessary to compute conditional expected regrets for each act and for each value of λ considered. Unconditional expected regrets for each act are computed using the probabilities on λ provided by the gamma distribution. These probabilities are given in Table 20.13.

Table 20.13 Gamma probabilities on the Poisson parameter

$\tilde{\lambda}$	$(\lambda_0 < \tilde{\lambda} < \lambda_1)$	$P_0(\lambda)$
0.1	0.0–0.2	0.27
0.3	0.2–0.4	0.33
0.5	0.4–0.6	0.21
0.7	0.6–0.8	0.11
0.9	0.8–1.0	0.05
1.1	1.0–1.2	0.02
1.3	1.2–1.4	0.01

Having conducted an experiment and observed the results, two failures in 2,300 operating hours, the prior distribution must be revised to reflect the new information from the sampling experiment. Rather than compute the likelihoods, joint probabilities, and posterior probabilities for each possible value of λ considered, we compute instead the new parameters of the posterior gamma distribution and use the new distribution to obtain the individual probabilities on the specific discrete values of λ. From the previous discussion of the gamma distribution we know that the parameters of the posterior distribution are

$$t_1 = t_0 + t$$

$$r_1 = r_0 + r$$

where t_0 and r_0 are the parameters of the prior distribution and t and r are the sample values. In this example, $t_0 = 5$, $r_0 = 2$, $t = 2.3$, and $r = 2$. Therefore, $t_1 = 7.3$, and $r_1 = 4$. The actual posterior probabilities for each specific discrete value of λ are given in Table 20.14.

Table 20.14 Posterior gamma probabilities

$\tilde{\lambda}$	$(\lambda_0 < \tilde{\lambda} < \lambda_1)$	$P_1(\tilde{\lambda})$
0.1	0.0–0.2	0.08
0.3	0.2–0.4	0.25
0.5	0.4–0.6	0.31
0.7	0.6–0.8	0.19
0.9	0.8–1.0	0.10
1.1	1.0–1.2	0.05
1.3	1.2–1.4	0.02

Once again, unconditional expected regrets would be computed for each act using the posterior gamma probabilities, and that act would then be selected for which the unconditional expected regret was the minimum.

20.5 SUMMARY

When the unknown state of nature is the value of the Poisson parameter and when the sampling is from a Poisson process, the appropriate conjugate distribution is the gamma distribution with parameters r and t. The gamma is a continuous distribution and is used to model the decision maker's uncertainties about the value of λ or μ. When the decision maker's prior distribution is gamma with parameters r_0 and t_0, and when r and t are sample values, the posterior distribution is gamma with parameters $r_1 = r_0 + r$ and $t_1 = t_0 + t$.

The decision-making process utilizing the gamma distribution is the same as that discussed for other distributions such as the beta and the normal. Unconditional expected regrets are determined for each act, and the act is selected for which the expected regret is a minimum.

PROBLEMS

20.1. Complete the solution to the example in Sec. 20.4 using the posterior distribution on λ given in Table 20.14 to compute the unconditional expected regret for each act.

20.2. In assessing his prior distribution on λ, suppose a decision maker states that his expected value of λ is 2.5 with a variance of 1.25. Specify the parameters of the appropriate gamma distribution.

20.3. For the prior distribution specified in the previous problem, determine the parameters of the posterior distribution after having observed an experiment in which the event of interest occurred as follows:

(*a*) Three times in 10 hr.
(*b*) Nine times in 5 hr.
(*c*) Five times in 18 hr.

20.4. For the posterior distribution specified in the answer to Prob. 20.3*a*, what is the expected number of occurrences of the event of interest in:

(*a*) 10 hr?
(*b*) 100 hr?
(*c*) 1,000 hr?

20.5. For the posterior distribution specified in the answer to Prob. 20.3*b*, what is the expected number of occurrences of the event of interest in:

(*a*) 20 hr?
(*b*) 50 hr?
(*c*) 100 hr?

20.6. For the posterior distribution in the answer to Prob. 20.3*c*, what is the expected number of occurrences of the event of interest in:

(*a*) 1,000 hr?
(*b*) 20,000 hr?
(*c*) 100,000 hr?

20.7. Consider the gamma distribution with parameters $r = 1.0$ and $t = 20$. Find the following probabilities utilizing the relationship between the gamma and the Poisson distributions:

(*a*) $P(\tilde{\lambda} < 0.05)$

(*b*) $P(\tilde{\lambda} < 0.25)$

(*c*) $P(\tilde{\lambda} > 0.30)$

(*d*) $P(0.01 < \tilde{\lambda} < 0.10)$

20.8. Consider the gamma distribution with parameters $r = 3$ and $t = 15$. Find the following probabilities:

(*a*) $P(\tilde{\lambda} < 0.60)$

(*b*) $P(\tilde{\lambda} > 0.50)$

(*c*) $P(\tilde{\lambda} < 0.40)$

(*d*) $P(0.30 < \lambda < 0.60)$

20.9. A company has just accepted a production contract requiring delivery to the customer in 90 days. In order to meet the delivery date, the production manager estimates that he must have a work force of 80 people working from the start date until the delivery date. Past records indicate that the average rate of absenteeism is approximately $2\frac{1}{2}$ percent of the work force on any given 8-hr work day.

(*a*) In order to have a probability of approximately 0.95 that there will never be less than 80 workers on the job, how many extra workers should be hired?

(*b*) What are the parameters of his prior distribution on λ, the daily absenteeism rate?

20.10. Because he is uncertain about his estimate of the rate of absenteeism, the production manager in the previous problem observed the workers whom he intends to assign to the new contract for a period of 5 days. The number of absentees on each of the five days was 1, 0, 3, 2, and 1, respectively.

(*a*) What are the parameters of his posterior distribution on λ?

(*b*) In order to have a probability of approximately 0.95 that there will never be less than 80 workers on the job, how many extra workers should be assigned to this job?

21
Decision Trees and Sequential Decisions

In previous sections, decision problems have been modeled graphically in order that all factors bearing upon a complex decision situation could be identified and so that the effects of each of these factors or components upon the overall decision situation could be determined and clearly illustrated. These models, both logical and probability, however, related only to the uncontrollable factors which are referred to in a typical decision problem as the state of nature. Aside from oversimplified textbook examples, the state of nature bearing upon a particular decision or upon a sequence of decisions is seldom a single factor or entity but is more usually a composite of several components. The probability model, discussed previously, assigned probability values to individual pertinent system components, and by the rules of mathematical probability allowed probabilities to be assigned to the total system state or to this composite state of nature.

It is from this point that another dimension of the decision problem must be considered, and that is the consequences to the decision maker of making a wrong decision. The combination of probabilities and economic consequences leads to the concept of an expected value or Bayes' criterion for selecting the best act from among the set of acts available to the decision maker. The previous few chapters grouped under the general heading of decision theory addressed themselves to the problem of combining economic consequences and probabilities in such a way as to optimize the expected outcome of a decision process. One further extension of the problem remains to be considered, and that is the problem of sequential decisions. The sequential-decision problem is one in which the decision maker may postpone his decision which involves the selection of an act from among a set of possible acts in order to gain additional information about the state of nature, and he may do so indefinitely.

We shall use the tree diagram to model a sequential-decision problem but we shall begin developing our model with the no-sampling case, follow with the single-sample case, and conclude with the general case.

21.1 THE NO-SAMPLING CASE

Consider the manufacturer's problem first discussed in Chap. 16. This is a two-action problem, the acts being a_1 (inspect each lot 100 percent) or a_2 (ship each lot as is). The payoff, in this case the cost of each act, is dependent upon the unknown fraction defective in each lot, which will be designated θ.

The prior probability distribution on θ and the payoff and regret tables for the problem are given in Table 21.1. Different values from those used in this example appeared in the original example in Chaps. 16 and 17.

A decision tree presentation of this problem is given in Fig. 21.1*a* in terms of cost and in Fig. 21.1*b* in terms of regret.

The first branching point or *node* in each tree is a *decision node*, and by convention is represented by a small square. At the decision node the decision maker makes a choice between alternate acts, in this case between a_1 and a_2. A line or path representing each available act leads from the decision node. The next node or branching point along each of the paths in the tree is a *chance node* and is represented by a small circle. The decision

Table 21.1

		Payoff (cost), dollars		*Regret, dollars*	
θ	$P_0(\theta)$	a_1	a_2	a_1	a_2
0.01	0.2	100.00	2.50	97.50	0
0.40	0.6	100.00	100.00	0	0
0.90	0.2	100.00	225.00	0	125.00
Expected values		100.00	105.50	19.50	25.00

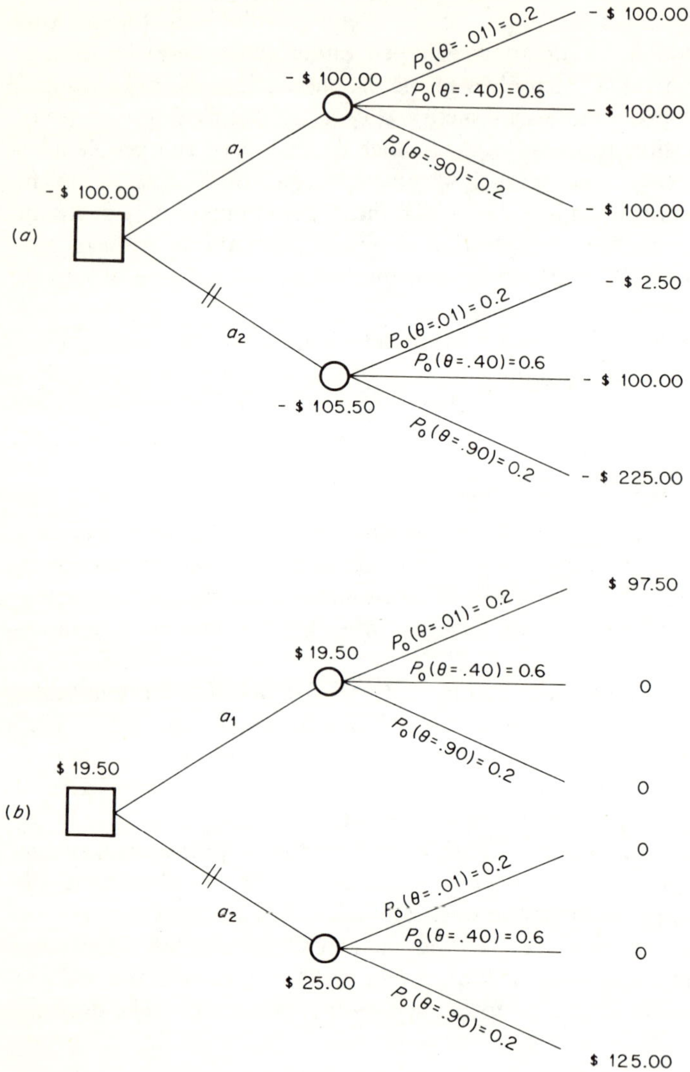

Fig. 21.1

maker having selected an act, either a_1 or a_2, nature now selects one of its possible states. In this example, nature, which is the proportion defective in a lot, has three possible values, $\theta = 0.01$, 0.40, or 0.90. Consequently, three paths issue from each chance node, each path corresponding to one of the possible states of nature. At the end of each chance path the payoff resulting from each possible combination of act and state of nature is designated.

In Fig. 21.1*a*, these figures are costs and are prefixed with a minus sign. In Fig. 21.1*b*, the figures are regrets or opportunity losses, and the minus sign is omitted. Keep in mind that small values of regret are more desirable than larger values.

In analyzing a decision problem under uncertainty, it is the prevailing state of nature, or the state that will prevail, that the decision maker is uncertain about. The information at his disposal regarding the likelihood of the occurrence of any specific state of nature is in terms of probabilities. Consequently, on each path leading from a chance node, we have noted the probability that chance or nature will select that path or state. This probability is a *prior* probability.

By using the ultimate payoffs or regrets which have been listed at the end of each path on the decision tree and the probabilities associated with each path, it is possible by working backward to assign a value at each chance node. That value represents the expected value to the decision maker of proceeding to that particular node but as yet with no knowledge of the path that nature will pick except as a probability. This expected value is computed in exactly the same way that expected payoffs and expected regrets were computed from the tabular arrangement of data such as given in Table 21.1. Each consequence (payoff or regret) is multiplied by its probability of occurrence, and the products are summed. These values, $-\$100$ and $-\$105.50$ in Fig. 21.1*a* and \$19.50 and \$25 in Fig. 21.1*b*, appear at the appropriate chance nodes.

Now let us place the decision maker at the origin of the problem, that is, at the decision node. *Before* nature makes its selection of a state, or what is essentially the same thing to the decision maker, before nature's selection becomes apparent to him, the decision maker sees an expected value of $-\$100$ along path a_1 and an expected value of $-\$105.50$ along path a_2 in Fig. 21.1*a*. Seeking to minimize cost, his logical choice should be act a_1. Having made this decision, path a_2 is blocked off with a double line. The same decision would be made in Fig. 21.1*b* in terms of expected regrets.

For a problem such as this one which involves no sampling, the decision tree approach is somewhat superfluous. The same decision could be made more simply and quickly by referring only to Table 21.1. However, we have used the tree diagram or decision tree with this very simple example with the intention of complicating it as we proceed.

21.2 THE SINGLE-SAMPLE CASE

Let us assume the same facts as in the previous example with one exception. We shall now provide the decision maker with an additional option. He will be allowed to defer his decision whether to inspect or accept the lot until after taking a sample of size $n = 1$ and observing the outcome. Let us assume that the cost of a sample of size 1 is \$4.50. Note again that in both sample size and sample cost this problem differs from the similar example used in Chap. 17.

The decision tree for the single-sample case is given in Fig. 21.2. Beginning at the first decision node, the decision maker may select a_1 or a_2 immediately, or he may select an act which we have designated s_1, which involves a decision to sample one item from the lot. The first chance node on branch s_1 results either in $r = 0$ or $r = 1$, where the letter r represents the number of defectives. Each path from this first chance node leads to another decision node where the decision maker must now make his selection between acts a_1 and a_2. Selecting path s_1 has not absolved the decision maker from choosing between inspecting or accepting; it has merely allowed him to delay this selection until a sample was taken. It should be apparent that once sampling is allowed, we might also provide the decision maker with the option of taking a second sample, a third sample, etc. However, in this example, the decision maker is limited to a single sample.

After he has made his selection between acts a_1 and a_2, nature then selects one of the possible states, and the outcomes or payoffs in terms of cost are listed at the end of each path. The chance nodes on the initial a_1 and a_2 branches lead to the same payoffs that were given in Fig. 21.1*a*.

The likelihood of nature selecting any one of the possible states is noted as a probability value on the appropriate branch. The probabilities leading from the chance nodes after an immediate decision to inspect or accept, that is, if the decision is made without sampling, are labeled $P_0(\theta)$, since these are the prior probabilities assigned to the states of nature. The probabilities on θ after sampling are labeled $P_1(\theta)$, since they are the new probability values assessed after the sample has been taken and the outcome has been observed. The posterior probabilities assigned after the sample outcome $r = 0$ differ from the posterior probabilities assigned after the sample outcome $r = 1$, and of course they both differ from the prior probabilities. The computation of the posterior probabilities for each sample outcome is shown in Table 21.2*a* and *b*.

Starting from the extreme right-hand side of the decision tree shown in Fig. 21.2 and working toward the left, the expected value at each chance node is noted. At the node $\{s_1,0,a_1\}$* that value is $-\$100$. At $\{s_1,0,a_2\}$ the value is $-\$71.85$. Since the decision maker should attempt to minimize cost in this particular case, the a_1 branch is ruled out with a double line, and the value $-\$71.85$ is placed at the decision node. The same procedure results in ruling out the a_2 branch at $\{s_1,1\}$ and placing the value $-\$100$ at that decision node.

Moving again to the left, we arrive at another chance node. Here

* The node is located by the designations of the branches leading to it.

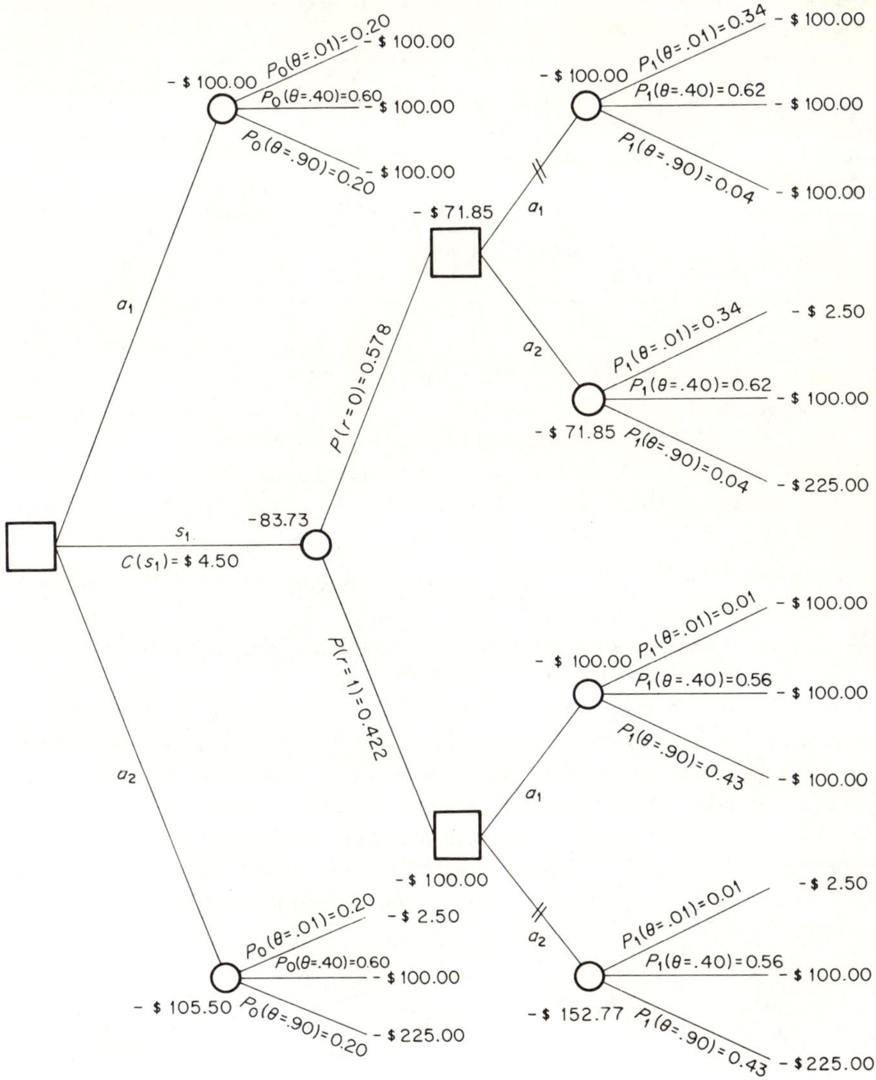

Fig. 21.2

nature selects an outcome of the sample, either $r = 0$ or $r = 1$. Although the decision maker, prior to the sample, does not know what the outcome will be, he can assess the probability of each possible outcome. The marginal probability of the sample outcome is the sum of the joint probabilities as determined from Table 21.2*a* and *b*. There it is shown that $P(r = 0) = 0.578$ and $P(r = 1) = 0.422$. The decision maker assessing the act s_1 prior to

Table 21.2*a* Posterior distribution, expected cost, and regret resulting from first-sample outcome $r_1 = 0$

θ	$P_0(\theta)$	*Likelihood*	*Joint*	$P_1(\theta)$	*Cost, dollars* a_1	*Cost, dollars* a_2	*Regret, dollars* a_1	*Regret, dollars* a_2
0.01	0.2	0.99	0.198	0.34	100.00	2.50	97.50	0
0.40	0.6	0.60	0.360	0.62	100.00	100.00	0	0
0.90	0.2	0.10	0.020	0.04	100.00	225.00	0	125
			0.578	1.00				
	Expected values				100.00	71.85	33.15	5

reaching the first chance node must assign an expected value to that node. In computing this expected value, the probabilities used are the marginal probabilities of each possible sample outcome, and the economic consequences are the values assigned at the next decision nodes. For the chance node at the end of the s_1 branch, the expected value results from the following calculation:

$$(0.578)(-\$71.85) + (0.422)(-\$100) = -\$83.73$$

This value, $-\$83.73$, is placed at the chance node at the end of the s_1 branch.

With the expected costs now available for each action, branch a_1, a_2, and s_1, the total decision tree shown in Fig. 21.2 can be reduced to the one in Fig. 21.3 by simply replacing all chance nodes with their expected values.

Using the criterion of least-expected cost in selecting an act leads to a decision to take a sample of size 1 since the expected cost of the act s_1 is \$83.73 plus the cost of taking the sample, which is \$4.50, leading to a total expected cost of \$88.23. This is less than the expected cost of either of the other acts. The complete solution to this decision problem which can be

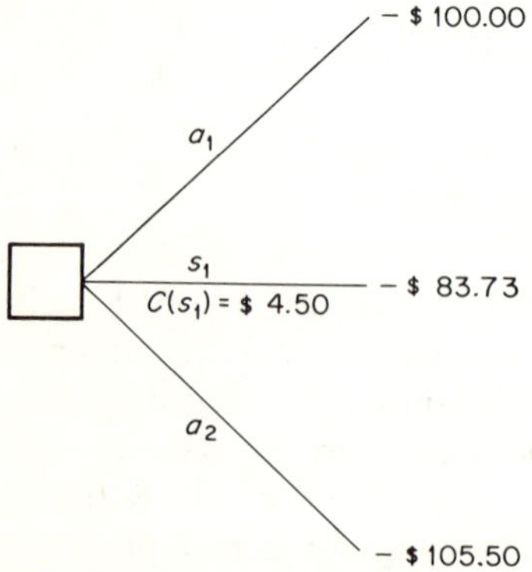

Fig. 21.3

Table 21.2*b* Posterior distribution, expected cost, and regret resulting from first-sample outcome $r_1 = 1$

θ	$P_0(\theta)$	*Likelihood*	*Joint*	$P_1(\theta)$	*Cost, dollars* a_1	*Cost, dollars* a_2	*Regret, dollars* a_1	*Regret, dollars* a_2
0.01	0.2	0.01	0.002	0.01	100.00	2.50	97.50	0
0.40	0.6	0.40	0.240	0.56	100.00	100.00	0	0
0.90	0.2	0.90	0.180	0.43	100.00	225.00	0	125
			0.422	1.00				
		Expected values			100.00	152.77	0.98	53.75

determined from Fig. 21.2 is to sample and then select act a_1 if $r = 1$ and select act a_2 if $r = 0$.

21.3 THE SEQUENTIAL CASE

In many situations, the manufacturer in the previous example would not necessarily be limited to a single sample of size 1. He would, no doubt, have the option of selecting between various sample sizes and the option of taking more than one sample. The problem of selecting an optimum sample size has been discussed previously.

Consider now, however, that the decision maker has the additional option of continuing to sample. In other words, he is no longer limited to a single sample but may, after a sample is taken, select either act a_1, "inspect the entire lot"; act a_2, "accept the lot as is"; or act s_1, "take another sample of size $n = 1$." Whenever the decision maker selects either a_1 or a_2, this particular decision sequence is terminated. But by continuing to select s_1, the procedure could be prolonged indefinitely. There should, however, be some rule for determining the maximum number of times that a decision to sample would constitute a rational act under the given circumstances. We can always determine the expected payoff or regret for either of the two terminating acts a_1 or a_2 at any stage of the process. However, the expected payoff or regret resulting from the act of continuing to sample is not known unless some stopping rule can first be established.

One such rule that can be established is that whenever a terminating act such as a_1 or a_2 has an expected cost or regret that is less than the cost of taking an additional sample, then that terminating act is preferable to sampling. Consequently, the s_1 branch issuing from that decision node should be barred in accordance with the procedure established previously.

To continue, then, with the previous example, we illustrate a decision tree in Fig. 21.4 which provides the decision maker with the option of continuing to sample. The tree begins with a single decision node at the extreme left-hand side of the diagram with the branches a_1, a_2, and s_1 issuing from it.

The expected regrets of an immediate decision to select either a_1 or a_2 are \$19.50 and \$25, respectively, as computed from Table 21.1. These values can be found on Fig. 21.4 at the ends of the a_1 and a_2 branches. At this point, if an immediate terminal decision were to be made between acts a_1 and a_2, a_1 would be the better act under the criterion already established and a_2 would be barred. The only thing known about the act s_1 at this point is that there is a cost of \$4.50 associated with the act of taking a sample.

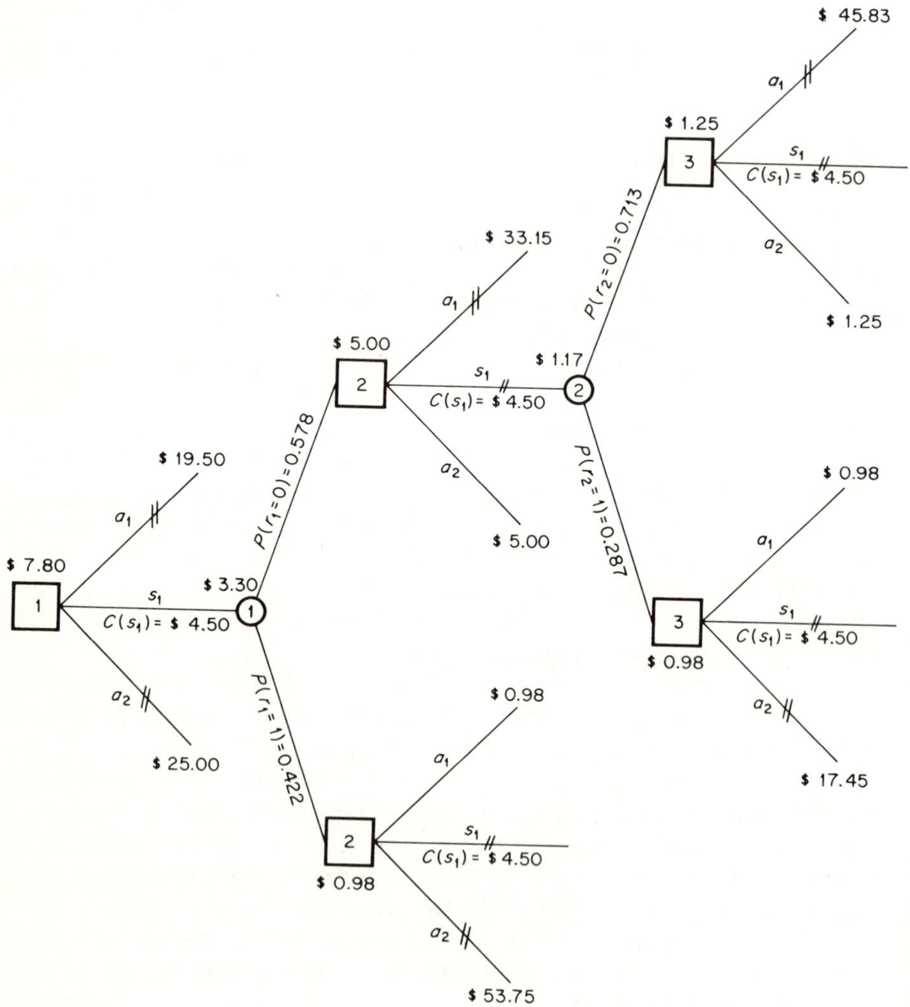

Fig. 21.4

At the end of the initial branch s_1 is a chance node indicating that at this point nature is in control of the sampling process, and the two paths leading from this chance node are labeled $r_1 = 0$ and $r_1 = 1$ corresponding to the outcomes of zero defectives and one defective on the first sample taken. Each of these paths leads to the second level of decision nodes where the decision maker must once again choose between the acts a_1, a_2, and s_1. The decision, at this point, must be based as before upon the expected value of each of these acts, given the outcome of the first sample.

Let us consider the $r_1 = 0$ branch first. If a sample of size 1 is taken resulting in no defectives, then the *posterior distribution* of θ and the expected regrets of acts a_1 and a_2 can be determined as in Table 21.2*a*. After consideration of the $r_1 = 1$ branch, the posterior distribution of θ given $r_1 = 1$ and the expected regrets of the acts a_1 and a_2 are calculated in Table 21.2*b*.

Looking at decision node $\boxed{2}$ following $r_1 = 0$, we readily see that a_2 with an expected regret of \$5 is preferable to a_1 with an expected regret of \$33.15. Consequently, the a_1 branch is barred. It is not known, at this point, whether a_2 is also preferable to s_1 since the cost of taking another sample of size 1 is only \$4.50, which is less than the expected regret of a_2.

Looking now at decision node $\boxed{2}$ following the outcome $r_1 = 1$, a_1 is obviously preferable to a_2 since 98 cents is less than \$53.75. However, since no amount of sampling can reduce expected regret below zero, a decision to sample at this point would at the very best cost the decision maker \$4.50 in sampling cost, while a_1 has an expected regret of only 98 cents. This branch of the decision tree should therefore be terminated at this point with the selection of act a_1 and the barring of both acts a_2 and s_1.

Going back to decision node $\boxed{2}$ following $r_1 = 0$, we take another sample, and the expected regrets for a_1 and a_2 must again be determined given all the possible outcomes of the second sample. These new expectations will be based on a new posterior distribution, which we label $P_2(\theta)$ since it is posterior to the second sample. $P_1(\theta)$ given $r_1 = 0$ is the prior distribution to $P_2(\theta)$. $P_2(\theta)$ and the expected regrets of the available acts are computed in Table 21.3*a* and *b* for $r_2 = 0$ and $r_2 = 1$, respectively.

Given that the first sample results in no defectives and that the second sample is taken, we progress to a third decision node. At decision node $\boxed{3}$ following $r_2 = 1$, the expected regret of $a_1 = 98$ cents is less than both the expected regret of a_2 and the known immediate cost of s_1, and therefore both a_2 and s_1 are barred. At node $\boxed{3}$ following $r_2 = 0$, the expected regret of $a_2 = \$1.25$ is less than the expected regret or known immediate cost of a_1 and s_1, and therefore the latter two acts are barred. The sequential procedure has terminated at this point since for each possible sample outcome one of the available acts is preferable to any further sampling.

We have not, at this point, yet achieved a solution to the decision

Table 21.3*a* Posterior distribution and expected regret resulting from second-sample outcome $r_2 = 0$ given $r_1 = 0$

θ	$P_1(\theta)$	*Likelihood*	*Joint*	$P_2(\theta)$	*Regret, dollars* a_1	a_2
0.01	0.34	0.99	0.337	0.47	97.50	0
0.40	0.62	0.60	0.372	0.52	0	0
0.90	0.04	0.10	0.004	0.01	0	125
			0.713	1.00		
		Expected values			45.83	1.25

problem. We have only carried the sequence of possible actions to a point where further sampling would cost more than the value of the information which it could possibly provide. We still do not know whether a_2 or s_1 is the better act at decision node [2] following $r_1 = 0$ or whether a_1 or s_1 is the better act at decision node [1]. In order to answer these questions and to arrive at a solution to the decision problem, we shall use the method of *backward induction,* which we previously used in the single-sample case without identifying the procedure by that name.

Consider node [3] after $r_2 = 0$. Acts a_1 and s_1 are barred, and therefore the value placed at [3] is \$1.25, which is the expected value of the best act at that point. This amount is marked on the decision tree adjacent to the node. Similarly, 98 cents is marked adjacent to node [3] following $r_2 = 1$.

Now if the decision maker is at node [2] following $r_1 = 0$ and is looking down the three paths a_1, a_2, and a_3, what does he see? The a_1 branch results in an expected regret of \$33.15, the a_2 branch in an expected regret of \$5, and looking down the s_1 branch, he sees a certain cost of \$4.50 plus an expected regret of \$1.25 if $r_2 = 0$ or 98 cents if $r_2 = 1$. The value at chance node (2) should be the expectation at that point considering both possible sample outcomes and the probability of each occurring, that is, the expected

Table 21.3*b* Posterior distribution and expected regret resulting from second-sample outcome $r_2 = 1$ given $r_1 = 0$

θ	$P_1(\theta)$	*Likelihood*	*Joint*	$P_2(\theta)$	*Regret, dollars* a_1	a_2
0.01	0.34	0.01	0.003	0.01	97.50	0
0.40	0.62	0.40	0.248	0.86	0	0
0.90	0.04	0.90	0.036	0.13	0	125
			0.287	1.00		
		Expected values			0.98	17.25

regret which results from choosing the better act given the sample outcome. The expected value is determined from the following:

$$(\$1.25)P(r_2 = 0) + (\$0.98)P(r_2 = 1)$$

The probability that $r_2 = 0$ is simply $1 - \sum \theta P_1(\theta)$, while the probability that $r_2 = 1$ is $\sum \theta P_1(\theta)$. More simply, these are the marginal probabilities of each sample outcome and can be obtained from Tables 21.3*a* and *b*. $P(r_2 = 0|r_1 = 0) = 0.713$ and $P(r_2 = 1|r_2 = 0) = 0.287$.

The expected value at ② is then

$$(\$1.25)(0.713) + (\$0.98)(0.287) = \$1.17$$

This amount is placed on the decision tree adjacent to ②.

The decision maker at decision node [2] following $r_1 = 0$ sees an expected regret of \$33.15 at the end of the a_1 branch, an expected regret of \$5 at the end of the a_2 branch, and an expected regret of \$1.17 plus \$4.50 in sampling cost for a total of \$5.67 when he looks down the s_1 branch. Consequently, at this decision node, a_2 is the best act, and both a_1 and s_1 are barred. The expected regret of a_2 which is \$5 is noted on the decision tree adjacent to decision node [2] following $r_1 = 0$.

At decision node [2] following $r_1 = 1$, s_1 and a_2 had previously been barred, and the value adjacent to that node is 98 cents.

We now proceed to find a value for chance node ①. Since a \$5 regret will occur if $r_1 = 0$ and an expected regret of 98 cents if $r_1 = 1$, the expected value at this chance node is:

$$(\$5)P(r_1 = 0) + (\$0.98)P(r_1 = 1)$$

Since no sampling has as yet taken place, these probabilities are based on the prior distribution on θ, that is, on $P_0(\theta)$. The marginal probabilities of each sample outcome from Tables 21.2*a* and *b* are:

$$P(r_1 = 0) = 0.578$$

and

$$P(r_1 = 1) = 0.422$$

The expected value at ① is

$$(\$5)(0.578) + (\$0.98)(0.422) = \$2.89 + 0.41 = \$3.30$$

At decision node [1], the decision maker sees an expected regret of \$19.50 at the end of path a_1, \$25 at the end of path a_2, and \$3.30 plus a sampling cost of \$4.50 for a total of \$7.80 looking down s_1. The act s_1 is obviously the best decision at this point, and a_1 can be barred. The expected regret at [1] is therefore \$7.80.

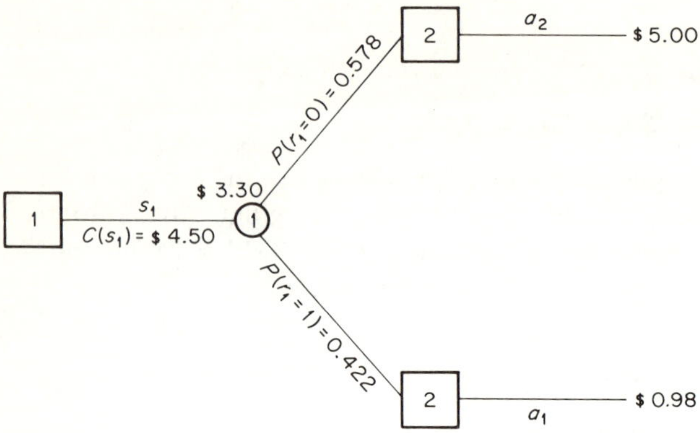

Fig. 21.5

The solution to the decision problem resulting in an expected regret of \$7.80 is as follows: Take a single sample of size $n = 1$; if $r_1 = 0$, select a (accept the lot as is); if $r_1 = 1$, select a_1 (inspect the lot 100 percent).

A reduced decision tree which eliminates all paths or branches that have been barred is shown in Fig. 21.5.

21.4 SUMMARY

A decision tree is a device for displaying the choices available to the decision maker together with the consequences in terms of expectations resulting from the decision maker's choice. Decision trees are most useful in situations where the decision maker has the option of continuing the sampling or information-gathering process. It has been shown that even where a specific number of sampling actions are not specified in advance, the process eventually terminates so long as there is a cost associated with sampling and so long as a rule is established that a terminating act is preferable to sampling whenever the expected cost or regret of that act is less than the cost of taking another sample.

PROBLEMS

21.1. For the single-sample problem illustrated in Fig. 21.2, what would the optimum decision be if the cost of a single sample were \$18.50? Why?

21.2. Consider a decision situation for which the regret table and the prior probabilities are as follows:

$P_0(S)$	*States*	*Regret* a_1	a_2
0.30	S_1	0	15
0.70	S_2	20	0

A single sample of size $n = 1$ can be taken. The sampling distribution of X, the statistic resulting from the sample $f(x,S)$, is given by

$$P(X = S_1|S_1) = 1 - e^{-n} \qquad P(X = S_1|S_2) = e^{-n}$$
$$P(X = S_2|S_1) = e^{-n} \qquad P(X = S_2|S_2) = 1 - e^{-n}$$

Assume that the cost of a single sample of size 1 is \$1. Perform the decision analysis and answer the following:

(*a*) What is $P_1(S)$?
(*b*) What are the expected costs (regrets) of the acts available?
(*c*) Should the sample be taken?
(*d*) If the sample should be taken, specify the decision rule.

21.3. If the regret table in the previous problem were as follows:

	Regret	
States	a_1	a_2
S_1	0	20
S_2	10	0

but all other data were identical, answer the same questions.

21.4. Using the regret table of Prob. 21.3 and the prior probabilities and the sampling distribution of X as given in Prob. 21.2, answer the following questions under the assumptions that sequential samples of size 1 are permitted and the cost of a sample of size 1 is \$6.

(*a*) How many samples will be taken?
(*b*) What is the decision rule?
(*c*) What is the total expected cost of the decision rule?

21.5. Do Prob. 21.4 under the assumption that the cost of a sample of size 1 is \$5.

22
Case Study: Decision Analysis

Two previous cases considered the Pennwood Corporation problem regarding the manufacture and marketing of a new heat pump. The first case study involved only a logical model of the uncontrollable factors which would affect the consequences of a decision either to market or not to market the heat pump. A logical analysis which involved an assessment of all major factors bearing upon the problem led to an assessment of the overall decision situation which in this case happened to be *good*. At this point, and if no further analysis were to be done, the logical decision would be to market the new product.

In the second case, also relating to Pennwood, it was decided to estimate probabilities for each decision component being good and then using the rules of probability to assign a probability to the condition that the decision system is in a good state. The result of this probability analysis led to an estimate that the probability that the system was good, equivalent to the probability that a decision to go ahead and market the product would be successful, was approximately 0.75. At this point, management must decide whether a probability of 0.75 is sufficiently high to warrant going ahead with the project.

Although management might make a decision based solely on this probability estimate that the venture will be profitable, it would be a great deal more reasonable if the costs of making a wrong decision were also considered before a decision was made. Let us consider what these costs might be and fit them into the decision framework.

22.1 ANALYSIS

Management will measure success or failure of the heat pump venture on the basis of contribution to profit. However, since several component states of nature relate to profit contribution with different weights, it is necessary to determine what the profit will be for the various possible combinations of component states. However, for a problem of any complexity, and we assume that most practical problems are *at least* as complex as this one, computing success measures, in this instance profit contribution for every possible combination of component states, would be a lengthy process. For that reason, we shall compute expected consequences for the *good* state and for the *bad* state and use these in arriving at the decision. There are two alternative acts: a_1 (market the heat pump) and a_2 (do not market the heat pump). We also consider two overall system states: S, which represents the *good* state, and S', which corresponds to the system being *bad*.

CONSEQUENCES OF a_1 IF S

Consider the probability model of the system in Fig. 9.2, which is reproduced below as Fig. 22.1. In this configuration, components A, B, and C are grouped together into a major subsystem designated E.

D and E together then constitute the system S. The logical equation for E is:

$$E = A \cdot B \cdot C' + C \tag{22.1}$$

This was reduced from the canonical form of the expression which was:

$$E = A \cdot B \cdot C + A \cdot B \cdot C' + A \cdot B' \cdot C + A' \cdot B \cdot C + A' \cdot B' \cdot C^* \tag{22.2}$$

Table 22.1 provides the contribution to profit which would result from each combination of the components and the probabilities of each combination occurring. The former comes from Chap. 4, and the latter from Chap. 9.

This expected contribution of subsystem E if a_1 is selected and E is good is \$362,250. The probability that E is good is the sum of the probabilities of the various combinations of component states that make E good, which is

* See Chap. 4.

Table 22.1

Component states	*Probability*	*Contribution to profit, dollars*	*Conditional contribution, dollars*
$A \cdot B \cdot C$	0.1350	600,000	81,000
$A \cdot B \cdot C'$	0.0450	450,000	20,250
$A \cdot B' \cdot C$	0.0150	600,000	9,000
$A' \cdot B \cdot C$	0.5400	420,000	226,800
$A' \cdot B' \cdot C$	0.0600	420,000	25,200
	0.7950		
		Expected value	362,250

0.795. However, in order for the system to be good, both D and E must be good, and the probability that D is good is $P(D) = 0.9$. We must also consider the contribution of D to profit.

D, representing the reliability of the heat pump, makes no direct contribution to profit. If D is bad, future profits can be affected detrimentally, and, therefore, there is a future cost associated with D'. But D makes no contribution, either positive or negative, to the first-year profit in this case. However, the probability that D is good must be considered, since for the system state to be good, D *must* be good.

$$\begin{aligned} P(S) &= P(D)P(E) \\ &= P(D)P(A \cdot B \cdot C' + C) \end{aligned}$$

All the probabilities in Table 22.1 should, therefore, be multiplied by $P(D) = 0.9$. This would have resulted in a reduction of the expected contribution to profit. Since D is, however, being considered separately, the expected contribution to profit for a_1 given S is:

$$P(D) \times \$362{,}250 = (0.9)(\$362{,}250) = \$326{,}025$$

and

$$P(S) = P(D)P(E) = (0.9)(0.795) = 0.7155$$

Since the expected contribution to profit if the project is undertaken and the system state is good turns out to be \$326,025, which is less than the \$400,000 criterion established previously, this would seem to indicate that the project should be abandoned.

The payoff of act a_1 if the system is good is simply the difference between the out-of-pocket costs of \$400,000 and the contribution to profit of \$326,025 or a loss of \$73,975. However, before making the decision to drop the project, we should at least determine the consequences of the other possible acts and states.

CONSEQUENCES OF a_1 IF S'

Let us again consider major subsystem E by itself for the time being. Since $E = A \cdot B \cdot C + A \cdot B \cdot C' + A \cdot B' \cdot C + A' \cdot B' \cdot C$, then E' must be equal to

$$E' = A \cdot B' \cdot C' + A' \cdot B \cdot C' + A' \cdot B' \cdot C' \qquad (22.3)$$

Table 22.2 provides the contributions to profit which would result from each combination of component states leading to E', and their probabilities are taken from Chaps. 4 and 9, respectively.

However, the system is bad if either D or E is bad. If D is bad, the reliability of the system is poor. This will affect Pennwood in two ways. There will be high warranty costs for repairing systems which break down, and there will be a loss of goodwill which could affect future sales. It is difficult to assess the cost of poor reliability at this point, but Pennwood assigns a cost of \$50,000 to this eventuality. How will this affect contribution to profit if

$$S' = E' \cdot D + E \cdot D' + E' \cdot D'$$

that is, S is bad if either D or E or both are bad?

If E is bad and D is good, contribution to profit will be \$62,400 as shown in Table 22.2. The probability of this occurrence is $P(D)P(E') = (0.9)(0.205) = 0.1845$.

If E is good and D is bad, contributions to profit will be \$362,500 as shown in Table 22.1, less the \$50,000 cost of poor reliability of \$312,500. The probability of this occurrence is $P(D')P(E) = (0.1)(0.795) = 0.0795$.

If D and E are both bad, the contribution to profit is \$62,400 − \$50,000 = \$12,400, and this probability is $P(D')P(E') = (0.1)(0.205) = 0.0205$.

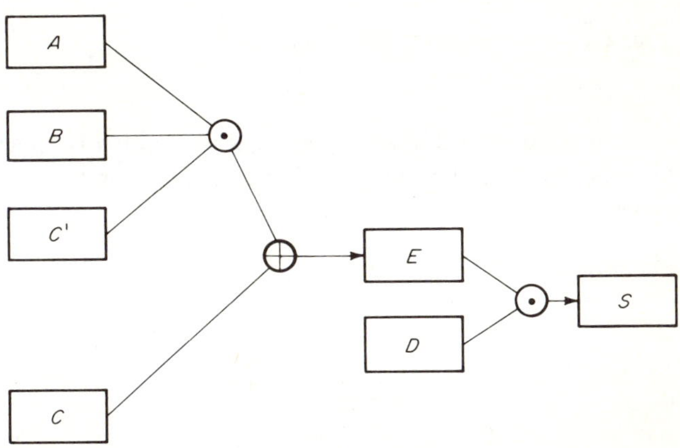

Fig. 22.1

Table 22.2

Component states	*Probability*	*Contribution to profit, dollars*	*Conditional contribution, dollars*
$A \cdot B' \cdot C'$	0.005	300,000	1,500
$A' \cdot B \cdot C'$	0.180	315,000	56,700
$A' \cdot B' \cdot C'$	0.020	210,000	4,200
	0.205		
		Expected value	62,400

Therefore, the expected contribution to profit if S is bad is:

$$\begin{aligned} (0.1845)(\$62{,}400) &= \$11{,}512.80 \\ (0.0795)(\$312{,}500) &= 24{,}843.65 \\ (0.0205)(\$12{,}400) &= 254.20 \\ &\overline{\$36{,}610.65} \end{aligned}$$

and the *cost* of act a_1 if S', that is, if S is bad, equals \$400,000 − \$36,610.65 = \$363,389.35.

CONSEQUENCES OF a_2 IF S OR S'

If the act a_2, "do not proceed with project," is selected, then contribution to profit is zero regardless of the state of the system.

COST FUNCTION OF ACTS

The cost function of a_1 is

$$C(a_1) = -\$400{,}000 + R$$

where R = profit contribution.

$$C(a_2) = 0$$

It is obvious that act a_2 is preferable with an expected loss of zero versus an expected loss of \$156,313 for a_1; the result in terms of regret would be the same.

Payoff table

S	$P(S)$	*Cost table* a_1	a_2
Good	0.7155	−\$ 73,975	0
Bad	0.2845	− 363,389	0
	Expected cost	−\$156,313	0

22.2 SUMMARY

The complete analysis of the Pennwood Corporation case involved the use of a logical model, a probability model, and finally a bayesian decision model which utilized both probabilities and economic consequences in arriving at a decision.

This study shows that although a_1 appeared to be the better act when only logical possibilities were considered and when probabilities were used, a_2 turned out to be better when economic consequences were included in the model. The fact that a_2 was the better act became apparent very early in the analysis when the evaluation of the act a_1 given a good system state indicated that under the *best circumstances*, the contribution to profit would be less than the company's investment.

If a decision in this case could have been deferred, for example, until the results of the labor negotiations were known and/or until information on the plans of the competition became available, then a sequential decision process could have been used in arriving at a decision.

SUGGESTED REFERENCES

Logic and sets

Birkhoff, G., and S. MacLane: "A Survey of Modern Algebra," Macmillan, New York, 1953.

Boole, G.: "An Investigation of the Laws of Thought," Dover, New York.

Brewer, J.: "Introduction to the Theory of Sets," Prentice-Hall, Englewood Cliffs, N.J., 1958.

Cangelosi, V. E.: "Compound Statements and Mathematical Logic," Merrill, Columbus, Ohio, 1967.

Rosenbloom, P. C.: "The Elements of Mathematical Logic," Dover, New York, 1950.

Suppes, P.: "Introduction to Mathematical Logic," Van Nostrand, Princeton, N.J., 1957.

Probability

Feller, W.: "An Introduction to Probability Theory and Its Application," Wiley, New York, 1950.

Harris, B.: "Theory of Probability," Addison-Wesley, Reading, Mass., 1966.

Mosteller, F., R. Rourke, and G. Thomas: "Probability with Statistical Applications," Addison-Wesley, Reading, Mass., 1965.

Parzen, E.: "Modern Probability Theory and Its Applications," Wiley, New York, 1960.

Thompson, W.: "Applied Probability," Holt, Rinehart, and Winston, New York, 1969.

Applied statistics

Dixon, W., and F. Massey: "Introduction to Statistical Analysis," 3d ed., McGraw-Hill, New York, 1969.

Freund, J., and F. Williams: "Elementary Business Statistics: The Modern Approach," Prentice-Hall, Englewood Cliffs, N.J., 1964.

Osthe, B.: "Statistics in Research," 2d ed., Iowa State University Press, Ames, Iowa, 1963.

Mathematical statistics

Freeman, H.: "Introduction to Statistical Inference," Addison-Wesley, Reading, Mass., 1963.

Freund, J.: "Mathematical Statistics," Prentice-Hall, Englewood Cliffs, N.J., 1962.

Hoel, P.: "Introduction to Mathematical Statistics," 2d Ed., Wiley, New York, 1954.

Mood, A., and F. Greybill: "Introduction to the Theory of Statistics," 2d ed., McGraw-Hill, New York, 1950.

Statistical decision theory

DeGroat, M.: "Optimal Statistical Decisions," McGraw-Hill, New York, 1970.

Sasaki, K.: "Statistics for Modern Business Decision Making," Wadsworth, Belmont, Calif., 1968.

Schlaiffer, R., and H. Raiffa: "Applied Statistical Decision Theory," Harvard, Cambridge, Mass., 1961.

Schlaiffer, R.: "Introduction to Statistics for Business Decisions," McGraw-Hill, New York, 1961.

Schlaiffer, R.: "Probability and Statistics for Business Decisions," McGraw-Hill, New York, 1959.

Schmitt, S.: "Measuring Uncertainty. An Elementary Introduction to Bayesian Statistics," Addison-Wesley, Reading, Mass., 1969.

Appendix Tables

Table A.1 Cumulative binomial probabilities

Table A.1 gives the cumulative binomial probabilities $P(\mathbf{x} \leq k)$ for selected values of n and π. The probability of obtaining at least 7 successes in 15 trials when $\pi = .40$ equals .78690. The probability of exactly 7 successes is $P(\mathbf{x} \leq 7) - P(\mathbf{x} \leq 6) = .78690 - .60981 = .17709$.

n	k	$\pi = .10$	$\pi = .20$	$\pi = .25$	$\pi = .30$	$\pi = .40$	$\pi = .50$
5	0	.59049	.32768	.23730	.16807	.07776	.03125
	1	.91854	.73728	.63281	.52822	.33696	.18750
	2	.99144	.94208	.89648	.83692	.68256	.50000
	3	.99954	.99328	.98437	.96922	.91296	.81250
	4	.99999	.99968	.99902	.99757	.98976	.96875
	5	1.00000	1.00000	1.00000	1.00000	1.00000	1.00000
10	0	.34868	.10737	.05631	.02825	.00605	.00098
	1	.73610	.37581	.24403	.14931	.04636	.01074
	2	.92981	.67780	.52559	.38278	.16729	.05469
	3	.98720	.87913	.77588	.64961	.38228	.17187
	4	.99837	.96721	.92187	.84973	.63310	.37695
	5	.99985	.99363	.98027	.95265	.83376	.62305
	6	.99999	.99914	.99649	.98941	.94524	.82812
	7	1.00000	.99992	.99958	.99841	.98771	.94531
	8		1.00000	.99997	.99986	.99832	.98926
	9			1.00000	.99999	.99990	.99902
	10				1.00000	1.00000	1.00000
15	0	.20589	.03518	.01336	.00475	.00047	.00003
	1	.54904	.16713	.08018	.03527	.00517	.00049
	2	.81594	.39802	.23609	.12683	.02711	.00369
	3	.94444	.64816	.46129	.29687	.09050	.01758
	4	.98728	.83577	.68649	.51549	.21728	.05923
	5	.99775	.93895	.85163	.72162	.40322	.15088
	6	.99969	.98194	.94338	.86886	.60981	.30362
	7	.99997	.99576	.98270	.94999	.78690	.50000
	8	1.00000	.99921	.99581	.98476	.90495	.69638
	9		.99989	.99921	.99635	.96617	.84912
	10		.99999	.99988	.99933	.99065	.94077
	11		1.00000	.99999	.99991	.99807	.98242
	12			1.00000	.99999	.99972	.99631
	13				1.00000	.99997	.99951
	14					1.00000	.99997
	15						1.00000

* Used by permission from W. C. Guenther, "Concepts of Statistical Inference," McGraw-Hill Book Company, New York, 1965.

Table A.1 (continued)

n	k	$\pi = .10$	$\pi = .20$	$\pi = .25$	$\pi = .30$	$\pi = .40$	$\pi = .50$
20	0	.12158	.01153	.00317	.00080	.00004	.00000
	1	.39175	.06918	.02431	.00764	.00052	.00002
	2	.67693	.20608	.09126	.03548	.00361	.00020
	3	.86705	.41145	.22516	.10709	.01596	.00129
	4	.95683	.62965	.41484	.23751	.05095	.00591
	5	.98875	.80421	.61717	.41637	.12560	.02069
	6	.99761	.91331	.78578	.60801	.25001	.05766
	7	.99958	.96786	.89819	.77227	.41589	.13159
	8	.99994	.99002	.95907	.88667	.59560	.25172
	9	.99999	.99741	.98614	.95204	.75534	.41190
	10	1.00000	.99944	.99606	.98286	.87248	.58810
	11		.99990	.99906	.99486	.94347	.74828
	12		.99998	.99982	.99872	.97897	.86841
	13		1.00000	.99997	.99974	.99353	.94234
	14			1.00000	.99996	.99839	.97931
	15				.99999	.99968	.99409
	16				1.00000	.99995	.99871
	17					.99999	.99980
	18					1.00000	.99998
	19						1.00000
25	0	.07179	.00378	.00075	.00013	.00000	.00000
	1	.27121	.02739	.00702	.00157	.00005	.00000
	2	.53709	.09823	.03211	.00896	.00043	.00001
	3	.76359	.23399	.09621	.03324	.00237	.00008
	4	.90201	.42067	.21374	.09047	.00947	.00046
	5	.96660	.61669	.37828	.19349	.02936	.00204
	6	.99052	.78004	.56110	.34065	.07357	.00732
	7	.99774	.89088	.72651	.51185	.15355	.02164
	8	.99954	.95323	.85056	.67693	.27353	.05388
	9	.99992	.98267	.92867	.81056	.42462	.11476
	10	.99999	.99445	.97033	.90220	.58577	.21218
	11	1.00000	.99846	.98027	.95575	.73228	.34502
	12		.99963	.99663	.98253	.84623	.50000
	13		.99992	.99908	.99401	.92220	.65498
	14		.99999	.99979	.99822	.96561	.78782
	15		1.00000	.99996	.99955	.98683	.88524
	16			.99999	.99990	.99567	.94612
	17			1.00000	.99998	.99879	.97836
	18				1.00000	.99972	.99268
	19					.99995	.99796
	20					.99999	.99954
	21					1.00000	.99992
	22						.99999
	23						1.00000

Table A.1 (continued)

n	k	$\pi = .10$	$\pi = .20$	$\pi = .25$	$\pi = .30$	$\pi = .40$	$\pi = .50$
50	0	.00515	.00001	.00000	.00000		
	1	.03379	.00019	.00001	.00000		
	2	.11173	.00129	.00009	.00000		
	3	.25029	.00566	.00050	.00003		
	4	.43120	.01850	.00211	.00017		
	5	.61612	.04803	.00705	.00072	.00000	
	6	.77023	.10340	.01939	.00249	.00001	
	7	.87785	.19041	.04526	.00726	.00006	
	8	.94213	.30733	.09160	.01825	.00023	
	9	.97546	.44374	.16368	.04023	.00076	.00000
	10	.99065	.58356	.26220	.07885	.00220	.00001
	11	.99678	.71067	.38162	.13904	.00569	.00005
	12	.99900	.81394	.51099	.22287	.01325	.00015
	13	.99971	.88941	.63704	.32788	.02799	.00047
	14	.99993	.93928	.74808	.44683	.05396	.00130
	15	.99998	.96920	.83692	.56918	.09550	.00330
	16	1.00000	.98556	.90169	.68388	.15609	.00767
	17		.99374	.94488	.78219	.23688	.01642
	18		.99749	.97127	.85944	.33561	.03245
	19		.99907	.98608	.91520	.44648	.05946
	20		.99968	.99374	.95224	.56103	.10132
	21		.99990	.99738	.97491	.67014	.16112
	22		.99997	.99898	.98772	.76602	.23994
	23		.99999	.99963	.99441	.84383	.33591
	24		1.00000	.99988	.99763	.90219	.44386
	25			.99996	.99907	.94266	.55614
	26			.99999	.99966	.96859	.66409
	27			1.00000	.99988	.98397	.76006
	28				.99996	.99238	.83888
	29				.99999	.99664	.89868
	30				1.00000	.99863	.94054
	31					.99948	.96755
	32					.99982	.98358
	33					.99994	.99233
	34					.99998	.99670
	35					1.00000	.99870
	36						.99953
	37						.99985
	38						.99995
	39						.99999
	40						1.00000

Table A.2 Areas under the normal curve

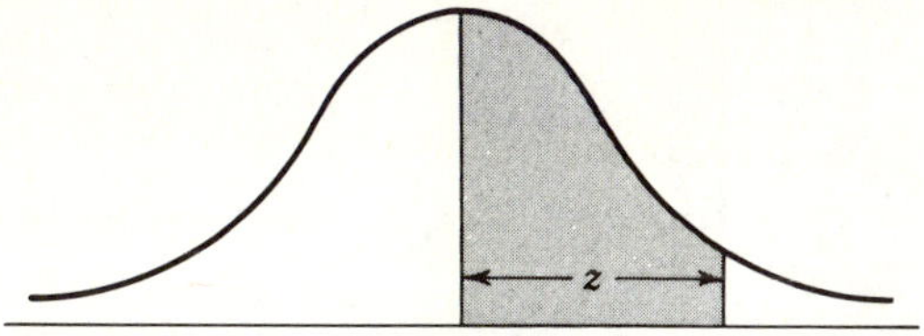

Mean

Example: For $z = 1.64$, the shaded area is .4495 out of a total area under the curve of 1.

z	.00	.01	.02	.03	.04	.05	.06	.07	.08	.09
0.0	.0000	.0040	.0080	.0120	.0160	.0199	.0239	.0279	.0319	.0359
0.1	.0398	.0438	.0478	.0517	.0557	.0596	.0636	.0675	.0714	.0753
0.2	.0793	.0832	.0871	.0910	.0948	.0987	.1026	.1064	.1103	.1141
0.3	.1179	.1217	.1255	.1293	.1331	.1368	.1406	.1443	.1480	.1517
0.4	.1554	.1591	.1628	.1664	.1700	.1736	.1772	.1808	.1844	.1879
0.5	.1915	.1950	.1985	.2019	.2054	.2088	.2123	.2157	.2190	.2224
0.6	.2257	.2291	.2324	.2357	.2389	.2422	.2454	.2486	.2518	.2549
0.7	.2580	.2612	.2642	.2673	.2704	.2734	.2764	.2794	.2823	.2852
0.8	.2881	.2910	.2939	.2967	.2995	.3023	.3051	.3078	.3106	.3133
0.9	.3159	.3186	.3212	.3238	.3264	.3289	.3315	.3340	.3365	.3389
1.0	.3413	.3438	.3461	.3485	.3508	.3531	.3554	.3577	.3599	.3621
1.1	.3643	.3665	.3686	.3708	.3729	.3749	.3770	.3790	.3810	.3830
1.2	.3849	.3869	.3888	.3907	.3925	.3944	.3962	.3980	.3997	.4015
1.3	.4032	.4049	.4066	.4082	.4099	.4115	.4131	.4147	.4162	.4177
1.4	.4192	.4207	.4222	.4236	.4251	.4265	.4279	.4292	.4306	.4319
1.5	.4332	.4345	.4357	.4370	.4382	.4394	.4406	.4418	.4429	.4441
1.6	.4452	.4463	.4474	.4484	.4495	.4505	.4515	.4525	.4535	.4545
1.7	.4554	.4564	.4573	.4582	.4591	.4599	.4608	.4616	.4625	.4633
1.8	.4641	.4649	.4656	.4664	.4671	.4678	.4686	.4693	.4699	.4706
1.9	.4713	.4719	.4726	.4732	.4738	.4744	.4750	.4756	.4761	.4767
2.0	.4772	.4778	.4783	.4788	.4793	.4798	.4803	.4808	.4812	.4817
2.1	.4821	.4826	.4830	.4834	.4838	.4842	.4846	.4850	.4854	.4857
2.2	.4861	.4864	.4868	.4871	.4875	.4878	.4881	.4884	.4887	.4890
2.3	.4893	.4896	.4898	.4901	.4904	.4906	.4909	.4911	.4913	.4916
2.4	.4918	.4920	.4922	.4925	.4927	.4929	.4931	.4932	.4934	.4936
2.5	.4938	.4940	.4941	.4943	.4945	.4946	.4948	.4949	.4951	.4952
2.6	.4953	.4955	.4956	.4957	.4959	.4960	.4961	.4962	.4963	.4964
2.7	.4965	.4966	.4967	.4968	.4969	.4970	.4971	.4972	.4973	.4974
2.8	.4974	.4975	.4976	.4977	.4977	.4978	.4979	.4979	.4980	.4981
2.9	.4981	.4982	.4982	.4983	.4984	.4984	.4985	.4985	.4986	.4986
3.0	.49865	.4987	.4987	.4988	.4988	.4989	.4989	.4989	.4990	.4990
4.0	.4999683									

SOURCE: From Jedamus and Frame, "Business Decision Theory," McGraw-Hill Book Company, with permission of the publisher.

Table A.3 Unit normal loss function*

The values in the body of the table $N(D)$ are expected opportunity losses for linear loss functions and a normal distribution with a mean of 0 and a standard deviation of 1. The value D represents the standardized deviation of the break-even value from μ.

Example: Given $\mu_o = 250$, $\mu_b = 200$ and $\sigma = 150$, $D = \left|\frac{\mu_o - \mu_b}{\sigma}\right| = .33$ and $N(D) = .2555$

D	.00	.01	.02	.03	.04	.05	.06	.07	.08	.09
.0	.3989	.3940	.3890	.3841	.3793	.3744	.3697	.3649	.3602	.3556
.1	.3509	.3464	.3418	.3373	.3328	.3284	.3240	.3197	.3154	.3111
.2	.3069	.3027	.2986	.2944	.2904	.2863	.2824	.2784	.2745	.2706
.3	.2668	.2630	.2592	.2555	.2518	.2481	.2445	.2409	.2374	.2339
.4	.2304	.2270	.2236	.2203	.2169	.2137	.2104	.2072	.2040	.2009

Table A.3 (continued)

D	.00	.01	.02	.03	.04	.05	.06	.07	.08	.09
.5	.1978	.1947	.1917	.1887	.1857	.1828	.1799	.1771	.1742	.1714
.6	.1687	.1659	.1633	.1606	.1580	.1554	.1528	.1503	.1478	.1453
.7	.1429	.1405	.1381	.1358	.1334	.1312	.1289	.1267	.1245	.1223
.8	.1202	.1181	.1160	.1140	.1120	.1100	.1080	.1061	.1042	.1023
.9	.1004	.09860	.09680	.09503	.09328	.09156	.08986	.08819	.08654	.08491
1.0	.08332	.08174	.08019	.07866	.07716	.07568	.07422	.07279	.07138	.06999
1.1	.06862	.06727	.06595	.06465	.06336	.06210	.06086	.05964	.05844	.05726
1.2	.05610	.05496	.05384	.05274	.05165	.05059	.04954	.04851	.04750	.04650
1.3	.04553	.04457	.04363	.04270	.04179	.04090	.04002	.03916	.03831	.03748
1.4	.03667	.03587	.03508	.03431	.03356	.03281	.03208	.03137	.03067	.02998
1.5	.02931	.02865	.02800	.02736	.02674	.02612	.02552	.02494	.02436	.02380
1.6	.02324	.02270	.02217	.02165	.02114	.02064	.02015	.01967	.01920	.01874
1.7	.01829	.01785	.01742	.01699	.01658	.01617	.01578	.01539	.01501	.01464
1.8	.01428	.01392	.01357	.01323	.01290	.01257	.01226	.01195	.01164	.01134
1.9	.01105	.01077	.01049	.01022	$.0^{2}9957$	$.0^{2}9698$	$.0^{2}9445$	$.0^{2}9198$	$.0^{2}8957$	$.0^{2}8721$
2.0	$.0^{2}8491$	$.0^{2}8266$	$.0^{2}8046$	$.0^{2}7832$	$.0^{2}7623$	$.0^{2}7418$	$.0^{2}7219$	$.0^{2}7024$	$.0^{2}6835$	$.0^{2}6649$
2.1	$.0^{2}6468$	$.0^{2}6292$	$.0^{2}6120$	$.0^{2}5952$	$.0^{2}5788$	$.0^{2}5628$	$.0^{2}5472$	$.0^{2}5320$	$.0^{2}5172$	$.0^{2}5028$
2.2	$.0^{2}4887$	$.0^{2}4750$	$.0^{2}4616$	$.0^{2}4486$	$.0^{2}4358$	$.0^{2}4235$	$.0^{2}4114$	$.0^{2}3996$	$.0^{2}3882$	$.0^{2}3770$
2.3	$.0^{2}3662$	$.0^{2}3556$	$.0^{2}3453$	$.0^{2}3352$	$.0^{2}3255$	$.0^{2}3159$	$.0^{2}3067$	$.0^{2}2977$	$.0^{2}2889$	$.0^{2}2804$
2.4	$.0^{2}2720$	$.0^{2}2640$	$.0^{2}2561$	$.0^{2}2484$	$.0^{2}2410$	$.0^{2}2337$	$.0^{2}2267$	$.0^{2}2199$	$.0^{2}2132$	$.0^{2}2067$
2.5	$.0^{2}2004$	$.0^{2}1943$	$.0^{2}1883$	$.0^{2}1826$	$.0^{2}1769$	$.0^{2}1715$	$.0^{2}1662$	$.0^{2}1610$	$.0^{2}1560$	$.0^{2}1511$
3.0	$.0^{3}3822$	$.0^{3}3689$	$.0^{3}3560$	$.0^{3}3436$	$.0^{3}3316$	$.0^{3}3199$	$.0^{3}3087$	$.0^{3}2978$	$.0^{3}2873$	$.0^{3}2771$
3.5	$.0^{4}5848$	$.0^{4}5620$	$.0^{4}5400$	$.0^{4}5188$	$.0^{4}4984$	$.0^{4}4788$	$.0^{4}4599$	$.0^{4}4417$	$.0^{4}4242$	$.0^{4}4073$
4.0	$.0^{5}7145$	$.0^{5}6835$	$.0^{5}6538$	$.0^{5}6253$	$.0^{5}5980$	$.0^{5}5718$	$.0^{5}5468$	$.0^{5}5227$	$.0^{5}4997$	$.0^{5}4777$

Table A.4 Cumulative Poisson probabilities

1,000 × probability of c or less occurrences of event that has average number of occurrences equal to c' or np'

c' or np' \ c	0	1	2	3	4	5	6	7	8	9
0.02	980	1,000								
0.04	961	999	1,000							
0.06	942	998	1,000							
0.08	923	997	1,000							
0.10	905	995	1,000							
0.15	861	990	999	1,000						
0.20	819	982	999	1,000						
0.25	779	974	998	1,000						
0.30	741	963	996	1,000						
0.35	705	951	994	1,000						
0.40	670	938	992	999	1,000					
0.45	638	925	989	999	1,000					
0.50	607	910	986	998	1,000					
0.55	577	894	982	998	1,000					
0.60	549	878	977	997	1,000					
0.65	522	861	972	996	999	1,000				
0.70	497	844	966	994	999	1,000				
0.75	472	827	959	993	999	1,000				
0.80	449	809	953	991	999	1,000				
0.85	427	791	945	989	998	1,000				
0.90	407	772	937	987	998	1,000				
0.95	387	754	929	984	997	1,000				
1.00	368	736	920	981	996	999	1,000			
1.1	333	699	900	974	995	999	1,000			
1.2	301	663	879	966	992	998	1,000			
1.3	273	627	857	957	989	998	1,000			
1.4	247	592	833	946	986	997	999	1,000		
1.5	223	558	809	934	981	996	999	1,000		
1.6	202	525	783	921	976	994	999	1,000		
1.7	183	493	757	907	970	992	998	1,000		
1.8	165	463	731	891	964	990	997	999	1,000	
1.9	150	434	704	875	956	987	997	999	1,000	
2.0	135	406	677	857	947	983	995	999	1,000	

SOURCE: From Eugene Grant, "Statistical Quality Control," 3d ed., McGraw-Hill Book Company, New York, 1964.

Table A.4 (continued)

c' or np' \ c	0	1	2	3	4	5	6	7	8	9
2.2	111	355	623	819	928	975	993	998	1,000	
2.4	091	308	570	779	904	964	988	997	999	1,000
2.6	074	267	518	736	877	951	983	995	999	1,000
2.8	061	231	469	692	848	935	976	992	998	999
3.0	050	199	423	647	815	916	966	988	996	999
3.2	041	171	380	603	781	895	955	983	994	998
3.4	033	147	340	558	744	871	942	977	992	997
3.6	027	126	303	515	706	844	927	969	988	996
3.8	022	107	269	473	668	816	909	960	984	994
4.0	018	092	238	433	629	785	889	949	979	992
4.2	015	078	210	395	590	753	867	936	972	989
4.4	012	066	185	359	551	720	844	921	964	985
4.6	010	056	163	326	513	686	818	905	955	980
4.8	008	048	143	294	476	651	791	887	944	975
5.0	007	040	125	265	440	616	762	867	932	968
5.2	006	034	109	238	406	581	732	845	918	960
5.4	005	029	095	213	373	546	702	822	903	951
5.6	004	024	082	191	342	512	670	797	886	941
5.8	003	021	072	170	313	478	638	771	867	929
6.0	002	017	062	151	285	446	606	744	847	916

c' or np' \ c	10	11	12	13	14	15	16
2.8	1,000						
3.0	1,000						
3.2	1,000						
3.4	999	1,000					
3.6	999	1,000					
3.8	998	999	1,000				
4.0	997	999	1,000				
4.2	996	999	1,000				
4.4	994	998	999	1,000			
4.6	992	997	999	1,000			
4.8	990	996	999	1,000			
5.0	986	995	998	999	1,000		
5.2	982	993	997	999	1,000		
5.4	977	990	996	999	1,000		
5.6	972	988	995	998	999	1,000	
5.8	965	984	993	997	999	1,000	
6.0	957	980	991	996	999	999	1,000

Table A.4 (continued)

c' or np' \ c	0	1	2	3	4	5	6	7	8	9
6.2	002	015	054	134	259	414	574	716	826	902
6.4	002	012	046	119	235	384	542	687	803	886
6.6	001	010	040	105	213	355	511	658	780	869
6.8	001	009	034	093	192	327	480	628	755	850
7.0	001	007	030	082	173	301	450	599	729	830
7.2	001	006	025	072	156	276	420	569	703	810
7.4	001	005	022	063	140	253	392	539	676	788
7.6	001	004	019	055	125	231	365	510	648	765
7.8	000	004	016	048	112	210	338	481	620	741
8.0	000	003	014	042	100	191	313	453	593	717
8.5	000	002	009	030	074	150	256	386	523	653
9.0	000	001	006	021	055	116	207	324	456	587
9.5	000	001	004	015	040	089	165	269	392	522
10.0	000	000	003	010	029	067	130	220	333	458

	10	11	12	13	14	15	16	17	18	19
6.2	949	975	989	995	998	999	1,000			
6.4	939	969	986	994	997	999	1,000			
6.6	927	963	982	992	997	999	999	1,000		
6.8	915	955	978	990	996	998	999	1,000		
7.0	901	947	973	987	994	998	999	1,000		
7.2	887	937	967	984	993	997	999	999	1,000	
7.4	871	926	961	980	991	996	998	999	1,000	
7.6	854	915	954	976	989	995	998	999	1,000	
7.8	835	902	945	971	986	993	997	999	1,000	
8.0	816	888	936	966	983	992	996	998	999	1,000
8.5	763	849	909	949	973	986	993	997	999	999
9.0	706	803	876	926	959	978	989	995	998	999
9.5	645	752	836	898	940	967	982	991	996	998
10.0	583	697	792	864	917	951	973	986	993	997

	20	21	22
8.5	1,000		
9.0	1,000		
9.5	999	1,000	
10.0	998	999	1,000

Table A.4 (continued)

c' or np' \ c	0	1	2	3	4	5	6	7	8	9
10.5	000	000	002	007	021	050	102	179	279	397
11.0	000	000	001	005	015	038	079	143	232	341
11.5	000	000	001	003	011	028	060	114	191	289
12.0	000	000	001	002	008	020	046	090	155	242
12.5	000	000	000	002	005	015	035	070	125	201
13.0	000	000	000	001	004	011	026	054	100	166
13.5	000	000	000	001	003	008	019	041	079	135
14.0	000	000	000	000	002	006	014	032	062	109
14.5	000	000	000	000	001	004	010	024	048	088
15.0	000	000	000	000	001	003	008	018	037	070

c' or np' \ c	10	11	12	13	14	15	16	17	18	19
10.5	521	639	742	825	888	932	960	978	988	994
11.0	460	579	689	781	854	907	944	968	982	991
11.5	402	520	633	733	815	878	924	954	974	986
12.0	347	462	576	682	772	844	899	937	963	979
12.5	297	406	519	628	725	806	869	916	948	969
13.0	252	353	463	573	675	764	835	890	930	957
13.5	211	304	409	518	623	718	798	861	908	942
14.0	176	260	358	464	570	669	756	827	883	923
14.5	145	220	311	413	518	619	711	790	853	901
15.0	118	185	268	363	466	568	664	749	819	875

c' or np' \ c	20	21	22	23	24	25	26	27	28	29
10.5	997	999	999	1,000						
11.0	995	998	999	1,000						
11.5	992	996	998	999	1,000					
12.0	988	994	997	999	999	1,000				
12.5	983	991	995	998	999	999	1,000			
13.0	975	986	992	996	998	999	1,000			
13.5	965	980	989	994	997	998	999	1,000		
14.0	952	971	983	991	995	997	999	999	1,000	
14.5	936	960	976	986	992	996	998	999	999	1,000
15.0	917	947	967	981	989	994	997	998	999	1,000

Table A.4 (continued)

c' or np' \ c	4	5	6	7	8	9	10	11	12	13
16	000	001	004	010	022	043	077	127	193	275
17	000	001	002	005	013	026	049	085	135	201
18	000	000	001	003	007	015	030	055	092	143
19	000	000	001	002	004	009	018	035	061	098
20	000	000	000	001	002	005	011	021	039	066
21	000	000	000	000	001	003	006	013	025	043
22	000	000	000	000	001	002	004	008	015	028
23	000	000	000	000	000	001	002	004	009	017
24	000	000	000	000	000	000	001	003	005	011
25	000	000	000	000	000	000	001	001	003	006
	14	15	16	17	18	19	20	21	22	23
16	368	467	566	659	742	812	868	911	942	963
17	281	371	468	564	655	736	805	861	905	937
18	208	287	375	469	562	651	731	799	855	899
19	150	215	292	378	469	561	647	725	793	849
20	105	157	221	297	381	470	559	644	721	787
21	072	111	163	227	302	384	471	558	640	716
22	048	077	117	169	232	306	387	472	556	637
23	031	052	082	123	175	238	310	389	472	555
24	020	034	056	087	128	180	243	314	392	473
25	012	022	038	060	092	134	185	247	318	394
	24	25	26	27	28	29	30	31	32	33
16	978	987	993	996	998	999	999	1,000		
17	959	975	985	991	995	997	999	999	1,000	
18	932	955	972	983	990	994	997	998	999	1,000
19	893	927	951	969	980	988	993	996	998	999
20	843	888	922	948	966	978	987	992	995	997
21	782	838	883	917	944	963	976	985	991	994
22	712	777	832	877	913	940	959	973	983	989
23	635	708	772	827	873	908	936	956	971	981
24	554	632	704	768	823	868	904	932	953	969
25	473	553	629	700	763	818	863	900	929	950
	34	35	36	37	38	39	40	41	42	43
19	999	1,000								
20	999	999	1,000							
21	997	998	999	999	1,000					
22	994	996	998	999	999	1,000				
23	988	993	996	997	999	999	1,000			
24	979	987	992	995	997	998	999	999	1,000	
25	966	978	985	991	994	997	998	999	999	1,000

Table A.5 Values of Student's *t* distribution*

The value at the head of each column indicates the probability of obtaining a value of t as large as that shown, for different degrees of freedom, purely as a result of random sampling variations. For example, with 10 degrees of freedom, a value of t as high as 2.228 would be expected to occur 5 times out of 100 purely as a result of chance. Note that these are two-tailed probabilities.

n	Level of Significance (P)											
	0.9	0.8	0.7	0.6	0.5	0.4	0.3	0.2	0.1	0.05	0.02	0.01
1	0.158	0.325	0.510	0.727	1.000	1.376	1.963	3.078	6.314	12.706	31.821	63.657
2	0.142	0.289	0.445	0.617	0.816	1.061	1.386	1.886	2.920	4.303	6.695	9.925
3	0.137	0.277	0.424	0.584	0.765	0.978	1.250	1.638	2.353	3.182	4.541	5.841
4	0.134	0.271	0.414	0.569	0.741	0.941	1.190	1.533	2.132	2.776	3.747	4.604
5	0.132	0.267	0.408	0.559	0.727	0.920	1.156	1.476	2.015	2.571	3.365	4.032
6	0.131	0.265	0.404	0.553	0.718	0.906	1.134	1.440	1.943	2.447	3.143	3.707
7	0.130	0.263	0.402	0.549	0.711	0.896	1.119	1.415	1.895	2.365	2.998	3.499
8	0.130	0.262	0.399	0.546	0.706	0.889	1.108	1.397	1.860	2.306	2.896	3.355
9	0.129	0.261	0.398	0.543	0.703	0.883	1.100	1.383	1.833	2.262	2.821	3.250
10	0.129	0.260	0.397	0.542	0.700	0.879	1.093	1.372	1.812	2.228	2.764	3.169
11	0.129	0.260	0.396	0.540	0.697	0.876	1.088	1.363	1.796	2.201	2.718	3.106
12	0.128	0.259	0.395	0.539	0.695	0.873	1.083	1.356	1.782	2.179	2.681	3.055
13	0.128	0.259	0.394	0.538	0.694	0.870	1.079	1.350	1.771	2.160	2.650	3.012
14	0.128	0.258	0.393	0.537	0.692	0.868	1.076	1.345	1.761	2.145	2.624	2.977
15	0.128	0.258	0.393	0.536	0.691	0.866	1.074	1.341	1.753	2.131	2.602	2.947
16	0.128	0.258	0.392	0.535	0.690	0.865	1.071	1.337	1.746	2.120	2.583	2.921
17	0.128	0.257	0.392	0.534	0.689	0.863	1.069	1.333	1.740	2.110	2.567	2.898
18	0.127	0.257	0.392	0.534	0.688	0.862	1.067	1.330	1.734	2.101	2.552	2.878
19	0.127	0.257	0.391	0.533	0.688	0.861	1.066	1.328	1.729	2.093	2.539	2.861
20	0.127	0.257	0.391	0.533	0.687	0.860	1.064	1.325	1.725	2.086	2.528	2.845
21	0.127	0.257	0.391	0.532	0.686	0.859	1.063	1.323	1.721	2.080	2.518	2.831
22	0.127	0.256	0.390	0.532	0.686	0.858	1.061	1.321	1.717	2.074	2.508	2.819
23	0.127	0.256	0.390	0.532	0.685	0.858	1.060	1.319	1.714	2.069	2.500	2.807
24	0.127	0.256	0.390	0.531	0.685	0.857	1.059	1.318	1.711	2.064	2.492	2.797
25	0.127	0.256	0.390	0.531	0.684	0.856	1.058	1.316	1.708	2.060	2.485	2.787
26	0.127	0.256	0.390	0.531	0.684	0.856	1.058	1.315	1.706	2.056	2.479	2.779
27	0.127	0.256	0.389	0.531	0.684	0.855	1.057	1.314	1.703	2.052	2.473	2.771
28	0.127	0.256	0.389	0.530	0.683	0.855	1.056	1.313	1.701	2.048	2.467	2.763
29	0.127	0.256	0.389	0.530	0.683	0.854	1.055	1.311	1.699	2.045	2.462	2.756
30	0.127	0.256	0.389	0.530	0.683	0.854	1.055	1.310	1.697	2.042	2.457	2.750
40	0.126	0.255	0.388	0.529	0.681	0.851	1.050	1.303	1.684	2.022	2.423	2.704
60	0.126	0.254	0.387	0.527	0.679	0.848	1.046	1.296	1.671	2.000	2.390	2.660
130	0.126	0.254	0.386	0.526	0.677	0.845	1.041	1.289	1.658	1.980	2.358	2.617
∞	0.126	0.253	0.385	0.524	0.674	0.842	1.036	1.282	1.645	1.960	2.326	2.576

SOURCE: Abridged from Table III of Fisher and Yates, *Statistical Tables for Biological, Agricultural and Medical Research*, 4th ed., Oliver & Boyd, Ltd., Edinburgh and London, by permission of the authors and publishers.

* Reprinted from Alva Tuttle, "Elementary Business and Economic Statistics," McGraw-Hill Book Company, New York, 1957.

Table A.6. Values of the chi-square distribution

Degrees of freedom	P = 0.99	0.98	0.95	0.90	0.80	0.70	0.50	0.30	0.20	0.10	0.05	0.02	0.01
1	0.000157	0.000628	0.00393	0.0158	0.0642	0.148	0.455	1.074	1.642	2.706	3.841	5.412	6.635
2	0.0201	0.0404	0.103	0.211	0.446	0.713	1.386	2.408	3.219	4.605	5.991	7.824	9.210
3	0.115	0.185	0.352	0.584	1.005	1.424	2.366	3.665	4.642	6.251	7.815	9.837	11.341
4	0.297	0.429	0.711	1.064	1.649	2.195	3.357	4.878	5.989	7.779	9.488	11.668	13.277
5	0.554	0.752	1.145	1.610	2.343	3.000	4.351	6.064	7.289	9.236	11.070	13.388	15.086
6	0.872	1.134	1.635	2.204	3.070	3.828	5.348	7.231	8.558	10.645	12.592	15.033	16.812
7	1.239	1.564	2.167	2.833	3.822	4.671	6.346	8.383	9.803	12.017	14.067	16.622	18.475
8	1.646	2.032	2.733	3.490	4.594	5.527	7.344	9.524	11.030	13.362	15.507	18.168	20.090
9	2.088	2.532	3.325	4.168	5.380	6.393	8.343	10.656	12.242	14.684	16.919	19.679	21.666
10	2.558	3.059	3.940	4.865	6.179	7.267	9.342	11.781	13.442	15.987	18.307	21.161	23.209
11	3.053	3.609	4.575	5.578	6.989	8.148	10.341	12.899	14.631	17.275	19.675	22.618	24.725
12	3.571	4.178	5.226	6.304	7.807	9.034	11.340	14.011	15.812	18.549	21.026	24.054	26.217
13	4.107	4.765	5.892	7.042	8.634	9.926	12.340	15.119	16.985	19.812	22.362	25.472	27.688
14	4.660	5.368	6.571	7.790	9.467	10.821	13.339	16.222	18.151	21.064	23.685	26.873	29.141
15	5.229	5.985	7.261	8.547	10.307	11.721	14.339	17.322	19.311	22.307	24.996	28.259	30.578
16	5.812	6.614	7.962	9.312	11.152	12.624	15.338	18.418	20.465	23.542	26.296	29.633	32.000
17	6.408	7.255	8.672	10.085	12.002	13.531	16.338	19.511	21.615	24.769	27.587	30.995	33.409
18	7.015	7.906	9.390	10.865	12.857	14.440	17.338	20.601	22.760	25.989	28.869	32.346	34.805
19	7.633	8.567	10.117	11.651	13.716	15.352	18.338	21.689	23.900	27.204	30.144	33.687	36.191
20	8.260	9.237	10.851	12.443	14.578	16.266	19.337	22.775	25.038	28.412	31.410	35.020	37.566
21	8.897	9.915	11.591	13.240	15.445	17.182	20.337	23.858	26.171	29.615	32.671	36.343	38.932
22	9.542	10.600	12.338	14.041	16.314	18.101	21.337	24.939	27.301	30.813	33.924	37.659	40.289
23	10.196	11.293	13.091	14.848	17.187	19.021	22.337	26.018	28.429	32.007	35.172	38.968	41.638
24	10.856	11.992	13.848	15.659	18.062	19.943	23.337	27.096	29.553	33.196	36.415	40.270	42.980
25	11.524	12.697	14.611	16.473	18.940	20.867	24.337	28.172	30.675	34.382	37.652	41.566	44.314
26	12.198	13.409	15.379	17.292	19.820	21.792	25.336	29.246	31.795	35.563	38.885	42.856	45.642
27	12.879	14.125	16.151	18.114	20.703	22.719	26.336	30.319	32.912	36.741	40.113	44.140	46.963
28	13.565	14.847	16.928	18.939	21.588	23.647	27.336	31.391	34.027	37.916	41.337	45.419	48.278
29	14.256	15.574	17.708	19.768	22.475	24.577	28.336	32.461	35.139	39.087	42.557	46.693	49.588
30	14.953	16.306	18.493	20.599	23.364	25.508	29.336	33.530	36.250	40.256	43.773	47.962	50.892

For degrees of freedom greater than 30, the expression $\sqrt{2\chi^2} - \sqrt{2n' - 1}$ may be used as a standard normal variable, where n' is the number of degrees of freedom.

SOURCE: From Fisher, "Statistical Methods for Research Workers," published by Oliver & Boyd Ltd. Edinburgh, and used by permission of the author and publishers. Reprinted from Frank Wolf, "Elements of Probability and Statistics," McGraw-Hill Book Company, New York, 1962.

Table A.7 Values of the F distribution

If Z has an F distribution with r degrees of freedom in the numerator and s degrees of freedom in the denominator, this table gives the value of z for which $P(Z \geq z) = 0.05$ (in regular type) and the value of z for which $P(Z \geq z) = 0.01$ (in boldface type), for the values of r listed along the top of the table and the values of s listed along the side of the table.

Value of s	Value of r: 1	2	3	4	5	6	7	8	9	10	11	12	14	16	20	24	30	40	50	75	100	200	500	∞
1	161 **4,052**	200 **4,999**	216 **5,403**	225 **5,625**	230 **5,764**	234 **5,859**	237 **5,928**	239 **5,981**	241 **6,022**	242 **6,056**	243 **6,082**	244 **6,106**	245 **6,142**	246 **6,169**	248 **6,208**	249 **6,234**	250 **6,258**	251 **6,286**	252 **6,302**	253 **6,323**	253 **6,334**	254 **6,352**	254 **6,361**	254 **6,366**
2	18.51 **98.49**	19.00 **99.00**	19.16 **99.17**	19.25 **99.25**	19.30 **99.30**	19.33 **99.33**	19.36 **99.34**	19.37 **99.36**	19.38 **99.38**	19.39 **99.40**	19.40 **99.41**	19.41 **99.42**	19.42 **99.43**	19.43 **99.44**	19.44 **99.45**	19.45 **99.46**	19.46 **99.47**	19.47 **99.48**	19.47 **99.48**	19.48 **99.49**	19.49 **99.49**	19.49 **99.49**	19.50 **99.50**	19.50 **99.50**
3	10.13 **34.12**	9.55 **30.82**	9.28 **29.46**	9.12 **28.71**	9.01 **28.24**	8.94 **27.91**	8.88 **27.67**	8.84 **27.49**	8.81 **27.34**	8.78 **27.23**	8.76 **27.13**	8.74 **27.05**	8.71 **26.92**	8.69 **26.83**	8.66 **26.69**	8.64 **26.60**	8.62 **26.50**	8.60 **26.41**	8.58 **26.35**	8.57 **26.27**	8.56 **26.23**	8.54 **26.18**	8.54 **26.14**	8.53 **26.12**
4	7.71 **21.20**	6.94 **18.00**	6.59 **16.69**	6.39 **15.98**	6.26 **15.52**	6.16 **15.21**	6.09 **14.98**	6.04 **14.80**	6.00 **14.66**	5.96 **14.54**	5.93 **14.45**	5.91 **14.37**	5.87 **14.24**	5.84 **14.15**	5.80 **14.02**	5.77 **13.93**	5.74 **13.83**	5.71 **13.74**	5.70 **13.69**	5.68 **13.61**	5.66 **13.57**	5.65 **13.52**	5.64 **13.48**	5.63 **13.46**
5	6.61 **16.26**	5.79 **13.27**	5.41 **12.06**	5.19 **11.39**	5.05 **10.97**	4.95 **10.67**	4.88 **10.45**	4.82 **10.27**	4.78 **10.15**	4.74 **10.05**	4.70 **9.96**	4.68 **9.89**	4.64 **9.77**	4.60 **9.68**	4.56 **9.55**	4.53 **9.47**	4.50 **9.38**	4.46 **9.29**	4.44 **9.24**	4.42 **9.17**	4.40 **9.13**	4.38 **9.07**	4.37 **9.04**	4.36 **9.02**
6	5.99 **13.74**	5.14 **10.92**	4.76 **9.78**	4.53 **9.15**	4.39 **8.75**	4.28 **8.47**	4.21 **8.26**	4.15 **8.10**	4.10 **7.98**	4.06 **7.87**	4.03 **7.79**	4.00 **7.72**	3.96 **7.60**	3.92 **7.52**	3.87 **7.39**	3.84 **7.31**	3.81 **7.23**	3.77 **7.14**	3.75 **7.09**	3.72 **7.02**	3.71 **6.99**	3.69 **6.94**	3.68 **6.90**	3.67 **6.88**
7	5.59 **12.25**	4.74 **9.55**	4.35 **8.45**	4.12 **7.85**	3.97 **7.46**	3.87 **7.19**	3.79 **7.00**	3.73 **6.84**	3.68 **6.71**	3.63 **6.62**	3.60 **6.54**	3.57 **6.47**	3.52 **6.35**	3.49 **6.27**	3.44 **6.15**	3.41 **6.07**	3.38 **5.98**	3.34 **5.90**	3.32 **5.85**	3.29 **5.78**	3.28 **5.75**	3.25 **5.70**	3.24 **5.67**	3.23 **5.65**
8	5.32 **11.26**	4.46 **8.65**	4.07 **7.59**	3.84 **7.01**	3.69 **6.63**	3.58 **6.37**	3.50 **6.19**	3.44 **6.03**	3.39 **5.91**	3.34 **5.82**	3.31 **5.74**	3.28 **5.67**	3.23 **5.56**	3.20 **5.48**	3.15 **5.36**	3.12 **5.28**	3.08 **5.20**	3.05 **5.11**	3.03 **5.06**	3.00 **5.00**	2.98 **4.96**	2.96 **4.91**	2.94 **4.88**	2.93 **4.86**
9	5.12 **10.56**	4.26 **8.02**	3.86 **6.99**	3.63 **6.42**	3.48 **6.06**	3.37 **5.80**	3.29 **5.62**	3.23 **5.47**	3.18 **5.35**	3.13 **5.26**	3.10 **5.18**	3.07 **5.11**	3.02 **5.00**	2.98 **4.92**	2.93 **4.80**	2.90 **4.73**	2.86 **4.64**	2.82 **4.56**	2.80 **4.51**	2.77 **4.45**	2.76 **4.41**	2.73 **4.36**	2.72 **4.33**	2.71 **4.31**
10	4.96 **10.04**	4.10 **7.56**	3.71 **6.55**	3.48 **5.99**	3.33 **5.64**	3.22 **5.39**	3.14 **5.21**	3.07 **5.06**	3.02 **4.95**	2.97 **4.85**	2.94 **4.78**	2.91 **4.71**	2.86 **4.60**	2.82 **4.52**	2.77 **4.41**	2.74 **4.33**	2.70 **4.25**	2.67 **4.17**	2.64 **4.12**	2.61 **4.05**	2.59 **4.01**	2.56 **3.96**	2.55 **3.93**	2.54 **3.91**
11	4.84 **9.65**	3.98 **7.20**	3.59 **6.22**	3.36 **5.67**	3.20 **5.32**	3.09 **5.07**	3.01 **4.88**	2.95 **4.74**	2.90 **4.63**	2.86 **4.54**	2.82 **4.46**	2.79 **4.40**	2.74 **4.29**	2.70 **4.21**	2.65 **4.10**	2.61 **4.02**	2.57 **3.94**	2.53 **3.86**	2.50 **3.80**	2.47 **3.74**	2.45 **3.70**	2.42 **3.66**	2.41 **3.62**	2.40 **3.60**
12	4.75 **9.33**	3.88 **6.93**	3.49 **5.95**	3.26 **5.41**	3.11 **5.06**	3.00 **4.82**	2.92 **4.65**	2.85 **4.50**	2.80 **4.39**	2.76 **4.30**	2.72 **4.22**	2.69 **4.16**	2.64 **4.05**	2.60 **3.98**	2.54 **3.86**	2.50 **3.78**	2.46 **3.70**	2.42 **3.61**	2.40 **3.56**	2.36 **3.49**	2.35 **3.46**	2.32 **3.41**	2.31 **3.38**	2.30 **3.36**
13	4.67 **9.07**	3.80 **6.70**	3.41 **5.74**	3.18 **5.20**	3.02 **4.86**	2.92 **4.62**	2.84 **4.44**	2.77 **4.30**	2.72 **4.19**	2.67 **4.10**	2.63 **4.02**	2.60 **3.96**	2.55 **3.85**	2.51 **3.78**	2.46 **3.67**	2.42 **3.59**	2.38 **3.51**	2.34 **3.42**	2.32 **3.37**	2.28 **3.30**	2.26 **3.27**	2.24 **3.21**	2.22 **3.18**	2.21 **3.16**
14	4.60 **8.86**	3.74 **6.51**	3.34 **5.56**	3.11 **5.03**	2.96 **4.69**	2.85 **4.46**	2.77 **4.28**	2.70 **4.14**	2.65 **4.03**	2.60 **3.94**	2.56 **3.86**	2.53 **3.80**	2.48 **3.70**	2.44 **3.62**	2.39 **3.51**	2.35 **3.43**	2.31 **3.34**	2.27 **3.26**	2.24 **3.21**	2.21 **3.14**	2.19 **3.11**	2.16 **3.06**	2.14 **3.02**	2.13 **3.00**
15	4.54 **8.68**	3.68 **6.36**	3.29 **5.42**	3.06 **4.89**	2.90 **4.56**	2.79 **4.32**	2.70 **4.14**	2.64 **4.00**	2.59 **3.89**	2.55 **3.80**	2.51 **3.73**	2.48 **3.67**	2.43 **3.56**	2.39 **3.48**	2.33 **3.36**	2.29 **3.29**	2.25 **3.20**	2.21 **3.12**	2.18 **3.07**	2.15 **3.00**	2.12 **2.97**	2.10 **2.92**	2.08 **2.89**	2.07 **2.87**

SOURCE: Reproduced by permission from George W. Snedecor, "Statistical Methods," 5th ed., 1956, copyright, Iowa State University Press, Ames, Iowa.
* Reprinted from Lionel Weiss, "Statistical Decision Theory," McGraw-Hill Book Company, New York, 1961.

Table A.7 (continued)

Value of s	Value of r: 1	2	3	4	5	6	7	8	9	10	11	12	14	16	20	24	30	40	50	75	100	200	500	∞
16	4.49	3.63	3.24	3.01	2.85	2.74	2.66	2.59	2.54	2.49	2.45	2.42	2.37	2.33	2.28	2.24	2.20	2.16	2.13	2.09	2.07	2.04	2.02	2.01
	8.53	**6.23**	**5.29**	**4.77**	**4.44**	**4.20**	**4.03**	**3.89**	**3.78**	**3.69**	**3.61**	**3.55**	**3.45**	**3.37**	**3.25**	**3.18**	**3.10**	**3.01**	**2.96**	**2.89**	**2.86**	**2.80**	**2.77**	**2.75**
17	4.45	3.59	3.20	2.96	2.81	2.70	2.62	2.55	2.50	2.45	2.41	2.38	2.33	2.29	2.23	2.19	2.15	2.11	2.08	2.04	2.02	1.99	1.97	1.96
	8.40	**6.11**	**5.18**	**4.67**	**4.34**	**4.10**	**3.93**	**3.79**	**3.68**	**3.59**	**3.52**	**3.45**	**3.35**	**3.27**	**3.16**	**3.08**	**3.00**	**2.92**	**2.86**	**2.79**	**2.76**	**2.70**	**2.67**	**2.65**
18	4.41	3.55	3.16	2.93	2.77	2.66	2.58	2.51	2.46	2.41	2.37	2.34	2.29	2.25	2.19	2.15	2.11	2.07	2.04	2.00	1.98	1.95	1.93	1.92
	8.28	**6.01**	**5.09**	**4.58**	**4.25**	**4.01**	**3.85**	**3.71**	**3.60**	**3.51**	**3.44**	**3.37**	**3.27**	**3.19**	**3.07**	**3.00**	**2.91**	**2.83**	**2.78**	**2.71**	**2.68**	**2.62**	**2.59**	**2.57**
19	4.38	3.52	3.13	2.90	2.74	2.63	2.55	2.48	2.43	2.38	2.34	2.31	2.26	2.21	2.15	2.11	2.07	2.02	2.00	1.96	1.94	1.91	1.90	1.88
	8.18	**5.93**	**5.01**	**4.50**	**4.17**	**3.94**	**3.77**	**3.63**	**3.52**	**3.43**	**3.36**	**3.30**	**3.19**	**3.12**	**3.00**	**2.92**	**2.84**	**2.76**	**2.70**	**2.63**	**2.60**	**2.54**	**2.51**	**2.49**
20	4.35	3.49	3.10	2.87	2.71	2.60	2.52	2.45	2.40	2.35	2.31	2.28	2.23	2.18	2.12	2.08	2.04	1.99	1.96	1.92	1.90	1.87	1.85	1.84
	8.10	**5.85**	**4.94**	**4.43**	**4.10**	**3.87**	**3.71**	**3.56**	**3.45**	**3.37**	**3.30**	**3.23**	**3.13**	**3.05**	**2.94**	**2.86**	**2.77**	**2.69**	**2.63**	**2.56**	**2.53**	**2.47**	**2.44**	**2.42**
21	4.32	3.47	3.07	2.84	2.68	2.57	2.49	2.42	2.37	2.32	2.28	2.25	2.20	2.15	2.09	2.05	2.00	1.96	1.93	1.89	1.87	1.84	1.82	1.81
	8.02	**5.78**	**4.87**	**4.37**	**4.04**	**3.81**	**3.65**	**3.51**	**3.40**	**3.31**	**3.24**	**3.17**	**3.07**	**2.99**	**2.88**	**2.80**	**2.72**	**2.63**	**2.58**	**2.51**	**2.47**	**2.42**	**2.38**	**2.36**
22	4.30	3.44	3.05	2.82	2.66	2.55	2.47	2.40	2.35	2.30	2.26	2.23	2.18	2.13	2.07	2.03	1.98	1.93	1.91	1.87	1.84	1.81	1.80	1.78
	7.94	**5.72**	**4.82**	**4.31**	**3.99**	**3.76**	**3.59**	**3.45**	**3.35**	**3.26**	**3.18**	**3.12**	**3.02**	**2.94**	**2.83**	**2.75**	**2.67**	**2.58**	**2.53**	**2.46**	**2.42**	**2.37**	**2.33**	**2.31**
23	4.28	3.42	3.03	2.80	2.64	2.53	2.45	2.38	2.32	2.28	2.24	2.20	2.14	2.10	2.04	2.00	1.96	1.91	1.88	1.84	1.82	1.79	1.77	1.76
	7.88	**5.66**	**4.76**	**4.26**	**3.94**	**3.71**	**3.54**	**3.41**	**3.30**	**3.21**	**3.14**	**3.07**	**2.97**	**2.89**	**2.78**	**2.70**	**2.62**	**2.53**	**2.48**	**2.41**	**2.37**	**2.32**	**2.28**	**2.26**
24	4.26	3.40	3.01	2.78	2.62	2.51	2.43	2.36	2.30	2.26	2.22	2.18	2.13	2.09	2.02	1.98	1.94	1.89	1.86	1.82	1.80	1.76	1.74	1.73
	7.82	**5.61**	**4.72**	**4.22**	**3.90**	**3.67**	**3.50**	**3.36**	**3.25**	**3.17**	**3.09**	**3.03**	**2.93**	**2.85**	**2.74**	**2.66**	**2.58**	**2.49**	**2.44**	**2.36**	**2.33**	**2.27**	**2.23**	**2.21**
25	4.24	3.38	2.99	2.76	2.60	2.49	2.41	2.34	2.28	2.24	2.20	2.16	2.11	2.06	2.00	1.96	1.92	1.87	1.84	1.80	1.77	1.74	1.72	1.71
	7.77	**5.57**	**4.68**	**4.18**	**3.86**	**3.63**	**3.46**	**3.32**	**3.21**	**3.13**	**3.05**	**2.99**	**2.89**	**2.81**	**2.70**	**2.62**	**2.54**	**2.45**	**2.40**	**2.32**	**2.29**	**2.23**	**2.19**	**2.17**
26	4.22	3.37	2.89	2.74	2.59	2.47	2.39	2.32	2.27	2.22	2.18	2.15	2.10	2.05	1.99	1.95	1.90	1.85	1.82	1.78	1.76	1.72	1.70	1.69
	7.72	**5.53**	**4.64**	**4.14**	**3.82**	**3.59**	**3.42**	**3.29**	**3.17**	**3.09**	**3.02**	**2.96**	**2.86**	**2.77**	**2.66**	**2.58**	**2.50**	**2.41**	**2.36**	**2.28**	**2.25**	**2.19**	**2.15**	**2.13**
27	4.21	3.35	2.96	2.73	2.57	2.46	2.37	2.30	2.25	2.20	2.16	2.13	2.08	2.03	1.97	1.93	1.88	1.84	1.80	1.76	1.74	1.71	1.68	1.67
	7.68	**5.49**	**4.60**	**4.11**	**3.79**	**3.56**	**3.39**	**3.26**	**3.14**	**3.06**	**2.98**	**2.93**	**2.83**	**2.74**	**2.63**	**2.55**	**2.47**	**2.38**	**2.33**	**2.25**	**2.21**	**2.16**	**2.12**	**2.10**
28	4.20	3.34	2.95	2.71	2.56	2.44	2.36	2.29	2.24	2.19	2.15	2.12	2.06	2.02	1.96	1.91	1.87	1.81	1.78	1.75	1.72	1.69	1.67	1.65
	7.64	**5.45**	**4.57**	**4.07**	**3.76**	**3.53**	**3.36**	**3.23**	**3.11**	**3.03**	**2.95**	**2.90**	**2.80**	**2.71**	**2.60**	**2.52**	**2.44**	**2.35**	**2.30**	**2.22**	**2.18**	**2.13**	**2.09**	**2.06**
29	4.18	3.33	2.93	2.70	2.54	2.43	2.35	2.28	2.22	2.18	2.14	2.10	2.05	2.00	1.94	1.90	1.85	1.80	1.77	1.73	1.71	1.68	1.65	1.64
	7.60	**5.42**	**4.54**	**4.04**	**3.73**	**3.50**	**3.33**	**3.20**	**3.08**	**3.00**	**2.92**	**2.87**	**2.77**	**2.68**	**2.57**	**2.49**	**2.41**	**2.32**	**2.27**	**2.19**	**2.15**	**2.10**	**2.06**	**2.03**
30	4.17	3.32	2.92	2.69	2.53	2.42	2.34	2.27	2.21	2.16	2.12	2.09	2.04	1.99	1.93	1.89	1.84	1.79	1.76	1.72	1.69	1.66	1.64	1.62
	7.56	**5.39**	**4.51**	**4.02**	**3.70**	**3.47**	**3.30**	**3.17**	**3.06**	**2.98**	**2.90**	**2.84**	**2.74**	**2.66**	**2.55**	**2.47**	**2.38**	**2.29**	**2.24**	**2.16**	**2.13**	**2.07**	**2.03**	**2.01**
32	4.15	3.30	2.90	2.67	2.51	2.40	2.32	2.25	2.19	2.14	2.10	2.07	2.02	1.97	1.91	1.86	1.82	1.76	1.74	1.69	1.67	1.64	1.61	1.59
	7.50	**5.34**	**4.46**	**3.97**	**3.66**	**3.42**	**3.25**	**3.12**	**3.01**	**2.94**	**2.86**	**2.80**	**2.70**	**2.62**	**2.51**	**2.42**	**2.34**	**2.25**	**2.20**	**2.12**	**2.08**	**2.02**	**1.98**	**1.96**
34	4.13	3.28	2.88	2.65	2.49	2.38	2.30	2.23	2.17	2.12	2.08	2.05	2.00	1.95	1.89	1.84	1.80	1.74	1.71	1.67	1.64	1.61	1.59	1.57
	7.44	**5.29**	**4.42**	**3.93**	**3.61**	**3.38**	**3.21**	**3.08**	**2.97**	**2.89**	**2.82**	**2.76**	**2.66**	**2.58**	**2.47**	**2.38**	**2.30**	**2.21**	**2.15**	**2.08**	**2.04**	**1.98**	**1.94**	**1.91**
36	4.11	3.26	2.86	2.63	2.48	2.36	2.28	2.21	2.15	2.10	2.06	2.03	1.98	1.93	1.87	1.82	1.78	1.72	1.69	1.65	1.62	1.59	1.56	1.55
	7.39	**5.25**	**4.38**	**3.89**	**3.58**	**3.35**	**3.18**	**3.04**	**2.94**	**2.86**	**2.78**	**2.72**	**2.62**	**2.54**	**2.43**	**2.35**	**2.26**	**2.17**	**2.12**	**2.04**	**2.00**	**1.94**	**1.90**	**1.87**
38	4.10	3.25	2.85	2.62	2.46	2.35	2.26	2.19	2.14	2.09	2.05	2.02	1.96	1.92	1.85	1.80	1.76	1.71	1.67	1.63	1.60	1.57	1.54	1.53
	7.35	**5.21**	**4.34**	**3.86**	**3.54**	**3.32**	**3.15**	**3.02**	**2.91**	**2.82**	**2.75**	**2.69**	**2.59**	**2.51**	**2.40**	**2.32**	**2.22**	**2.14**	**2.08**	**2.00**	**1.97**	**1.90**	**1.86**	**1.84**

Table A.7 (continued)

Value of *s*	Value of *r*: 1	2	3	4	5	6	7	8	9	10	11	12	14	16	20	24	30	40	50	75	100	200	500	∞
40	4.08	3.23	2.84	2.61	2.45	2.34	2.25	2.18	2.12	2.07	2.04	2.00	1.95	1.90	1.84	1.79	1.74	1.69	1.66	1.61	1.59	1.55	1.53	1.51
	7.31	**5.18**	**4.31**	**3.83**	**3.51**	**3.29**	**3.12**	**2.99**	**2.88**	**2.80**	**2.73**	**2.66**	**2.56**	**2.49**	**2.37**	**2.29**	**2.20**	**2.11**	**2.05**	**1.97**	**1.94**	**1.88**	**1.84**	**1.81**
42	4.07	3.22	2.83	2.59	2.44	2.32	2.24	2.17	2.11	2.06	2.02	1.99	1.94	1.89	1.82	1.78	1.73	1.68	1.64	1.60	1.57	1.54	1.51	1.49
	7.27	**5.15**	**4.29**	**3.80**	**3.49**	**3.26**	**3.10**	**2.96**	**2.86**	**2.77**	**2.70**	**2.64**	**2.54**	**2.46**	**2.35**	**2.26**	**2.17**	**2.08**	**2.02**	**1.94**	**1.91**	**1.85**	**1.80**	**1.78**
44	4.06	3.21	2.82	2.58	2.43	2.31	2.23	2.16	2.10	2.05	2.01	1.98	1.92	1.88	1.81	1.76	1.72	1.66	1.63	1.58	1.56	1.52	1.50	1.48
	7.24	**5.12**	**4.26**	**3.78**	**3.46**	**3.24**	**3.07**	**2.94**	**2.84**	**2.75**	**2.68**	**2.62**	**2.52**	**2.44**	**2.32**	**2.24**	**2.15**	**2.06**	**2.00**	**1.92**	**1.88**	**1.82**	**1.78**	**1.75**
46	4.05	3.20	2.81	2.57	2.42	2.30	2.22	2.14	2.09	2.04	2.00	1.97	1.91	1.87	1.80	1.75	1.71	1.65	1.62	1.57	1.54	1.51	1.48	1.46
	7.21	**5.10**	**4.24**	**3.76**	**3.44**	**3.22**	**3.05**	**2.92**	**2.82**	**2.73**	**2.66**	**2.60**	**2.50**	**2.42**	**2.30**	**2.22**	**2.13**	**2.04**	**1.98**	**1.90**	**1.86**	**1.80**	**1.76**	**1.72**
48	4.04	3.19	2.80	2.56	2.41	2.30	2.21	2.14	2.08	2.03	1.99	1.96	1.90	1.86	1.79	1.74	1.70	1.64	1.61	1.56	1.53	1.50	1.47	1.45
	7.19	**5.08**	**4.22**	**3.74**	**3.42**	**3.20**	**3.04**	**2.90**	**2.80**	**2.71**	**2.64**	**2.58**	**2.48**	**2.40**	**2.28**	**2.20**	**2.11**	**2.02**	**1.96**	**1.88**	**1.84**	**1.78**	**1.73**	**1.70**
50	4.03	3.18	2.79	2.56	2.40	2.29	2.20	2.13	2.07	2.02	1.98	1.95	1.90	1.85	1.78	1.74	1.69	1.63	1.60	1.55	1.52	1.48	1.46	1.44
	7.17	**5.06**	**4.20**	**3.72**	**3.41**	**3.18**	**3.02**	**2.88**	**2.78**	**2.70**	**2.62**	**2.56**	**2.46**	**2.39**	**2.26**	**2.18**	**2.10**	**2.00**	**1.94**	**1.86**	**1.82**	**1.76**	**1.71**	**1.68**
55	4.02	3.17	2.78	2.54	2.38	2.27	2.18	2.11	2.05	2.00	1.97	1.93	1.88	1.83	1.76	1.72	1.67	1.61	1.58	1.52	1.50	1.46	1.43	1.41
	7.12	**5.01**	**4.16**	**3.68**	**3.37**	**3.15**	**2.98**	**2.85**	**2.75**	**2.66**	**2.59**	**2.53**	**2.43**	**2.35**	**2.23**	**2.15**	**2.06**	**1.96**	**1.90**	**1.82**	**1.78**	**1.71**	**1.66**	**1.64**
60	4.00	3.15	2.76	2.52	2.37	2.25	2.17	2.10	2.04	1.99	1.95	1.92	1.86	1.81	1.75	1.70	1.65	1.59	1.56	1.50	1.48	1.44	1.41	1.39
	7.08	**4.98**	**4.13**	**3.65**	**3.34**	**3.12**	**2.95**	**2.82**	**2.72**	**2.63**	**2.56**	**2.50**	**2.40**	**2.32**	**2.20**	**2.12**	**2.03**	**1.93**	**1.87**	**1.79**	**1.74**	**1.68**	**1.63**	**1.60**
65	3.99	3.14	2.75	2.51	2.36	2.24	2.15	2.08	2.02	1.98	1.94	1.90	1.85	1.80	1.73	1.68	1.63	1.57	1.54	1.49	1.46	1.42	1.39	1.37
	7.04	**4.95**	**4.10**	**3.62**	**3.31**	**3.09**	**2.93**	**2.79**	**2.70**	**2.61**	**2.54**	**2.47**	**2.37**	**2.30**	**2.18**	**2.09**	**2.00**	**1.90**	**1.84**	**1.76**	**1.71**	**1.64**	**1.60**	**1.56**
70	3.98	3.13	2.74	2.50	2.35	2.32	2.14	2.07	2.01	1.97	1.93	1.89	1.84	1.79	1.72	1.67	1.62	1.56	1.53	1.47	1.45	1.40	1.37	1.35
	7.01	**4.92**	**4.08**	**3.60**	**3.29**	**3.07**	**2.91**	**2.77**	**2.67**	**2.59**	**2.51**	**2.45**	**2.35**	**2.28**	**2.15**	**2.07**	**1.98**	**1.88**	**1.82**	**1.74**	**1.69**	**1.62**	**1.56**	**1.53**
80	3.96	3.11	2.72	2.48	2.33	2.21	2.12	2.05	1.99	1.95	1.91	1.88	1.82	1.77	1.70	1.65	1.60	1.54	1.51	1.45	1.42	1.38	1.35	1.32
	6.96	**4.88**	**4.04**	**3.56**	**3.25**	**3.04**	**2.87**	**2.74**	**2.64**	**2.55**	**2.48**	**2.41**	**2.32**	**2.24**	**2.11**	**2.03**	**1.94**	**1.84**	**1.78**	**1.70**	**1.65**	**1.57**	**1.52**	**1.49**
100	3.94	3.09	2.70	2.46	2.30	2.19	2.10	2.03	1.97	1.92	1.88	1.85	1.79	1.75	1.68	1.63	1.57	1.51	1.48	1.42	1.39	1.34	1.30	1.28
	6.90	**4.82**	**3.98**	**3.51**	**3.20**	**2.99**	**2.82**	**2.69**	**2.59**	**2.51**	**2.43**	**2.36**	**2.26**	**2.19**	**2.06**	**1.98**	**1.89**	**1.79**	**1.73**	**1.64**	**1.59**	**1.51**	**1.46**	**1.43**
125	3.92	3.07	2.68	2.44	2.29	2.17	2.08	2.01	1.95	1.90	1.86	1.83	1.77	1.72	1.65	1.60	1.55	1.49	1.45	1.39	1.36	1.31	1.27	1.25
	6.84	**4.78**	**3.94**	**3.47**	**3.17**	**2.95**	**2.79**	**2.65**	**2.56**	**2.47**	**2.40**	**2.33**	**2.23**	**2.15**	**2.03**	**1.94**	**1.85**	**1.75**	**1.68**	**1.59**	**1.54**	**1.46**	**1.40**	**1.37**
150	3.91	3.06	2.67	2.43	2.27	2.16	2.07	2.00	1.94	1.89	1.85	1.82	1.76	1.71	1.64	1.59	1.54	1.47	1.44	1.37	1.34	1.29	1.25	1.22
	6.81	**4.75**	**3.91**	**3.44**	**3.13**	**2.92**	**2.76**	**2.62**	**2.53**	**2.44**	**2.37**	**2.30**	**2.20**	**2.12**	**2.00**	**1.91**	**1.83**	**1.72**	**1.66**	**1.56**	**1.51**	**1.43**	**1.37**	**1.33**
200	3.89	3.04	2.65	2.41	2.26	2.14	2.05	1.98	1.92	1.87	1.83	1.80	1.74	1.69	1.62	1.57	1.52	1.45	1.42	1.35	1.32	1.26	1.22	1.19
	6.76	**4.71**	**3.88**	**3.41**	**3.11**	**2.90**	**2.73**	**2.60**	**2.50**	**2.41**	**2.34**	**2.28**	**1.17**	**2.09**	**1.97**	**1.88**	**1.79**	**1.69**	**1.62**	**1.53**	**1.48**	**1.39**	**1.33**	**1.28**
400	3.86	3.02	2.62	2.39	2.23	2.12	2.03	1.96	1.90	1.85	1.81	1.78	1.72	1.67	1.60	1.54	1.49	1.42	1.38	1.32	1.28	1.22	1.16	1.13
	6.70	**4.66**	**3.83**	**3.36**	**3.06**	**2.85**	**2.69**	**2.55**	**2.46**	**2.37**	**2.29**	**2.23**	**2.12**	**2.04**	**1.92**	**1.84**	**1.74**	**1.64**	**1.57**	**1.47**	**1.42**	**1.32**	**1.24**	**1.19**
1,000	3.85	3.00	2.61	2.38	2.22	2.10	2.02	1.95	1.89	1.84	1.80	1.76	1.70	1.65	1.58	1.53	1.47	1.41	1.36	1.30	1.26	1.19	1.13	1.08
	6.66	**4.62**	**3.80**	**3.34**	**3.04**	**2.82**	**2.66**	**2.53**	**2.43**	**2.34**	**2.26**	**2.20**	**2.09**	**2.01**	**1.89**	**1.81**	**1.71**	**1.61**	**1.54**	**1.44**	**1.38**	**1.28**	**1.19**	**1.11**
∞	3.84	2.99	2.60	2.37	2.21	2.09	2.01	1.94	1.88	1.83	1.79	1.75	1.69	1.64	1.57	1.52	1.46	1.40	1.35	1.28	1.24	1.17	1.11	1.00
	6.64	**4.60**	**3.78**	**3.32**	**3.02**	**2.80**	**2.64**	**2.51**	**2.41**	**2.32**	**2.24**	**2.18**	**2.07**	**1.99**	**1.87**	**1.79**	**1.69**	**1.59**	**1.52**	**1.41**	**1.36**	**1.25**	**1.15**	**1.00**

Table A.8 Values of e^{-x}

x	e^{-x} (value)	x	e^{-x} (value)	x	e^{-x} (value)	x	e^{-x} (value)
0.00	1.00000	0.50	0.60653	1.00	0.36788	1.50	0.22313
0.01	0.99005	0.51	.60050	1.01	.36422	1.51	.22091
0.02	.98020	0.52	.59452	1.02	.36060	1.52	.21871
0.03	.97045	0.53	.58860	1.03	.35701	1.53	.21654
0.04	.96079	0.54	.58275	1.04	.35345	1.54	.21438
0.05	.95123	0.55	.57695	1.05	.34994	1.55	.21225
0.06	.94176	0.56	.57121	1.06	.34646	1.56	.21014
0.07	.93239	0.57	.56553	1.07	.34301	1.57	.20805
0.08	.92312	0.58	.55990	1.08	.33960	1.58	.20598
0.09	.91393	0.59	.55433	1.09	.33622	1.59	.20393
0.10	.90484	0.60	.54881	1.10	.33287	1.60	.20190
0.11	.89583	0.61	.54335	1.11	.32956	1.61	.19989
0.12	.88692	0.62	.53794	1.12	.32628	1.62	.19790
0.13	.87809	0.63	.53259	1.13	.32303	1.63	.19593
0.14	.86936	0.64	.52729	1.14	.31982	1.64	.19398
0.15	.86071	0.65	.52205	1.15	.31664	1.65	.19205
0.16	.85214	0.66	.51685	1.16	.31349	1.66	.19014
0.17	.84366	0.67	.51171	1.17	.31037	1.67	.18825
0.18	.83527	0.68	.50662	1.18	.30728	1.68	.18637
0.19	.82696	0.69	.50158	1.19	.30422	1.69	.18452
0.20	.81873	0.70	.49659	1.20	.30119	1.70	.18268
0.21	.81058	0.71	.49164	1.21	.29820	1.71	.18087
0.22	.80252	0.72	.48675	1.22	.29523	1.72	.17907
0.23	.79453	0.73	.48191	1.23	.29229	1.73	.17728
0.24	.78663	0.74	.47711	1.24	.28938	1.74	.17552
0.25	.77880	0.75	.47237	1.25	.28650	1.75	.17377
0.26	.77105	0.76	.46767	1.26	.28365	1.76	.17204
0.27	.76338	0.77	.46301	1.27	.28083	1.77	.17033
0.28	.75578	0.78	.45841	1.28	.27804	1.78	.16864
0.29	.74826	0.79	.45384	1.29	.27527	1.79	.16696
0.30	.74082	0.80	.44933	1.30	.27253	1.80	.16530
0.31	.73345	0.81	.44486	1.31	.26982	1.81	.16365
0.32	.72615	0.82	.44043	1.32	.26714	1.82	.16203
0.33	.71892	0.83	.43605	1.33	.26448	1.83	.16041
0.34	.71177	0.84	.43171	1.34	.26185	1.84	.15882
0.35	.70469	0.85	.42741	1.35	.25924	1.85	.15724
0.36	.69768	0.86	.42316	1.36	.25666	1.86	.15567
0.37	.69073	0.87	.41895	1.37	.25411	1.87	.15412
0.38	.68386	0.88	.41478	1.38	.25158	1.88	.15259
0.39	.67706	0.89	.41066	1.39	.24908	1.89	.15107
0.40	.67032	0.90	.40657	1.40	.24660	1.90	.14957
0.41	.66365	0.91	.40252	1.41	.24414	1.91	.14808
0.42	.65705	0.92	.39852	1.42	.24171	1.92	.14661
0.43	.65051	0.93	.39455	1.43	.23931	1.93	.14515
0.44	.64404	0.94	.39063	1.44	.23693	1.94	.14370
0.45	.63763	0.95	.38674	1.45	.23457	1.95	.14227
0.46	.63128	0.96	.38289	1.46	.23224	1.96	.14086
0.47	.62500	0.97	.37908	1.47	.22993	1.97	.13946
0.48	.61878	0.98	.37531	1.48	.22764	1.98	.13807
0.49	.61263	0.99	.37158	1.49	.22537	1.99	.13670
0.50	.60653	1.00	.36788	1.50	.22313	2.00	.13534

SOURCE: From Cox, "Basic Tables in Business and Economics," McGraw-Hill Book Company, New York, with permission of the publisher.

Table A.8 (continued)

x	e^{-x} (value)	x	e^{-x} (value)	x	e^{-x} (value)
2.00	0.13534	2.50	0.08208	3.00	0.04979
2.01	.13399	2.51	.08127	3.05	.04736
2.02	.13266	2.52	.08046	3.10	.04505
2.03	.13134	2.53	.07966	3.15	.04285
2.04	.13003	2.54	.07887	3.20	.04076
2.05	.12873	2.55	.07808	3.25	.03877
2.06	.12745	2.56	.07730	3.30	.03688
2.07	.12619	2.57	.07654	3.35	.03508
2.08	.12493	2.58	.07577	3.40	.03337
2.09	.12369	2.59	.07502	3.45	.03175
2.10	.12246	2.60	.07427	3.50	.03020
2.11	.12124	2.61	.07353	3.55	.02872
2.12	.12003	2.62	.07280	3.60	.02732
2.13	.11884	2.63	.07208	3.65	.02599
2.14	.11765	2.64	.07136	3.70	.02472
2.15	.11648	2.65	.07065	3.75	.02352
2.16	.11533	2.66	.06995	3.80	.02237
2.17	.11418	2.67	.06925	3.85	.02128
2.18	.11304	2.68	.06856	3.90	.02024
2.19	.11192	2.69	.06788	3.95	.01925
2.20	.11080	2.70	.06721	4.00	.01832
2.21	.10970	2.71	.06654	4.10	.01657
2.22	.10861	2.72	.06587	4.20	.01500
2.23	.10753	2.73	.06522	4.30	.01357
2.24	.10646	2.74	.06457	4.40	.01227
2.25	.10540	2.75	.06393	4.50	.01111
2.26	.10435	2.76	.06329	4.60	.01005
2.27	.10331	2.77	.06266	4.70	.00910
2.28	.10228	2.78	.06204	4.80	.00823
2.29	.10127	2.79	.06142	4.90	.00745
2.30	.10026	2.80	.06081	5.00	.00674
2.31	.09926	2.81	.06020	5.10	.00610
2.32	.09827	2.82	.05961	5.20	.00552
2.33	.09730	2.83	.05901	5.30	.00499
2.34	.09633	2.84	.05843	5.40	.00452
2.35	.09537	2.85	.05784	5.50	.00409
2.36	.09442	2.86	.05727	5.60	.00370
2.37	.09348	2.87	.05670	5.70	.00335
2.38	.09255	2.88	.05613	5.80	.00303
2.39	.09163	2.89	.05558	5.90	.00274
2.40	.09072	2.90	.05502	6.00	.00248
2.41	.08982	2.91	.05448	6.25	.00193
2.42	.08892	2.92	.05393	6.50	.00150
2.43	.08804	2.93	.05340	6.75	.00117
2.44	.08716	2.94	.05287	7.00	.00091
2.45	.08629	2.95	.05234	7.50	.00055
2.46	.08543	2.96	.05182	8.00	.00034
2.47	.08458	2.97	.05130	8.50	.00020
2.48	.08374	2.98	.05079	9.00	.00012
2.49	.08291	2.99	.05029	9.50	.00007
2.50	.08208	3.00	.04979	10.00	.00005

Table A.9 Beta distribution: highest density regions for 50% probability

r	n	P_l	P_u	r	n	P_l	P_u	r	n	P_l	P_u
1	2	.250	.750	3	4	.607	.909	6	10	.498	.710
1	3	.133	.500	3	5	.456	.757	6	15	.311	.485
1	4	.092	.379	3	10	.196	.392	6	20	.224	.368
1	5	.069	.293	3	15	.125	.263	6	25	.180	.295
1	10	.032	.143	3	20	.091	.196				
1	15	.020	.095	3	25	.072	.157	7	10	.391	.805
1	20	.015	.072					7	15	.377	.554
1	25	.012	.056	4	5	.707	.931	7	20	.274	.422
				4	10	.290	.512	7	25	.216	.339
2	3	.500	.867	4	15	.184	.339				
2	4	.326	.674	4	20	.135	.255	8	10	.726	.886
2	5	.243	.544	4	25	.102	.204	8	15	.446	.623
2	10	.107	.274					8	20	.322	.475
2	15	.001	.180	5	10	.350	.650	8	25	.258	.383
2	20	.051	.136	5	15	.249	.413				
2	25	.040	.109	5	20	.180	.312	9	10	.857	.968
				5	25	.142	.250	9	15	.515	.689
								9	20	.372	.526
								9	25	.292	.425

Table A.10. Values of $z = \frac{1}{2} \ln \frac{1 + r}{1 - r}$*

r	.00	.01	.02	.03	.04
0	0.00000	0.01000	0.02000	0.03001	0.04002
.1	0.10034	0.11045	0.12058	0.13074	0.14093
.2	0.20273	0.21317	0.22366	0.23419	0.24477
.3	0.30952	0.32055	0.33165	0.34283	0.35409
.4	0.42365	0.43561	0.44769	0.45990	0.47223
.5	0.54931	0.56273	0.57634	0.59014	0.60415
.6	0.69315	0.70892	0.72500	0.74142	0.75817
.7	0.86730	0.88718	0.90764	0.92873	0.95048
.8	1.09861	1.12703	1.15682	1.18813	1.22117
.9	1.47222	1.52752	1.58902	1.65839	1.73805

r	.05	.06	.07	.08	.09
0	0.05004	0.06007	0.07012	0.08017	0.09024
.1	0.15114	0.16139	0.17167	0.08017	0.09024
.2	0.25541	0.26611	0.27686	0.28768	0.29856
.3	0.36544	0.37688	0.38842	0.40006	0.41180
.4	0.48470	0.49731	0.51007	0.52298	0.53606
.5	0.61838	0.63283	0.64752	0.66246	0.67767
.6	0.77530	0.79281	0.81074	0.82911	0.84795
.7	0.97295	0.99621	1.02033	1.04537	1.07143
.8	1.25615	1.29334	1.33308	1.37577	1.42192
.9	1.83178	1.94591	2.09229	2.29756	2.64665

* For negative values of r, the values in the table are negative.

Index